S0-AHX-736

1800–1849	1850–1899

1827 Elizabeth Gurney Fry, *Observations in Visiting, Superintendence and Government of Female Prisons*

1833 Alexis de Tocqueville and Gustave de Beaumont, *On the Penitentiary System in the United States*

1870 *Declaration of Principles*, Cincinnati, Ohio; creation of National Prison Association

1860 Cesare Lombroso, *Criminal Man*

1825 New York House of Refuge
Western State Penitentiary, Pittsburgh

1829 Eastern Penitentiary, Cherry Hill, Pennsylvania

1840 Alexander Maconochie and Walter Crofton develop the concept of parole

1841 John Augustus develops the concept of probation

1859 New York State Lunatic Asylum for Insane Convicts, Auburn, New York

1864 Halfway house for women, Boston

1865 House of Shelter, a reformatory for women run by Zebulon Brockway

1873 Indiana State Reformatory, first independent, female-run prison for women

1876 Elmira Reformatory, Elmira, New York

1877 Massachusetts Reformatory Prison for Women, Framingham

1899 Law establishes first juvenile court, Cook County (Chicago)

1817 New York Good Time law

1868 Amendment 14 to the Constitution guarantees due process of law and equal protection of law

1871 Civil Rights Act
Ruffin v. *Commonwealth:* Upholds judicial "hands off" policy

1878 Massachusetts Probation Act

1899 Illinois Juvenile Court Act

1812–1815 War of 1812
1848 Beginning of California Gold Rush
1846–1848 Mexican War

1860-1865 American Civil War
1895 First automobile patent
1898 Spanish-American War

Continues on inside back cover

DATE DUE

PRINTED IN U.S.A.

merican Corrections

ions

KALAMAZOO VALLEY COMMUNITY COLLEGE
LIBRARY
KALAMAZOO, MICHIGAN 49009

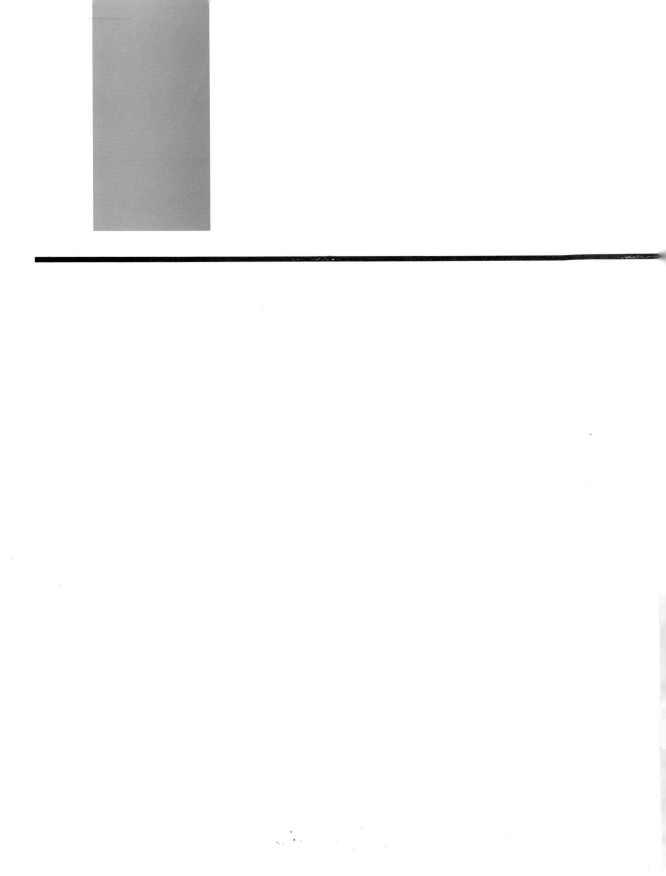

HV
9471
.C57
1994

American Corrections

THIRD EDITION

Todd R. Clear
Rutgers University

George F. Cole
University of Connecticut

Wadsworth Publishing Company
Belmont California
A Division of Wadsworth, Inc.

 KALAMAZOO VALLEY
COMMUNITY COLLEGE
LIBRARY

AUG 1 7 1995

Criminal Justice Editor: Brian Gore
Development Editor: Jan Hunter
Editorial Assistant: Jennifer Dunning
Production Editor: Deborah Cogan
Managing Designer: Andrew Ogus
Print Buyer: Randy Hurst
Art Editor: Kelly Murphy
Permissions Editor: Jeanne Bosschart
Text and Cover Designer: MaryEllen Podgorski
Copy Editor: Jean Mann
Photo Researcher: Photosearch
Technical Illustrator: Precision Graphics
Compositor: Brandon Carson,
    Wadsworth Digital Productions
Printer: R. R. Donelley and Sons
Cover Photo: © Wally McNamee/Woodfin Camp &
    Associates

 This book is printed on recycled paper.

International Thomson Publishing
The trademark ITP is used under license.

© 1994 by Wadsworth, Inc. All rights reserved. No part
of this book may be reproduced, stored in a retrieval system, or transcribed, in any form or by any means, without
the prior written permission of the publisher, Wadsworth
Publishing Company, Belmont, California 94002.

1 2 3 4 5 6 7 8 9 10—97 96 95 94 93

Printed in the United States of America

Library of Congress Cataloging-in-Publication Data

Clear, Todd R.
    American corrections / Todd R. Clear, George
F. Cole.—3rd ed.
        p.   cm.
    Includes bibliographical references and index.
    ISBN 0-534-18972-5
    1. Corrections—United States.   I. Cole,
George F., 1935–   .
II. Title.
HV9471.C57   1993
365′ .973—dc20   93-27757

Todd R. Clear is Professor and Faculty Chair at the School of Criminal Justice, Rutgers University. He has conducted extensive research on a range of topics in corrections, including sentencing policy, probation and parole supervision, institutional programs, and corrections administration. He has received awards from the American Probation and Parole Association and the National Council of Juvenile and Family Court Judges for his work on penal policy. Among his recent books are *Issues in Corrections* (with M. Schwartz and L. Travis) and *Controlling the Offender in the Community* (with V. O'Leary). He is currently completing *Punishment in America: The Penal Harm Experiment, 1973–1993.*

George F. Cole is Professor and Head of the Department of Political Science at the University of Connecticut. A specialist on the administration of criminal justice, he has published extensively on such topics as prosecution, the courts, and corrections. He developed and directed the graduate corrections program at Connecticut. He has been granted two awards under the Fulbright-Hays Program to conduct research in England and Yugoslavia. In 1988 he was a Fellow at the National Institute of Justice. In addition to his scholarly publications he is the author of the widely used introductory textbook *The American System of Criminal Justice,* 6th edition (Brooks/Cole, 1992), and is the editor of *Criminal Justice: Law and Politics,* 6th edition (Wadsworth, 1993). He and Todd Clear have been collaborators since 1985.

Brief Contents

Preface   xiv
Introduction   xvii

PART ONE   *The Correctional Context   2*

CHAPTER 1
The Corrections System   4

CHAPTER 2
The Early History of Correctional
Thought and Practice   29

CHAPTER 3
History of Corrections in America   47

CHAPTER 4
The Punishment of Offenders   71

CHAPTER 5
The Correctional Client   101

PART TWO   *Correctional Practice   138*

CHAPTER 6
Jails: Detention and Short-Term Incarceration   140

CHAPTER 7
Probation   171

CHAPTER 8
Intermediate Sanctions and Community Corrections   207

CHAPTER 9
Incarceration   235

CHAPTER 10
The Prison Experience   256

CHAPTER 11

Incarceration of Women   283

CHAPTER 12

Institutional Management   309

CHAPTER 13

Institutional Programs   344

CHAPTER 14

Prisoners' Rights   374

CHAPTER 15

Release from Incarceration   400

CHAPTER 16

Making It: Supervision in the Community   427

PART THREE   *Correctional Issues and Perspectives   460*

CHAPTER 17

Incarceration Trends   462

CHAPTER 18

Death Penalty   477

CHAPTER 19

Surveillance and Control in the Community   496

CHAPTER 20

American Corrections Today and Tomorrow   507

APPENDIX

Career Opportunities in Corrections   525

GLOSSARY   528

INDEX   536

PHOTO CREDITS   551

Detailed Contents

Preface   xiv

Introduction   xvii

PART ONE

The Correctional Context   2

CHAPTER 1

The Corrections System   4

The Purpose of Corrections   5
The Complexity of Corrections   8
Developing a Comprehensive Perspective on Corrections   9
    Corrections as a System   10
    The Organizations of Corrections   11
    The Administration of Corrections   12
    The Complex and Competing Goals of Corrections   14
    The Implementation of Correctional Programs   18
    The Interconnectedness of Corrections   23
What Makes Corrections Tick?   26
Summary   27

CHAPTER 2

The Early History of Correctional Thought and Practice   29

The Development of Corrections   30
From the Middle Ages to the American Revolution   31
    Galley Slavery   32
    Imprisonment   32
    Transportation   34
    Corporal Punishment and Death   37
On the Eve of Reform   37

The Age of Reason and Correctional Reform   38
   Beccaria and the Classical School   39
   Bentham and the "Hedonic Calculus"   41
   John Howard: Father of the Penitentiary   42
Summary   44

CHAPTER 3
History of Corrections in America   47

The Colonial Period   48
The Arrival of the Penitentiary   49
   The Pennsylvania System   51
   The New York System   53
   Debating the Systems   54
The Reformatory Movement   55
   Cincinnati, 1870   56
   Elmira Reformatory   58
   Juvenile Corrections   59
   Lasting Reforms   60
The Rise of the Progressives   61
   Individualized Treatment   61
   Modern Criminology   62
   Progressive Reforms   62
The Rise of the Medical Model   65
From Medical Model to Community Model   67
Crime Control Model: The Pendulum
Swings Again   68
   Rehabilitation Recedes   68
   Crime Control Comes to the Fore   68
Where Are We Today?   69
Summary   69

CHAPTER 4
The Punishment of Offenders   71

The Purpose of Corrections   72
   Retribution (Deserved Punishment)   73
   Deterrence   74
   Incapacitation   75
   Rehabilitation   77
   Criminal Sanctions: A Mixed Bag?   78
Forms of the Criminal Sanction   79
   Incarceration   80
   Intermediate Sanctions   86
   Probation   89
   Death   90
The Sentencing Process   91
   Attitudes and Background   92
   The Administrative Context   93

   Sentence Disparity: One Result
   of the Process   94
   The Presentence Report   94
The Politics of Sentencing Reform   95
   Legislative Action   95
   Impact of Reform   98
Summary   98

CHAPTER 5
The Correctional Client   101

Selection for the Correctional System   102
Special Types of Offenders and Their Problems   106
   The Situational Offender   106
   The Career Criminal   108
   The Sex Offender   110
   The Substance Abuser   113
   The Mentally Ill Offender   118
   The Mentally Handicapped Offender   122
   The Offender with AIDS   124
   The Elderly Offender   127
   The Juvenile Offender   128
Classifying Offenders: Some Issues   131
   Overlap and Ambiguity in
   Classification Systems   131
   Offense Classifications and
   Correctional Programming   131
   Behavioral Probabilities in Classification   131
   Sociopolitical Pressures and Classification   132
   Distinctions in the Criteria
   for Classifying Offenders   133
Summary   134

PART TWO
Correctional Practice   138

CHAPTER 6
**Jails: Detention and
Short-Term Incarceration   140**

The Contemporary Jail:
Entrance to the System   142
   Origins   142
   Population Characteristics   143
   Administration   144
   The Jail and Local Politics   145
   Regional Jails   147

Pretrial Detention   152
  Special Problems of Detainees   153
  Release from Detention   157
The Sentenced Jail Inmate   160
Alternatives to Incarceration   162
Issues in Jail Management   162
  Legal Liability   162
  Jail Standards   163
  Personnel Matters   163
  Jail Crowding   165
  The Jail Facility   166
The Future of the Jail   168
Summary   169

CHAPTER 7

Probation   171

The History and Development of Probation   172
  Benefit of Clergy   173
  Judicial Reprieve   173
  Recognizance   174
  John Augustus   174
  The Modernization of Probation   175
The Organization of Probation Today   177
  *Should Probation Be Centralized
  or Decentralized?   177*
  Who Should Administer Probation?   178
  *Should Probation Be Combined
  with Parole?   179*
The Dual Role of Probation: Investigation
and Supervision   180
The Investigation Function   187
  Purpose   188
  Contents   188
  Recommendations   189
  Disclosure   190
  Private PSIs   190
The Supervision Function   191
  The Officer   192
  The Offender   194
  The Bureaucracy   195
The Effectiveness of Supervision   197
  Case Management Systems   197
  Special Supervision Programs   198
Revocation and Termination of Probation   199
Probation in the Coming Decade   202
Summary   203

CHAPTER 8

Intermediate Sanctions
and Community Corrections   207

The Case for Intermediate Sanctions   208
  Unnecessary Imprisonment   209
  Limitations of Probation   209
  Improving Justice   209
The Continuum of Sanctions Concept   210
Problems with Intermediate Sanctions   210
  Agencies   210
  Offenders   211
  Widening the Net   213
Varieties of Intermediate Sanctions   214
  Judicial Programs   215
  Probation Supervision Programs   217
  Corrections-Administered Programs   222
Making Intermediate Sanctions Work   223
  Sentencing Issues   224
  Selection of Offenders   224
  Surveillance and Control   226
  The New Corrections Professional   226
Community Corrections: Past, Present,
and Future   227
  Community Corrections Legislation   228
The Future of Intermediate Sanctions
and Community Corrections   232
Summary   232

CHAPTER 9

Incarceration   235

Links to the Past   236
The Goals of Incarceration   238
Organization for Incarceration   240
  Federal Bureau of Prisons   240
  State Prison Systems   242
The Design and Classification of Prisons   243
  Today's Designs   244
  Location of Prisons   246
  Classification of Prisons   246
  Private Prisons   248
  Correctional Facilities Today   250
Who Is in Prison?   250
Summary   253

CHAPTER 10

The Prison Experience 256

Prison Society 257
  Norms and Values 259
  Indigenous or Imported? 260
  Adaptive Roles 262
The Prison Economy 263
Prison Violence 271
  Causes of Prison Violence 271
  Prisoner-Prisoner Violence 271
  Prisoner-Officer Violence 275
  Officer-Prisoner Violence 275
  Institutional Structure 276
  *What Can Be Done
  About Prison Violence?* 277
Discipline of Prisoners 277
  The Disciplinary Process 278
Summary 279

CHAPTER 11

Incarceration of Women 283

Forgotten Offenders 284
Historical Perspective 287
  *The Incarceration of Women
  in the United States* 287
  The Reformatory Movement 288
  The Past Sixty Years 291
Incarceration 293
  Women in Prison 293
  The Subculture of Women's Prisons 296
  Male Versus Female Subcultures 298
  Programs 299
  Co-Corrections 301
  Services 302
  Mothers and Their Children 303
Release to the Community 305
Summary 305

CHAPTER 12

Institutional Management 309

Formal Organization 311
  Structure 312
  The Impact of Structure 320
Governing Prisons 325
  The Defects of Total Power 327
  Rewards and Punishments 328

  Co-optation of Correctional Officers 328
  Inmate Leadership 329
  *Leadership: The Crucial Element
  of Governance* 329
Correctional Officers: The Linchpin
of Management 330
  Who Are the Officers? 334
  Problems with the Officer's Role 340
  Unionism 340
Summary 341

CHAPTER 13

Institutional Programs 344

Managing Time 345
  Time and Security 346
  The Principle of Least Eligibility 347
Classification 347
  The Classification Process 348
  Objective Classification Systems 350
  Classification and the Inmate 350
Rehabilitative Programs 352
  Psychological Programs 352
  Behavior Therapy 355
  Social Therapy 357
  Vocational Rehabilitation 359
  Religious Programs 361
The Rediscovery of Correctional Rehabilitation 362
Prison Industry 362
  *The Contract Labor, Piece-Price,
  and Lease Systems* 363
  The Public Account System 364
  The State Use System 364
  The Public Works and Ways System 365
Prison Industry Today 365
Prison Maintenance Programs 367
Prison Recreation Programs 370
Prison Programming Reconsidered 371
Summary 371

CHAPTER 14

Prisoners' Rights 374

The End of the Hands-Off Policy 376
The Foundations of Prisoners' Rights 377
  The Constitution of the United States 377
  State Constitutions 377
  State Statutes 378
  Federal Statutes 378

Constitutional Rights   378
   First Amendment   379
   Fourth Amendment   381
   Eighth Amendment   381
   Fourteenth Amendment   383
   A Slowing of the Pace?   385
The Problem of Compliance   387
Prisoner Litigation: The Best Route?   388
Alternatives to Litigation   390
   Inmate Grievance Procedures   391
   The Ombudsman   392
   Mediation   393
   Legal Assistance   393
The Impact of the Prisoners' Rights Movement   394
Summary   397

CHAPTER 15

Release from Incarceration   400

Release: From One Part of
the System to Another   401
Contemporary Methods of Release   403
Origins of Parole   404
The Decision to Release   407
   Discretionary Release   408
   Mandatory Release   411
   The Consequences of the Release Decision   414
   The Effect on Sentencing   415
The Organization of Releasing Authorities   417
   Autonomous Versus Consolidated   417
   Field Services   421
   Full-Time Versus Part-Time   421
   Appointment   421
Release to the Community   422
Summary   424

CHAPTER 16

**Making It: Supervision
in the Community   427**

Overview of the Postrelease Function   428
   Community Supervision   429
   Revocation   429
The Structure of Community Supervision   434
   Agents of Community Supervision   436
   The Community Supervision Bureaucracy   439
Residential Programs   443
The Offender's Experience of
Postrelease Life   445
   The Strangeness of Reentry   445

   The Problem of Unmet Personal Needs   450
   Barriers to Success   450
Making It As a Game   452
Postrelease Supervision   455
   How Effective Is It?   455
   What Are Its Prospects?   456
Summary   457

PART THREE

*Correctional Issues
and Perspectives   460*

CHAPTER 17

Incarceration Trends   462

Explaining Prison Population Trends   463
   Regional Factors   464
   Demographic Changes   464
   Better Police and Prosecution   466
   Tougher Sentencing Practices   466
   Construction   467
   War on Drugs   468
Dealing with the Population Crisis   469
   The Null Strategy   469
   The Selective Incapacitation Strategy   469
   The Population-Reduction Strategy   470
   *The Population-Sensitive
Flow-Control Strategy   470*
   The Construction Strategy   471
The Impact of Prison Crowding   472
Does Incarceration Pay?   474
Summary   475

CHAPTER 18

Death Penalty   477

Justification for the Death Penalty   478
The Death Penalty in America   480
The Death Penalty and the Constitution   482
   Continuing Legal Issues   484
Who Is on Death Row?   487
A Continuing Debate?   491
Summary   494

CHAPTER 19

Surveillance and Control in the Community   496

The Growth of Surveillance   497
The Techniques of Surveillance and Control   498
   Drug Controls   *498*
   Electronic Controls   *499*
   Human Surveillance   *500*
   Programmatic Controls   *500*
The Goals of Surveillance   501
   Communities and Community Protection   *501*
   Control: A Double-Edged Sword   *501*
The Politics of Surveillance and
Community Protection   502
The Limits of Control   503
   Technology   *504*
   Human Responses   *504*
   Moral and Ethical Limits   *505*
Toward an Acceptable Community Control   505
Summary   506

CHAPTER 20

American Corrections Today and Tomorrow   507

Five Correctional Dilemmas   509
   Mission   *509*
   Methods   *510*
   Structure   *510*
   Personnel   *511*
   Costs   *512*

Issues in the Profession   513
   Education   *514*
   Training and Continuing Education   *515*
   Civil Service Versus Professionalism   *516*
   Career Opportunities for Women   *517*
   Insider Versus Outsider Promotions   *518*
   Technology   *518*
Directions and Counterdirections   519
   De-escalation   *519*
   Demystification   *520*
   Devaluation   *521*
   Development   *522*
Changing Corrections: A Summary   523

APPENDIX

Career Opportunities in Corrections   525

GLOSSARY   **528**

INDEX   **536**

PHOTO CREDITS   **551**

Preface

This book was inspired by our shared belief that undergraduates must be exposed to the dynamics of corrections in a manner that captures their attention and encourages their entering the field. Because corrections is rich in history, innovative in practice, and challenged by societal problems, it deserves to be taught interestingly and accurately. Happily, our teaching and research are in different areas of corrections, so each of us was able to focus on the aspects he knows best, without forgetting that the other is equally expert and thus qualified to challenge interpretations. Ours has been a pleasurable intellectual and writing experience; we hope that our feelings about our field and the satisfaction we have had in it are reflected in the book. For complete descriptions of our approach and of the organization and features of the text, please see the Introduction. Here, let us describe some of the major revisions that we have made so as to make *American Corrections* current, interesting, and classroom-friendly.

Revision Highlights

In this third edition, the book has been completely updated and rewritten on a line-by-line basis. We have added new chapters and reaaranged others. More than twenty instructors reviewed chapters of the second edition. They pointed out portions of the text their students found difficult, made suggestions as to additional topics that should be covered, and noted those sections that should be dropped. A focus group of eight faculty met with our editor at the meetings of the Academy of Criminal Justice Sciences. Their taped comments, often painful to our ears, forced us to recognize some of the problems they had experienced teaching corrections—and in using our text in the classroom. However, their positive comments about the book provided the stimulus to write the best corrections text on the market. Drafts of revisions were submitted for review, and further suggestions were incorporated into the final product.

Although the revisions in the third edition are too extensive to describe completely here, the following examples illustrate some of the changes that have been made:

l. **New organization, new topics.** Reviewers noted that in earlier editions some chapters repeated materials presented in other courses. They also suggested new topics to be included in the text. In response, we have eliminated several chapters, added several new chapters, and reordered all of the chapters. In so doing, we have divided the book into three parts: The Correctional Context, Correctional Practice, and Correctional Issues and Perspectives. We believe that professors and students alike will now find the textual material ordered in a logical manner.

2. **Real-life examples.** Corrections is an exciting field in the 1990s. Approaches to dealing with offenders in ways that are just and that meet society's demands for deserved punishment are constantly being rethought. We have tried to instill in the text the dynamic qualities of corrections by using real-life examples, by having practitioners describe their work, and by including graphics and photographs that drive home the excitement of the field.

3. **Coverage of prison alternatives.** With prison crowding and overwhelming probation caseloads has come a search for intermediate punishments more restrictive than probation but less restrictive than incarceration. Chapter 8 is a new chapter that introduces such sanctions as house arrest, boot camps, restitution, and intensive probation supervision.

4. **Contemporary policy issues.** Certain correctional policy issues are now being debated by professionals and are of interest to students of corrections. Four chapters exploring correctional issues and perspectives—incarceration trends, the death penalty, surveillance in the community, and the future of American corrections—are found in Part III. Each of these chapters has been written so as to provoke class discussion and to involve students in the issues that will greatly affect their futures either as correctional professionals or as citizens.

5. **Strong graphics.** Special care and attention has been paid to selecting and preparing the graphic features in this edition. Today's students have been greatly influenced by television. They are attuned to images that convey not only information but also values and emotions. We worked directly with a group of outstanding graphic artists to develop an extensive program of illustrations. Wherever possible, quantitative data have been converted into bar graphs, pie charts, and other graphic forms so that they will be clearly understood. Explanatory summaries of the graphic presentations make them easier to grasp. Special care has been taken with regard to the placement of photographs and their captions so that the images are tied directly to the message of the text.

6. **Expanded Instructor's Resource Manual.** Many faculty have told us that they would like to have the assistance of teaching resources beyond a set of test items. We recognize these needs and have worked at fulfilling them. Harry Dammer,

Jr., of Utica College of Syracuse University and Peter Benekos of Mercyhurst College have developed a comprehensive resource manual that includes suggestions for course syllabi, lecture outlines, teaching aids, and class projects. In addition, essay, identification, true/false, and multiple-choice questions are provided for each chapter.

Acknowledgments

I n writing this third edition of *American Corrections*, we were greatly assisted by people who merit special recognition. Instructors and students who used the second edition were most helpful in pointing out its strengths and weaknesses; we took their comments seriously and hope that new readers will find their educational needs met more fully. We also gratefully acknowledge the valuable contributions of the following reviewers: Hugh J. B. Casidy, Adelphi University; Robert Fossen, American University; Ken Gallagher, University of Nebraska; Mike Green, Black Hawk College; Harvey Kushner, Long Island University; Neal Lippold, Waubonsee Community College; Anthony W. Salerno, Glassboro State College; and Georgia Smith, Jacksonville State University.

Jan Hunter served as developmental editor and helped us to tighten our prose, made suggestions to make the text come alive, and created the "wish list" for our graphics program. Fine editors at Wadsworth Publishing Company gave us support and encouragement throughout the undertaking. We also wish to thank Deborah Cogan, production editor; Andrew Ogus, managing designer; and MaryEllen Podgorski, text and cover designer.

Introduction

There have been major changes in American corrections during the past few years. After a decade that focused on crime control through incarceration, experts in the field have shifted to a new (or renewed) emphasis on community corrections through the use of intermediate sanctions. This shift in philosophy corresponds to increased public recognition that the crime problem is not being solved. Legislatures in many states have passed new sentencing laws, mandated prison terms for certain offenders, and stipulated that new priorities should guide corrections. Yet they have recently become aware of the high cost of incarceration. As the judiciary responds to rising public sentiment for strong punishments, probation caseloads and prison populations continue to grow. Increased public and professional attention is given to research by scholars who have evaluated correctional practices. Many scholars have found these practices wanting and have urged alternatives.

In learning about corrections, students gain a unique understanding of the ways in which social and political forces affect the way organizations and institutions respond to a particular segment of the community. Social values come to the fore in the corrections arena because the criminal sanction reflects those values. In a democracy, corrections must operate not only within the framework of law but also within the boundaries set by public opinion. As a public activity corrections is accountable to elected representatives, but it must compete politically with other agencies for resources and "turf."

Academically, corrections is interdisciplinary. Sociology, psychology, history, law, and political science contribute significantly. The cross-fertilization is enriching, yet it requires both writer and teacher to be familiar with a vast literature. Because students often find the breadth of the field confusing, we have structured our text in the interests of coherence.

The Corrections System

Corrections is a system composed of large and small organizations, administered by various levels of government, seeking to achieve complex and sometimes competing goals through professional and nonprofessional employees who are put in contact with one another in direct authority over offenders. We examine this framework as we discuss each element of the subject. Diverse aspects of this complex yet dynamic field are unified for readers as students, as correctional researchers or practitioners, and as citizens.

The failure to perceive corrections as a system sometimes distorts our understanding of correctional practices and their context. Problems are often defined in terms that reflect the political or social attitudes of the observer. If a more analytic approach were taken, correctional policies would be more carefully planned, discrediting the crisis orientation that so often seems to characterize correctional leadership. For example, the current crisis of prison crowding should have been anticipated, given what we know of demographic shifts, changing public attitudes, and reforms in sentencing policy. But it was not until prison populations reached record levels that efforts were made to alleviate the situation.

The main advantage of the system perspective is that it allows for a dispassionate analysis in which concepts developed by various human service agencies illuminate corrections. This is not a small advantage, for a weakness of corrections is its susceptibility to fads: A new panacea seems to be discovered every year or so. Group treatment is popular one year, and scaring delinquents the next. By maintaining a clear view of what is essential to the tasks of corrections, we can differentiate between the short-term, less consequential fluctuations in correctional practice and its continuing themes and struggles. Although the former make for interesting reading and are worth discussing, they can be understood properly only in the context of the more fundamental problems of corrections.

Organization of the Text

We explore the context, practices, and special interests of corrections in three major sections. In Part I we describe the historic problems that frame our contemporary experience: by examining the context of the correctional system (Chapter 1); by examining the early history of correctional thought and practice (Chapter 2); by focusing on the distinctive aspects of correctional history in America (Chapter 3); and by analyzing current theory and evidence on methods of punishment (Chapter 4). In Chapter 5, we portray the correctional client: the offender. We consider the offender in relation to criminal legislation, criminal justice processing, and larger societal forces that are associated with crime. Part I is thus a delineation of the underpinnings—the constants—of American corrections: context, history, goals, organizations, and offenders.

In Part II we look at the current state of the major components and practices of the system. The complexity of correctional organization results in fragmentation and ambivalence in correctional services. Jails and other short-term facilities are scrutinized in Chapter 6; probation in the community, by which most offenders are handled, in Chapter 7, and the new focus on intermediate sanctions in Chapter 8. Because imprisonment remains the core symbolic and punitive mechanism of corrections, we examine it in detail. We discuss incarceration (Chapter 9); the prison experience (Chapter 10); incarceration for women (Chapter 11); institutional management (Chapter 12); educational, industrial, and treatment programs in correctional institutions (Chapter 13); and prisoners' rights (Chapter 14). Our perspective is both descriptive and critical, for we hope to raise questions about current incarceration policies. In Chapters 15 and 16, we examine the process of releasing prisoners from incarceration and the ways in which offenders adjust to supervised life in the community. Thus, in each of the chapters in Part II we consider closely a functional area of the existing correctional system. We focus on the development, structure, and methods of each area, portraying them in light of the continuing issues described in Part I.

In Part III we analyze issues that have become prominent relatively recently in the history of corrections and are of such importance that they deserve individual attention: incarceration trends (Chapter 17); the death penalty (Chapter 18); and surveillance in the community (Chapter 19). In Chapter 20 we conclude by taking both a retrospective view of American corrections and a look toward its future. These chapters are designed to raise questions in the minds of readers so that they can examine and deal with these important issues.

Special Features

everal special features make this introduction to American corrections both informative and enjoyable.

1. **Workperspectives:** We asked correctional practitioners—and offenders—to describe their roles and give their views of their field. Among these, a judge, a sheriff, a correctional administrator, a probation officer, a correctional officer, and an offender have written about what they do and what they think about it; through their eyes we can see how corrections actually operates.

2. **Biographies:** Many people have contributed to the development of corrections. We present biographical sketches of some of the most important, because familiarity with the lives of leaders helps us to appreciate their work.

3. **Focus sections:** The real-world relevance of the issues discussed in the text is made clear by vivid in-depth accounts by journalists, prisoners and parolees and their relatives, and corrections workers.

4. **Glossary:** One goal of an introductory course is to familiarize students with the terminology of the field. We have avoided jargon in the text but naturally include terms that are in common use. Such indispensable words and phrases are set in bold type at their first appearance in the text. There is a full glossary, with definitions of all terms, located at the back of the book.

5. **Graphics:** We have created tables and figures that clarify and enliven information so that it can be perceived easily and grasped accurately.

6. **Photographs:** A full program of dynamic photographs are spread throughout the book. These reveal many aspects of corrections that ordinarily are concealed from the public eye.

7. **Careers in corrections:** Since many readers of this book are considering corrections as their profession, we have gathered information in the Appendix to help students guide their decision.

8. **Other student aids:** At the beginning of each chapter is an outline of the topics to

be covered, to help students prepare and review; at the end of each chapter are a summary, discussion questions, and suggestions for further reading.

In *American Corrections,* Third Edition, we offer an accurate analysis of contemporary corrections that is based on up-to-date research. We acknowledge the problems with the system, and we hope that our exposition will inspire suggestions for change. We are aware, however, that corrections professionals tend to grasp at one proposed innovation after another. We believe that when human freedom is at stake, policies must reflect research and must be formulated only after their potential effects have been considered carefully. We hope that a new generation of students will decide that a career in corrections is for them. We also hope that they will have a solid understanding of all the aspects of their complex field.

American Corrections

As we begin our study of American corrections, it is first necessary to understand the social, historical, and political context within which it operates. What do we mean by corrections? How has punishment been used in Europe and in the United States to maintain social control? What are the goals of the corrections? Who are the clients of corrections? Part One explores such questions with a twofold aim: to give the reader (1) a broad, general framework within which to analyze the correctional system and (2) a perspective on the history of corrections within the criminal justice system.

CHAPTER 1

The Corrections System

CHAPTER 2

The Early History of Correctional Thought and Practice

CHAPTER 3

History of Corrections in America

CHAPTER 4

The Punishment of Offenders

CHAPTER 5

The Correctional Client

The Corrections System

Corrections remains a world almost unknown to law-abiding citizens, and even those within it often know only their own particular corner.

President's Commission on Law Enforcement and Administration of Justice, 1967

The Purpose of Corrections
The Complexity of Corrections
**Developing a Comprehensive Perspective
    on Corrections**
Corrections as a System
The Organizations of Corrections
The Administration of Corrections
The Complex and Competing Goals of Corrections
The Implementation of Correctional Programs
The Interconnectedness of Corrections
What Makes Corrections Tick?
Summary

I t is 11:00 A.M. in New York City. A five-man crew has been removing trash from a park in the Bronx for several hours. Across town in Rikers Island, the view down a corridor of jail cells is of the hands of the incarcerated, gesturing through the bars as they converse, play cards, share cigarettes—the hands of people doing time. About a thousand miles to the south, over two hundred inmates sit on Florida's death row. In the same state, a woman on probation reports to a "community-control officer." She is wearing an electronic monitoring device on her ankle; it signals the officer if she leaves her home at night. On the other side of the Gulf of Mexico, crops are tended by sun-burned Texans dressed in stained work clothes. Almost due north in Kansas, an inmate grievance committee in a maximum security prison reviews complaints of guard harassment. Beside the Pacific, in San Francisco, a young man leaves a center-city office building on his way to work after dropping off a urine sample and talking with his parole officer. All of these activities are part of corrections. And all of the central actors are offenders.

The Purpose of Corrections

T he need to punish citizens who violate society's rules is an unfortunate but necessary part of life. From the earliest accounts of humankind one finds examples of the use of punishment as one means of **social control,** ways in which individuals or the state get people to conform to certain types of behaviors that are consistent with the norms and rules of society. Parents chastise their children when they disobey family rules, individuals ostracize

those who deviate from expected social norms, colleges and universities expel students who cheat, and governments impose punishments on those who break the criminal laws.

Of the various ways that societies and their members try to control behavior, criminal punishment is the most formal, for criminal behavior is perhaps the most serious type of behavior over which a society must gain control. Criminal justice is designed to aid society in the prevention and control of criminal behavior.

Three basic concepts of law—offense, guilt, and punishment—define the purpose and procedures of criminal justice. In the United States, Congress and state legislatures define what conduct is considered criminal; they define the offenses. The police, prosecutors, and courts are involved in processes to determine guilt, the determinations that must be made before a person can be found to have committed a criminal offense. The postconviction process then focuses on what should be done with a person who has been found guilty of a criminal offense.

The central purpose of corrections is to carry out the criminal sentence. Ordinarily, the term **corrections** refers to actions applied to offenders after they have been convicted and implies that some "corrective" action is being taken to punish these convicted offenders according to society's needs. In our discussion of corrections, we also include those who have been accused—but not yet convicted—of criminal offenses since they are often under correctional supervision awaiting disposition of their case—sitting in jail, undergoing drug or alcohol treatment, or living in the community on bail.

Corrections encompasses all of the legal responses of society to those members of the community who engage in prohibited behavior. To a large extent, a society is defined by the actions it does or does not tolerate and by the

social control   Actions and practices of individuals and social institutions designed to induce conformity with social norms and rules.

corrections   The variety of programs, services, facilities, and organizations responsible for the management of people who have been accused or convicted of criminal offenses.

Figure 1.1 ■ **Correctional Populations in the United States, 1980–1991.** Although there has been much publicity about the increase in prison populations, a greater portion of correctional growth has occurred in probation and parole. From year-end 1980 to year-end 1990, the number of adults on probation grew 126 percent, on parole grew 107 percent, and in jails or prison grew 114 percent.

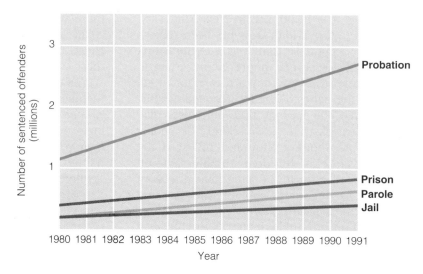

Source: U.S. Department of Justice, Bureau of Justice Statistics, National Update (Washington, D.C.: Government Printing Office, January 1992), p. 4.

steps it takes to enforce behavioral norms. For example, most Americans would probably find it amazing that in the 1990s in Indonesia, public flogging is being used to enforce laws prohibiting premarital sex and in the Muslim world, certain Bedouin cultures enforce laws against thievery by cutting off the offender's hand. Yet people from non-Western countries would also be amazed (or amused) that in the United States drug users are incarcerated and some convicted murderers spend the rest of their days in a mental hospital. In each instance, the correctional practice tells us a great deal about the society embracing it; our reactions tell us a little bit about our own society's values.

Thus, in addition to serving to protect society, corrections also helps to define the boundaries of the community by emphasizing acceptable types of behavior. This was stressed by the nineteenth-century sociologist Emile Durkheim. He argued that crime is normal in society and that it performs an important function by spotlighting the rules and values of the community. When a law is broken, citizens come together to express their outrage. The deviant supplies a focus for group feeling. As people unite against the offender, a sense of mutuality or community is created.

Offenders thus make people more alert to their shared interests and values. In our complex, heterogeneous society, a wide range of actions, from speeding to committing arson to defrauding consumers and polluting, violate the law. Depending on the nature and seriousness of the offense, together with such factors as the character of the offender, sanctions may be chosen from among the options (for example, fine, probation, prison, or death) stipulated by law. Because it reflects our values, corrections is every bit as complex and challenging as the society in which we live today.

The postconviction activities that we touched on in opening this chapter give some idea of the breadth of corrections in the United States. In fact, the Department of Justice estimates that more than four million adults and juveniles are under some form of correctional care, custody, or supervision. This means that 1 out of every 43 adults (1 of every 24 men and 1 of every 162 women) in America either is being supervised in the community (on probation or parole) or is incarcerated. As noted in Figure 1.1, there has been extensive growth in the correctional population since 1980.

The corrections system employs more than 500,000 administrators, psychologists, officers, counselors, social workers, and others to care for

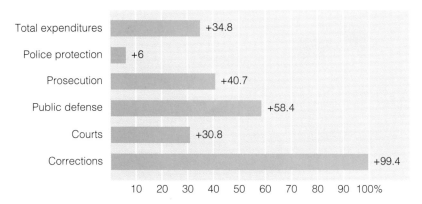

Total expenditures	+34.8
Police protection	+6
Prosecution	+40.7
Public defense	+58.4
Courts	+30.8
Corrections	+99.4

10 20 30 40 50 60 70 80 90 100%

Figure 1.2 ■ **Percentage Change in Expenditures for Justice Activities, All Governments, 1979–1991.** Among the agencies of criminal justice, corrections has had the greatest increase in expenditures expressed in constant 1990 dollars.

Source: U.S. Department of Justice, Bureau of Justice Statistics, Bulletin (Washington, D.C.: Government Printing Office, September 1992), p. 4.

these people. Authorized by the laws of the federal government, fifty states, over three thousand counties, and uncounted municipalities, corrections is administered by public and private organizations and costs about $25 billion yearly.[1] Since 1979, correctional spending by all levels of government has increased about 100 percent, as seen in Figure 1.2.[2]

Clearly, corrections encompasses a major commitment on the part of American society to deal with persons who are convicted of criminal law violations. The increase of offenders under supervision during the past decade has caused a major expansion of correctional facilities, staff, and budgets; some might say that corrections is now a "big business." Spending for corrections has risen more dramatically than any other state function, jumping more than 328 percent between 1979 and 1990.[3] Today, some states spend more on prisons than they do for all of public higher education. Table 1.1 shows some of the costs of providing correctional services. For all its size and complexity, the essential business of corrections is punishment administered under law, whether designed to deter, to rehabilitate, to incapacitate, or simply to achieve retribution.

Table 1.1 ■ **What Do Correctional Dollars Buy?** Providing correctional services is expensive. Compare the average cost for the items listed below with the costs of a college education.

Average cost ($)	
One adult offender, annually	
In federal prison	13,162
In state prison	11,302
In state community-based facility	7,951
On federal probation or parole	1,316
On nonfederal probation or parole	584–702
One unsentenced federal prisoner, daily	
In local jail	36
In halfway house	30
In prison or jail	33
Construction per bed	
Maximum security state prison	71,000
Medium security state prison	53,000
Minimum security state prison	30,000
Constitutional jail	43,000

Source: Adapted from U.S. Department of Justice, Bureau of Justice Statistics, *Report to the Nation on Crime and Justice*, 2nd ed., (Washington, D.C.: Government Printing Office, 1988).

Corrections is much more than just prisons and jails. It involves dealing with offenders in a variety of ways.

The Complexity of Corrections

Although the general public may believe that corrections is mainly concerned with the agencies that deal with criminal offenders—probation, parole, prisons, and jails—this is too general an observation and not a true depiction of reality. It must be emphasized that not all people with whom corrections deals are offenders. Increasingly, such correctional agencies as jails and probation departments are called on to perform duties in relation to people who have yet to be—and may never be—convicted of crimes. For example, in many jurisdictions, accused persons are diverted from prosecution and trial if they agree to undergo alcohol, drug, or mental illness treatments. If they successfully complete the treatment and do not commit another criminal offense during a specified time period, their cases will be dropped from the system.

The theory inherent in the term *corrections*—the assumption that offenders can be "corrected"—is itself much in dispute. For example, there are those who believe that only the aging process influences some people to abide by the law and it is not possible to rehabilitate most offenders. Others argue that corrections should not be concerned with the future behavior of criminals, that punishment should be applied only for past wrongdoing.[4] Yet until the 1970s, the corrective function of rehabilitative programs was so widely accepted that treatment and reform of the offender were virtually the only issues deemed worthy of serious attention in the whole field of criminal justice.

Adding to the complexity of corrections is the fact that the United States operates under **federalism,** a system of government in which

federalism A system of government in which power and responsibilities are divided between a national government and state governments.

One of every forty-three Americans is under some form of correctional supervision. Most offenders live in the community.

power is divided between the national government and the states. Citizens must obey the criminal laws of both the federal government and their own state. Despite the similarity of behaviors that are labeled criminal from state to state, there are important differences in specific definitions of offenses, the types and severity of sanctions, and the procedures governing the finding of guilt and the treatment of offenders. In fact, most criminal justice and correctional activity takes place at the state level. Correctional supervision under federal authority covers only 2 percent of those on probation, 5 percent of those on parole, and 9 percent of those in prison.[5]

The fact that the United States is a democracy adds a further dimension to the complexity

of corrections. Officials are elected; legislatures determine the objectives of the criminal law system and appropriate the resources to carry out those objectives; and political parties channel public opinion on such issues as law and order to officeholders. From time to time there have been shifts in the goals of correctional policies. For example, from about 1940 to 1970, corrections was oriented toward liberal rehabilitative policies; since about 1970, conservative crime control policies have influenced corrections. Questions of crime and justice are thus inescapably public questions, subject to all the pressures and vagaries of the political process.

Finally, corrections is only one of many governmental systems providing services to citizens. Being a part of this governmental setting directly affects the people responsible for carrying out the work of corrections. Corrections thus refers to the procedures, facilities, and philosophies of various organizations and institutions and the individuals operating within them.

To summarize, when criminal justice researchers, officials, and practitioners speak of corrections, they may be referring to any number of programs, processes, and agencies. Corrections activities are performed by public and private organizations; involve federal, state, and local governments; and occur in a variety of community and closed settings. We can speak of corrections as a department of the government, a subfield of the academic discipline of criminal justice, an approach to the treatment of offenders, and a part of the criminal justice system. Corrections is all of these things and more.

Developing a Comprehensive Perspective on Corrections

I s there some way that we can develop a framework to sort out the complex and multidimensional nature of corrections? As students of criminal justice, we are seeking answers to a number of questions concerning the role of corrections in the administration of justice, the practices of corrections as they relate to crime control, and the ways in which correctional practitioners go about their business. How can we gather and organize information about all facets of this complex and dynamic enterprise so that we can address these and other questions?

When social scientists and policy analysts seek to make sense out of a lot of information, they use the concept of **paradigm,** which refers to a set of assumptions supporting a field of inquiry.[6] It defines the boundaries of the field, the key concepts and theories used to explain phenomena, the research methodologies for gathering and analyzing data, and the tools for the practical application of research findings. Paradigms change over time as theoretical approaches prove unsatisfactory and as technological or societal factors shift the direction of research interest. At any one time there may be competing paradigms, each claimed to be the best means to study the field.

The field of corrections has followed several paradigms over its history. In the nineteenth century, for example, religious assumptions about the causes of criminal behavior and the ways to deal with it served as the paradigm for corrections. During the 1950s and 1960s, psychological theories shaped the field. In subsequent years, rehabilitation has been deemphasized, the focus on deserved punishment has been sharpened, and greater emphasis has been placed on incarceration. Contemporary corrections seems now to be in a period of flux, with no dominant paradigm.

Corrections as a System

In this book we use the paradigm of the *correctional system* as a framework to help guide our study. We chose this paradigm because it seems to describe the field best and to focus attention for research and understanding on the dynamic aspects of tasks performed in the overall interests of justice. The system paradigm also allows us to draw on the insights of several disciplines of the social and behavioral sciences, and thus to benefit from all relevant research.

The concept of **system** evokes images of interconnected processes operating toward a common purpose. Interstate highways, for example, constitute a transportation system. We refer to the various portions of criminal justice— police, prosecutors, courts, and corrections—as a system. But what does this term really mean? Can systems be used as a comprehensive paradigm for the study of corrections?

If a *system* is defined as a complex whole consisting of interdependent parts whose operations are directed toward common goals and influenced by the environment within which they function, then the systems paradigm can be used for studying corrections. In America today, corrections is certainly a complicated web of operations working simultaneously on the goals of fair punishment and community protection. At the same time, all corrections agencies must deal with environmental forces such as public opinion, fiscal constraint, and law. Thus, this definition is somewhat unsatisfying when applied to corrections. Do corrections agencies really pursue common goals in their operations? Is corrections truly a whole?

When we use the term *system* in describing corrections, we use it in a particular way. The correctional system is concerned with the management and supervision of criminal offenders. Corrections includes a variety of organizations administered by various levels of government. Those who implement corrections must attempt to satisfy complex and sometimes competing

---

paradigm   A model; a set of assumptions about the boundaries, theories, methodologies, and research tools supporting a field of inquiry.

system   A complex whole consisting of interdependent parts whose operations are directed toward common goals and influenced by the environment within which they function.

The corrections system is composed of several loosely related agencies that are themselves bureaucracies. This means that there must be coordination and cooperation among the heads of these agencies.

goals. In short, corrections is interconnected and complex, for the actions of any subpart affect all other parts.

The Organizations of Corrections

Corrections is composed of many subunits, each with its own functions and responsibilities. These subunits—probation offices, halfway houses, prisons, and others—vary in size, goals, clientele, and organizational structure. Some are agencies of government; others are private organizations contracted by government to provide specific services to correctional clients. A probation office is organized differently from a halfway house or a prison, yet all three are part of the correctional system and pursue an overriding common goal. There are, however, important differences among subunits of the same general type. A five-person probation office working closely with one judge in a rural setting, for example, has an organizational life different from that of the more bureaucratized 100-person office in a large metropolitan system. That organizational life may help or hinder the system of justice.

The management of correctional agencies is all the more problematic because most correc-

tions systems comprise several loosely related organizations that are themselves bureaucracies. Decision making is thus dispersed, and no one person can implement the full range of correctional practice. The sheriff who runs the jail and the chief probation officer who runs the pretrial release program are both affected by the problem of jail crowding and delays in sentencing hearings. Even so, it can often be extremely difficult to get them to work together because each is busy protecting an area of managerial control. Line workers in corrections, those in direct contact with offenders, seldom have influence on organizational policies, even though they are the people responsible for implementing those policies on a day-to-day basis. Corrections itself is in the unfortunate position of being unable to determine the type and number of its clients. Others in the criminal justice system, primarily judges, do that, and correctional officials are not able to halt or regulate the flow. Thus, the efforts of correctional workers are sometimes sporadic, uncoordinated, or inconsistent merely because of the looseness with which bureaucracies are connected.

The complexity of the corrections system is illustrated by the variety of public and private agencies that are part of the correctional system of Philadelphia County, Pennsylvania, shown in Table 1.2. Note that offenders are supervised by various service agencies operating at different levels of government—state, county, municipal—and in different branches of government—executive, judicial. What are the correctional agencies of your own community?

Further, any organization develops routines simply to operate. Like most people, workers in corrections organizations want regular and predictable responsibilities. They do not want to venture into uncharted seas where they may make an uninformed decision and then be penalized by superiors. Uncertainty is decreased when operations are reduced to routines—patterns that are repeated and thus become familiar. Recognizing the routines of the organization is essential if one wishes to understand corrections.

Table 1.2 ■ **The Distribution of Correctional Responsibilities in Philadelphia County, Pennsylvania.** Note the various correctional functions performed at different levels of government by different government agencies.

Correctional function	Level and branch of government	Responsible agency
Adult corrections		
Pretrial detention	Municipal/executive	Department of Human Services
Probation supervision	County/courts	Court of Common Pleas
Halfway houses	Municipal/executive	Department of Human Services
Houses of corrections	Municipal/executive	Department of Human Services
County prisons	Municipal/executive	Department of Human Services
State prisons	State/executive	Department of Corrections
County parole	County/executive	Court of Common Pleas
State parole	State/executive	Board of Probation and Parole
Juvenile corrections		
Detention	Municipal/executive	Department of Public Welfare
Probation supervision	County/courts	Court of Common Pleas
Dependent/neglect	State/executive	Department of Human Services
Training schools	State/executive	Department of Public Welfare
Private placements	Private	Many
Juvenile aftercare	State/executive	Department of Public Welfare
Federal corrections		
Probation/parole	Federal/courts	U.S. Courts
Incarceration	Federal/executive	Bureau of Prisons

Source: Taken from the 1983 and 1984 annual reports of the responsible agencies.

The Administration of Corrections

In our federalist system of government, some powers are delegated to the national government, some are reserved to the states, and some are shared by both. All levels of government—national, state, county, and municipal—are involved in one or more aspects of the correctional system. The national government operates the full range of correctional organizations to deal with the people who have been convicted of breaking federal laws; likewise, state and local governments provide correctional services for those who have broken their laws. As noted in Figure 1.3, criminal justice costs are borne by each level of government, with most correctional costs falling on state and local governments.

The extent to which the different levels of government are involved in corrections varies. The scope of the criminal laws of the states is much broader than the criminal laws of the national government; as a result, only about 150,000 adults are under federal correctional supervision. There are 67 federal **prisons;** 521 prisons are run by the states. **Jails** are operated mainly by local governments, but in six states

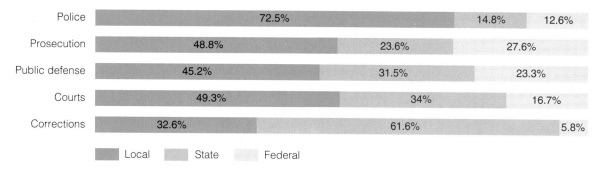

Figure 1.3 ■ **Distribution of Justice System Expenditures by Level of Government.** State and local governments bear the brunt of the costs of correctional activities.

Source: U.S. Department of Justice, Bureau of Justice Statistics, Bulletin (Washington, D.C.: Government Printing Office, September 1992), p. 3.

they are integrated with the state prison system. State and local governments pay for 95 percent of all correctional activities in the nation. In most states, the agencies of community corrections—probation and intermediate sanctions—are run by the county government and are usually part of the judicial branch, yet in some jurisdictions they are run by the executive branch. In still other states, this part of corrections is run by statewide organizations.

It is important to note that there are many variations in the ways that corrections is formally organized at the state and local levels. Four state corrections systems—California, Florida, New York, and Texas—handle nearly one-third of all the offenders under correctional control in the United States. As you read the Focus box, "The Big Four in Corrections" (pp. 16–17), note the differing organizational configurations that have been developed to provide correctional services.

prison An institution for the incarceration of persons convicted of serious crimes, usually felonies.

jail A facility authorized to hold pretrial detainees and sentenced misdemeanants for periods longer than forty-eight hours. Most jails are administered by county governments; sometimes they are part of the state government.

At all political levels, the correctional system is only one of many services operated by government and paid for by tax revenues. Thus, corrections must vie for funding, not only with other criminal justice agencies, but also with such departments as those dealing with education, transportation, and social welfare. Per capita spending on all criminal justice activities ranges from less than $100 in West Virginia to more than $400 in Alaska and New York. As shown by Table 1.3, criminal justice as a whole and corrections in particular take differing portions of the federal, state, and local budgets.

Understandably, corrections does not always get the funding it needs; people may want garbage collected with regularity more than they want quality correctional work performed. This competitive position is made more difficult by the fact that corrections is largely invisible until a problem occurs, such as when a parolee commits a heinous crime or a prison riot breaks out. An even greater difficulty stems from the perceived undesirability of its clientele; it is not easy to gain larger budgets to provide assistance to people who have broken the law.

Like all other government services, corrections is buffeted by frequently shifting social and political forces that greatly complicate the problem of administration. Any correctional client

Table 1.3 ■ **Percentage of Direct Spending for Selected Governmental Functions.** Corrections must compete with other governmental agencies for its share of public spending. What may account for low levels of spending for corrections as compared to other governmental services?

Activity	Level of government			
	All	Federal	State	Local
Social insurance payments	20.5%	31.4%	13.7%	1.5%
National defense and international relations	15.5	27.6	—	—
Education and libraries	14.0	1.4	19.1	37.6
Interest on debt	10.7	15.1	5.4	4.9
Housing and environment	7.1	7.0	3.8	9.6
Public welfare	6.3	2.7	21.0	4.2
Hospitals and health	4.2	1.4	8.9	6.8
Transportation	3.5	.6	9.5	5.7
Justice	3.3	.7	6.4	6.9
Police protection	1.4	.3	1.2	4.0
Judicial and legal	.7	.3	1.3	1.4
Corrections	1.1	.1	3.9	1.4
Space research and technology	.5	1.0	—	—

Source: U.S. Department of Justice, Bureau of Justice Statistics, *Bulletin* (Washington, D.C.: Government Printing Office, September, 1992), p. 3.

who commits a serious crime can become the centerpiece of a political crisis. That helps explain why the turnover rate among top state correctional administrators is so high. As many as two-thirds resign or are dismissed in any one year.

Conflict among the branches and levels of government also creates problems for corrections. Local governments are often responsible for correctional programs for minor offenders; state governments handle longer-term, more serious offenders. Often, the two levels vie for operating funds, and each seeks to avoid responsibility for offenders under supervision by the other. With fragmented government correctional services, there is normally some overlap of services and programs.

Officials of the executive branch often complain that legislatures enact correctional codes and prescribe operational responsibilities without providing sufficient funds to carry them out. Both branches complain that court rulings set unfair constraints on the flexibility they feel they need to handle assigned offenders. In developing and implementing policies, correctional agents must consider not only the sociopolitical environment but also the government setting in which corrections functions.

The Complex and Competing Goals of Corrections

Every system has a set of goals that provides a rationale for its existence. The goals of corrections are by no means clear and absolute. Is the purpose of corrections to rehabilitate offenders? To punish them? To keep society safe from dangerous individuals? Different answers to these questions suggest important differences in policies and tactics. Yet, in practice, there is an uncoordinated attempt to satisfy all of these competing goals at once.

Goal ambiguity Ambiguity of goals is a constant problem for corrections. Which goals should be served? Conflict over goals occurs precisely because of the shifting forces that bear directly on corrections. Political ideology, for example, often colors the analysis and development of correctional policy. Liberals believe that corrections should follow one path; conservatives believe it should follow another. Because it is nearly impossible to separate correctional policy from political interests, correctional goals must often reflect various ideologies that do not always fit well together.

The organizational "turf" of criminal justice and other human service agencies is often unclear because there is a blurring around the edges as to who is responsible for what type of actions. Most probation offices are attached to the judiciary and paid for by county governments; are they then within the domain of corrections or of the judiciary? Should the sheriff be in charge of transporting offenders from jail to prison, or should the administrators of the prison to which the offenders are being transported? To what extent should social service agencies become involved with the needs of correctional clients in a halfway house? Is it the obligation of parole officers or the police to find offenders who have violated the conditions of their release?

Goal conflict The work of corrections requires that practices be developed that are acceptable to the general public so that they will receive support. The problem is that different people have quite different expectations in regard to correctional goals. Consequently, correctional leaders frequently find it necessary to offer conflicting (or at least divergent) justifications for a given policy in order to maintain a veneer of consensus for the organization. A program of private-industry employment for prison inmates, for instance, can be commended to liberals as reha-

bilitative training, to free enterprise advocates as expansion of the private sector's responsibility for government, and to conservatives as a get-tough policy designed to make prisoners pay the costs of their imprisonment. While this tactic helps to preserve support for the prison's industrial operations, it creates managerial problems for correctional leaders because the goals of treatment, profit, and punishment may well be in conflict when the program is actually put into practice.

This kind of goal conflict has often been noted in studies of parole officers. Research has shown that some officers seem to emphasize the goal of law enforcement; others give much more attention to the aims of social casework. Because of this conflict, little credence can be given to the general idea of "organizational goals" as applied to parole because, in fact, the goals as carried out in daily operations were determined by line staff, who themselves disagreed about the purpose of their work.

Since there is so much uncertainty about correctional goals and the extent to which they are supported by other governmental officials and the general public, correctional leaders enunciate clear and precise objectives at their own risk. Thus, goals tend to be framed in such vague general terms as "to protect the public" or "to rehabilitate offenders." The effects of this imprecision extend well beyond the realm of public relations; often, it is difficult for staff members to make goal-oriented choices because they are unsure of what the leaders want. Examine the Focus box, "Vermont's New Vision" (p. 20). How do the "new" goals set by Commissioner Gorczyk reflect the problems of restructuring an ongoing correctional system?

Because of conflicts over goals and rivalry for scarce resources, it may be in corrections' interest to employ alternative strategies. For example, programs may be designed and implemented, not as a means of advancing correctional goals (which are vague and conflicting), but as a way of preserving and advancing organizational needs—perhaps because of a perceived threat to the organization's domain from some other human service agency.

The Big Four in Corrections

California

Not only does California have the largest prison population in the United States, it has one of the highest rates of growth in number of prisoners. Much of this growth has been attributed to landmark "get tough" sentencing reform combined with a gradual increase in severity of sentencing by judges.

The California correctional system is decentralized. Adult institutional corrections is administered by the Adult Authority, which is a part of the state executive branch of government. Juvenile institutions are administered by the Youth Authority. Adult and juvenile probation services are county executive branch functions headed by a chief probation officer. A portion of the county probation costs is subsidized by the state, but these subsidies are not as large a part of the budget now as they once were.

In California, local taxes pay for jails and probation services, and predictably these services have been hit very hard by caps in tax revenues. Jails and probation compete with schools and hospitals for scarce funds. One result is that jails are filled to capacity and priority is given to sending prisoners to the state facilities, which are themselves overcrowded (but funded by a different tax base). Probation caseloads have also grown: for example, from 100 per officer a decade ago to over 300 per officer now in Los Angeles County. The California citizen seems to want to be tough on law violators but does not want to pay for it. The most pressing question in California, especially given the state's huge budget deficit, is how to reconcile these divergent themes.

Florida

The state of Florida is a newcomer to the correctional elite—an ominous sign given that the current age profile in Florida represents what the nation as a whole will be in the year 2010. If Florida is painting a picture of U.S corrections of the future, corrections will continue to be a growth industry.

The state administers all correctional services regionally, with regional directors having considerable autonomy. The five adult regional administrators report to the secretary of the Department of Corrections and manage all institutional and field services. Juvenile corrections is housed within the Department of Health and Rehabilitative Services and operates in eleven districts. Thus, Florida operates under a unified model under state control, with separate adult and juvenile functions.

In 1984, Florida enacted sentencing guidelines as a way of overcoming widespread sentencing disparity. Institutional admissions then shifted from a slow increase to a skyrocketing increase in numbers. Alarmed by this trend, Florida administrators started the Community Control Project, providing close supervision (often with electronic monitoring) to serve as a diversion for prison-bound offenders. The program is the largest diversion effort of its kind in the nation, taking in about 1,000 new offenders per month. But still the prison populations—and the rate of prison admissions—continue to climb.

New York

The corrections system in New York was for many decades a leader in innovation. The reformatory was a New York invention, as was modern parole. Adult institutional corrections is managed by the Department of Corrections; juvenile institutions and aftercare, by the Division of Youth Services. Probation is a county function; adult and juvenile services are combined under a single chief probation officer, who is accountable to the county chief executive. A coordinating function for probation is carried out by the State Division of Probation. Parole release and supervision are both administered by the Division of Parole. New York is a decentralized model with strong state coordination functions.

As is true for almost all other states in the United States, the New York correctional system is overcrowded. However, there is the added burden created by New York City corrections, which itself includes jails and prisons. New York City corrections populations are larger than the corrections system of many states and are also seriously overcrowded and strapped for funds. This creates pressures for the state operations, since many New York City prisoners are awaiting sentence to state facilities.

The burden of correctional population growth in New York in the latter half of the 1980s has been eased by fiscal prosperity during that same time period. There are signs, however, that the revenues are tightening up, and this provokes concern among the correctional leaders in New York. As it gets tougher to find dollars to provide correctional services, how will the state deal with the ever-growing numbers of prisoners, especially those from New York City, which is always under fiscal restraint?

Texas

Over 250,000 adult Texans are on probation, and more than 100,000 are in jail or prison or on parole. All adult corrections in Texas are housed under the Department of Criminal Justice, which is supervised by a nine-person board appointed by the governor. The Department administers corrections through three separate divisions: institutions, parole supervision, and probation. In addition, the parole board reports to the Board of Criminal Justice. The Institutional Division, in addition to managing all state custodial facilities, monitors the local jails. The Texas Youth Commission handles all juvenile institutions and aftercare.

Adult and juvenile probation are organized on a county basis and are run separately by chief probation officers locally appointed by the county judiciary. Standards for both probation functions are established and monitored by state authority. Adult probation is accountable to the Department of Criminal Justice; juvenile probation practices are monitored by the Juvenile Probation Commission. (There has been a recent effort to bring all juvenile corrections under the umbrella of the Department of Human Services.) Because there are over two hundred counties in Texas, the coordination work of these commissions is immense and often complicated.

Over the past decade, Texas corrections has operated under something of a siege mentality. As a result of a series of lawsuits, Texas prisons have a tightly established population cap, and this has been forcing the rest of the system to be more cautious in commitments to prison. The obvious decision-making fragmentation means that it is nearly impossible to develop a coordinated response to the prison overcrowding problem. Action finally occurred when a federal judge promised to fine the state over $500,000 a day if it failed to operate in compliance with court-ordered standards. An emergency legislative session was called, and all parts of the system were pressured to develop responses to control prison crowding.

One can imagine a department of corrections setting itself against a department of mental health in a contest for funds to set up a drug rehabilitation program; both departments may view the new resources as a way to expand. Such empire-building actions are often designed merely to keep a corrections department strong and viable.

This kind of tactic has led some observers to argue that corrections does not seek to achieve an overriding goal; rather, it seeks to maintain a balance among stated and unstated goals so that no particular goal is sacrificed. Thus, correctional workers cannot rely on a stable formation of work goals but must keep several objectives in mind. In this way, for instance, parole officers learn to provide services to their clients (one goal) while avoiding the appearance of putting the community at inordinate risk (a second goal).

The Implementation of Correctional Programs

"People work" is central to corrections since the raw material of the system consists of people— the staff and the offenders. *Staff* is the collective term that designates the probation officers, correctional officers, counselors, and others who have been assigned responsibility for the daily management and supervision of offenders.

The correctional staff includes both professional and nonprofessional employees. Psychologists, counselors, and administrators are among those staff members who are college educated, usually holders of at least one degree. They view themselves as members of a profession, with all of the rights that adhere to such callings. They believe that they should be able to carry out their work without supervision and that they are capable of making decisions without always consulting rulebooks or guidelines. These professional employees work closely with nonprofessional staff, such as jail or prison corrections officers. The formal education of the nonprofessional staff has frequently stopped at high school; they function under close, often military-

Corrections is "people work" in which uncertain technologies are applied by professionals and nonprofessionals to offenders. It is difficult to measure the impact of such uncertain technologies as counseling.

style supervision and are prepared to use physical force to enforce rules. The different perspectives of these two groups and the ways in which they communicate with one another have caused problems in some types of corrections organizations.

Uncertain technologies   A major difficulty facing corrections is that the way of effectively dealing with offenders is highly uncertain, since knowledge does not exist to support a belief in *one* approach. **Technology** refers to a method of applying scientific knowledge to practical purposes in a particular field. Unfortunately, the technologies of corrections are not at the level of sophistication and scientific confidence achieved by, for example, engineering.

Engineers have reasonably exact methods of design and measurement. By contrast, correctional organizations are expected to be able to make decisions about the classification of offenders, placing those needing treatment services into appropriate residential or outclient programs, and about the release of offenders from prison or community supervision. Although knowledge of human behavior has increased during the past century, there remains much uncertainty about the validity of the various approaches for treating offenders, such as group therapy, behavior modification, and anger management.

The fact that corrections is expected to implement programs of questionable value presents organizations with a serious problem: Not all prison releasees adjust successfully to free society; not all mental health referrals of offenders result in emotional adjustment; not all probationers prove trustworthy. Correctional decisions are prone to error. In fact, the technical problem facing corrections organizations may be characterized as selecting types of error for reduction rather than eliminating error altogether.

In the chapters that follow, the highly uncertain choices that must be made by corrections workers and managers will emerge as an important theme. How does the correctional official organize staff, choose programs, and manage offenders when the consequences of the actions taken are not at all clear? Given this element of uncertainty, organizational theorists say that the environment of corrections is unstable and that, as a result, one of management's major concerns is avoiding negative feedback from sources in the community, such as the courts, political leaders, and the public.

Because the effectiveness of correctional strategies in dealing with offenders is so uncertain, organizations often give greater emphasis to secondary technologies of which they are more confident—the design of a prison's security apparatus, a computer-based offender tracking system for probation, and so on. But the core work of corrections concerns the interactions of people—staff and offenders—about which there is much uncertainty to be managed.

Exchange One of the most important points that emerges when corrections is examined is the degree of interdependence that exists between staff and offenders. The correctional officer assigned to a prison or jail, unarmed, outnumbered, and with much to lose, has surprisingly little raw power with which to exact cooperative behavior. Likewise, a probation officer can do little with a client who resists the officer's influence. On the other side, the prisoner depends on the work of the correctional officer, while the parolee often experiences a sense of powerlessness in regard to the conditions of supervision. Thus, staff and offenders are part of an interdependent relationship; each depends on the other for the achievement of personal goals. The officer needs the cooperation of the offender to convince superiors that the officer is performing properly in the job; the offender needs the recommendation of the officer so that parole release will be granted.

The interdependence of correctional people makes the concept of **exchange** important to our understanding of their daily world. Exchange occurs when two parties engage in a trade of promises or concessions that have the effect of making each person's work easier or more predictable. A probationer, for example, cooperates by reporting regularly and attending an alcohol treatment program; in return, the officer is more likely to overlook incidental,

---

technology A method of applying scientific knowledge to practical purposes in a particular field.

exchange A mutual transfer of resources; hence, a balance of benefits and deficits that flow from behavior based on decisions as to the values and costs of alternatives.

Vermont's New Vision

The Vermont Department of Corrections is changing the way it does business. The "old" way of doing business is familiar to people in the corrections system: More people are sent to prison than the system's capacity allows, so a large number have to be released early to accommodate the influx of new cases. In fact, every Thursday, decisions have to be made about which offenders, taken from a list of those who are eligible, will be granted emergency furlough in order to stay within a certain limit of overcrowdedness.

Nobody likes this arrangement. Conservatives know that it reduces the certainty of punishment—sometimes, staying in prison can seem like losing the lottery. Professionals know that the old way is like a time bomb—with over four hundred "furlough" cases on the streets, there's bound to be a problem sooner or later. To make matters worse, every projection indicates the demand for prison space will continue to grow over the next several years, and Vermont cannot afford to build enough new prisons to stem the tide of overcrowding.

John Gorczyk, the new commissioner of corrections, believes it is time for a new vision of the corrections system in his state. He has begun the implementation of a "restructuring" project that aims to make the emergency furlough program obsolete within two years. The new approach has the following elements:

1. Expanded sentencing options. Currently, half of Vermont's sentenced offenders go to prison, half to probation. The goal is to devise a new array of intermediate sanctions that will change this pattern. By 1996, the plan is to shift into these programs up to one-half of the prison-bound offenders. The programs will be designed for offenders whose profile shows them to be low risk to the community and who have committed crimes of low seriousness.

2. Returned value to the community. Offenders sentenced to correctional terms will be expected to perform public work in Vermont's communities. Serious offenders who are sentenced to institutions will spend a portion of their sentence in "work camps," where they will labor in crews that work to improve public facilities. Less serious offenders will be sentenced to "reparative probation" terms of community service and restitution.

3. Reduced risk of re-offending. An array of proven treatment programs will be implemented for those offenders having problems that indicate a risk of new criminal behavior. These programs will be managed under a "supervised community sentence," and offenders will be assigned to programs that offer relapse prevention training, drug treatment, cognitive restructuring groups, and so forth. These programs are designed for offenders who are not serious enough to require imprisonment but represent too much of a risk for regular probation terms.

minor violations of the conditions of supervision. Each party's situation is made easier by the voluntary decisions of the other.

Because exchange relations between staff and offenders are very important, they often are subject to informal enforcement. A rowdy inmate is removed from his cell and placed in solitary until he "settles down" and recognizes the officials' authority. A juvenile on probation is arrested and "detained" (locked up) for the weekend while awaiting a hearing on her truancy from school, even though the officials have no intention of revoking her probationary status. Conversely, a guard whose tone and demeanor with inmates are hostile or condescending finds it takes much longer to return prisoners to their cells for the morning count or to quiet down a noisy group of prisoners. Subtle and not-so-subtle pressures unceasingly reinforce the need for the keepers and the kept to be aware of each other's needs.

Street-level bureaucrats Michael Lipsky has provided perhaps the most vivid portrait of the problems of the correctional worker. He coined the term **street-level bureaucrats** to refer to "public service workers who interact directly with citizens in the course of their jobs, [including] teachers, police officers and other law enforcement personnel, social workers, judges, public lawyers and other court officers, health workers and many other public employees who grant access to government programs and provide services within them."[7] Lipsky's provocative generalizations about street-level bureaucrats apply to virtually all those who have face-to-face contact with offenders. They work with inadequate resources—and ever-increasing demands. Frequently, officials face a situation in which they are theoretically obligated to provide higher-quality treatment for their clients than is

---

street-level bureaucrats Public service workers who interact directly with citizens in the course of their work, granting access to government programs and providing services within them.

possible given the high cost of such service. Street-level bureaucrats soon learn that "with any single client they probably could interact flexibly and responsibly. But if they did this with too many clients, their capacity to respond flexibly would disappear."[8] Probation officers may believe, for example, that they have an obligation to find jobs for their clients, but if they took the time necessary to do so, they would have no opportunity to provide other services. An officer may have a real desire to work hard for those probationers who have promise, though not for others. Officers faced with these conflicts may become alienated from their clients because they cannot satisfy their clients' needs.

Limited resources also create the necessity for administrators of service bureaucracies to monitor carefully the way workers apply their time and energies. Bureaucracies that process people develop a set of categories for working with their clients in an attempt to best use personal or agency resources and to succeed with some clients, even though they cannot succeed with all of them.[9]

After analyzing the several problems and constraints of government services, Lipsky concludes that there is a contradiction in the delivery of street-level policy through bureaucracy. The idea of service delivered by people to people suggests a model of human interaction, caring, and responsibility; the delivery of the service through a bureaucracy suggests a model of detachment and equal treatment for clients under conditions of limited resources. Conflicting and ambiguous goals combined with difficulties in measuring and evaluating work performance may reduce effectiveness and commitment to the work. Thus, the bureaucratic model guarantees that services are delivered only up to a point and that goals are not achieved.

Whether Lipsky's conclusion is pessimistic or simply realistic is difficult to say. Certainly, the tasks facing correctional workers and their clients are formidable. Workers must make daily decisions under conditions of technical uncertainty and sporadic negative feedback; offenders must comply with both the legal mandates concerning

Corrections has links with other criminal justice agencies. The police, sheriff, prosecutor, and judiciary all play roles with regard to correctional clients. What are some of the problems that develop out of these necessary links?

their behavior and the less explicit parameters established by the needs of the correctional organization. Yet there are positive benefits to bureaucratic worker–client relations. The need to structure the workers' use of time makes abuses of unfettered discretion less probable. Limited organizational resources force agencies to clarify their goals and to direct services toward persons who most seriously require staff time. Offenders are in a vulnerable position, given the extensive power of correctional agencies. Per-

haps the conditions found in bureaucracies are a check on the abuse of state power.

In sum, the transactions of corrections people almost uniformly involve some aspect of worker–client contact and interaction. This process must be managed through screening and processing routines, staff training and evaluation programs, and so forth. The clients of corrections agencies, unlike those of many other organizations, are both the input and the output of those agencies. Changes resulting from clients' contact with the organization are a product of their interactions with correctional workers. Because worker and offender depend on each other to achieve their goals, each person can influence evaluations made by the other.

The Interconnectedness of Corrections

In many respects, corrections can be viewed as a series of processes: sentencing, classification, supervision, programming, and revocation, to name but a few. Throughout, it is important to realize that the processes used in one part of the corrections system will affect in ways both large and small the processes of the rest of the system.

Examples of this principle of interconnectedness abound. When a local jail changes its classification policies for eligibility for work release, the caseload of probation will be affected. When a parole agency decides to improve its supervision practices by implementing new drug-screening practices, the increased rate of technical violators uncovered by the new policy will have an impact on the jails and prisons within the system. If presentence investigation report writers fail to verify their facts, poorly reasoned correctional assignments may result.

These processes affect one another because of the flow of offenders through the corrections process. The process is a type of assembly-line system with return loops. Once a criminal is set for sentencing, a selection process determines which offender goes where, and why. This sifting process is itself uncertain and often hard to understand. Most, but not all, violent offenders will be sent to prison. Most, but not all, violators of the rules of probation or parole will be given a second chance. Most, but not all, offenders who are caught committing crimes while under the supervision of correctional authorities will be slated for more severe punishment. Figure 1.4 provides examples of the interconnections of correctional agencies as they deal with offenders who have been given different sentences.

There are two points of interest here. First, offenders obviously are handled in a variety of ways. Who determines what happens to offenders and how they make this determination is a major consideration of this book. Second, and even more central, corrections not only gets its business from the courts, but it derives some of the business from itself. Policies and their routine practice determine how strictly the rules will be enforced, how dire the consequences will be when they are broken, and how much latitude staff will have in assigning offenders to programs.

Within the system of corrections there is a great deal of formal interconnection of policy. In most states, as many as one-fourth or more of all prison inmates are people sent there because they have violated a requirement of probation or parole. In other words, the enforcement policies of the supervision agencies determine a large portion of the caseload. Yet in most systems, the prison authorities have little basis for controlling policies concerning those who violate rules. Similarly, the caseload size of a probation officer is determined by the number of people placed on probation and the length of time those people are to be supervised. Even though there is a finite amount of time for supervision, officers normally have little or no control over the number of cases they are given for supervision. As offenders flow through the system—probation to revocation to prison to work release to parole—the work load of the system is created by one agency for the others.

The existence of informal interconnections creates an uneasy tension. It may make sense for agency directors to take whatever steps are necessary to protect their piece of the system from encroachment by the rest of the system. Accordingly, it is common for each corrections unit to insulate itself from the pressures faced by the other units, since the others are often the source of unwanted work load increases. Ironically, that very isolation makes it more likely that the other units will experience the problems that occur with lack of cooperation, and these problems will haunt all units when criticisms of all corrections are received.

Case 1: Two years probation, drug treatment, and fifty hours of community service.

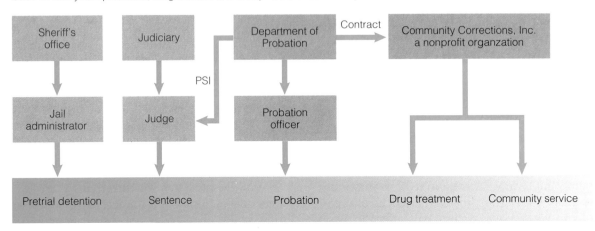

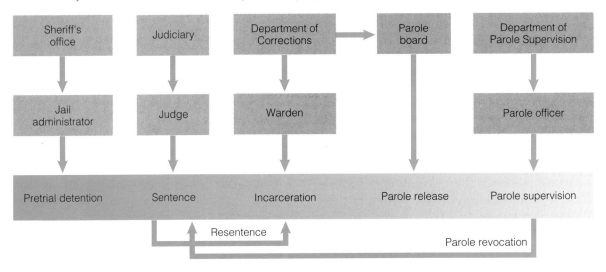

Case 2: Two years incarceration to be followed by community supervision on parole.

Figure 1.4 ■ Interconnectedness of Correctional Agencies in Implementing Sentences. Note the number and variety of agencies that deal with these two offenders. Would you expect these agencies to cooperate effectively with each other?

WORKPERSPECTIVE

Being a Director of Corrections in the 1990s

Chase Riveland

A corrections director today is faced with a fascinating array of challenges. Legislators, courts, inmates, citizens, correctional staff, and others all have enhanced interest as stakeholders in the administration of corrections agencies. The list of priorities includes siting of correctional facilities; designing and building of facilities (cheaper and quicker); containing health care costs; managing overcrowding; developing alternatives; addressing issues of gangs, AIDS, and staff safety and training; continuing to satisfy old court orders and consent decrees; avoiding new court orders and consent decrees; avoiding new court oversight due to burgeoning institution populations; enhancing security and programs, while facing a reduction in resources; and addressing a series of daily "mini priorities."

Ten to twenty years ago the corrections director who was a solid manager could survive quite well. Today corrections directors must spend large amounts of their time in the public policy arena. The political process a few years ago adopted the credo of "tough on crime." As sentencing policy became more politicized, we once again experienced overcrowded prisons and jails. The corrections director must enter the political arena, at a minimum, as a harbinger projecting the resources that will be required and preferably as one who can shape a course of sound public policy through the political process.

As correctional systems have grown sharply in size over the last few years, the ability of the system to keep pace with trained and experienced staff at all levels has also been a challenge. Although such an expanding environment does offer optimism in terms of upward mobility, the absence of solid experience and strong professional training is of major concern.

Technology creates dilemmas for correctional administrators. On one hand, the demands, both externally and internally, for a greater quality and quantity of information are desirable. Collaterally, maintaining the "human connection" in a business dealing with humans sometimes becomes more difficult when the demands and priorities of technology compete for available time.

Yet, corrections suffers from a lack of sufficient information. The field is devoid of strong research and, therefore, lacks new methodologies to use in either controlling or changing the behavior of its charges. Too frequently, we rely solely on aggregate numbers and summation of historical data, without strong inquiry into what works and what doesn't. Therefore, the correctional administrator is redundantly challenged to mimic or develop programs that are generally advertised as "cheaper" and inevitably hold some "political charm." Seldom do we have qualitative data with which to support or reject such challenges. In recent years boot camps, intensive supervision, day fines, community service, work release, and several other programs have hit jurisdiction after jurisdiction, proposed as less expensive solutions to corrections problems. Only recently have legitimate research efforts trailed the development of many programs.

The correctional administrator of today must also deal with the political heritage left by Willie Horton. On any given day, the probation, parole, or work release case that reoffends in a highly visible manner may well completely change the public and political winds in a juris-

. . .

Continued

WORKPERSPECTIVE, *Continued*

diction. An escape from an institution, a failure to "properly supervise" a serious reoffender, or difficulty in siting new facilities may also lead to the same end. Governors, legislators, and other officials have all learned the political lesson of Willie Horton. Few around the country have been willing to challenge the perceived public feeling that "tough on crime" is an essential political cornerstone. Therefore, the correctional administrator remains caught between the pragmatic knowledge that many persons in our prisons can safely be dealt with elsewhere and the requirement to remain politically consistent and loyal to an administration's desires.

. . .

Being a correctional administrator today is exciting. The field is being challenged at the federal, state, and local levels. Federal courts continue their vigilance, and the combined pressure of mandated massive growth and a tight economy provides challenges to management techniques and opportunities for leader-

ship. The political fear of the offender and the costs of incarcerating him or her are creating an environment where a return to "a balanced system" appears achievable. The ravages of the "drug scene," resulting in a large new class of offenders with attendant gang, health, and economic competition problems, have challenged us to consider new means of safety and behavior for field staff and an addition of new technologies to our prison security systems....

. . .

Being a correctional administrator in the 1990s will fulfill the "challenge needs" of anyone so inclined. Leadership, management, and political skills will be requisite to holding systems together, weathering the economy, and hopefully evolving into more rational, balanced, and professional correctional systems.

Chase Riveland is secretary (commissioner), Washington Department of Corrections.

Source: Chase Riveland, "Being a Director of Corrections in the 1990s," *Federal Probation,* June 1990, pp. 10–11. Reprinted by permission.

What Makes Corrections Tick?

All of these problems combine to make the field of corrections controversial and therefore engrossing for those who study it. Yet as fascinating as these problems may be, they are but a sidelight to the central reason for the appeal of field of corrections. The questions that corrections raises concerning social control are fundamental to defining our society and its values. Seemingly every aspect of the field raises questions that concern deeply held values about social relations. A few examples suffice:

■ What kinds of free services and treatment facilities are to be provided to inmates infected with AIDS?

■ Should we be more concerned with punishing offenders for their crimes or with providing programs to help them overcome the problems in their lives that contribute to crime?

■ Is placing surveillance devices in people's homes a good idea or an invasion of privacy?

The questions of interest to researchers, students, and citizens hardly end with these, yet these questions are illustrative. Crucial public and private controversies abide at every turn.

We cannot answer the questions inherent in these controversies without reference to our values and those of our society.

People who undertake careers in corrections often do so because they find the field a captivating place to express their most cherished values. Probation and parole officers frequently report that their original desire to work in these jobs came from a sense of the importance of helping people. Correctional officers often say that the aspect of their work they like best is "working with people who are in trouble and want to improve their lives." Administrators report that they value the challenge of building effective policies and helping staff to become better at their jobs. All of these individuals are saying that the field of corrections helps them to be fully involved with the key questions of public service and social life. Corrections is interesting to them in part because it deals with a core conflict of values in our society—freedom and social control—and it does so in ways that require people to work together.

Summary

Corrections is composed of a great number of programs, services, facilities, and organizations responsible for the management of people who have been accused or convicted of criminal offenses. It is complex because it encompasses broad responsibilities concerned with the formal, legal responses of society to those of its members who engage in prohibited behavior.

We use the concept of the correctional system to provide a framework or comprehensive theme for our study. The correctional system is a composite of large and small organizations administered by various levels of government. The staff of these organizations are put in contact with one another and in direct authority over offenders. In these actions, these employees must strive to achieve the organizations' complex goals.

Correctional workers, like others in the human service field, are street-level bureaucrats. They interact with citizens and are in a position to grant access to government programs and to furnish services within those programs. Correctional officials are theoretically obligated to provide their clients with services of higher quality than is possible in practice because the costs of such services are politically out of the question. Officials are therefore unable to maintain the standards set for the service of their clients and must devise strategies to work within the limited resources available to them. The problem is exacerbated by the fact that the techniques used in the system are of uncertain value and, further, offenders have not voluntarily sought the services. Despite these problems, corrections holds interest because it is concerned with fundamental societal values.

For Discussion

1. What do you see as some of the advantages and disadvantages of the system concept?

2. Corrections is a system in which technologies of uncertain validity are used. What are some of the dangers of using these technologies? Are there safeguards that should be applied?

3. Assume that the legislature has stipulated that rehabilitation should be the goal of corrections in your state. Why may this goal be displaced by persons working in the system?

4. What does Lipsky mean by the term *street-level bureaucrat?* Give some examples of how street-level bureaucrats act.

5. As the commissioner of corrections for your state, which correctional activities might come within your domain? Which might not?

For Further Reading

Cole, George F. *The American System of Criminal Justice.* 6th ed. Pacific Grove, Calif.: Brooks/Cole, 1992. Provides an introduction to the American system of criminal justice.

DiIulio, John J., Jr. *No Escape: The Future of American Corrections.* New York: Basic Books, 1991. States that we should adopt neither a conservative nor a liberal approach to correctional policy but should learn to listen to those who work on the front lines.

Garland, David. *Punishment and Modern Society.* Chicago: University of Chicago Press, 1990. Argues that the social meaning of punishment is badly understood and that we need to discover ways to punish that are more in keeping with our social ideals.

Goldfarb, Ronald L., and Singer, Linda R. *After Conviction.* New York: Simon & Schuster, 1973. One of the first works to really describe the processes of corrections. Still a useful source.

Walker, Samuel. *Sense and Nonsense about Crime: A Policy Guide.* 2nd ed. Pacific Grove, Calif.: Brooks/Cole, 1989. An examination of those crime control practices that don't work (the "nonsense") and those that appear to have some potential for success (the "sense").

Notes

1. U.S. Department of Justice, Bureau of Justice Statistics, *National Update,* (Washington, D.C.: Government Printing Office, January 1992), p. 4; U.S. Department of Justice, Bureau of Justice Statistics, *Sourcebook of Criminal Justice Statistics, 1990* (Washington, D.C.: Government Printing Office, 1991), p. 19.

2. U.S. Department of Justice, *Bulletin* (Washington, D.C.: Government Printing Office, September 1992), p. 4.

3. Ibid., p. 6.

4. Andrew von Hirsch, *Past or Future Crimes* (New Brunswick, N.J.: Rutgers University Press, 1985).

5. U.S. Department of Justice, Bureau of Justice Statistics, *Bulletin* (Washington, D.C.: Government Printing Office, November 1991), p. 3; U.S. Department of Justice, Bureau of Justice Statistics, *Bulletin* (Washington, D.C.: Government Printing Office, May 1992), p. 6.

6. See Thomas S. Kuhn, *The Structure of Scientific Revolutions* (Chicago: University of Chicago Press, 1970).

7. Michael Lipsky, *Street-Level Bureaucracy* (New York: Russell Sage Foundation, 1980), p. 3.

8. Ibid., pp. 37–38, 81, 99.

9. Ibid., p. 107.

The Early History of Correctional Thought and Practice

2

The sight of whippings, thumb cuttings, and hangings is not part of the experience of the average inhabitant of the Western world.

Pieter Spierenburg

The Development of Corrections
**From the Middle Ages to the American
    Revolution**
Galley Slavery
Imprisonment
Transportation
Corporal Punishment and Death
On the Eve of Reform
The Age of Reason and Correctional Reform
Beccaria and the Classical School
Bentham and the "Hedonic Calculus"
John Howard: Father of the Penitentiary
Summary

A hush came over the French court-room as the chief judge rose to read the sentence to be imposed on Robert-François Damiens, convicted of unsuccessfully attempting to kill King Louis XV:

> He is to be taken and conveyed in a cart, wearing nothing but a shift, holding a torch of burning wax weighing two pounds; in the said cart to the Place de Greve, where on a scaffold that will be erected there, the flesh will be torn from his breasts, arms, thighs and calves with red-hot pinchers, his right hand, holding the knife with which he committed the said parricide, burnt with sulphur, and, on those places where the flesh will be torn away, poured molten lead, boiling oil, burning resin, wax and sulphur melted together and then his body drawn and quartered by four horses and his limbs and body consumed by fire, reduced to ashes and his ashes thrown to the winds.[1]

Newspaper accounts recorded that Damien's death was even more horrible than the sentence required. Since the horses were not able to pull him limb from limb, the executioners came to their assistance by hacking Damien's arms and legs. All of this occurred while the man was still alive.

What was the point of this punishment? What did the state hope to achieve through this atrocity? Why does this execution seem so horrible to us today? After all, public corporal punishment was normal for thousands of years, and it was pursued with gusto. In the twentieth century, however, public spectacle has been replaced by punishments carried out within the confines of prisons or in the community under the supervision of a correctional staff that sees itself not as instruments of suffering but as technicians of reform, managers, and social workers.

Until the nineteenth century, throughout Europe and even America, punishments were public occasions and street spectacles. Crowds taunted the condemned as the executioner or sheriff conducted whippings, burnings, pillory-ings, and hangings on orders of the king or court. Punishment-as-spectacle was used to control crime and to exhibit the sovereign's power. Yet only a few decades after Damien's 1757 execution, a major change had taken place in Europe and the United States. Efforts were made to devise a rational and reformative model of the penal sanction focused on the mind and soul, not the body. With the rise of the penitentiary as the place where offenders could reflect on their misdeeds, repent, and prepare for life as crime-free citizens, torture as a public spectacle disappeared.

In this chapter we will examine the European antecedents of American correctional thought and practice. In Chapter 3 we will continue this historical coverage by looking at corrections in the United States from colonial times to the present. In these chapters we will present the broad trends. In other portions of the book we will discuss the history of such specific correctional practices as prison industry, probation, and parole in greater detail.

The Development of Corrections

How did American corrections come to where it is today? Why are offenders now incarcerated or placed on probation rather than whipped or branded? The current system did not just spring up full-blown; instead, the goals and practices of corrections have undergone marked shifts over time.

Like other social institutions, corrections is affected by concerns of the larger community. In fact, it is often said that a society can be measured by the way it treats those at the bottom. Thus, it is not surprising that during the idealism of the postrevolutionary period, for example, Americans strongly believed that crime could be eliminated from this rich new land if offenders were isolated from bad influences and encouraged to repent. Neither is it

During the Middle Ages various punishments were imposed upon the body of the offender. These punishments were harsh and were used extensively.

surprising that twentieth-century penology veered sharply toward a psychological orientation to offender behavior, since the rise of the behavioral sciences lent credence to the belief that offenders could be rehabilitated. Likewise, with crime rising in the late 1960s, public opinion demanded another shift in correctional policy with greater emphasis on crime control.

Why do the hopes of one period, the thought that one method is *the* answer to the crime problem, seem to turn into the dismay of another? Let us examine correctional practices of earlier times before we explore their role in America.

From the Middle Ages to the American Revolution

lthough scholars point to the Hammurabic Code, developed by the king of Babylon in 1750 B.C., as the first

comprehensive statement of prohibited behavior, it is not until the beginning of the European Middle Ages, in the thirteenth century, that forms of legal sanctions appeared that are familiar to us. Response to crime was initially looked on as a private affair; wrongs were avenged in accordance with the *lex talionis,* or law of retaliation. This principle underlay the laws of the Anglo-Saxon societies until the time of the Norman Conquest in 1066. Vengeance was a duty that was expected to be carried out by the person wronged or by a family member. In England by the year 1200, a system of *wergild,* or payment of money as compensation for a wrong, was developed as a way of reducing the frequency of violent blood feuds. During this period the view that offenses were personal matters to be settled by individuals gradually gave way to the view that the peace of society required the public to participate in determining guilt or innocence and in exacting a penalty.

The church, as the dominant institution of the Middle Ages, maintained its own system of ecclesiastical punishments, which had a great impact on society as a whole. Especially during the Inquisition of the fourteenth and fifteenth centuries, the church zealously punished those who violated its laws. At the same time, it gave refuge from secular prosecution to those who could claim **benefit of clergy.** In time, benefit of clergy was extended to all literate persons, and its tie to the ecclesiastical courts lessened.

lex talionis   Law of retaliation; the principle that punishment should correspond in degree and kind to the offense, as in "an eye for an eye, a tooth for a tooth."

wergild   "Man money"; money paid to relatives of a murdered person or to the victim of a crime to compensate them and to prevent a blood feud.

benefit of clergy   The right to be tried in an ecclesiastical court, where punishments were less severe than those meted out by civil courts, given the religious focus on penance and salvation.

During the Middle Ages the **secular law** of England and the Continent was organized according to the feudal system of the times. In the absence of a strong central government, crimes among neighbors took on the character of war: The public peace was endangered as one feudal lord attempted to avenge the transgression of another. The main emphasis of criminal law was thus on public order among people of equal status and wealth. Georg Rüsche and Otto Kirchheimer describe the procedure:

> If, in the heat of the moment, or in a state of intoxication, someone committed an offense against decency, accepted morality, or religion, or severely injured or killed his neighbor … a solemn gathering of free men would be held to pronounce judgment and make the culprit pay *Wergild* or do penance so that the vengeance of the injured parties should not develop into blood feud and anarchy.[2]

Given the parties involved, the main criminal punishments during this period were penance and the payment of fines or restitution. Lower-class offenders without money received physical punishment at the hands of their masters.

During the later Middle Ages, especially during the fifteenth and sixteenth centuries, governmental authority was extended and the criminal law system more fully developed. With the rise of trade, the breakdown of the feudal order, and the emergence of a middle class, other punishments appropriate to the existing conditions were developed. In addition to fines, five punishments were common in Europe prior to the nineteenth century: galley slavery, imprisonment, transportation, corporal punishment, and death. As we will discuss, each of these punishments had a specific purpose, and the development of each was linked to ongoing forces in the society. It is important to recognize that at the time, with no police force or other centralized instruments of order, deterrence was the dominant purpose of the criminal sanction. Thus, before the nineteenth century it was believed that one of the best ways to keep order was to torture the convicted person in public so that the entire population might see what lay in store for lawbreakers.

Galley Slavery

Although **galley slavery**, the practice by which men were forced to power ships by rowing, is often associated with ancient Rome or Greece, the practice was not formally abolished throughout Europe until the latter part of the eighteenth century. It had, however, begun to wane by the sixteenth century, with the advent of heavy sailing ships. Originally the exclusive function of slaves or men captured in battle, galley slavery came to be the lot of some convicts, often as a reprieve from the gallows. According to a proclamation of Queen Elizabeth I in 1602, the galleys were considered more merciful than ordinary civil punishments, even though the oarsmen might be chained in bondage for life.[3]

Imprisonment

Until the nineteenth century, jails were used primarily for the detention of people awaiting trial. It is true that some sentenced political criminals and lower-class persons who could not pay their fines or debts were also imprisoned, but these groups represented a small proportion of all those under penal sanction.

The conditions were appalling. Men, women, and children, healthy and sick, were all mixed together; the strong preyed on the weak, sanitation was nonexistent, and disease was epidemic. Further, the authorities made no provision for the inmates' upkeep. Often the warden

---

secular law   The law of the civil society, as distinguished from church law.

galley slavery   Forced rowing of large ships, called galleys.

Bridewell houses were workhouses built throughout England for the employment and housing of offenders. Here prisoners work at the treadwheel while others exercise in the yard of the vagrants' prison.

viewed his job as a business proposition; he sold food and accommodations to his charges. The poor thus had to rely for survival on alms given by charitable persons and religious groups.

Attempts to reform prisons began in various European countries in the sixteenth century. With the disintegration of feudalism, political power became more centralized and economies began to shift from agriculture to the production of goods. Without links to the feudal landlords, the rural poor wandered about the countryside or drifted to the cities. The emphasis of the Protestant Reformation on the duty to labor and the sinfulness of sloth stirred English reformers to urge that some means be found to provide work for the idle poor. It was out of these concerns that the house of correction was born.

In 1553 London's Bishop Nicholas Ridley persuaded Edward VI to donate Bridewell Palace as the first house of correction. The inmates, primarily prostitutes, beggars, minor criminals, and the idle poor, were to be disciplined and set to work. Given the nature of its population, the house of correction combined the major elements of a workhouse, poorhouse, and penal institution. In 1576 Elizabeth I promulgated a law providing for the estab-lishment of a similar institution in every county. By providing employment for people who were not contributing to the economy through socially useful work, these institutions were expected to instill the habits of industry and prepare the inmates to be productive upon their release. The products made in the house of correction were to be sold on the market, so that it would be self-sufficient and not need government subsidy.[4]

Institutions similar to the English house of correction appeared in Holland, France, Germany, and Italy. Visiting these places in 1775, the English reformer John Howard was impressed by their cleanliness, discipline, and emphasis on rehabilitation through Bible reading and regularity of habits. A motto carved over the doorway to one institution offered Howard a succinct definition of the authority of the law with regard to the inmates: "My hand is severe but my intention benevolent." This motto was to influence the development of the penitentiary.

Of the European institutions, the Milan House of Correction, built in 1755, and a similar institution in Ghent, the Maison de Force, built in 1772, attracted attention, the latter because of its design. It was an octagonal building surrounding a central octagonal yard. Eight long pavilions radiated from the center, allowing for the separation of inmates by the seriousness of crime, sex, or status as a member of the noncriminal poor. The prisoners worked in common areas during the day and were segregated at night.

Conditions in England's houses of correction deteriorated as the houses assumed increased responsibility for the incarceration of criminals and less for the poor, orphans, and the sick. In the eighteenth century, the labor power provided by the inmates was no longer economically profitable and the reformative aim of the institution vanished. But, as we'll see, elements of the houses of correction were later incorporated in the penitentiary and the industrial prison of the nineteenth century.

Transportation

From ancient times people who have disobeyed the rules have been cast out, or banished, from the community. This practice was maintained in Europe until the Middle Ages. With the breakdown of feudalism and the worsening of economic conditions in the seventeenth century, prisons and houses of correction in England and Europe became filled. The New World caught the overflow. It was now possible to send offenders to places from which there was little or no possibility that they would return.

Initially **transportation** was chosen by English prisoners in place of the gallows or the whipping post. The Vagrancy Act of 1597, however, prescribed transportation for the first time. By 1606, with the settlement of Virginia, the transportation of convicts to North America became economically important for the colonial companies for whom they labored for the remainder of their terms. It also helped relive the overcrowded prisons of England.

After England lost America through revolution, it began to use abandoned ships as a "temporary" solution to house offenders. The settling of Australia helped put an end to the use of hulks. More recently, New York City used a decommissioned U.S. Navy ship as a temporary solution to their crowding problem during the 1980s.

Transportation seemed such a successful policy that in 1717 a statute was passed allowing convicts to be given over to private contractors, who then shipped them to the colonies and sold their services. Any prisoners who returned to England before their terms expired were to be executed. Transportation was the standard sanction during this period for about 90 percent of convicted felons. It is estimated that from 1596 to 1776 up to two thousand convicts a year were shipped to the American colonies.[5]

With the onset of the American Revolution, transportation from England came to a halt. By this time, questions had been raised about the policy. Some critics argued that it was not just to send convicts to live in a country where their lives would be easier than at home. But perhaps more important, by the beginning of the eighteenth century American planters had discovered that African slaves

---

transportation   The practice of removing offenders from the community to another region or land, often a penal colony.

WORKPERSPECTIVE

A Historian Looks at Corrections

John A. Conley

For any topic of study, the historian's job is to do more than record past events or tell a story about great people and great moments of history. The historian seeks to learn about the past in order to explain why things happened the way they did. Through the analysis of original documents and data from the period under study, the historian attempts to determine the underlying causes of patterns, trends, and changes in society. By describing and analyzing the past, historians provide us with a long-term perspective that allows us to understand the complexities of current social issues. For example, in spite of the current alarm about crime levels generated by the news media and political leaders, historians remind us that levels of disorder were higher in the past and that the concept of crime is elastic, shrinking and expanding as society defines and redefines order at different times throughout history. In this case, the historian is interested in what social forces influenced those changes and why.

The chapters on the history of corrections in this book give you a broad overview of the story of corrections and summarize some of the issues that are of interest to historians. I will not retell the history of punishment here, but I will try to illustrate what the historian attempts to accomplish. For a long time, criminologists thought that punishment was barbaric in premodern societies that relied on torture. Over time, punishment changed to a rational system of fines and imprisonment as societies matured in the modern era, culminating in the rehabilitative model of the twentieth century known as "corrections." This development from torture to corrections suggests that we have progressed in a linear way from bad to better, from cruel to humanitarian. But historians ask, if this is progress, why are prisons so destructive, why has rehabilitation apparently failed, what can we learn from the past, and how can that knowledge influence options available to us today?

To answer these questions, historians focus on the social factors that influence change. Through historical research we have learned that there is no single historical era where one form of punishment was used exclusively. As far back as ancient times in Greece and Rome, through the medieval period and up to the present, individuals, the state, and the church used a wide variety of punishments to maintain order, to control people, to influence behavior, and to serve powerful interests. Historians have learned that although certain forms of punishment became primary tools of social control during different periods, such as corporal punishment during the medieval period, fines in the later medieval period, and imprisonment in the eighteenth century, there was no single form of punishment. Punishments varied from community to community depending on such factors as religious philosophy, economic needs, class relationships, and level of state development. Historians have learned that most of these shifts in punishment methods reflect long-term changes in the larger society and that the relationship between punishment and social change is much more complex than simply associating punishment modes to crime levels.

For example, the rapidly growing population of vagrants and beggars caused by the decay of the feudal economy in sixteenth-

Continued

WORKPERSPECTIVE, *Continued*

century Europe brought about a reliance on houses of corrections in the belief that, by instilling discipline and good work habits, these people would become productive workers. In the late nineteenth century in the United States, the Eastern states built large prisons to discipline the marginal population of immigrants and the "dangerous classes." Southern states relied on a lease system that allowed convicts to work for private contractors, which relieved the states from building prisons. The Western states developed a combined model of large prisons and private contracts to serve their frontier needs. In each of these regions, complex and differing economic, political, and social forces shaped the development of prisons and the region's particular response to punishment.

So what perspective does the historian provide on punishment and corrections as we approach the twenty-first century? The first is that we should be cautious as we embrace and implement any change in current penal philosophy because it is shaped by complex societal pressures that have little relationship to crime control strategies. Second, we should acknowledge that shifting forms of corrections are the norm as society changes and that whatever replaces the current approach more than likely has been tried in the past. Finally, we should continue to seek an understanding of the past because that knowledge will contribute to a better understanding of where our society may be heading as it responds to social change in the twenty-first century.

John A. Conley is professor and chair of the Department of Criminal Justice at Buffalo State College, Buffalo, New York. This Workperspective was written especially for this book.

were better workers and economically more viable than English convicts. The importation of black slaves increased dramatically, the prisons of England again became overcrowded, and large numbers of convicts were assigned to live in **hulks** (abandoned ships) along the banks of the Thames.

Transportation began again in 1787 to different locales. In the next eighty years, 160,000 prisoners were transported from Great Britain and Ireland to New South Wales and other parts of Australia. As discussed by historian Robert Hughes in *The Fatal Shore*, "Every convict faced the same social prospects. He or she served the Crown or, on the Crown's behalf, some private person, for a given span of years. Then came a pardon or a ticket-of-leave, either of which permitted him to sell his labor freely and choose his place of work."[6]

But in 1837 a select committee of Parliament studied transportation and reported that, far from reforming criminals, it created thoroughly depraved societies. Critics of transportation argued that the Crown was forcing Englishmen to be "slaves until they were judged fit to become peasants."[7] The committee recommended that transportation be abolished and that a penitentiary system with confinement and hard labor be substituted. This recommendation was only partially adopted; it was not until 1868 that all transportation from England ceased.[8]

hulks Abandoned ships converted by the English to hold convicts during a period of prison crowding between 1776 and 1790.

Corporal Punishment and Death

Although capital punishment and **corporal punishment** have been used throughout history, the sixteenth through the eighteenth centuries in Great Britain and Europe were particularly brutal in these respects. Punishments were carried out in the market square for all to see and were thus considered useful instruments of deterrence. The punishments themselves were harsh: Whipping, mutilation, and branding were used extensively, and death became the common sentence for a host of felonies. It is recorded that 72,000 people were hanged during the reign of Henry VIII (1509–1547), and that during the Elizabethan period (1558–1603) vagabonds were strung up in rows of 300–400 at a time.[9] Today's equivalent would be 15,000–23,000 Americans strung up at once. Those criminals who were not hanged were subjected to various forms of mutilation so that they could be publicly identified. Removing of a hand or finger, slitting the nostrils, severing an ear, or branding usually made it impossible for the marked individual to find honest employment.

We need not wallow in descriptions of the excesses of the period; almost every imaginable torture was used in the name of retribution, deterrence, the sovereignty of the authorities, and the public good. Further, the mob of spectators often added its own punishment, throwing rocks or other objects at the offender.

The reasons for the rise in the severity of punishments during this period are unclear but are thought to reflect the expansion of criminal law, the enhanced power of secular authorities, an increase in crime (especially during the eighteenth century), and changes in the economic system. It is known, for example, that the number of crimes for which the English authorized the death penalty swelled from 50

---

corporal punishment Punishment inflicted on the body of the offender with whips or other devices that cause pain.

---

in 1688 to 160 in 1765, and reached 225 by 1800. Some of the new statutes made capital crimes of offenses that had previously been treated more lightly; other laws made certain activities criminal for the first time. But the criminal law, popularly known as the "Bloody Code," was less rigid than it seemed; it allowed for judicial discretion and lesser punishments were often given.[10]

London and other cities doubled in population from 1600 to 1700, while the entire population of England and Wales rose by only 25 percent. As might be expected, the incidence of crime in the cities ballooned. It has been estimated that in London, for example, from 1805 to 1833 there was a 540 percent increase in the number of convictions.[11] The crime wave was undoubtedly related to the desperate poverty and the overwhelming increase in the city's population. The rise in the number of prosecutions and convictions may also have represented a response by government and the elite to the threat posed to public order by the suddenly outsized working-class population. As Rüsche and Kirchheimer have argued, the rise of capitalism led to economic, rather than penal, considerations as the basis for punishment.[12]

On the Eve of Reform

We can arbitrarily designate 1770 as the eve of a crucial period of correctional reform on both sides of the North Atlantic. As we have noted, corrections in the Middle Ages consisted of the extensive imposition of fines; as time passed, fines were supplemented by corporal punishment, confinement in houses of correction, and transportation. Economic and social factors, particularly with regard to labor, had a bearing on the nature of the penal sanction. Altered political relationships, the roles of the church, and the organization of secular authority helped to restructure the allocation of punishment. It is of special interest that in the middle of the eighteenth century, England was inflicting capital and corporal punishment extensively, transporting large numbers of subjects overseas, and facing the problem of overcrowded prisons; yet crime continued its upward curve. England, the most advanced and powerful country in the world, was ready for correctional reform. The revolutionaries in the American colonies, with their liberal ideas about the relationship between citizen and government and their belief in human perfectibility, also set the stage for a shift in penal policies.

The Age of Reason and Correctional Reform

During the eighteenth century, scholars and social activists, particularly in England and France, engaged in an almost complete rethinking of the nature of society. In this period, known as **the Enlightenment**, or **the Age of Reason,** traditional assumptions were challenged; the individual, limitations of government, and rationalism were emphasized. Revolutions took place in America and France, advances were made in science, and the Industrial Revolution came into full swing. It was truly a remarkable period.

Until the eighteenth century, life in Europe had been generally static and closed; individuals had their place in a hierarchy of fixed social relationships. The Enlightenment may be viewed as a liberal reaction against this feudal and monarchical tradition. The Reformation had already ended the monopoly of religion held by the Catholic church, and the writings of such Protestant thinkers as Martin Luther and John Calvin encouraged a new emphasis

the Enlightenment or the Age of Reason   During the eighteenth century in England and France, concepts of liberalism, rationality, equality, and individualism dominated social and political thinking.

on individualism and the social contract between government and the governed. The triumph of William of Orange in the Glorious Revolution of 1688 brought increased power to the English Parliament, and the institutions of representative government were strengthened. The publication in 1690 of John Locke's two treatises on government further developed the ideas of a liberal society, as did the writings of the French thinkers Montesquieu and Voltaire.

Finally, advances in scientific thinking led to a questioning attitude that emphasized observation, experimentation, and technological development. Sir Isaac Newton argued that the world could be known and reduced to a set of rules. The revolution in science had a direct impact on social and political thought because it encouraged the questioning of established institutions, the belief that the use of reason could remake society, and the idea that progress would ultimately bring about a just community.

What impact did these political and social thinkers of the Enlightenment have on corrections? As we have emphasized, ideas about crime and justice are part of larger philosophical and scientific movements. Because of the ideas that gained currency in the eighteenth century, people in England, in America, and on the Continent began to think about such matters as the procedures to be used to determine guilt, the limits on a government's power to punish, the nature of criminal behavior, and the best ways to correct offenders. Enlightenment thought had a direct impact on views of the way the criminal law should be administered and on the goals and practices of corrections. It was during this period that the classical school of criminology emerged, with its insistence on a rational link between the gravity of the crime and the severity of the punishment. The social contract and utilitarian philosophers emphasized limitations on the power of government and the need to erect a system of graduated criminal penalties so that people would be deterred from crime. Further, political liberals and religious groups encouraged great reform of the prison system.

BIOGRAPHY

Cesare Beccaria (1738–1794)

Born into an aristocratic family in Milan, Cesare Bonesana, marquis of Beccaria, graduated from the University of Pavia in 1758. Publication in 1764 of Beccaria's book *Essay on Crimes and Punishments* ignited an interest in the reform of criminal justice throughout Europe. He listed the essential principles that should guide reform of the

criminal justice system. Beccaria was the first to integrate these aims into a consistent penological system. It was from this focus that the classical school of criminology emerged. After publication of the book, Beccaria's interest in criminal justice seems to have waned. His only other scholarly work was a series of lectures on political economy that were collected and published in 1804.

During this period of correctional reform, a major shift took place with regard to penal thought and practice. Penal codes were rewritten to emphasize the adaptation of punishment to the offender. There was a move away from the infliction of pain on the body of the offender to correctional practices that would set the individual on a path of honesty and right living. Finally, there was the development of the penitentiary, an institution in which criminals could be isolated from the temptations of society, reflect on their offenses, and thus be reformed.

Of the many persons who actively promoted the reform of corrections, three stand out: Cesare Beccaria (1738–1794), the founder of what is now called the classical school of criminological thought; Jeremy Bentham (1748–1832), a leader of reform in England and the developer of a utilitarian approach to crime and punishment; and John Howard (1726–1790), sheriff of Bedfordshire, England, whose book *The State of the Prisons in England and Wales* (1777) served to bring about changes that resulted in the development of the penitentiary.

Beccaria and the Classical School

The rationalist philosophy of the Enlightenment, with its emphasis on individual rights, was applied to the practices of criminal justice by Cesare Beccaria in his book *Essays on Crimes and Punishments*, published in 1764. He argued that the true aim and only justification for punishment is utility: the safety it affords society by preventing crime. Beccaria was particularly concerned that there seemed to be little rational link between the gravity of a crime and the severity of punishment. Six principles underlie the reforms Beccaria advocated; it is from these principles that the classical school of criminology emerged:

1. The basis of all social action must be the utilitarian concept of the greatest happiness for the greatest number.

2. Crime must be considered an injury to society, and the only rational measure of crime is the extent of the injury.

3. Prevention of crime is more important

BIOGRAPHY

Jeremy Bentham (1748–1832)

Born in London, Jeremy Bentham was the foremost writer on jurisprudence and criminology of his time. He earned a master's degree in law at Oxford and was admitted to the bar in 1767 but spent little time in the practice of law.

Instead, he soon became well known for pursuit of his three major interests: politics, jurisprudence, and criminology.

Wishing to depart from the social-control jurisprudence of his day, Bentham substi-

tuted a new theory termed *utilitarianism*. He applied these principles to prison management and discipline. His *Introduction to the Principles of Morals and Legislation* (1789) contains the basis for many reforms in the treatment of prisoners, including reform of their morals, preservation of their health, and the provision of education so that society would be relieved of their burden. His design for a penitentiary, called a panopticon, never became a reality in England, although two prisons based on his design were later constructed in the United States.

than punishment for crimes. In preventing crime, it is necessary to improve and publish the laws so that the nation can understand and support them.

4. Secret accusations and torture should be abolished. There should be speedy trials. The accused should be treated humanely before trial and must have every right to bring forward evidence in his or her behalf.

5. The purpose of punishment is to deter persons from crime, not social revenge. Certainty and swiftness in punishment rather than severity best secure this result.

6. Imprisonment should be more widely employed, but better physical quarters and classification of prisoners by age, sex, and degree of criminality should be provided.

In his conclusion, Beccaria summarized the thinking of those who wanted to rational-

ize the law: "In order for punishment not to be, in every instance, an act of violence of one or many against a private citizen, it must be essentially public, prompt, necessary, the least possible in the given circumstances, proportionate to the crime, dictated by laws."[13]

Beccaria's ideas took hold especially in France; many of them were incorporated in the French Code of 1791, in which crimes were organized on a scale and a penalty was affixed to each. In the United States, James Wilson, the leading legal scholar of the postrevolutionary period, credited Beccaria with having influenced his thinking, notably with regard to the deterrent purpose of punishment. Through Wilson, Beccaria's principles had an important effect on reform of the penal laws of Pennsylvania, which laid the foundation for the penitentiary movement.[14] Beccaria is remembered for his emphasis on certain and speedy punishment in accordance with the social wrong committed.

Bentham and the "Hedonic Calculus"

Jeremy Bentham, one of the most fascinating thinkers and reformers of English criminal law, is best known for his utilitarian theories, often referred to as his "hedonic calculus." By this term, Bentham meant that it was possible to categorize all human actions and through either incentives or punishment to direct individuals to activities considered desirable. Undergirding this idea was his concept of **utilitarianism**, the doctrine that the aim of all action should be "the greatest happiness of the greatest number." As he said, an act possesses utility "if it tends to produce benefit, advantage, pleasure, good or happiness … or to prevent the happening of mischief, pain, evil or unhappiness to the party whose interest is considered."[15] Thus, according to Bentham, intelligent persons behave in ways that achieve the most pleasure while bringing the least pain; they are constantly calculating the pluses and minuses of potential actions.

The impact of Bentham's theories on criminology and reform of the penal law are obvious. He viewed criminals as somewhat like children or people of unsound mind who lack the self-discipline to control their passions by reason. Behavior was not preordained but an exercise of free will. Thus, crime was not sinful but the result of improper calculation. Accordingly, the criminal law should be organized so that the offender would derive more pain than pleasure from a wrongful act. Potential offenders, recognizing that legal sanctions were organized according to this scheme, would be deterred from committing antisocial acts.

---

utilitarianism The doctorine that the aim of all action should be the greatest possible balance of pleasure over pain; hence, the belief that a punishment inflicted on an offender must achieve enough good to outweigh the pain inflicted.

Bentham sought to reform the criminal laws of England so that they would emphasize deterrence and prevention. They were to be designed not to avenge an illegal act but to prevent the commission of such an act in the first place. Because excessive punishment is unjustified, the punishment should not be more severe than necessary to deter crime. It should not be "an act of wrath or vengeance" but one of calculation that was tempered by considerations of the social good and the offender's needs.[16]

Bentham wrote at a time when John Howard, Elizabeth Fry, and others were attempting to reform the English criminal code by reducing the level of corporal punishment and by developing the penitentiary. He sought to end the capriciousness, barbarity, and inconsistency of punishment; to improve the prison system; and to abolish transportation. Like Beccaria, Bentham urged that criminal justice be administered according to rules and that punishment be tempered so that the rehabilitation of the offender would have greater priority.

Always interested in putting his theories into practice, Bentham developed plans for a penitentiary designed according to his utilitarian principles; his "panopticon," or "inspection house," called for a circular building with a glass roof and cells on each story around the circumference. This arrangement would permit a prison inspector in the center of the building to keep out of sight of the prisoners yet view their individual actions through a system of blinds. Bentham wanted this structure of unique design to be located near the center of the city so that it would serve also as a reminder and deterrent to citizens. In keeping with the reform ideas of the time, prisoners were to be kept busy with work; were to be segregated by age, sex, and criminal category; and were to be provided with the religious services that would help them toward rehabilitation.

The panopticon was never constructed in England; one was proposed for France but never adopted, as was one for Ireland. Two panopticon-type prisons were actually constructed in the United States. In 1825 Western

John Howard's investigations of conditions in English jails served to rally legislative interest in reform. Howard was a major proponent of the penitentiary.

State Penitentiary was opened in Pittsburgh, modeled to some extent on Bentham's ideas; it was found to be unsuitable and was ordered rebuilt in 1833. The fullest expression of the style was the prison in Stateville, Illinois, where four circular cellhouses were built from 1916 to 1924. Described by an architect as "the most awful receptacle of gloom ever devised and put together with good stone and brick and mortar,"[17] the panopticon model was abandoned as the state constructed additional buildings in Stateville according to a more conventional design.

John Howard: Father of the Penitentiary

Probably no individual did more for penal reform in England than John Howard—county squire, social activist, and sheriff of Bedfordshire. Like many members of the new merchant class, Howard had a social conscience and was concerned about conditions among the poor. On being appointed high sheriff of Bedfordshire in 1773, he exercised the traditional but usually neglected responsibility of visiting the local prisons and institutions. He was shocked by what he saw, especially when he learned that the jailers received no regular salary but made their living from the prisoners and that many persons who had been discharged by the grand jury or acquitted at their trials were still detained because they could not pay their discharge fees.[18]

Howard expanded his inspections to the prisons, hulks, and houses of correction outside his jurisdiction, and then to those on the Continent. The prisons of England were overcrowded, discipline was lacking, and sanitation was unheard of—thousands died yearly from disease. Even among members of the free community, "prison fever" was feared, for the disease often infected personnel of the courthouse and others in contact with offenders. At the time, a sentence of seven years' imprisonment was viewed as a de facto penalty of death.

Howard thought some of the prisons that he visited in Belgium, Holland, Germany, and Italy could be emulated in England. In particular, the separate confinement of inmates at night after their work at common tasks during

BIOGRAPHY

John Howard (1726–1790)

The son of a merchant, John Howard was brought up within the culture of the emerging middle class. Upon his father's death, Howard used a portion of his inheritance for travel abroad. In 1756 the ship on which he was traveling to Portugal was captured by a privateer. The crew and passengers were incarcerated in France under extreme conditions. Howard returned to England on parole and secured the release of his fellow prisoners through negotiations with the French government. His experience likely influenced his lifelong concern with the conditions of incarceration.

As sheriff, Howard suggested that jailers be paid a salary rather than depend on fees. Told that this was unprecedented, Howard then was determined to find a jailer paid by a fixed salary. He found none but did view the many abuses of prisoners and the conditions in which they lived. He described his findings to a committee of the House of Commons in 1774. Legislation was soon passed abolishing jailers' fees and requiring improvements in the sanitary conditions of prisons.

Howard continued his self-appointed task of inspecting correctional facilities, visiting Scotland, Ireland, Holland, Germany, and France in 1775. These investigations led to his book, *The State of the Prisons in England and Wales with Preliminary Observations and an Account of Some Foreign Prisons,* which was published in 1777.

What distinguished Howard from other reformers was the care with which he recorded his observations of prison conditions. His book is an unsentimental, unsensationalized, factual account based on an approach that may be viewed as a precursor of modern social-scientific investigation. For every prison in the country, Howard recorded the dimensions of the buildings, the diet of the inmates, the number incarcerated at the time of his visit, the discharge fees paid, and other details that seemed important to his inquiring mind. The book was well reviewed and widely read, and aroused much interest in the cause of penal reform.

During the rest of his life, Howard continued to visit prisons and hospitals in England and on the Continent, updating and publishing new editions of his book. The final edition was published in 1789. Soon afterward he set out to visit Holland, Germany, and Russia, where the defective state of the Russian military hospitals drew his attention. While with the Russian army in Turkey, he caught "camp fever" and died on January 20, 1790.

the day impressed him. Of the Maison de Force in Ghent he wrote, "The convicts were properly lodged—fed—clothed—instructed—worked. The utmost regularity, order, cleanliness prevailed; there was no drunkenness; no riot; no excessive misery; no irons, no starvation."[19]

Howard's descriptions of conditions in English penal institutions horrified society. Of particular concern was the lack of discipline. Subsequent to his report before the House of Commons, Howard, along with Sir William Blackstone and William Eden (later Lord Auckland), drafted the Penitentiary Act of 1779, a curious amalgam of traditional and progressive ideas that had a great impact on penology.

The Penitentiary Act originally called for the creation of houses of hard labor where people convicted of crimes that would otherwise have earned them a sentence of transportation would be imprisoned for up to two years. The act was based on four principles set down by Howard: (1) secure and sanitary structure, (2) systematic inspection, (3) abolition of fees, and (4) a reformatory regimen. Prisoners were to be confined in solitary cells at night but were to labor silently in common rooms during the day. The labor was to be "of the hardest and most servile kind, in which Drudgery is chiefly required and where the Work is little liable to be spoiled by Ignorance, Neglect or Obstinancy"—such work as sawing stone, polishing marble, beating hemp, and chopping rags.[20] The legislation further specified in detail such items as the diet, uniforms, and conditions of hygiene for the prisoners.

Perhaps influenced by his Quaker friends, Howard came to believe that the new institution should be not merely a place of industry but also one for contrition and penance. The twofold purpose of the penitentiary was to punish and to reform offenders through solitary confinement between intervals of work, the inculcation of good habits, and religious instruction so that inmates could reflect on their moral duties.

The Penitentiary Act and follow-up legislation passed in 1782 and 1791 attracted political support from a variety of sources. Legalists sought to deter crime; philanthropists wanted to save humanity; conservatives thought that the products made by convict labor would save money; and pragmatic politicians wanted a solution to the disquieting prison situation. In particular, the philanthropists and other social reformers believed that solitary confinement was the best way to end the evil of inmate association and provide opportunity for reflection. Bentham agreed, since he believed that the penitentiary would contribute to the deterrence of crime by being onerous to but not destructive of the offender.

But what was behind this era of criminal law reform? It appears that reform was brought about as much by the emergence of the middle class as by the humanistic concerns of the Quakers and Jeremy Bentham. It can be argued that the new industrialists were concerned about the existing criminal law because its harshness was paradoxically helping some offenders to escape punishment: Jurors would not convict persons accused of petty property offenses for which death was the prescribed sanction. In petitions sent to Parliament, groups of businessmen asserted that their property was not protected if offenders could expect to escape punishment.[21] They wanted sanctions that were swift and certain, and their demands fell on the fertile soil of moral indignation prepared by Bentham, Howard, Peel, and their fellow reformers.

Changes were made in England's prisons, and new institutions were constructed along lines suggested by Howard and Bentham, but it was not until 1842, with the opening of Pentonville in North London, that the penitentiary plan came to fruition. Meanwhile, the concept of the penitentiary had traveled across the Atlantic and was planted in the more fertile soil of Pennsylvania and New York, where it blossomed.

Summary

This chapter has described the types of punishments that existed in Europe prior to the American Revolution. From the Middle Ages to the American Revolution, galley slavery, imprisonment, transportation, corporal punishment, and death dominated the correctional landscape. But with the Enlightenment, changes began to be made in penal policy. A shift of focus occurred during the later part of the eighteenth century.

Rather than stressing physical punishment of the offender, efforts began to be directed to the reformation of the offender. These changes were first proposed in Europe and later brought to fruition in America.

Traditional scholarship on correctional thought and practice has emphasized the humanitarian motives of reformers toward a system of benevolent justice. Some scholars have sought to revise the traditional view by looking at the underlying economic or social factors that account for shifts in correctional policies. They have been unwilling to accept the standard version that such persons as Beccaria, Bentham, and Howard were motivated by their concern for fellow humans when they advocated a particular perspective on the problem of criminality.

The work of some of these revisionists shows, for example, that up to the year 1700, the size of the incarcerated population in England was linked to the economic demand for workers. Perhaps the invention of the penitentiary represented not the workings of the humanitarian instincts unleashed by the Enlightenment but a means of disciplining the working class to serve a new industrial society.

For Discussion

1. In what ways are changes in the social, economic, and political environment of a society reflected in policies concerning corrections?

2. How might developments discussed in this chapter have eventually brought about the separation of children from others in the prison system?

3. How have the interests of administrators and the organizations they manage distorted the ideals of penal reformers?

4. Some people believe that the history of corrections shows a continuous movement toward more humane treatment of prisoners as society in general has progressed. How do you react to that assumption?

5. Explain how specific underlying social factors may have influenced the development of correctional philosophies.

For Further Reading

Foucault, Michel. *Discipline and Punish.* New York: Pantheon, 1977. Describes the transition from a focus of correctional punishment on the body of the offender to the use of the penitentiary to reform the individual.

Hughes, Robert. *The Fatal Shore.* New York: Knopf, 1987. Traces the colonization of New South Wales and the impact of transportation.

Ignatieff, Michael. *A Just Measure of Pain.* New York: Pantheon, 1978. Recounts the coming of penal institutions to England during the latter part of the eighteenth century.

Spierenburg, Pieter. *The Spectacle of Suffering.* New York: Cambridge University Press, 1987. Examines of the role of public punishment in preindustrial Europe and its ultimate disappearance by the middle of the nineteenth century.

Notes

1. Michel Foucault, *Discipline and Punish* (New York: Pantheon, 1977), pp. 4, 8.

2. Georg Rüsche and Otto Kirchheimer, *Punishment and Social Structure* (New York: Russell & Russell, [1939] 1968), p. 9.

3. For a description of the treatment of galley slaves, see George Ives, *A History of Penal Methods* (Montclair, N.J.: Patterson Smith, 1970), p. 104.

4. Thorsten Sellin, *Slavery and the Penal System* (New York: Elsevier, 1976), p. 94.

5. Ibid., p. 97.

6. Robert Hughes, *The Fatal Shore* (New York: Knopf, 1987), p. 282.

7. Ibid.

8. Ibid., p. 162.

9. Rüsche and Kirchheimer, *Punishment and Social Structure,* p. 19.

10. Michael Ignatieff, *A Just Measure of Pain* (New York: Pantheon, 1978), p. 27.

11. Rüsche and Kirchheimer, *Punishment and Social Structure,* p. 96.

12. Ibid., p. 55.

13. Harry E. Barnes and Negley K. Teeters, *New Horizons in Criminology* (New York: Prentice-Hall, 1944), p. 461.

14. Francis Edward Devine, "Cesare Beccaria and the Theoretical Foundation of Modern Penal Jurisprudence," *New England Journal of Prison Law* 7 (1981): 8.

15. Gilbert Geis, "Jeremy Bentham," in *Pioneers in Criminology,* ed. Herman Mannheim (Montclair, N.J.: Patterson Smith, 1973), p. 54.

16. Ignatieff, *A Just Measure of Pain,* p. 27.

17. Geis, "Jeremy Bentham," p. 65.

18. Anthony Babington, *The English Bastille* (New York: St. Martin's Press, 1971), p. 103.

19. Barnes and Teeters, *New Horizons in Criminology,* p. 481.

20. Ignatieff, *A Just Measure of Pain,* p. 93.

21. Michael Russigan, "A Reinterpretation of Criminal Law Reform in Nineteenth-Century England," *Journal of Criminal Justice* 8 (1980): 205.

3

History of Corrections in America

While society in the United States gives the example of the most extended liberty, the prisons of the same country offer the spectacle of the most complete despotism.

Gustave de Beaumont
and Alexis de Tocqueville, 1833

The Colonial Period
The Arrival of the Penitentiary
The Pennsylvania System
The New York System
Debating the Systems
The Reformatory Movement
Cincinnati, 1870
Elmira Reformatory
Juvenile Corrections
Lasting Reforms
The Rise of the Progressives
Individualized Treatment
Modern Criminology
Progressive Reforms
The Rise of the Medical Model
From Medical Model to Community Model
**Crime Control Model: The Pendulum
    Swings Again**
Rehabilitation Recedes
Crime Control Comes to the Fore
Where Are We Today?
Summary

On October 25, 1829, Charles Williams, an eighteen-year-old African American from Delaware County, Pennsylvania, began serving a two-year sentence for larceny at the Eastern Penitentiary located in Cherry Hill outside of Philadelphia. The newly constructed facility was described at the time as "the most imposing in the United States."[1] Williams was assigned to a cell measuring twelve-by-eight-by-ten feet with an attached eighteen-foot long exercise yard. The cell was furnished with a fold-up metal bedstead, a simple toilet, a wooden stool, a workbench, and eating utensils. Light came from an eight-inch window in the ceiling that could be blocked to plunge the cell into darkness should disciplinary actions be needed.

Charles Williams became Prisoner Number l at Eastern, a model of the separate confinement penitentiary viewed at the time as a great advance in penology. For the two years of his sentence, Williams could expect to be confined to his cell and exercise yard, his only human contact being a weekly visit by the chaplain. Every measure was taken to ensure that the prisoner would not be distracted from his moral rehabilitation. Officials could inspect the interior of the cell through a peephole, without the resident knowing. Food was inserted through an opening in the wall designed so that the resident could not see the guard. Solitary labor, Bible reading, and reflection were viewed as the keys to providing the offender with the opportunities to reflect on his behavior and repent.

Few Americans realize that their country gave the world the first penitentiary, an institution created to reform offenders within an environment designed to focus their full attention on their moral rehabilitation. This idea of reform reflects major changes. Remember that brutal public punishments such as the dismemberment of Damiens had occurred with some regularity just sixty years prior to the time that Williams entered Eastern. The passage of time had brought dramatic changes in thought, with respect to both the nature of man and the purpose of punishment.

Especially during its formative years, American corrections was greatly influenced by English trends and practices. To be sure, the work of Cesare Beccaria and the development of the Milan House of Correction had a bearing on penal policies throughout the Western world, but it was from English policies and thought that corrections in the American colonial period drew. The transatlantic ties have continued over the years. Yet over the past two centuries, correctional institutions and practices have responded to social and political pressures and developed in ways that are decidedly American.

Let us survey the changes in correctional thought and practices in the United States. We'll focus on seven periods: the colonial period, the arrival of the penitentiary, the reformatory movement, the progressive movement, the rise of the medical model, the community model, and the crime control model.

As we discuss each period we will emphasize the ways in which correctional goals reflected current ideas.

The Colonial Period

During the colonial period most Americans lived under laws and practices that had been transferred from England and adapted to local conditions. In New England the Puritans maintained a tight society governed by religious principles well into the middle of the eighteenth century, and they strictly punished violations of religious laws. As in England, banishment, corporal punishment, the pillory, and death were the common penalties. In 1682, with the arrival of William Penn, Pennsylvania adopted "The Great Law," which was based on humane Quaker principles and emphasized hard labor in a house of correction as punishment for most crimes. Death was reserved for premeditated murder. The Quaker Code survived until 1718, when it was replaced by the Anglican Code, in force in other colonies.

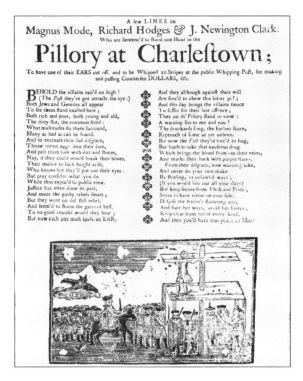

During the colonial period punishments in America were similar to those being carried out in England. Broadsides were used to publicize public gatherings to observe such punishment.

The latter code listed thirteen capital offenses; larceny was the only felony not punishable by death. Whipping, branding, mutilation, and other corporal punishments were prescribed for other offenses, as were fines. This situation continued throughout the colonies until the Revolution.

Unlike the mother country, with its crowded houses of correction, hulks, and prisons, the colonies seldom used institutions for confinement. Banishment from the community was imposed, as were fines and the other punishments just mentioned. The death penalty was widely used. David Rothman writes:

> The New York Supreme Court in the pre-Revolutionary era regularly sentenced criminals to death, with slightly more than twenty percent of all its penalties capital ones. When magistrates believed that the

fundamental security of the city was in danger, as in the case of a slave revolt in 1741, the court responded with great severity (burning to death thirteen of the rebellion's leaders and hanging nineteen others). Even in less critical times the court had frequent recourse to the scaffold—for those convicted of pickpocketing, burglary, robbery, counterfeiting, horse stealing, and grand larceny as well as murder.[2]

Jails were maintained to hold persons awaiting court action or those unable to discharge their debts. Only on rare occasions were convicted offenders incarcerated for the duration of their sentences; the stocks, whipping post, or gallows were the places for punishment. In keeping with Calvinist doctrine of predestination, there was little thought about reforming offenders—such people were considered naturally depraved.

The Arrival of the Penitentiary

Until the beginning of the nineteenth century, American society was small and predominantly rural. In 1790 the entire population numbered less than four million, and no town had more than fifty thousand inhabitants. By 1830 the rural population had more than doubled and the urban population had more than tripled. Growth was accompanied by very rapid social and economic changes that affected all aspects of life. Colonial life had been oriented toward the local community; everyone knew everyone else, neighbors gave help when it was needed, and social control was a matter for the local clergy and elite. After 1800 life was more urban; there were thousands of new immigrants. No longer could social problems be handled through the assistance of neighbors. In an increasingly heterogeneous urban and industrial society, responsibility for the poor, insane, and criminal became the province of the state and the institutions it developed.

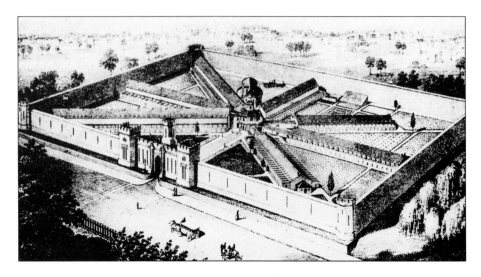

Eastern State Penitentiary located outside of Philadelphia became the model for the Pennsylvania system of "separate" confinement. The building was designed to ensure that each offender was separated from all human contact so that he could reflect upon his misdeeds.

With the Revolution, the ideas of the Enlightenment, as discussed in Chapter 2, gained currency and a new concept of criminal punishment came to the fore. This correctional philosophy, based very much on the ideas of Beccaria, Bentham, and Howard, coincided with the ideals of the Declaration of Independence, which stressed an optimistic view of human nature and a belief in each person's perfectibility.[3] Accordingly, social progress was thought to be possible through reforms carried out in line with the dictates of "pure reason." In addition, emphasis shifted from the assumption that deviance was part of human nature to a view that crime was a result of forces operating in the environment. The punitive colonial penal system based on retribution was held to be incompatible with a society committed to the idea of human perfectibility. It was argued that if Americans were to give more than lip service to the humane and optimistic idea of human beings' improvability, they had to remove the barbarism and vindictiveness from their penal codes and admit that one great

objective of punishment for crime must be the reformation of the criminal.

Although the idea of the **penitentiary** had its origin with the English reformers, the concept was first implemented in America. The penitentiary differed markedly from the prison, house of correction, and jail. The penitentiary was conceived as a place where criminal offenders could be isolated from the bad influences of society and of one another so that, by reflecting on their misdeeds while engaged in productive labor, they could be reformed. As the word *penitentiary* indicates, while offenders were being punished, they would become penitent, see the error of their ways, and want to place themselves on the right path. Thus, they could reenter the community as useful citizens.

---

penitentiary An institution intended to isolate prisoners from society and from one another so that they could reflect on their past misdeeds, repent, and thus undergo reformation.

The penitentiary concept was implemented first in the Walnut Street Jail, Philadelphia, in 1790. A portion of the jail was converted to create an environment based on the assumptions of the penitentiary.

The American example attracted the world's attention, and the penitentiary was transported back across the Atlantic to be incorporated in Millbank and Pentonville in England and in various other locales in Europe. By 1830 foreign observers were coming to America to see this innovation in penology; they were excited by the changes that were being made in the United States. France sent Alexis de Tocqueville and Gustave Auguste de Beaumont, England sent William Crawford, and Prussia dispatched Nicholas Julius. By the middle of the century the U.S. penitentiary in its various forms had indeed become world famous.

The Pennsylvania System

As in England, Quakers set about to implement their humanistic and religious ideas in the new nation; in Philadelphia, their efforts came to fruition. The Quaker philosophy emphasizes that the Inner Light (God's grace) is available to all, but it must be individually achieved; receiving it is directly dependent on the ways in which one behaves in the world. For Quakers, penance and silent contemplation were the means to move from the state of sin toward perfection. The penitentiary thus provided a place where individuals, on their own, could be reformed.

Quakers were among the Philadelphia elite who in 1787 formed the reformist Society for Alleviating the Miseries of Public Prisoners. Under the leadership of Dr. Benjamin Rush and such non-Quakers as Benjamin Franklin, the society urged replacement of capital and corporal punishment with incarceration. Members had been in communication with John Howard, and their ideals in many ways reflected his.

In 1790 the group was instrumental in passage of legislation almost identical to England's Penitentiary Act of 1779. The 1790 legislation specified that an institution was to be established in which "solitary confinement to hard labour and a total abstinence from spirituous liquors will prove the most effectual means of reforming these unhappy creatures."[4]

To implement the new legislation, it was stipulated that the existing three-story, stone Walnut Street Jail in Philadelphia should be expanded for the solitary confinement of "hardened and atrocious offenders." The plain building housed eight cells on each floor, and there was an attached yard. Each cell was dark and small (only six-by-eight feet, and nine feet high). From a small grated window high on the outside wall, the inmate "could perceive neither heaven nor earth." Inmates were classified by offense: Serious offenders were placed in solitary confinement without labor; those with minor records worked together in shops during the day under a strict rule of silence and were confined separately at night.

The Walnut Street Jail soon became overcrowded. The legislature was then persuaded to build additional institutions for the state: Western Penitentiary on the outskirts of Pittsburgh and Eastern Penitentiary in Cherry Hill, near Philadelphia. The opening of Eastern in 1829 marked the full development of the penitentiary system based on **separate confinement**. In the years between Walnut Street and Eastern, other states had adopted aspects of the

---

BIOGRAPHY

Benjamin Rush (1745–1813)

Physician, patriot, signer of the Declaration of Independence, and social reformer, Benjamin Rush was born in Pennsylvania and began practicing medicine in Philadelphia in 1769. Widely recognized for his work in medicine, particularly his insistence on the importance of personal hygiene, Rush was also a humanitarian. He helped to organize the Pennsylvania Society for the Abolition of Slavery and served as surgeon general under Washington during the Revolutionary War.

Following his military career, Rush became active in various reform movements, especially those concerned with treatment of the mentally ill and with prisoners. His interest in methods then being used to punish criminals led him to protest laws assigning such punishments as shaved heads, whippings, and other public displays. In *An Enquiry into the Effects of Public Punishment upon Criminals* (1787), he maintained that such excesses served only to harden criminals. Opposed to capital punishment, he wrote *On Punishing Murder by Death* (1792), condemning the practice as an offspring of monarchical divine right, a principle contrary to a republican form of government. With publication of *On the Diseases of the Mind* (1816), Rush argued for development of asylums for the treatment not only of the mentally ill but also of criminals. He is probably best known for advocating the penitentiary as a replacement for capital and corporal punishment.

Pennsylvania model. Separate confinement was introduced by Maryland in 1809, by Massachusetts in 1811, by New Jersey in 1820, and by Maine in 1824, but Eastern was the fullest expression of the concept of rehabilitation through separate confinement.

Eastern Penitentiary was designed by John Haviland, an English immigrant and an acquaintance of John Howard. The facility was one of the most imposing and expensive public structures for its day. In many respects, the shape of the buildings seems to have been influenced by the Maison de Force at Ghent. Cell blocks extended from a central hub like the spokes of a wheel. Each prisoner ate, slept, worked, and received religious instruction in his own cell. The inmates did not see peers; in fact, their only human contact was the occasional visit of a clergyman or prison official.

As described by Robert Vaux, one of the original reformers, the Pennsylvania system was based on the following principles:

1. Prisoners should be treated not vengefully but in ways designed to convince them that through hard and selective forms of suffering, they could change their lives.

2. To prevent the prison from being a corrupting influence, solitary confinement of all inmates should be practiced.

---

separate confinement   A penitentiary system developed in Pennsylvania in which each inmate was held in isolation from other inmates. All activities, including craftwork, were carried on in the cells.

3. In their seclusion the offenders were to have opportunities to reflect on their transgressions so that they might repent.

4. Solitary confinement is a punishing discipline because humans are by nature social beings.

5. Solitary confinement is economical because prisoners do not need long periods of time to benefit from the penitential experience, fewer keepers are required, and the costs of clothing are reduced.[5]

The question as to whether the Pennsylvania system of separate confinement could achieve its goals was instantly controversial. In 1831 de Tocqueville and de Beaumont wrote that "nothing distracts in Philadelphia, the mind of the convicts from their meditations; and as they are always isolated, the presence of a person who comes to converse with them is the greatest benefit."[6] By contrast, after visiting Eastern in 1842, the English novelist Charles Dickens argued that "very few men are capable of estimating the immense amount of torture and agony which this dreadful punishment, prolonged for years, inflicts upon the sufferers."[7]

Within five years after it opened, Eastern was subjected to the first of investigations carried out over the years by a judicially appointed board of inspectors. The inspection reports detail the extent to which the goal of separate confinement was not fully observed, physical punishments were used to maintain discipline, and prisoners suffered mental breakdowns as a result of the isolation. Separate confinement declined by the 1860s when crowding required double-celling, yet it was not abolished by the Commonwealth of Pennsylvania until 1913.[8]

The New York System

Faced with the overcrowding of existing facilities such as Newgate Prison, built in 1797, the New York legislature in 1816 authorized a new state prison in Auburn. Influenced by the reported success of the separate confinement of some prisoners in the Walnut Street Jail, the New York building commission decided that a portion of the new facility should be erected on that model, and that an experiment should be undertaken to test its effectiveness. The concept proved a failure, for there was a marked increase in sickness, insanity, and suicide among the prisoners. It was discontinued in 1822, and those then held in solitary were pardoned by the governor.

In 1831 Elam Lynds was installed as the warden at Auburn, and he worked out a new **congregate system** of prison discipline. Instead of duplicating the complete isolation practiced in Pennsylvania, Lynds decreed that inmates should be kept in individual cells at night but congregate in workshops during the day. The inmates were forbidden to talk or even to exchange glances while on the job or at meals. Lynds was thoroughly convinced that convicts were hopelessly incorrigible and that industrial efficiency should be the overriding purpose of the prison. He instituted a reign of discipline and obedience that included the lock-step and the wearing of prison stripes. Furthermore, he considered it "impossible to govern a large prison without a whip. Those who know human nature from books only may say the contrary."[9]

Inmates of the Pennsylvania penitentiaries worked in their cells, but those in New York engaged in industry both as therapy and as a way to pay for the institution. The state negotiated contracts with manufacturers, who then delivered raw materials to the prison for conversion into finished goods. By the 1840s Auburn was producing footwear, barrels, carpets, carpentry tools, harnesses, furniture, and clothing. Thus, Auburn, and the prisons like it in other states, reflected some of the growing emphases of the Industrial Revolution in that

————

congregate system A penitentiary system developed in Auburn, New York, where each inmate was held in isolation during the night but worked with fellow prisoners during the day under a rule of silence.

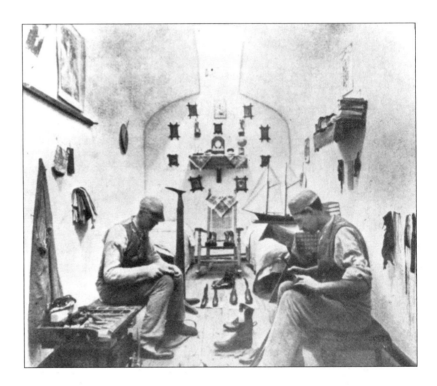

It has been said that the Pennsylvania model was oriented primarily toward an earlier religious craft society and that the New York model looked forward to the emerging industrial age.

the inmates were to have the benefits of labor as well as meditation. They were to live under tight control, on a simple diet, and according to an undeviating routine, but they also would work to pay for a portion of their keep. There was a greater concern for instilling good work habits and thus preventing recidivism than for the moral rehabilitation of the prisoner.

Debating the Systems

During this period of reform, the preferred structure of prison systems was hotly debated. Advocates of both the Pennsylvania and the New York plans argued on public platforms and in the nation's periodicals over methods of punishment. Underlying the debates were questions about the disciplining of citizens in a democracy and the maintenance of social peace in a community emphasizing individualism. Participants in this contest included some of the leading figures of the time: For example, Samuel Gridley Howe (a Pennsylvania advo-

cate) was pitted against Matthew Carey (for New York). As each state considered new penal construction, it joined in the debate.

It has often been noted that the Quaker method in Pennsylvania (the separate system) aimed to produce honest persons while the New York method (the congregate system) sought to mold obedient citizens. Advocates of both systems agreed that the prisoner must be isolated from society and subjected to a disciplined routine. They believed that deviance was a result of pervasive corruption in the community and that such institutions as the family and the church were not effectively countering corrupt influences. Only by removing offenders from temptations and substituting a steady and regular regimen could society make them into useful citizens. The convicts were not inherently depraved; rather, they were the victims of a society that had not protected them from vice.

What divided the two camps was the way in which reformation was to be brought about.

Proponents of the New York system maintained that inmates first had to be "broken" and then socialized by means of a rigid discipline of congregate but silent labor. Those who pushed for the separate system of Pennsylvania rejected such harshness and, following Howard, renounced physical punishments and any other form of human degradation. The New Yorkers countered that the silent system cost less, was an efficient use of convict labor, and developed individuals who eventually would be able to return to the community imbued with the discipline necessary for the industrial age. The Pennsylvanians responded that New York had sacrificed the principal goal of the penitentiary (reformation) to the accessory goal (cost-effectiveness), and contended that the exploitation of inmates through large-scale industry embittered them and failed to promote the work ethic.

It can be said that the Pennsylvania model was predominantly oriented toward an earlier religious craft society and that the New York model looked forward to the emerging industrial age. Conley has argued that the Pennsylvania model lost out because it embraced an outdated labor system. In contrast, the New York system, as practiced at Auburn, was consistent with the new demands and challenges of factory production, which "would provide the state with a means of exploiting the labor of inmates to defray the expenses of the institution and possibly earn a profit for the state."[10] In this sense, Auburn was the forerunner of the industrial prison that was dominant until the rise of organized labor in the twentieth century.

In helping to clarify some of the issues left hazy in the writings of Bentham and Howard, the debate contributed to decisions in a number of states and in Europe on the way penitentiaries should be designed and run. Of the prisons constructed in the United States during this period, the New York style was the overwhelming choice. Most European visitors, however, favored the Pennsylvania model, and the First International Prison Congress, held in 1846 in Frankfurt, endorsed it by a large major-

ity. The separate system was soon incorporated in correctional facilities in Germany, France, Belgium, and Holland. But as prison populations increased in the United States, the Pennsylvania system proved to be too expensive. In addition, the public became aroused by reports that prisoners were going insane because they were unable to endure long-term solitary confinement. Yet it was not until the end of the century that Pennsylvania, the birthplace of the penitentiary, finally converted to the congregate system.

The Reformatory Movement

Unfortunately, ways in which reforms are implemented often do not match the high ideals of social activists. Legislators and governors may be willing to support the espoused goals of change, but putting the ideals into practice requires leadership, money, public support, and innovative administrators. Soon after an innovation, corrections facilities become overcrowded, discipline becomes lax, programs are abandoned, and charges of official misconduct erupt. An investigation typically recommends changes that may or may not be implemented—and the cycle continues.

In the post–Civil War period American reformers became disillusioned with the results of the penitentiary movement. Deterrence and reform had not been achieved in the New York or Pennsylvania systems, nor in their copies. The failure of the penitentiaries, however, was seen as a problem of poor administration rather than an indictment of the concept of incarceration. Within forty years of their advocates' optimistic proclamations, penitentiaries were bulging, understaffed, and minimally financed. Discipline was neglected, administrators were viewed as corrupt, and the institutions were places of brutality; the reality was a far cry from the vision of John Howard and Benjamin Rush.

The reformatory movement emphasized education and training, such as this machine class at Elmira Reformatory in 1898. On the basis of their achievement and conduct offenders moved forward toward release.

Across the Atlantic, controversy developed surrounding penal policy. In England, Alexander Maconochie, warden of the Birmingham Borough Prison, challenged the corrections establishment by urging that the "mark system" of graduated terms of confinement be established. Penalties should be graded according to the severity of the crime, and offenders released from incarceration according to their performance within the institution. A certain number of marks were to be given at the time of sentencing, and prisoners could reduce the number by voluntary labor, participation in educational and religious programs, and good behavior. Thus Maconochie was arguing for sentences of indeterminate length and a system of rewards. Through these incentives the offenders would be reformed so that they could return to society.

Maconochie's ideas were not implemented in England, but they were incorporated into the penal system of Ireland. In 1854 Sir Walter Crofton adopted practices similar to the mark system that were known as the Irish or intermediate system. Marks were awarded for industry, attention and improvement at school, and general conduct, and the offenders moved through stages of confinement with varying levels of discipline and privileges. Upon conviction prisoners spent a period in solitary confinement and then were sent to public work prisons where they could earn marks. When they accumulated sufficient marks, they were transferred to the intermediate stage and housed in what today might be called a halfway house. The final test was a ticket-of-leave, a conditional release that was the precursor of the modern parole system.[11] Again, cross-pollination worked between the continents. Maconochie's and Crofton's ideas traveled back across the Atlantic and became part of a reform begun at a convention in Cincinnati, Ohio.

Cincinnati, 1870

By 1870 a new generation of American penal reformers had arisen. Among them were Gay-

BIOGRAPHY

Enoch Cobb Wines (1806–1879)

Born in New Jersey, Enoch Cobb Wines was the guiding force of American corrections from 1862, when he became the secretary of the New York Prison Association, until his death in 1879. He was the central figure in the organization of the National Prison Association, led its important Cincinnati meeting in 1870, and remained its secretary until his death. His thinking about corrections is reflected in the Cincinnati Declaration of Principles. In 1872 he served as the U.S. representative to the International Penitentiary Congress, attended by the spokesmen of twenty-six nations. He was appointed by the Congress to the chair of a permanent international commission on corrections.

For the first portion of his professional career, Wines was an educator, teaching in and administering public schools. Later he became a Congregational minister, serving churches in Vermont and New York before returning to the world of education in 1859 as president of the City University of St. Louis. He resigned that position to enter the prison reform movement in 1862.

Wines epitomizes the ties of education, religion, and penology in the United States during the latter part of the nineteenth century. In *The State of Prisons and of Child-Saving Institutions in the Civilized World* (1880), he wrote that of all the reformatory agencies, religion is the most important because it is the most powerful in its action on the human heart and life. He emphasized that moral forces should replace physical force. Wines believed that intemperate use of alcohol was the basis of much criminal behavior, but that the "wretched home-life or lack of home-life" in cities was also a significant source of crime.

lord Hubbell, warden of Sing Sing, who had observed the Irish system in operation in 1863; Enoch C. Wines, secretary of the New York Prison Association; Franklin Sanborn, secretary of the Massachusetts State Board of Charities; and Zebulon Brockway, head of Detroit's Michigan House of Correction. These penologists, like the Quakers, were motivated by humanitarian concerns, but they also understood the way prisons operated.

The National Prison Association (predecessor of the American Correctional Association) and its 1870 meeting in Cincinnati embodied the new spirit of reform. In its famous Declaration of Principles the association advocated a new design for penology. The goal should be the treatment of criminals through their moral regeneration, that is, the reformation of criminals and "not the infliction of vindictive suffering." The declaration asserted that prisons should be operated on a philosophy of inmate change; reformation would be rewarded by release. Fixed sentences should be replaced by sentences of indeterminate length, and proof of reformation—rather than the mere lapse of time—should be a requirement for a prisoner's release. The reformation program should be encouraged through the classification of prisoners on the basis of character and improvement. Penitentiary practices that had evolved during the first half of the nineteenth century—the fixed sentence, the lockstep, rules of silence, and isolation—were now seen as debasing, humiliating, and destructive of initiative.

BIOGRAPHY

Zebulon Brockway (1827–1920)

Zebulon Brockway of Connecticut began his distinguished career in penology at the age of twenty-one as a clerk at the Wethersfield Prison. In 1852 he became superintendent of the Albany Municipal and County Almshouse, where he founded the first county hospital for the insane. In 1854, at the age of twenty-seven, he became superintendent of the Monroe County Penitentiary in Rochester, New York, where he began to experiment with ideas on making prisons more humane and rehabilitative. Believing that his energies should be devoted to youthful offenders, who offered the greatest possibility for reformation, Brockway moved to Detroit in 1861 to head the Michigan House of Correction, an institution for young men between the ages of sixteen and twenty-one.

Brockway welcomed the opportunity to put his theories into practice as superintendent of Elmira State Reformatory, New York, in 1876. In the following twenty-five years he made it a model for other institutions through the development of educational instruction and training for trades. He persuaded the New York legislature to enact indeterminate sentences and ran Elmira on a graded system that rewarded inmates for their progress. He believed that incarceration had one purpose—to protect society against crime—but that reform of the criminal should be the ultimate goal.

Brockway retired from Elmira in 1900 and served in a variety of public and charitable offices for the next twenty years. He was a charter member of the National Prison Association and was its president in 1898. His autobiography, *Fifty Years of Prison Service*, was published in 1912.

Given the leadership roles of distinguished clergymen in the National Prison Association, it is not surprising that, like the activists who had promoted the penitentiary in the 1830s, those gathered at Cincinnati still saw crime as a sort of moral disease that should be treated by efforts at moral regeneration.

The 1870 reformers, like the Quakers before them, looked to institutional life as the way to effect rehabilitation. Inmates should be made into well-adjusted citizens, but the process should take place behind walls. The Cincinnati Declaration could thus in good faith insist that "reformation is a work of time; and a benevolent regard to the good of the criminal himself, as well as to the protection of society, requires that his sentence be long enough for the reformatory process to take effect."[12]

Elmira Reformatory

The new approach took shape in 1876 at Elmira Reformatory in New York where Zebulon Brockway was superintendent. According to Brockway the key to reform and rehabilitation lay in education. To this end, an attempt was made at Elmira to create a school-like atmosphere with courses in academic, vocational, and moral subjects.

Designed for first-time felons between the ages of sixteen and thirty, the approach at Elmira incorporated a mark system of classification, indeterminate sentences, and parole.

Like their counterparts in adult reformatories, juveniles incarcerated at the turn of the century were supposed to learn a trade that would assist them on the outside.

When a judge committed an offender to Elmira, the administrators could determine the release date as long as the time served did not exceed the maximum prescribed by law for the particular offense.

A three-grade system of classification was linked to the indeterminate sentence. The inmate entered the institution at grade 2, and if he earned nine marks a month for six months by completing school assignments and causing no problems, he could be moved up to grade 1—necessary for release. If, however, he did not cooperate and violated bans of crookedness, quarreling, and disregard for rules of propriety, thus demonstrating indifference to progress and lack of self-control, he would be demoted to grade 3. Only after three months' satisfactory behavior there could he then embark on his upward climb toward eventual release. This system echoed the reform principles and placed "the prisoner's fate, as far as possible, in his own hands."[13]

Elmira's proclaimed success at reforming young felons was widely heralded, and during the next several decades its program was emu-lated in more than fifteen states. Brockway's annual reports claimed that 81 percent of inmates released from Elmira underwent "probable reformation." His optimism was echoed in an article that appeared in the journal of the American Social Science Association, "How Far May We Abolish Prisons?" The author's answer: "to the degree that we put men into reformatories like Elmira, for it reforms more than 80 percent of those who are sent there."[14] Brockway even weathered a state investigation into charges of brutality at Elmira, which revealed that the whip and solitary confinement were used there regularly.

The reformatory movement had spread throughout much of the nation by 1900, but it was short-lived. By the outbreak of World War I in 1914, the movement was already in decline. Although the Cincinnati Declaration had not been specific with regard to age, reformatories were actually only for young offenders, a small fraction of convicted criminals.

This point is of particular relevance in discussing the reformatory movement. As we will see, in reality, the treatment of adults differed little from what it had been, but treatment of juveniles changed markedly. To understand these changes, we need to look back a bit to corrections for juveniles in the nineteenth century.

Juvenile Corrections

In the United States, as in England, until the early nineteenth century, juveniles over the age of seven who engaged in serious misbehavior were treated as adults if the state could show they knew the difference between right and wrong. As a result, children were often treated very brutally for simple acts of mischief. They were confined in workhouses (sometimes with their parents) or in jails and prisons, where they served out their sentences alongside convicted adults. Older juveniles frequently were subjected to sexual exploitation or harassment by other prisoners. The juvenile who was apprehended for a crime faced a bleak set of alternatives: punishment, forced apprenticeship, or (for girls) indentured servitude.

In 1838 the doctrine of **parens patriae** was adopted by the Supreme Court of the Commonwealth of Pennsylvania in *Ex parte Crouse*. The suit was brought by a father who objected to his daughter's commitment (by his wife, without his knowledge) to the Philadelphia House of Refuge after a finding that she was "incorrigible." The court approved the commitment, asking rhetorically, "May not the natural parents, when unequal to the task of education, or unworthy of it, be superseded by the *parens patriae* or common guardian of the community?" It justified its affirmative answer on grounds that still have much support: Parents' main responsibility in the rearing of children is to enable them to become fully functioning, productive adults. If parents fail in that responsibility, the state should assume it by training the children "to industry; by imbuing their minds with the principles of morality and religion; by furnishing them with means to earn a living; and, above all, by separating them from the corrupting influences of improper associates."[15] Thus, the state claimed to be acting in the child's best interest by taking over the role of parent.

The reformers of the day looked to the *parens patriae* philosophy to bring the disruptive child to a less damaging way of life. Houses of refuge were established in Philadelphia and New York, and children sent to them were indentured to farm communities as laborers. The general idea was to remove them from evil metropolitan influences and instruct them in the virtues of the simple life on the land.

Throughout the latter half of the nineteenth century, private reformers sought to aid juveniles who were in trouble. Industrial schools (built mostly in the country) were established for wayward youths, and New York's Children's Aid Society (still in operation

today) placed nearly 100,000 vagrant or wayward children.[16] But the reformers were increasingly troubled by the inapplicability of the adult criminal law to the kinds of problems they were attempting to address and the means that they wished to use.

Even though the doctrine of *parens patriae* has fallen on hard times in the latter half of the twentieth century, the legitimacy of the nineteenth-century reformers' aims is not in dispute. There were mounting numbers of unsupervised children and crimes committed by youths in the larger cities. No reasonable way to handle these problems seemed to exist: The adult criminal justice system was too harsh, and in any event the problem was not criminal but social.

Several reforms consistent with the ideals then current were implemented. Massachusetts provided for separate trials of juveniles in 1870 and separated the dockets and records in 1877; in 1898 Rhode Island provided for segregation of persons under sixteen who were awaiting trial. Separate training schools and industrial homes were common, and probation had been extended to juveniles by 1880. Thus, throughout the latter nineteenth century, there was a widening legal consensus that juvenile offenders should be treated differently (and separately) from adult offenders.

Aside from these differences with respect to the treatment of juveniles, what was the effect of the reform movement? Did it have other lasting effects?

Lasting Reforms

Talk of reforms notwithstanding, the architecture of most institutions, the attitudes of the guards, and the emphasis on discipline differed little from the orientations of the past. Too often the educational and rehabilitation efforts took a back seat to the traditional punitive methods. Even Brockway admitted difficulty in distinguishing inmates whose attitudes had changed from those who superficially conformed to prison rules. Being a good prisoner,

---

parens patriae   The "parent of the country"; the state as guardian and protector of all persons (particularly juveniles) who are unable to protect themselves.

the traditional emphasis, became the way to win parole in most of these institutions.

Although the ideals of Wines, Brockway, and the other leaders of the reformatory movement were not realized, these men did make major contributions to American corrections. The indeterminate sentence, classification, rehabilitative programs, and parole were all first developed at Elmira. The Declaration of Principles of the 1870 meeting in Cincinnati set goals that inspired prison reformers well into the twentieth century. Still more changes were to come before that, however. In the mid-nineteenth century, the United States was entering a period of significant social change. The nation was coming to grips with two forces: the gradual shift of the population from the countryside to the cities and the cultural threat posed by a flood of immigrants.

The Rise of the Progressives

T he first two decades of the twentieth century, called the "Age of Reform," set the dominant tone for American social thought and political action until the 1960s.[17] It was an age of response to the industrialization, urbanization, technological change, and advancement of science that had revolutionized the landscape. A group known as Progressives attacked the excesses of this revolution, especially big business, and placed their faith in state action to deal with the social problems of slums, adulterated food, dangerous occupational conditions, vice, and crime.

The Progressives, most of whom came from upper-status backgrounds, were optimistic about the possibility of solving the problems of modern society. They were concerned in particular about conditions of cities whose large immigrant populations were beginning to develop political power. They believed that civic-minded people could apply the findings of science to social problems, including penol-ogy, in ways that would benefit all. Correctional reformers believed that the new penology would succeed in rehabilitating criminals.

Individualized Treatment

The Progressive programs, according to David Rothman, can be epitomized in two words: *conscience* and *convenience*. The reforms were promoted by benevolent and philanthropic men and women who aimed to understand and cure crime through a case-by-case approach. They believed that the reformers of the penitentiary era were wrong in assuming that all deviants were "victims of social disorder" and that the deviants "could all be rehabilitated with a single program, the well-ordered routine" of the prison.[18] The Progressives thought it necessary to know the life history of each offender and then devise a treatment program specific to that individual. However, in order to diagnose each criminal, prescribe treatment, and determine when release to the community was possible, correctional administrators had to be given discretion. It was from this orientation that the phrase "treatment according to the needs of the offender" came into vogue, in contrast to "punishment according to the severity of the crime," which had been the hallmark of Beccaria and the reformers of the early nineteenth century.

Rothman argues that because discretion was required for the day-to-day practice of the new penology, correctional administrators responded favorably to it. The new discretionary authority made it more convenient for administrators to carry out their daily assignments. He also notes that although the Progressives were not committed to incarceration, as supporters of the penitentiary were, and in fact were instrumental in promoting acceptance of probation and parole, the requirement of discretion served to expand the size of the prison population.

The Progressives had faith that the state would carry out their reforms with justice. In the same way that they looked to government programs to secure social justice, they assumed that the agents of the state would help offenders. Rothman notes:

> In criminal justice, the issue was not how to protect the offender from the arbitrariness of the state, but how to bring the state more effectively to the aid of the offender. The state was not a behemoth to be chained and fettered, but an agent capable of fulfilling an ambitious program. Thus, a policy that called for the state's exercise of discretionary authority in finely tuned responses was, at its core, Progressive.[19]

Modern Criminology

Although many of the reforms advocated by the Progressives were first stated in the 1870 Declaration of Principles, the new activists looked to social, biological, and psychological rather than religious or moral explanations for the causes of crime and for treatment therapies. They relied on the modern criminological developments associated with a scientific approach to crime and human behavior known as the **positivist school**.

The classical school of Beccaria and Bentham had emphasized a legal approach to the problem, focusing on the act rather than the criminal. By applying the scientific method, positivist scholars changed the focus of inquiry from the criminal law to the behavior of the offender. By the beginning of the twentieth century, advances in the biological and social sciences provided the framework that contributed to the reforms proposed by the Progressives.

Though several theoretical perspectives can be found within the positivist school, three

---

positivist school An approach to criminology and other social sciences based on the assumption that human behavior is a product of biological, economic, psychological, and social factors, and that the scientific method can be applied to ascertain the cause of the behavior of any individual.

---

basic assumptions are shared by most of its practitioners.

1. Criminal behavior is not the result of free will but stems from factors over which the individual has no control: biological characteristics, psychological maladjustments, sociological conditions.

2. Criminals can be treated so that they can lead crime-free lives.

3. Treatment must be focused on the individual and the individual's problem.

Progressive Reforms

Armed with their views about the nature of criminal behavior and the need for state action to reform offenders, the Progressives fought for changes in correctional methods. Their efforts centered on two strategies: One was designed to improve conditions in those environments they believed to be breeding grounds for crime; the other emphasized ways to rehabilitate the individual deviant. Because they looked on crime as primarily an urban problem, one that was concentrated especially among the immigrant lower class, the Progressives sought through political action to bring about changes that would improve ghetto conditions: better public health, landlord–tenant laws, public housing, playgrounds, settlement houses, education. But because they also believed that criminal behavior varied among individuals, a case-by-case approach was required.[20] Through such instruments as the presentence report, with its extensive personal history, judges and correctional officials could analyze individuals' problems and take action to rehabilitate them.

By the 1920s the Progressives had succeeded in getting wide acceptance of four portions of their program: probation, indeterminate sentences, parole, and juvenile courts. These elements had been proposed at the 1870 Cincinnati meeting, but the Progressives and their allies in corrections were instrumental in spreading their use throughout the country.

BIOGRAPHY

Julian W. Mack (1866–1943)

A federal judge for thirty years, Julian Mack ranks as one of the foremost innovators in juvenile justice. Born in San Francisco, he received his law degree at Harvard and went into practice in Chicago in 1890. He was elected to a judgeship for the Circuit Court of Cook County, Illinois, in 1903, and between 1904 and 1907 he presided over Chicago's juvenile court, the first in the world. This court had been established by the Illinois legislature in 1899. Under Mack, the court dealt with neglected and abused children, runaways, school dropouts, and juveniles who had committed crimes. Juveniles were to be seen not as criminals but as wards of the state, thereby achieving a new legal status. The court was to become a social agency mixing services, discipline, probation, and the use of reformatories.

Mack believed that the proper work of the system depended to a large extent on the judge and the support that judge received from probation officers, caseworkers, and psychologists. The judge and the staff had to be intellectually and temperamentally suited for work with juveniles; they had to be professionals and not political hacks. To this end, Mack supported the founding of the National Probation Officers Association. He sought as much as possible to avoid using reformatories and tried to bring the expertise of social service professionals to work for the courts.

In 1907 Mack was promoted to the Illinois Appeals Court, and in 1911 he was appointed by President William Howard Taft to a seat on the U.S. Court of Appeals for the Seventh Circuit, from which he retired in 1941.

Probation Probation had its origin in the work of John Augustus in the Boston Police Court in 1841 (see Chapter 7). This alternative to incarceration fitted nicely into the Progressive scheme, for it recognized individual differences and allowed offenders to be treated in the community under supervision. Massachusetts passed a probation law in 1878, yet no other state took the step until 1897, and in 1900 only six states provided for probation. But by 1920 every state permitted it for juveniles and thirty-three states permitted it for adults. In 1930 the federal government and thirty-six states, including every industrial state, had adult probation laws on their books.

Much as this rapid expansion of probation appears to attest to the strength of the Progressives' argument, a closer look is needed.

Probation remained primarily an urban strategy; it never took root in rural or small-town America. The reason may lie in beliefs about the cost-effectiveness of the approach in areas where populations are scattered, or perhaps it lies in a different mind-set among rural people.

In urban areas problems of staffing, caseload size, and the quality of supervision never permitted probation to approach the reformers' expectations. Almost no jurisdiction met the 50:1 ratio of clients to supervisors then advocated by penologists. Perhaps more important, probation officers were given an almost impossible task: With very little scientifically based theory to guide their actions, they were expected to keep their charges crime-free. What passed as ways to reform probationers often turned out to be little more than attempts to indoctrinate them with a set of middle-class moral injunctions—work, go to church, keep clean, get ahead, be good—attitudes that were not consistent with the reality of life in city slums.

From time to time politicians in one state or another attacked probation as the "coddling" of criminals, yet the system prevailed. For one thing, probation was a useful device for inducing the guilty plea, then thought to be necessary for the functioning of overcrowded courts.[21]

Indeterminate sentence and parole Although the idea of parole release had been developed in Ireland and Australia in the 1850s and Zebulon Brockway had instituted it at Elmira in 1876, it was not until the mid-1920s that it really caught on in the United States. By then thirty-seven states had indeterminate sentencing laws and forty-four provided for release on parole. Flat sentences were retained for lesser offenses, but during this period more than three-quarters of convicted offenders whose maximum terms exceeded five years were serving indeterminate sentences.

The sentences were called "indeterminate," but nearly always there were minimum and maximum terms, within which the correctional process of rehabilitation could operate. At no time were state legislatures willing to give correctional officials unbridled authority to decide when (or if) a prisoner could be released. Yet over time, legislatures tended to expand the outer limits of sentences. Especially when they wanted to respond to public outcries over crime, politicians would often increase the maximum penalties, thus giving parole decision makers wider discretion.

Like probation, parole expanded greatly during the Progressive period. By the middle of the 1920s, well over 80 percent of felons sentenced in the major industrial states left prison via the parole gate. What once had been a procedure for the release of deserving offenders in a few reformatories became the means by which the overwhelming majority of inmates went back into the community. As parole expanded, so did public criticism of it, especially when newspapers reported that a particularly heinous crime had been committed by someone released from prison under supervision. Studies conducted in the 1920s and 1930s showed that recidivism was high among parolees, and that the purported "diagnostic evaluation" by parole boards usually meant little more than speculation and a reflection of the prejudices of their members.

Rothman argues that because these reforms included wide discretionary authority for criminal justice officials and affirmed the vitality of the rehabilitative ideal, they were retained and extended.[22] But when probation, indeterminate sentences, and parole were put into practice, they fell far short of expectations; yet they have been retained in the face of many doubts about them, and they remain dominant elements of corrections to this day. Another of the Progressive's reforms, juvenile court, has been subject to less questioning over the years.

Juvenile court By 1899 the stage was set for the most significant justice reform since the invention of the penitentiary in Philadelphia barely a century earlier: the creation of the juvenile court. The 1899 law by which the first juvenile court was established (in Cook County [Chicago], Illinois) was an all but inevitable result of the philosophy that dominated the reform period. The law defined the jurisdiction of the juvenile court to include both the delinquent child—the child under sixteen who violated the law—and the dependent and neglected child. The law described the court's charges as

> any child who for any reason is destitute or homeless or abandoned; or dependent upon the public for support; or has not proper parental care or guardianship; or who habitually begs or receives alms; or who is found living in any house of ill fame or with any vicious or disreputable person; or whose home, by reason of neglect, cruelty or depravity on the part of

its parents, guardian or other person in whose care it may be, is an unfit place for such a child.[23]

The law did not differentiate between the delinquent, neglected, or dependent child. All were troubled; all needed the benevolent intervention of the state. Because the court existed to help children in trouble, differentiation served no purpose. By 1925 all but two states had followed this model; by 1945 every state had a complete juvenile code.

The reformers were quite right in believing that children reared in brutalizing conditions were likely to turn into problem adults. Where they may have been wrong was in assuming that the state could be an effective surrogate parent under the sociopolitical pressures of the day. Recent critics of the juvenile reform movement have pointed out that the reformers' motives were mixed: Police wanted children removed from the streets; the upper class wanted immigrants to be inculcated with traditional American values; industrialists wanted youth to be taught discipline and basic skills; and some reformers sought a way to add meaning to their lives through social action.[24] In practice, the pure desire to help children may have been far outweighed by forces linked to urbanization and industrialization. Subsequently, these and other forces promoted yet another change in corrections.

The Rise of the Medical Model

Even before psychiatry assumed its influential role in American society, the idea that crimes are committed by people who are ill was current in correctional circles. At the 1870 Cincinnati congress one speaker described a criminal as "a man who has suffered under a disease evinced by the perpetration of a crime, and who may reasonably be held to be under the dominion of such disease until his conduct has afforded very strong presumption not only that he is free from its immediate influence, but that the chances of its recurrence have become exceedingly remote."[25] Certainly, much of the reform activity of the Progressives was based on the idea that criminals could be rehabilitated through treatment, but it was not until the 1930s that serious attempts were made to implement what became known as the **medical model** of corrections. Under the banner of the newly prestigious social and behavioral sciences, the emphasis of corrections shifted to treatment of criminals as persons whose social, intellectual, or biological deficiencies had caused them to engage in illegal activity.

Rehabilitation as the primary purpose of incarceration became national policy in 1929, when the new Federal Bureau of Prisons was authorized by Congress to develop institutions that would ensure the proper classification, care, and treatment of offenders. Many states, particularly New Jersey, New York, Illinois, and California, soon fell in line with new programs designed to reform through treatment. Most other states and political leaders everywhere adopted at least the rhetoric of rehabilitation, changing statutes to specify that treatment was the goal of their correctional system and that punishment was an outworn concept. Prisons were thus to become something like mental hospitals that would rehabilitate and test the inmate for readiness to reenter society. In many states, however, the medical model was often honored in name only: Departments of prisons became departments of corrections, but the budgets for treatment programs remained about the same.

It is not surprising that corrections moved in the direction of a medical model when it did. In the 1920s the field of social work had gained

---

medical model   A model of corrections based on the assumption that criminal behavior is caused by biological or psychological conditions that require treatment.

intellectual and professional status; its practitioners were no longer viewed as merely deliverers of charity to the poor. Through the casework approach, social workers attempted to diagnose and help the unfortunate. Following World War I, psychology had developed new ways of measuring mental fitness and assessing personality. The theories of Sigmund Freud and Carl Jung dominated American psychiatry, and these approaches began to take their place alongside biological explanations for illness. Advocates of the medical model sought to bring about change through treatment programs, most often with a psychological base. As psychiatrist Karl Menninger was to say, criminal acts are "signals of distress, signals of failure … the spasms of struggles and convulsions of a submarginal human being trying to make it in our complex society with inadequate equipment and inadequate preparation."[26]

Since the essential structural elements of parole, probation, and the indeterminate sentence were already in place in most states, incorporation of the medical model required only the addition of classification systems to diagnose offenders and treatment programs to cure them. Tests were developed to assist psychologists, psychiatrists, and social workers to determine the cause of the inmate's problem and indicate appropriate treatment. Recognizing that the prison environment would have an influence on the effectiveness of treatment, it was argued that different types of institutions should be developed for different types of inmates. Envisioned were institutions not merely with differing levels of security but prisons that would be devoted primarily to vocational training, agricultural work, or psychiatric care. Classification thus became the crucial first step in treatment; the individual was to be differentiated from the masses and a program of educational, medical, and psychological care prescribed.

The systems of classification varied greatly from state to state. Generally, attempts were made to differentiate inmates who were likely to benefit from treatment from those who were

not. In some states recidivists, the feebleminded, and the physically impaired might get only the "treatment" of custody or labor at a prison farm or industry. A most extensive classification scheme was promulgated in Wisconsin in 1937. Inmates were placed into one of seven groupings that were exclusively psychiatric:

1. mentally deficient: arrested intellectual development; "feebleminded";
2. mentally defective: inadequate personality; "criminal";
3. mentally diseased: psychotic; "insane";
4. mentally deviate: neurotic; "borderline insane";
5. mentally distorted: inadequate state; "morally aberrant";
6. mentally delayed (minors); or
7. atypical or unclassifiable…[27]

Although initially the number of psychiatrists and therapeutic treatment programs was limited, they increased greatly after World War II. California set a national standard of commitment to treatment programs. Group therapy, behavior modification, shock therapy, individual counseling, psychotherapy, guided group interaction, and numerous other approaches all became part of the "new penology." Competing schools of psychological thought debated the usefulness of many of these techniques, many of which were adopted or discarded before their worth had been evaluated. Further, the administrative needs of the institution often superseded the treatment needs of the inmate; prisoners tended to be assigned to facilities, jobs, and programs that had openings rather than to those that would provide the prescribed treatment.

Maryland's Patuxent Institution, which opened in 1955, is probably the best example of a prison built on the principles of the medical model. Patuxent was founded to treat adults given indeterminate sentences and adjudged to be "defective delinquents." Its administrators had broad authority to control intake, to experiment with a treatment milieu, and to decide when to release "patients." Throughout the period of incarceration, a patient was diagnosed and treated through a variety of programs and therapies.

By the 1970s, as criticism rose about the lack of success with the medical model, the Maryland legislature undertook a critical examination of Patuxent's mission. Changes were made that reduced the authority of the administrators, especially with regard to the release decision. By 1991 the legislature had also changed the institution's goal from rehabilitation to remediation—helping inmates overcome such deficits as lack of reading skills, poor behavior controls, or substance abuse.[28]

Critics of treatment programs in American prisons pointed out that even during the 1950s, when the medical model was at its zenith, only 5 percent of state correctional budgets was allocated for rehabilitation. Although states adopted the rhetoric of the medical model, the institutions were still being run with custody as an overriding goal. Some people argued that it was impossible to develop the rapport with inmates needed to cure their personality difficulties, and others asserted that custody always took precedence over treatment in the day-to-day running of prisons.

From Medical Model to Community Model

As we have seen, correctional thought and practices are greatly influenced by the social and political values of particular periods. During the 1960s and 1970s, U.S. society experienced the civil rights movement, the war on poverty, and resistance to the war in Vietnam. Governmental institutions dealing with education, mental health, juvenile delinquency, and adult corrections were challenged. In 1967 the President's Commission on Law Enforcement and Administration of Justice reported that

> crime and delinquency are symptoms of failures and disorganization of the community.... The task of corrections, therefore, includes building or rebuilding social ties,

> obtaining employment and education, securing in the larger senses a place for the offender in the routine functioning of society.[29]

This analysis was consistent with the views of advocates of **community corrections** who felt that the goal of the criminal justice system should be the reintegration of the offender in the community.

Community corrections called for a radical departure from the medical model's emphasis on treatment in the prison. Instead, prisons were to be avoided since they were viewed as artificial institutions that interfered with the offender's ability to develop a crime-free lifestyle. It was argued that corrections should turn away from psychological treatment to programs that would increase offender opportunities to become successful citizens. Probation should be the sentence of choice for nonviolent offenders so that they could engage in vocational and educational programs that increased their chances of adjusting to society. For the small portion of offenders who had to be incarcerated, the amount of time in prison should be only a short interval until release on parole. To further the goal of reintegration, correctional workers were to serve as advocates for offenders as they dealt with governmental agencies providing employment counseling, medical treatment, and financial assistance.

The reintegration idea was dominant in corrections for about a decade, until the late 1970s. It gave way to a new punitiveness in conjunction with the rebirth of the determinate sentence. Advocates of reintegration would say, as advocates of earlier reform proposals had said, that the idea was never given a complete testing. Nevertheless, community programming for offenders remains one of the significant ideas and practices in the recent history of corrections.

community corrections A model of corrections based on the assumption that the reintegration of the offender into the community should be the goal of the criminal justice system.

Crime Control Model: The Pendulum Swings Again

Beginning in the late 1960s the public became concerned about rising crime rates, studies of treatment programs were published challenging their worth, and the Progressive assumption that state officials would exercise discretion in a positive manner proved to be unfounded. The rethinking of corrections emphasized the need to move away from the goal of rehabilitation toward a greater concern for crime control. Critics of rehabilitation attacked the indeterminate sentence and parole, urging that treatment be available on a voluntary basis but that it not be tied to release. In addition, advocates of a greater emphasis on crime control called for longer sentences, especially for career criminals and for those who had committed violent offenses.

James Q. Wilson summarized the "new realism" in regard to treatment programs and crime rates when he declared that our efforts to understand and curb the rise in crime have been frustrated by "our optimistic and unrealistic assumptions about human nature."[30] Addressing the fact that the United States experienced an upsurge in crime during the prosperity of the 1960s and early 1970s, Wilson found it strange that "we should persist in the view that we can find and alleviate the 'causes' of crime, [and] that serious criminals can be rehabilitated."[31]

Rehabilitation Recedes

One of the most frequently voiced criticisms of the rehabilitation model concerns the effectiveness of treatment. It has been said that if recidivism is the criterion, then correctional treatment has worked in only a small proportion of cases. Probably the most thorough analysis of research data from treatment programs was undertaken by Robert Martinson for the New York State Governor's Special Committee on Criminal Offenders. Using rigorous standards, he surveyed all studies of rehabilitation programs in correctional systems written in the English language; 231 met his criteria. Included in Martinson's analysis were such standard rehabilitative programs as educational and vocational training, individual counseling, group counseling, milieu therapy, medical treatment (plastic surgery, drugs), parole, and supervision. Martinson summarized his findings by saying: "With few and isolated exceptions, the rehabilitative efforts that have been reported so far have had no appreciable effect on recidivism."[32]

Critics of the rehabilitation model pointed out that discretion is required by decision makers so that the criminal sanction may be tailored to meet the special needs of each offender. Critics say that such discretion is unwarranted. In particular, they have argued that the discretion given to parole boards to release offenders was based more on the whim of individual members than on the scientific criteria espoused by the medical model.

Crime Control Comes to the Fore

During the late 1970s and the 1980s, the crime rate was at historic levels and policies designed to enhance crime control came to the fore. The critique of the rehabilitative model led to changes in the sentencing structures of more than half of the states and the abolition of parole release in many. One result was that the new determinate sentencing laws were designed to incarcerate offenders for longer periods of time. In conjunction with other forms of punishment, the thrust of the 1980s was for crime control through risk containment.

The punitive ethos of the 1980s can be seen in the emphasis on the need to deal more strictly with those offenders who had committed violent crimes and those viewed as career criminals. Supplementing these efforts was a greater stress on the intensive supervision of probationers, the holding without bail of accused persons thought to present a danger to the community, reinstitution of the death penalty in thirty-seven states, and the requirement that judges impose mandatory penalties for persons convicted of certain offenses or having extensive criminal records. By the end of the decade, the success of these policies was evidenced by the record numbers of persons incarcerated, the greater amount of time being served, and the size of the probation population. Some observers point to these policies as the reason that the crime rate has begun to fall. Others question whether the crime control policies have really made a difference given demographic and other changes in the United States.

Where Are We Today?

As the United States moves toward a new century, the time may be ripe for another look at correctional policy. The language now used in journals of corrections is quite different from that found on their pages twenty years ago. The optimism that once suffused corrections has waned. The costs, both financial and human, of the retributive crime control policies of the 1980s are now being scrutinized. Critics have asked if the costs of incarceration and surveillance are justified. They ask, Has crime been reduced? Are we safer today? Many researchers have answered both of these questions in the negative. As we look to the future, we wonder if there will be a new direction for corrections. If so, what will be the new focus?

Summary

Social change is brought about by diverse elements in society that place questions on the political agenda, lobby for new policies, and urge an end to existing practices. The history of correctional thought and practice has been one of periodic shifts, marked by enthusiasm for new approaches, disillusionment with these approaches, and then substitution of yet another tactic.

Each of the reform movements through which American corrections has passed seems to have resulted from the efforts of well-intentioned people working in the name of humanity. As society has changed, the assumptions underlying corrections changed from one period to the next. Regardless of the assumptions, the reformers' ideals were never fully achieved and the changes they effected often produced unsatisfactory results. In most cases, political and bureaucratic influences won out, prisons quickly became poorly managed, and probation and parole cases became too numerous. And always the stone walls of the prisons remained.

For Discussion

1. Why do you think that the idea of the penitentiary first caught on in the United States?

2. What changes in society might be behind the shift in attitudes about *parens patriae* since the nineteenth century?

3. To what extent have developments in American corrections mirrored shifts in the organization and management of other human services institutions? Provide specific examples to support your answer.

4. The prison seems to hold continuing fascination in American culture. What other methods might the general public find acceptable as ways to punish offenders?

5. How do you think offenders will be punished in the United States in the future? What philosophical and technical developments would buttress the approaches you foresee?

6. We seem to be constantly driven by images of a crime-free society. As a result, we adopt drastic solutions as though "crime-free" is a possibility. Is it?

For Further Reading

McKelvey, Blake. *American Prisons.* Montclair, N.J.: Patterson Smith, 1977. A classic history of the development of American prisons.

Platt, Anthony. *The Child Savers: The Invention of Delinquency.* Chicago: University of Chicago Press, 1970. A history of the Progressive "child saver" movement.

Rothman, David J. *Conscience and Convenience.* Boston: Little, Brown, 1980. Examines Progressive Era reforms to individualize cure and treatment for deviants and therefore solve the problems of crime and mental illness.

————. *The Discovery of the Asylum.* Boston: Little, Brown, 1971. Describes changes in the ways Americans treated criminals, the mentally ill, and the poor during the eighteenth and early part of the nineteenth centuries.

Teeters, Negley K., and Shearer, John D. *The Prison at Philadelphia Cherry Hill.* New York: Columbia University Press, 1957. A history of Eastern Penitentiary, the first correctional facility organized around the concept of separate confinement.

Notes

1. Negley K. Teeters and John D. Shearer, *The Prison at Philadelphia Cherry Hill* (New York: Columbia University Press, 1957), p. 63.

2. David J. Rothman, *The Discovery of the Asylum* (Boston: Little, Brown, 1971), p. 51.

3. Louis P. Masur, *Rites of Execution* (New York: Oxford University Press, 1989), p. 24.

4. Blake McKelvey, *American Prisons* (Montclair, N.J.: Patterson Smith, 1977), p. 8.

5. Thorsten Sellin, "The Origin of the Pennsylvania System of Prison Discipline," *Prison Journal* 50 (Spring-Summer 1970): 15–17.

6. Gustav de Beaumont and Alexis de Tocqueville, *On the Penitentiary System in the United States and Its Application to France* (Carbondale: Southern Illinois University Press, [1833] 1964), p. 146.

7. Charles Dickens, *American Notes,* vol. 1 (London: Chapman & Hall, 1842), p. 238.

8. Teeters and Shearer, *Prison at Philadelphia,* ch. 4.

9. de Beaumont and de Tocqueville, *On the Penitentiary System,* p. 201.

10. John A. Conley, "Prisons, Production, and Profit: Reconsidering the Importance of Prison Industries," *Journal of Social History* 14 (Winter 1980): 257–75.

11. Elizabeth Eileen Dooley, "Sir Walter Crofton and the Irish or Intermediate System of Prison Discipline," *New England Journal of Prison Law* 575 (Winter 1981): 55.

12. David J. Rothman, *Conscience and Convenience* (Boston: Little, Brown, 1980), p. 18.

13. Ibid., p. 41.

14. W. M. F. Round, "How Far May We Abolish Prisons?" *Journal of the American Social Science Association* 325 (1897): 200–201. As cited in Rothman, *Conscience and Convenience,* p. 55.

15. *Ex parte Crouse,* 4 Wharton (Pa.) 9 (1838).

16. Enoch C. Wines, *The State of Prisons and Child Saving Institutions in the Western World* (Montclair, N.J.: Patterson Smith, [1880] 1968).

17. Richard Hofstader, *The Age of Reform* (New York: Knopf, 1974).

18. Rothman, *Conscience and Convenience,* p. 5.

19. Ibid., p. 60.

20. Ibid., p. 53.

21. Ibid., p. 99.

22. Ibid.

23. *Illinois Laws,* April 21, 1899, pp. 131–32.

24. Jameson W. Doig, "For the Salvation of Children: The Search for Juvenile Justice in the United States," in *Crime and Criminal Justice,* ed. John A. Gardiner and Michael A. Mulkey (Lexington, Mass.: D.C. Heath, 1975), pp. 141–42.

25. Quoted in Jessica Mitford, *Kind and Usual Punishment* (New York: Knopf, 1973), p. 96.

26. Karl Menninger, *The Crime of Punishment* (New York: Viking, 1969), p. 19.

27. Harry E. Barnes and Negley K. Teeters, *New Horizons in Criminology* (New York: Prentice-Hall, 1944), p. 768.

28. Thomas F. Courtless, "Maryland's Flirtation with Positive Penology: Patuxent Institution from Cutting Edge Back to the Drawing Board." Paper given at the annual meeting of the American Society of Criminology, San Francisco, November, 1991.

29. U.S. President's Commission on Law Enforcement and Administration of Justice, *The Challenge of Crime in a Free Society* (Washington, D.C.: Government Printing Office, 1967), p. 7.

30. James Q. Wilson, "Lock 'Em Up and Other Thoughts on Crime," *New York Times Magazine,* 9 March 1982, p. 11.

31. Ibid.

32. Robert Martinson, "What Works? Questions and Answers About Prison Reform," *Public Interest* 35 (Spring 1974): 22.

4

The Punishment of Offenders

When my assignment is changed from the civil to the criminal side of the superior court, I know I am in for a grim time.

Judge Robert Satter

The Purpose of Corrections
Retribution (Deserved Punishment)
Deterrence
Incapacitation
Rehabilitation
Criminal Sanctions: A Mixed Bag?
Forms of the Criminal Sanction
Incarceration
Intermediate Sanctions
Probation
Death
The Sentencing Process
Attitudes and Background
The Administrative Context
Sentence Disparity: One Result of the Process
The Presentence Report
The Politics of Sentencing Reform
Legislative Action
Impact of Reform
Summary

As she lay sleeping in her Scarsdale, New York, home, Bonnie Garland's college sweetheart killed her by hitting her with a hammer. Hours later, Garland's killer, Richard Herrin, said, "Her head broke open like a watermelon."[1]

The tragic ending to their love affair raised difficult questions of justice as Herrin's Catholic supporters, the psychiatrists, and the lawyers all looked at the crime through different perceptual lenses and prescribed different dispositions of the case consistent with their own values. With so much attention focused on Herrin, a Yale University graduate from the Hispanic barrio of Los Angeles, it seemed that the victim had been pushed aside and forgotten, the crime forgiven.

After a trial dominated by often contradictory psychiatric testimony in which it was argued that Herrin acted under the influence of extreme emotional disturbance, the jury found him guilty of manslaughter. They did not find that he acted with malice, required for the verdict of murder that was sought by the state. Herrin was sentenced to a minimum of eight and one-third years to a maximum of twenty-five years in prison.

In *The Killing of Bonnie Garland,* Willard Gaylin asks, "Where is justice?" Should Richard Herrin have been executed, sentenced to imprisonment, treated in a mental hospital, placed under house arrest with electronic monitoring, or released on probation? Did justice serve Bonnie Garland and her parents? Were the needs of society for the maintenance of right conduct supported by the sentence? What rationale buttresses the punishment handed down?

These age-old questions are central to our consideration of the corrections system, which is charged with carrying out the sanction that society has deemed just for those who violate its rules. In this chapter we examine the goals of corrections, the forms of the criminal sanction, and the sentencing process. As we explore these topics, we will examine their links to one another and to the historical and philosophical issues developed in Chapter 2 and 3.

The Purpose of Corrections

Theories of punishment are very much influenced by the broad philosophical, political, and social themes that have come to prominence at various times in Western history. Prevailing ideas about the causes of crime are closely tied to questions of individual responsibility and hence to the rationale for specific sanctions. The ideas of the classical school of criminology, founded by Beccaria, fitted nicely with the concepts of the Age of Reason, and Bentham's utilitarianism meshed with the rationalistic approaches. Under the leadership of the German philosopher Immanuel Kant, efforts were made to balance the degree of punishment with the gravity of the offense. In the context of the times, "make the punishment fit the crime" was a humanistic advance in that it sought to do away with the horrible punishments often inflicted for trivial offenses. With the rise of science and the development of the positivist school in the nineteenth century, new beliefs emerged as to the nature of criminal responsibility and the extent to which punishment should be designed to meet the needs of the offender. With criminal behavior increasingly viewed as resulting from sociological, psychological, or biological factors, the focus of punishment was directed toward the correction of these problems. Rehabilitation of the offender thus became dominant for both humanitarian and utilitarian reasons.

Before we further examine the goals of the criminal sanction, we must consider the term *punishment.* What does it mean? Does it encompass all actions taken under law against an offender, or only retribution? Is a person enrolled in a rehabilitative program being punished? These questions must be asked, for in twentieth-century America the term often has an ideological connotation linking it to retribution and not to the other justifications for the criminal sanction.

Herbert Packer argues that punishment may be described as all ways of dealing with people that are marked by these features:

1. the presence of an offense;

2. the infliction of pain on account of the commission of the offense; and

3. a dominant purpose that is neither to compensate someone injured by the offense nor to better the offender's condition but to prevent further offenses or to inflict what is thought to be deserved pain on the offender.[2]

This definition reflects much of the philosophical and criminological debate about the sanctions imposed by law. Note that Packer emphasizes two major goals of criminal punishment: the deserved infliction of suffering on evildoers and the prevention of crime.

During the twentieth century four goals of the criminal sanction are acknowledged in the United States: retribution (deserved punishment), deterrence, incapacitation, and rehabilitation. As we discuss each of the four justifications for punishment, bear in mind that the reality of criminal justice may result in a mixture of sanctions including incarceration, intermediate sanctions, probation, or death. It is common for judges to stress publicly that their sentencing practices are in accord with a particular goal, yet conditions in correctional institutions or the actions of probation officers may be inconsistent with that goal. A close examination may reveal that sentencing and correctional policies are carried out in such a way that no one goal dominates. The criminal sanction may be administered in ways that confuse the purposes to such an extent that justice does not win out.

Retribution (Deserved Punishment)

When someone violates the law, the immediate response often is that the offender deserves to be punished for disregarding the rights of others or upsetting the moral order. **Retribution** is the oldest justification for punishment; "an eye for an eye, a tooth for a tooth" goes back to biblical times. Although the ancient saying may sound barbaric, it can be thought of as a definition of retribution: Those who do a wrong should be punished alike, in proportion to the gravity of the offense or to the extent to which others have been made to suffer. Retribution is punishment that is deserved; offenders should "pay their debts." It focuses on past behavior, and on the offense, and has no concern with the future acts of the criminal or with some utilitarian purpose such as reform or deterrence. According to retribution, offenders should be penalized for their wrongful acts because fairness and justice require that they be punished.

As discussed in Chapter 2, with the Age of Reason and the development of utilitarian approaches to punishment, the idea of retribution lost much of its influence. However, some philosophers held to the idea of retribution. In about the year 1800, Immanuel Kant wrote that even an island society that was about to disband should punish its last offender. Society, he asserted, has not only a right to punish violators of the law but a duty to do so. If the public fails to carry out its duty, it is an accomplice in the violation.

It has also been argued that the desire for retribution is a basic human emotion and that if the state does not provide a means for the community to express its revulsion against offensive acts, individuals will take the law into their own hands. Retribution helps the community to emphasize the standards it expects all of its members to uphold.

After about one hundred and fifty years of having taken a backseat to such utilitarian justifications as deterrence and rehabilitation, retribution has again caught the interest of scholars and criminal justice reformers. Beginning in the early 1970s, a sharp reaction to the dominant emphasis on rehabilitation brought efforts

---

retribution (deserved punishment) Punishment inflicted on a person who has infringed the rights of others and so deserves to be penalized to a degree commensurate with the crime.

to change those sentencing, treatment, and release structures that had been incorporated in all American correctional systems as a result of the positivist and reform orientation. These efforts returned retribution to the foreground. Now, however, it is often referred to more delicately as *deserved punishment* or *just deserts.*

In *Doing Justice,* one of the leading statements of the just deserts approach, Andrew von Hirsch writes, "Someone who infringes the rights of others...does wrong and deserves blame for his conduct. It is because he deserves blame that the sanctioning authority is entitled to choose a response that expresses moral disapproval; namely, punishment."[3] The severity of the sanction should be proportionate to the gravity of the defendant's criminal conduct. The punishment is therefore backward looking, its severity based only on the seriousness of the offense. It is not based on such utilitarian considerations as the offender's need for treatment, the likelihood that the offender will commit crimes in the future, or the possible deterrent effect of the punishment on others. Offenders should be penalized for their wrongful acts because fairness and justice dictate that they receive the punishment they deserve.

Deterrence

With the increasing influence of utilitarian rationales in the nineteenth century, emphasis began to shift to the idea that some "good" should result from the infliction of punishment. Retribution, it was argued, was pointless and unjustifiable except as it could be shown that more good would result from pain inflicted than from pain withheld. The presumed good of the punishment was the prevention of crime. Thus, the utilitarian goal of deterrence is enhanced by the extent to which the punishment, either actual or threatened, will limit those who might otherwise be disposed to commit crimes. Thus, offenders are useful to society as they provide examples to others; the fear of punishment is at the base of deterrence.

Modern ideas of deterrence have incorporated two subsidiary concepts: **general deterrence**, which is most directly linked to Bentham's ideas, and **special deterrence** (often called *specific* or *individual deterrence*). General deterrence is the idea that the population at large is dissuaded from criminal behavior when it can be seen that punishment necessarily follows commission of a crime. It is assumed that rational individuals weigh the fact that the pain of the sanction is greater than the benefits that may stem from the illegal act. General deterrence thus requires that punishment be severe enough to have an impact, that the population may be certain that the sanction will be carried out, and that examples be numerous enough to remind people constantly of what lies ahead if they break the law. The public punishments of the seventeenth and eighteenth centuries described in Chapters 2 and 3 were justified in terms of retribution but were also designed as deterrents. But clearly, some people are difficult to deter.

Special deterrence is concerned with changes in the behavior of the convicted. It is individualized in that the correct amount and kind of punishment must be prescribed so that the criminal will not repeat the offense. Theoretically, the pain of punishment conditions the individual to avoid criminal behavior in the future. What the criminal needs for this to be effective becomes the most important question.

There are obvious difficulties with the concepts of general and special deterrence. In many cases, the two goals are incompatible. The level of punishment needed to impress the populace may not be what the offender needs.

---

general deterrence Punishment of criminals intended to serve as an example to the general public and thus to discourage the commission of offenses.

special deterrence (specific or individual deterrence) Punishment administered to criminals with the intent to discourage them from committing crimes in the future.

For example, public disgrace of upper-status professionals who have stolen may have the desired effect on them. But if these offenders are not incarcerated, the public may believe that they "got off" or that the sanction violated the concept of equity because a working-class person would have been sent to prison for the same crime.

From a scientific point of view, there is a more important problem: It is difficult to obtain empirical data to prove or disprove the effectiveness of deterrence. Although common sense may tell us that general deterrence is plausible, social science is unable to measure its effects; only those who are *not* deterred come to the attention of criminal justice researchers. Research has tended to support the idea that the certainty of punishment has a greater deterrent effect than does the severity of the sanction. But it is not clear whether deterrence plays *any* role in persuading some people to obey the law.

If potential criminals know that only five of a hundred robberies will result in prison sentences, will these people be deterred? In a study of self-reports of a California sample of incarcerated robbers Peter Greenwood found that the probability of arrest and conviction in that state is .03; for convictions the probability of incarceration is .86. Thus, the probability of incarceration for a given robbery is only .0258—odds that are not likely to provide a deterrent effect, if they are known.[4]

For deterrence to be effective, sentencing policies must depend heavily on the efficiency of the police and prosecution. Increases in the percentage of crimes solved by the police, the probabilities of arrest, and the level of police expenditures have been found to be associated with decreases in crime; in contrast, the relationship is not as strong between the severity of sentences and crime rates.[5] Presumably, if people know that they can commit an offense with a small chance of being caught, they will not be deterred. Deterrence may be less effective in preventing crimes that are difficult to solve than those that are associated with high rates of conviction.

The utilitarian basis of deterrence assumes that people will rationally consider the pluses and minuses of being punished before they commit an offense. Deterrence thus rests on the assumption that criminal behavior is not impulsive and that individuals make the necessary calculations before they act. Research has shown, however, that much crime, especially violent crime, is committed on the spur of the moment. In such situations deterrence has little effect.

While deterrence is believed to be a prominent purpose of the criminal sanction, the exact nature of the role it plays and the extent to which sentencing policies should be altered to effect that purpose have not been scientifically proved. Research findings are generally consistent with the deterrence hypothesis; jurisdictions with several penalties, for example, generally have lower rates of crime.[6] Yet the data do not prove the effect of deterrence or indicate its magnitude. As the Norwegian legal scholar Johannes Andenaes has said, however, "It is still a fundamental fact of social life that the risk of unpleasant consequences is a very strong motivational factor for most people in most situations."[7]

Incapacitation

The goal of preventing crime would certainly be enhanced if all criminals and potential criminals were rendered physically unable to ply their trade. Such measures, of course, would violate their civil rights; the penal law is directed only at individuals who have committed crimes, not those who may commit crimes in the future. In any case, our knowledge of criminal behavior is so primitive that it would be impossible to designate those who are going to violate the law. Still, even though such a policy of total **incapacitation** is not possible, the sanction has been used since ancient times

incapacitation Deprivation of capacity to commit crimes against society by detention in prison.

and has been the focus of renewed interest by criminal justice scholars since the mid-1970s.

The assumption behind the use of incapacitation is that crime may be prevented if offenders are physically restrained. By locking them up, banishing them, or killing them, society averts the crimes that those offenders would commit if they were at large in the community. Proponents of incapacitation assume that criminals do not just extend their careers when they are released from prison to make up the lost time, and that other individuals are not recruited to take their place in the criminal world.

As we saw earlier, the English policy of transportation had an incapacitative effect, at least in regard to crime in the mother country. In early America, agreement to move to the frontier or to join the army was often presented as an alternative to some other form of punishment. Today, prison is the most typical mode of incapacitation. But, given the schooling in crime that the young offender may receive there, does it truly serve to prevent future crimes? The ultimate method of incapacitation is capital punishment. Some states have even resorted to castration and other medical procedures in the belief that those measures will prevent offenders from committing additional sex crimes.

Any policy that incarcerates or in some other way physically restricts the offender will have some incapacitative effect. This effect can occur even when retribution, deterrence, or rehabilitation is the espoused goal. But incapacitation differs from these other sanctions in that it is future-oriented (unlike retribution); is based on the personal characteristics of the offender, not on those of the crime (unlike general deterrence); and carries no intent to reform (unlike rehabilitation). A person is thus subjected to incapacitation because he or she has committed a crime of a particular type and seems likely to repeat the offense.

A problem with the concept of incapacitation is that of severity. If the object is prevention, incapacitation may be justified for both trivial and serious offenses. Shoplifting, for example, is an offense that some people commit frequently, yet prolonged incapacitation of such persons would violate our sense of justice; murder is a crime that is rarely repeated, yet we would not want murderers to go unpunished. It is important, then, to note that what we are discussing is **selective incapacitation** and not general incapacitation, which would require the incarceration of all offenders.

Selective incapacitation The concept of selective incapacitation has been given increased attention by scholars in recent years. Research has suggested that a relatively small number of offenders are responsible for a large number of violent and property crimes; burglars, for example, commit many such offenses before they are caught. It is argued that these career criminals should be locked up for long periods of time.

Some researchers estimate that the crime rate in New York State could be reduced by two-thirds if every person convicted of a serious crime were incarcerated for three years.[8] This estimate may be overly optimistic, but experience in other countries does suggest that certainty of incapacitation would have considerable impact. James Q. Wilson argues that conviction for certain crimes should result in imprisonment and that the result would be a 20 percent—or greater—reduction in crime.[9]

Not all researchers agree that selective incapacitation will greatly reduce crime. Some argue that even if the most stringent penalties were imposed, the crime rate would be reduced by no more than 25 percent and that the level of sanctions now in general use affects the rate by less than 5 percent.[10] Al-

---

selective incapacitation The strategy of making optimum use of expensive and limited prison space by targeting for incarceration those individuals whose incapacitation will do the most to reduce crime.

though some offenders may be incapacitated, others are ready to take their places. Regarding costs to the community, a great increase in the number and length of prison terms would require correctional facilities to be expanded. In addition, it would be more difficult to obtain guilty pleas if the accused were aware of long prison terms in the offing, and policing activities would have to be upgraded to secure the evidence required to convict these serious offenders.

We have mentioned that certain offenders look at short periods of incarceration as a cost of doing business. Presumably, incapacitation of these professionals would enhance crime control, but how are they to be singled out? Do we have the technology to make accurate predictions? Much as selective incapacitation may appear to be a logical policy, the implementation of that policy could lead to incarcerating an unwarranted number of **false positives**—persons whom the prediction tables designate as candidates for long incarceration but who would, in fact, commit no further crimes if they were released. Since individual freedom and civil liberties are involved, such schemes raise serious moral and ethical questions.

Incapacitation as a goal of the criminal sanction is taken more seriously today than it was a decade ago. The idea of confining or closely supervising repeat offenders is appealing, yet it involves costs to the criminal justice system. In addition, selective incapacitation raises disturbing moral questions. Because the theory looks at aggregates—the total harm of a certain type of crime and the amount of suffering to be inflicted to reduce its incidence—the cost–benefit comparison can appear to outweigh questions of justice. But we must keep the idea of due process in mind: Is it right to punish persons for predicted future behavior—especially when the predictions might be wrong?

Rehabilitation

The concept of **rehabilitation**, which has dominated American corrections for much of the twentieth century, can be traced to classical Greece: Plato envisaged a system of "reform centers" in which offenders could be kept until they were cured. In the period following World War II, the idea of rehabilitation became dominant. Many criminal justice scholars and correctional practitioners believed that techniques had been developed to identify and treat the causes of criminal behavior. This idea that the offender may be treated and resocialized while under the care of the state is an engaging justification for punishment. As positivist theories of criminality came to the fore, rehabilitation of the offender was seen to contribute to the utilitarian goal of crime prevention. Rehabilitation is thus future-oriented; the sanction is applied so that the offender will not commit new crimes.

Rehabilitation is oriented toward the offender rather than the offense. A sentence should promote the offender's resocialization, and the judge should take into consideration the likelihood of future criminality. Because offenders are being treated, it follows that they should return to society when they are well.

Objections to the emphasis on rehabilitation in American corrections reached a peak in the 1970s, when critics pointed to the ineffectiveness of treatment programs on recidivism, the lengthy incarceration of offenders in states with extensive treatment programs, and the misuse of discretion by parole and other correctional officials.

Rehabilitation as a goal of the criminal sanction has been criticized as unjust on two principal grounds: individualized and predictive restraint. If a sentence is seen as an instrument of treatment, then the amount of punishment

---

false positive An individual incorrectly classified because of imperfections in the method used.

rehabilitation The process of restoring a convicted offender to a constructive place in society through some form of vocational, educational, or therapeutic treatment.

required depends on the offender's individual need rather than on the character of the crime. It is therefore likely that two people who have committed the same crime will require different levels of treatment. Perhaps one will receive outpatient care at a local clinic while the other is incarcerated to undergo milieu therapy. The difference between the sentences may be seen as manifestly unfair, yet it is quite logical if the goal is to return to society an individual who is unlikely to commit a crime again.

A related problem with the individualization of sentences under the rehabilitation model is that there is little correspondence between the gravity of the offense and the kind of treatment an offender may need. Studies have shown that murderers do not usually murder again and may be very good parole risks. Drug addicts who steal to support their habits, however, may require extensive incarceration and treatment and be unlikely prospects for successful parole. But to release murderers before thieves would probably strike the general public as unjust.

The criticism of predictive restraint centers on the fact that under the rehabilitation model, correctional officials are given discretion to determine when it is probable that a prisoner's future behavior will be free of crime. Such predictions are decried as unjust: Since accurate predictions cannot be made, persons who will not repeat their offenses are often held longer than necessary.

Defenders of the treatment model argue that a large number of rehabilitative programs have achieved positive results, though they concede that only certain programs seem to work for certain offenders. They also argue that even if some treatment programs do not reduce recidivism, rehabilitation is a moral and humanitarian responsibility of society toward those unfortunates who clash with the law.[11] These arguments seem to come from another era, when a large number of people were ready to promote the ideal of rehabilitation. Today these ideas fall on deaf ears.

Criminal Sanctions: A Mixed Bag?

Which should it be: retribution, deterrence, incapacitation, or rehabilitation? The justifications for each of the criminal sanctions overlap to a considerable extent. A term of imprisonment may be philosophically justified in terms of its primary goal of retribution, but the secondary functions of deterrence and incapacitation are also present. Deterrence is such a broad concept that it mixes well with the other goals, with the possible exception of rehabilitation, to which logically only special deterrence applies.

Only rehabilitation, if carried out according to its model, does not overlap with the stated goals of the correctional process. The emphasis on treatment and rehabilitation may diminish the capacity of the criminal justice system to serve as a general deterrent to crime: To the extent that imprisonment is unpleasant, it may be less than an ideal environment in which to conduct treatment. To the extent that it becomes a therapeutic environment, its deterrent effect may diminish.

For the trial judge the burden of determining a sentence that accommodates these values in a particular case is extremely difficult. A forger may be sentenced to prison as an example to others, even though she is no threat to community safety and is probably not in need of correctional treatment. The same judge may impose a light sentence on a youthful offender who, although he has committed a serious crime, may be a good risk for rehabilitation if he can move quickly back into society.

To see how these goals might be enacted in real life, consider Richard Herrin's sentencing for the murder of Bonnie Garland. Various hypothetical sentencing statements that might have been given, depending upon which of these goals took precedence, are set forth in Table 4.1.

Table 4.1 ■ **Punishment of Richard Herrin.** At sentencing the judge usually gives reasons for the punishment imposed. Here are possible statements that Judge Richard J. Daronco might have given depending upon the goal of the sanction that he wanted to promote.

Goal	Judge's statement
Retribution	I am imposing this sentence because you deserve to be punished for killing Bonnie Garland. Your criminal behavior in this case is the basis for your punishment. A young woman was killed. Justice requires that I impose a sanction at a level that illustrates the importance that the community places on human life.
Deterrence	I am imposing this sentence so that your punishment for killing Bonnie Garland will serve as an example and deter others who may contemplate similar actions. In addition, I hope that the sentence will deter you from ever again committing such an illegal act.
Incapacitation	I am imposing this sentence so that you will be incapacitated and hence unable to kill another during the length of this term. Since you have not committed prior offenses, selective incapacitation is not warranted.
Rehabilitation	The trial testimony of your psychiatrist and information contained in the presentence report make me believe that there are aspects of your personality that led you to kill Bonnie Garland. I am therefore imposing this sentence so that you can be treated in ways that will rectify your behavior so that you will not commit another criminal act. With proper treatment you should be able to return to society and lead a crime-free life.

Source: Adapted from U.S. Department of Justice, Bureau of Justice Statistics Report to the Nation on Crime and Justice, 2nd ed., 1988 (Washington D.C.: Government Printing Office, 1988).

On July 27, 1978, Judge Richard J. Daronco sentenced Richard Herrin to prison for the manslaughter death of Bonnie Garland. Calling the killing a "needless, heartless, and brutal act," the judge said that "even under the stress of extreme emotional disturbance the act of killing another is inexcusable. The court must come to the inescapable conclusion that the maximum penalty must be imposed."[12]

We noted earlier that Richard Herrin was sentenced to eight and one-third to twenty-five years as prescribed by the New York Penal Code. Such an indeterminate sentence was developed to advance the ideals of rehabilitation: There is leeway within the minimum and maximum terms for correctional officials to determine when Herrin could be returned to the community on parole. So perhaps a combination of goals was incorporated into the sentence, a combination that would address the needs of justice for the offender, the victim, and society.

Forms of the Criminal Sanction

From 1935 until the mid-1970s, every American state, the District of Columbia, and the federal system had an indeterminate sentencing system. Since 1975 the laws and practices of almost every jurisdiction have undergone major changes; there is now great diversity. Many states retained the indeterminate sentences that they had used throughout most of this century, while others moved to determinate sentences. Some states abolished release on parole; some retained the supervision function of parole. Mandatory sentences for certain offenses were imposed by legislatures in many states. And, as we discuss later in this chapter, sentencing guidelines were incorporated in several jurisdictions on either a voluntary or required basis. What was once possible to describe as "the American system of sentencing" has disappeared, replaced by a buffet of sentencing forms that are used in various combinations in individual states. Where once there was broad agreement as to the forms and structures of the sentences to be imposed on offenders, there is now diversity, with no single approach dominant.[13]

Incarceration, **intermediate sanctions**, probation, and death are the basic forms used to achieve the criminal sanction. But throughout most of American history, incarceration has been the expected fate of most felons and serious misdemeanants. This public attitude is widely held even though only a small portion of offenders ever see the inside of a jail or prison. We have been brought up hearing about prisons as the place where "bad people are sent," and this image has been maintained through books, songs, and films. As a consequence, much of the public views the use of nonincarcerative sanctions as allowing offenders to "get off."

Many judges, criminal justice planners, and researchers believe that the sentencing structures in the United States are both too severe and too lenient: Many offenders who do not warrant incarceration are sent to prison, and many who should be given more restrictive punishments receive little probation supervision. Because sanctions more severe than probation but less severe than incarceration are not often applied, advocates have urged greater use of such intermediate sanctions as fines, house arrest, intensive probation supervision, restitution, and community service.

While he or she is incarcerated, the offender is not on the streets committing crimes. The amount of time actually served in prison varies not only with the sentence but also with such other factors as "good time" and the level of crowding.

As we examine the various forms of the criminal sanctions, bear in mind that complex problems are associated with the application of these legally authorized punishments. Although the penal code defines the behaviors that are considered illegal and specifies the punishment, the legal standards for sentencing—applying the punishment—have not been as well developed as either the definitions of the offenses or the procedures used to determine guilt. In the United States there is no common law of sentencing. Thus, judges are given wide discretion in determining the appropriate sentence within the parameters of the penal code.

Incarceration

Imprisonment is the most visible penalty imposed by the American criminal justice system and is almost the exclusive means employed to punish violent and serious offenders. Because of its severity, imprisonment is

---

intermediate sanctions A variety of punishments that are more restrictive than traditional probation but less stringent and less costly than incarceration.

thought to have the greatest effect in deterring potential offenders, but it is expensive for the state to carry out and may prevent the offender's later reintegration into society.

The sanction of imprisonment is more complicated than a statutory rule specifying a certain number of years based on the gravity of the crime and the characteristics of the offender. Usually, legislatures specify a range of terms within which a judge may choose. The court also has the discretion to stipulate where the sentence is to be served and whether sentences for more than one charge are to be served concurrently or consecutively.

The length of actual incarceration can vary from the sentence announced in the courtroom. Written into the penal codes of all states are various mechanisms—such as discretionary parole release, good-time credits, and emergency release when crowding becomes intolerable—that provide for reductions in the sentence. Thus, sentencing structures constitute only one of several elements that determine the length of incarceration.

Penal codes vary as to the structure of the sentences permitted and the procedures that judges follow in determining the length of incarceration. Four sentencing structures are prominent: indeterminate, determinate, mandatory, and guidelines. Each makes certain assumptions about the goals of the criminal sanction. Each allocates the extent and location of discretionary authority differently. In addition, an aspect of penal law that has an impact on sentencing is good-time provisions. The length of incarceration can be shortened if the offender lives according to the rules set by the correctional officials.

Indeterminate sentences Consistent with the goal of rehabilitation, which dominated corrections from the 1930s to the 1970s, state legislatures adopted indeterminate (often termed *indefinite*) sentences, based on the idea that correctional personnel must have the discretion to release an offender if treatment has been successful. Penal codes with **indeterminate sen-** tences stipulate a minimum and maximum amount of time to be served in prison: one to five years, three to ten years, twenty years to life, and so on. At the time of sentencing, the offender knows the range of the sentence and the possibility of parole at some point after the minimum term (minus good time) has been served.

Determinate sentences Growing disaffection from the rehabilitative goal has brought renewed efforts toward **determinate sentences**, based on the assumption of deserved punishment. Determinate sentences consist of a specific number of years rather than a range of years. At the end of this term, minus credited good time, the prisoner is automatically freed. There is no parole board, and release is not tied to participation in treatment programs or a prediction of future criminality.

As states have moved toward determinate sentences, some have adopted penal codes that stipulate a specific term for each crime category; others still allow the judge to choose (from a range) the time to be served. Some states emphasize a determinate presumptive sentence; the legislature or often a commission specifies a term from a range into which it assumes most cases will fall. Only in special circumstances should judges veer from the presumptive sentence. Whichever variant is used, however, the offender knows at sentencing the amount of time to be served. One result of

indeterminate sentence A period of incarceration set by a judge as a minimum term that must be served before a decision on parole eligibility is made and a maximum term at the conclusion of which the sentence has been completed (for example, five to ten years). This type of sentence is closely associated with the rehabilitation concept, which holds that the time necessary for treatment cannot be predetermined.

determinate sentence A sentence of a fixed period of incarceration imposed by a court. This type of sentence is associated with the concept of retribution or deserved punishment.

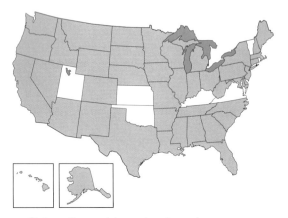

a States with mandatory prison terms for violent crimes

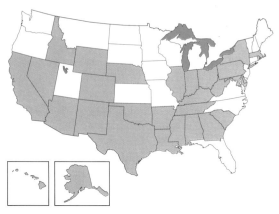

b States with mandatory prison terms for habitual offenders

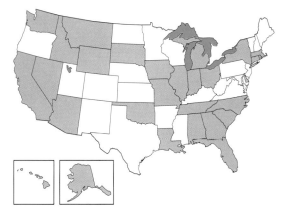

c States with mandatory prison terms for narcotic/drug law violations

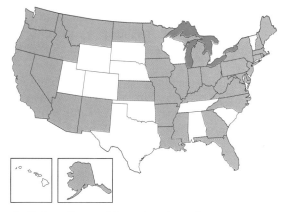

d States with mandatory prison terms for crimes with handguns or other firearms

Figure 4.1 ■ **Jurisdictions Requiring Mandatory Prison Terms in Four Crime Categories.** States with mandatory prison terms are shown in blue for each category. Although researchers have cast doubt on the effectiveness of mandatory sentences, they are part of the penal codes of most states. Why?

Source: U.S. Department of Justice, Bureau of Justice Statistics, *Bulletin* (Washington, D.C.: Government Printing Office, 1983), p. 3.

determinate sentencing is that legislatures have tended to reduce the discretion of the judiciary as a means of limiting sentencing disparities and ensuring that terms will correspond to those deemed appropriate by the elected body.

Mandatory sentences Recent years have brought allegations by legislators and other public officials that many offenders are being permitted to go free by lenient judges and that crime control requires greater certainty that criminals will be incarcerated. All but two states now require **mandatory sentences**, stipulating some minimum period of incarceration that must be served by persons convicted of selected crimes. No regard may be given to the circumstances of the offense or to the background of the individual; the judge has no discretion and is not allowed to suspend the sentence.

Mandatory prison terms are most often legislated for violent crimes, habitual offenders, drug violations, and crimes involving the possession or use of a firearm, as indicated in Figure 4.1. Experience has shown that these laws have had little effect, however. Defense attorneys work hard to arrive at a plea bargain by which the charge is changed to one without the mandatory requirement.

Studies of the 1973 Rockefeller drug law of New York and the Bartley-Fox gun control law of Massachusetts have shown that the mandatory sentence provisions have had no deterrent or incapacitative effects.[14] The draconian sentences prescribed by the New York law merely raised the stakes for the defense so high that the prosecution had to bargain to move cases. Punishment became more severe only for the small percentage of drug dealers who were actually convicted. Although Massachusetts publicized its law with the statement "If you are caught with a gun, you will go to prison for a year and nobody can get you out," evidence indicates that criminal justice officials were able to adjust to the mandatory provision in a way that undermined its impact. Police officers modified their frisking of suspects so that "otherwise innocent" persons would not be caught with a gun. Because the number of persons who appealed convictions soared, prosecutors had second thoughts about pressing for the mandatory provisions.

Research in several states shows that the mandatory sentence is imposed in only a small portion of the cases in which it could be used. What appears to happen is that, since the prosecutors and defense attorneys view the mandatory penalties as too harsh given the circumstances of many cases, they avoid the mandatory provisions by exacting a guilty plea to a lesser charge or by interpreting the record so that the requirements do not apply.

Do mandatory sentences achieve their purpose? Research conducted on Florida's mandatory minimum sentences, designed to ensure that certain categories of offenders are not released early through good time and other provisions before a certain portion of their sentence has been served, supports their effectiveness.[15] Eleven categories of offenders—for example, those convicted of capital offenses and of certain drug and firearms offenses, and those designated habitual offenders—come under the mandatory minimum provisions. The impact of these laws has been cited as a major cause for increased incarceration lengths with a resulting growth in the prison population.

Sentencing guidelines In recent years **sentencing guidelines** have been established in the federal courts, in several states, and in selected jurisdictions in other states. Guidelines are designed to reduce the sentencing discretion of judges so that there is less variation among sentences for offenders with similar

---

mandatory sentence   A sentence required by statute to be imposed and executed on certain offenders.

sentencing guidelines   An instrument developed to indicate to judges the usual sanction given in the past in particular types of cases.

charges and criminal histories. After voluntary experimentation in several courts during the 1970s, Minnesota adopted guidelines in 1980. Since then, guidelines have also been adopted by Pennsylvania and Washington. Congress created the U.S. Sentencing Commission in 1984 and directed that it produce guidelines that would avoid unwarranted sentencing disparities while retaining enough flexibility to permit individualized sentencing when called for by mitigating or aggravating factors. The commission guidelines went into effect on November 1, 1987. Most observers view sentencing guidelines as a constructive middle ground between legislatively mandated determinate sentences and indeterminate sentences.

Sentencing guidelines are designed to constrain the discretion of judges. Although statutes provide a variety of sentencing options for particular crimes, the guidelines attempt to direct the judge to more specific actions that *should* be taken. Sentence ranges provided for most offenses are based on seriousness of the crime and the criminal history of the offender. The guidelines specify the presumptive sentence; some jurisdictions require that judges explain the special circumstances of a case that led them to impose a sanction out of the expected range.

For sentencing guidelines, as for parole guidelines, a grid is constructed on the basis of two scores, one related to the seriousness of the offense, the other to characteristics of the offender that indicate the likelihood of recidivism. (See Table 4.2, in which the guidelines grid used in Minnesota is set forth.) The offender score is arrived at by adding the points allocated to the number of juvenile, adult misdemeanor, and adult felony convictions; the number of times incarcerated; probation or parole status; escape from confinement at the time of the last offense; and employment status or educational achievement. The judge locates the recommended sentence by finding the appropriate cell.

Sentencing guidelines are expected to be reviewed and modified periodically so that decisions in the most recent past will be included. Some critics argue that because the guidelines reflect only what has happened, they in no way really reform sentencing. Others question the choice of characteristics included in the offender scale and wonder whether some are used to mask racial criteria. Unlike some reforms designed to limit the discretion of judges, guidelines attempt to reflect the collective experience of sentencing in a particular jurisdiction. Some prefer the use of guidelines to legislative enactment of a penal code based on mandatory or definite sentences.

Good time Although not a type of sentence, **good time** has quite an impact on sentencing. In all but four states, prisoners are awarded days off their minimum or maximum terms for maintaining good behavior or participating in various types of vocational, educational, and treatment programs. Other states give good-time reductions for only one of the two categories of behavior. Correctional officials view these sentence-reduction policies as necessary for the maintenance of institutional order and as a mechanism to reduce overcrowding. Good time is also taken into consideration by prosecutors and defense attorneys during plea bargaining. Offenders who plead guilty are often encouraged to accept the expected sentence by being told that the time served will be greatly reduced by the accumulation of good-time credits.

The amount of good time that can be earned varies from five to fifteen days a month. The amounts are written into the penal codes of some states, stipulated in department of corrections policy directives in others. Of importance is the extent to which good time can be vested, that is, the amount that cannot be taken away because of misbehavior. In some

----

good time   A reduction of time to be served in a correctional institution awarded at the discretion of correctional officials to inmates whose behavior conforms to the rules or whose activities deserve to be rewarded.

Table 4.2 ■ **Sentencing Guidelines Grid Used in Minnesota** (presumptive sentence length in months). The italicized numbers within the grid denote the range within which a judge may sentence without the sentence being deemed a departure. The criminal history score is computed by adding one point for each prior felony conviction, one-half point for each prior gross misdemeanor conviction, and one-quarter point for each prior misdemeanor conviction. First-degree murder is excluded from the guidelines by law and is punished by life imprisonment.

Severity levels of conviction offense		Criminal history score						
		0	1	2	3	4	5	6 or more
Unauthorized use of motor vehicle Possession of marijuana	I	12	12	12	15	18	21	24 *23–25*
Theft-related crimes ($150–$2500) Sale of marijuana	II	12	12	14	17	20	23	27 *25–29*
Theft crimes ($150–$2500)	III	12	13	16	19	22 *21–23*	27 *25–29*	32 *30–34*
Burglary—felony intent Receiving stolen goods ($150–$2500)	IV	12	15	18	21	25 *24–26*	32 *30–34*	41 *37-45*
Simple robbery	V	18	23	27	30 *29–31*	38 *36–40*	46 *43–49*	54 *50–58*
Assault, second degree	VI	21	26	30	34 *33–35*	44 *42–46*	54 *50–58*	65 *60–70*
Aggravated robbery	VII	24 *23–25*	32 *30–34*	41 *38–44*	49 *45–53*	65 *60–70*	81 *75–87*	97 *90–104*
Assault, first degree Criminal sexual conduct, first degree	VIII	43 *41–45*	54 *50–58*	65 *60–70*	76 *71–81*	95 *89–101*	113 *106–120*	132 *124–140*
Murder, third degree	IX	97 *94–100*	119 *116–122*	127 *124–130*	149 *143–155*	176 *168–184*	205 *195–215*	230 *218–242*
Murder, second degree	X	116 *111–121*	140 *133–147*	162 *153–171*	203 *192–214*	243 *231–255*	284 *270–298*	324 *309–339*

Source: Minnesota Sentencing Guidelines Commission, *Report to the Legislature,* 1983.

states, once ninety days of credit is earned, it is vested. Prisoners in those systems are in danger of losing only amounts not vested if they violate the rules.

The sentence versus actual time served If you relied only on the length of sentences as reported in the news, you would think that judges in the United States prescribe long periods of incarceration for serious crimes. But there is a great difference between the length of the sentence and the amount of time actually served. Credit for time spent in jail awaiting the sentence, the application of good time, and—in most states—release to the community on parole greatly reduce the period of incarceration.

Because of the variation in sentencing and releasing laws, it is difficult to compare the amount of time served with the length of sentence imposed throughout the United States. It is possible, however, to make comparisons in regard to different offenses in the same state. The Bureau of Justice Statistics has brought to light an interesting phenomenon: The more serious the offense, the smaller the proportion of the sentence served (see Figure 4.2). An auto thief, for example, may be sentenced to twenty-four months in prison but actually serves twenty months, or 83.3 percent of the sentence; a murderer may well be sentenced to thirty years but be released after fifteen years, or 50 percent of the sentence. These examples are not atypical. In states with indeterminate sentences, release on parole is possible after good-time and jail-time credits have been deducted from the minimum term.

Intermediate Sanctions

Prison crowding and the low levels of probation supervision have spurred interest in the development of intermediate sanctions, those punishments that are less severe than prison and more restrictive than probation. It has been estimated that if murderers and rapists, plus those who had been previously incarcerated and who

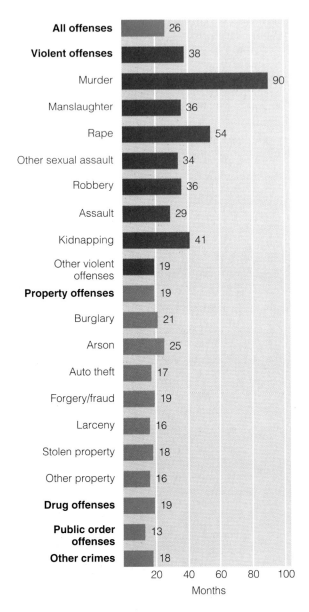

Figure 4.2 ■ **Average Time Served by State Inmates by Offense Type.** The data give credibility to the observation that the average felony offender spends about two years in prison. This time served includes jail credits. What would be the public's reaction to this fact?

Source: Adapted from U.S. Department of Justice, Bureau of Justice Statistics, *Report to the Nation on Crime and Justice,* 2nd ed. (Washington D.C.: Government Printing Office, 1988), p. 100.

Some judges are creative in their imposition of intermediate sanctions. For his failure to clean up slum-like conditions in buildings he owned, this neurosurgeon was sentenced to live for a time in one of his rat-infested apartments.

had a prior conviction for violence, are excluded from consideration for intermediate sanctions, 29 percent of those who are now prison bound would be punished in the community.[16] Punishments such as fines, house arrest, intensive probation supervision, restitution and community service, boot camp, and forfeiture are among the sentencing forms that fit this category. Here we will briefly describe each of these forms. Later,

in Chapter 8, we will more fully examine these punishments and their implementation.

Fines Fines are routinely imposed today for offenses ranging from traffic violations to felonies; probably well over one billion dollars in fines are collected annually by courts across the country.[17] But fines are rarely used as the *sole* punishment for crimes more serious than motor vehicle violations; typically, they are used in conjunction with other sanctions, such as probation and incarceration. For example, it is not unusual for a judge to impose two years' probation and a $500 fine.

Greater use of the fine is gaining increased attention from judges and criminal justice planners as they struggle with overcrowded jails and prisons and overwhelming probation caseloads. Yet, as will be discussed in Chapter 8, there are problems with regard to the use of fines, such as issues of equity between poor and rich defendants, collection, and enforcement. However, as argued by the National Advisory Commission, "Properly employed, the fine is less drastic, far less costly to the public, and perhaps more effective than imprisonment or community service."[18]

House arrest With the increase in prison crowding and technological innovations that provide for electronic monitoring, **house arrest** has gained new attention from criminal justice planners. House arrest is a sentence imposed by a court requiring convicted offenders to spend all or part of the time in their own residence. Conditions are placed on permissible actions; some offenders are allowed to go to a place of employment during the day but must return to their residence by a specific hour. The development of electronic monitoring equipment makes house arrest in its contemporary version a viable sentencing alternative.

———

house arrest   A sentence requiring the convicted offender to remain inside his or her home during specific periods.

House arrest has the advantage of flexibility, since it can be used as a sole sanction or in combination with other penalties and can be imposed at almost any point in the criminal justice process: during the pretrial period, after a short term in jail or prison, or as a condition of probation or parole. Electronic monitoring is not foolproof, however, and studies have shown that it is hard to keep offenders inside their residence for more than six weeks before they violate the conditions of their sentence.

Restitution and community service In its simplest form, **restitution** is repayment to a victim who has suffered some form of financial loss as a result of the offender's crime. In the Middle Ages it was a common way to settle a criminal case: The offender was ordered to do the victim's work or to give the victim money. The growth of the modern state meant that less attention was given to "private" arrangements between offender and victim, and greater attention to the wrong done to the community by the offender.

Restitution has always been a part of the U.S. criminal justice system, but a largely unpublicized one, effected by informal agreements between enforcement officials and offenders, at the station house and during plea bargaining, and by sentence recommendations. Only during the past decade has it been institutionalized in many areas. It is usually carried out as one of the conditions of probation.

Community service is unpaid service to the public to overcome or compensate society for some of the harm caused by the crime. It takes the form of, for example, working for a social service agency, cleaning parks, or assisting the poor. It can be tailored to the economic and ability levels of offenders. The person convicted thus serves the community in some public manner, thereby "overcoming" some of the harm caused by the crime. There is also symbolic value in the offender's effort to make reparation to the community offended by the crime.

Forfeiture With passage of the Racketeer Influence and Corrupt Organizations Act (RICO) and the Continuing Criminal Enterprise Act (CCE) in 1970, Congress resurrected **forfeiture**, a criminal sanction that had lain dormant since the American Revolution. Through amendments in 1984 and 1986, Congress improved procedures for implementing the forfeiture provisions of the law.[19] Similar laws are now found in a number of states, particularly with respect to controlled substances and organized crime. Forfeiture proceedings, by which the government seizes property derived from or used in criminal activity, can take both a civil and a criminal form. Using the civil law, property used in criminal activity (equipment to manufacture illegal drugs, automobiles, boats) can be seized without a finding of guilt. Criminal forfeiture is a punishment imposed as a result of a conviction at the time of sentencing. It requires that the offender relinquish various assets related to the crime. These assets can be quite considerable: An estimated one billion dollars' worth of assets was confiscated from drug dealers by state and federal officials during the five years ending in 1990.[20]

Boot camp/shock incarceration Among the most publicized of intermediate sanctions are **boot camps**, now operated in more than fourteen

---

restitution Compensation for financial, physical, or emotional loss caused by an offender, in the form of either a payment of money to the victim or work at a service project in the community, as stipulated by the court.

community service Compensation for injury to society by the performance of service to the community.

forfeiture Seizure by the government of property and other assets derived from or used in criminal activity.

boot camp A physically rigorous, disciplined, and demanding regimen emphasizing conditioning, education, and job training. Designed for young offenders.

Probation is the oldest alternative to incarceration. Offenders live in the community under the supervision of an officer of the court.

states. Although programs vary, they are all based on the belief that young offenders can be "shocked" out of their criminal ways if they undergo a physically rigorous, disciplined, and demanding regimen for a short period, usually three or four months, before being returned to the community for supervision. The boot camp concept is drawn from the military, but most boot camps also include educational and job training programs as well as other rehabilitative services.

Although boot camps have proved to be popular with the general public, critics charge that their effectiveness has yet to be proved. It has been argued that often offenders simply develop leadership skills and physical prowess in the boot camp that are transferred to the streets upon return to the community.

Intensive probation supervision During the past decade **intensive probation supervision** (IPS) has been added to the sentencing menu of intermediate punishments. Often referred to

as "old style" probation, the major characteristic of this sanction is strict and frequent reporting to a probation officer who carries a limited caseload. Other restrictions are often placed on probationers receiving intensive supervision, such as required drug treatment, curfew, community service, and electronic monitoring. It is thought that through this approach the number of rearrests may be cut and offenders who might otherwise go to prison can be released to the community. But questions have been raised about how much difference constant surveillance can make to probationers who also need help to secure employment and to deal with emotional and family situations as well as their own drug or alcohol problems.

Probation

Nearly 65 percent of adults under correctional supervision are on **probation**. Probation is designed to maintain control and to assist offenders while permitting them to live in the community under supervision. We will discuss probation more fully in Chapter 7; here it is important to note that this form of the criminal sanction is a judicial act and is given by grace of the state, not as a right.

Although probationers serve their sentences in the community and not in prison, the sanction is often tied to incarceration. If the conditions of probation are not met, the supervising officer may bring the offender back to court and recommend that the probation be revoked and that the sentence be served in prison. Judges may set a prison term but suspend it upon successful completion of a period of probation. In some jurisdictions the court may modify an offender's prison sentence after a portion is

intensive probation supervision Probation granted as an alternative to incarceration under conditions of strict reporting to a probation officer with a limited caseload.

probation A sentence the offender serves in the community while under supervision.

Death by hanging was the method of execution used in most states well into the twentieth century. Although executions were usually shielded from the general public by the time of the Civil War, officials often allowed some observers to be present.

served by changing it to probation. This is often referred to as "shock probation" (also called "split sentence"); an offender who is sentenced to incarceration is released after a period of incarceration (the shock) and resentenced to probation. An offender on probation may be required to spend intermittent periods, such as weekends or nights, in jail. Whatever the specific terms of the probationary sentence, its emphasis is on guidance and supervision in the community.

Probation is generally advocated as a way of rehabilitating offenders whose crimes have not been serious or whose past records are clean. It is viewed as less expensive and more effective than imprisonment, which may embitter youthful or first-time offenders and mix them with hardened criminals so that they learn more sophisticated criminal techniques.

Death

As we write this chapter, more than 2,600 incarcerated persons are awaiting execution in thirty-three of thirty-six death penalty states. Yet since 1976, when the Supreme Court upheld Georgia's capital punishment law, the number of executions has been less than twenty-seven in any one year.[21] From 1930 through 1967, in contrast, more than 3,800 men and women were executed in the United States, 199 of them in 1935, the deadliest year.

The number of persons under sentence of death has increased dramatically in the past decade (see Figure 4.3). Two-thirds of those on death row in 1992 were in the South, with the greatest number concentrated in Florida, Georgia, and Texas. From 1977 to 1990, during which time a total of 3,451 death sentences were handed out, 143 people were executed but 1,335 were removed from death row as a result of appeal, a time-consuming and expensive process; commutation by a governor; or death while awaiting execution.[22]

More than two hundred and fifty new death sentences are now being given out each year, yet executions are comparatively few. Is this situa-

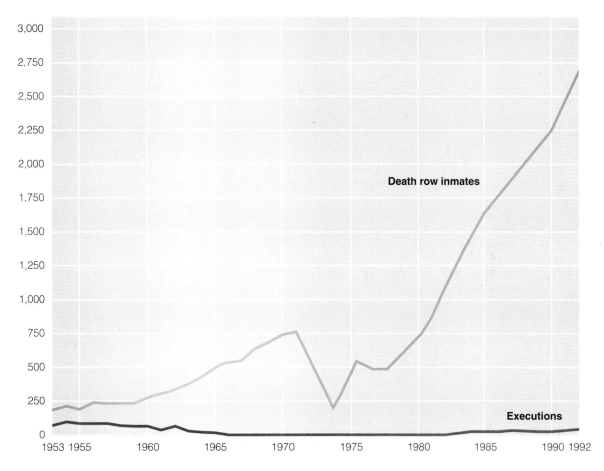

Figure 4.3 ■ **Persons Under Sentence of Death and Persons Executed, 1953–1992.** Since 1976 approximately two hundred and fifty new offenders have been added to death row each year, yet the number of executions has never been greater than twenty-seven. What explains this situation?

Source: NAACP Legal Defense and Educational Fund, *Death Row, U.S.A.,* Winter 1992, p. 5.

tion the result of the appeals process or of lack of will on the part of political leaders and a society that is perhaps uncertain about the taking of human life? It may be that the death penalty has more significance as a political symbol than as a deterrent to crime. Is it possible that in the future the United States will join the other industrial democracies (South Africa is the exception) and stop executing criminal offenders? These are questions to consider, and in Chapter 18 we will discuss the death penalty more fully.

The Sentencing Process

As the judge looks down at the offender and intones the sentence, what has gone into the decision? What factors have been considered? To what extent is the sentence individualized to fit the offender and the crime? As reflected in Judge Forer's thoughts on sentencing (see the Workperspec-

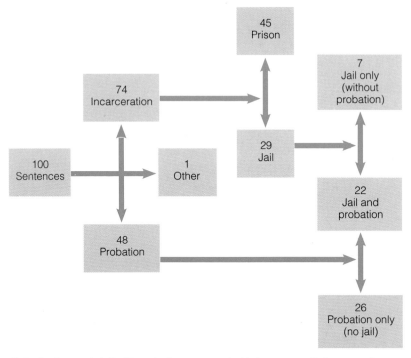

Figure 4.4 ■ Types of Sentences Imposed on 100 Typical Cases in Felony Court. Judges have wide discretion with regard to the type of sentence imposed. Note that among these felony convictions, not everyone is incarcerated.

Source: U.S. Department of Justice, Bureau of Justice Statistics, *Sentencing Outcomes in Twenty-Eight Felony Courts* (Washington, D.C.: Government Printing Office, 1987), p. 5.

Note: Sentences to jail with probation are counted twice, once with incarceration and again with probation. For this reason, the sum of incarceration, probation, and other exceeds 100. "Other" includes such sentences as restitution to the victim or a fine.

tive on pp. 96–97), these questions are very hard to answer.

A study of sentencing practices in twenty-eight felony courts provides data on the type of sanction imposed on 100 typical offenders. Figure 4.4 graphically portrays the sentencing options used by judges in these felony cases. Figure 4.5 relates the conviction offense to the type of sentence imposed. It must be emphasized that these are outcomes in typical felony convictions; *misdemeanor* sentences would show much greater use of probation and much less of incarceration. In deciding the punishment, the judge will have the presentence report prepared by the probation officer as a guide, but the decision will also be influenced by his or her own attitudes and the administrative context.

Research by social scientists suggests that the background and attitudes of the judge, the administrative context of the criminal courts, and the contents of the presentence investigation are important factors in determining the fate of the offender. To some extent, each of these factors structures the judge's exercise of discretion in sentencing. In addition, the judge's perception of them is dependent on his or her own attitudes toward the law, toward a particular crime, or toward a type of offender. As one example, consider what influence Judge Daronco's attitudes and background might have played in his sentencing of Richard Herrin.

Attitudes and Background

That each judge has a distinctive sentencing tendency is taken as a fact of life by defense

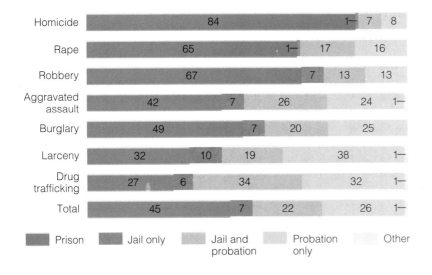

Figure 4.5 ■ **Percentages of Types of Sentences Imposed for Various Conviction Offenses.** Note the various sentencing options used by judges for the different conviction offenses. What other factors might be taken into account by the judges in making this decision?

Source: U.S. Department of Justice, Bureau of Justice Statistics, *Sentencing Outcomes in Twenty-Eight Felony Courts* (Washington, D.C.: Government Printing Office, 1987), p. 5.

attorneys and most recidivists. People who are familiar with courthouse operations and know the judges often attempt to manipulate the system so that a favored jurist hears the case. Knowledge of the sentencing record of the judge also influences plea bargainers.

Disparities among judges may be explained in part by the fact that judges are products of different backgrounds and have different social values. Martin A. Levin's study of the criminal courts of Pittsburgh and Minneapolis showed the influence of these factors on sentencing behavior. He found that Pittsburgh judges, all of whom came from humble backgrounds, exhibited a greater empathy toward defendants than did their brethren in Minneapolis, who tended to come from upper-class backgrounds. Where the Pittsburgh judges tried to base their decisions on what they believed was best for the defendants, Minneapolis judges were more legally oriented and considered society's need for protection from criminal behavior.[23]

Some studies have shown that members of racial minorities and the poor are treated more harshly by the system; other research has been unable to demonstrate a direct link between harshness of sentence and race or social class. Further, although some evidence supports the belief that blacks and poor people receive the longest prison terms and are least likely to be placed on probation, the research is not conclusive. Yet the prison populations of most states do contain a higher percentage of minority group members than the general population. Is this the result of the prejudicial attitudes of judges, police officers, and prosecutors? Are poor people more likely to commit violations that elicit a strong response from society? Unfortunately, the research evidence on these and similar questions is inconclusive.

The Administrative Context

In the organizational and administrative context of the criminal courts, judges often do not have the time to consider all the crucial elements of an offense and the special characteristics of a defendant before imposing a sentence. Especially when the offenses are minor, judges tend to routinize decisions and announce sentences that they believe fit certain categories of crime without paying too much attention to the particular offenders. There are also certain norms or "tariffs" that develop as to the expected sentences for certain offenses. With plea bargaining as extensive as it is, the judge may merely articulate and legitimize the sentence that has been agreed on

The sentence imposed by the judge can be viewed as the beginning of corrections. What punishment would you impose on a young, college-educated male who pleads guilty to killing his girlfriend? What if the offender was a female who kills her spouse?

between counsel and prosecutor. Most judges try to maintain a distance from plea bargaining and in the courtroom are usually careful to emphasize that they are merely receiving sentencing recommendations from counsel.

Sentence Disparity: One Result of the Process

One result of the wide discretion of judges is **sentence disparity**: Widely divergent penalties may be imposed on offenders with similar backgrounds who have committed the same offense. This situation not only raises constitutional issues about the idea of equal justice under the law but often presents problems for correctional administrators. Prisoners and probationers compare their sentences; those who have received the harsher sanctions believe that they have been the objects of prejudice and become embittered and less cooperative. In addition, if there are consistent differences among judges within an urban court system, scheduling and process-

ing may become snarled as defense attorneys try to get their cases before the more easygoing judges. The need to rein in the discretion of judges has been one of the major stimuli for reform of the sentencing system, including development of sentencing guidelines.

The Presentence Report

Although sentencing is the judge's responsibility, other persons may participate in the decision-making process. In most states the presentence investigation has become an important ingredient in the judicial mix, especially when the offender has been convicted of a felony. Usually, the probation officer looks into the convicted person's background, criminal record, job status, and social situation in order to suggest a sentence that is in the interests of both the offender and society. The probation officer may consider hearsay as well as firsthand information, and the offender generally has no opportunity to challenge the contents of the report or the recommendation.

Although presentence reports are represented as diagnostic evaluations, critics point out that there are no scientific tools for such evaluations and that the reports end up as the application of stereotyped labels. Rosecrance

---

sentence disparity   Divergence in the lengths and types of sentences imposed for the same crime or for crimes of comparable seriousness when no reasonable justification can be discerned.

has argued that in actual practice, the presentence report primarily serves to maintain the myth of individualized justice; he found that the present offense and the prior criminal record determine the probation officer's final sentencing recommendation.[24] He learned that probation officers begin by reviewing a case and typing the defendant as one who should fit into a particular sentencing category. Their investigations are then conducted mainly to gather further information to buttress this early decision so that the sentence recommendation will later become the official designation of the judge.

Regardless of how they construct their reports, probation officers are made uneasy by the possibility that their reports may be merely the window dressing that helps the judge to shift the responsibility for the sentence onto them. Or, if the judge relies heavily on the recommendation of the attorneys as they transmit the terms of the plea bargain, probation officers may come to believe that their work is of little value. Yet research has shown that in 90 percent of cases the sentence conforms to the recommendation of the probation officer.

Questions are often raised as to whether this reliance on the presentence report is just—and whether the time spent preparing it is an appropriate use of a probation officer's time. In considering these and other questions concerning sentencing, we need to look at the politics of sentencing reform.

The Politics of Sentencing Reform

Michael Tonry has argued that from about 1935 to 1975 the United States had a national sentencing system. Anchored to the goal of rehabilitation, every state, the District of Columbia, and the federal system had indeterminate sentences and parole. But the reform movement of the 1970s and 1980s raised questions about the effectiveness of rehabilitation and the forms of sentencing—indeterminate terms and release on parole—linked to it.

Beginning in 1969 the need for reform of corrections and sentencing was brought to the attention of legislators and opinion leaders primarily by a series of books and articles written by criminal justice scholars. These works pointed to problems resulting from the heavy focus on rehabilitation. They pointed to (1) the failure of treatment programs to reduce recidivism and (2) disparities in the sentences received by similar offenders that were a product of the broad discretion exercised by judges and parole boards. Political leaders pushed to change the sentencing process by "toughening" criminal penalties, making greater use of incarceration, and ending or limiting parole release. There are now major differences among the states as to the stated goals, forms, and practices of sentencing offenders.

Legislative Action

Are legislators able to translate politically the concepts of the criminal sanction into a correctional policy addressed to sentencing and parole? Arthur Rosett and Donald R. Cressey suggest that sentencing policy is influenced by a severity-softening-severity process by which legislators and criminal justice officials attempt to achieve their own ends. The authors believe that to a considerable degree the legislature becomes an agency of harshness, especially for defendants who do not acquiesce to pressures from the courthouse to plead guilty. The six steps of this process of legislative action and reaction seem to follow an established pattern:

1. Laws calling for severe punishments are passed by legislatures on the assumption that fear of pain will cow the citizenry into conformity.

2. Criminal justice personnel soften these severe penalties for most offenders in the interests of (a) serving justice, (b) limiting bureaucracy, and (c) gaining acquiescence.

WORKPERSPECTIVE

From Where I Sit

Judge Lois G. Forer

Some may argue that the accused has too many rights and that the guilty escape punishment by reason of legal technicalities. This has not been my experience. On the contrary, I find that the poor and ignorant rarely exercise their legal and constitutional rights; [they] do not understand their rights and frequently waive them through ignorance. Most accused persons—rich and powerful as well as poor and ignorant—plead guilty.... To lawyers and appellate courts, a trial is of great importance. To the defendant, the sentence is really all that matters.

The sentence imposed on convicted criminals and those who plead guilty means the difference between freedom and prison. In a limited number of cases, it means the difference between life and death. Obviously, the sentence is the most important part of the entire criminal justice system. But it receives the least consideration under the law. Until recently, there were few regulations or limitations on the sentence that might be imposed and few restrictions or rules regulating the procedures to be followed in imposing sentence. The law governing the sentence to be imposed is still vague, the options limited, and the purposes of criminal penalties diffuse and contradictory.... Naturally, there has been tremendous dissatisfaction with disparities in sentencing.

Numerous proposals for change have been offered by bar association committees, law professors, and criminologists. These proposals have been concerned with two issues: (1) How long a prison sentence should be imposed? and (2) Who should make that determination?... Little thought has been given to other options. There are several basic assumptions underlying these discussions: that the choice of "in" or "out" is the only one; that if the crime is violent or the defendant has a prior record, then a prison sentence is appropriate no matter what the nature of the crime, the circumstances surrounding it, or the condition of the offenders; that if the offense is not violent and the offender has no prior record, "out" is appropriate regardless of the amount of money involved, the harm done to the public, or the intent of the offender....

A judge who tries major criminal cases and accepts guilty pleas sees the actual criminals, hundreds of them if not thousands. A trial judge also sees the victims of crime. Most judges are so burdened with simply getting through the day and "disposing" of the allotted quota of cases that they are usually too weary to undertake the painful examination of the justice, morality, or common sense of the sentences that they impose....

3. The few defendants who then insist on a trial and are found guilty, or who in other ways refuse to cooperate, are punished more severely than those who acquiesce.

4. Legislatures, noting that most criminals by acquiescing avoid "the punishment prescribed by law," (a) increase the prescribed punishments and (b) try to limit the range of discretionary decision making that permits the harsh penalties to be softened.

5. The more severe punishments introduced in step 4 are again softened for most offenders, as in step 2, with the result that the defendants who do not acquiesce are

A judge deals with specific cases and individuals, one at a time. What may be true of 90 percent of the population does not concern the judge. His duty is to deal with the individual in court who may or may not be average or typical, who may indeed be the rare, aberrant, and statistically insignificant individual who deviates from the norm of criminals. In each case, a judge is faced with a unique individual and a specific crime. The judge must be concerned with the rights of the accused, protection of society, and promotion of the rule of law....

It is not easy to look any human being in the eye and say, "I am placing you behind bars for two years or ten years, sending you to a place where you will not be able to see your spouse and family except under degrading circumstances, a place that may not be physically safe, where you may be beaten or sexually abused, where most of your time will be spent in idleness or performing boring routine tasks for pay of perhaps fifteen cents an hour, where you will have no privacy, little opportunity to study, no opportunity to do meaningful work or support your family or make amends for the wrong you have committed." How does one justify such an action taken in the name of law and government? What are the facts and the theories that impel courts to impose sentences of imprisonment on tens of thousands of men, women, and children every year? Is there a choice other than prison that will vindicate the law, protect society and the victim, and do justice to the offender? These are the questions that sentencing judges ask themselves....

My conclusions are based on the belief that every human being is responsible for his acts.... We must also assume that every offender owes a debt for the wrong he has done. The maintenance of a civilized society depends on this responsible interrelationship among people.

In sentencing an offender, a judge should strive for proportionality between the penalty and the offense. A judge should also recognize the inequalities and differences among individuals and their rights to equality of treatment. I do not suggest that any one form of penalty is appropriate for all offenses and all offenders. I do, however, believe that every penalty must provide for the needs of the victim, society, and the offender. A penalty that requires restitution or reparation is, I believe, congruent with a humanistic and democratic concept of society and with decent treatment of criminals. It would provide a feasible alternative to prison and probation for many offenders.

Lois G. Forer is a judge of the Court of Common Pleas of Philadelphia. She has been active in efforts to reform the criminal justice system. Among her published works are No One Will Listen: How Our Legal System Brutalizes the Poor *(1970) and* The Death of the Law *(1975).*

Source: L. G. Forer, *Criminals and Victims: A Trial Judge Reflects on Crime and Punishment* (New York: W. W. Norton, 1980), pp. 1–14. Copyright © 1980 by Lois G. Forer Reprinted by permission of the author and the publisher.

---

punished even more severely than they were in step 3.

6. The severity-softening-severity process is repeated.[25]

It is too soon to test this hypothesis against the sentencing reforms. It does, however, make us aware of the links between the actions of legislatures in structuring the laws of sentencing and the actions of correctional administrators and judges in carrying out those requirements.

Even though reformers all voiced the same basic set of criticisms, their proposals for sentencing changes met a mixed fate. Many of the proponents argued that the new laws should not result in an increase in the length of incarceration. A goodly number of the legislators, in contrast, responded to the public demand for crime control by structuring penal codes to ensure that most offenders would stay in prison for longer periods. Correctional officials, although content to have the discretion of independent parole boards restricted, were concerned that they would not have the resources to manage the expected increase in prison populations. Judges, who might have responded favorably to attempts to reduce sentence disparities, became alarmed when it appeared that the new schemes would shift power away from the judiciary to prosecutors, whose plea bargaining leverage would thereby increase. In short, the well-thought-out schemes of the reformers to constrain discretion and shift criminal justice to the goal of deserved punishment came face to face with the political reality of legislatures and governmental bureaucracies. Compromise, that key element of politics and policy change, came to guide reform attempts.

Impact of Reform

After a decade of sentencing innovation, what has been the impact of changes in the penal codes? Is there more consistency in sentencing? Have the new laws resulted in longer prison terms and, hence, prison crowding? Have the costs to the criminal justice system increased or decreased? Finally, what have the changes meant with respect to crime control?

Researchers have provided only tentative answers to these questions. If we posit that the goals of the sentencing reforms were "consistency and predictability in outcomes, accountability on the part of decision makers, (and) reduction of disparities and anomalies," some of the innovations can be judged as successes and some as failures.[26] Tonry lists parole guidelines, comprehensive plea bargaining bans, and presumptive sentencing guidelines as having achieved these stated goals; voluntary sentencing guidelines, mandatory sentencing laws, and partial plea bargaining bans have largely failed; determinate sentencing laws defy easy generalization.[27]

With regard to the other questions posed—about lengths of prison terms, crowding, costs, and crime control—the answers are either not available or unclear. A major problem that criminal justice researchers must face in carrying out impact studies is the difficulty of isolating the change being tested from other factors at work in the system. Prison terms have grown longer, but is that because of determinate sentencing or public pressure for judges to dole out stiffer penalties? If the number and duration of trials have increased since reform, is the new penal code the main cause, or are changes in prosecution policies? Crime rates for most offenses have leveled off since the early 1980s. Is this a result of sentencing reforms or demographic changes in the crime-prone age group?

Summary

Sentencing—the specification of the sanction—may be viewed as the beginning of the postconviction process and corrections. Although many of the actions taken by criminal justice officials from the time of arrest to a plea or verdict are based on assumptions about the ultimate sanction, sentencing formalizes the punishment that the state imposes on the convicted.

The goals of retribution, deterrence, incapacitation, and rehabilitation may be viewed as distinct, but they overlap in many areas. Rehabilitation appears to be the one goal that, if carried out according to its model, requires the creation of distinctive sentencing, correctional, and releasing structures.

Punishment may take a variety of forms, but public attention is focused on incarceration. Only a small proportion of adult offenders go to prison; most receive fines or probation. The recent campaign to shift the goal of the criminal sanction away from rehabilitation to deserved punishment has resulted in actions by a number of legislatures to reduce the discretion of judges and parole boards by moving to determinate sentences.

The attitudes and background of the judge, the administrative context of decision making, the presentence report, and the agreed-on plea bargain have great influence on the actual sentence handed down. One of the problems with sentencing in the United States is that disparities exist in the severity of punishment accorded offenders who have committed the same crime.

Efforts at reform alert us to various aspects of the correctional system. Policies are not merely the outcomes of decisions made by correctional officials; they have their basis in laws passed by legislatures, whose members are attuned to public opinion and political pressures. Through the political process of compromise, laws may incorporate elements unanticipated by the promoters of reform.

For Discussion

1. What should be the dominant goal of the criminal sanction? Why?

2. What are the prospects for the rehabilitation of offenders? How should the correctional system respond to this prospect?

3. How much discretion should judges and members of parole boards have in administering the criminal sanction? What justifies the latitude currently given these individuals?

4. You are a state legislator. What considerations will influence your vote on the process by which criminal sanctions are set?

5. Is selective incarceration a good idea? What are the implications of the concept for crime control? For due process?

For Further Reading

American Friends Service Committee. *Struggle for Justice.* New York: Hill & Wang, 1971. A critique of indeterminate sentences and discretionary parole release. The book that raised the battle cry for sentencing reform in the 1970s.

Cullen, Francis T., and Gilbert, Karen E. *Reaffirming Rehabilitation.* Cincinnati: Anderson, 1982. A defense of the rehabilitative goal of corrections and a critique of the justice model.

Gaylin, Willard. *The Killing of Bonnie Garland.* New York: Simon & Schuster, 1982. The true story of the murder of a Yale student by her boyfriend and the reaction of the criminal justice system to the crime. Raises important questions about the goals of the criminal sanction and the role of the victim in the process.

Satter, Robert. *Doing Justice: A Trial Judge at Work.* New York: Simon & Schuster, 1990. A judge's view of the cases he faces daily and the factors influencing the decisions.

von Hirsch, Andrew. *Doing Justice.* New York: Hill & Wang, 1976. The best statement of the "just desserts" model, with recommendations for implementing it.

Notes

1. Willard Gaylin, *The Killing of Bonnie Garland* (New York: Simon & Schuster, 1982), p. 10.

2. Herbert L. Packer, *The Limits of the Criminal Sanction* (Stanford, Calif.: Stanford University Press, 1968), pp. 33–34.

3. Andrew von Hirsch, *Doing Justice* (New York: Hill & Wang, 1976), p. 49.

4. Peter Greenwood, *Selective Incapacitation* (Santa Monica, Calif.: Rand Corporation, 1982), p. xiv.

5. Daniel Nagin, "General Deterrence: A Review of the Empirical Evidence," in *Deterrence and Incapacitation: Estimating the Effects of Criminal Sanctions on Crime Rates*, eds. Alfred Blumstein, Jacqueline Cohen, and Daniel Nagin (Washington, D.C.: National Academy of Sciences, 1978), pp. 95–139.

6. Peter Greenwood, "Controlling the Crime Rate Through Imprisonment," in *Crime and Public Policy*, ed. James Q. Wilson (San Francisco: Institute for Contemporary Studies Press, 1983), p. 255.

7. Johannes Andenaes, "The Morality of Deterrence," *University of Chicago Law Review* 37 (1970): 644.

8. Shlomo Shinnar and Reuel Shinnar, "The Effects of the Criminal Justice System on the Control of Crime: A Quantitative Approach," *Law and Society Review* 9 (1975): 581–611.

9. James Q. Wilson, *Thinking About Crime* (New York: Basic Books, 1975), p. 199.

10. Stephen Van Dine, John P. Conrad, and Simon Dinitz, *Restraining the Wicked* (Lexington, Mass.: Lexington Books, 1979), p. 92.

11. See Ted Palmer, *Correctional Invention and Research* (Lexington, Mass.: Lexington Books, 1978); Francis T. Cullen and Karen E. Gilbert, *Reaffirming Rehabilitation* (Cincinnati: Anderson, 1982).

12. *New York Times,* 28 July 1978, p. l.

13. Michael Tonry, "Structuring Sentencing," in *Crime and Justice,* vol. 10, eds. Michael Tonry and Norval Morris (Chicago: University of Chicago Press, 1988), p. 267.

14. "Mandatory Sentencing: The Experience of Two States," *Policy Briefs* (Washington, D.C.: Government Printing Office, 1982).

15. Florida Department of Corrections, "Mandatory Minimum Sentences in Florida: Past Trends and Future Implications," 11 February 1991.

16. Joan Petersilia and Susan Turner, "The Potential of Intermediate Sanctions," *State Government* (March/April 1989): 65.

17. Sally T. Hillsman, Joyce L. Sichel, and Barry Mahoney, *Fines in Sentencing* (New York: Vera Institute of Justice, 1983). A national survey discovered that judges in the lower courts were more positively disposed to fines than were judges of higher courts, yet fines are extensively imposed by courts that handle only felonies.

18. National Advisory Commission on Criminal Justice Standards and Goals, Task Force on Corrections, *Report* (Washington, D.C.: Government Printing Office, 1973), p. 154.

19. Karla R. Spaulding, "'Hit Them Where It Hurts': RICO Criminal Forfeitures and White-Collar Crime," *Journal of Criminal Law and Criminology* 80 (1989): 197.

20. *New York Times,* 16 July 1990.

21. NAACP Legal Defense and Educational Fund, *Death Row, U.S.A.* (New York: NAACP Legal Defense and Educational Fund, Winter 1992), p. 5.

22. U.S. Department of Justice, Bureau of Justice Statistics, "Capital Punishment, 1990," *Bulletin* (Washington, D.C.: Government Printing Office, September 1991), p. 11.

23. Martin A. Levin, "Urban Politics and Policy Outcomes: The Criminal Courts," in *Criminal Justice: Law and Politics,* 6th ed., ed. George F. Cole (Belmont, Calif.: Wadsworth, 1993).

24. John Rosecrance, "Maintaining the Myth of Individualized Justice: Probation Presentence Reports," *Justice Quarterly* 5 (June 1988): 235.

25. Arthur Rosett and Donald R. Cressey, *Justice by Consent: Plea Bargains in the American Courthouse* (Philadelphia: Lippincott, 1976), p. 159.

26. Michael H. Tonry, *Sentencing Reform Impacts* (Washington, D.C.: Government Printing Office, 1987), p. 1.

27. Ibid., p. 98. See also Sandra Shane-Dubow, Alice P. Brown, and Erik Olsen, *Sentencing Reform in the United States: History, Content and Effect* (Washington, D.C.: Government Printing Office, 1985).

The Correctional Client

5

We'll get a better class of
prisons as we get a better
class of prisoners.

Lester Maddox,
Former Governor of Georgia

Selection for the Correctional System
Special Types of Offenders and Their Problems
The Situational Offender
The Career Criminal
The Sex Offender
The Substance Abuser
The Mentally Ill Offender
The Mentally Handicapped Offender
The Offender with AIDS
The Elderly Offender
The Juvenile Offender
Classifying Offenders: Some Issues
Overlap and Ambiguity in Classification Systems
Offense Classifications and Correctional
     Programming
Behavioral Probabilities in Classification
Sociopolitical Pressures and Classification
Distinctions in the Criteria for Classifying Offenders
Summary

In his acclaimed novel, *The Bonfire of the Vanities*, Tom Wolfe tells the story of Sherman McCoy, a Wall Street stockbroker and self-styled "Master of the Universe," who, through a series of unusual events, gets caught up in the criminal justice system and is accused of murder. Wolfe's description of the everyday indignities in the justice system's detention and prosecution of suspects is accurate and compelling. At one point, for example, Sherman finds himself in a holding tank, surrounded and terrified by a routine collection of drunks and thugs. Later, there is the dreadful frustration of being utterly unable to get anyone—even his own lawyer— to listen to his side of the story. His friends see him as a social outcast and shun him; his wife deserts him. Sherman's anguish grows throughout the novel, until he finally admits that being accused of a crime has changed his life forever, remaking him from a "master" to a common criminal.

The novel works so well partly because its protagonist is so wealthy and powerful. Sherman McCoy, classic beneficiary of The American Dream, is strangely impotent when faced with the awesome power of The American Penal System. Readers may find the novel a bit suffocating: They can imagine themselves being carried away by an irresistible tide of accusation and prosecution, drowned in the overwhelming volume of schedules, procedures, and legal maneuvers. The irony of seeing Sherman, once a master of the universe, brought down by the inexorable forces of the criminal law, is a criticism of both the powerfully wealthy and our system of justice.

In truth, however, the powerful and wealthy are rarely the subject matter of the criminal justice system. Whenever it happens that a "famous" person is brought into the courts, it is always big news. But for every person of means or reputation who enters the justice system, there are tens of thousands of nameless and faceless who are processed through the same decision apparatus. Where the wealthy can afford the most expensive counsel and can arrange for tac-

tical delay and strategic legal gambits, the ordinary person caught up in the justice process experiences it much as did Sherman McCoy: a demeaning, life-changing, isolating, and ultimately disabling experience.

Except for the occasional Sherman McCoy, the person who faces the justice system is primarily a young, minority male from a poor neighborhood. African Americans make up less than one-seventh of the U.S. population; they are nearly one-half of the accused and convicted people in the justice system. Males are one-half the general population but as much as nine-tenths of the justice system population. Half of those entering state prisons are between eighteen and twenty-seven years old.[1]

How does it come about that correctional clients, as a group, appear to be so different from the general population? The answer is not obvious, but it has to do with the selection process that operates to determine who gets charged, prosecuted, and convicted. Exactly how this selection process produces the clientele for corrections is a matter of some controversy.

Selection for the Correctional System

In the preceding chapter we described the decision-making process of the criminal justice system through which each offender must go before becoming a client of corrections. The nature of the process may make it seem that it is almost difficult to become a correctional client—that corrections has to be "broken into"—and there is a bit of truth to that idea. The criminal justice system operates as a large offender-selection bureaucracy, removing some offenders at each stage while passing others on to the next decision point.

The ones who go to the corrections system do not look like a random sample of our population. It is estimated that almost one of four black men aged twenty to twenty-nine years is

Table 5.1 ■ **Percentage of Men and Women Who Admitted Committing Offenses, by Type of Crime.** Most adults have committed a serious offense in their lifetime.

Type of crime	Men	Women
Petty Theft	89%	83%
Disorderly Conduct	85	76
Malicious Mischief	84	81
Assault	49	5
Tax Evasion	57	40
Robbery	11	1
Falsification and Fraud	46	34
Criminal Libel	36	29
Concealed Weapons	35	3
Auto Theft	26	8
Other Grand Theft	13	11
Burglary	17	4

Source: Adapted from James Wallerstein and Clement J. Wyle, "Our Law-Abiding Law-Breakers," *Probation* 35 (April 1947): 112. Reprinted by permission.

in prison, in jail, or on probation on any given day.[2] For many black males, prison is a probable experience. This situation has led Alvin Bronstein, director of the National Prison Project of the American Civil Liberties Union, to observe that "blacks are treated differently than whites at every stage of the criminal justice process. They are treated more harshly. The criminal justice system is a predominantly white, upper-middle/middle-class instrument that treats black people as an underclass.... Racism pervades the prison system as it does the rest of society."[3]

Other scholars disagree with Bronstein's view. In 1983 the National Research Council of the National Academy of Sciences (NAS) commissioned a major review of sentencing research. The review of more than seventy reports on race and criminal justice found them ambiguous; some seemed to uncover racism, while others did not. Most studies had significant methodological flaws. Overall, the NAS scholars asserted that "factors other than racial

discrimination in sentencing account for most of the disproportionate representation of blacks in U.S. prisons."[4]

If discrimination is not at the root of the overrepresentation of blacks, the poor, and men in U.S. corrections, something else must be. Is it that persons with these characteristics are more prone to crime? Do they have psychological or behavioral defects that make them commit crimes? Does their social condition impel them to break the law as a way of breaking out of poverty? Answers to these questions are neither obvious nor uncontroversial.

Self-report studies, which ask private citizens to report on their own criminal behavior, have shown that nearly everyone admits to having committed a crime during his or her lifetime, though most people are never caught. The results of these studies have been criticized because people doubt the validity or reliability of data furnished by respondents who admit to crimes, yet the numbers are often astounding. In the first self-report study, conducted on a cross section of citizens in 1947, an astonishing 99 percent of respondents admitted at least one criminal offense since turning sixteen (see Table 5.1).[5] A more recent study of 4,000 students found that 49 percent of black youths and 44 percent of white youths reported having committed a delinquent act during the preceding year.[6]

Because lower-class males tend to report more frequent and more serious delinquency, some scholars have reasoned that the higher representation of lower social classes in the corrections system may result more from their greater rates of criminality than from any special biases in the decision making of the justice system.

Even so, the rate of incarceration of lower-class and minority citizens is far greater than

self-report study An investigation of behavior (such as criminal activity) based on subjects' responses to questions concerning activities in which they have engaged.

their higher rates of offending would justify. For example, 27 percent of victims of violent crimes report that their assailant was black, but 31 percent of persons committed to prison for violent crimes are black, and 47 percent of all prisoners are black.[7] One recent study in New York State found that differences in incarceration rates of blacks and whites constituted "significant disparities…that could not be attributed to arrest charges [or] prior criminal charges."[8]

Some argue that this pattern occurs because of court policies that tend to work unintentionally to the detriment of the disadvantaged defendant. Pretrial release programs take into account factors such as employment status and living arrangements, and thus the unemployed tend to languish in jail awaiting trial. Ultimately, some critics say prosecutors are less likely to dismiss charges against poor, unemployed, single men—many of whom are black—simply because such people are in jail before trial and thus less able to build a good defense.

It is at the point of sentencing that the justice system completes its function as a huge, if uncoordinated, screening device to select the most serious offenders for punishment. The distribution of offenses for which people are arrested and for which they are incarcerated is shown in Figure 5.1. Although such crimes as burglary, robbery, and homicide account for less than 15 percent of all arrests (less than a third if "public order" crimes are excluded), they are the charges for which almost half of all jail inmates and three-fourths of all prison inmates are convicted.

If studies normally find that blacks, the unemployed, and the poor are more likely to receive prison terms, these findings seem to result largely from the more serious crimes and more extensive prior records these people present at the time of sentencing. The evidence on discrimination in sentencing is disputable and ambiguous; the National Academy of Sciences recently summarized it with these words: "Some studies find statistical evidence of…discrimination; others find none. While there is no evidence of a widespread systematic pattern of discrimination in sentencing, some pockets of discrimination are found for particular judges, particular crime types, and in particular settings."[9]

Thus it would be unfair to the justice system to leave the impression that intentional discrimination is a major factor in the decisions that produce correctional populations. A more reasonable interpretation is that justice system officials, acting under the daily pressures and routines of bureaucratic decision making, use filtering criteria to move cases along through the process. The filtering criteria are difficult to dispute: When a crime is not serious, when the suspect or defendant appears contrite and unlikely to repeat the offense, when the evidence is weak or contradictory, when the prior history of the accused is respectable, then the justice system chooses not to proceed with the case.

If these policies seem defensible and reasonable—and few people seriously advocate we abandon them—then they must be seen as a double-edged sword: Those unfortunate enough to have few resources and to have had prior contacts with the justice system are generally treated more harshly. The result is a population of offenders in corrections that is different from the general population at large.

The distinctiveness of the correctional population is not lost on the inmates themselves. They recognize that many other offenders' charges were dropped or reduced and theirs were not, that other offenders were able to avoid the full penalties of the law by using resources they did not have. Herein lies one of the significant results of the filtering process in criminal justice: Despite their guilt, many offenders feel unjustly treated in comparison with others. It is perhaps not surprising that offenders who feel this way are often not easy to manage in the correctional setting.

The obvious contrast between prison populations and the general community also leads some critics to think of prisons as a mechanism for control of minorities and the lower social

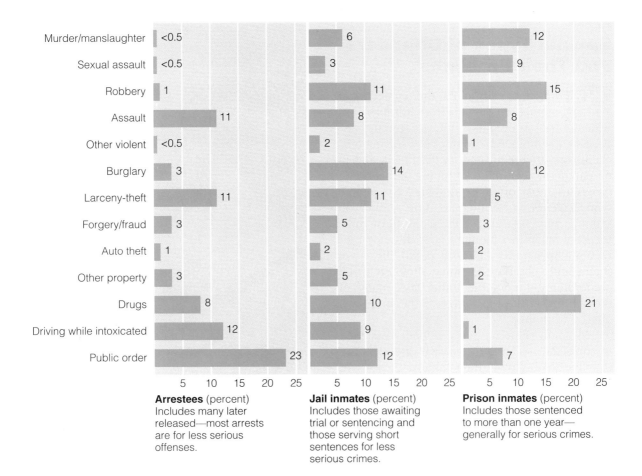

Figure 5.1 ■ **Percentage of Persons Arrested, Jailed, and Imprisoned for Offenses in Thirteen Categories.** The justice system acts as a selection filter, increasingly bringing more serious cases forward for more severe punishments.

Sources: U.S. Department of Justice, Bureau of Justice Statistics, *Report to the Nation on Crime and Justice,* 2nd ed. (Washington, D.C.: Government Printing Office, 1988), p. 40; Bureau of Justice Statistics, *Survey of State Prison Inmates, 1991* (Washington, D.C.: U.S. Department of Justice, March 1993), p. 4; Bureau of Justice Statistics, Sourcebook of Criminal Justice Statistics, 1991 (Washington, D.C.: U.S. Department of Justice, 1992).

classes. Historical studies of American corrections have shown that in earlier eras it was the newest immigrant groups who filled the prisons out of proportion to their numbers in the general population. Although blacks have made up the largest group in southern prisons in all periods since the Civil War, in the rest of the country the largest group has changed over time: first Germans, Irish, and Italians, and now blacks and Hispanics. This idea of ethnic succession is not entirely consistent with more contemporary research, but it remains undeniable that our prisons and jails hold many poor, disadvantaged, and minority citizens.

Special Types of Offenders and Their Problems

The composition of the correctional population has a direct influence on the programs and treatment approaches employed. Many of corrections' clients are undereducated, underskilled, and ill prepared for legitimate lifestyles. Educational programs must often be designed for people who have only minimal reading skills. Job training must be undertaken at the most rudimentary level. In Chapter 13 we describe correctional programs in more detail; here we shall simply observe that since offenders come predominantly from the underclass, many of them bring little preparation to the programs offered to them.

In some respects, every offender assigned to corrections is unique; no two offenders are exactly alike. In writing about "types" of offenders, we may then group individuals because they share an important characteristic (such as type of offense) when they differ in some other vital characteristic (such as prior record or intelligence). Any attempt to describe groups of offenders is a decision to generalize about people at the potential cost of specific accuracy. Thus when we talk about groups of offenders, we are really talking about individuals who, although unique, share some characteristic, even though we know quite well that not all persons in that group are alike.

When offenders are discussed, however, this point is too often forgotten. We tend to talk about "sex offenders" or "professional criminals" as though they all behaved in the past (and will behave in the future) in the same way. This approach simplifies policy making and correctional programming, but it bears little resemblance to reality. Therein lies the peril of grouping offenders. We forget that the grouping is done only to enable correctional officials to take action, and that groupings in some respects inevitably offer distorted portraits of the individual offenders.

Jean Harris, private school headmistress, was convicted of the 1980 killing of her lover, Dr. Herman Tarnower. Her incarceration ended in 1993. Do you expect Ms. Harris to recidivate?

To be honest then, our discussion of criminal categories will contain inaccurate statements about groups of offenders with whom corrections must work. Keep this in mind as you learn about offenders. Whether situational offender or career criminal, some individuals will fit in a group nicely; others are more difficult to place, and all individuals within a group will vary in some respects. The groupings are made for our convenience, to help us understand the types of clients corrections manages and the way their characteristics influence the work of corrections.

The Situational Offender

Most individuals who are caught and convicted of a felony are not arrested again. This statement

Ruth's Story

The argument started as a trivial incident but ended in tragedy. As he had on countless other evenings, Jack came home at about nine after spending the time since the end of work drinking with the boys. Unsteady on his feet, he demanded that his wife, Ruth, prepare his supper.

"Supper was cooked and over hours ago. The kids and I got tired of waiting for you and finally ate."

"Don't raise your voice at me, you bitch! Get me some food!" Jack yelled as he pushed Ruth against the sink.

Crying, she pushed him away. "Don't touch me! You're drunk."

"I'm not drunk. I want some food. Get it."

He approached her menacingly, but she ran out of the kitchen, across the hallway, and into the bedroom of their small apartment, slamming the door. "Keep away from me, Jack Moore! Get out of this house!" The words seemed only to antagonize Jack further. He rushed at the door, broke the latch, and stormed into the bedroom.

He stopped short. Ruth was standing by the nightstand, the drawer was open, and she was holding the Saturday-night special purchased for her protection when he was away. "Don't you come near me, I'm warning you!" she said as she backed away.

"Put that fucking thing down!"

The shot reverberated throughout the building. Jack fell to the floor. Ruth slumped at his side, sobbing, "I didn't mean to. I didn't mean to."

In court Ruth pleaded guilty to manslaughter. Her attorney urged that because of the circumstances of the offense, and especially because of "the provocative behavior of her husband," Ruth be given probation. Ruth tearfully told the judge that she had not meant to kill Jack and that on other occasions he had come home drunk and abused her. But the judge did not accept the recommendation of the defense attorney, citing the loss of life and the requirement that justice be done. "The court can well understand your feelings, Mrs. Moore, but a man is dead at your hand." Ruth was sentenced to a five-year term, to be suspended after two years.

At the state correctional institution for women, Ruth distanced herself from most of the other prisoners, whom she found frightening. Barbara, a bookkeeper serving time for embezzlement, was her only confidante. Because she had been a hairdresser, Ruth was assigned as an assistant to the civilian in charge of the beautician course. She went to chapel daily and sang in the choir on Sundays. After ten months Ruth was moved to a halfway house, and she was granted release with supervision after serving twelve months. She now works in a department store as a salesperson, having lost her beautician's license because she is a former felon.

is carefully worded, because it may be that some people who are not rearrested simply are not caught a second time. Yet some studies suggest that up to 80 percent of first-time felony offenders are never arrested again. There are probably many reasons for this. One explanation offered is the idea of the **situational offender,** described by Haskell and Yablonsky as one who

1. is confronted with a problem that requires action

2. took action that was in violation of the criminal law

3. was apprehended and given the status of criminal

4. until the time of the offense, was committed to the normative system of our society and who, prior to the offense, was indistinguishable from other persons[10]

Thus the situational offender "made a mistake" and "paid a debt to society" for that mistake. But this offender presents many problems for corrections, for several reasons. First, the crime is usually a serious, violent crime (often murder or aggravated assault), and the offender usually knew the victim well (the victim is often a spouse or other family member). For such a crime, a severe punishment is often thought to be appropriate.

Yet once the situational offender reaches the institution, there is little for corrections to do. The person has a positive orientation toward accepted social values, ordinarily a solid work history, and good basic employment skills. Other than assistance in adjusting to the life crisis of imprisonment, few positive programming options exist for the situational offender. The prognosis for a good adjustment on parole is extremely high. Nevertheless, soci-

ety fears all violent criminals, including the situational offender (whose crime may have been the most violent of all). Even though only an extremely small percentage of murderers commit murder again, the fear of the situational offender together with outrage at the offense often results in lengthy incarceration. Managing the time served by these essentially adjusted offenders is troublesome for corrections because there are few positive actions that can be taken. Although situational offenders may participate in programs as a means of self-improvement, they are not in need of rehabilitation. Their time in prison is mainly a matter of simply serving the sentence.

Under conditions of crowding, moreover, it is precisely the situational offenders whom correctional officials and parole boards believe are most appropriate for release because they pose very little threat to the public. The space they vacate can house far more serious criminals. The decision to give early release to a situational offender leaves the corrections system vulnerable, however. There is inevitable citizen reaction to what may appear to be coddling. It may seem to observers that justice has not been served. Even more important, in the case of the one person out of twenty who murders again, public outcry can end the careers of the officials involved.[11] Therefore, situational offenders often remain in prison while other felons, those who actually represent a greater threat to society but a lesser threat to corrections, are released.

The Career Criminal

One of the most slippery concepts in the classification of offenders is the so-called **career criminal.** Originally the term was applied to a small proportion of all offenders, but more

---

situational offender A person who in a particular set of circumstances has violated the law but who is not given to criminal behavior in normal circumstances and is unlikely to repeat the offense.

career criminal A person for whom crime is a way of earning a living. Over time the career criminal has numerous contacts with the justice system and may come to look upon the criminal sanction as a normal part of life.

Archie's Story

Archie left home at age thirteen and traveled around the country as a transient, sometimes supporting himself as a truck driver. Archie claims to have committed about five hundred burglaries, five hundred auto thefts, and five robberies before his eighteenth birthday. Of them, he was arrested for only one robbery. As he was not convicted, however, he has no juvenile record. Even in this early phase of his criminal career, Archie was quite sophisticated in his MO. He used theatrical makeup to disguise himself for his burglaries and robberies, including contact lenses of various colors. He recalls being fairly violent and obsessed about his small size. He injured one of his robbery victims when the man tried to resist.

Archie's first incarceration did not come until his mid-thirties. For this conviction he served several years in a California prison. Although his rap sheet shows nine arrests for drug violations and petty theft, the only serious prison time he served before his present term was for an auto-theft conviction.

Before his first incarceration, Archie was employed much of the time, but his main source of income was crime. His wife was a heroin addict. Between his eighteenth birthday and his first incarceration, he estimates that he committed about one hundred grand thefts, one hundred burglaries, and twelve robberies. His average take per robbery was about $2,500. He was never arrested for any of these crimes. He used the loot mainly to support his wife's drug habit and for partying.

The main targets of Archie's robberies were savings and loan banks or payroll offices. His MO was to disguise himself in full theatrical makeup and to enter the savings and loan carrying a sawed-off shotgun, which he would point at a young female employee.

The main targets of Archie's burglaries were pawnshops or businesses. His few residential burglaries were at private homes where an informer had told him a valuable collection or large sums of money were kept. His typical MO was to make the acquaintance of the prospective victim and gain access to his home to learn where the valuables were kept. Within a month after befriending the victim, Archie would burglarize his house. He also performed insurance-fraud burglaries in which the victim would indicate the articles he wanted stolen. Archie would burglarize the house at a prearranged time, stealing the articles that had been specified and selling them to a fence. The fence would profit, Archie would profit, and the insurance company would reimburse the victim for the items stolen.

Archie reports having shot victims in both burglaries and robberies when they tried to resist. He also mentions having retaliated against two heroin addicts who were friends of his wife and who apparently had tried to kill him. Archie says that both were seriously injured. Archie relates that his first conviction and incarceration occurred because his wife informed on him when he was trying to stop her from using drugs.

After release from the first incarceration, in his late thirties, Archie remained on the street about five years before being incarcerated for his present term. During this period he committed only four robberies, at large stores or markets, and they yielded very large amounts of money. As in his earlier years, he engaged in elaborate planning for each crime. Archie was convicted by a jury on two counts of armed robbery with a prior felony conviction, and he is serving two concurrent sentences of five-to-life; he is also serving two consecutive five-to-life sentences for the use of a firearm in these robberies.

Source: Joan Petersilia, Peter W. Greenwood, and Marvin Lavin, *Criminal Careers of Habitual Felons* (Washington, D.C.: Government Printing Office, 1978), pp. 100–101.

recently it has been used to include a much broader variety of persons.

When Walter Reckless first developed the idea of the career criminal, he had in mind a specific set of attributes:

1. Crime is his way of earning a living, his main occupation.

2. He develops technical skills useful to the commission of his crimes.

3. He started as a delinquent child and progressed in favorable skills and attitudes toward criminality.

4. He expects to do some time in prison as a "cost" of doing this type of work.

5. He is psychologically normal.[12]

These characteristics are attributed to a more or less undifferentiated group of offenders who work at crime. They include members of organized crime, white-collar criminals, and professional criminals who work continuously at an illegal occupation.

The consistent scholarly finding that a small proportion of offenders accounts for a large percentage of crime has led to a more inclusive definition of career criminal. From studies of a group of males born in Philadelphia in 1958 to interviews of convicted and imprisoned adults in California, Texas, and Michigan, the results of a wide range of studies has led scholars to believe that a small group of active criminals commits a majority of all crimes.[13]

This led to a significant shift in thinking about career criminals. Instead of using the term to refer to someone whose *work* is crime, policymakers began to refer to any offender with several convictions or arrests as a career criminal. Thus a person with as few as three or four convictions is commonly labeled a career criminal. This may seem a bit odd to most of us; we would hardly call our own jobs a career if we had been seen at work only three or four times.

Of course, many of those who are repeatedly convicted actually do admit to more crimes, sometimes many more than the handful for which they are being punished. Peter Greenwood's famous study of robbers, for example,

found that as many as half of those with multiple convictions for robbery admitted to having committed a large number of robberies for which they were not caught.[14] Undeniably, this small minority made something of a career out of that crime. Many repeaters—almost half of Greenwood's sample, for example—are not high-rate offenders. That is, the mere existence of multiple convictions does not mean that the person is working at crime as a career; it may mean that the person is a frequent offender (has committed several crimes in the past few years) who shifts from one type of crime to another.

Why, then, this recent trend to paint the picture of the career criminal with such a broad brush? The answer has to do partly with political pressures. With the devaluation of rehabilitation in the 1970s came renewed confidence in incapacitation as the appropriate correctional course. But if incapacitation was to be the political catchword, what group would be the target? Earlier studies of the career criminal found so few that this notion was not promising for correctional administrators. Yet if the career criminal concept could be expanded to include virtually all multiple repeaters, then the target group for this newly popular policy would be large indeed.

Corrections has borne the cost of this conceptual shift. Much as in the case of violent situational criminals, pressure has grown to keep repeaters in prison longer to prevent them from pursuing their predatory "careers." Yet these criteria result in nonprofessional but intermittent offenders being misclassified as career criminals. One result is serious crowding.

Without question our prisons hold some career criminals, professional offenders committed to lives of crime. But we must examine the accuracy of the overall label and recognize that the decision to classify offenders has social and political significance.

The Sex Offender

Although a wide array of legislation regulates sexual conduct in most jurisdictions, corrections commonly deals with three basic types of **sex offenders:** rapists (sexual assaulters), child molesters (pedophiles), and, to a lesser extent, prostitutes. In the case of each of these subclasses of sex offenders, the correctional response is deeply influenced by prevailing public opinion about the crimes themselves.

The rapist With the rise of the new feminism in the 1960s and 1970s, the justice system's response to the crime of rape became a major political issue. Indeed, to discuss the crime of rape under the heading of "sex offenses" is to risk ignoring that it is primarily an act of violence against women. Susan Brownmiller's classic study, *Against Our Will*, persuasively argued that the crime of rape needs to be reconceptualized; it is not a sex crime but a brutal personal assault: "To a woman the definition of rape is fairly simple.... A deliberate violation of emotional, physical and rational integrity and ... a hostile, degrading act of violence...."[15] When rape is placed where it truly belongs, within the context of modern criminal violence and not within the purview of ancient masculine codes, the crime retains its unique dimensions, taking its place among armed robbery and aggravated assault.

The wide recognition that rape is not a crime motivated by sexuality but a physical intrusion motivated by a desire for violent coercion led to two general changes in the criminal justice system. The first was a move to redefine the crime of "rape" as a gender-neutral "sexual assault" or even as a special case of the general crime of assault. The second change was a trend toward harsher treatment of convicted rapists.

The sexual assaulter presents particular difficulties for correctional management. The truly violent offender may well be a security risk

inside the prison, for the same irrational attitudes and unpredictable behavior patterns may occur during incarceration. It is more likely, however, that the rapist will become a target for inmate violence. In the prisoner subculture, "crazies," including many rapists, are near the bottom of the pecking order. It is common for such persons to be subjected to humiliating physical and sexual attacks as a form of prisoner domination. Thus, whether unpredictably violent or predictably vulnerable to attack, the sexual assaulter in prison is a security risk.

The child molester Few offenses have received such uniform disapprobation as child molestation. Public revulsion against it is so high that great stigma is attached to the act. Only in recent years, with more open discussion of sexuality, has significant scholarly attention been given to convicted child molesters.

The picture of the child molester that emerges from various studies is more tragic than disgusting. Estimates are that most—perhaps as many as 90 percent—child molesters were themselves molested as children.[16] Child molestation is a complex crime involving many factors, but it ordinarily stems from deep feelings of personal inadequacy on the part of the offender. As many as 20 percent of child molesters are over fifty years old, and many cases involve ambivalent feelings of attachment between adults and children that gradually become converted into sexual contact.

Most victims of molestation are confused by the crime and feel guilty about it because the emotional attachment to their molesters is quite real. They are usually aware that the act is "wrong" or "bad." If the act arouses pleasurable feelings, the situation is further complicated.

The child molester is often the most despised offender in the court and in the prison. An incarcerated molester is almost certain to be the target of repeated threats, actual violence, and routine hostility from other prisoners. Moreover, because most prison systems have very little treatment to offer the molester, this offender's experience in prison is normally bleak indeed.

sex offender A person who has committed a sexual act prohibited by law. Such acts may be committed for a variety of reasons, including economic, psychological, and even situational.

Nevin's Story

For as long as he can remember, Nevin has relived in his dreams the experience of being forced to have oral sex with a man when he was about five years old. Now, at the age of forty-nine and serving a five- to ten-year term for sexual assault of a ten-year-old boy, Nevin has confronted correctional authorities in Connecticut with a problem. He has filed a lawsuit to force the state to provide treatment for him after his release from the maximum security prison in Somers. He has no money to pay for treatment, and he says flatly that he will never be able to resist the attraction he feels toward young boys.

Nevin's criminal record stretches back thirty-five years. He has been in and out of prisons in Connecticut, New York, and Pennsylvania for all but five of those years. He estimates that he has sexually assaulted about a thousand boys during his lifetime, and he has said that he has never had any difficulty finding willing partners. "I hang out where the prostitutes hang out, and they [boys] approach me. That solves the problem. I walk down Forty-Second Street in New York City, and in fifteen minutes I have five kids asking if they can go home with me, because I'm known as that type of person." Nevin prefers dark-haired, dark-skinned youngsters and says that he has paid various fees. "I'd pay twenty dollars. I'd pay fifty cents."

Pedophilia, preference for children as sexual objects, is an extremely difficult abnormality to cure. Psychologists believe pedophiles are generally sane and in all other respects are good citizens, but they cannot control this one aspect of their lives. Sexual aversion therapy has been used in some cases. At the Somers Prison it was used until 1975, when it was stopped as a result of a lawsuit filed by child molesters who said that they were being denied parole release unless they underwent the treatment. The technique involved the application of electric shocks to the genital area when photographs of nude children were flashed on a screen. Injections of Depo-Provera are also being used with some pedophiles at the Sexual Disorders Clinic at Johns Hopkins Hospital, Baltimore. The drug blunts the male sexual drive, and success has been reported when its use is accompanied by therapy. Depo-Provera, however, is not approved for use in the prison setting.

Nevin has written to the Superior Court asking for treatment upon release. The Department of Correction says that it has given him treatment, cannot hold him longer than his sentence, and cannot provide treatment after release. Should Nevin be able to prove that the state has an obligation to provide treatment, provision of that treatment would be up to another state agency, such as the Department of Mental Health.

Nevin acknowledges that he has a responsibility "not to engage in this type of behavior." Nevin is more concerned with the rights of the boys he fears will become his next victims than he is with the protection of his own rights. In his letter to the court he wrote, "I believe it is time we consider the rights of the people to be safe in their homes and to be secure in the knowledge that their children can go to school safely without being molested."

Because he is sane, Nevin cannot be involuntarily committed to a state mental hospital. What should be done? What of the pedophiles who are not so concerned about their problem as Nevin is?

Source: Adapted from *Hartford Courant,* 12, 13, and 14 October 1984. Reprinted by permission.

Alcoholism and drug abuse often lead to crime. Because alcohol is legally available there is not the direct crime link that there is with drug abuse.

As a result, some states have to set aside special institutions or cell blocks for molesters in order to ensure them better security.

The prostitute Prostitution is more an economic than a sexual crime; that is, it is an illegal economic transaction between a service provider and a customer. Public opinion about prostitution is ambivalent; public policy seems to fluctuate between "reform" legislation designed to legalize and regulate prostitution and wholesale police roundups of hookers and pimps designed to "clean up" the streets. During the current AIDS epidemic there is renewed concern that prostitutes are major transmission agents for the disease. Some courts have ordered infected prostitutes brought before them to refrain from practicing their trade. In any event, prostitution exists (even flourishes) in virtually every section of the country, and when prostitutes or their pimps are punished, the sentence generally is probation.

Because prostitution is an economic crime, correctional caseworkers are forced to find a substitute vocation for offenders. This is not an easy task, for many prostitutes lack other salable skills or education, and many are addicted to drugs. Many have little desire to change their

lifestyle. Because prostitution is more public nuisance than public threat, caseworkers are likely to accord such cases low priority, as do the courts and prosecutors. The result is that prostitution is a crime that often receives marginal enforcement and indifferent punishment.

The Substance Abuser

The criminal law typically distinguishes between the use of illegal drugs and the illegal use of alcohol. In the case of drugs, any unauthorized possession of a controlled substance is prohibited. Laws against the mere possession of some drugs are so severe that in the federal system, as well as many states, prison terms are mandatory for these offenders. By contrast, possession of alcohol is prohibited only for minors. The criminal justice system becomes involved in alcohol offenders' lives primarily because of their conduct under the influence of alcohol. The difference between these two types of offenders is important for correctional policy, so we describe them separately.

The drug abuser Our culture is a drug-using culture, from aspirin and caffeine to marijuana and heroin. It is not surprising, then, that substance abuse figures prominently in criminal behavior. A national survey of state prisoners found that over half (54 percent) of those serving time for violent offenses admitted they were under the influence of an illegal drug when they committed the crime.[19] In 36 percent of all criminal victimizations, the victim perceives the offender as under the influence of drugs or alcohol.[18] It is estimated that 23 percent of all inmates in local jails are there for drug crimes.[19] As shown in Figure 5.2, from 42 percent to 79 percent of offenders arrested in twenty-three U.S. cities tested positive for an illegal drug at the time of their arrest.[20]

The **drug abuser** presents two problems for corrections. First, the person is an offender because of the role drugs played in the commission of the crime. The offender may have been convicted for possession or sale of drugs

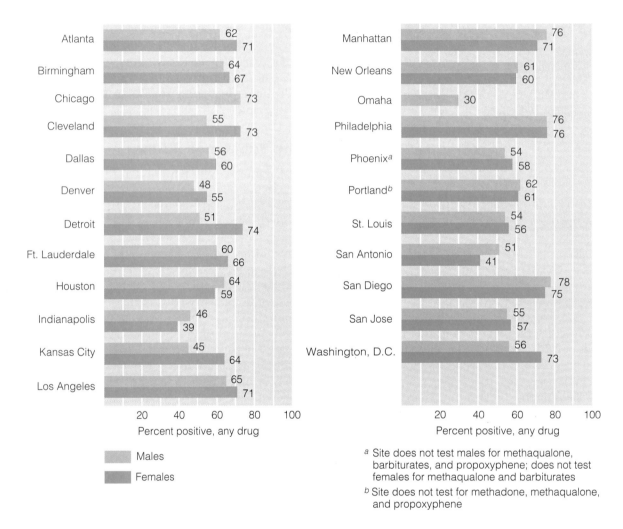

Figure 5.2 ■ Drug Use by Booked Arrestees in Twenty-Three U.S. Cities. A large proportion of felony arrestees are under the influence of drugs at the time of their arrest.

Source: National Institute of Justice, *Drug Use Forecasting* (Washington, D.C.: U.S. Department of Justice, November 1991), p. 2.

or for some other offense committed as a result of their use. Second, the effects of drug dependency must be addressed by correctional personnel while the client is in detention, on probation,

drug abuser A person whose use of a chemical substance disrupts normal living patterns to the extent that social problems develop, often leading to criminal behavior.

in prison, or on parole. Whether in prison or on the streets, the drug abuser, because of the likelihood of rearrest, represents a potential control problem for correctional staff.

The street addict's life is structured by the need to get money to support the habit, and that need often leads to property crime. In studies of the relationship between drugs and crime, it has been found that although a substantial part of the expenditures for the support of a

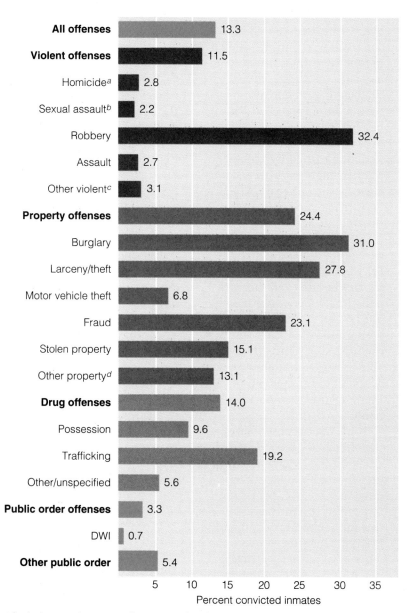

Offense	Percent
All offenses	13.3
Violent offenses	11.5
Homicide[a]	2.8
Sexual assault[b]	2.2
Robbery	32.4
Assault	2.7
Other violent[c]	3.1
Property offenses	24.4
Burglary	31.0
Larceny/theft	27.8
Motor vehicle theft	6.8
Fraud	23.1
Stolen property	15.1
Other property[d]	13.1
Drug offenses	14.0
Possession	9.6
Trafficking	19.2
Other/unspecified	5.6
Public order offenses	3.3
DWI	0.7
Other public order	5.4

Percent convicted inmates

[a] Includes murder, nonnegligent manslaughter, and negligent manslaughter
[b] Includes rape
[c] Includes kidnapping
[d] Includes arson

Figure 5.3 ■ **Percent of Convicted Jail Inmates Who Committed Their Offenses to Support a Drug Habit.** Drugs and crime are closely connected for addicts.

Source: Office of Justice Programs, *Drugs and Crime* (Washington, D.C.: U.S. Department of Justice, September, 1992), p. 7.

drug habit may be legitimately obtained, a high proportion of drug users admit engaging in income-generating crimes. Even if an addict supports only a small fraction of the habit's cost through crime, this fraction can eventually be translated into large amounts of crime.

Habits costing $50 to $150 a day are not uncommon. Because stolen goods are fenced at much less than their market value, an addict has to steal goods worth several times the cost of the habit just to survive. Figure 5.3 shows some of the crimes that are committed to support a drug

Mary Lou's Story

Mary Lou looks much older than her twenty-five years. She was brought up in a family of six children, and the only income was her mother's monthly welfare check. She is now approaching the time of her release from prison after serving a sentence for driving the getaway car involved in the armed robbery of a drugstore.

A school dropout at sixteen, Mary Lou met Frankie, a flashy dude who seemed to have money to spend yet was always on the street. Soon she was taking dope with Frankie, and even though her girlfriends warned her that he was a junkie and a pimp, she moved into his apartment; by then she had graduated to heroin. During their first weeks together they were high much of the time—sleeping most of the morning, taking a fix, then cruising the streets in Frankie's Olds, dropping in at bars and apartments to visit what seemed like an endless number of his friends.

When Frankie's money ran low, he told Mary Lou that she was going to have to "hustle" if she expected to live with him. She told him she wouldn't, and she moved in with a girlfriend. Within a day she was feeling so bad that she had to borrow money for a fix. Faced with her habit and an empty pocketbook, Mary Lou hustled. She turned two tricks the first night, but her second customer beat her up. Shaken by the experience and hurting for heroin, she returned to the only person she thought could help her— Frankie. He was not happy to see her because another girl had already taken her place, but he agreed to help if she would hustle for him. During the next six months she was able to make enough money to retain the protection of Frankie and to support her habit.

With the onset of winter, the streets of Chicago turned cold and the supply of heroin on the streets suddenly tightened in response to a strong law enforcement effort. By this time both Mary Lou and Frankie were heavy users. After two frantic days of trying to find heroin at a price they could afford, Frankie decided to rob a drugstore. In a haze Mary Lou drove him to the store, parked in an alley, and waited. Frankie entered the store with a gun in his pocket. Within minutes he was back and they took off. A burglar alarm sounded as the Olds careened down the alley and into the street, where it hit another car.

Frankie jumped out and ran off. A stunned Mary Lou just sat behind the steering wheel as a crowd formed and an officer arrived to investigate the accident.

It took little detective work for the police to link the collision to the robbery. They arrested Frankie back at his apartment and took him to the stationhouse for booking. Mary Lou was already there when he came in. Held in the Cook County Jail awaiting court action, she endured withdrawal as her body reacted to the absence of heroin.

At the suggestion of her public defender, Mary Lou pleaded guilty to a reduced charge of abetting an armed robbery and was sentenced to a three- to five-year term.

habit. Robbery is more directly lucrative than theft but also more chancy: There is always a risk of violence, and the victim may have little cash.

Treatment programs for those who compulsively or habitually use drugs are not highly successful and some are controversial. As the social movement against heroin grew in the 1950s and 1960s, the support for clinical treatment of addiction also grew, and special drug treatment facilities were opened to house addicts as a special population of incarcerated offenders. Civil commitment procedures were often used to send convicted offenders to such facilities, where their incarceration term frequently exceeded what they would otherwise have received. Evaluation studies of these programs yielded dismal results. A twenty-year follow-up study of a hundred releases from one program found only ten instances of five or more consecutive years of abstinence following hospitalization.[21]

Thus substance abusers represent a serious dilemma for corrections. By definition their behavior is compulsive and likely to be repeated. Although the mere act of abuse of drugs is not considered a serious offense, the collateral acts of predatory crime and violence are considered very serious. The lack of effective treatment alternatives for this control problem often puts corrections in a bind: The punishments imposed seem to outweigh the seriousness of the acts being punished. Nonetheless, repeated criminality by addicts found in possession of drugs often makes corrections appear inordinately lenient and ineffectual.

The alcohol abuser Unlike marijuana, heroin, and other controlled substances, alcohol is widely available and relatively inexpensive, and its consumption is an integral part of life in the United States. It is only when alcohol leads to problems such as unemployment, family disorganization, and crime that society becomes concerned. The **alcohol abuser's** problem translates into crime much less directly than that of the drug user. Because alcohol is legal, no criminal subculture attends its use. Where many addicts must engage in a criminal act just to obtain the drug of their choice, the alcoholic need only go to the corner store. But in getting there the alcoholic may produce disastrous consequences that are far in excess of those of the heroin addict: It is estimated that alcohol use contributes to almost 100,000 deaths annually, five times the total number of homicides reported to the police. Moreover, large proportions of all automobile injuries and personal offenses are at least in part products of intoxication: A drunk's drive home becomes vehicular homicide; a domestic dispute becomes aggravated assault; a political debate or quarrel over money becomes disorderly conduct; a night of drinking leads to a burglary or an auto theft. Alcohol use produces loss of coordination, impairment of judgment, reduction of inhibitions, and confused understanding; criminal acts can easily follow.

Although research on alcoholic offenders has focused on those who are incarcerated, alcoholic offenders appear in other correctional environments as well. Like drug abusers, alcoholics present problems for probation officers, community treatment providers, and parole officers. Because some alcoholics become assaultive when they drink, dealing with them is not a pleasant or safe experience.

There are other problems related to the treatment of alcohol abusers. To some extent, the problems stem from Americans' generally ambivalent attitudes toward alcohol use—it is seen as recreational behavior rather than deviance. Consequently, treatment programs seem to work when they focus on getting the individual to recognize the nature of his or her own patterns of alcohol use rather than on alcohol use per se. This is one reason that the program of Alcoholics Anonymous (AA) has consistently proved to be the most successful of

---

alcohol abuser   A person whose use of alcohol is difficult to control, disrupting normal living patterns. Such persons frequently violate the law while under the influence of alcohol or in attempts to secure it.

alcohol treatment methods: It provides intensive peer support to help individuals face their personal inability to manage alcohol use.

Despite its general success, AA may be of limited usefulness to criminal offenders, many of whom come from lower social classes that appear to be less responsive to its middle-class orientation. Moreover, AA views itself as a strictly voluntary treatment; individuals must want to help themselves to subscribe to it. This characteristic often clashes with the coercive nature of treatment in corrections, which can require attendance at AA as a condition of the sentence. The poor fit between AA's voluntary peer-group structure and the involuntariness of corrections may explain why studies find these programs are not particularly effective with public-drunkenness offenders.

The Mentally Ill Offender

Few images disturb us more than that of the "crazy," violence-prone criminal whose random, senseless acts seem to lack explanation or rationale. To help us understand such people better, we often roughly classify them as "disturbed" offenders—persons whose rational processes do not seem to operate in normal ways. Such a person might be called a "psychopath" and thought of as a **mentally ill offender.**

Mentally ill offenders are those who have a diminished capacity to think realistically about their conduct, including criminal conduct. Psychopaths are mentally ill, but there are many kinds of mental illness. Not all mentally ill offenders are violent or psychopathic—though those who are may present the most problems for corrections.

------

mentally ill offender A person whose criminal behavior may be traced to diminished or otherwise abnormal capacity to think or reason as a result of psychological or neurological disturbance, or who exhibits such diminished capacity while under correctional authority.

Recently, we have come to recognize that the classification of violent offenders as "mentally ill" is an excessive generalization and a social issue. It is excessive because not all violent offenders are demonstrably mentally ill. It is a social issue because the decision to apply the label "sick" (which is implied by the term *psychopath* or *sociopath*) makes the person seem somehow less whole and makes it easier to justify extreme correctional measures.

There is some overlap between what we described as the career criminal and the so-called psychopath. Both engage in frequent criminal activity, but the distinction between them is made clear in the original description of the psychopath: "an asocial, aggressive, highly impulsive person, who feels little or no guilt and is unable to form lasting bonds of affection with other human beings."[22] Thus the psychopath is motivated by a lack of attachment to people or rules, whereas a career criminal is motivated by gain. But even this distinction is insufficient. Who is to say that a person never feels love, affection, or guilt? Is not the gain to be achieved by a crime at least part of the amoral motivation of the psychopath?

The problem with definitive identification of psychopaths applies to any offender whose behavior is unusual: How can anyone say with certainty that the mind of the offender is abnormal or dysfunctional? The general problem of a mental health model of criminality is that the mind cannot be observed; what goes on in a person's feelings and thoughts can only be inferred from behavior. When we observe someone engaging in outrageous or bizarre behavior, we are tempted to infer that his or her mind or emotions work in strange ways—the mind is "sick." We call these people "emotionally ill" even when there is no way to prove an illness comparable to the flu or any other physical disease. In earlier times, deities, witches, and instincts were considered to be behind a variety of odd or criminal behaviors. As Thomas Szasz has argued, today we use the term *mental illness* to explain behaviors we do not understand, even if the behavior is not caused by a "disease of the brain."[23]

Bill's Story

Bill Gunderson is only thirty-nine years old but he looks sixty. His eyes are sunken; his face is bony, pockmarked, and stubbly. He is bundled up in layer upon layer of clothing, topped by a grease-stained, military-green overcoat. His hair, clotted in bunches and standing out all over his head, combines with his physique to give him the appearance of a scarecrow. On this day in late December, Gunderson is stumbling among the crowd of affluent holiday shoppers on King Street in Alexandria, Virginia, looking for handouts and having little success. They can immediately tell that he is drunk.

Being drunk is Gunderson's normal state. Because he has no home, he is often drunk in public and has been arrested repeatedly on this charge since he arrived in Alexandria two months before. "The cops pick me up whenever I get too drunk, not because they want to," Gunderson says. "A couple of times they just took my bottle and poured it on the street. But usually they pick me up. It's for my own health, I reckon."

After his first arrest, Gunderson was driven directly to the city's detoxification center, a six-bed facility designed to relieve some of the burden on the Alexandria Correctional Center. "They gave me a bed, let me take a shower, and gave me some coffee," Gunderson says. But after a few hours he began to go into withdrawal, and because the detox center is not staffed or equipped to administer sedatives to ease the pain, Gunderson left in search of the only relief he knows—another bottle of wine. "I was shaking so bad, but the only thing they told me was, 'Hey, you gotta go through it.'"

The second time Gunderson was arrested, the detox center refused to admit him and the police took him to jail. Every time after that—Gunderson guesses it has happened 16 times in a month and a half—he has gone straight to jail. He is always released after a few hours and told to appear later for trial. Gunderson says he has never appeared in court and has no intention of doing so. "They don't care," he says with a toothless grin. "Why should they?"

Sheriff Michael Norris of Alexandria admits that the police do not track down drunks like Gunderson for court appearances. The offense is punishable only by a $10 fine, and no matter what the police do, they are likely to pick up the same offender on the same charge a few days later. "It's just a merry-go-round," Sheriff Norris says.

Source: D. Whitford, "Despite Decriminalization, Drunks Still Clog Our Nation's Jails," *Corrections Magazine* (April 1983): 31. Reprinted by permission of the Edna McConnell Clark Foundation.

Our need to understand criminal behavior by explaining it as "mental illness" leads us to overgeneralize criminal behavior as mental illness and ascribe mental illness to criminals. The National Commission on the Causes and Prevention of Violence recognized the problem when it concluded:

1. The popular idea that the mentally ill are overrepresented in the population of violent criminals is not suggested by research evidence.

2. Generally, persons identified as mentally ill represent no greater risk of committing violent crimes than the population as a whole.[24]

This conclusion underscores the problem for corrections represented by mentally ill offenders: Their mental illness is often a separate issue from their criminality, and dealing with their criminality may not require treatment of their mental illness. In other words, the fact that a person has mental or emotional problems and is an offender does not necessarily mean that the person will continue to offend until the mental or emotional problems are resolved.

The general public links mental illness, crime, and the insanity defense because of a very few highly publicized trials, such as that of John Hinckley, the would-be assassin of Ronald Reagan. But only about 8 percent of convicted or accused persons in mental hospitals are there because they were found to be not guilty by reason of insanity. Another 6 percent are in hospitals because they have been judged mentally disordered sex offenders, and 32 percent have been found incompetent to stand trial. The largest group (54 percent), and the group of greatest concern to corrections, is made up of offenders who became mentally ill after having been imprisoned.[25]

Why is it that some offenders become mentally ill while serving their terms? We must recognize that incarceration is a stressful experience—even for those who are emotionally strong. Prisoners lose contact with families and other sources of emotional support. Often, they have been humiliated by being convicted and sentenced to prison. Then they must face the strains of prison life, which are often augmented by unsafe and burdensome prison conditions. For some prisoners, the strain proves too much to bear; the result is a loss of emotional stability.

Corrections for the mentally ill offender

Institutional care for mentally ill offenders has paralleled historical shifts in corrections. There were early efforts to separate the mentally ill from other incarcerated offenders, but it was not until 1859 that the first institution built specially for such people, the New York State Lunatic Asylum for Insane Convicts, was opened in Auburn, near Auburn Prison. The facility held both convicted and unconvicted patients, and later received patients judicially transferred from civil hospitals.

Mentally ill offenders present a problem for corrections since their illness is often unrelated to their criminality. How should mentally ill offenders be cared for? Should they be placed in prisons or in mental hospitals?

New York's pioneering efforts were soon copied by other states, but rules governing the types of populations to be admitted varied. In some states, a separate section of the state mental hospital was set aside for mentally ill offenders, and in other jurisdictions patients who had been civilly admitted were transferred to the more secure facility for the criminally insane when they could not be controlled in the less structured environment.

Today all states have either separate facilities for mentally ill criminals or a section of a mental hospital for them. In some states, these institutions are under the control of the department of correction, and in others, the department of mental health.

The effect of deinstitutionalization Corrections in the coming decade will face an increased number of mentally ill clients. Much of the increase is related to a major policy shift in the mental health field: **deinstitutionalization.** With the availability of drugs that

deinstitutionalization The release of mental patients from mental hospitals and their return to the community.

Johnnie's Story

Johnnie Baxstrom was a black male, born on August 12, 1918, in Greensboro, North Carolina. He was the youngest of nine children. He quit school when he was seventeen, while he was in the eleventh grade. As described by his hospital notes, throughout his childhood "he had what he termed `fainting headaches.'" He said it felt as though someone were beating on the side of his temple and that he would black out in school. He was hospitalized from May 29, 1956, to June 8, 1956, for head injury. Diagnosis: "Idiopathic Epilepsy and residuals from Bilateral Subdural Hematoma, following skull fracture."

Baxstrom had a very irregular job record showing that he worked only for short times at a variety of unskilled positions. He did have a good military record; he entered the armed forces in September 1943 and received an honorable discharge in March 1946. He was married three times. His first marriage was in 1939 to a woman who bore him four children. She died giving birth to their fifth child. Baxstrom remarried in late 1946. No children resulted from this marriage, and they separated after a brief time. He then entered a common-law arrangement with a third woman with whom he had five children. He left this woman in 1951.

Baxstrom's criminal record is a lengthy list of drinking and property offenses. However, his first offense did not occur until he was thirty, which was two years after his getting out of the military service and while he was living with his second wife. It occurred on February 23, 1948, in Greensboro. He was charged with assaulting a female with a dangerous weapon, but the case was never disposed of in the courts. Again in 1950, he was arrested on two counts of assault and one of larceny in Baltimore, where his sister lived. He was found not guilty of all charges. His first conviction occurred six months later, in June 1950, in Greensboro, where he received a twelve-month sentence on the road gang for an "affray assault on a female." He was discharged on March 26, 1951.

Over the next few years, Baxstrom appears to have taken up a wandering lifestyle involving no work. Between 1951 and 1958, when he was sentenced to Attica, Baxstrom was arrested twelve times … for such things as trespassing on Southern Railway property, drunkenness, vagrancy, disorderly conduct, intoxication, and one time for robbery for which he received and served a one-year sentence in the Maryland House of Corrections.

On October 21, 1958, Baxstrom was arrested in Rochester, New York, for attacking a police officer with an ice pick. According to hospital records, he stabbed the officer in the face, forehead, and collarbone. Little else about the incident is found in the hospital record. However, in a personal communication, Dr. A. L. Halpern, who examined Baxstrom extensively in 1966, reports Baxstrom's account of the incident, which is corroborated by the police report. Apparently Baxstrom was drinking in a bar where he got into a fight with another patron. During the fight Baxstrom pulled a knife or ice pick and stabbed the other combatant. This other combatant turned out to be a police officer in civilian clothes. For this act, he received a two-and-a-half- to three-year sentence in the Monroe County Court on April 9, 1959. The conviction was for assault, second-degree. He was admitted to Attica State Prison on the same day with his full sentence to expire on December 18, 1961.

While in Attica, Baxstrom was reported to "often have epileptic fits during which he was aggressive, assaultive toward guards and inmates. He also used obscene language." Because of this, he was transferred to Dannemora on June 1, 1961.

Source: H. J. Steadman and J. J. Cocozza, *Careers of the Criminally Insane* (Lexington, Mass.: Lexington Books, 1974, 43–45). Reprinted by permission.

inhibit aberrant behavior, it became possible to discharge a multitude of mental patients from hospitals to the community. After being given prescriptions for the medicines that permit them to maintain their behavior at a socially acceptable level, patients have been released to live alone or in groups, often with little or no supervision.

Undersupervised or without supervision, former patients often fail to take their medication and then commit deviant or criminal acts that come to the attention of the police. The acts are usually related to public order or larceny, but assaultive behavior often erupts as well. Because the acts are minor, the mentally ill offenders generally receive correctional services during their detention while they await disposition of their cases or from probation officers working cooperatively with mental health workers.

The Mentally Handicapped Offender

The forty-three-year-old man entered the Dunkin' Donuts shop, approached the counter, and demanded, "All your money and a dozen doughnuts." With his finger pointed inside his pocket, he announced that he had a gun and would use it. When the police arrived, they found the man standing outside the shop eating the doughnuts—just as they had found him after several previous holdups. The man's name is Eddie; he has an IQ of 61. He has served prison sentences for this type of offense, but almost immediately upon release he commits another such crime.

Ron, a thirty-three-year-old man who functions at the level of a ten-year-old, was sentenced to a five-year prison term for bank robbery. He was easily identified by the police because he signed his name on the note he gave to the teller demanding money.

Charlie set fire to a trash barrel in the hallway of his apartment building. A psychotic woman tenant, panicked by the smoke, jumped out of the window and was killed by the fall. Charlie is awaiting trial for murder.[26]

These cases point to a type of person who is a special problem for the correctional system: the **mentally handicapped offender.** It is estimated that about 2 percent of the U.S. population are mentally handicapped or developmentally disabled (they have IQs below 70). Among the incarcerated population, about 5 percent (25,000) are in this category, and countless others are on probation or under juvenile care. Perhaps another 300,000 incarcerated individuals are classified as being on the borderline that separates the handicapped or disabled from the average.[27]

Like other Americans, mentally handicapped people commit crimes, but there is no proven link between their disability and a propensity for criminal behavior. Their criminality may result from the fact that they do not know how to obtain what they want without breaking the law. It may also result from the fact that they are easily led into becoming patsies for persons who think deviant behavior is a joke or who use the mentally handicapped to secure something for themselves. Mentally handicapped people may break the law unknowingly. They are also disproportionately poor, so if they need or want something, they may commit a crime to get it. And because they cannot think quickly, they get caught more often than other criminals do.

The majority of the offenses committed by mentally handicapped people are classified as property or public-order crimes. This is not to say that they do not also commit serious violent crimes, for among the incarcerated, a higher proportion of mentally handicapped than others have been sentenced for homicide and other crimes against persons.

Deinstitutionalization has been a recent focus of programs to deal with mentally handicapped individuals. Like the mentally ill, mentally handicapped persons have been returned

---

mentally handicapped offender A person whose limited mental development prevents adjustment to the rules of society.

Donald's Story

Donald stole to survive. Often he took food from grocery stores. Sometimes he broke into diners to cook meals for himself in the middle of the night.

"I'd never break into anybody's house," Donald said. "That would be wrong. People have to work too hard for their money. I only break into stores." He doesn't understand that when he steals from businesses, he hurts the people who own them. He is mentally retarded.

Donald, whose IQ is in the 60s (100 is normal), spent most of his life in Ladd School, Rhode Island's institution for the retarded. In 1967, when he was twenty-four years old, he was released and given a job washing dishes in an East Greenwich, Rhode Island, restaurant.

"It wasn't enough money," said Donald. "It was only $30 a week. If I paid for my room, I couldn't eat. So I quit. I had to survive somehow, so I would go out and steal. I didn't know how to do no job."

Asked why he didn't go on welfare, he replied, "I didn't know about that stuff. Nobody ever told me anything about it. It's hard to get on welfare. You have to write stuff on papers."

Arrests came one after the other, Donald's court records show. One was for breaking into a diner and stealing thirty-five cents.

At one point, Donald found a job at a Providence laundry and for a few months the break-ins stopped. "All I did was fold clothes from the dryer," he recalled. "There was me and another guy. Then they decided one person could do it, and they got rid of my helper. I got scared. I couldn't do it alone. So I just quit."

So it was back to the break-ins.

Donald often got caught and was continually before the courts. But the judges never knew what to do with him; Rhode Island has no program for retarded offenders. Sometimes they put him on probation, and on several occasions they sent him to the state mental hospital for observation.

"The patient," one psychiatrist wrote in a report to the court, "said he cannot read the newspapers to find a job himself. He said that he would not do any breaking and entering if he had work and money."

But no one helped Donald get a job. Finally, the judges lost patience and started sending Donald to prison. He has served at least three prison sentences, although court records are unclear and Donald is not sure there were not more. He is not good with numbers. When asked, he didn't know his age, which is thirty-seven.

On July 30, 1978, police records show that Donald was out of prison again. At 10:02 that night, a burglar alarm went off at a Providence factory building. Police found Donald hiding behind a door with a glass cutter in his pocket. As usual, Donald confessed. "I felt like getting some money," he told police. "I didn't know where to get it. Then I tried to get it in there."

A sympathetic judge put Donald on probation on the condition that he voluntarily live at the state mental hospital until a better arrangement could be made for him. Since then, Donald hasn't done any stealing. "Don't need to," he said. "I eat for free now."

Every weekday, after breakfast at the mental hospital, Donald takes the bus to downtown Providence and walks the streets looking for a job. He's been doing it for more than a year now, without success.

"If only I can get a job, maybe I can get out of the hospital," he said. "But I can't read and write. I can't do the forms. They ask you where you live. I live in a nuthouse. They ask about your last job...."

What's his future? "I don't know," he said. "I don't want to steal no more. It ain't worth it. I wish when I got in trouble a cop had shot me. So I wouldn't have to do it no more."

Source: B. DeSilva, "Donald's Story," *Corrections Magazine* (August 1980): 27. Reprinted by permission of the Edna McConnell Clark Foundation.

to the community, where they are expected to live, work, and care for themselves with a minimum of supervision. Because they have difficulty adjusting to the social rules of the community, they often become part of the caseload of the criminal justice system.

What can corrections do for or with this special category of offender? It seems obvious that the usual routines of probation, diversion, incarceration, and community service will not work. Mentally handicapped individuals are not comfortable with change, are usually difficult to employ outside of sheltered workshops, and are not likely to improve significantly in mental condition or social habits. And so they break probation or prison rules and are further penalized. While incarcerated, they are often the butts of practical jokes and exploited as scapegoats or sexual objects.

Some observers believe that mentally handicapped offenders are less criminals than misfits who lack training in the ways to live in a complex society; they belong not in prison but in a treatment facility where they could learn the rudimentary skills necessary to survive. Criminal justice practitioners often argue that mentally handicapped offenders constitute a mental health problem, but because they have committed crimes, mental health agencies do not want them. They are shunned by both camps and get little help from either.

The Offender with AIDS

For the foreseeable future, acquired immune deficiency syndrome (AIDS) is going to play a major role in American corrections. By 1991 it was the leading cause of death in the United States among males between the ages of twenty-five and forty-four, which is the same group that makes up almost three-quarters of the adults under correctional supervision. The potential impact of AIDS on corrections is further heightened by the fact that the probation, parole, jail, and prison populations contain a high concentration of individuals at particular risk for the disease—those with histories of

intravenous drug use and, to a lesser extent, homosexual behavior.

Although the offender with AIDS, either a person with the illness itself or a person who has been infected with the human immunodeficiency virus (HIV), confronts probation and parole officers with a number of problems, jail and prison administrators are most affected by questions and policy issues concerning the people under their supervision. Institutional administrators must develop policies covering such matters as methods to prevent transmission of the disease, the housing of those infected, and medical care for inmates who have the full range of symptoms found in the end stage of AIDS. In determining what actions should be taken, administrators have found that a host of legal, political, budgetary, and attitudinal factors impinge on their ability to make what they believe are the best decisions.

Prevention AIDS is a communicable disease that occurs when the human immune defenses are broken down by the HIV virus and the body becomes unable to combat infections. The virus is transmitted by means of contaminated blood and semen, primarily through needle sharing related to intravenous drug use and sexual activity. The virus is difficult to transmit, and scientific evidence shows that it is not passed on through casual contact.

Preventing the spread of AIDS is made difficult because there is a long period of incubation between time of infection and first indication of the disease's symptoms. Thus, carriers may engage in unsafe drug and sexual activities without knowing that they are infecting others. Although for corrections this indicates that the overwhelming number of infected offenders received the virus before they were incarcerated, transmission within the institution remains a problem.

In most prisons, educational programs now inform staff and inmates about the disease and the ways in which it is spread. It has been suggested that hypodermic needles and condoms be made available to prisoners so that

Mike's Story

On July 15, 1986, at 9:30 A.M., Mike Camargo lay in his hospital bed in the prison ward of Bellevue Hospital in New York City. Camargo was a pretrial detainee accused of selling drugs to an undercover police officer the previous summer. When he was conscious, he felt sharp, stabbing pains in his arms and feet. He could hardly move, much less sit up. Camargo was told that he suffered from pneumonia and toxoplasmosis.

Six weeks later he was transferred to an intensive care unit of the hospital. He had gone into shock because the bacteria growing in his brain deprived his nervous system of necessary oxygen. His inability to breathe was also caused by other bacteria clogging his heart valves. Mike Camargo's life had been spent in petty crime as a small-time drug dealer. The cops had caught him more than once, and he had served several sentences. Now he was dying of AIDS.

On December 8, 1986, Camargo's presence was required for a court appearance before Justice Sheindlin of the Supreme Court of New York in the Bronx. Dr. Jonathan Cohn, Camargo's attending physician at Bellevue Hospital, was subpoenaed by Camargo's lawyer to explain the defendant's absence. Cohn was placed under oath, and he then graphically explained to the court why he believed Camargo's deteriorating condition made production of the prisoner, much less continued prosecution, a futility.

Over the prosecutor's objection, the court granted the defendant's motion to dismiss in the interest of justice. Justice Sheindlin explained to the prosecutor that although the defendant was a recidivist, it was doubtful that he could be regarded in the future as a threat to the safety or welfare of society. For the court to impose a sentence of incarceration on this defendant, a minor drug dealer, would be absurd in view of the doctor's prognosis of imminent death. Further, the court noted that no sentence that could be imposed would compare with the severity of the many diseases that were attacking the defendant.

The profile of the typical AIDS prisoner could easily have been that of Mike Camargo. He was in his early thirties. He was an intravenous drug user who had been incarcerated for a drug-related crime. He died of AIDS-related pneumonia on January 19, 1987.

Source: Adapted from Patricia Raburn, "Prisoners with AIDS: The Use of Electronic Processing," *Criminal Law Bulletin* (May-June 1988): 213–14. Reprinted by permission. © 1988 Warren, Gorham, & Lamont Inc., 210 South Street, Boston MA 02111.

if they do engage in intravenous drug taking and homosexual behavior, they will be protected. However, because these behaviors are against prison rules, administrators believe they should not be legitimized. Testing all residents and new inmates for the presence of the HIV antibody has been widely debated. Mass screening on a systemwide basis is used in Colorado, Iowa, Missouri, and Nevada, and at individual institutions in other states. Opponents of the programs argue that there is no proof of higher transmission in prisons than in the free community, and thus there is no reason to screen. It is also said that it is impossible to keep test results confidential; hence infected individuals will be stigmatized while incarcerated and discriminated against in connection with insurance, housing, and employment upon release. Finally, policies have been developed to ensure that correctional personnel and inmates do not become infected while handling blood or body fluids in the course of their duties. The use of protective coverings, avoidance of needle injuries, and care in the handling of diseased bodies have all become standard operating procedures.

Housing If inmates are found to be carriers of the AIDS virus, what should be done? When they become ill as a result of the virus, there is no question that they should be cared for in a medical facility. But what about inmates who test positive yet may not become ill for several years? Should they be housed in a segregated facility or remain in the general population? Should they be protected from the hostility of other inmates and staff?

Correctional administrators have selected among various housing options, depending upon such factors as number of infected inmates in a given population and the availability and cost of separate facilities. A survey of correctional systems sponsored by the National Institution of Justice found that most systems segregate inmates with the AIDS disease but maintain those with the virus—but not yet symptomatic—in the general population.[28] On a case-by-case basis, most administrators will segregate prisoners who display high-risk behavior, or who have a need for protection, or whose medical condition calls for separate housing.

In some systems, persons who are infected with the virus are kept in the general population but given special programs to reduce the possibility that they will transmit the virus to others. In Nebraska and New Hampshire, they are assigned single cells; in Nevada and Texas, they are housed together in double cells. These policies have been criticized at some institutions because the designation of particular cell arrangements for AIDS-infected inmates announces their condition to staff and to other inmates.

When inmates become ill from the AIDS virus, they are usually confined in a hospital or infirmary setting. In some states (New Jersey among them), such inmates are placed in a hospital in the community; in other states (California among them), they are placed in correctional medical facilities. In states with a large number of prisoners carrying the virus—even when they do not have an illness from the disease—segregated housing is the policy. California, for example, now houses all HIV-infected inmates in a wing of the Correctional Medical Facility at Vacaville, to prevent transmission and to most effectively provide medical and counseling services to the group.

Medical care Corrections has a legal responsibility to furnish medical care to persons under supervision. Because AIDS patients experience serious psychological problems in addition to physical problems, they require counseling and support services for themselves and their families.

Medical services for AIDS patients are costly: Estimates range from $50,000 to $145,000 annually per patient; for each New York City inmate, the cost of extended acute medical care could be as high as $300,000.[29] States with a large number of HIV and AIDS prisoners are facing costs that could easily constitute a major portion of the entire correctional budget.

The release of inmates with AIDS at termination of their sentences also presents medical issues. On humanitarian grounds it might be argued that executive clemency or parole should be granted so that AIDS patients do not spend their last days in prison, yet there is a moral—and probably a legal—obligation to ensure that they are not "dumped" onto the street.

AIDS and the law Several correctional systems and judges believe that inmates with AIDS should be kept in the system as long as possible to enable better medical care and to prevent transmission of the disease. Although the mentally ill may be kept in a hospital until

An increasing portion of persons under correctional supervision are elderly. In some states their numbers have grown to such a degree that nursing home wings have been added to prisons. How should these offenders be treated?

they do not pose a threat to themselves or society, a legal question exists with regard to AIDS patients and those who carry the virus. The resolution of this question is still in the future.

Existing case law on AIDS in correctional facilities falls into three major categories:

1. *Equal protection:* Cases filed by inmates alleging denial of equal protection based solely on the fact that they had AIDS.[30]

2. *Quality of care:* Cases filed by inmates alleging inadequacies in medical care and associated services.[31]

3. *Failure to protect others from AIDS:* Cases filed by inmates, and potentially also by staff, alleging inadequate protective measures and seeking additional steps, such as mass screening of inmates and segregation of inmates with AIDS or HIV seropositivity.[32]

The Elderly Offender

Crime—at least predatory street crime—is an activity of young males more than of any other group. Upon visiting a prison, a person is usu-ally struck by the predominant numbers of young men, especially minorities. America's prison population has always been young and poor, but in recent years, it is changing. The U.S. prison population is aging. In 1991, there were 19,581 men and 812 women in prisons who were over fifty-five years old. This was a 41 percent increase in the elderly population over the last three years.[33]

The prison population is growing older for two reasons. First, the U.S. population in general is aging, so the overall citizenry from which we sample is becoming older. This is a minor reason for the change. A much more powerful explanation for this change is the recent use of long sentences to punish offenders. The popularity of consecutive lengthy sentences for heinous crimes, and the particular impact of life sentences without parole, mean that some men enter prison young, with the full expectation of living all or most of their remaining lives incarcerated.

The prison population of elderly can be divided into three general groups. Most elderly offenders were young when they first entered prison facing a long, long sentence because of a particularly serious crime. Often the crimes were murders or heinous sexual assaults. A few enter prison in their old age for the first time, convicted either of financial crimes such as embezzlement, or an older man's crime such as molestation or pedophilia. Then there are the experienced committed criminals, those who have been in prison before (usually more than once) but who are returning again because they cannot stay crime-free upon release. Obviously, then, elderly offenders can vary in terms of criminal history and prison sophistication. But there are some ways in which older prisoners are quite different from their younger peers.

The most obvious difference has to do with health. Aging prisoners handle the physical strains of prison life with greater difficulty than young people, and they need the increased medical care that normally comes with age. Elderly offenders also have different social interests. While young men in prison enjoy physical sports and competitive recreation, older men may prefer solitude and less strenuous interaction while incarcerated. Older inmates prefer activities that differ little from older people in the free world.[34]

Even though many elderly inmates have committed quite serious crimes, studies indicate that with age comes a reduced chance that the prisoner will break the rules of the prison. Older prisoners often are more stable and dependable than their youthful counterparts, and they frequently occupy positions of trust within the prison. Upon release, these inmates typically pose little risk to the public.

The adjustment problem facing most elderly offenders has to do with the way extended prison terms tend to institutionalize them. When a person spends a large number of years in prison, the routines of the prison become debilitating. The prison regime controls all time and takes away most personal autonomy and decision making. After years of being told what to do almost every waking hour, it becomes difficult for a person to relearn how to make even the simplest decision. This is a point to which we return in Chapter 13.

The Juvenile Offender

Juveniles come under the authority of the juvenile justice system in one of two ways: They may be adjudicated guilty of an offense that would be criminal had they been adults, or they may be found to have engaged in behavior (or lived in a situation) that indicates they are candidates for personal or legal trouble. The kind of presenting problem that results in the child's being referred to the juvenile court often determines the way the child is eventually handled, although the decision on whether to treat the child as a delinquent or as a status offender is often somewhat arbitrary. The child who comes to the attention of the juvenile authorities usually is both a delinquent and a status offender, and either label could be applied.

The delinquent offender The average age of offending juveniles parallels the trend in arrest ages for the overall population. For the two decades preceding 1980, the arrest age was slowly getting younger, but in the last few years there has been an increase in the average age at arrest. Among juvenile offenders, sixteen-year-old boys display the highest arrest rate for serious crimes, and sixteen- and seventeen-year-olds appear to be more active than people of other age groups in robbery, aggravated assault, burglary, and larceny. The peak arrest-rate age has shifted from fifteen to sixteen to seventeen in recent years, accompanying a surge in the seriousness of juvenile crime.

Girls commit offenses that are significantly less serious, on the whole, than those of boys. Their rate of arrest is lower, comprising 23 percent of juvenile arrests as compared with 77 percent for boys. Yet there is some evidence that female delinquents are engaging in more serious crimes than they did in earlier years and that the rate of increase in arrests of girls for violent crimes is rising slightly faster than that for boys. It is also clear that girls who are arrested are more likely than adult women to be accused of serious violent crimes. Female

Most juvenile offenders are placed in the community under the supervision of a probation officer trained to address their needs.

delinquency is rising, but it is still far outrun by male delinquency.

Officially processed delinquents are still predominantly youngsters with limited life opportunities. They tend to be from the lower socioeconomic classes, to have dropped out of school, and to be living under conditions of financial hardship. Several factors seem to heighten their chances of being labeled delinquent: academic failure, family disruption (divorce and other strains), and association with other delinquents.[35]

The status offender Considerably less study has been devoted to **status offenders** than to delinquent offenders. A juvenile may be desig-

nated a status offender in two ways. About half the states take a traditional approach: They designate as offenses—not as crimes—certain kinds of behavior when they are engaged in by juveniles. The behaviors are named in the delinquency statute itself, a type of legislation that has come under criticism for two reasons. First, the language is overly broad; at one time as many as thirty defined behaviors subjected a juvenile to intervention by the court in one state or another. Second, the defining language is very vague, generally not much different from the ambiguous language associated with the original Chicago juvenile court (see Chapter 3). Many states have taken steps to remove the status offender provisions from the delinquency statute and to create a separate legislative title covering status offenders, who are designated either minors, children, juveniles, or persons in need of supervision.

Studies of status offenders find them to be demographically very similar to delinquency populations, with two exceptions. First, delinquent juveniles are predominantly male; most female juvenile offenders are processed as status offenders. Second, status offenders tend to lack the prior juvenile court involvement that is common among older delinquents. The two exceptions are perhaps best understood as results of juvenile justice system policies rather than innate differences between the two groups of offenders. Status offenders and delinquent offenders are alike in terms of presenting behavior. Perhaps, then, the chivalry factor causes the petitions of girls to be couched in terms of status offenses, as are those of first-time referrals generally (subsequent referrals normally involve formal processing as delinquents).

Recent research has also dispelled one common myth: that delinquents begin their careers with status offenses and graduate to criminal conduct. The juvenile court's policy of handling first-time referrals as status offenders fosters this impression, but studies reveal that most status offenders never go on to delinquent careers, and many delinquents present no evidence of prior status offenses.[36] The idea that delinquent

---

status offenders Juveniles who are made subjects of the juvenile court because of behavior that, although not criminal, calls for the supervision of official authorities.

careers need to be nipped in the bud at the status offender stage is simply erroneous.

The violent offender The violence of some juvenile offenders is arousing growing concern. Juvenile courts are perceived to treat violent offenders with such leniency that serious violent juveniles often escape adequate punishment. On the basis of this perception, as we have seen, many states have passed legislation making it easier to handle juveniles accused of serious crimes as adults and subject them to the adult system's punishments.

Evidence supports the idea that serious violent juvenile offenders are a problem. Juveniles' arrest rates for violent crimes in 1992, although lower overall than those for adults, were high, and juveniles' burglary arrest rates were even greater than those for adults. Juveniles are predominantly property offenders (even more so than adults), but they also demonstrate a fairly high rate of serious predatory crime. Recently, drug-related crime in inner cities has involved more juveniles, and it has become more violent.

Aside from the few widely publicized incidents, the crimes committed by juveniles tend to be less violent than those committed by adults. Findings such as those presented in Figure 5.4 have led some observers to question the immediacy and significance of the problem of the violent juvenile offender. Relatively few juveniles are violent, they say; a kind of get-tough hysteria, not logical policymaking, is leading to the legislation that allows juveniles accused of serious crimes to be subjected to the adult system. They point out that of the first 2,500 juveniles thirteen to fifteen years old arrested in New York for the crimes of murder, kidnapping, manslaughter, rape, sodomy, burglary, robbery, and assault under a new law that provided for handling in adult court, fewer than 250 were retained there; the remainder were returned to the juvenile court for prosecution. Even when serious juvenile offenders are waived to adult court, studies show they

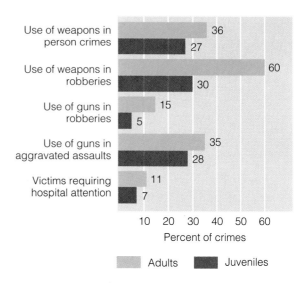

Figure 5.4 ■ **Serious Crimes as Committed by Adults Versus Juveniles.** When committing serious crimes, juveniles, compared to adults, tend to use fewer and less dangerous weapons.

Source: Donna M. Hampurian, Linda K. Estep, Susan M. Muntean, Ramon R. Prestino, Robert G. Swasher, Paul L. Wallace, and Joseph L. White, *Youth in Adult Courts: Between Two Worlds* (Columbus, Ohio: Academy for Contemporary Problems, 1982), p. 16.

get fines or probation about half the time anyway, because adult court judges do not consider their cases to be as serious as those of the normal adult offender.[37]

Other experts find these data unconvincing. They point out that court caseloads of serious juvenile offenders appear to be growing, and public concern about the problem has never been greater. News coverage of gang violence, drive-by shootings, and armed carjackings by juveniles underscores an intense public concern about this problem. It is this kind of thinking that led to the 1978 Washington State law that requires that all serious violent juvenile offenders be committed to the state's training school for at least some period. The purpose of the law was not preventive but punitive—to get tough with the serious delinquents. Early evaluations suggest that the law has increased punitive handling of juveniles and decreased disparity of dispositions. Its effects have not been confined to violent juveniles; harsh treatment seems to have been accorded to juvenile offenders in general, including those who earlier would have been handled simply as status offenders.[38]

Classifying Offenders: Some Issues

Our descriptions of the categories of offenders should make it clear that several problems frustrate attempts to classify correctional clients.

Overlap and Ambiguity in Classification Systems

Some sex offenders may also be alcoholics; some situational offenders may have emotional problems (perhaps even stemming from their new status as offender); some career criminals may be addicts. A classification system that has so much overlap can furnish correctional decision makers with little guidance as to appropriate treatment. Should an addicted multiple burglar be treated as a career criminal or as an addict?

Offense Classifications and Correctional Programming

Some critics have argued that the most important requirement for any correctional classification system is that it should improve our ability to manage and treat offenders effectively. If the categories we have described leave many of these correctional programming decisions unresolved, of what use are they? When one considers offenders, the normal temptation is to ask first, What is the person's crime? and second, What is the person's criminal history? The nine classes of offenders we have described probably constitute 80 percent or more of the felony offenders managed by corrections, yet in

each case the category is so broad that it leaves the important question—How shall this offender be managed?—unanswered. Broad categories may be useful for portraying the nature of offenders, but much more narrow and definite classification systems are required for the programmatic needs of corrections. In particular, we must be able to identify the offender's potential risk to correctional security and to the community.

Behavioral Probabilities in Classification

Much as human behavior is impossible to predict, we can certainly make educated guesses about future behaviors that are likely to occur. Thus a five-time check forger may be likely to commit a similar offense again, even though we know that he or she may not do so. This is often thought of as a probabilistic approach to classification. Similarly, a first offender may be unlikely to commit any crime again, even though we know that he or she may do so.

Recent advances in classification systems have taken advantage of the probabilistic approach. Rather than rely on guesswork, officials try to see what offender characteristics are associated with reinvolvement in crime. The approach is similar to that used by automobile insurance companies, whose actuaries know that even though many teenagers do not have accidents, teenagers as a group have much higher rates of accidents than do adult drivers. And so teenagers are required to pay higher premiums because they represent a greater risk.

In the same way, offenders who have characteristics associated with higher risk can be classified as more likely to pose a threat and so can be required to pay a penological "premium": closer supervision on probation or parole, tighter security in institutions. Even though we know that most offenders, even those of the highest risk, will not commit more offenses, the use of probabilistic classification is more directly related to the action needs of corrections.

Raymond's Story

Raymond's school history was marked by turbulence; he was suspended at age nine for repeatedly fighting with other students, and the suspension ran several weeks past the legally permitted period because his mother never responded to written requests to discuss the situation. There was no follow-up by the school, and the home was never visited.

The only available report card from Raymond's school was from the second grade. He received a marking of S (for Satisfactory) in all subjects, including deportment.

At age ten, Raymond was arrested inside a sporting goods store; he had apparently been boosted over the transom by older boys, but he refused to identify them to the police. Taken to the detention center, he was attacked by a group of older inmates who were awaiting trial on armed robbery. The actual motivation for this attack is still unknown; however, Raymond acquitted himself so favorably that the other inmates desisted without the need for intervention by the guards.

Because of his "recalcitrant attitude" and because his mother told the juvenile court judge that she "couldn't do nothing with him," Raymond was sentenced to a state train-ing school. His training school record shows repeated "disciplinary action" (unspecified) for fighting, and Raymond once spent ten days in "isolation" for another unspecified offense. He was paroled at age twelve and returned to his home.

Raymond was returned to the same training school about six months later; this time the charge was mugging. Again acting in concert with older boys, Raymond was attacking elderly people on the streets of the downtown business district. Although linked to a series of such crimes and a suspect in a number of push-in muggings within his housing project, Raymond was actually convicted ("found to be delinquent") of only one offense. Again he refused to name the other participants.

Sociopolitical Pressures and Classification

One of the most frustrating aspects of offender classification is that the public response to crime frequently makes classification a highly charged emotional issue. As a result, corrections is often forced to respond to changing public demands in its management of offenders.

Each of the groups of offenders we described has been subjected to intense public hostility. In the 1940s and 1950s, public outrage over the use of narcotics led to the establishment of stiff penalties for their sale and the establishment of addiction hospitals in several regions across the United States. Public attention to the "psychopath" in the 1950s and 1960s led to the establishment of long-term treatment facilities just for the "dangerous" offender, such as Maryland's famous Patuxent Institution. A recent version of this recurrent theme has been the attention drawn to "high-rate" offenders and the resulting policies oriented toward selective or collective incapacitation of recidivists.

In each of these cases, public alarm about crime has produced a labeling response on the part of the criminal justice system, with special handling given to all those who fit the label.

Back in the training school, Raymond was moving up in the institutional hierarchy. He had grown considerably since his last incarceration, and the crime for which he was returned was higher in status than his original offense. This institutional period was marked by his overt membership in an exploitive institutional gang, and he spent almost half of his two-year incarceration in the school's disciplinary cottage. According to the training school's records, he was too disruptive to be allowed to attend classes, and he was a suspect in the gang rape of another inmate. Again paroled, Raymond returned to his home community.

Returned to the same institution for a violation of his parole (being a passenger in a stolen car), Raymond quickly proved to be beyond the control of the institutional authorities, and he was transferred to a high-security installation in another part of the state. Once more he joined an institutional gang, and once more he became totally enmeshed in the institutional subculture. Raymond now sported tattoos on both arms (his initials on one arm, the name of the institutional gang on the other), and he continued to mature physically. When asked about his period of adjustment to the new training school, Raymond told an interviewer: "When I first got to [the training school], I was the littlest there, but I wasn't the littlest with my hands. ... I had to show those suckers that I wasn't goin' for lollipops [sexual seduction] or rip-offs [forceful sexual threats or actual rape], and I knowed how to do that. But when I got to [the "secure" training school] I already had a rep behind the Dragons [the gang from the first institution] and there was like already a place for me."

At age sixteen, Raymond shot and killed a rival gang member in a dispute over the proceeds of a narcotics transaction. He had been out on parole less than three months.

Source: Adapted from A. H. Vachss and Y. Bakal, *The Life-Style Violent Juvenile*, Lexington, Mass.: Lexington Books, 1979, pp. 3–4. Reprinted by permission.

The difficulty is that the labels are often broadly applied (partly because of the overlap in any classification system) and the handling is ordinarily more severe than necessary. Those who object to the frequent "reform" movements in corrections recognize that great harm can be done by the misapplication of labels. Yet in many instances the accuracy of the label and the appropriateness of the new offender-management method the label calls for are of little concern to correctional policymakers, who face a more severe problem in the public demand for "action" to "crack down" on some type of crime or another. The problem is more political than penological.

Distinctions in the Criteria for Classifying Offenders

All of us classify people around us. We think, John is a Democrat, Nancy is a nice person, Tim is untrustworthy, and so on. We realize that these terms do not fully describe those persons but serve only as rough labels that help us to gauge how they may behave or think in a given situation. In reality, we know that on some occasions John may sound like a Republican, Nancy may be grumpy, and Tim may keep his word. A person's behavior may be characterized by certain tendencies, but it is seldom fixed.

The variability of human behavior makes it critically important to understand offender classification as a rough way of grouping people. It is equally important to be precise about the criteria used for grouping. Three general kinds of criteria are used to classify offenders:

1. Offense criteria classify offenders as to the seriousness of the crime the person committed.

2. Risk criteria classify offenders as to the probability of future criminal conduct.

3. Program criteria classify offenders as to the nature of correctional treatment appropriate to the person's needs and situation.

These criteria do not lead to the same correctional consequences. Many offenders who committed serious crimes are not likely to do so again; many offenders who have few treatment needs still represent a risk to the community; and so on. Correctional systems need to use a range of classification systems to determine the most appropriate way to manage any given offender.

Summary

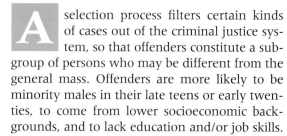

A selection process filters certain kinds of cases out of the criminal justice system, so that offenders constitute a subgroup of persons who may be different from the general mass. Offenders are more likely to be minority males in their late teens or early twenties, to come from lower socioeconomic backgrounds, and to lack education and/or job skills.

The composition of the correctional population has a direct impact on corrections and its ability to achieve its goals. Because much of the correctional clientele is undereducated, underskilled, and ill-prepared for legitimate lifestyles, programs have been developed to correct the deficiencies.

The client population includes several general categories of offenders: the situational of-

fender, the career criminal, the sex offender, the drug abuser, the alcohol abuser, the mentally ill, the mentally handicapped, the offenders with AIDS, the elderly offender, and the juvenile offender. Each group has distinctive characteristics and problems that are related to offense situations and basic needs. When one understands these differences, one can see that it is impossible to talk of "the offender" as if all criminals were similar. Offender classification is influenced by the public's response to certain crimes at particular times. Public attitudes target certain groups for more severe or specialized punishment, and corrections must respond to this concern.

For Discussion

1. Is the process by which correctional clients are selected discriminatory? What might be done to reduce at least the appearance of discrimination?

2. In what ways does the classification of correctional clients reflect the fragmentation of corrections?

3. What role should public opinion play in categorizing various offenders for the purpose of punishing them?

4. Is classification of offenders according to the probability of future criminal conduct a good idea? What are the dangers of the practice? What are its advantages?

5. What policy recommendations would you make with regard to the way career criminals are handled?

For Further Reading

Blumstein, Alfred; Cohen, Jacqueline; Roth, Jeffrey; and Visher, Christy. *Criminal Careers and "Career Criminals."* Washington, D.C.: National Academy of Sciences, 1986. Comprehensive study of policy aspects regarding career criminals.

Cameron, Mary Owen. *The Booster and the Snitch.* New York: Free Press of Glencoe, 1964. Classic study of working criminals.

Hammett, Theodore H. *AIDS in Correctional Facilities: Issues and Options.* Washington, D.C.: U.S. Department of Justice, 1988. Survey of management practices regarding the AIDS inmate.

Klockars, Carl. *The Professional Fence.* New York: Free

Press, 1976. Detailed study of the financial and practical aspects of burglary and fencing.

McCarthy, Belinda, and Langworthy, Robert. *Older Offenders.* New York: Praeger, 1988. Summary of studies of elderly offenders.

Notes

1. James Austin and John Irwin, *Who Goes to Prison?* (San Francisco: National Council on Crime and Delinquency, 1990).

2. Marc Mauer, *Black Men in Prison* (report to the Edna McConnell Clark Foundation by the Sentencing Project, Washington, D.C., 1992), p. 1.

3. Interviewed by Scott Christianson, quoted in "Racially Differential Imprisonment," *Jericho* 32 (January 1983): 9.

4. Steven Klepper, Daniel Nagin, and Luke-Jon Tierney, "Discrimination in the Criminal Justice System: A Critical Appraisal of the Literature," in *Research on Sentencing: The Search for Reform*, vol. 2, ed. Alfred Blumstein, Jacqueline Cohen, Susan E. Martin, and Michael H. Tonry (Washington, D.C.: National Academy Press, 1983), p. 65.

5. James F. Wallerstein and Clement J. Wyle, "Our Law-Abiding Law-Breakers," *Probation* 35 (April 1947): 107–19, 147.

6. Travis Hirschi, *Causes of Delinquency* (Berkeley: University of California Press, 1969).

7. Compare U.S. Department of Justice, *Criminal Victimization in the United States* (Washington, D.C.: U.S. Department of Justice, February 1992), p. 60; to U.S. Department of Justice, *National Corrections Reporting System, 1988* (Washington, D.C.: U.S. Department of Justice, April 1992), p. 12; to U.S. Department of Justice, *Prisons and Prisoners in the United States* (Washington, D.C.: U.S. Department of Justice, April 1992), p. 13.

8. New York State Office of Justice Systems Analysis, *The Incarceration of Minority Defendants: An Identification of Disparity in New York State, 1985–1986* (Albany, N.Y.: New York State Division of Criminal Justice Services, July 1991), p. i.

9. Blumstein et al., eds., *Research on Sentencing*, p. 93.

10. Martin R. Haskell and Lewis Yablonsky, *Criminology: Crime and Criminality* (Chicago: Rand McNally, 1974), p. 264.

11. Patrick A. Langan and Mark A. Cuniff, *Recidivism of Felons on Probation, 1986–89* (Washington, D.C.: Bureau of Justice Statistics, 1992), p. 6.

12. Walter C. Reckless, *The Crime Problem* (New York: Appleton-Century-Crofts, 1961), pp. 153–77.

13. Alfred Blumstein, Jacqueline Cohen, Jeffrey Roth, and Christy Visher, *Criminal Careers and "Career Criminals"* (Washington, D.C.: National Academy of Sciences, 1986).

14. Peter Greenwood, *Selective Incapacitation* (Santa Monica, Calif.: Rand Corporation, 1982).

15. Susan Brownmiller, *Against Our Will: Men, Women, and Rape* (New York: Simon & Schuster, 1975), pp. 376–77.

16. David Finkelhor, "The Trauma of Child Sexual Abuse—Two Models," in *Lasting Effects of Child Sexual Abuse*, ed. G. E. Wyatt and G. J. Powell (Newbury Park, Calif.: Sage, 1988), pp. 61–82.

17. National Institute of Justice, *Drugs and Jail Inmates, 1989* (Washington, D.C.: U.S. Department of Justice, 1990), p. 4.

18. National Institute of Justice, *Criminal Victimization in the United States* (Washington, D.C.: U.S. Department of Justice, 1990), p. 33.

19. National Institute of Justice, *Profile of Jail Inmates, 1989* (Washington, D.C.: U.S. Department of Justice, 1990), p. 3.

20. National Institute of Justice, *Drug Use Forecasting* (Washington, D.C.: U.S. Department of Justice November 1991), p. 2.

21. George E. Vaillant, "A 20-Year Follow-Up of New York Narcotic Addicts," *Archives of General Psychiatry* 29 (August 1973): 237–41.

22. William McCord and Joan McCord, *The Psychopath* (New York: Van Nostrand, 1964), p. 2.

23. Thomas S. Szasz, *Law, Liberty, and Psychiatry* (New York: Macmillan, 1963), p. 12.

24. National Commission on the Causes and Prevention of Violence, *Crimes of Violence* (Washington, D.C.: Government Printing Office, 1969), p. 444.

25. U.S. Department of Justice, Bureau of Justice Statistics, *Report to the Nation on Crime and Justice* (Washington, D.C.: Government Printing Office, 1983), p. 68.

26. For descriptions of retarded offenders, see Miles B. Santamour and Patricia S. Watson, *The Retarded Offender* (New York: Praeger, 1982).

27. Sheilagh Hodgins, "The Criminality of Mentally Disordered Persons," in *Mental Disorder and Crime,* ed. Sheilagh Hodgins (Newbury Park, Calif.: Sage, 1993), pp. 3–22.

28. Theodore M. Hammett, *AIDS in Correctional Facilities: Issues and Options,* 3d ed., publication of U.S. Department of Justice, National Institute of Justice (Washington, D.C.: Government Printing Office, 1988), pp. 82–84.

29. Susan Darst Williams, "Corrections' New Balancing Act: AIDS," *Corrections Compendium* 11 (August 1987): 1.

30. *Cordero* v. *Coughlin,* 607 F. Supp. 9 (S.D.N.Y., 1984).

31. *Thagard* v. *County of Cook,* No. 85C–4429 (N.D. Ill., May 20, 1985).

32. *Mtr LaRocco* v. *Dalsheim,* 120 Misc. 2d 697 (N.Y., 1983).

33. American Correctional Association, *Directory: Adult and Juvenile Correctional Departments, Institutions, Agencies and Paroling Authorities* (Laurel, Md.: American Correctional Association, 1992), p. xxxii.

34. Michael J. Sabath, "Factors Affecting the Adjustment of Elderly Inmates to Prison," in *Older Offenders,* ed. Belinda McCarthy and Robert Langworthy (New York: Praeger, 1988), p. 185.

35. Michael Gottfredson and Travis Hirschi, *A General Theory of Crime* (Stanford, Calif.: Stanford University Press, 1990).

36. Charles P. Smith, Paul S. Alexander, David J. Beckman, and Donald E. Pehlke, *A Preliminary National Assessment of the Status Offender and the Juvenile Justice System: Role Conflicts, Constraints, and Information Gaps* (Washington, D.C.: Government Printing Office, April 1980).

37. Michael J. Hindelang and M. Joan McDermott, *Juvenile Criminal Behavior: An Analysis of Rates and Victim Behavior* (Albany, N.Y.: Criminal Justice Research Center, 1981), p. 19.

38. Gordon Bazemor, "Washington Juvenile Law Reform: Problems in Implementation and Impact on Disparity," *Criminal Justice Newsletter* 14 (10 October 1983): 1–3.

PART TWO

Correctional Practice

Part II may be viewed as dealing with the heart of corrections. Here we will be examining the different correctional practices as they relate to the major institutions of community corrections and incarceration. As you read each of the chapters, consider how you would act if you should find yourself in the position of either offender or officer.

CHAPTER 6

Jails: Detention and
Short-Term Incarceration

CHAPTER 7

Probation

CHAPTER 8

Intermediate Sanctions
and Community Corrections

CHAPTER 9

Incarceration

CHAPTER 10

The Prison Experience

CHAPTER 11

Incarceration of Women

CHAPTER 12

Institutional Management

CHAPTER 13

Institutional Programs

CHAPTER 14

Prisoners' Rights

CHAPTER 15

Release from Incarceration

CHAPTER 16

Making It: Supervision in the Community

6

Jails: Detention and Short-Term Incarceration

People familiar with the American jail scene realize that jails rank at the bottom of the criminal justice hierarchy in influence.

Kenneth E. Kerle, American Jail Association

The Contemporary Jail: Entrance to the System
Origins
Population Characteristics
Administration
The Jail and Local Politics
Regional Jails
Pretrial Detention
Special Problems of Detainees
Release from Detention
The Sentenced Jail Inmate
Alternatives to Incarceration
Issues in Jail Management
Legal Liability
Jail Standards
Personnel Matters
Jail Crowding
The Jail Facility
The Future of the Jail
Summary

San Francisco's jails are over-crowded—as are almost all jails in the big cities of America. Sheriff Michael Hennessey decided to try a new idea: He sought to house fifty prisoners in the Pontiac Hotel, a transient hotel in south San Francisco, a low-income area bordering the city's business district. The idea seemed to have merit. Specially selected "low-risk" prisoners would be removed from the jail, social services would be provided to these prisoners and others in the neighborhood from the hotel's ground floor, and the overall cost would be much cheaper than jail.

There was only one hitch: Most of the hotel's neighbors objected. One anxious nearby resident worried that the program would worsen "alcohol and drug problems on a street already deluged with both." Another asked, "Why does everything get pushed off here in the armpit of the city?" To get his new and innovative program going, the sheriff would have to disregard the objections of people whose votes he needs to stay in office—an act of grave political risk.[1]

Jails are not very popular, even when they are not in your neighborhood. They are a strange correctional hybrid: part detention center for people awaiting trial, part penal institution for sentenced misdemeanants, part refuge for social misfits taken off the streets. There are men, women, and juveniles, people of all colors; and one characteristic most of them share is that they are poor and in need. They are there because they have committed, or have been accused of, a violation of the law. Jail is also the traditional dumping ground not only for criminals but also for petty hustlers, derelicts, junkies, prostitutes, the mentally ill, and disturbers of the peace, mainly from the poorer sections of cities. Thus, jail's functions include those of the workhouse of the past.

Students interested in improving corrections during their future careers could find no area in more obvious need of reform than this country's jails. Among the institutions and programs of the corrections system, the jail is the one most neglected by scholars and officials, and least known to the public. Uniformly jam-packed and frequently brutalizing, jails are almost never life-enhancing. Many criminal justice researchers would say that of all correctional agencies, jails are the oldest, most numerous, most criticized, and most stubbornly resistant to reform.

Jails are in such a state of decline that the estimated cost to bring them up to acceptable standards is more than the nation can pay, at least in the foreseeable future. The price tag of jail construction and renovation was estimated at over a half-billion dollars more than a decade ago, and that figure covered improvements in only about 10 percent of existing facilities.[2] Today jails are even worse off because of crowding in state prisons: Sentenced felons are being held in jails while they await vacancies in prisons. These circumstances lead scholars, administrators, policymakers, and elected officials to agree that the use of jail for any offender should be avoided whenever possible. Yet if an American is to have some personal contact with corrections, it will first occur in jail. For a high percentage this will be their only time in a correctional institution, and the impression it leaves will greatly influence their views of the criminal justice system.

The turnover in the jail population is so great that in one year more citizens directly experience jails than experience prisons, mental hospitals, and halfway houses combined: The estimate is more than eight million jail admissions per year.[3] Even if we take into account the fact that some portion of this total is admitted more than once, probably as many as six to seven million people are detained at some time during the year.

In this chapter we examine the problems associated with the operation of jails and look at the means by which some individuals avoid pretrial detention. We also raise questions about the role of corrections in this type of facility, where prisoners generally sit idle, without opportunities for programs.

The Contemporary Jail: Entrance to the System

A s we begin our examination of correctional institutions and practices, it is fitting that we consider jails first because they are the entryway to the correctional structure. Jails house accused individuals awaiting trial and sentenced offenders serving terms usually of one year or less. Persons appealing sentences are often held in jail too, as are those awaiting transfer to other jurisdictions. Nationally, almost 400,000 people are in jail on any one day, as shown in Figure 6.1.

Some people argue that jails are outside the boundaries of corrections. They say that most of the 3,300 jails are really a part of law enforcement because they are administered by sheriffs. They also note that sentenced offenders make up only about half of the jail population and that it is not proper to consider pretrial detainees, roughly the other half, as within the scope of correctional responsibility. Further, the fact that most jails have neither treatment nor rehabilitative programs is used as another argument for excluding jails from corrections.

We believe that jails are an important part of corrections and that they illustrate many of the complexities of the system. Because they are administered by locally elected officials, jails are buffeted by the local politics of taxation, party patronage, and law enforcement. Jail practices also affect probation, parole, and prison policies.

Jails are perhaps the most frustrating component of corrections for people who want to apply technologies or treatment modalities in efforts to help offenders. Of the enormous numbers of people who come through the jail, many need a helping hand. But the unceasing human flow usually does not allow time for such help—nor are the resources available in most instances.

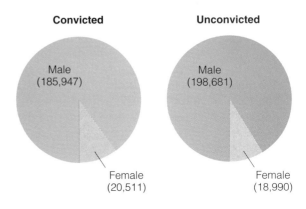

Figure 6.1 ■ **Adult Male and Female Jail Inmates in the United States.** Jails serve a number of purposes and hold both convicted and unconvicted inmates.

Source: U.S. Department of Justice, Bureau of Justice Statistics, "Jail Inmates, 1991," *Bulletin* (Washington, D.C.: Government Printing Office, June 1992), p. 2.

Origins

Jails in the United States are direct descendants of feudal practices in twelfth-century England. At that time an officer of the crown, the *reeve*, was appointed in each *shire* (what we call a county) to collect taxes, keep the peace, and operate the gaol (jail). Among other duties, the *shire reeve* (from which term the designation *sheriff* evolved) was called upon to apprehend and hold in custody persons accused of breaches of the king's law until a formal court hearing could be arranged to determine guilt or innocence. With the development of the workhouse in the sixteenth century, the sheriff took on added responsibilities for the vagrants and unemployed who were sent there. The sheriff made a living by collecting fees for holding inmates and by hiring out prison labor.

English settlers brought these traditions and institutions with them to the American colonies. After the American Revolution, the responsible officials—particularly sheriffs and constables—were elected by the local community, but the functions of the colonial jail re-

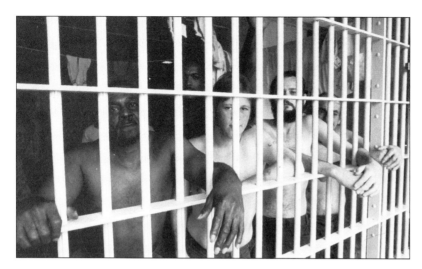

The American jail has been called the ultimate ghetto because most of the 350,000 people in jails are poor. They are held in jail awaiting disposition of their cases, serving sentences of under one year, or awaiting transfer to state prison.

mained unchanged. It was used to make certain that accused persons stayed in town to appear at their trials. It also provided shelter for misfits who could not be taken care of by their families, churches, or others.

The jails, which were often a part of sheriffs' homes, were run like the sheriffs' households. Detainees were free to dress as they desired and to contribute their own food and necessities. The historian David Rothman notes, "So long as they did not cost the town money, inmates could make living arrangements as pleasant and homelike as they wished."[4] Some detainees could not make independent contributions, and fees for their room and board were paid to the jailer from local revenues.

In the nineteenth century the jail began to change in response to the penitentiary movement. The jail retained its pretrial detention function but also became a facility for offenders serving short terms. It continued to hold vagrants, debtors, beggars, prostitutes, and the mentally ill. The fee system survived. But changes did take place. The juvenile reformatory movement and the creation of hospitals for the criminally insane during the latter part of the nineteenth century siphoned off some of the people previously sent to jail. The

development of probation also removed some offenders, as did adult reformatories and state farms. Inmates were segregated by gender. But even with these innovations, the jail was still the place where the overwhelming majority of accused and convicted misdemeanants were held.

Population Characteristics

Not until 1978 was a complete nationwide enumeration of jails conducted by the Bureau of the Census for the Bureau of Justice Statistics. To be repeated every five years, the census collects information on those incarcerated in jails that hold inmates beyond arraignment (usually more than forty-eight hours) and are administered by local officials. Excluded from the count are persons in federal and state-administered facilities. These nationwide counts are supplemented by an annual survey of the top one-third largest jails, in which about 75 percent of the inmate population is held.

The 1991 National Jail Census shows that about 91 percent of inmates are males, most are under thirty years of age, a little more than half are white, and most have very low incomes.[5] The demographic characteristics of the jail population diverge from those of the national population in many ways: People in jail are younger and disproportionately black, and most are unmarried (see Figure 6.2).

As with prisons, jail populations vary among the regions of the country and from state to state. The proportion of a state's population who are in jail, known as the jail rate, is high in the West and South (see Figure 6.3). In many states where prisons are at full capacity, sentenced felons are backed up in jails awaiting transfer.

Administration

There are about 3,300 jails in the United States. Of these, 2,700 have a county jurisdiction and most are administered by an elected sheriff. There are also about 600 municipal jails. Only in six states—Alaska, Connecticut, Delaware, Hawaii, Rhode Island, Vermont—are jails for adults administered by state government. There are also an estimated 13,500 police **lockups,** drunk tanks, and similar holding facilities authorized to detain people for up to forty-eight hours.[6] The Federal Bureau of Prisons has only four detention facilities (in New York, Chicago, San Diego, and Florence, Arizona) and contracts with local governments to hold more than a thousand persons awaiting trial or sentence.

The capacity of jails varies greatly. As shown in Table 6.1, the ten largest jail jurisdictions alone hold nearly 20 percent of the nation's jailed inmates. The Los Angeles County Men's Central Jail holds more than eight thousand inmates. Most jails are much smaller; 63 percent hold fewer than fifty persons.[7] These small facilities are becoming fewer because of new construction and the creation of regional, multicounty facilities.

lockup   A facility authorized to hold persons prior to court appearance for periods of up to forty-eight hours. Most lockups (also referred to as *drunk tanks* or *holding tanks*) are administered by local police agencies.

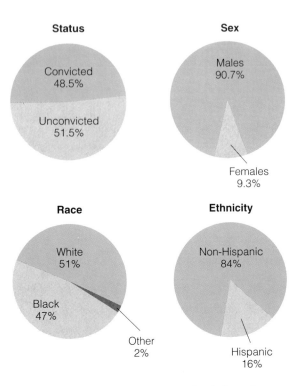

Figure 6.2 ■ **Characteristics of Adult Jail Inmates in U.S. Jails, June 30, 1991.** Compared with the American population as a whole, jails are disproportionately inhabited by males, minorities, the poorly educated, and those with low income.

Source: U.S. Department of Justice, Bureau of Justice Statistics, *Bulletin* (Washington, D.C.: Government Printing Office, 1992), pp. 2–3.

As facilities to detain accused persons awaiting trial, jails have customarily been run by law enforcement agencies. It seems reasonable that the agency that arrests and transports defendants to court should also administer the facility that holds them. Typically, however, neither the sheriff nor the deputies have much interest in corrections. They often think of themselves as police officers and of the jail as merely an extension of their law enforcement activities. In some of the largest cities, municipal departments of correction, rather than the police, manage the jails.

Many experts argue that the jail has outgrown the logic of police administration. It is no longer simply a holding place but one of the

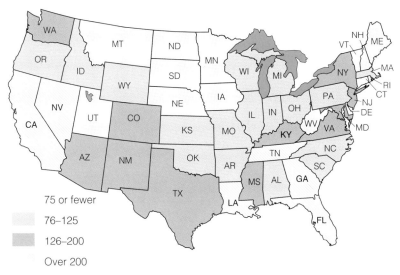

Figure 6.3 ■ **Persons Incarcerated in Local Jails per 100,000 Civilian Population, by State, as of June 30, 1988.** What accounts for the fact that incarceration rates in jails differ from state to state?

Source: U.S. Department of Justice, Bureau of Justice Statistics, *Bulletin* (Washington, D.C.: Government Printing Office, 1990), p. 2.

75 or fewer

76–125

126–200

Over 200

Note: Five states—Connecticut, Rhode Island, Vermont, Delaware, and Hawaii—have integrated jail-prison systems; therefore, information for these states is not given.

primary correctional facilities in the criminal justice system. In fact, much correctional work is directed toward jail inmates. Probation officers conduct presentence investigations in jails, treatment for alcohol and drug abuse is carried on in many facilities, and forms of community service or reintegration operate in some facilities. The effective administration of jails requires skills in offender management and rehabilitation that are not generally included in law enforcement training. This point was well made twenty-five years ago by the President's Commission on Law Enforcement and Administration of Justice: "The basic police mission of apprehending offenders usually leaves little time, commitment, or expertise for the development of rehabilitative programs, although notable exceptions demonstrate that jails can indeed be settings for correctional treatment."[8]

Good management practices may not always overcome several problems that face jail administrators. One problem is that some jails cannot send their prisoners to state facilities after they are sentenced. Many state prisons are so crowded that they refuse to accept sentenced jail cases until space becomes available.

In fact, over 12,000 offenders remained in local jails in 1991 as they awaited space to open up in the prison. Three states—Alabama, New Jersey, and Tennessee—accounted for more than half of the inmates sentenced to prison but incarcerated locally.[9]

Another problem is that many jails are still budgeted under a **fee system,** where the costs of housing, food, and services are averaged and a standard fee (say, $10 a day per prisoner) is set. This creates an incentive for poor jails: inadequate food, services, and prisoner support. Often the sheriff uses money saved on housing prisoners to augment the kinds of law enforcement services that attract public support and are therefore helpful at the polls.

The Jail and Local Politics

Because of the close links between the administration of the jail and local politics, fiscal and

fee system A system by which jail operations are funded by a set amount paid for each prisoner held per day.

Table 6.1 ■ **Capacities and Inmate Populations of the Twenty-Five Largest Jail Systems in the United States, 1991.** Our nation's largest cities have multiple jails that house large numbers of inmates.

Jurisdiction	Number of jails	Average daily population	Population on June 28
Los Angeles County, Calif.	9	20,799	20,885
New York City, N.Y.	17	20,419	20,563
Cook County, Ill.	—	7,257	8,356
Harris County, Tex.	3	6,751	6,808
Dade County, Fla.	7	5,343	5,493
Dallas County, Tex.	4	5,247	4,686
Shelby County, Tenn.	2	5,008	5,755
Philadelphia County, Penn.	7	4,897	4,589
San Diego County, Calif.	12	4,660	4,303
Orange County, Calif.	3	4,378	4,390
Maricopa County, Ariz.	6	4,312	4,480
Santa Clara County, Calif.	7	4,072	4,166
Tarrant County, Tex.	4	3,779	4,000
Orleans Parish, La.	—	3,677	4,481
Broward County, Fla.	3	3,502	3,584
Orange County, Fla.	2	3,267	3,225
Sacramento County, Calif.	3	3,170	2,980
Fulton County, Ga.	4	2,983	2,969
Alameda County, Calif.	3	2,912	2,891
Baltimore City, Md.	4	2,828	2,894
San Bernardino County, Calif.	2	2,735	2,929
Washington, D.C.	1	2,365	2,356
Bexar County, Tex.	1	2,313	1,981
Riverside County, Calif.	4	2,240	2,174
Kern County, Calif.	3	2,076	1,770

Source: U.S. Department of Justice, Bureau of Justice Statistics, *Bulletin* (Washington, D.C.: Government Printing Office, June 1992), p. 4.

political conservatism have a powerful effect on jails. Measures that are fiscally sound are often out of bounds because of political pressures. For example, pretrial release programs are cost-efficient and a proven means of reducing institutional crowding, yet the public's fear of crime often makes the programs politically infeasible. Political support may exist for expanded use of the jail for misdemeanant offenders or violators of probation rules, particularly when crime is such a potent electoral issue. But the money to expand or upgrade the jail's capacity to handle additional offenders is often lacking; the jail is a crime-control service and a drain on revenues. The tension between these two public interests is often expressed in local debate, particularly when capital expenditures for jail construction are being considered. And the issues

Do you think it makes a difference to the judge and jury whether the defendant approaches the bench from the courtroom audience or is led in from the jail by a bailiff?

remain, for many jails are unable to house all the inmates assigned to their supervision, because of overcrowding, special needs of some prisoners, and the absence of facilities to house females or juveniles.

It is very hard to take control of local facilities away from a politically sensitive office, such as that of sheriff or police chief. The more than seventy thousand jobs in jails constitute a large block of political patronage for elected officials to distribute to political supporters. Sometimes it is acknowledged that such appointees need not spend their working hours at the facility when there is political work to be done. Even when jail employees are under civil service, political considerations can be a factor in hiring and promotion. Few politicians would willingly surrender control over such a potential political force as the jail. As a result, change is slow to come.[10]

Regional Jails

Most regional jails are located away from major population centers, and capacities are small, often as few as thirty persons. Frequently, the state provides a portion of the operating funds. Even so, they lack essential services such as medical care that must be provided no matter how few persons may need them.

A recent trend, designed to remedy these problems, has been to push for regionalization: the creation of combined municipal-county or multicounty jails. This multijurisdictional or **regional jail,** fiscally sound though it may be, has been slow to catch on because several interest groups are negatively affected by it. Local political and correctional leaders do not want to give up their autonomy and control over patronage jobs, and reformers often object to moving inmates away from their communities. Finally, people object to having regional jails "in their backyard," as did the San Franciscans described at the beginning of this chapter.

----

regional jail Facility operated under a joint agreement by two or more governmental units, usually with a jail board drawn from representatives of the participating jurisdictions with varying authority over policy, budget, operations, and personnel matters.

Rite of Passage

Michael Knoll

Between the booking desk and the holding tank, the corridor is a fluorescent tunnel, rank with the smell of vomit and old piss. The jailer keeps behind me, walking slow, his boot heels clicking ominously on the gray linoleum. He stops at the last door, slips his key into the lock. The heavy iron grinds open and my whole body goes rigid. For a moment I want to drop the towel and plastic mattress, turn and run. But I don't. I hesitate for a moment and then allow him, with one fat hand, to shove me into the smoky dimness of the holding tank.

The door slams and I blink my eyes twice against the dirty light, straining to see through the shadows. The tank might be a dozen feet across, windowless, the ceiling light screened with an iron grillwork and a shredded towel that reads Santa Cruz County Jail. Below it, covering the iron bunks and the floor between them, are a half dozen men, each glancing up to look me over. I turn to the closest man, a heavyset guy with greasy hair and a Harley Davidson tee shirt, and ask what I should do with my mattress. "It's my first time in jail," I announce. "They just booked me in."

He looks back without speaking, his expression suggesting a vague annoyance. He stares, his face hard, and I stare back, a slow chill forming at the base of my spine. "Will you check this one out?" he says to the man at his right.

The other man, a skinny guy with elaborate dragons tattooed on both arms, answers with a trace of derision. "Looks like another fish, don't he? Don't he look like a fish, fellas?"

"He's a pretty one though," says a Chicano over in the corner. "Long hair, nice buns...."

When they laugh, my whole body tenses and I edge backward, retreating until the bars of the cell push against my back, ice-cold. For a second I consider yelling for the guard—the fat cop who booked me in, read me my Miranda rights, made me strip naked and spread my ass, joking about the fun I'd have in the holding tank. Remembering the hostility in his voice, I decide against yelling. Instead, I move with my mattress still dragging into the center of the tank. The others arrange themselves around me as if preparing for an inquisition.

Each of their expressions is curious or hostile, indifferent or angry. Looking them over, I wonder suddenly what it is I've done.

I don't ask them that though, afraid of what they'd say. I keep silent, listening while the silence grows and becomes painful: the kind of silence that might precede an execution, the silence of a gas chamber.

From the sink on the back wall I can hear a faucet dripping, each drop a small explosion. Out in the hall I can hear someone's laughter, a cop maybe, oblivious to anything going on inside. I look again at the faces: the stocky man in the Harley shirt, the skinny guy with the dragon arms, two Chicanos in white tee shirts, a black man wearing sunglasses, a few others lost in shadows along the far wall. I examine each face for a sign of recognition, a potential ally or supporter. Each expression though is blank, mute, closed. I could be in jail in Turkey or Morocco, some place where another language was spoken.

When the tattooed man spits something near my foot, every nerve in my body convulses. I look away sharply, aware that my fear has given me away, has become visible here under the dirty light.

"Why don't you tell us what you're in here for?" begins the one in the Harley shirt. His voice is cold and mocking. Before I can answer, a second voice, dripping venom, joins the first.

"He's probably in for sniffin' bicycle seats," snaps the skinny guy, his tattoos livid in the dim light.

"That, or staying out past curfew," laughs the man in the dark glasses. He flips a cigarette butt past my leg and adds, "I don't know why they put him with us adults."

Becoming impatient, the one in the Harley shirt shifts on his bunk, his voice rising. "You gonna tell us about your beef, kid, what you're in here for? Or do you have something to hide?"

I make myself look him in the eye, my face level with his. "I'm in for drugs," I answer, wondering if I should have lied, told him kidnapping or robbery. "I'm in for possession." I say it again for emphasis, though my voice is shaking now like my hands.

"Possession of what, oregano?" cracks the biker. A moment ago, walking into the tank, I thought the biker might be on my side, a source of support. His voice now is without sympathy, sarcastic, unrelenting.

"Possession of marijuana." I hear my voice waver, crack, slip out of control.

"How much marijuana?"

I wet my lips, stalling, then continue. "A pound and a half. Colombian weed." I emphasize the word *Colombian,* as if it might impress one of them, as if I were speaking to potential buyers.

"A pound and a half of weed isn't shit. It ain't nothin'—except to a kid. And say, does your mommy and daddy know you're down here in jail?"

"My parents are dead." They aren't, but I say they are, hoping to buy time, wanting them to ease up. The fear is rising like warm lava up my spine.

"Poor baby. All alone with us criminals. Who do you got to bail you out of here?"

Nobody, I think, or nobody close enough to go my bond. A year ago, a few hundred miles from here, there was a girl, Susan, who I might have called. For a while we'd thought we loved each other. Drugs were the thing we'd argued about. We argued and she told me I'd end up here, busted, that I'd have nobody to turn to. My parents had sided with her, making the same prediction. It had been a year since I'd seen any of them. I wasn't even sure of their phone numbers, whether they'd accept my call.

"C'mon, hot shit, talk up," taunts the biker. "Think you're big time? Big time dealer? Think you're pretty hot shit?"

"No—" I say it without conviction, my voice wilting and becoming smaller. "No, I don't think I'm hot shit."

"Just shit, huh? Ordinary shit. Like us. That what you mean?"

And I become still smaller. I want to ask why they're doing this, what the point is and how far they're going to go.

"I think this kid's scared. I think he's scared to death."

"That right?" questions the biker, leading the others with his voice. "And what is it you're scared of exactly?"

I want to say nothing, deny that I'm scared of them. I can't though, and they know it. With that realization I can feel my chest constrict—as if the walls of the tank were closing in, like the cell was becoming smaller. I can feel my heart pounding like a fist against my ribs. Abruptly I think back to the place where I was busted, the highway where I'd been hitchhiking: a black strip of asphalt rising over a slope of mountains, the sky above the high peaks a crystalline blue, and above them sunlight like lemon meringue over everything. How could I have imagined there'd be a sheriff's car cruising that highway, that I'd be stopped and frisked?

The man with the tattoos breaks the silence. "You know you'll probably get

Continued

prison time for that much weed. Maybe years, a nickel or so. Think you can handle that? Think you'll like doing time?"

"I'm not going to consider it until I know—"

"Look on the bright side of that though," interrupts the one in sunglasses. "When you hit the joint, you'll make somebody a fine kid. Anybody as young and pretty as you will be real popular with all those men."

I ignore the insinuation, trying not to think about the penitentiary. I remember instead the beauty of the mountains, the western desert rolling out to the horizon. Against the ugliness of their voices, the shadowy iron of the holding tank, the memory becomes vivid, nearly exquisite.

The one in the biker shirt resumes. "How you think you'll like that? Being somebody's kid? Somebody's punk? Some lifer that ain't had no real woman in ten years?"

I leer back at him. I try to appear indifferent.

"Hear what the man asked you?" questions the skinny Chicano. "He said they'll turn you out down there, that you'll hit the joint and turn *puta!*"

I know the word *puta,* the Mexican word for whore, applied now to a sissy, queer, homosexual. I heard it first

in a bar where one Chicano was trying to insult another. I saw the man stabbed for saying that. Now I want to ask the kid what he's trying to prove, and why he's chosen me for this ordeal.

"You'll turn *puta* and like it," declares a Latin voice near the back. "You'll sell your ass for candy and cigarettes."

"Is that right, kid?" teases the biker. "You'd trade your manhood for a candy bar?"

With each insult I can feel something tightening in my chest, winding there like a spring. My hands have begun to sweat and I realize suddenly that I've been holding my mattress the whole time, my arm going gradually numb. I let the mattress fall, watching as it strikes the foot of the Chicano who's been yelling the loudest.

He jerks back as if he's been slapped, exaggerating the effect of my action. "You trying to break my foot with that mattress? You loco? You tryin' to start something?" Turning to the other he shouts: "Did you all see that? This guy threw a mattress on me! I think he wants a fight."

"I saw it," yells the Harley shirt, wanting a confrontation. "He's trying to provoke you, Martinez. He's looking to start something."

"No, he ain't," someone in back yells. "He's too *puta.*"

The tension in the tank is almost physical, the lust for blood ringing in their voices.

I flash back to the last time I fought. Ten years ago on the playground of some grade school. I'd won the fight and broken some kid's jaw. Afterwards I'd felt lousy. The violence had been for nothing. I'd promised myself I'd never hurt anyone again. There were other ways to settle things, more reasonable ways.

"What about it, kid?" demands the man with the dragon tattoo. "You too scared to fight? You rather turn *puta* than fight Martinez?"

The Mexican moves directly in front of me now, a yard or two separating our bodies. I can see the contempt on his face, his arrogance, his eagerness to fight. It seems absurd—he knows almost nothing about me, where I'm from, what my name is, how I feel.

"Or maybe you'd enjoy that," chants the black man. "Maybe you got some girl in you. Maybe you'd like Martinez to rip you off. You'd make it sweet to him, wouldn't you, Martinez?"

In response, the Mexican pushes closer. "I'd make it real nice, just like I'd do a woman. And I wouldn't have to raise a finger, would I? Huh, gringo?" He inches closer, breathing hard, rocking on the balls of his feet.

"Answer him, kid," demands the biker. "You gonna fight him or not?"

Martinez is just an arms'

length away, his jaw cocked, body tense. Positioned under the light, he appears younger than I'd imagined, his eyes flashing old anger. On his right arm I notice a small tattoo: a yellow rose stenciled above a woman's name, Juanita. The beauty of the small tattoo, its testament to his love for a woman, seems out of character on an arm tensed now for fighting.

"What's it gonna be, kid?" yells an old man in back, someone who hasn't spoken until now. "You better hurt him—or get hurt yourself. Come out of here a sissy."

They take turns screaming ultimatums, each one trying to outdo the others. In front of me, Martinez prances back and forth like a prizefighter, as if he'd been preparing all his life for this moment. When he levels his fists in anticipation, the others go wild.

"Can I get a wager on this?" yells the biker. "I'll bet a pack of Camel filters on Martinez."

"I'll double that," calls the man with the dragon tattoo. "I'll bet you breakfast and dinner."

Someone else shouts louder. "I'll go two packs of smokes and four meals. But I want a knockout. I want to see some blood."

The skinny man near the toilet, his voice like ice, yells over all of them. "You're wasting our time, kid. You gonna defend yourself? You

gonna fight the man—or get your ass kicked?"

Fight him for what? I want to tell them this is pointless, that we have no reason to fight. The man called Martinez has nothing against me and I've done nothing to harm him. I want to remind them we're in this tank together, that we shouldn't make it harder on ourselves, shouldn't act like animals because we're caged. Searching for words I remember Gandhi's line: *It is possible to live in peace.* I have no words to tell them that though, and I am not Gandhi.

The Mexican's first jab catches me off guard, a warning, his fist floating slowly past my jaw. He feints twice with short jabs, baiting me to fight, teasing me. He swings again with his right, the fist coming closer, and then dances back, turning to the others for encouragement.

The biker yells first: "You've cut him enough slack, Martinez. Let him have it."

The black in sunglasses: "Down him, Martinez."

The tattooed man, his voice rabid: "He's a punk. He's got it coming."

Their voices run together now, a scramble of noise demanding blood. Watching Martinez's fists, their rapid movement, I feel myself going dizzy. I raise my hands in fear, wanting to protect

my eyes and mouth, wanting just to get through this. When the Mexican spits on my cheek, I'm not sure at first what it is. I hesitate, glancing around uncertainly.

"He spit in your god damn face, kid. How'd you like that?"

"You're a sissy if you take that."

"Puta!"

When he spits again, something tightens and then snaps in my chest: my fear becoming rage, something primitive that precludes reason. I watch my fists fly at him. Once, twice, again. I swing like I want to kill him, every muscle in my body rigid. I swing like my life depends on it. Wanting his blood on my hands, wanting to see him go down. And wanting them to shut up, all of them, and leave me alone. I swing like a machine, not sure whether I'm hurting him or not.

When someone's arms lock around my shoulders, forcing my own arms in against my chest, I know I've had it. The man's standing behind me, his arms like steel bands around my own body. I yell that this isn't fair, then feel my legs go weak and buckle, caving in beneath me, my body slipping heavily to the floor. Lying motionless on the concrete, I look up at the circle of faces gathered above.

Continued

When Martinez extends his hand again I cringe in terror, expecting to be knocked unconscious.

"Grab my hand," he says, his voice neutral as he lifts me awkwardly from the floor. "The fight's over. No *puta.*"

"You did all right," states the biker, patting my back with one big hand. "You fought back."

"You stood up to him," says the black man.

"You done all right," admits another. "You need to work on that right hook though…"

Their arms around my shoulders, we walk together to one of the benches. I listen as each one tells me his name, and then I announce mine. Taking turns, we relate our stories. How we got busted, why we shouldn't have been, how we're going to beat our cases. A. J., the biker, rolls me a cigarette and we smoke it together like old comrades. Later, we're playing poker when someone turns to the door, says abruptly: "Shut up—there's someone walking in the hall, a fish maybe. Get ready."

We wait together then, one group, none of us daring to speak, each anxious for the next new prisoner to appear at the door, hoping for a very young one, somebody scared, each of us hungry for the ritual to begin again.

Source: Adapted from M. Knoll, "Rite of Passage," *Greenfield Review* 11 (Winter-Spring 1984): 121–27. Reprinted by permission.

Pretrial Detention

Imagine yourself picked up by the police and accused of a serious crime. You are warned of your rights, probably handcuffed, and taken to the station house for booking. You have a hundred questions; few answers are given. You are frightened; the police treat you as if your fears are irrelevant to their work. You may feel angry at yourself for something you have done. You are frustrated that you cannot seem to stem the flow of procedure: fingerprints, mug shots, sitting while detectives and officers discuss you without acknowledging your presence. Slowly you begin to understand that you have taken on a label: accused offender.

Then you are taken to the detention section of the jail. If it is an advanced facility, you are taken to a holding room for an intake interview. There you are asked questions about your background that will help determine the best way to manage you while you are in jail, your situation is explained to you, and you are told what you can expect next.

If, however, you are in one of many jails with no formal intake procedure, you are simply put in the holding tank. If you are a man, there are three or more strangers in the cell with you, men whose stories you do not know and whose behavior you cannot predict. If you are a woman, you are probably by yourself. In either case, once the guard leaves, you are on your own. You now have time to think and to worry about your situation.

Many people begin to panic in such circumstances. In fact, the first hours following arrest are often a time of crisis for the defendant. The vulnerability, the sense of hopelessness and fright, the threat of lost freedom are never more stressful. During 1991, 24 percent of deaths that occurred in jail were the result of suicide.[11] It is understandable that most of these suicides happened within the first six to ten hours after lockup, and that most psychotic episodes occur during or just after jail intake.

The crisis nature of arrest and detention can be exacerbated by other factors. Often the newly arrested person is intoxicated or on drugs, a state that may have contributed to the crime for which the person is being held. Sometimes the criminal behavior stems from an emotional instability that may deteriorate further in detention. Especially for young offenders, the oppressive reality can set off debilitating depression. Without question, one of the most crucial times for the defendant is the period immediately following arrest.

Detainees differ in their need for help during this period. Those under the influence of mind-altering substances need time to overcome their effects; others need to be left alone; still others need communication and advice. Jails lack the programmatic flexibility to accommodate the range of needs that exist. But the early confinement period is a mental health opportunity: During a crisis, help can be most effective because the person is most likely to respond positively to it. Unfortunately, the jail is not ordinarily well suited to provide help in the first hours of detention. Elaborate mental health measures are not feasible, nor are they necessarily required. Simple human contact—conversation with corrections staff, involvement in some activity, communication that is responsive to what the detainee is likely to be experiencing—is frequently sufficient to reduce many initial anxieties.

Special Problems of Detainees

Aside from the crisis experience of being arrested and jailed, serious problems arise for many people who are detained for an extended period. As we will discuss, the most significant are mental health problems, substance dependency, medical needs, and legal problems. Because so many jail inmates have these problems, the jail has often been referred to as the social agency of last resort. Studies underscore this opinion:

■   Of 545 inmates at the Denver County Jail, 22 percent were diagnosed as psychotic, and 23 percent had a history of long-term or multiple hospitalization for mental illness.

■   Research conducted in March and April 1979 at the Milwaukee House of Corrections showed that 17 percent of the total jail population had been diagnosed by the facility's consulting psychiatrist as mentally ill.

■   A survey of 150 inmates in the Fairfax County, Virginia, jail on a typical weekday in December 1980 revealed that more than 33 percent of the inmates whose records were checked had had serious alcohol, drug, or mental problems.

■   At any given time, 10 percent of the roughly 380 inmates at the Montgomery County Detention Center in Maryland are mentally ill, emotionally disturbed, or mentally handicapped.[12]

Mental health problems Growing attention is being paid to the mental health of many arrested people whose behavior is not seriously criminal but socially bizarre—those who are only partially clothed, who speak gibberish or talk loudly to themselves, who make hostile gestures. These people, whose behavior is unpredictable and to some extent uncontrollable, formerly were taken to mental institutions where they could be treated. But with the nationwide deinstitutionalization movement, they have become outpatients in the general society and they often spend time in jail instead of receiving psychiatric treatment as they once did.

Observers say that "the number of inmates generally considered as mentally ill is increasing."[13] Police have few alternatives to confinement when they come across people engaging in odd or self-destructive behavior that is more a nuisance than a crime. Moreover, persons of fragile stability often respond to the stress of jail with emotional outbursts and irrational behavior. Jails draw from and add to the mentally disturbed group.

Managing the World's Largest Municipal Jail

Catherine Abate

As commissioner of the world's largest municipal jail system—a system that is bigger than the prison systems of forty states—I have had a unique opportunity to view the challenge of providing criminal justice services as we move ever so quickly into the twenty-first century.

. . .

A modern correction system should aspire to living up to its true name and mission, that of correction.

That's the direction in which I am taking my agency of 14,000 dedicated uniformed and civilian employees. For if there is no hope or care expressed by the Department of Corrections, our jobs will never be about correction and we will see the same people coming in and out of our institutions year after year.

How to facilitate this directional change is no easy task, for we must never give the impression that we are coddling or being "soft" on inmates or crime. Yet, we must be

about care … care for needs such as substance abuse intervention, AIDS treatment, parenting skills, vocational training and educational advancement. These are social needs that may mean the difference between people returning to jail or becoming responsible and productive members of society. We must create an environment where we show offenders they have the power to change.

Can everyone be helped? Of course not. Surely there are those who are the chronic career criminals who cannot be reached, no matter how supportive the correction system. But that number is truly a fraction of the overall human equation we deal with day in and day out.

. . .

The system I manage has grown from 7,000 beds in 1980 to nearly 20,000 today. Unfortunately, those incarcerated soon were replaced by too many others on the street who were willing to follow in their footsteps. Too many released from jail returned to their communities no better prepared to live a law-abiding life.

. . .

Fiscal constraints will also define future policy. It costs New York City $58,000 per year to maintain a defendant on Rikers Island, a 400-acre jail complex with ten separate and distinctly different detention centers.

The typical offender is a minority male, between the ages of nineteen and twenty-

Most jails lack resources to provide care for mentally ill offenders. Three-fourths of all jails have no rehabilitative staff, and among the remainder the vast majority of rehabilitation personnel are not trained to deal with severe cases of mental and emotional stress, particularly when threats of self-injury are involved. Consequently, mentally disturbed inmates

often languish in jails, abused by other inmates, misunderstood by corrections workers, and untreated by professional personnel.

The news is not all bad, however; some positive steps have been taken to divert the mentally ill from jail. Many jails screen new arrivals for mental health problems, with specially trained counselors interviewing and eval-

nine, who is charged with a drug-related offense. He is abusing either drugs or alcohol. He is a high school dropout and unemployed, and he is functionally illiterate with few, if any, job skills. Of course, we've also seen a growth in female offenders, up from 450 women per day ten years ago to 1,600 per day on the average—all of them requiring some kind of special services or treatment.

. . .

We recognize that the community and victims throughout this city are our primary clients. If we effectively treat and then monitor offenders, our streets and our neighborhoods will become safer. To accomplish this, however, corrections must become a part of the community it serves. We must bring correction into the community.

Community corrections … will improve our ability to provide support and discharge planning to offenders and link them to appropriate aftercare services in their own neighborhoods … services that more often than not are offered by the very same people who live in these communities.

It is imperative that we make every attempt to encourage those in our custody to take advantage of the special programs we offer so that they can try and reintegrate themselves into their communities in a more meaningful way. We have initiated several innovative programs geared toward making that reintegration more feasible. They include a pilot literacy program that utilizes a multimedia teaching network operating in two jails on Rikers Island and at community centers. We also have worked with the city's university system to create educational and career opportunities for discharged inmates. Professionals and entrepreneurs offer vocational training in the jail and jobs upon release. Perhaps our most innovative community outreach encourages recently released females to call a special "help line" in our Self-Taught Empowerment and Pride (STEP) program. Many of the incarcerated women are being linked to a community network of health and housing providers.

. . .

Not only do we have the responsibility to see that those who leave our system do not return, but we must encourage young people to stay in school and not enter jail in the first instance.

We must keep the glimmer of hope and opportunity alive in the hearts and minds of the incarcerated. Our failure to do so will be measured in enormous human and financial costs.

Catherine Abate is Commissioner of the Department of Corrections in New York City. Previously, she was head of the New York State Office of Victim Services and also served as Commissioner of New York City Probation Department.

uating pretrial detainees. Inmates with mental health problems are usually referred to local social service agencies for treatment and may be diverted from criminal prosecution in order to allow treatment to proceed.[14]

Substance dependency From over 40 percent to nearly 90 percent of people arrested test positive for drug use at the time of their arrest.[15] Many of these offenders are drug dependent. The most dramatic of the problems posed by offenders' drug abuse occurs during withdrawal, when the addict's body reacts to the loss of the substance on which it has grown dependent. Both alcoholics and narcotics addicts suffer withdrawal, but it is especially painful for the latter and may last as long as a week. It is not uncommon for addicts to attempt suicide to escape the pains of withdrawal. In fact, a higher percentage of drug addicts are successful in ending their lives than nonaddicts. Early identification of the narcotics addict is a high priority in urban jails, for withdrawal symptoms can be assuaged by methadone maintenance or the offender can be released to an addiction treatment facility.

Every jail regularly houses alcoholic offenders, many of whom are physically sick during the initial hours of confinement, hallucinating, and paranoid. These symptoms tend to be looked upon as inconveniences rather than as conditions requiring treatment. Few jails provide any real form of treatment, and treatment furnished by outside agencies is often just as rare because agencies prefer voluntary clients to offenders.

Since the first detoxification center was established in St. Louis in 1966, there has been a national trend toward treating public drunkenness as more of a medical than a criminal problem. Detoxification centers are designed as quasi-voluntary facilities for recidivist inebriates, many of whom have no other place to go. The centers provide shelter, medical care, food, clothing, and counseling for residents, most of whom are taken there by police.

Medical needs The medical needs of detainees are numerous and range from treatment of minor scrapes and bruises sustained in the process of arrest and booking to major injuries sustained during the crime and its aftermath. To these injuries can be added the routine health deficiencies of any sample of poor minority citizens: lack of dental care, infections, poor nutrition, and so forth. Even so, over three-quarters of the jails in the United States offer neither medical facilities nor sound medical services.

Today the most pressing medical need in jails is presented by the offender with AIDS. As we described in Chapter 5, there are treatments for AIDS that jail officials should be in a position to provide, and there are standard precautions that all workers should take around clients with AIDS. The main problems have to do with staff training, for many jail staff have misconceptions about the spread of AIDS, and this can lead to mishandling of AIDS-infected inmates.

Legal needs Access to an attorney is one of the most frequently cited concerns of detainees. Pretrial detainees are people in trouble, and they need legal assistance to get out of it. In the emotionally stressful period after arrest, suspects need information about the processes they will undergo during the pretrial period. They also want legal help in securing release through bail or diversion. If release is not possible, they must have assistance in preparing their case, negotiating with the prosecutor about the charges, or directing the attorney to people who may provide an alibi or exonerating evidence. Not surprisingly, research consistently shows that people kept in jail until trial are at a disadvantage in preparing their defense.

People in jail are likely to require the help of a public defender, an appointed counsel, or an attorney provided by contract. Unfortunately, attorneys involved in criminal defense work cannot spend much time on each case; they must process large numbers of cases for the relatively small fees they receive. As a general rule, they cannot spend substantial time locating witnesses, conducting investigative interviews, and preparing testimony; consequently, these essential defense plans are only partially pursued for many detainees.

Detainees can expect long periods during their incarceration when they will not see an attorney. In fact, most will probably have only one or two hurried conversations with their attorneys before they appear in court. Then, as if to add insult to injury, detained offenders are brought to the courtroom in handcuffs and jail-issue clothing, in dramatic contrast to well-groomed defendants who have had the advantage of remaining free. If detainees once were employed, they have long since been fired. In short, detainees can entertain little hope for leniency.

Pretrial detainees' rights Unlike prisoners, pretrial detainees have not been convicted of the crimes for which they are held; they are technically innocent yet are being detained under some of the worst conditions of incarceration. In the 1970s several courts reasoned that such persons should suffer no more restrictions than are necessary to ensure their presence at trial and that legal protections of detainees should exceed those of sentenced prisoners. Thus a Michigan federal district judge ruled that a detainee had the right to receive any publication available to the general public, and other judges ruled that there should be few constraints on contact visits with friends and relatives.[16]

In 1979 the U.S. Supreme Court viewed the matter of pretrial detainees' rights in a more limited way and overruled the lower courts. In *Bell* v. *Wolfish* it ruled that conditions can be created to make certain that detainees are available for trial and that administrative practices designed to manage the institution and maintain security and order are constitutional.[17] The justices said that restrictions other than those that ensure court appearance may legitimately be imposed on detainees and that when jail security, discipline, and order are at stake, detainees may be treated like other prisoners.

Release from Detention

One of the most startling facts about U.S. jails is that about half of the persons in them are awaiting trial. For many, this pretrial detention will be long: The average delay between arrest and trial is six months or more in many states. In urban jails the wait is often longer because of heavy backlogs in trials. Remarkably, in some court systems defendants can expect to wait in jail for up to a year or more before their cases will be tried.

The hardship of detention before trial exerts pressure on defendants to waive their rights and plead guilty. Further, as we've seen, it undermines their defense. And delay, often a useful defense tactic because it can weaken the prosecutor's case, imposes a further penalty on the detained defendant.

Small wonder, then, that recent years have seen a major emphasis on programs to facilitate the release of offenders awaiting trial. The programs have been highly successful. One study of twenty cities found that the pretrial release rate had been only 48 percent in 1962 but was 67 percent in 1971.[18] More recently, it was found that in 1981, 87 percent of defendants in eight cities were released before trial.[19] In some cities, a high percentage of defendants are detained at the time of arraignment, but most are eventually released prior to trial. The growing crisis of jail crowding is accelerating the development of new mechanisms for pretrial release, for this is one of the most rapid ways to reduce a jail's population.

The bail problem When someone is arrested for a crime, the primary interest of the court is that that person appear at the appointed time to face charges. Judges have traditionally responded to this need by requiring that the person post a **bail** bond, normally ranging from $1,000 to $25,000 (although higher amounts may be required), to be forfeited if the accused fails to appear.

Defendants have two principal ways to make bail. They may post the full amount to the court, where it is held until the case is decided. Or they may pay a set fee to a **bondsman,** who posts the amount with the court; the fee varies, depending on the jurisdiction.

bail An amount of money specified by a judge to be posted as a condition for pretrial release for the purpose of ensuring the appearance of the accused in court as required.

bondsman An independent business person who provides bail money for a fee, usually 5 to 10 percent of the total.

Dissatisfaction with the bail process stems from several factors. First, far too many defendants are practically indigent and cannot afford bail. A survey of 88,120 pretrial detainees in 1983 found that of the 87 percent whose bail had been set, 94 percent were incarcerated simply because they could not afford bail or a bondsman's fee.[20] Second, money is a weak incentive for appearance in court in many cases: Persons who can most easily afford bail are likely to appear at trial without the threat of its forfeiture. Perhaps the most disquieting factor is that the precious commodity of human freedom can be had for a price. For people to be imprisoned merely because they are too poor to pay for their release seems antithetical to our culture and our concept of justice.

Alternatives to traditional bail To avoid the problems of bail, some jurisdictions have increased the use of *citations and summonses.* For nonserious offenses, police can give the accused a "ticket" with a court appearance date and thus avoid bringing the accused into custody. Experiments with this approach suggest that it is a useful way to reduce demands for short-term detention space.

By far the most successful programs have been those that allow defendants to be released solely upon their promise that they will appear at trial, a practice known as **release on recognizance (ROR).** ROR programs assume that ties to the community (residence, family, employment) give people an incentive to keep their promise to appear and to retain their status in the community.

Evaluators of ROR programs have shown that community ties actually play an insignificant role in judicial decisions in regard to ROR. Instead, ROR seems to be connected to the seriousness of the offense and the defendant's prior record. These are questionable criteria to use for unconvicted persons. Moreover, surveys of jail inmates disclose that few are likely to meet the traditional ROR standards of community ties. A composite picture of jail detainees shows that, in effect, detention is an institution for those without economic resources. The apparent deficiencies of ROR programs lead many observers to conclude that the programs are not enough.

In some respects, however, ROR programs have been highly successful. ROR defendants frequently have better rates of appearance than defendants freed in various bail programs, lower rearrest rates, and higher rates of sentences to probation rather than prison. ROR programs have demonstrated clearly that the vast majority of accused persons can be safely and responsibly released into the community on their promise to return for trial. Loss of bail is an unnecessary threat. In all, the rate of willful failure to appear is normally less than 5 percent.[21]

Preventive detention The heightened public concern about crime over the past decade has led to a political movement to prevent pretrial release, especially release on bail. In **preventive detention,** defendants who are thought to be dangerous or who are thought to be likely to commit crimes while awaiting trial are kept in prison to protect society from them. The Comprehensive Crime Control Act of 1984 authorizes the holding of an allegedly dangerous defendant without bail if the judge finds that no conditions of release would ensure the defendant's appearance at trial and at the same time ensure the safety of the community.

The notion of protection from accused criminals has been subjected to sustained analysis. Many scholars believe that holding in

release on recognizance (ROR) Pretrial release granted on the defendant's promise to appear in court because the judge believes that the defendant's ties in the community are sufficient to guarantee the required appearance.

preventive detention Detention of an accused person in jail for the purpose of protecting the community from crimes the accused is considered likely to commit if set free pending trial.

custody a person who has not been convicted of committing a crime but who someone thinks might commit a crime is a violation of the due process provisions of the Constitution. Others argue that the practice is impractical and potentially nefarious. In reality, less than 16 percent of all defendants who are released pending trial are arrested for another crime before trial, and less than half of those are eventually convicted of the new crime.[22] It is exceedingly difficult to identify in advance the one in twelve who will be found to have violated the law while awaiting trial on an earlier charge.

Nonetheless, political pressure to incorporate public safety concerns into release decisions had become so strong by 1982 that well over half of the states had enacted laws that reflected the notion of preventive detention. The United States Supreme Court, in *Schall* v. *Martin* (1984) and *United States* v. *Salerno* (1987), approved preventive detention practices.[23]

Pretrial diversion **Pretrial diversion** had its genesis in the belief that formal processing of people through the criminal justice system is not always beneficial. Each of the three main reasons advanced in its support has provoked controversy.

1. Many offenders' crimes are caused by special problems—vagrancy, alcoholism, emotional distress—that cannot be managed effectively through the criminal justice system.

2. The stigma attached to formal criminal labeling often works against rehabilitation and promotes an unnecessarily harsh or long-term penalty for a relatively minor offense.

3. Diversion is cheaper than criminal justice processing.

For the most part, correctional leaders agree that jails can do very little for those in its charge who have mental, emotional, or alcohol-related disabilities. For such people, social programs are more suitable than jails. There is less agreement about how to appropriately treat those whose problems are less clearly beyond their own control: unemployed and unskilled youths, multiple drug users, and episodic offenders, to name a few. Their marginal criminality may stem primarily from their disadvantaged status, and their status can be thought to be at least partly their own fault. For these people, diversion from the criminal justice system is controversial because it looks as though they are getting off. Yet the logic of diverting them is attractive. The jail sanction does little to alter their disadvantaged status; indeed, the stigma of a conviction often decreases their chances of becoming productive citizens. A more enlightened policy would deflect them from criminal justice processes and instead put them into reparative programs. That is, in fact, the precise aim of most pretrial diversion.

The mixed success of pretrial diversion programs highlights one of the persistent problems of criminal justice reforms. Innovations designed to reduce the overall intrusiveness of the system, no matter how well intentioned, often backfire and instead add to its capacity for social control. The process, called **widening the net,** occurs when a new program is applied to less serious offenders than those for whom it was originally designed; rather than focusing its efforts on the more serious offenders, it increases the scope of corrections.

---

pretrial diversion An alternative to adjudication in which the defendant agrees to conditions set by the prosecutor (for example, to receive counseling or drug rehabilitation) in exchange for withdrawal of charges.

widening the net Increasing the scope of corrections by applying a diversion program to persons charged with offenses less serious than those of the persons the program was originally intended to serve.

If pretrial diversion programs are to meet their objectives, they must be applied to offenders who otherwise would be treated more harshly. This is not easy to accomplish because many justice system officials distrust programs that are more lenient or more oriented to service than their current practices.

The Sentenced Jail Inmate

The sentenced jail inmate presents special difficulties for the correctional administrator, most of which stem from two factors: the duration of the term and the limitations of the jail's physical plant. By definition, jail terms are short. Some are as long as six months, even a year in a county jail, but such terms are unusual and may have been designed as a way to avoid early release programs from crowded state prisons. The more usual sentence is thirty, sixty, or ninety days for a misdemeanor. In many cases, the sentence ultimately imposed is "time served"; the judge believes that the time already spent in pretrial detention—when under law, the person was innocent—is sufficient, or more than sufficient, punishment for the offense committed. The real punishment is not the sentence but rather the impact on the offender of the unpleasant, costly, and harmful conditions from arrest up to case disposition: the process is the punishment.

Of those sentenced to additional time, misdemeanants constitute the forgotten component of most local criminal justice operations. Their short terms make treatment difficult. Most inmates have not graduated from high school and many are illiterate, yet educational programming is unlikely to yield results in such short time periods, especially with adults. For example, it is the rare offender who can earn a high school equivalency diploma in one or two months, and prospects for continued educational advancement after release are dim. Similar drawbacks are inherent in job training

Most jails lack recreation areas and educational or treatment programs. Offenders must while away the days with board games and television.

programs, which may require twenty-five to thirty weeks to complete. Job placement prospects are spotty for the former inmate, and a parole or probation officer may not be assigned to the case in order to help in the search.

Treatment programs for the mentally ill and emotionally disturbed suffer from the same time constraints. General therapies often must go on for years. Drug and alcohol treatment programs also require substantial blocks of time to be effective. When treatment programs are run in jails, they tend to be based on more short-term psychotherapeutic approaches, such as group therapy, transactional analysis, reality therapy, and contingency contracting (see Chapter 13).

The facility also places limits on programming. Job assignments within the institution are few, and most inmates go without any real work to occupy their time. Those who are assigned to work details find the labor menial and monotonous: janitorial, kitchen, and laundry tasks. Still, they are lucky; the

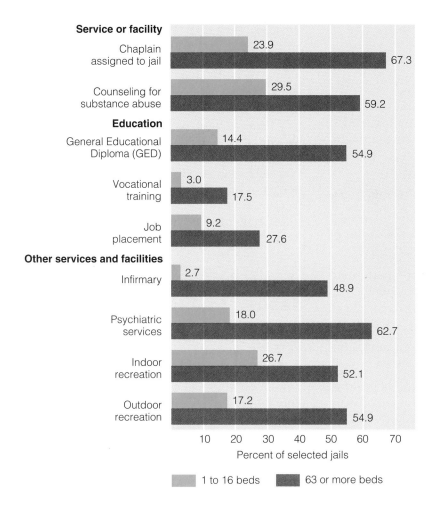

Figure 6.4 ■ **Percentage of Selected Jails That Provide Certain Services and Facilities.** Small jails find it difficult to provide inmate services.

Source: Adapted from U. S. Department of Justice, Bureau of Justice Statistics, *Sourcebook on Criminal Justice Statistics* (Washington, D.C.: Government Printing Office, 1983), p. 129.

vast majority of inmates have to sit through idle hours in a small cell. Recreation may depend on a library of donated books, a Ping-Pong table, and a few card tables. Only occasionally might there be a jail that has a basketball court or a weight room. Whatever the resources, recreational time is carefully rationed.

The kinds of programs available in jails, as reported by sheriffs, are listed in Figure 6.4. Two facts are immediately apparent. First, small jails, which constitute the majority of jails, provide minimal services and programs to help prisoners pass the time. Second, the lack of certain programs, even in large facilities, is

astounding. About half of the largest jails lack infirmaries, group counseling, educational opportunities, and both indoor and outdoor recreation. Without these basic amenities, jail time can be dead time.

Contact with friends and relatives is the only thing that sustains many prisoners in jail. And opportunities for visiting are often confined to a few minutes each week.

With isolated exceptions, jail time is the worst kind of time to serve as a correctional client. For corrections, it is an expensive and largely ineffective proposition; in many cases, jails are proving to be expensive revolving doors.

Alternatives to Incarceration

Nearly all of the wide array of nonincarcerative correctional methods used to reduce prison crowding are also used as ways to reduce jail crowding. The most common jail alternatives are as follows:

- *Fines:* Financial penalties set to reflect the seriousness of the offense.

- *Restitution:* Reimbursement to the victim of the losses resulting from the crime.

- *Community service:* Public labor performed by the offender as compensation for the offense.

- *Intensive probation:* Close surveillance of the offender, often combined with drug testing and employment checks.

- *Work release:* Freedom from the jail during work hours, with return to jail during non-work periods.

- *House arrest:* Restriction to the home, often combined with electronic monitoring.

Since we will describe these alternatives in detail in Chapters 7 and 8, we will only summarize some main issues about them here. First, the jail population is often not well suited for the structure these programs require. For example, offenders who do not have jobs are seldom able to pay fines or restitution, and they have no chance to receive work release. Offenders without places to live (or without telephones for electronic monitors) cannot be sentenced to house arrest.

Second, the strictness of these programs often makes it difficult to abide by all the rules. When offenders do violate the rules, they normally receive additional jail time—often completely erasing the original savings of the "alternative" sentence.

Third, judges are often reluctant to sentence difficult offenders to these programs.

Instead, they sort through the less serious offenders to find candidates the judges believe will do well, if assigned to the jail alternative. Often, the offender selected would not have been placed in jail in the first place—hence another instance of "widening the net."

Finally, with severe problems of prison crowding in virtually every prison in the United States, alternatives are at a premium. Much of the time, they are focused not on jail inmates, for whom the "savings" in diverting them from jail amounts to days or months because of the short sentence, but on prison inmates, where savings can be counted in years.

Issues in Jail Management

American jails are faced with numerous problems, many of them age-old—lack of programs, poor financial resources, antiquated facilities, and so on. But four issues are of particular importance now: legal liability, jail standards, personnel matters, and crowding.

Legal Liability

Under the Civil Rights Act of 1871 (codified as 42 U.S. Code 1983) jail employees may be legally liable for their actions. Whenever a governmental official (such as a corrections officer) uses his or her authority to deprive a citizen of rights, that official can personally be sued in court to stop the violation and to pay damages (both actual and punitive) and legal costs to the person whose rights were violated. Supervisors (including wardens) may be liable as well for actions of staff members—even if they were not aware of those actions—if it can be shown that they should have been aware had they been adequately performing their jobs. Lack of funds does not excuse an administrator from liability for failure to train staff sufficiently well or to provide basic constitutionally required custodial arrangements. Local governments that administer the jails are also liable for injurious conduct.

Many people believe that court decisions awarding civil judgments under the act are an open invitation for prisoners to sue, and sue they have. Prisoners have litigated just about every conceivable aspect of the conditions of incarceration, from hours of recreation to quality of food. The most successful suits have been those that show that an action of an employee has contributed to a situation that resulted in harm to a prisoner.

The threat of litigation has forced jails to develop basic humane practices for managing offenders. Civil damages and legal fees in excess of $1 million have been awarded often enough to draw the attention of sheriffs, jail managers, and local government officials. Budgets for jails have been increased to reflect the additional costs of developing training and classification procedures and managerial policies to prevent liability actions.

Jail Standards

One of the best ways to deflect the problem of litigation is to develop standards for jail operation that indicate the routine practices and procedures.[24] Standards are important for at least three reasons. First, they indicate proactive criteria for jail management, and this helps to eliminate the "Monday morning quarterback" aspect of much litigation. If jails are following standard procedures, it is less reasonable to hold them accountable for problems inmates experience during incarceration. Second, standards provide a basis by which administrators can evaluate staff performance. They need merely ask whether staff are in compliance with operational standards. Third, standards facilitate planning and evaluation of jail programs, since they provide a target that program managers can consider in their work.

Authorities are unclear as to the best way to design and implement jail standards. Some experts argue that standards should be *binding.*

Usually, this means that an oversight agency will have responsibility for visiting each jail in the state and determining whether its programs are consistent with the standards. Those jails that fail to comply with standards are given a deadline by which to meet them: If they do not, they may be fined—or even closed.

Other experts argue that jails are so different in size and needs, and so many jails suffer from underfunding and inadequate facilities, that to hold all jails accountable for meeting the same, inflexible standards is not reasonable. These experts argue for *voluntary guidelines,* in which program goals would be set for jail operations. Table 6.2 shows the types of jail operation standards used in the various states.

The bottom line is that if jail administrators do not implement standard practices, courts will intervene. In one recent study of 612 jails, more than one-fourth were already under court order to eliminate unconstitutional conditions of confinement, and 20 percent had been ordered by the court to reduce jail population to eliminate overcrowding.[25] Even new jails are not immune to this problem: In the late 1980s it became common for jails to come under court order soon after opening, sometimes even before opening.

Personnel Matters

Local corrections workers are among the most poorly trained, least educated, and worst paid employees in the criminal justice system. Many take custodial positions only as a temporary measure until an opening occurs in the ranks of the sheriff's law enforcement officers. Of the approximately 100,000 jail employees noted in the 1988 census, about 73 percent performed direct custody functions, 12 percent were involved in clerical or maintenance tasks, 7 percent had administrative positions, and 1 percent were in educational areas.[26]

The personnel issues facing jail administrators stem from several factors, but the primary source is probably a combination of low pay

Table 6.2 ■ **Jail Management Standards of the Various States.** No particular strategy for jail standards appears to work without a problem.

State	Mandatory standards	Voluntary standards	Developed but not implemented standards	No standards
Alabama				X
Arizona			X	
Arkansas	X			
California		X		
Colorado			X	
Florida	X			
Georgia		X		
Idaho		X		
Illinois	X			
Indiana	X			
Iowa	X			
Kansas		X		
Kentucky	X			
Louisiana				X
Maine	X			
Maryland	X			
Massachusetts	X			
Michigan	X			
Minnesota	X			
Mississippi				X
Missouri			X	
Montana			X	
Nebraska	X			
Nevada				X
New Hampshire				X
New Jersey	X			
New Mexico			X	
New York	X			
North Carolina	X			
North Dakota	X			
Ohio	X			
Oklahoma	X			
Oregon	X			
Pennsylvania	X			
South Carolina	X			
South Dakota			X	
Tennessee		X		
Texas	X			
Utah		X		
Virginia	X			
Washington	X			
West Virginia				X
Wisconsin	X			
Wyoming			X	

Source: G. Larry Mays and Joel A. Thompson, "The Political and Organizational Context of American Jails," in *American Jails: Public Policy Issues,* ed. J. A. Thompson and G. L. Mays (Chicago: Nelson-Hall, 1991), pp.19–20.

Note: For states not listed, no information regarding standards is available.

and poor working conditions. Local correctional workers make an average annual salary substantially less than firefighters and police officers in the same jurisdiction. Few people with high school educations seek employment with local corrections. And whenever corrections workers can, they leave for more highly paid jobs with less stressful working conditions. Many corrections employees, however, do not fare well in competition for better positions and hence must stay where they are.

The working conditions in most jails are made even worse by understaffing. Jails are twenty-four-hour operations. When a jurisdiction has a forty-hour workweek with normal holidays and leave time, nearly five full-time employees are required to fill one position around the clock. The national ratio of prisoners to jail custodial employees is about 5:1, or over 25:1 for "full-time" posts. In essence, each jail employee must be able to control twenty-five inmates or more—hence the frequent practice of simply locking the doors and leaving inmates in their cells all day.

Local corrections workers are often an unhappy lot. Turnover is extraordinarily high; many jails report complete staff turnover once each two or three years. The effects are disastrous. No matter what the level of staffing, proper security must be maintained in the jail, so there is pressure to move a new employee into the ranks. But liability for employee error rests with the administrator. And training at a state academy may last thirty to sixty days—and classes may not start for several months. The dilemma is obvious and has prompted the National Jail Center of the National Institute of Corrections in Boulder, Colorado, to make the training of jail staff instructors a high national priority. This strategy seeks to increase the number of qualified trainers for jail workers so that no new employee is without the necessary preparation for the assignment. But at best, this is a stopgap measure. A more long-range solution requires jails to be made a more attractive employment option by improving pay and working conditions.

Jail Crowding

The number of people confined in jails reached nearly crisis proportions in the early 1980s. The jail population, which had remained fairly stable during the 1970s, rose by over 80 percent from 1978 to 1990. Much of the crowding is a result of the fact that the jail is expected to handle a wide range of people, including drug addicts, the mentally ill, and alcoholics. Further, more than 150 jails have been forced to close as a result of litigation, and ten times that number are operating under court orders.

Recently jail crowding has worsened because of yet another cause: The state corrections system does not immediately accept sentenced offenders who should be serving time in prisons but for whom there is no space. This situation has led to problems for sheriffs and jail administrators. One sheriff in Arkansas chained inmates to the state penitentiary fence and tried to abandon them. State officials armed with shotguns and a court order made him take the inmates back.[27]

Cells intended to hold one or two persons are holding three, four, even five. It is not uncommon for prisoners to sleep in hallways, with or without mattresses. Direct and immediate consequences of overcrowding are violence, rape, and a variety of health disorders. There is some evidence that prolonged exposure to seriously crowded conditions reduces the expected life span of inmates. Certainly tempers flare in close quarters, and the vulnerable inmate becomes a more likely victim. And remember: Many of the persons subjected to these conditions have not yet been tried and must be presumed to be innocent.

There are numerous possible solutions to jail crowding. Two center on persons detained before trial: increasing the availability of release options, such as ROR and supervised release, and speeding up trials. Other ameliorative measures are directed toward persons serving time, and include work release sentences, which at least relieve crowding for part of the day. Yet less than half of all jails currently have some form of work release, and barely a third have provisions for weekend sentences.

Oddly, building new jails—or increasing the capacity of existing facilities—appears to have little effect on the problem of crowding. Instead, it seems that policies regarding the use of jail, combined with crime rates in the jurisdiction served by the jail, determine the amount of crowding. In a study of a national sample of jails, wide variations were found among jurisdictions in patterns of jail usage, controlling for population served. Some jails were heavily used; others were relied on less. The most crowded jails tended to be those relied on more to house "pass through" populations—arrestees and detainees—and these tended to be larger facilities as well.[28] This may explain the common occurrence that new jails with expanded capacities are opened, only to suffer renewed conditions of crowding. The solution to crowding is not so much jail capacity as it is jail policy.

The Jail Facility

According to a survey of sheriffs, almost 30 percent of all jail cells are fifty years old or more, despite an unprecedented construction boom in jails to replace old facilities. Jails are expensive structures, costing as much as $100,000 per cell to build and perhaps $200,000 per cell when financing is taken into consideration. But running a physically outmoded jail can be more expensive still. Even such basic items as radios and television sets were lacking in over half of all jails in 1983. With idle time, poor physical security, and little or no program space, prisoners are often cheek by jowl day in and day out. Crowded cells make for threatening environments and may translate into lawsuits and potentially large awards. Often the only way to counteract poor security in older jails is to hire extra staff. For these reasons and others, many jurisdictions have turned toward what is called the **new-generation jail.**

Jail crowding has meant that many pretrial detainees must await their trials in close quarters, without recreation facilities or programs.

The new-generation jail is both a design and a set of programs. This approach attempts to use the physical plant to improve the staff's ability to manage the inmate population. Three general concepts are employed: podular design, interaction space, and personal space.

The **podular unit** (the term is derived from *pod* and *modular*) is a living area for a group of inmates that defines a post or a watch. The pod replaces the old cell ranges. Twelve to twenty-five individual cells are orga-

---

new-generation jail A facility of podular architectural design and management policies that emphasizes interaction of inmates and staff and provision of services.

podular unit Self-contained living areas, for twelve to twenty-four inmates, composed of individual cells for privacy and open areas for social interaction. "New-generation jails" are made up of two or more pods.

The new generation jails are designed to increase the interaction of inmates with correctional officers. How might this type of jail influence your work as a correctional officer?

nized into a unit (the pod) that serves as something like a self-contained mini-jail. Typically the cell doors open into a common living area where the inmates of the pod are allowed to congregate.

The new jail tends to reinforce interaction of various sorts: Inmates have greater freedom to interact recreationally, and corrections staff are in direct contact with them. In older jails, corrections officers were separated from inmates by bars and doors; the new-generation jail places them in the same rooms with inmates. This is called the **direct supervision** approach. The inmates are also given personal space, and they may stay in their individual cells to pursue their own interests when they wish. They may even have keys to their own quarters within the pod.

The new structure has several advantages over older jails. First, its economics are flexible. When populations are low, whole pods can be temporarily shut down, saving personnel and operational costs. Minimum standards for recreation time and nonlockup time can be met routinely without costly construction or renovation. Supervision of staff is less demanding, for staff have greater autonomy to manage their pods. Research also indicates new-generation jails are as much as 20 percent cheaper to construct.

The greatest advantages, however, are programmatic. In larger jails, pods can serve specialized offender groups who share a need, such as for remedial educational services, or who for any reason (for example, AIDS, gang affiliation, or type of offense) should be separated from the rest of the jail population. Thus the needs of the inmate can become a more significant factor in the nature of the confinement.

Placing the correctional staff in closer contact with the inmates carries advantages as well. Prisoners often show symptoms of depression or acting out, which may become more troublesome if they are not responded to appropriately by staff. When corrections officers are physically closer to inmates, they can more readily become aware of feelings or behavior that may require attention.

direct supervision   A method of correctional supervision in which staff members are in direct physical interaction with inmates throughout the day.

The physical structure can also be a potential moderator of the conflict between staff and inmates. Each group can know the other better, and individuals can come to live on easier terms with one another. Thus in the long run the new-generation jail can help to overcome the correction officer's alienation from inmates and the kinds of false stereotypes that alienation allows to develop. The officer in proximity to inmates learns to rely on communication skills and judgment rather than force in controlling the inmate population. This is one reason studies have found the direct supervision jail results in improved staff morale, reduced staff sick leave, less injury to staff and inmates—and even reduced maintenance costs.[29]

Despite its advantages, all is not well with the new-generation jail. For one thing, it is hard to sell the jail to a public that underestimates the painfulness of jail and sees the new system as a means of coddling offenders. The fact that usually more than half the inmates are not yet convicted does not lessen the public's desire for harsh punishment of offenders. Jail administrators need to inform political decision makers of the fiscal and programmatic advantages of the new jail.

A second problem is more troubling: Many new jails become outmoded between the time they are planned and the time they are completed. Standards of law may change, creating new requirements for cell space, recreation space, visitation, and the like. Inadequate attention may have been given to possible programmatic needs. Often the very existence of a new jail leads to such enthusiastic response by judges and other criminal justice officials that the new facility quickly becomes crowded.

Finally, the number of cells that should be built into a new jail is controversial. Planners often argue that new jails need to be more capacious than old jails to accommodate growing numbers of offenders. Architects, pleading for large jails, often use projections of burgeoning populations to support expansion. Critics respond that jail populations grow to meet available capacity, and they cite numerous new jails of doubled capacities that were overcrowded on the day they opened. The need, they say, is for policies to keep jail populations under control as well as for facilities to house those populations.

The Future of the Jail

Few government functions in the United States are under assault from as many directions as the jail. Reform groups call for jail conditions to become more humane; the media expose them as cruel, crowded, and counterproductive; inmates sue their keepers for mistreatment, often successfully; and experts describe jails as failures.

In some respects, the jail's importance to the criminal justice system has seldom been greater than it is today. With many prisons more crowded than they are legally permitted to be, the jail is a backup resource for managing the many offenders for whom the state lacks space. As local governments experiment with ways to improve the credibility of criminal justice, solutions seem inevitably to involve the jail—for work release, to enforce court orders, for new laws against drunkenness, and for other initiatives. Local decision makers have more control over jails and jail policy than the alternative facilities operated by state corrections agencies.

Perhaps because of the jail's centrality, two general trends—if they continue—bode well for its future. First, many jurisdictions have renovated or replaced jail facilities since the early 1970s. The overwhelming difficulties of decrepit physical plants are at least partially overcome by new construction. Second, many jurisdictions are joining with others to build and maintain a single jail to serve the needs of each. Though political problems abound in such an arrangement—politicians resist giving up authority over jail budgets—this movement seems to be gaining adherents.

Summary

As the entrance to corrections, the jail holds a mixed and changing population. Sentenced offenders make up only about half of the jail population; the rest are pretrial detainees. In urban areas the jail holds persons with long criminal histories alongside alcoholics and released mental patients.

In most parts of the United States the operation of jails is a county responsibility. The jail administrator thus feels the force of local political pressures. In most places the jail is poorly funded and the facility is inadequate for the functions it is expected to serve.

Persons awaiting trial in jail are those who are unable to obtain their release on bail or by some other pretrial release mechanism. Many of these people have alcohol- or drug-abuse problems and must suffer the pangs of withdrawal in jail with minimal medical assistance. In recent years a variety of release mechanisms have been developed as alternatives to traditional bail. Citations and summonses and release on recognizance are among the new approaches.

Most jails incarcerate sentenced offenders for periods of no more than one year. For these misdemeanants, alternatives to jail have been developed, including community service, work release, intensive supervision probation, and home detention.

The administrators and staffs of American jails must be aware of current issues that affect their performance. The prisoners' rights movement, for example, has raised the question of the legal liability of officials. Personnel problems stemming from low pay and poor working conditions require constant attention. The problem of jail crowding, caused in part by prison crowding, results in heightened costs and tension.

The new-generation jail has been designed as a secure environment that allows for the interaction of staff and inmates while providing personal space. Though these facilities are controversial, the advantages they offer to administrators, staff, and inmates have won them many adherents.

For Discussion

1. How does local politics affect the administration of jails? Should political influence be as extensive as it is? Is it a help or a hindrance to good corrections?

2. What special problems and needs do jail detainees have? Why? What problems do these needs pose for jail administrators?

3. Discuss the pros and cons of preventive detention. How may it affect crime control? Due process?

4. How would you propose balancing the tensions between jail management and public safety?

5. What are some of the problems you would expect to encounter if you were in charge of providing rehabilitative programs in a jail?

For Further Reading

Braly, Malcolm. *Felony Tank.* New York: Pocket Books, 1976. Describes the problems of pretrial detention.

Goldfarb, Ronald. *Jails: The Ultimate Ghetto.* Garden City, N.Y.: Doubleday, 1975. Presents a powerful critique of the American jail.

Irwin, John. *The Jail.* Berkeley: University of California Press, 1985. Describes the jail experience and how inmates react to jail.

Moynahan, J. M., and Stewart, Earle K. *The American Jail: Its Development and Growth.* Chicago: Nelson-Hall, 1980. Provides a critical history of jails in the United States.

Thompson, Joel A., and Mays, G. Larry, eds., *American Jails: Public Policy Issues.* Chicago: Nelson-Hall, 1991. Provides a series of papers on contemporary jail issues.

Notes

1. Gerald D. Adams, "Sixth Street Jail Proposed," *San Francisco Examiner,* 7 January 1993, pp. B4–5.

2. Richard Allinson, "Crisis in the Jails," *Corrections Magazine* 8 (April 1982): 20.

3. Bureau of Justice Statistics, *Census of Local Jails, 1988, Vol. 1* (Washington, D.C.: U.S. Department of Justice, 1991), p. 5.

4. David Rothman, *Discovery of the Asylum* (Boston: Little, Brown, 1971), p. 56.

5. U.S. Department of Justice, Bureau of Justice Statistics, *Bulletin* (Washington, D.C.: Government Printing Office, 1992), pp. 2–3.

6. Bureau of Justice Statistics, *Census of Local Jails,* p. 19.

7. U.S. Department of Justice, Bureau of Justice Statistics, *Bulletin* (Washington, D.C.: Government Printing Office, February 1990), p. 6.

8. U.S. President's Commission on Law Enforcement and the Administration of Justice, *Task Force Report: Corrections* (Washington, D.C.: Government Printing Office, 1967), p. 79.

9. U.S. Department of Justice, Bureau of Justice Statistics, *Bulletin* (Washington, D.C.: Government Printing Office, May 1992), p. 4.

10. Wayne N. Welsh, Henry N. Pontell, Matthew C. Leone, and Patrick Kincade, "Jail Overcrowding: An Analysis of Policymakers' Perceptions," *Justice Quarterly* 7 (June 1990): 341.

11. U.S. Department of Justice, Bureau of Justice Statistics, *Bulletin* (Washington, D.C.: Government Printing Office, December 1991), p. 2.

12. U.S. Advisory Commission on Intergovernmental Relations, *Jails: Intergovernmental Dimensions of a Local Problem* (Washington, D.C.: Government Printing Office, 1984), p. 13.

13. Dave Kalinich, Paul Embert, and Jeffrey D. Senese, "Integrating Community Mental Health Services in Local Jails: A Policy Perspective," *Policy Studies Review* 7(3) (1988): 660–70.

14. *Jail: The New Mental Institution* (Washington, D.C.: National Coalition for Jail Reform, n.d.), p. 2.

15. National Institute of Justice, *Research in Action: Drug Use Forecasting* (Washington, D.C.: U.S. Department of Justice, November 1991), pp. 2–3.

16. O'Bryan v. Saginaw County, Michigan, 437 F. Supp. 567 (D. Neb. 1976); Jones v. Diamond, 594 F. 2d 997, 1013 (5th Cir. 1979).

17. Bell v. Wolfish, 441 U.S. 520 (1979).

18. Wayne Thomas, *Bail Reform in America* (Berkeley: University of California Press, 1976), p. 45.

19. Mary A. Toborg, *Pretrial Release: A National Evaluation of Practices and Outcomes* (Washington, D.C.: Government Printing Office, 1981), p. 41.

20. National Institute of Justice, *Report to the Nation on Crime and Justice* (Washington, D.C.: U.S. Department of Justice, 1988), p. 76.

21. Donald E. Pryn and Walter F. Smith, "Significant Research Findings Concerning Pretrial Release," in *Pretrial Issues* 2(2) (Washington, D.C.: Pretrial Services Resource Center, February 1982).

22. Toborg, *Pretrial Release,* p. 6.

23. Schall v. Martin 467 U.S. 253 (1984); United States. v. Salerno 481 U.S. 739 (1987).

24. Joel A. Thompson and G. Larry Mays, "State-Local Relations and the American Jail Crisis: An Assessment of State Jail Mandates," *Policy Studies Review* 7(3) (1988): 567–80.

25. Bureau of Justice Statistics, *Jail Inmates, 1986* (Washington, D.C.: Government Printing Office, 1987), p. 36.

26. Bureau of Justice Statistics, *Census of Local Jails, 1988* (Washington, D.C.: U.S. Department of Justice, July 1988).

27. *Overcrowded Time: Why Our Prisons Are So Overcrowded and What Can Be Done* (New York: Edna McConnell Clark Foundation, 1982), p. 5.

28. John M. Klofas, "Disaggregating Jail Use: Variety and Change in Local Corrections over a Ten-Year Period," in *American Jails: Public Policy Issues,* ed. Joel A. Thompson and G. Larry Mays (Chicago: Nelson-Hall, 1991), pp. 40–58.

29. W. Raymond Nelson, "Cost Savings in New Generation Jails: The Direct Supervision Approach," *Construction Bulletin,* publication of U.S. Department of Justice, National Institute of Justice (Washington, D.C.: Government Printing Office, July 1988), p. 2.

7

Probation

The nation's prisons have become so critically over-crowded that the courts must now consider alter-native sentence for an increasing number of convicted felons. Probation is the major— and, in many cases, the only—alternative.

Granting Felons Probation, a report of the Rand Corporation

The History and Development of Probation
Benefit of Clergy
Judicial Reprieve
Recognizance
John Augustus
The Modernization of Probation
The Organization of Probation Today
Should Probation Be Centralized or Decentralized?
Who Should Administer Probation?
Should Probation Be Combined with Parole?
The Dual Role of Probation: Investigation and Supervision
The Investigation Function
Purpose
Contents
Recommendations
Disclosure
Private PSIs
The Supervision Function
The Officer
The Offender
The Bureaucracy
The Effectiveness of Supervision
Case Management Systems
Special Supervision Programs
Revocation and Termination of Probation
Probation in the Coming Decade
Summary

New York City Probation Department faces a problem. With over 44,000 probationers and caseloads already approaching two hundred per probation officer, the city budget office has advised the department that over the next three years, probation must absorb an unprecedented budget cut. Because the budget mostly pays for probation officers, their number will have to be reduced.

Faced with this crisis, the probation leaders have undertaken what the *New York Times* has called "a bold experiment." The new approach calls for a two-tier system of supervision: Violent offenders will be seen in lengthy group sessions designed to deal with the attitudes that lead to violence; nonviolent offenders will not see a probation officer but instead will report electronically, using machines that read fingerprints with laser techniques.[1] If the experiment works, probation in New York and in other big cities will never be the same.

Some people would say that probation needs to change, for it seems to get the worst of two worlds: Few citizens or political leaders give it much respect; yet it is by far the most extensively used form of corrections in the United States. Nearly 65 percent of all adults under correctional authority are serving probation sentences. In 1991 this figure represented more than 2,700,000 persons, or nearly four times the number of adults in felony prisons and over two and a half times the number of adults in all penal institutions combined.[2] Even though escalating prison growth gets the public's attention, since 1985 the U.S. probation population has actually grown at an even higher rate than the incarcerated population.

Despite the wide use of probation, it is frequently given short shrift by media critics, who tend to portray it as "a slap on the wrist." This notion is so widespread that even a scholarly work on correctional policy referred to probation as "a kind of standing joke."[3] These views contrast with official policies:

1. Government devoted over a quarter of a billion dollars in federal funds to improve and expand probation in the last decade alone.

2. Advocates of intermediate sanctions point to probation as the base from which more severe punishments can be built.

3. Supervision in the community is being used as the sanction for more and more offenders.

What is the reality of probation? How effective is it? How important is it today? In this chapter we describe the function of probation in corrections and review numerous studies of probation supervision and court services. We shall see that, as in most other areas of corrections, the work of probation agencies is carried out in an atmosphere of social and political ambivalence about punishment. This ambivalence, together with uncertainty about treatment methods, leaves probation in a quandary: We ordinarily rely heavily on it in sentencing offenders, but we seem to have limited confidence in its corrective capacities.

The History and Development of Probation

Probation is basically the idea that in lieu of imprisonment, the offender is given the chance to remain within the community and demonstrate a willingness to abide by its laws. In this country, probation began with the innovative work of John Augustus, a Boston bootmaker who was the first to **stand bail** for defendants under authority of the Boston Police Court. But the roots of probation lie in earlier attempts, primarily in England, to mitigate the harshness of the criminal law.

stand bail   The practice, by a private citizen, of posting bail for a defendant and promising to make certain that the defendant will appear for trial.

Benefit of Clergy

From the thirteenth century until the practice was abolished by statute in 1827, persons accused of serious offenses in England could appeal to the judge for leniency by reading in court the text of the Fifty-First Psalm. As we saw in Chapter 2, the original purpose of this practice was to protect persons who were under church authority, such as monks and nuns, from the awesome punitive power of the state represented by the king's law. Because this benefit was gradually extended to protect ordinary citizens from capital punishment—the predominant sanction for serious offenses under English law in those days—the Fifty-First Psalm came to be known as the "neck verse."

Originally, the invocation of the Fifty-First Psalm required that the person be able to read, and thus it discriminated in favor of the upper social classes. Eventually, common thugs memorized the verse so they could pretend to read it before the court and avail themselves of its protection. Consequently, judges became arbitrary in their application of the benefit.

For a short period the benefit of clergy was practiced in the United States, but it "eventually fell into disrepute because of its unequal application and confused legal character."[4] Criticisms once leveled against it—arbitrariness and invidious favoritism—are often directed today at probation. Probation's detractors assert that the cynical penance of the privileged and socially advantaged affords them a leniency denied to lower-class and less reputable offenders.

Judicial Reprieve

The statutes written by legislatures are often based on an image of the offender as evil or dangerous. But in reality, many offenders are neither. Most are more or less ordinary individuals whose problems or circumstances have led to confrontations with the law. Judges have long understood the need for leniency with some offenders, and they regularly seek avenues of punishment that deflect the full punitive force of the law.

In England a common law practice called **judicial reprieve** became widespread in the nineteenth century. If a convicted offender requested, the judge could elect to suspend either the imposition or execution of a sentence for a specified length of time, on condition of good behavior. At the expiration of that time, the offender could apply to the Crown for a pardon.

In the United States judicial reprieve took a different form and led to a series of legal controversies. Rather than limiting the duration of the reprieve, many judges suspended imposition of punishment indefinitely, so long as the offender's behavior remained satisfactory. The idea was that the reprieved offender who remained crime-free need not fear the power of the court; the offender who committed another crime, however, was subject to punishment for both crimes.

The discretionary use of such indefinite reprieves was declared unconstitutional by the Supreme Court in 1916.[5] The Court recognized the occasional need to suspend a sentence temporarily because of appeals and other circumstances, but it found that indefinite suspension impinged on the powers of the legislative and executive branches to write and enforce laws. With this opinion, the practices of probation became subject to the provisions of the states' penal codes.

The uneasy balance between the legislature and the judiciary in selective mitigation of the harshness of the law continues today. While the judiciary seeks discretion to avoid imposing the full sentences specified by law on all defendants, legislatures increasingly pass mandatory penalties that make probation unavailable to certain offenders. The innovation of judicial reprieve, which essentially forgave offenders on condition of good behavior, no longer seems a legitimate sentencing alternative.

---

judicial reprieve A practice under English common law whereby a judge might suspend imposition or execution of a sentence on condition of good behavior on the part of the offender.

It was in the Boston Police Court that John Augustus convinced Judge Peter Oxenbridge Thatcher to place an offender on probation.

Recognizance

In a search for alternative means to exercise leniency in sentencing, judges began to experiment with extralegal forms of release. Much of this innovation occurred among the Massachusetts judiciary, whose influence on modern probation was enormous.

One of the most famous trailblazers was Boston Municipal Court Judge Peter Oxenbridge Thatcher, the originator of the practice of **recognizance.** In 1830 Thatcher sentenced Jerusha Chase "upon her own recognizance for her appearance in this court whenever she was called for."[6] The idea of recognizance with monetary sureties was made law in Massachusetts in 1837. What made recognizance important was the implied supervision of the court—the fact that the whereabouts and actions of the offender were subject to court involvement.

The main thrust of reprieve and recognizance was to humanize the criminal law and mitigate the law's harshness. They foreshadowed the movement toward individualized punishment that would dominate corrections a century later. All the major justifications for probation—the need for flexibility in sentencing and individualized punishment—already had strong support. Yet an institutionalized way of performing recognizance functions was still needed. This formalization of court leniency is the main contribution of John Augustus.

John Augustus

Virtually every basic practice of probation was originally conceived by John Augustus, the first probation officer. He was the first person to use the term *probation*, and he developed the ideas of the presentence investigation, supervision conditions, social casework, reports to the court, and revocation of probation.

Augustus's story is one of admirable humanitarianism combined with reformist zeal. He was a man of substantial financial resources, and he had the intent of putting into practice the principles of philanthropy espoused by the nationwide temperance movement. Over several years'

recognizance   A formally recorded obligation to perform some act (such as keep the peace, pay a debt, or appear in court when called) entered by a judge to permit an offender to live in the community, often upon posting a sum of money as surety, which is forfeited by nonperformance.

BIOGRAPHY

John Augustus (1785–1859)

John Augustus was a Boston bootmaker who became a self-appointed probation officer, thereby developing the concept of probation as an alternative to incarceration. His initial probation effort occurred in the Boston Police Court in 1841 when he posted bail for a man charged with being a common drunkard. Because his philanthropic activities made Augustus a frequent observer in the courts, the judge was willing to defer sentencing for three weeks and the man was released into Augustus's custody. At the end of this brief probationary period, the man convinced the judge of his reform and therefore received a nominal fine. The concept of probation had been born.

Continuing his interest in criminal justice reform, Augustus was frequently present in Boston courts, acting as counsel and furnishing bail. He found homes for juvenile offenders and frequently obtained lodging and employment for adults accused or convicted of violating Boston's vice or temperance laws. Between 1842 and 1858 he bailed out 1,152 men and 794 women, making himself liable to the extent of $243,235 and preventing these individuals from being held in jail to await trial. He reported great success with his charges—of the first 1,100 offenders he discussed in his autobiography, he claimed only one had forfeited bond—and asserted that, with help, most of them eventually led upright lives. Since Augustus belonged to no charitable or philanthropic society, his primary sources of financial support were his own business and voluntary contributions. He never received a salary from any organization. As a result of Augustus's efforts, criminal justice gained a new practice that has since become commonplace.

---

work, the methods used by Augustus came to parallel those of modern probation. He was careful to screen his cases "to ascertain whether the prisoners were promising subjects for probation, and to this end it was necessary to take into consideration the previous character of the person, his age, and the influences by which he would in future be likely to be surrounded."[7] His supervision methods were analogous to casework strategies: He obtained the convicts' confidence and friendship, and by helping the offender obtain a job or aiding the family in various ways, he helped the offender to reform.

Do not assume, however, that Augustus's work received uniform support from his fellow Bostonians. The public and officials of the court were skeptical of and even hostile to much of his work. Since the local correctional officer received seventy-five cents for each prisoner, some of the objections were due to finances. Eventually, Augustus extended his work to the municipal court, where the supportiveness of the judiciary made his probation practice a little easier.

The Modernization of Probation

The probation concept eventually extended to every state and federal jurisdiction. In the course of its development, the field underwent a curious split. The heritage left by Augustus and his followers was a humanitarian orientation that focused on reformation. The new officers hired under the enabling legislation were drawn largely from the law enforcement community—retired sheriffs and policemen—whose orientation they shared.

The strain between the so-called law enforcer role of probation, which emphasizes surveillance of the offender and close controls on behavior, and the social worker role, which emphasizes provision of supportive services to meet offenders' needs, continues today. No easy resolution exists. Advocates of the law enforcement model argue that conditions for community control must be realistic, tailored to the individual, and enforced. Those who favor the social worker model believe that supervision must have a treatment component so that the offender can be helped to become a worthwhile citizen. Each view has been dominant at one time or another in the last half century.

In the 1940s, leaders in probation and other aspects of corrections began to embrace ideas about personality and human development current in the field of psychology. Heavily influenced by the pioneering work of Sigmund Freud and other early psychoanalysts, probation began to emphasize rehabilitation as its overriding goal. This new focus moved probation work into the realm of the professions, at least in the field's rhetoric. While it is questionable that the ideas of psychiatry were ever fully implemented by even a small number of probation departments, the logic of this approach certainly dominated the professional literature.

The orientation toward a medical model of criminality and its treatment remained strong through the 1960s, when a new set of ideas emphasizing reintegration came to the fore. This model was based on the notion that crime is a product of poverty, racism, unemployment, unequal opportunities, and other community processes. Probation was seen as a central correctional method because it was the primary existing means of working with the offender in the problem context—the offender's community. The methods of probation began to change from direct service (by psychological counseling) to service brokerage: After their needs were assessed, the clients were put in touch with appropriate community service agencies. The reintegrative approach was heralded by government studies, and federal funds were shifted to community-based corrections agencies (discussed in the following chapter), including probation agencies.

In the latter part of the 1970s, thinking about probation changed again. Now the goals of rehabilitation and reintegration have given way to an orientation widely referred to as risk management. This orientation tries to minimize the probability that an offender will commit a new offense, especially by use of tight controls over the probationer's activities reinforced by careful surveillance. Risk management combines values of the just deserts model of the criminal sanction with the commonly accepted idea that the community deserves protection.

Another recent development in the field of probation is the "probation fee." This is a requirement that the probationer pay a monthly charge (normally $15 to $25) for the privilege of being on probation. The probation fee was originally developed as a way of offsetting the costs of probation. It was based upon the argument that offenders assigned to probation are getting "a break," and they ought to be assessed the costs of that break.

The idea that people should pay the costs of their supervision is an appealing one. But there are problems with the plan. The main problem has been that once the fee is assessed, it has to be collected. Critics argue that the probation officer is forced to turn attention away from the supervision of the offender's adjustment and focus instead upon the collection of the fees—a difficult task, given that actual collection rates are as low as 40 percent.

Even when the money comes in, it may work to the detriment of the agency. In many places, the probation fees collected in one year are deducted from the next year's budget. The result is continually building pressure to collect the fees as the first act of supervision. No wonder many administrators are against the idea of probation fees.

The problem may not be intractable. Studies show that collection rates can be improved by "feedback systems" that enable probation officers to compare their rates with those of their peers.[8] Critics, of course, say that this is exactly the point: Probation officers pay attention to their "scores" instead of their clients. On the other hand, probation fee systems raise literally millions of dollars each year to support probation services.

But one of the main ways probation has changed in the 1990s is that it no longer is exclusively a sentence imposed in lieu of incarceration, through one of the following:

- *Split sentence:* The court specifies a period of incarceration to be followed by a period of probation.

- *Modification of sentence:* The original sentencing court may reconsider an offender's prison sentence within a limited time and modify it to probation.

- *Shock incarceration:* An offender sentenced to incarceration is released after a period of time in confinement (the shock) and resentenced to probation.

- *Intermittent incarceration:* An offender on probation may spend weekends or nights in a local jail.

Each of these probation trends has been a product of social forces operating across the country. The emphasis on psychiatric social work was a natural outcome of the conceptualization of corrections as reformative, a vision held by religious and social reformers of the day. The reintegration movement represented a shift in emphasis away from imprisonment toward more direct services, such as job training and education. This approach was consistent with President Lyndon Johnson's idea of the Great Society, in which equal opportunities would be available for all citizens and discrimination and poverty would be eliminated. When the Great Society failed to materialize, attention turned to the fundamental responsibility of a society to protect its citizens from crime. Thus the recent emphasis on risk management is an outgrowth of widespread public demands that the justice system be streamlined and that it direct its attention to reduction of crime. Combining probation with periods of incarceration is seen by many as a way to make it "tougher" and more effective against crime.

The Organization of Probation Today

Probation originated in a court, and the initial probation agencies were units of the judicial branches of city and county governments, primarily in the eastern United States. As the idea of probation caught on and moved westward, variations in its organization were attempted. Probation has been placed in the executive branch, it has been subjected to statewide unification, and it has been consolidated with parole. By 1991, seven types of probation organization existed, as shown in Figure 7.1.

Three general issues are involved in the organization of probation: whether it should be centralized or decentralized, whether it should be administered by the judiciary or the executive, and whether or not it should be combined with parole services. We discuss these issues in the following sections.

Should Probation Be Centralized or Decentralized?

The centralization issue concerns the location of authority to administer probation services. Proponents of decentralization argue that an agency administered by a city or county instead of a state is smaller, more flexible, and better able to respond to the unique problems of the

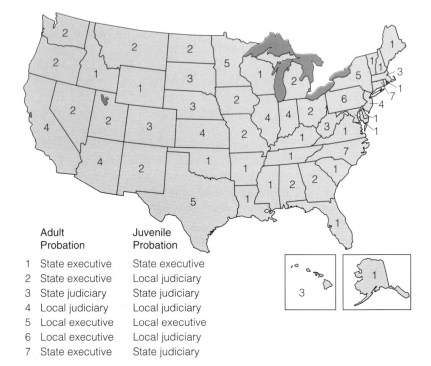

Figure 7.1 ■ **Seven Jurisdictional Arrangements for Probation Exist in the Fifty States.** The organization of probation varies depending on the traditions and politics of state and local governments.

Source: American Correctional Association, *ACA Directory 1992* (College Park, Md.: American Correctional Association, 1992).

	Adult Probation	Juvenile Probation
1	State executive	State executive
2	State executive	Local judiciary
3	State judiciary	State judiciary
4	Local judiciary	Local judiciary
5	Local executive	Local executive
6	Local executive	Local judiciary
7	State executive	State judiciary

community. Because decentralized probation draws its support from the community and from its city or county governments, it is able to provide more appropriate supervision for its clients and to make better use of existing community resources.

In contrast, centralization places authority for a state's probation activities with a single administrative body. Proponents of this approach assert that local probation has been characterized by low professionalism and a tendency to lag behind the times. State agencies, they argue, are larger, can train staff to take a variety of roles, and can implement broader programs with greater equality in supervision and services.

Who Should Administer Probation?

Though the recent trend has been away from judicially administered probation, many observers (especially those who seek greater accountability in probation) believe the proba-tion function rightfully belongs under the judiciary. The usual claim is that under judicial administration, probation is more responsive to the desires of the sentencing judge, who is more likely to scrutinize supervision when it is performed by judicial employees. It is also believed that probation officers' morale is higher when they work closely with judges.

Proponents of placing probation under the executive branch argue that the judiciary is ill prepared to manage a human service operation. To coordinate and upgrade the quality of human services, of which probation is a part, requires the full attention of professional public administrators. As the National Advisory Commission said in 1973, placing probation under the executive branch would result in better allocation of probation services, increased interaction and administrative coordination with corrections and allied human services, increased access to the budget process (legislature), and more appropriate service priorities.[9]

Probation officers work closely with judges, especially regarding sentencing options. In many jurisdictions judges want to know the progress of the offenders being supervised.

Should Probation Be Combined with Parole?

Because probation and parole are analogous services with similar investigation and supervision functions, many states have combined the two into a single agency. This approach takes advantage of efficiencies in hiring, training, and developing staff. It is believed that the professionalization of community supervision officers is promoted by such comprehensive community corrections approaches.

There are, however, subtle but important distinctions between probationers and parolees that some experts say are hard to sustain in a unified system. Probation clients ordinarily are less deeply involved in criminal lifestyles, and parole clients face the serious problems involved in reentering the community after incarceration (see Chapter 16).

These differences call for different handling, which some people believe can best be accomplished by separate agencies.

No solution to the problem of how to organize probation is at hand. Rather than searching for a single "best" way to organize probation, it may be more fruitful to look at how criminal justice services are generally operated in a state or region. In jurisdictions with a tradition of strong local government, decentralized probation under the executive branch may be the best alternative. In states that have typically provided services through centralized, large-scale bureaucracies, perhaps probation should be a part of such services. Likewise, a strong judiciary with a history of administrative competence may be the place to rest authority for probation if it is to be effective.

The Dual Role of Probation: Investigation and Supervision

Probation officers have traditionally performed two major functions: investigation and supervision. Investigation involves the preparation of a **presentence investigation (PSI)** to be used by the judge in sentencing an offender. Typically, the PSI is ordered by the court following the offender's conviction (often on a guilty plea). A date is set for sentencing the offender, and in the interim the probation officer conducts the investigation and prepares a report.

The PSI process typically begins with an interview of the newly convicted offender to obtain basic background information. The probation officer then seeks to verify, clarify, and explore the information derived from (or left out of) the initial interview. The final PSI document is a summary of what has been learned and an evaluation of the offender, often with a sentence recommendation.

Supervision begins once an offender is sentenced to probation. There is no standard way to describe the supervision process, because the policies and practices vary greatly from agency to agency. In general, supervision involves three steps:

1. A relationship is established with the offender and the roles of officer and offender are defined.

2. Certain supervision aims are pursued to help the offender comply with conditions established by the court (often directed at helping the offender confront significant needs or problems in his or her life).

3. On the basis of the offender's response to supervision, a decision is made on how to terminate probation. This decision may be early termination based on satisfactory adjustment, termination because the sentence has expired, or revocation because of a new conviction or violation of probation conditions set by the judge or probation officer.

This description of supervision is, of course, very general. As we point out later in this chapter, the leeway typically given officers in carrying out supervision makes management of this function very difficult. For this reason, many probation administrators have recently begun to require officers to use standardized offender classification and supervision techniques.

Investigation and supervision are divergent functions. In investigating the client and preparing a PSI, the probation officer is working primarily with other human service professionals—teachers, officials, psychologists, and so forth. There is often a sense of partnership with the judge: Both parties seek the best sentence and therefore value useful, accurate information on which to base the disposition. These relationships may reinforce the self-esteem of the officer. Moreover, there is a tangible product—the report—that can be a well-written, high-quality piece of work. Supervision, by contrast, is fraught with uncertainty and error. There are no standard solutions to the problems faced by most probationers, and the daily interactions with clients, many of whom are troubled and hard to manage, may provide little sense of worthwhile accomplishment. Further, there is seldom a tangible product; instead, work consists of a series of tasks loosely connected to eventual rehabilitative results.

This difference in the task structures of the two functions often puts informal pressure on probation officers to give investigation a higher priority than supervision. The quality of the investigation is more visible to superiors than the quality of supervision; in effect, then, "producing a sound, professionally appealing report has become more important than serving the client who is the subject of that report."[10]

---

presentence investigation (PSI)   An investigation and summary report of the background of a convicted offender, prepared to help the judge decide on an appropriate sentence.

Presentence Investigation Report

Date: May 13, 1994
Name: Matthew Martin
Address: Metropolis, Jefferson
County: Jefferson
Court #: 1775-1
Offense: Burglary I
Class: Felony A
Custody Status: Jail
Maximum Penalty: 20 years/$2,500
Detainers or Pending Charges: None known
Judge: Wilson Morgan
D.A.: Paula Harrison
Counsel: David Acorn
Plea: Not Guilty
Verdict: Guilty
Birth Date: 8/19/69
Height: 5'11"
Eyes: Brown
Age: 25
Weight: 198
Hair: Red
Race: White
Sex: Male
Marital Status: Single
Education: 3 years college
Citizenship: U.S.A.
Employment Status: Temporary leave
Concerned Agencies: None known
Place of Birth: Delta, Louisiana
Marks: Tattoo, right arm: "Born to Raise Hell"
No. of Dependents: None

Report Submitted by: Leslie Blue

Jefferson County Probation Department
State of Jefferson

The Honorable
Wilson Morgan   May 13, 1994

Jefferson County
Circuit Court   Court #1775-1
10 Main Avenue
Metropolis, Jefferson   99999

Dear Judge Morgan:

The following is the presentence report on Matthew Martin that you ordered on April 15, 1994.

Offense Summary

On February 13, 1994, Jefferson Police arrested Matthew Martin at the scene of a burglary. He was subsequently charged with Burglary I. On April 15, 1994, Jefferson County Circuit Court Jury found Mr. Martin guilty of the charge. He is in custody and sentencing is set for May 20, 1994, at 9:00 a.m.

Plea Bargain/Negotiations and Stipulations

N.A.

Official Version

On February 13, 1994, at approximately 7:09 p.m. Jefferson Police responded to a silent alarm at Petcare Animal Clinic, located at 17 Maybelle Dr. Upon arrival, the responding officers discovered Mr. Martin and Arthur James on the roof of the building. Mr. Martin had a pair of gloves, a screwdriver, and a pocketknife. The defendant refused to answer any questions without his attorney present. Mr. Martin and Mr. James were taken into custody.

Further investigation revealed that entry was made through a plastic-covered window. The plastic was cut away

Continued

FOCUS, *Continued*

from the window frame. Drawers and cabinets had been rummaged through, a wooden box had been pried open, and numerous burnt matches were found on the floor.

During an interview, Mr. Martin reported that he burglarized the veterinarian clinic to obtain records on his cat. He explained that he had brought his cat to the clinic a couple of weeks ago and did not have the money to pay the bill. It was his intention to remove the records on his cat, but he found the bookkeeping system to be very extensive and he was unable to find the file. He admitted to gaining entry by cutting the plastic on the window but refused to answer any further questioning. The police confirmed the fact that Mr. Martin's cat was treated at the Petcare Animal Clinic from 2/2/94 to 2/4/94.

Defendant's Version

Mr. Martin admitted to breaking into the animal clinic, but explained that he became "petrified" and decided to leave the building. At that point, the police came and he stated that he lay down and waited for them. The defendant related that he had been unemployed and was behind in rent. His cat acquired a respiratory disease and he took her to the veterinarian. Mr. Martin indicated that he gave the clinic $10 and was to pay them $40 at a later date. One evening, he and Mr. James were sitting around "chewing the fat" and he came up with the idea to break in the office and get the records. He admitted to entering the animal clinic by ripping the plastic-covered window.

Mr. Martin expressed his remorse and stated, "I don't blame anyone but myself." He related that he did not take the stand at his court hearing upon his attorney's suggestion and feels that this may jeopardize his position at the time of sentencing.

Accomplices/Codefendants

Criminal Circuit Court records indicate that on 4/10/94 Judge Carey issued a bench warrant for Mr. James's arrest. As of 5/8/94, the Court had not received a return of services.

Victim's Statement/Damages

Dale Rector, the receptionist at Petcare Animal Clinic, reported that although the office was badly vandalized, no items were noted to be missing with the exception of a screwdriver.

Prior Record

Conviction summary
Juvenile:

1. 11/3/83: Metropolis, Jefferson—Incorrigible, Beyond Parental Control—Committed to Danville School for Boys.

2. 6/27/84: Metropolis, Jefferson—Child Molesting—Returned to Danville School for Boys. The defendant had a five-year-old girl's clothes off and was fondling her genitals.

3. 8/29/85: Metropolis, Jefferson—Runaway, Burglary I—Returned to Danville School for Boys. Mr. Martin had run away from Danville and committed burglary.

4. 4/5/86: Bequinta, California—Carrying a Concealed Weapon and Runaway—Returned to School for Boys. Mr. Martin went to California and was picked up by police for carrying a concealed weapon.

Adult:

1. 1/5/89: Metropolis, Jefferson—Resisting Arrest, Theft II—The defendant indicated that he received ten days County Jail time.

2. 2/11/91: Metropolis, Jefferson—Burglary I—Pled guilty to Burglary II, sentenced to five years jail.

Records reveal that Mr. Martin broke into the Rialto Theater, took $900 and flew to Texas with the stolen money.

3. 3/15/91: Metropolis, Jefferson—Sodomy I—The defendant was sentenced to ten years jail to run concurrently with item number 2. The defendant engaged in sexual intercourse with a seven-year-old boy while he was released on recognizance for his burglary charge.

4. 3/25/91: Metropolis, Jefferson—Theft II, Menacing with a Knife. The defendant was found guilty of Theft II and sentenced to nine days County Jail time.

5. 2/13/94: Metropolis, Jefferson—Burglary I—Present offense, disposition pending.

Arrests not resulting in conviction

Juvenile:

1. 5/9/84: Metropolis, Jefferson—Vandalism and Burglary in a School—Disposition unknown.

2. 12/26/84: Metropolis, Jefferson—Shoplifting—No complaint.

3. 1/21/85: Metropolis, Jefferson—Unauthorized Use of a Vehicle—Released.

Adult:

1. 2/12/89: Metropolis, Jefferson—Theft II—Dismissed.

2. 10/26/90: Metropolis, Jefferson—Schedule IV Drug Possession—No misdemeanor complaint.

Driving record

Division of Motor Vehicle records reveal that Mr. Martin's driver's license is currently invalid. His license was suspended for Failure to Appear at a Hearing. He incurred citations for Expired Registration, No Driver's License, and Failure to Obey Traffic Control Device.

Prior Parole, Probation, and Institutional Performance

Mr. Martin was committed to Danville School for Boys 11/3/83 for Incorrigibility and Beyond Parental Control. During the five years he spent at Danville School for Boys, he had at least two runaways and incurred new charges each time.

Mr. Martin was received at Jefferson State Correctional Institution on 4/11/91 and again on 6/27/91, for a period of five years and ten years concurrent on charges of Burglary II and Sodomy I. He was paroled to Washington County on 10/5/92 with conditions. On 2/13/93, his parole officer, Larry Prouse, submitted a special report to the Parole Board informing them that Mr. Martin was arrested and charged with Theft II. The charges were later dismissed. The defendant's parole was continued on February 28, 1993. The defendant had been receiving mental health treatment with Dr. Cathart. Through Dr. Cathart's recommendation, Mr. Martin reported to the State Hospital on 3/8/93. The hospital would not admit the defendant, and he was subsequently referred to the Division of Mental Health. During his parole supervision he was enrolled as a student at Metropolis Community College.

On 3/25/93, Mr. Martin was again arrested. He was charged with Theft II and Menacing with a Knife. A special report was again submitted by his probation officer, and Mr. Martin's parole program evaluation was considered as "poor." Washington County detectives indicated that Mr. Martin was involved in at least twenty-five burglaries and thefts in Lincoln and Washington counties. His former parole officer, Larry, recommends that Mr. Martin be sent back to the penitentiary. While Mr. Martin was incarcerated, he was involved in the sex offender group. Dr. Williams, psychiatrist, indicated that Mr. Martin "has learned some insight, and through some college classes in psychology and sexual education and school, he has

Continued

learned that he is pretty much like everyone else except for his acting out with pedophilia. Apparently he has made a great deal of growth in this institution, especially in the last eight months."

Family History

Father: Bernard Martin died in 1974 from chronic alcoholism. The defendant related that his father was in the United States Army for twenty-eight years.

Stepfather: Willie Olsen, age unknown, is currently unemployed. The defendant related that his stepfather and his mother had been living together since 1979 and were divorced only recently.

Mother: Bernice Olsen, 51, lives in Delbarten, Jefferson, and is employed as a waitress. The defendant indicated that she and his natural father were divorced when he was very young.

Sister: Lucy Daly, 30, lives in Wilson, Jefferson. She is employed as a secretary. She is divorced and has three children.

Sister: Dettie Conwald, 28, also lives in Wilson, Jefferson. She is a housewife and has a part-time job with a dentist. She is married and has three children.

Brother: Barry Martin, 27, lives in Jefferson; address and employment are unknown to the defendant. The defendant related that his brother is married and has one child.

Brother: David Martin, 20, lives in Metropolis, Jefferson. The defendant related that he is employed as a painter, is single, and has no children.

Stepsister: Melissa Olsen, 12, lives with her mother in Wilson, Jefferson. She attends junior high school.

The Defendant: Matthew Martin was born to the union of Bernard Martin and Bernice Cathwall in Delta, Louisiana, on August 19, 1969. His parents were divorced when he was approximately five years old, and the defendant remained with his mother. The defendant's mother married Willie Olsen when the defendant was twelve years old. His stepfather was described as a "strict disciplinarian" and his mother as an "extremely permissive, indulgent person." Correctional files indicate that Mr. Martin's deviant behavior began at the age of twelve. State Prison files report that Mr. Martin had been kidnapped and sexually molested for three days when he was six years old. The defendant related that this "messed up" his sexual orientations since that time. He indicated that he does not remember this episode, which he learned of from his psychologist.

Mr. Martin moved to Metropolis in 1974 and indicates that he has lived within the area in various residences since that time.

Marital History

Mr. Martin has never been married.

Education

The defendant reports that he has received forty-four college credit hours, being registered in educational courses at Jefferson State Prison and college courses at Metropolis Community College subsequent to his release. He relates that he was enrolled in General Studies courses. He related that, prior to his college credits, he received his high school diploma while incarcerated at State Prison.

Health

Physical: The defendant related that his physical health is good and that he suffers from no handicaps. He stated that he is allergic to penicillin.

Mental: A psychiatric evaluation stated, "He does not appear to be psychologically ill, only anxious, and has a grossly immoral character." Another psychological report indicated that "Matthew does not belong in Danville School for Boys. He is certainly much more a candidate for State Hospital."

Mr. Martin was involved in the Sexual Offenders Program while incarcerated. He related that his psychologists gave him a "clean bill of health." He related that he saw Dr. Cathart for nine months while he was incarcerated and two months subsequent to his release. Dr. Cathart believes that Mr. Martin no longer needs mental health treatment.

Alcohol: The defendant related that he began alcohol consumption at the age of seventeen. He related that he drinks once a week "at the most." He stated that he has never had an alcohol problem and has never received any alcohol abuse counseling.

Drugs: The defendant related that he began experimenting with drugs at the age of seventeen. He indicated that he received drug abuse counseling while he was incarcerated and explained that his attorney told him to admit to a drug abuse problem to get him into a treatment program. He indicated that this did not work out the way he wanted it, since he had no drug abuse problem. Mr. Martin denies any current usage of illicit drugs.

Employment

October 15, 1992 to Present (Approximately two and one-half years, intermittently)—Paint Contractor. The defendant related that he and his brother-in-law are painting subcontractors. He related that when he is working, he earns $5.00 per hour working 55 hours a week. We were unable to verify employment information at the time of this writing. His parole officer related that this job was only part-time and described it as "fishy."

June 1992 to August 1992 (Approximately three months)—Camp Counselor. The defendant related that he was a youth camp counselor for the summer, earning $800.00 per month. This information was verified on 5/11/94.

October 1991 to January 1992 (Approximately four months)—Nurse's Aide. His employer indicated that he was employed as a nurse's aide, earning $3.25 per hour. The defendant indicated that he quit subsequent to being accused of stealing a purse. Employment verification was made on 5/11/94.

Military Service

Mr. Martin has never been in the military.

Financial Condition

Mr. Martin reported that his income averages between $400.00 and $600.00 per month. He related that he pays $250.00 per month in rent and $80.00 per month in utilities. He indicated that he has no car and stated that he has no other assets nor outstanding debts.

Current Situation

Mr. Martin lives by himself but also spends a great deal of time with his girlfriend, Sheila Vettor. He says that they are considering marriage but that the prospect is unsettling to him. He reports he has few regular friends.

Psychological Evaluation

This twenty-five-year-old white male was interviewed and administered a battery of psychological tests in the Jefferson County Jail on May 12, 1994. During the psychological evaluation, he was initially somewhat sleepy, distracted, and wary. As the interview progressed, Mr. Martin became quite articulate, intelligent, and extraordinarily alert.

There is a high level of vigilance and distrust in this man's overt behavior that would be highly suggestive of underlying emotional or psychological problems. This perhaps is exemplified by the fact that Mr. Martin refused to complete any formal psychological tests presented to him by this examiner. He said he didn't trust psychologists and he didn't trust the criminal justice system; he believes

Continued

the type of questions and procedures that psychologists offered were stupid and of little value. He said he had taken many psychological tests in the past, and no one ever seemed to give him any help following these tests. He insisted that it was a waste of time.

Mr. Martin went on to say that he really didn't care what happened as the result of this refusing to take the tests. He noted, "I'm unique. I don't want to be categorized. I just want to be left alone. I never want to see another cop or another judge or another psychologist again. I hate tests. I am a unique individual. People may believe I am institutionalized. I am not institutionalized. I am not a criminal. Lots of things have changed in my life. I have stayed out of trouble for three years. I have a girlfriend. I don't hang around with the same kind of people I used to. I have taken all of the psychological tests before, and I refuse to be categorized."

Mr. Martin also indicated that he received an extended amount of psychotherapy from Dr. Cathart regarding some underlying sexual problems, and he signed a release indicating that I could talk to Dr. Cathart about his treatment. This examiner was unable to reach Dr. Cathart prior to the dictation of this report.

Mr. Martin was able to discuss some of his history. He explained that he was born in Delta, Louisiana, but traveled all over the country because his father was in the service. In 1974 he came to Metropolis and subsequently spent some time in Danville. He reported that he had a "nervous breakdown" in 1983 or 1984 when he was at Danville. According to his account, he was told by a staff member that he would never again return home. As the result of this information, he became extremely hysterical and in spite of injections of tranquilizing medication, they were unable to calm him and so he was transferred to the State Hospital where he spent some time. Mr. Martin also openly admitted that he spent much of a five-year sentence in the State Prison as the result of a burglary and sodomy conviction. He noted that while there, he participated in their sex offender program for about a year and then followed up with about four months of psychotherapy with Dr. Williams in the community.

This examiner's impression is that Mr. Martin is a stubborn, control-avoidant, and paranoid individual. It was also indicated that he probably has above-average intellectual abilities and he has taught himself to be highly tuned to the slightest intrusion upon his sense of independence and autonomy. Even though some of his suspicions and distrust of the mental health and criminal justice system may be justified, he seems unable to escape from the sweeping generalization that everybody that he meets is going to assume a persecutory role. He did indicate that he did have a considerable amount of trust in Dr. Cathart and that he would allow Dr. Cathart to report openly regarding his course in treatment.

Mr. Martin is the type of person who tends to provoke the most unsympathetic types of sentiments from people in the criminal justice system. As long as he remains in the system, neither he nor the system will have much relief from that antagonism. In many ways, Mr. Martin's desired outcome of being free from contact with the system is the most desirable one for the system as well. Unfortunately, the way in which he goes about trying to avoid the system is highly ineffective.

Diagnosis: Borderline personality

Prognosis: Guarded

Case Supervision Plan

Supervising Officer: Leslie Blue   **Client's Name: Matthew Martin**

Date: 6/12/94

Supervision Level _X_ Intensive ___ Regular ___ Minimal

Client's Supervision Objectives	Target Date	Resource
1. To obtain full-time employment	6/30/94	Probation Officer; Metropolis Employment Center
2. To enroll in college on a part-time basis; at least one course per semester	9/1/94	Probation Officer; Metropolis Junior College
3. To have no contact with Arthur James while on probation	N.A.	Probation Officer
4. To discuss with girlfriend the nature of their relationship in order to clarify whether to marry	N.A.	Metropolis Community Mental Health Center

Special Conditions:
1. Probationer will seek and cooperate with mental health treatment.
2. Probationer will make $500 restitution to victim.

To circumvent this problem, large probation departments often assign some officers exclusively to supervision and others to investigation only. While there are some obvious efficiencies in this approach, there are inefficiencies as well. The officer who supervises a client must learn much of the information that has already been discovered by the presentence officer. Similarly, when probationers are convicted of new offenses, it is easier for the supervisory officer to write a PSI, given his or her familiarity with the case. Ironically, specialization does not necessarily protect the supervision function: Many times the best staff members are assigned to the PSI units and top priority is given to maintaining an adequate PSI work force, even in the face of unwieldy supervision caseloads.

Nevertheless, it is much easier to manage a probation system whose workers are specialized. Accountability for the timeliness and accuracy of PSIs is enhanced, while the operation of supervision routines according to agency policies can be more easily ensured. Therefore, the trend is toward specialization of these functions, almost as if they were two different jobs.

The Investigation Function

The first role of probation we discuss is that of investigation. We examine the PSI—its purpose and content—and discuss its typical uses.

Purpose

The primary purpose of the presentence investigation is to help the judge select an appropriate sentence for the offender. Among its secondary purposes are to help with the eventual classification decisions regarding probation, institutions, and parole agencies that may encounter the offender; to aid in treatment planning; to aid parole decisions; and to serve as a document for systematic research.

Despite its many other uses, the true value of the PSI lies in its role in the sentencing process. Its importance is compounded by the fact that there are no uniformly accepted guidelines or rationales for sentencing. Individual judges, even those in the same court system, may vary in the weight they give to factors in the case. The PSI must therefore be comprehensive enough to meet the information needs of judges with a variety of sentencing perspectives.

The concept of rehabilitation requires an assessment of the offender's treatment needs. It is generally agreed that imprisonment has limited rehabilitative value, so in practice a commitment to rehabilitation poses two questions: Does the offender have special problems, circumstances, or needs that led to the criminal behavior? Can these problems be overcome by community services combined with careful supervision so as to prevent further criminal involvement?

Over and above a concern for the offender's rehabilitation, there has been growing interest in protection of the community. With the idea of risk control in mind, the probation officer assesses the likelihood that the offender will continue criminal behavior if allowed to remain in the community. Estimates of risk are based on degree of prior criminal involvement, stability of the offender's lifestyle, and pattern of prior adjustment to correctional treatment.

The just desserts orientation to sentencing requires that the probation officer take a completely different tack in preparing the PSI. Instead of emphasizing offender need or risk, the PSI must uncover the seriousness of the offense. Aggravating or mitigating factors in the offense, such as wanton violence or lack of harm to the victim, are described to present the degree of seriousness of the crime. A judge who takes this approach might then consider restitution and community service in setting a punishment commensurate with the offense.

In practice, two circumstances constrain the influence of the PSI in sentencing. For one thing, because goals are unclear, judges often use a mixture of the values of rehabilitation, risk control, and just deserts, maintaining a balance among these goals. Rather than pursue a single value in sentencing, judges ordinarily ask a complicated question: If this offender is not a risk to the community, is there some rehabilitative reason to keep him or her in the community—a reason strong enough to overcome the objection that probation tends to depreciate the seriousness of the offense?

The second constraint is plea bargaining. When the sentence has already been proposed in the process of negotiation between the prosecutor and the defense attorney, the role of the PSI is altered. It no longer serves as the basis of the judge's decision but is used instead to determine whether the negotiated agreement is appropriate.

Contents

For many years the ideal PSI was thought to be a lengthy narrative description of the offense and offender, culminating in a recommendation in regard to the sentence and a justification of that recommendation. Early manuals for the writing of PSIs stressed length and breadth of coverage. Now, however, people are questioning the assumption that more is better. While long PSIs make interesting reading and may be relatively satisfying to prepare, information theory suggests that short PSIs are not necessarily less useful.

A large body of research on human processing of information suggests that the number of information items (facts or data) a person can normally consider simultaneously in making a decision varies from five to nine, depending on the person and the problem. When this number of items is exceeded and so much information is included in a message that it interferes with the recipient's ability to process it, the person undergoes *information overload*. Information overload seems to be associated with both a decrease in the accuracy of judgments made and, interestingly, increased confidence in them. Under conditions of overload, apparently the decision maker perceives *redundant information* (information that simply repeats facts presented earlier) as new information and gives it more weight than it deserves. In addition, *noise* (information unrelated to the problem, although it may appear to be important) is not distinguished from relevant information. The implication is ominous: No judge is able to take all of the information contained in a lengthy, detailed PSI into consideration when determining a sentence. So different judges are likely to consider different information and assign inappropriate importance to some facts in the PSI. Further, a judge may have unwarranted confidence in the sentencing decision.

Information theory is supported by the experiences of probation officers who have seen the judges skim through the long PSIs they prepared. The judges search for a few pertinent items and then read the sentencing recommendation.

The recent trend has been toward a shortened, directed, and standardized PSI format. This approach may seem less professional, but in practice it places even greater responsibility on the probation officer. Early in the investigation process the officer will probably develop an idea of the disposition that fits the case. This disposition is then constantly tested against new data on the offender as the investigation continues. Should something call into question the original tentative judgment, the officer reviews the entire case. A detailed PSI will

occasionally be necessary, but usually the officer's summary of the key factors contains the information most significant to the judge. The process requires more skill than the commonly used large-form PSI, but it can be considerably more efficient.

Related to the amount of information in the PSI are its validity and reliability. Although the terms have more precise meanings in the social sciences, for our purposes we may think of *validity* as the degree to which information is an accurate representation of the reality of the situation and of *reliability* as the degree to which other investigators would come to the same conclusion about the facts (or the degree to which the same investigator would make the same sorts of observations and reach the same conclusions in similar cases). Validity and reliability are obviously important for the PSI, for the sentencing decision ought not to be based on invalid or unreliable information.

How do probation officers improve validity and reliability? There are two techniques. Validity is improved by the process of *verification:* Before information is put into the PSI, it is cross-checked with some other source for accuracy. If the offender states during the PSI interview that he or she has no problem with drinking, for example, the investigator questions the offender's family, companions, and employer before writing "No apparent problem" in the PSI. The officer can also improve reliability by avoiding vague conclusions about the case. For instance, rather than describe the offender as *immature* (a term that is subject to various interpretations and thus is of doubtful reliability), the PSI writer might describe the offender's observed behaviors that suggest immaturity: poor attendance at work, lack of understanding of the seriousness of the offense, and so forth.

Recommendations

The recommendation is a controversial aspect of the PSI because a person without authority to sentence the offender is nevertheless suggesting what the sentence should be. For this reason, not all probation systems include a recommendation in the PSI. Yet there is a well-established tradition of sentence recommendations by nonjudicial court actors; normally the judge solicits recommendations from the defense and prosecution. The probation officer's recommendation is but one of many that the judge routinely accepts. But what the probation officer says may carry extra weight because it is a presumably unbiased evaluation of the offender based on thorough research by someone who understands the usefulness of probation and is familiar with community resources. These considerations may explain why judges so often follow the recommendations in the PSI.

Studies of the congruence of the PSI recommendation and the judicial sentence find a range of agreement from 70 percent to over 90 percent.[11] Of course, it is hard to know whether judges are following the officers or whether the officers' experience has given them the ability to come up with recommendations the judges will select.

If the reason for the congruence between the probation officer's recommendation and the sentence imposed is the judge's confidence in the officer's analysis, that confidence may be misplaced. One evaluation found that "in only a few instances did the offenders they recommended for probation behave significantly better than those they recommended for prison."[12] Perhaps, the study speculated, this prognostic inaccuracy arose because officers did not have time to verify information reported in the PSI because of their heavy workloads. For data on the relationship between recidivism and PSI recommendations, see Table 7.1.

The recommendation may be most useful when there is a plea bargaining agreement that includes a sentence. In such a case, the PSI is a critical check on the acceptability of the negotiated settlement, permitting the judge to determine whether any factors in the offense or in the offender's background might indicate that the agreement should be rejected.

Disclosure

In view of the importance of the PSI to the sentencing decision, one would think that the defendant would have a right to see it. After all, it may contain inadvertent irrelevancies or inaccuracies that the defense would want to dispute at the sentencing hearing. Nevertheless, in many states the defense does not receive a copy of the report. The case most often cited in this regard is *Williams* v. *New York,* in which the judge imposed a death sentence on the basis of evidence in the confidential PSI despite the jury's recommendation of a life sentence.[13] The Supreme Court upheld the judge's decision to deny the defense access to the report, although without such access the defense was incapable of challenging its contents at the sentencing hearing.

Cases and state law since 1949 have reduced the original restrictive impact of *Williams*. At least one circuit court has held, for example, that illegally seized evidence excluded from a trial cannot be referred to in the PSI.[14] And legislation in sixteen states requires full disclosure of the PSI. In the other states, the practice is generally to "cleanse" the report and then disclose it. Cleansing involves the deletion of two kinds of statements: (1) confidential comments from a private citizen that, if known to the offender, might result in danger to the citizen, and (2) clinical statements or evaluations that might be damaging to the offender if disclosed. Moreover, many judges allow the defense to present a written challenge of any disclosed contents of the PSI.

Private PSIs

Private investigative firms have recently begun to provide judges with presentence investigation reports. These firms work in one of two ways. Some contract with defendants to conduct comprehensive background checks and provide judges with creative sentencing options as alternatives to incarceration. In this approach, often called *client-specific planning,* the

Table 7.1 ■ **Probationers Rearrested and Reconvicted Compared with the PSI Recommendation Concerning Probation.** These data raise questions about the sentencing recommendations of probation officers. Do you detect differences between their recommendation and the probationer's rearrest and reconviction?

Original conviction crime	Rearrested		Reconvicted of any crime		Reconvicted of violent crime	
	PSI recommends prison	PSI recommends probation	PSI recommends prison	PSI recommends probation	PSI recommends prison	PSI recommends probation
Drugs	65%	52%	35%	34%	5%	12%
Property	67	68	60[a]	51	19	13
Violent	65	56	53	44	29	27
All offenses combined	67	63	52	50	22	19

Source: Adapted from Joan Petersilia, Susan Turner, James Kahan, and Joyce Peterson, *Granting Felons Probation: Public Risks and Alternatives* (Santa Monica, Calif.: Rand Corporation, 1985), p. 40. Copyright by Rand Corporation.

[a]Difference between the percentage recommended for and against probation is significant at $p < .5$.

agency serves as an advocate for the defendant at the sentencing stage. In the second approach, the court contracts directly with a private investigator to provide a neutral PSI in lieu of the traditional version prepared by a probation officer.

Privately conducted PSIs have sparked controversy. Because client-specific planning is paid for by the defendant, many people view it as an advantage for upper- and middle-class offenders who can afford the special consideration the advocacy report provides. Often it is the white-collar offender who can make the best case for creative sentences. (Richard Nixon's convicted former aide John Ehrlichman offered to do free legal work with Native Americans in place of going to prison, but his suggestion was rejected.) Their concerns are well-taken; the advocates of private PSIs point out that their reports often result in less severe sentences for their clients.

The neutral PSI also raises serious issues. Advocates say that private investigators do what the probation department does—only better.[15] Yet critics question whether private firms ought to be involved in the quasi-judicial function of making sentence recommendations. Moreover, the liability of private investigators for the accuracy and relevance of the information they provide to government agencies such as courts is unclear. Finally, it is quite likely that private PSIs, when purchased by the court, cost the taxpayer more than the traditional public alternative.

The Supervision Function

Just as there are no universally accepted standards for the investigation of offenders by probation officers, neither are there universally accepted standards for their supervision. Indeed, nearly everywhere both probation officers and clients enjoy wide latitude. To help you understand

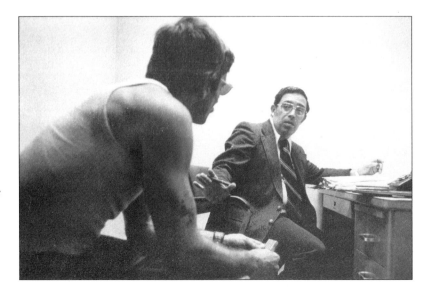

Probation supervision includes checking to see that the conditions of the sentence are being observed and providing assistance to offenders in the community.

how this latitude is exercised in practice, we will describe the three major elements of supervision: the officer, the offender, and the bureaucracy.

The Officer

The probation officer faces role conflict in virtually every aspect of the job. Most of this conflict has its genesis in the uneasy combination of two responsibilities: to enforce the law and to help the offender. While the responsibilities may often be compatible, just as frequently they do not fit together very well.

The chief conflict between the officer's two roles arises from the use of power and authority. In human relations, these terms have very specific meanings. *Power* is the ability to force a person to do something he or she does not want to do. *Authority* is the ability to influence a person's actions in a desired direction without resort to force. Thus a person who chooses to exercise power in a relationship can almost always be shown to lack authority.

The problem of power and authority is a thorny one for probation officers. Officers are expected to exercise the power of law in controlling offenders under their care. This is one reason that in many jurisdictions probation officers are legally classified as "peace officers," with the power of arrest. Yet the actual power of the role is less than it seems: Short of the formal power to arrest or hold probationers, there is normally little that probation officers can do to force compliance with the law.

The lack of substantive power explains why probation officers rely heavily on their authority in supervising offenders: It is a more efficient and ultimately more effective tool. The techniques of authority in probation are similar to those of social casework, but many people have questioned their applicability in a role that is permeated by the power of law. They point out that the principles of social work have long been based on the concept of self-determination, which allows clients to decide the nature, goals, and duration of the intervention—a condition that is not always feasible in the probation setting.

Despite such skepticism, professionals have tried to develop an understanding of how probation officers might use authority as a positive tool. Shankar Yelaja, for example, has identified various types of authority used by probation officers in their work.[16] *Irrational authority* is based solely on power. *Rational authority* derives from the officer's competence in deciding on the best approach to take. *Psychological authority,* the most influential type, is acceptance by the client and officer of each other's interest in jointly determined goals and strategies of supervision.

When the probation officer is most effective, a combination of types of authority is used in lieu of the formal power of the role to help the probationer to maintain a crime-free lifestyle. As one observer put it: "One of the first major accomplishments of treatment comes about when the offender becomes aware, both intellectually and emotionally, that the officer represents not only authority with the power to enforce certain restraints and restrictions but that [the officer] is also able to offer material, social and psychological adjustment aids."[17]

This concept is difficult to execute and often complicated. The officer is attempting to develop the offender's trust and confidence so that through a measure of rational or (it is hoped) psychological authority, the offender will be guided to change patterns of living that tend to promote involvement in crime. Yet both parties know that the officer has raw power to be exercised should the offender falter. Often the point comes across as "let me help you—or else!" This kind of mixed message leads to manipulation by both the officer and the probationer and may make the supervision relationship seem inconsistent.

Probation officers often take refuge from the complicated nature of their authority by defining their role conflict in very simplistic terms, as if they were forced to choose between two incompatible sets of values: protecting the public versus helping offenders, law enforcement versus social work, and so on. But any simplistic classification does not resolve the ambiguities of the probation officer's job. The officer is frequently given only vague guidance as to the competing aims of supervision; as a result, approaches to clients can indeed be inconsistent, and wide disparities exist.

These disparities can complicate the job since probation officers are now held accountable for any abridgment of the community's safety that occurs as a result of any act of theirs committed or neglected in the performance of their duties. In practice, this means that reasonable efforts must be taken to monitor the behavior of clients and to show particular care with those whose backgrounds make them potential risks to the community. The most famous case that establishes this principle involved a probationer who had been convicted of sexual assault. His probation officer helped him get a job as a maintenance worker in an apartment complex, a position that gave him access to keys to various apartments. In placing the probationer, the officer withheld his client's past record from the employer. The probationer sexually assaulted several apartment residents, who later sued the probation

Offenders sentenced to probation are told to report to their officer on a given date. During this initial interview the officer spells out the rules under which the probationer is to live and assesses his or her housing and employment situation.

officer for his cover-up of the probationer's record. The court held in favor of the victims, ruling probation officers liable for their conduct as government employees.[18]

The liability of probation officers (and parole officers as well) is a new area of law, one that is not yet well formulated. The chief significance of the emergence of this issue is that operational procedures in probation become even more important. To defend against possible allegations of misconduct, probation officers need more than ever to document in writing the actions they are taking with their clients so that they can meet a potential challenge of the reasonableness of the actions.

The Offender

The public tends to underestimate the influence of the offender's response to supervision and the nature and effectiveness of the supervision relationship. It should be obvious that offenders do not respond uniformly to supervision, but this fact has had little effect on probation operations. Some researchers believe

that the officer should tailor the style of supervision to the offender to bring about the most beneficial change.

One study of probationers' responses to supervision provides similar conclusions. The investigators identified four supervision strategies:

1. *Selective intervention strategies* are designed to help clients cope with the temporary situational crisis that led to involvement in crime.

2. *Environmental structure strategies* attempt to develop daily living skills so that clients can reduce their associations with criminal peers.

3. *Casework/control strategies* attempt to overcome serious problems with stability, particularly in emotional, personal, and substance-abuse areas.

4. *Limit-setting strategies* provide for close monitoring of conditions of probation and assertive enforcement of the requirements of supervision.[19]

This classification scheme underscores the importance of selecting appropriate ways to

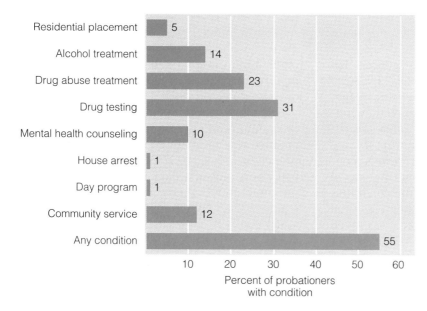

Figure 7.2 ■ **Special Conditions Imposed on Probationers.** The problems probationers bring to the probation system vary from one jurisdiction to the next.

Source: Mark Cuniff and Mary Shelton, "Variations in Felony Probation: Persons Under Supervision in Thirty-Two Urban and Suburban Counties" (Washington, D.C.: Criminal Justice Planners Association, March 1991), p. 24.

handle probationers. Consider, for example, how ineffective a supportive, nonaggressive selective intervention approach would be with an offender who needs the control implied by a limit-setting strategy.

Most probationers believe they have little influence on the supervision process. Though probation officers' power is limited, it often seems to offenders much greater than it actually is. Moreover, officers decide on the style of supervision—whether relatively supportive or controlling—and the offenders have few direct ways of influencing even this decision. Therefore, probationers often perceive themselves to be relatively impotent against the potentially arbitrary decisions of the officers.

It is not surprising, then, that probationers commonly resent their status, even when most people think they should be grateful for "another chance." Many probation officers try to blunt the indignity by involving the probationer in determining the goals and strategies of supervision. Rather than simply requiring the offender to seek assistance, the officer brings the client into a problem-solving process. Such strategies are aimed at reducing the perceived discrepancy between the power of the officer and the powerlessness of the client.

The Bureaucracy

Ultimately, all supervision activities take place in the context of an organization, and the organization imposes both formal and informal constraints on them. Formal constraints are the "legal conditions" of probation, whether standard, punitive, or treatment; these are set by the court or written into law. *Standard conditions*, imposed on all probationers, include such requirements as reporting to the probation office, notifying the agency of any change of address, remaining gainfully employed, and not leaving the jurisdiction without permission. *Punitive conditions*, including fines, community service, and some forms of restitution, are designed to increase the restrictiveness or painfulness of probation. A punitive condition is usually established to reflect the seriousness of the offense. *Treatment conditions* are imposed to force the probationer to deal with a significant problem or need, such as substance abuse (see Figure 7.2). An offender who fails to comply with a condition is usually subject to incarceration; thus, one main purpose of the officer's supervision is to enforce compliance with the conditions.

Until recently most probation agencies had to enforce large numbers of conditions of all types, perhaps because the sentencing judges believed that the more conditions they imposed, the greater the control over the offender. In fact, the reverse is often true: If there are numerous conditions, some quite meaningful to the offender, and others not at all meaningful, the credibility of all the conditions is reduced. If the offender disobeys a trivial condition, the probation officer may well choose to look the other way. The probationer may then wonder if any conditions will be enforced. Moreover, scattershot conditions confuse the supervision rationale and make the power of supervision and the officer's authority to assist the client even more vague.

The current trend is toward restricted imposition of conditions. It is thought that because probation conditions are both punishments imposed by the state and restrictions on personal liberty, they should reflect the purposes of law. A major consideration is that the conditions should be proportional to the seriousness of the offense. Treatment conditions should be made mandatory only after failure to cooperate. But how can a condition be "imposed voluntarily" and later be "made mandatory"? Its very existence is a mandate to both the offender and the officer. Which conditions should be set for which offenders? And why?

The formal constraints imposed by the organization often pale before the informal constraints imposed by the bureaucracy. Three such pressures have been identified: case control, case management structure, and competence.[20]

Case control pressures emerge because judges, prosecutors, administrators, and community members all expect probation officers somehow to "make" probationers abide by the conditions and legal requirements of probation. But there is little the officer can do to "make" the offender cooperate, for real power (such as

the threat of revocation) may be limited. Consequently, officers are forced to rely on their discretion and individualistic supervision style, often minimizing or deliberately ignoring formal requirements in order to persuade the offender to cooperate.

Similarly, the frequently large numbers of probationers and the unpredictability of the job produce a need for case management structure (see Figure 7.3). It is achieved by means of paperwork documenting the officer's activities on cases and by such routines as scheduled reporting days (when offenders come for office visits) and field days (when officers make home visits). But the demands of the caseload do not always correspond to the case management routines, nor do documented activities always lead to positive results. And so the management of work through regular schedules and operating procedures limits the creativity, intensity, and responsiveness of the supervision effort.

The pressure for competence can be demoralizing for probation staff. It is simply not possible for officers to be effective with all their cases. There is no surefire approach to take with offenders. At best, the officer is faced with a variety of approaches that may or may not work. Add to these uncertainties the fact that the officer typically receives little feedback about successes but much about failures, and what you have is an unintentional but systematic attack on the officer's sense of competence. Many officers react with cynical, defensive stances: Probationers cannot be changed unless they want to be; probationers are losers; and so forth. When several probation officers within an office develop this kind of cynicism, their negativism can pervade the entire working atmosphere.

In sum, the supervision role is best understood as a complex interaction between officers (who vary in style, knowledge, and philosophy) and offenders (who vary in responsiveness and need for supervision) in a bureaucratic organization that imposes significant formal and informal constraints on the work. In light of such complexity, it is not easy to assess the effectiveness of probation supervision.

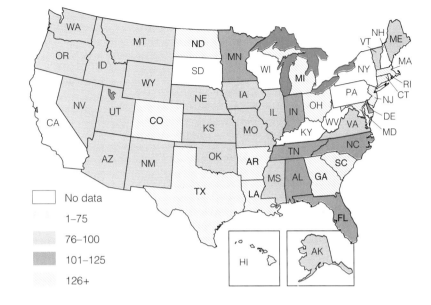

Figure 7.3 ■ **Probation Officer's Caseload Size, by State.** The size of a probation officer's caseload tells us something about how much probation is valued in a state or community.

Source: Bureau of Justice Statistics, *Sourcebook of Criminal Justice Statistics* (Washington, D.C.: U.S. Department of Justice, 1992), pp. 81–82.

No data
1–75
76–100
101–125
126+

The Effectiveness of Supervision

For many years experts believed that supervision could be made more effective by reducing the size of the caseloads being managed by probation officers. They reasoned that smaller caseloads would allow the officers to devote more attention to each client, thus improving the services provided. Frequently cited standards called for caseloads of thirty-five to fifty persons, though such figures had never been justified by empirical study. During the 1960s and 1970s dozens of experiments were conducted to find the most effective size of a caseload. Yet a review of those studies concluded that "caseload reduction alone does not significantly reduce recidivism in adult probationers."[21]

Why don't smaller caseloads improve the effectiveness of supervision? Perhaps the assumption that "more supervision is better supervision" is too simplistic, for it fails to take into account the significant elements of super-

vision. It seems that "the nature of the supervision experience, the classification of offenders, officers, and types of treatment, and the social systems of the corrections agency" have more impact than the size of the caseload.[22]

Case Management Systems

Case management systems have been developed to focus the supervision effort of probation officers on client's problems, identified using a standardized assessment of probationer risk and needs. In 1980 the National Institute of Corrections (a division of the Federal Bureau of Prisons) developed what it referred to as a "model system" of case management. This model has five principal components—statistical risk assessment, systematic needs assessment, contact supervision standards, case planning, and workload accounting—each of which is designed to increase the effectiveness of probation supervision.

1. *Statistical risk assessment:* Since fully accurate predictions are impossible, there is pressure to be conservative when assess-

ing risk, considering the client a risk even when the evidence is ambiguous. This tendency to *overprediction* (estimating that a person's chance of being arrested is greater than it actually is) means officers will spend their time with clients who really need very little supervision. The use of statistically developed risk assessment instruments reduces overprediction and improves the accuracy risk classifications.

2. *Systematic needs assessments:* Subjective assessments of clients' needs often suffer from lack of information and even biases on the part of the probation officer. Systematic needs assessments, which require an evaluation of the client on a list of potential needs areas, is a more comprehensive way to determine what problems the probation officer should address.

3. *Contact supervision standards:* Probation officers have an understandable tendency to avoid "problem" clients and spend more time with the ones who cooperate with supervision. In terms of the aims of probation, however, more time should be focused on the cases with the greatest risk and needs. Using the assessments, offenders are classified into supervision "levels." Each level has a minimum supervision contact requirement; those of the highest risk or need receive the most supervision.

4. *Case planning:* The broad discretion given probation officers to supervise their clients leads to idiosyncracies in approaches. By having the probation officer indicate the supervision plan in writing, a better fit is created between the client's problems and the officer's supervision strategy, and the officer's work is more easily evaluated.

5. *Workload accounting:* Since cases pose very different issues in the supervision they need, simply counting cases can misrepresent the overall work load of an agency. A better system for staffing the agency is provided by using time studies to estimate the number of staff needed to carry out the supervision policies.

The model has enjoyed widespread support from probation and parole administrators. In just over ten years since it was first announced, the model has been adopted in a number of countries and is now considered standard practice in virtually every large probation agency in the United States.

Structured case management systems also help the probation staff to determine more reliably which clients need intensive supervision, special services, or traditional probation monitoring. Research suggests that when all three components of the system are used in combination, probation can become more effective.

The results of an evaluation of this kind of system conducted in Texas are shown in Figure 7.4. The study compared matched jurisdictions, some of which used the new system. The structured case management system had lower revocation rates, especially for higher-risk cases. This finding suggests that the key to effective supervision does lie in differential supervision: giving some offenders more intensive supervision, and others less, and targeting the supervision effort to precise services and objectives for higher-risk probationers.

Special Supervision Programs

The needs of probationers vary dramatically. Sex offenders require different supervision strategies than do cocaine addicts; mentally ill offenders must be handled differently than embezzlers. With caseloads often exceeding 100 probationers per officer, it is unrealistic to expect the probation officer to tailor the supervision effort to fit each person on the caseload. Instead there has been a growing emphasis on specializing probation caseloads. Specialization groups probationers with similar problems into a single caseload. It allows the probation officer to develop better expertise in handling that problem, and it promotes a concentrated supervision effort to deal with that problem.

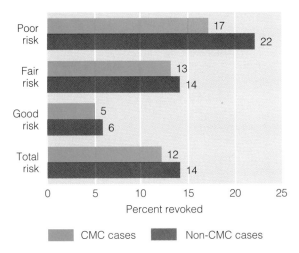

Figure 7.4 ■ Revocation Rates for Various Levels of Risk for Cases Receiving Structured Case Management System (CMC) and Those Not Receiving the Structured System (non-CMC). Structured case management systems work better—especially for high-risk clients.

Source: Adapted from Greg Markley and Michael Eisenberg, "Something Works in Community Supervision," *Federal Probation* 51(4) (1987): 28–32.

Studies of specialized supervision show this approach has promise. A program of employment counseling and support services failed to reduce recidivism, but it did have a positive effect on the employment status of its participants. Specialized treatment programs operated by probation agencies have reduced recidivism for sex offenders.[23] In general, targeted, specialized services have been found to be more effective than traditional services.

Recent interest in the problem of substance abuse has increased the attention given to offenders on probation who have problems with drugs and alcohol. Several special programs have been tried to combat the use of drugs by probationers. These programs typically take advantage of new techniques for drug surveillance and treatment. Urinalysis is used to determine if an offender is continuing to use drugs. **Antabuse,** a drug that stimulates nausea when combined with alcohol, is used to inhibit alcohol use. Methadone, a drug that overcomes the craving for heroin, is used to allow addicts to avoid withdrawal symptoms. These approaches are often combined with close surveillance to reinforce abstinence on the part of probationers.

Another new special program is to pair the probation officer more closely with the street police officers. Officers who work in tandem with the police are often given caseloads of especially tough probationers. The special police liaison makes for more effective searches and arrests and allows probation to take advantage of information available to the police about probationers.

The difficulty with special supervision programs is what to do with the "ordinary" offender who is slated for traditional services. There is often a feeling that "regular" probation is a less attractive function, and conflict among the specialized units can become a serious management problem. As a consequence, specialized service programs in probation, even when successful, require extensive managerial support.

Revocation and Termination of Probation

Probation status is ended in one of two ways: the person successfully completes the period of probation and is terminated, or the person's probationary status is revoked because of misbehavior. Revocation can result from a new arrest or conviction or from a rules violation—the probationer has failed to comply with a condition of probation. Rules violations that result in revocations are referred to as **technical violations.**

antabuse A drug that, when combined with alcohol, causes violent nausea; it is used to control a person's drinking.

Revocations for technical violations are somewhat controversial, because behaviors that are not ordinarily illegal— changing one's residence without permission, failing to attend a therapy program, neglecting to report to the probation office, and so forth—result in incarceration. Some years ago, technical violations were common whenever probationers were uncooperative or resistant to supervision. Today probation is revoked when the rules violation is persistent or poses a threat to the community. Otherwise, rules violations are handled by other means.

Although patterns vary across the country, the most common reason for a revocation is a new offense by the probationer. Sometimes the court will await conviction on the new offense before revoking probation, but if the offense is serious enough, probation is immediately revoked. In such a case, a technical violation is alleged, even though the real basis for revocation is the new offense.

Most studies of probation revocation have estimated that from one-fifth to one-third of probationers fail to abide by the terms of their probation (see Figures 7.5 and 7.6). A Rand Corporation study, however, makes these estimates seem low. A sample of probationers from two urban California counties who had been placed on probation for FBI index crimes was followed for forty months. It was found that 34 percent had been reincarcerated for technical violations or new offenses; 65 percent had been arrested for a felony or misdemeanor during their probation terms; and 51 percent were convicted of a crime during that period. Many of these probation "failures" were continued on probation after their convictions, even though the crimes were often serious. This study indicates that once a person is placed on probation, it is not necessarily the case that any serious

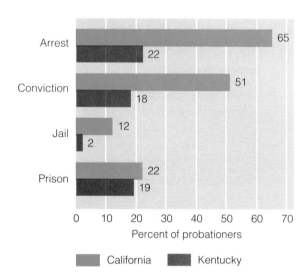

Figure 7.5 ■ **Comparison of Felony Probationer Recidivism Rates in California and Kentucky.** California's probation failure rates are higher than elsewhere in the country and may not be a good representation of the overall effectiveness of probation.

Source: Gennaro F. Vito, "Felony Probation and Recidivism: Replication and Response," *Federal Probation* 50(4) (December 1986): 17–25. Reprinted with permission of the author and the publisher.

misbehavior will result in removal from the community.[24] Although replications of this study outside of California have found far lower levels of serious misbehavior by probationers, the results of this study remain startling.[25]

Because the revocation of probation represents a serious change in the offender's status, the courts have ruled that the offender has several due process rights in the revocation procedure. The major case governing probationers was decided by the Supreme Court in 1967 in *Mempa* v. *Rhay*.[26] The suspension of Jerry Mempa's sentence for the offense of joyriding had been revoked after he admitted involvement in burglaries while on probation for the joyriding offense. The court ruled that sentences could not be imposed after a probation revocation without an attorney to represent the offender.

technical violation The revocation of the probation sentence due to the probationer's failure to abide by the rules and conditions of probation specified by the judge.

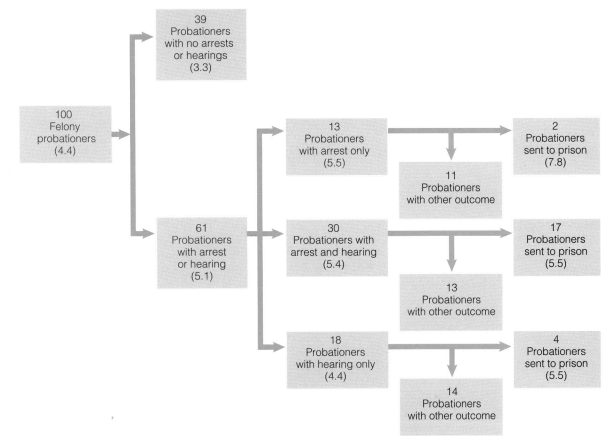

Note: The number in parentheses is the average risk score associated with each group.

Figure 7.6 ■ **Rates of Revocation and Return to Prison for 100 Typical Probationers.** The failure rate of probation depends upon the seriousness of the clientele and the effectiveness of the supervision program.

Source: Mark Cuniff and Mary K. Shilton, "Variations on Felony Probation: Persons Under Supervision in Thirty-Two Urban and Suburban Counties" (Washington, D.C.: Criminal Justice Planners Association, March 1991), p. 70.

In a subsequent decision, the Supreme Court further clarified the procedures for a revocation.[27] The approved practice is to handle the revocation in three stages.

1. In the first stage (sometimes waived), often called the preliminary hearing, the facts of the arrest are reviewed to determine if there is probable cause that a violation has occurred.

2. In the second stage, the facts of the allegation are heard and decided. The evidence to support the allegation is presented by the probation department, and the probationer has an opportunity to refute the evidence. The probationer has the right to written notice of the charges and the disclosure of evidence of the violation; the right to testify and to present witnesses and evidence to contradict the allegations; the right to cross-examine adverse witnesses; the right to a neutral

Dealing with the Drug Offender

Drug-involved offenders present problems and opportunities to probation. The problem is that many such offenders lead disorganized lives and consequently have trouble abiding by even the simplest rules of probation, such as reporting and remaining employed. The opportunity is that getting a drug offender to stay off drugs is one of the most effective ways to prevent crime.

There is no easy way to help drug-involved offenders stay clean. In developing a training program regarding the supervision of drug offenders, the American Probation and Parole Association identified several "principles" in the supervision of drug offenders:

1. *Use urine tests to confirm behavior*. Effective supervision is impossible unless the probation officer knows reliably whether the probationer is truly "clean." Drug testing—more frequent early in the sentence and gradually tailing off—is the best way to know the truth.

2. *Know the pharmacology of drugs*. Different drugs have different effects. Knowing those effects can help in the early identification of relapse, and it can help the officer understand the sometimes erratic behavior of the client.

3. *Expect "slips," especially at first*. Recovery from drug addiction is a lifelong process. Almost no one who is truly addicted walks away from drugs the first time. The probation officer needs to be prepared for "slips," even in the most motivated client.

4. *Have realistic goals*. Abstinence is the right goal, but it is more reasonable to aim the supervision strategy a bit lower: reduce the duration of "slips" and increase the time between them.

5. *Have a graduated program of enforcement sanctions*. When a client fails, don't start with prison as a first response. Instead, begin with a rapid response (say, a curfew) and gradually escalate the severity if the failures continue. Save prison or jail as a last resort.

Source: Todd R. Clear, Val B. Clear, and Anthony Braga, "Intermediate Sanctions for Drug Offenders," *The Prison Journal*, Summer, 1993.

---

and detached hearing officer; and the right to a written statement of findings. Unless unusual grounds exist to deny counsel, the probationer also has a right to an attorney.

3. The third stage is the sentencing stage. With an attorney present, the judge decides whether to impose a term of incarceration and, if so, the duration of the term. The third stage is more than a technicality because probation will often be reinstated with greater restrictions following a minor violation.

For those who successfully complete probation, the sentence is terminated. Ordinarily the probationer is then a completely free citizen again, without obligation to the court or to the probation department.

Probation in the Coming Decade

s we move toward the end of the twentieth century, there is evidence of dramatic change in probation. Caseloads of traditional probation are growing well beyond reasonable management: 200- and even 300-person caseloads are not unusual. At the same time, special and intensive programs with smaller caseloads and intense, high-quality services are also growing.

This leaves us with two increasingly divergent probations of the future. One is largely a paper exercise. Whatever services are provided will be done through brokerage: The probation officer serves as a referral agent, involving the probationer in single-focus community service agencies (such as drug treatment programs) that work with a variety of community clients, not just with offenders. The remaining probationers—a minority of all offenders, to be sure—will be watched closely and will receive first-rate supervision and control from highly trained professionals working with reasonable levels of funding and programmatic support.[28]

The use of brokerage is not necessarily a bad idea. Its proponents argue that persons with special skills in any problem area can provide treatment superior to what a generalist probation officer can give and that the community ought to be providing such assistance to its offenders. Yet community agencies are not always quick to offer services to offenders; they prefer to work with voluntary clients, not those who must avail themselves of services under threat of law.

In many respects, then, probation finds itself at a crossroads. While its credibility is probably as low as it has ever been, its work load is growing dramatically and, in view of the crowding in prisons and jails, will probably continue to do so. Under the strain of the work loads and on-again, off-again public support, probation faces a grave challenge: Can its methods of supervision and service be adapted to work effectively with high-risk offenders? There is no certain answer to this question, and trends are ambiguous. Many innovations are being attempted, but it is unclear whether such new programs actually strengthen probation or detract from it. Certainly they expand the variety of probation sanctions, making them more applicable to more offenders. But do they strengthen the mainstream functions of proba-

tion—investigation and supervision? These functions must be improved for probation to succeed in its current challenge.

Summary

Probation is the most extensively used form of punishment in the correctional system. About two-thirds of all adults under correctional supervision are on probation. Probation can be used in combination with incarceration or other punishments, such as fines, restitution, and community service. Probation allows offenders to serve the terms imposed by the court in the community under supervision.

Although probation in the United States began with the work of John Augustus, attempts had been made earlier to mitigate the harshness of criminal law through benefit of clergy, judicial reprieve, and recognizance.

Three general issues are argued with regard to the organization of probation: whether it should be centralized or decentralized; whether it should be administered by the judiciary or the executive; and whether or not it should be combined with parole services. Differences among the states with respect to these arrangements seem to reflect political traditions of strong local governments versus strong centralized state bureaucracies.

Probation officers serve two major functions: investigation and supervision. The presentence investigation helps judges determine the appropriate punishment for the offender. The extensiveness of the investigation varies, but increasingly there is a trend toward short reports that focus on the issue of risk. No general right is recognized for the defense to receive a copy of the presentence report, but sixteen states do require its disclosure. Such organizational problems as unclear sentencing goals, plea bargaining, and heavy work loads limit the influence of the PSI on the sentencing decision.

On Being a Chief Probation Officer in the 1990s

Norman Helber

There is no doubt that probation will continue to expand during the next ten years. Probation is a profession rich with opportunities for both its employees and the community. The role of the chief probation officer in this process is extremely exciting.

Since that first day in 1841 when John Augustus looked for a better way of working with criminals, probation has continued to grow. What was once known as an "alternative to incarceration" is now the number one sentencing option used by judges all across America. The phenomenal growth it has experienced in the last 150 years indicates the direction it will continue in the future. The chief probation officer is in a position to manage and direct this growth.

During the last twenty years probation has gone through some major changes, from an emphasis on rehabilitation to one of surveillance, and eventually to a concentration on risk management. Chief probation officers have been providing leadership for this transition.

Probation now finds itself on the brink of what could be another major directional change. More and more jurisdictions seem to be clearly saying that probation must take responsibility for the desired behavioral changes in probationers. Society is demanding that probation assist these individuals in changing behaviors as Augustus did with the inebriates in Boston. Society believes that probation can accomplish this task.

Our communities seem to be facing tremendous turmoil with respect to corrections. They are almost in a state of despair. Prisons are overcrowded. Jails are filled. The cost of corrections is escalating, taking monies that would otherwise be used for education or health services. And yet the crime rates are escalating and citizens do not feel safe. In the midst of all this negativism, probation stands as a symbol of hope. Probation says, "Let us have a chance with this individual. Maybe we can help him change his behavior. Maybe we can help him live productively in the community. Maybe we can help heal the wounds that he has inflicted on our community."

In a public opinion survey, residents of Arizona were asked whether they would favor "giving nonviolent offenders probation or home arrest instead of prison." This question was answered favorably by 72 percent, in a state that is considered to be extremely conservative. The public wants probation to work. The public supports the message of hope that probation brings to its community. Being a chief probation officer is being in a position to fill a real societal need.

Norman Helber is chief probation officer in Maricopa County, Arizona. He is also a past president of the American Probation and Parole Association.

The probation officer, required both to enforce the law and to help the offender, faces role conflict in virtually every aspect of the job. Because officers lack substantive power, they must rely heavily on their authority in supervising offenders. The offender's response to supervision greatly influences the nature and effectiveness of the relationship with the officer, as does the fact that all supervision activities take place in the context of the probation bureaucracy.

Probation may be revoked as the result of a new arrest or for violation of the conditions of community supervision. Most research reports that about a third of probationers do not complete probation successfully. A recent study in California, however, indicated a much higher rate.

For Discussion

1. How does the use of probation affect the corrections system? Why is it used so extensively?

2. How does the report of the presentence investigation contribute to the dispersion of accountability for the sentence that is imposed?

3. In your opinion, how could the investigative and supervision functions of probation be most effectively organized? What would the judges in your area say about your proposal? The department of correction?

4. Given the two major tasks of probation, how should officers spend their time? How do they spend their time?

5. Why might some probationers be kept in the community after a technical violation rather than have their status revoked?

For Further Reading

Carter, Robert M., and Wilkins, Leslie T., eds. *Probation, Parole, and Community Corrections.* New York: Wiley, 1976. A selection of classic essays on probation supervision.

Clear, Todd R., and O'Leary, Vincent. *Controlling the Offender in the Community,* Lexington, MA: Lexington, 1981. A presentation of the argument for risk management methods in probation.

Duffee, David, and McGarrell, Edward. *Community Corrections: A Community Field Approach.* Cincinnati: Anderson, 1990. A theoretical approach to probation that focuses upon the forces that surround it.

Petersilia, Joan, and Turner, Susan. *Granting Felons Probation: Public Risks and Alternatives.* Santa Monica, Calif.: Rand Corporation, 1985. A study of probation for serious offenders in California.

Vass, Anthony A. *Alternatives to the Community: Punishment Custody and the Community.* Newbury Park, Calif.: Sage, 1990. An up-to-date critique of imprisonment and defense of probation.

Notes

1. "Probation's Bold Experiment," *New York Times,* 14 February 1993, p. A–20.

2. U.S. Department of Justice, Bureau of Justice Statistics, *Bulletin* (Washington, D.C.: Government Printing Office, November 1991) p. 1.

3. Robert Martinson, "California Research at the Crossroads, *Crime and Delinquency* 22 (April 1976): 191.

4. Frederick A. Hussey and David E. Duffee, *Probation, Parole, and Community Field Services: Policy, Structure, and Process* (New York: Harper & Row, 1980), p. 36.

5. Ex parte United States, 242 U.S. 27 (1916); often referred to as Killits.

6. John Augustus, *A Report of the Labors of John Augustus, for the Last Ten Years, in Aid of the Unfortunate* (Boston: Wright & Hasty, 1852), reprinted as *John Augustus, First Probation Officer* (New York: Probation Association, 1939), p. 26.

7. Ibid., p. 34.

8. Mary Rudolph, "New Strategies to Improve Probation Officers' Fee Collection Rates: A Field Study in Performance Feedback," *Justice System Journal* 14 (1990): 78–94.

9. U.S. National Advisory Commission on Criminal Justice Standards and Goals, *Corrections* (Washington, D.C.: Government Printing Office, 1973), p. 314.

10. Hussey and Duffee, *Probation, Parole, and Community Field Services,* p. 134.

11. Comptroller General of the United States, *State and Local Probation: Systems in Crisis,* Report to Congress (Washington, D.C.: Government Printing Office, 1976).

12. Joan Petersilia, Susan Turner, James Kahan, and Joyce Peterson, *Granting Felons Probation: Public Risks and Alternatives* (Santa Monica, Calif.: Rand Corporation, 1985), pp. 39, 41.

13. Williams v. New York, 337 U.S. 241 (1949).

14. Verdugo v. United States, 402 F. Supp. 599 (1968).

15. James S. Granelli, "Presentence Reports Go Private," *National Law Journal* (May 2, 1983): 9.

16. Shankar A. Yelaja, "The Concept of Authority and its Use in Child Protective Services," in *Authority and Local Casework,* ed. Shankar A. Yelaja (Toronto: University of Toronto Press, 1971), p. 234.

17. Charles L. Newman, "Concepts of Treatment in Probation and Parole Supervision," *Federal Probation* (March 25, 1961): 38.

18. Rieser v. District of Columbia, 21 Cr.L. 2503 (1977).

19. Gary Arling and Ken Lerner, *Client Management Classification* (Washington, D.C.: National Institute of Corrections, 1980).

20. Todd R. Clear and Vincent O'Leary, *Controlling the Offender in the Community* (Lexington, Mass.: Lexington Books, 1983), pp. 55–61.

21. J. Banks, A. L. Porter, R. L. Rardin, T. R. Siler, and V. E. Unger, *Phase I Evaluation of Intensive Special Probation Projects* (Washington, D.C.: Government Printing Office, 1977), p. 13.

22. Robert M. Carter and Leslie T. Wilkins, "Caseloads: Some Conceptual Models," in *Probation, Parole, and Community Corrections,* ed. Carter and Wilkins, 2d ed. (New York: Wiley, 1976), p. 394.

23. The program for employment counseling and support services in Rochester, New York, is summarized and discussed in Don M. Gottfredson, James O. Finckenauer, and Carol Rauh, *Probation on Trial* (Newark, N.J.: Rutgers University School of Criminology, 1977), pp. 254–55; programs for sex offenders are discussed in James Olsson, *Final Evaluation Report: An Outpatient Treatment Clinic for Special Offenders* (Hunt Valley, Md.: Maryland Division of Parole and Probation, 1975).

24. Petersilia et al., *Granting Felons Probation,* p. 39.

25. Gennaro F. Vito, "Felony Probation and Recidivism: Replication and Response," *Federal Probation* 50 (4) (December 1986): 17–25.

26. Mempa v. Rhay, 389 U.S. 128 (1967).

27. Gagnon v. Scarpelli, 411 U.S. 778 (1973).

28. James M. Byrne, "The Future of Probation and the New Intermediate Sanctions," *Crime and Delinquency* 36 (1990): 6–14.

8

Intermediate Sanctions and Community Corrections

Effective and principled punishment requires the development of a range of punishments between imprisonment and probation.

Norval Morris and Michael Tonry, *Between Prison and Probation*

The Case for Intermediate Sanctions
Unnecessary Imprisonment
Limitations of Probation
Improving Justice
The Continuum of Sanctions Concept
Problems with Intermediate Sanctions
Agencies
Offenders
Widening the Net
Varieties of Intermediate Sanctions
Judicial Programs
Probation Supervision Programs
Corrections-Administered Programs
Making Intermediate Sanctions Work
Sentencing Issues
Selection of Offenders
Surveillance and Control
The New Corrections Professional
Community Corrections: Past, Present, and Future
Community Corrections Legislation
The Future of Intermediate Sanctions and Community Corrections
Summary

When it comes to working with criminal offenders, Peter Roesing doesn't have much use for pop psychology. Give him a convicted felon and he won't try to hypnotize him or lie him down on a leather couch to cure his errant behavior. He'll put him to work, put him in Alcoholics Anonymous, put him on a straight track. And if his client waivers off that track, Roesing will put him back in prison.

As case manager for Torrington, Connecticut's Alternative Incarceration Center, Roesing is primarily responsible for offering people who would otherwise be serving prison time a chance at a new start.

"We're going to work on what got you here," he said recently, discussing the center's philosophy. "I don't care when a guy was potty trained, I don't care what his first words were.... That's chasing the rainbow.... What happens to these people here is they tip their lives upside down, and we provide them with some structure."

The clientele consists mostly of people charged with crimes serious enough to land them in prison but focuses on those either in pretrial stages or at the start of their sentence. That allows prisons to keep serious offenders who are serving long sentences—people who would be first out in supervised releases or other programs aims at solving overcrowding problems.

Instead of lying in a prison cell or lifting weights—activities that have little chance of bringing about reform—clients at Torrington are given job and substance abuse counseling, must find a place to live, and are required to have daily contact with center staff, submit to regular drug testing, and contribute a minimum of twenty-five hours to community service projects.

Clients are not treated at Torrington as if they were at a summer camp. One offender asked to go to Niagara Falls to get married, and his request was quickly rejected.

"I told him, 'You wouldn't ask the warden to do that if you were in jail,'" Roesing said. "You can't give them too many breaks. It may seem hardhearted, but that's what this is all about.... I firmly believe that something good can happen to them."[1]

Many people believe that history will define the last years of the twentieth century as the beginning of the correctional era of intermediate sanctions. This move stems from a desire to find effective and fair ways to respond to criminal conduct that are less onerous than prison but more controlling than traditional probation.

The case for intermediate sanctions can be made on several grounds, but Norval Morris and Michael Tonry put it best in saying, "Prison is used excessively; probation is used even more excessively; between the two is a near vacuum of purposive and enforced punishments."[2]

In this chapter, we analyze what might be called the modern intermediate sanction movement. We call it the modern movement, because in the history of correctional reform there have been other times when leaders have called for similar changes. Since history never repeats itself exactly, we first present the main arguments for this approach in their contemporary context. We then explore how the current call for intermediate sanctions is a product of several developments, including the idea of community corrections.

The Case for Intermediate Sanctions

The realization that there is a need for correctional strategies that fall between probation and imprisonment is based on three related ideas: Imprisonment is an overly restrictive sanction for many offenders, traditional probation is ineffective with most offenders, and justice is well-served by having options between prison and probation. Let us now explore these arguments in more detail.

Unnecessary Imprisonment

By virtue of history and tradition, those in the United States tend to think of prison as equivalent to punishment. When offenders receive sentences other than prison, many are tempted to think they "got off." When a short prison sentence is imposed, many think that the offender "got a break." Yet to treat prison as though it is the primary means of punishment is wrong on two grounds.

First, most sanctions imposed in the United States and in other Western democracies do not involve imprisonment. In the United States probation is the most commonly imposed sanction: Three offenders are on probation or parole for every one in prison or jail. In reality, prison is not the centerpiece of American practice. In fact, most offenders experience quite different correctional sanctions.

In Europe this is even more true. Germany, for example, imposes fines as a sole sanction on two-thirds of its property offenders; in England, the figure approaches 50 percent.[3] Community service orders are seen as the option of choice for most property offenders in England.[4] In Sweden, The Netherlands, France, Austria— and virtually every other Common Market country—sanctions other than prison are used far more than incarceration. Since nonprison sanctions are a worldwide phenomenon, it makes little sense to think of them as nonpunishment.

There is a second reason why an inordinate focus on prison as punishment is unwise: Prison as punishment is not very effective. One expectation we have for punishment is that the offender will learn something from it and reject the life of crime. But considerable evidence shows that this does not happen for many offenders. One study suggests that only 45.l percent of all discharges from prison successfully complete their parole term.[5] Another study found that prisoners have a higher re-arrest rate than do similar offenders sentenced to probation.[6] The point is that prison punishes but does not educate.

If prison is neither the most common nor the most effective sanction, why does it dominate our thinking when it comes to punishment? Perhaps it is time to recognize that corrections can and should develop nonincarcerative sanctions that fill the gap between prison and probation.

Limitations of Probation

Many believe that probation has proved ineffective with serious offenders. As we saw in Chapter 7, there is a good basis for this concern. Caseloads are too large to allow meaningful probation supervision. With one hundred and more offenders per officer, the average probationer can get no more than fifteen minutes of contact per week, hardly what we would consider to be meaningful supervision.

In many cases, what happens between the probation officer and the offender is not very relevant to the offender's special problems. The probation officer may check the client's pay stubs; a urine sample may be taken to test for drug use. But in the limited time available, little may happen to help the probationer achieve a change in lifestyle.

Intermediate sanctions can improve on traditional probation supervision in two ways. First, they often can intensify the supervision of the offender. Second, they can provide for specialized programs that are better suited to address the offender's needs.

Improving Justice

Judges sometimes complain that their sentencing choices are too limited. They say they find themselves confronted with an offender whose crime does not warrant prison, but for whom probation seems inadequate as well. The development of an array of sanctions between these two extremes enables judges to better fit the sentence to the crime's seriousness.

A similar problem occurs when an offender fails to abide by the rules of probation or parole supervision. Some response is needed to maintain the credibility of the rules, but to send the rule violator to prison for behavior that is not otherwise criminal seems unwarranted.

Finally, intermediate sanctions allow a closer tailoring of the punishment to the offender's situation. Many offenders can be adequately punished by a fine. Others may be equally well punished by being required to complete a drug treatment program. Still others can be subjected to a period of house arrest. It is argued that intermediate sanctions, tailored to fit the offender's circumstances, can be more just.

The Continuum of Sanctions Concept

One way to establish intermediate sanctions is to use the **continuum of sanctions** approach. Continuum of sanctions refers to a range of correctional strategies that vary in terms of level of intrusiveness and control. Offenders are initially assigned to one of the levels based on the seriousness of their offense and their prior record. Offenders then may move to a less restrictive or a more restrictive level, depending on their conduct and their response to supervision. Delaware's sentencing accountability approach, presented in Table 8.1 (pp. 212–213), illustrates this idea. Under Delaware's model, all offenders are graded regarding risk of a new offense and seriousness of current offense. Their movement through the corrections systems depends on their performance at each level of sentencing accountability.

Many jurisdictions have made an effort to develop a continuum of sanctions, and the

continuum of sanctions   A range of correctional management strategies based on degree of intrusiveness and control over the offender, along which an offender is moved based on response to correctional programs.

advantages of this approach now seem plain. First, it makes the correctional system's capacity much more flexible. As the more costly and less elastic custodial portions of the corrections system become crowded, selected offenders can be moved to less restrictive options. For instance, jailed inmates can be placed in work release. Second, it allows a more responsive management of individual offenders, based on the needs of the corrections system. For example, if a person on regular probation is not reporting, a brief period of house arrest can be imposed, followed by a return to probation.

The continuum of sanctions idea is flexible enough that it can operate at both the state and the county level. It can be codified into law, or it can be operated as a practice agreed to by the various agencies responsible for correctional programs. For instance, in Maricopa County, Arizona, the combined resources of multiple agencies—the jail, treatment centers, and probation—are used to rationalize the punishment system along a continuum of sanctions, as shown in Figure 8.1. This approach accomplishes the same aims as Delaware's sentencing accountability system, but it is not a part of penal law, nor is it operated by a single state agency.

Problems with Intermediate Sanctions

Despite the growing range of available alternatives, all is not well with the intermediate sanctions movement. There are problems in the selection of agencies and offenders: which agencies should operate the process and which offenders should receive intermediate sanctions. Further, intermediate sanctions often bring up the issue of widening the net.

Agencies

Administrators of such traditional agencies as probation, parole, and institutional corrections

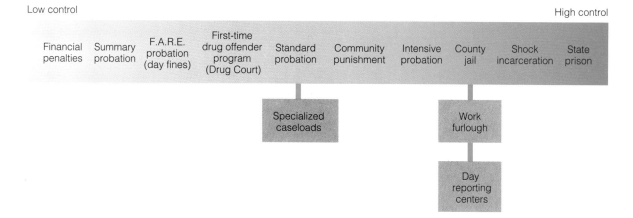

Figure 8.1 ■ Continuum of Sanctions System of Maricopa County, Arizona. Maricopa County uses interagency cooperation to establish its continuum of sanctions at the county level.

Source: Maricopa County Adult Probation Department, *Day Fine Demonstration Project (FARE Probation)* (Maricopa County Probation Department, 1993). Reprinted by permission.

often argue that they should be allowed to operate intermediate sanctions. They have the staff and the experience to design new programs to meet the requirements of special subgroups of offenders, they say, and if the system is to have programmatic coherence, they ought to operate all correctional processes. Critics of this point of view say that new agencies, public and private, ought to be charged with operating the new programs. Since traditional correctional organizations must give highest priority to traditional operations, it is argued, they cannot give the attention or support to a mid-range alternatives movement that is necessary to make it succeed. Inevitably, critics believe, intermediate sanctions programs will be controlled by the currently dominant probation and prison systems—especially as these systems need intermediate sanctions to resolve problems of overcrowding of caseloads and cells.

Offenders

A second issue has to do with the selection of appropriate offenders for alternative programs. One school of thought emphasizes the seriousness of the offense; the other concentrates on the problems of the offender. A focus on the offense usually results in the elimination of some crime categories from consideration for intermediate sanctions. It is often argued that violent or personal offenses and drug-marketing offenses are so abhorrent that a nonincarcerative program is not an appropriate form of punishment for such offenders. Yet these offenders are often the best able to adjust to these programs. Moreover, to the degree that these programs need to reduce prison overcrowding, they must include more serious offenders.

In practice, both the crime and the criminal are taken into consideration. Certain offenses are so serious that the public would not long tolerate intermediate punishments for them (even though numerous instances of successful community-based control of murderers and other serious offenders exist). Likewise, judges want programs to respond to the needs of the offenders they sentence.

Underlying this issue is the thorny problem of **stakes.**[7] The concept of stakes is easily illustrated. Most of us would be willing to bet $1 on a one-in-ten chance of winning $10, yet

Table 8.1 ■ Sentencing Accountability System of Delaware. In Delaware, offenders are assigned to a correctional accountability level based on their current offense and their prior record.

Restrictions	Accountability level				
	I 0–100	II 101–200	III 201–300	IV 301–400	V 401–500
Mobility in the community	100% (unrestricted)	100% (unrestricted)	90% (restricted 0–10 hours/week)	80% (restricted 10–30 hours/week)	60% (restricted 30–40 hours/week)
Amount of supervision	None	Written report monthly	1–2 face-to-face/month, 1–2 weekly phone contact	3–6 face-to-face/month, weekly phone contact	2–6 face-to-face/week, daily phone, weekly written reports
Privileges withheld or special conditions	(100%) same as prior offense conviction	(100%) same as prior conviction	1–2 privileges withheld	1–4 privileges withheld	1–7 privileges withheld
Financial obligations	Fine/costs may be applied (0–2 day fine)	Fine/costs/restitution/probation supervisory fee may be applied (1–3 day fine)	Same as II (increase probation fee by $5–10/month) (2–4 day fine)	Same as III (increase probation fee by $5–10/month) (3–5 day fine)	Same as IV (pay partial cost of food/lodging/supervisory fee) (4–7 day fine)
Examples[a]	$50 fine/court costs; 6 months unsupervised probation	$50 fine/restitution/court costs; 6 months supervised probation; $10/month fee; written report	Fine/costs/restitution; 1 year probation; weekend community service; no drinking	Weekend community service or mandatory treatment, 5 hours/day; $30/month probation fee; no drinking; no out-of-state trips	Mandatory rehabilitation skills program, 8 hours/day; restitution; probation fee of $40/month; no drinking; curfew

Source: Norval Morris and Michael Tonry, *Between Prison and Probation: Intermediate Punishments in a Rational Sentencing System* (New York: Oxford University Press, 1990), pp. 66–67. Copyright ©1990 Oxford University Press, Inc. Reprinted with permission.

[a]These are examples only—many other scenarios could be constructed meeting the requirements of each level.

few of us would be willing to bet $1,000 on a one-in-ten chance of winning $10,000. The odds are the same, but we stand to lose so much more that the bet may be unwise. In the same way,

stakes The potential losses to victims and to the system if offenders fail; stakes include injury from violent crimes and public pressure resulting from negative publicity.

intermediate sanctions officials are often unwilling to accept offenders convicted of serious crimes, particularly violent crimes, even though the chances of the offenders' successfully completing a program may be quite good. If those offenders commit serious new crimes, the damage to the community and—through negative publicity—to the corrections system can be substantial. With some offenders, the stakes are simply too high, regardless of the amount of risk.

Accountability level				
VI 501–600	VII 601–700	VIII 701–800	IX 801–900	X 901–1000
30% (restricted 50–100 hours/week)	20% (restricted 100–140 hours/week)	10% (90% of time restricted)	0% (incarcerated)	0% (incarcerated)
Daily phone, daily face-to-face, weekly written reports	Daily on-site supervision 8–16 hours/day	Daily on-site supervision 24 hours/day	Daily on-site supervision 24 hours/day	Daily on-site supervision 24 hours/day
1–10 withheld	1–12 withheld	5–15 withheld	15–19 withheld	20 or more withheld
Same as V (8–10 day fine)	Same as V (11–12 day fine)	Fine/costs/restitution payable upon release to VII or lower (12–15 day fine)	Same as VIII	Same as VIII
Work release; pay partial cost of room/board/restitution; no kitchen privileges outside mealtime; no drinking; no sex; weekends home	Residential treatment program; pay partial program costs; limited privileges	Minimum security prison	Medium security prison	Maximum security prison

Widening the Net

Ambivalence about the appropriate selection of offenders for intermediate sanctions has led to the third major problem of the movement: widening the net. In some ways this problem is potentially the most damaging because it strikes at the very core of the intermediate sanctions concept. Critics argue that instead of reducing the control exerted over offenders' lives, the new programs have in fact increased it. We can readily see how this might be so. The existence of an alternative at each possible point in the system makes it possible for the decision maker to impose a *more* intrusive option than ordinarily would have been imposed—rather than a *less* intrusive one. Community service, for instance, can be added to probation; shock incarceration can be substituted for the straight probation that might otherwise have been imposed.

Limited Risk Management and Intermediate Sanctions

Billy Wasson

The idea of an expanded range of correctional alternatives— a "continuum of intermediate sanctions"— was articulated by the President's Commission on Law Enforcement and Administration of Justice in 1967. Many have feared that the availability of an expanded number of alternatives may encourage overuse of the correctional system through net widening, exposing more offenders to unnecessarily intrusive measures of social control. A more recent challenge is the actual development and administration of a continuum of intermediate sanctions. This poses problems for those on the front line of the criminal justice system. Will they be empowered to respond to offender behavior in a timely manner?

The Marion County Department of Corrections has fashioned an answer to this perplexing problem by instituting a limited risk management model. The department has refined its classification and case management tools, installed a computerized management information system, and revised its policies and procedures so as to provide a full range of correctional sanctions while controlling and optimizing their use.

Limited risk management attempts to balance both public protection and fairness to the offender. Under the model, the seriousness of the offense established a range of penalties (the fairness dimension) within which decisions are based on the individual's risk of reoffending (the public protection dimension). The model is explicitly seen as reducing rather than widening the net of social control while containing costs and limiting the risk of new crime.

Limited risk management requires a continuum of intermediate sanctions, along with use of the least restrictive measure and progressive movement to lower levels. It means

Available evidence reveals that intermediate sanctions have created:

- *Wider nets:* Reforms increase the proportion of individuals in society whose behavior is regulated or controlled by the state.

- *Stronger nets:* Reforms augment the state's capacity to control individuals through intensification of the state's intervention powers.

- *Different nets:* Reforms transfer or create jurisdictional authority from one agency or control system to another.[8]

Varieties of Intermediate Sanctions

There are many different types of intermediate sanctions, and it is possible to identify only the main types here. How programs relate to each other is dependent upon the jurisdiction running them. For example, in one county intensive supervision can be used in lieu of a sentence to jail, whereas in another system it may be devoted to probation violators.

the imposition of only those conditions that are enforceable and necessary and the provision of only those kinds of assistance that are reasonably related to risk control. It assumes that decision making at both individual and organizational levels will be visible and regularly reviewed, based on specified kinds of information and directed toward accomplishment of measurable objectives and clearly stated goals. Perhaps most significant, the model assumes that the corrections organization will function as a learning system with information routinely used to assess and modify operations and goals.

The limited risk management model has important implications for the way in which a corrections agency is organized and managed. The model places substantial authority in the hands of the front-line staff since they are expected to organize their work with offenders around explicit and measurable goals of risk control. Supervisory review—of case plan objective as well as their achievement—is the primary mechanism by which the risk management philosophy of the organization is translated into action at the line level.

The system requires an information technology capable of tracking decisions, actions, and outcomes at the operational level and aggregating them in ways that allow measurement of success in meeting organizational objectives. It requires a reliable risk classification and case management scheme and the policies and procedures that govern their appropriate use. And because success depends so heavily on decisions made and actions taken at operational levels, it also requires a widely shared vision of what the organization is and ought to be.

In developing and managing our continuum of intermediate sanctions, have we expanded our level of social control and have we effectively used our intervention responsibility well?

These remain issues for continuous study based on information we routinely collect. But we've taken a stand in Marion County. We know what we believe in and generally agree on where we want to be. I am convinced we will act on new knowledge as it becomes available.

Billy Wasson is director of the Corrections Department in Marion County, Oregon. He is also a consultant to the National Institute of Corrections on management of community corrections agencies.

We have organized our description based on the agencies generally running the programs, whether the judiciary, probation departments, or corrections departments.

Judicial Programs

The need for intermediate sanctions is often driven by judges' dissatisfaction with the choices they have available. In courts that have managerial authority over probation, this discontent has translated into the kinds of new probation programs we describe later in this section. Other courts have sought to expand their sentencing options by greater reliance on programs they can operate under their own auspices. Two of these are *pretrial diversion* and *fines*. The aim of these programs is clearly to reduce the trial caseload, especially focusing upon the less serious offenders who ought not to tie up the court system.

Pretrial diversion The functions of pretrial diversion, especially as a jail alternative, are laid out in Chapter 6. Because courts have extremely broad discretion when it comes to

Fines are a very old sanction that has taken on increasing importance in recent years as an intermediate punishment. Fines are collected by court personnel who are now using installment plans to increase the likelihood of payment.

pretrial matters, some have sought to expand the uses of this discretion to a broader range of offenders.

Commonly, these new programs target petty drug offenders. A new strategy in Wayne County (Detroit), Michigan, exemplifies this idea. First-time arrestees for drug possession are "fast-tracked" into drug treatment programs within twenty-four hours of their arrest. They are promised that if they successfully complete the drug treatment program, the charges against them will be dropped. This kind of treatment-based diversion program is based on cooperation between the court and the prosecution. Judges indicate a willingness to delay trial under condition that prosecutors are willing to drop charges on minor offenders who show changes in their lives.

Fines   Compared with other Western democracies, the United States makes little use of fines. As we saw in Chapter 4, when they are used, it is typically as an add-on to another sanction, such as probation.

Many judges cite the difficulty of collecting and enforcing fines as the reason that they do not make greater use of this punishment. They say that offenders tend to be poor, and many judges fear that fines would be paid from the proceeds of additional illegal acts. Other judges are concerned that reliance on fines as an alternative to incarceration would mean that the affluent would be able to "buy" their way out of jail and that the poor would have to serve time.

In Europe fines are used extensively, are enforced, and are normally the sole sanction for a wide range of crimes. The amounts are geared to the severity of the offense and the resources of the offender. To deal with the concern that fines exact a heavier toll on the poor than on the wealthy, Sweden and Germany have developed the **day fine,** which takes into account the differing economic circumstances of offenders who have committed the same crime. The amount of the fine is determined in a two-stage process. First the number of units of punishment is ascertained according to the seriousness of the offense and such elements as the offender's prior record. Second, the monetary value of each unit of punishment is established in light of the offender's financial circumstances. Thus, the total penalty—the degree of punishment—should cause an equivalent level of economic burden to offenders of differing means who are convicted of similar offenses. For example, a person making $36,500 a year and sentenced to ten units of punishment would pay $3,650; a person making $3,650 and receiving the same penalty would pay $365. The day fine concept is currently being adapted to the U.S. system and tested in five jurisdictions in Arizona, Connecticut, Iowa, New York, and Washington.

Probation Supervision Programs

The basis for the intermediate sanction movement rests a great deal on the argument that probation, as traditionally practiced, is inadequate for large numbers of offenders. Probation leaders have responded to this criticism by developing new programs and expanding old ones. New programs often rely on increases in surveillance and control. Old programs are often revamped to become more efficient and expanded to fit more probationers.

Community service and restitution Community service and restitution have been around for years as an option for judges, but they were used heavily only in some jurisdictions. Recently, with the effects of prison over-

crowding and with judges searching for efficient sentencing options, the interest in these ideas has increased.

A community service condition requires the offender to provide a specified number of hours of free labor in some public service, such as street cleaning, repair of run-down housing, or hospital volunteer work. A restitution condition establishes a sum of money that must be paid by the offender either to the victim or to a public fund for victims of crime.

Both alternatives rest on the assumption that the offender can atone for his or her offense with a personal or financial contribution to the victim or to society. They have been referred to as reparative alternatives because they seek to repair in part the harm done by the offender. These approaches have become popular because they force the offender to make a positive contribution to offset the damage inflicted, and thus they satisfy a common public desire that offenders not "get away" with their crimes. They are also advocated as ways to reduce correctional overcrowding.

The evidence on the effectiveness of these programs is mixed. Most studies seem to find that in the absence of such programs, the vast majority of offenders who were ordered to provide community service and restitution would have been punished with a traditional probation sentence—this bodes poorly for community service as a real solution for correctional crowding.[9] Nor have community service and restitution programs proved especially effective at reducing the criminal behavior of their participants; in fact, studies have shown that they have somewhat higher failure rate than do the regular supervision cases.[10]

In sum, community service and restitution stand as an excellent illustration of the fact that simply implementing a so-called alternative does not always achieve the aims of intermediate sanctions. Careful attention must be paid to the selection of appropriate offenders so that the phenomenon of net widening is avoided. Judicial decision making must be controlled to ensure that persons who enter the programs

---

day fine A criminal penalty based on the amount of income an offender earns in a day's work.

Work in the community under supervision is often used as an intermediate sanction. How should such programs be managed?

are those who otherwise would have been incarcerated.

Probation day reporting (treatment) centers As prisons became more and more crowded, judges grew reluctant to place probation violators in jail or prison except when the violation involved a new crime. The result was that probationers in some jurisdictions began to learn they could disregard probation rules, with little consequence. Probation administrators found the lack of credibility with clients to be a severe detriment to effective supervision.

The solution seemed to be the development of probation-run enforcement programs. Georgia experimented with *probation centers,* which were residential facilities where persistent probation violators could be sent for short periods. Massachusetts and New York City have followed with *day reporting centers,* where violators go for day-long intervention and treatment. Minnesota and other states have established *restitution centers,* where those who fall behind in restitution are sent to make payments upon their debt.

All these forms of centers are usually referred to as day reporting centers. These facilities vary widely, but all have in common the desire to provide a credible option for probation agencies to enforce their conditions, when prisons are too overcrowded to accept them.[11] Most day reporting centers incorporate a potpourri of common correctional methods. For example, in some, the treatment regime is comparable to that of a halfway house—but without the problems of siting a residential facility. Others "provide contact levels equal to or greater than intensive supervision programs, in effect, creating a community equivalent to confinement."[12]

To date, no outcome evaluations have been conducted of these programs. One study of New York City's program found that its stiff eligibility requirements resulted in very small numbers of cases entering the program, a problem common to newly established intermediate sanctions programs.[13] The real test of these programs will involve two issues: How much do they improve probation's credibility as a sanction, and how well do they combat jail and prison crowding? These questions remain unanswered.

Table 8.2 ■ **Results of the Rand Studies of Intensive Supervision Probation.** These data show the average number of arrests per individual for one year of time on the street and the average court reprocessing costs for one year in the programs. Clients assigned to ISP were not less likely to be arrested than those assigned to routine probation.

| | Contra Costa | | Ventura | | Los Angeles | | |
	ISP	Routine probation	ISP	Community resource management team	Electronically supervised probation	ISP	Routine probation
Violent crimes	0.2	0.1	0.2	0.3	0.1	0.2	0.1
All crimes combined	1.0	0.7	2.1	2.5	1.4	1.3	0.8
Full costs	$7,240	$4,923	$8,548	$9,606	$8,633	$8,902	$7,123

Source: Joan Petersilia and Susan Turner, *Intensive Supervision for High-Risk Probationers: Findings from Three California Experiments* (Santa Monica, Calif.: Rand Corporation, 1990), pp. 77, 92.

Intensive supervision Intensive probation supervision programs have sprung up around the country, and they seem ideally suited to the pressures facing corrections today. Because they target offenders who are subject to incarceration, they should help to alleviate crowding; because they involve strict and close supervision, they are responsive to community pressures to control offenders. By 1990, over 70,000 offenders were under intensive supervision in the community.[14]

Early evaluations of programs in Georgia, New York, and Texas found evidence that intensive supervision can cut into the rearrests of probationers. The Georgia program, in particular, reported that the first thousand participants engaged in fewer than twenty-five serious offenses; and by its sixth year, the program had saved the state millions of dollars in corrections costs.[15]

Nevertheless, these programs are not without controversy. For one thing, the impact on rearrests comes at a cost. All evaluations of intensive supervision find that, probably because of the closer contact with the clients, probation officers uncover a larger number of rules violations than occur in regular probation. There-

fore, these programs often have higher failure rates than regular probation, even though their clients produce fewer arrests.

This was precisely what Rand researchers found in a series of experiments testing the effectiveness of intensive supervision probation (ISP). Offenders were randomly assigned to ISP versus regular probation. Results indicated no differences in overall arrest rates but substantial differences in probation failure rates. ISP clients did much worse under the stricter rules—possibly because ISP makes detecting rules violations easier.[16] The result was that these programs not only failed to reduce crime but actually cost the public *more* than if the programs had not been started in the first place. The results of the Rand studies are shown in Table 8.2.

What constitutes intensive supervision? Even the most ambitious programs require only once-a-day meetings between officers and offenders. Such meetings, which may last ten minutes or less, can never take up more than a minuscule portion of the offender's waking hours. So, no matter how intensive the supervision, a substantial element of trust must still be placed in the probationer.

Jail Moves into Probationer's Home

J. Nordheimer

Jay Match fidgets. He paces the floor, sits for a while at a kitchen table to flip the pages of a textbook for electrical contractors, walks back out into his living room.

In a corner near the telephone sits a black box about the size of an attaché case. The box is Mr. Match's jailer. In a classic way, the prisoner has come to hate his jailer.

It has been two weeks since Mr. Match was placed under three-month house confinement by a county judge. A three-ounce transmitter strapped to his leg above the ankle emits a radio signal every thirty-five seconds.

The electronic innards of the black box in the corner monitor the signals and report Mr. Match's movements over the telephone to a computer miles away in the offices of Pride Inc., a company that charges chronic misdemeanor defendants like Mr. Match a substantial fee for the right to be supervised at home.

Pride Inc. is a nonprofit private concern that in a few years has pioneered private supervising of traffic and misdemeanor probation cases. Like a medieval jailer, the monitor tells the IBM-PC computer downtown in electronic pulses the equivalent of "all is well; the prisoner is not in violation."

Law enforcement officials are monitoring the company to see how well it manages a program that allows chronic misdemeanor and traffic offenders to stay out of jail and how it does other probation work.

Company is also counselor

Most of the probationers, of whom there were more than 9,000 last year, are required to report in person to Pride Inc.'s offices on a regular basis for conferences with the concern's counselors. In the past, these duties were administered by local or state agencies.

Electronically monitored in-house confinement as an alternative to jail operates like a program in which the prisoner is released to work. But these offenders spend a sentence confined at home with time off during the day to go to a place of employment. It also allows single parents, like Mr. Match, to remain at home with their children rather than having to place them elsewhere.

Mr. Match's adjustment to nighttime and weekend confinement had not been as easy as he thought it would be. By the end of the first week, he said, he was studying ways to dismantle the monitoring equipment without being caught.

. . .

The puzzle sometimes keeps Mr. Match awake late at night when his jailer automatically dials the computer, making soft internal clicks and whirs in the black box.

"I hear that box kick in and I feel like tearing it from the wall," he said with a faint smile, newly mindful that iron bars do not a prison make.

Source: Adapted from J. Nordheimer, "Jail Moves into Probationer's Home," *New York Times,* 15 February 1985. Copyright ©1985 by The New York Times Company. Reprinted by permission.

Despite questions about the effectiveness of ISP, the approach has enjoyed wide support from corrections administrators, judges, and even prosecutors. The close supervision has revitalized the reputation of probation in the criminal justice system. It has also demonstrated probation's ability to enforce strict rules, ensure employment, support treatment programs, and so forth. Given the good public relations, it is likely that ISP is here to stay.

Much as intensive supervision may satisfy public demands for control measures, probationers continue to need various forms of assistance. Many offenders are buffeted by serious personal problems—unemployment, emotional and family crises, substance abuse—that cannot be addressed effectively without some form of service or treatment. So officers still have to juggle the roles of helper and controller. In intensive supervision programs the conflicts between these roles may seem less extreme on paper, but in practice they may well continue and perhaps be exacerbated by the mixed messages of the programs.

House arrest House arrest is a simple concept: Offenders are sentenced to terms of incarceration, but they serve those terms in their own homes. Variations on this theme are possible. Some offenders might, after a time, be allowed to venture out to work or for restricted periods of the day. Others might be allowed to maintain their employment for the entire duration of their sentence. Whatever the details, the concept has as its basic thrust the use of the offender's residence as the place of punishment.

On the surface, there is much to recommend the idea of house arrest. It costs the state nothing to house the offender; lodging, subsistence, and often even the cost of an electronic monitor are covered by the offender's own resources. More important, significant community ties—to family, friends (restricted visitation is ordinarily allowed), employers, and community groups—can be maintained. The punishment is more visible to the community than that of the person sent away to prison. In a sense, the goals of reintegration, deterrence, and financial responsibility are simultaneously served.

Evaluations of house arrest provide a few impressions of how the program works. One survey concluded that "most offenders placed in home confinement [e.g., house arrest] appear to be more similar to incarcerated offenders than to probationers and [it] does genuinely divert from incarceration at least half, and sometimes a much higher proportion, of those who receive it."[17]

Anecdotal evidence suggests the effectiveness of house arrest seems to wear off after a few months; it is increasingly difficult to enforce detention conditions as the sentence rounds into its second half-year. (This should come as no surprise: The impact of imprisonment on the offender seems to stabilize after about the same length of time.) The program appears to be best suited to low-risk offenders who have relatively stable residences in which to be detained.

Electronic monitoring One of the most popular new approaches to probation supervision is the use of electronic monitors to expand the surveillance capacity of supervision. Electronic monitoring is ordinarily combined with house arrest and is used to enforce its restrictions. In 1989 nearly 10,000 offenders were under electronic monitoring, over 40 percent of them in the states of California, Florida, and Michigan.[18]

As we've discussed in Chapters 4 and 6, the electronic monitor is a small mechanical device that emits an electronic signal. Two types of such devices exist. Passive monitors respond only to inquiries; most commonly, the offender receives an automated telephone call from the probation office and is told to place the device on a receiver attached to the phone. Active devices send continuous signals that are picked up by a receiver; a break in the signal is noted by the receiver computer.

Advocates of these systems point out that they are cheaper than incarceration (especially since the offender often pays to use the system) and tougher than probation. They are also more humane than prison or jail, since offenders keep their jobs and stay with their families. In addition, probation officers are free to address the needs of the clients. Others are more skeptical. They point out that only those offenders who own telephones and can afford the $25 to $100 per week these systems cost to rent are eligible. In addition, confinement to the home is no guarantee that crimes will not occur. Many crimes—child abuse, drug sales, and assaults, to name a few—commonly occur in offenders' residences.

Moreover, recent problems have arisen with the reliability of these devices. Some offenders have figured out how to remove the monitors without detection; others have been found in violation of the house arrest when they were arrested at the scene of a crime— even though the monitoring system indicated they were safely at home. Studies also suggest that the monitors have a significant negative side effect—they can intrude on the privacy of the family and may be demanding and stressful for the offender's family members.[19]

Despite its limits, the growth of electronic monitoring seems a safe bet. To date, only a few thousand of the millions of offenders in the community are under electronic monitors, but it is likely that the use of monitors in probation will continually increase.

Corrections–Administered Programs

Corrections agencies have been the hardest hit by problems of overcrowding. They have tried to develop intermediate sanctions as ways to manage a burgeoning load of offenders. While some corrections agencies rely on electronic monitoring to support an early release program, the two most common versions of corrections programs are shock incarceration and boot camps.

Shock incarceration The fact that the deterrent effect of incarceration wears off after a very short term of imprisonment has led to experimentation with shock incarceration in which the offender is sentenced to a term in jail or prison; then, after the offender has been incarcerated thirty to ninety days, the judge reduces the sentence. The assumption is that the offender will find the jail experience so distasteful that he or she will be motivated to work harder at staying free of crime.

Shock incarceration is a controversial program. Its critics argue that it combines the undesirable aspects of both probation and imprisonment. Offenders who are incarcerated lose their jobs, have their community relationships disrupted, and are exposed to the labeling and brutalizing experiences of the institution. The release to probation reinforces the idea that the system is arbitrary in its decision making and that probation is a "break" rather than a truly individualized supervision program. It is hard to see how this kind of treatment avoids demeaning and embittering offenders.

Yet studies of shock incarceration find that it has little effect one way or the other on the offender's adjustment in the community. A major study of Ohio's shock program found little or no difference in the performance of "shocked" probationers, regular probationers, and incarcerated offenders, suggesting that shock incarceration is of minimal effectiveness. This finding echoes those of other studies of programs designed to shock or scare offenders into complying with the law: At best they seem to have no effect; at worst they sometimes increase misbehavior.[20]

Boot camps One variation on the idea of shock incarceration is the boot camp. It is a short-term institutional sentence, usually followed by probation, that puts the offender through a physical regimen designed to develop discipline and respect for authority. The daily routine includes strenuous workouts, marching, military drills, and hard physical labor.

Proponents of the boot camp argue that many young offenders get involved in crime

On graduation day, the 5th Platoon of New York's Summitt Shock Incarceration Camp performs a precision march before the warden and other prison officials prior to receiving diplomas.

because they lack self-respect and are unable to order their lives. Consequently, the boot camp model targets young first offenders whose initial crimes seem to suggest a future of sustained criminality.

Evaluations do show that these offenders may experience improvements in self-esteem. But critics of boot camps argue that military-style physical training and the harshness of the boot camp experience do little to overcome the problems that get inner-city youth in trouble with the law in the first place. In fact, early follow-ups of boot camp graduates show they do no better than other offenders after release from the program.[21] Perhaps job training and education would be better than physical training. The intentionally harsh tactics of boot camp may seem brutal, especially for young offenders who are impressionable. Nevertheless, the approach has proved to be very popular with a public searching for new ways to handle offenders.

Making Intermediate Sanctions Work

Intermediate sanctions have been used for too brief a time to allow a complete evaluation of their effectiveness. Of the hundreds of intermediate sanctions programs that have been attempted since the mid-1980s, few have been studied, and fewer still have been subjected to evaluation.

One of the evaluation problems is that intermediate sanctions often profess lofty goals: improve justice, save money, and prevent crime. Any correctional strategy that can produce these results surely deserves broad support. Yet the limited record on intermediate sanctions suggests that these goals are not always accomplished. To make intermediate sanctions work, they must be carefully planned and implemented—and even then, there will be challenges to overcome if they are to be effective. In this concluding section on the topic of intermediate sanctions, we discuss some of the issues that these programs must resolve if they are to reach their potential as correctional approaches.

Sentencing Issues

The most important issues concerning use of intermediate sanctions have to do with the sentencing philosophy and practice. In recent years, there has been a trend toward the emphasis of deserved punishment in sentencing philosophy: Offenders convicted of similar offenses ought to be subjected to penalties of corresponding severity. Since intermediate sanctions fall between imprisonment and probation, they could potentially increase the number of mid-range severe punishments and thereby improve justice.

Yet advocates of deserved punishment argue that it is not automatically evident how intermediate sanctions compare with either prison or probation, in terms of severity, nor is it clear how they compare with each other.[22] For example, it may violate the equal punishment rationale of just deserts to allow one offender to be placed on intensive probation, while another is ordered to pay an extensive fine.

When intermediate sanctions are used to reduce prison crowding, the problem becomes even more serious. Using intermediate sanctions as sentencing alternatives for some offenders may raise serious concerns about equity. Is it fair for some offenders to receive prison terms while others receive the intermediate alternative?

For intermediate sanctions to be effective, exchange rates consistent with the **principle**

---

principle of interchangeability The intrusiveness of different forms of intermediate sanctions can be calibrated to make them equivalent as punishments despite their differences in approach.

of interchangeability must be developed so that one form can be substituted for or added to another form.[23] For example, two weeks of jail might be considered as equal to thirty days intermittent confinement or two months house arrest or a hundred hours community service or one month's salary.

Advocates say that a short prison sentence can be roughly equivalent to some intensive supervision programs or residential drug treatment, in terms of intrusiveness, and that various forms of intermediate sanctions can be made roughly equivalent to each other. Studies of intensive supervision support this contention when they find that some offenders would rather be in prison than be placed on the tough intermediate sanctions.[24] Thus it is possible to design intermediate sanctions so that they equate with incarceration in terms of intrusion, and they therefore do not violate principles of deserved punishment.

In practice, some have tried to structure this principle of interchangeability by describing punishment in terms of units: A month in prison might count as thirty units; a month on intensive supervision might count as ten. Thus a year on ISP would be about the same as a four-month prison stay. To date, no one has designed a full-blown system of interchangeability, though both the Federal Sentencing Guidelines and those in the state of Oregon embrace the punishment units concept. It is likely that future years will see attempts to create interchangeability, using strategies that provide for equivalence in punishments.

Selection of Offenders

If intermediate sanctions are to work, they must be reserved for appropriate offenders. Whichever offenders are appropriate for a given program depends upon the program's goals. Regardless of the program's goals, however, the availability of intermediate sanctions should not be biased against anyone because of race, sex, or age.

The target group There are two general goals of intermediate sanctions: to serve as a less costly alternative to prison and to serve as a more effective alternative to probation. To meet these two goals, intermediate sanctions managers search for appropriate offenders for their staff to supervise. It is not always easy to identify appropriate offenders and move them into these programs.

Prison alternatives are designed for offenders who would otherwise be sentenced to prison. But it is difficult to be certain that an offender given an alternative sanction would have otherwise been sentenced to prison. In most jurisdictions, a person who is sentenced to probation is legally *eligible* for a prison sentence. Research shows that even though many offenders who are sentenced to intermediate sanctions are eligible for prison, most—if not all—would actually have been on probation instead. Because of judges' reluctance to divert offenders from prison, many intermediate sanctions programs billed as prison alternatives actually serve as probation alternatives. As an example, consider boot camp programs, which are usually restricted to first-time property offenders who are sixteen to twenty-five years old. Boot camp, then, cannot be considered an effective prison alternative, since young, first-time property offenders seldom go to prison.

Probation alternatives (often called probation enhancements) face a similar problem. In theory, they should be restricted to the greatest risks on probation, those needing the most surveillance and control. Typically, however, the natural conservatism that accompanies new programs means that the true high risk is made ineligible for the program, which is instead afforded to better risks on probation.

It should be clear that when intermediate sanctions are applied to the wrong target group, they cannot achieve their goals. When prison alternatives are applied to nonprison cases, they cannot save money; when probation enhancement programs are provided to low-risk clients, they cannot reduce much crime.

One of the solutions advanced by some scholars is to use intermediate sanctions as backups for clients who fail on regular probation or parole. This makes it more likely that the target group is composed of high-risk, prison-bound offenders.

Problems of bias Race, sex, and/or age bias is a concern anywhere in the justice system, but it is a particular concern for intermediate sanctions. Since getting assigned to an intermediate sanction is usually a matter of official (usually judicial) discretion, the concern is that officials will be more likely to want to take a chance on white, middle-class offenders than on others. Many programs have found that nonwhites are more likely to stay in prison rather than receive alternative sanctions, and minorities are more likely to be subjected to tougher supervision instead of regular probation.

Alternative sanctions also tend to be designed for men, not for women. The understandable reason for this is that men make up over 80 percent of the corrections population. But if the result is that special programs are available to men but not to women, this is patently unfair. Moreover, the design of intermediate sanctions, which is often based on tough supervision, is questioned by some experts on female offenders. They are concerned that toughness may be inappropriate for many women offenders, whose problems require more of an emphasis on social services.[25]

The solution to problems of bias is neither obvious nor uncontroversial. Most observers recognize that some discretion is necessary to place offenders in specialized programs. They believe that without the confidence of program officials, offenders are likely to fail. This means that automatic eligibility for these programs may not be a good idea. It may be necessary to recognize the potential for bias and to control for it by designing programs especially for women, making certain that cultural factors are taken into account in selecting offenders for them.

Surveillance and Control

The new intermediate sanctions have, for the most part, been developed during a period in which correctional policy has been enmeshed in the politics of "getting tough on crime." It is not surprising, then, that most of these alternatives tend to emphasize, at least in their public relations, their toughness. Boot camps are described as providing no-nonsense discipline; intensive supervision is expressly designed to incorporate surveillance and control as primary strategies with offenders.

Certainly this rhetoric is useful in obtaining public support for the programs. But do the programs themselves benefit from being so unabashedly tough? James Finckenauer's classic evaluation of the "scared straight" program in Rahway Prison provides a good illustration. When popular actor Peter Falk served as narrator in describing the program's main tenet—prisoners serving life in Rahway would use threatening and confrontational techniques with first-time juvenile offenders, literally to try to scare them into giving up petty crime—the public was impressed. Finckenauer's evaluation found, however, that scare tactics may backfire: The juveniles who went through the program were actually arrested more than a matched sample not sent to the program.[26]

There is growing evidence that the tough aspects of intermediate sanctions may not be totally positive. As we've seen when both the requirements of supervision and the surveillance of offenders are increased, more violations occur. Whether it is in the interest of the system to increase violations by upgrading the supervision standards and their enforcement—by being tough—is an open question. If this tough approach has no impact on crime, but instead merely costs more money (through the need to process more violators), what is the benefit?

In many jurisdictions, violators are a serious management problem. In Oregon, over 60 percent of new prison admissions are probation or parole violators, many of whom have not been accused of a new crime.[27] In other states, such as California and New York, if the rate of violations could be reduced, the costs of the equivalent of an entire prison's population could be saved. The increase in violations has been in part a product of more stringent enforcement and in part a result of improved surveillance, especially drug testing. Some people wonder whether the benefits of these changes have outweighed the costs.

The New Corrections Professional

Without a doubt, the advent of intermediate sanctions has changed the work world of the professional in corrections. The long-standing choice between prison and probation has been expanded to include community and residential options that run the gamut from tough, surveillance-oriented operations to supportive, treatment-based programs. The kind of professional needed to staff these programs varies from recent college graduates to experienced and well-trained mental health clinicians. Central to this growth, however, are two major shifts in the working environment of the new corrections professional (see Chapter 20 for a more detailed discussion of these issues).

First, organizations have emerged to administer community corrections programs that are not governmental agencies. Rather, hundreds of nonprofit organizations, such as Connecticut Halfway Houses, Inc. described in the Focus box (pp. 228–229), now dot the correctional landscape. These organizations contract with agencies of probation and parole to provide services to clients in the community.

Second, there is an increased emphasis on accountability. The individualistic and discretionary work of past eras no longer exists. Instead, professionals use their discretion within boundaries, often defined as guidelines, that provide a set of rules for choosing actions with a case. For instance, a staff member may be told that each offender must be seen twice a month in the office and once a month in the community, and that in each contact, a urine sample must be taken. Rules such as these not

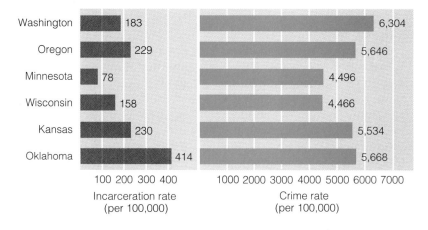

Figure 8.2 ■ **Incarceration and Crime Rates in Selected Contiguous States, 1991.** Community values vary as to how much emphasis should be given to the prison as a solution to crime.

Source: Adapted from U.S. Department of Justice, Bureau of Justice Statistics, *Bulletin* (Washington, D.C.: Government Printing Office, May 1992); U.S. Department of Justice, *Crime in the United States* (Washington, D.C.: U.S. Department of Justice, 1992).

only constrain discretion but also provide a basis for holding staff accountable for the way they handle offenders.

Third, the relationship between the professional and the client has become less important than the principles of criminal justice that underlie that relationship. Instead of training in psychology and counseling, for instance, the new corrections worker receives training in law and criminal justice decision making. This means that the sources of job satisfaction have shifted from helping offenders with their problems toward managing offenders through the system.

Thus, the new corrections professional is more accountable for decision making and is more oriented toward the system in carrying out agency policy. This has significant implications for motivation and training of staff, but it also means that in the traditional three-way balance between offender, staff, and agency, the latter has grown in importance.

Community Corrections: Past, Present, and Future

C orrections in the United States has always had a community focus. In Puritan society, the public, punitive use of the stock and the pillory was a direct

reflection of community values that were intolerant of religious and behavioral differences. When William Penn and his Quaker followers contemplated the tragedy of moral failure among fellow citizens of Philadelphia, their manifest aim was a deep reflection of Quaker religious beliefs: to construct facilities run by religious volunteers where the fallen might go to do penance and be reformed (see Chapter 3).

Even today, correctional systems that are but a few miles apart can vary dramatically in philosophy and practice because of differences in community values and interests. For instance, a person who crosses the border from Minnesota to Wisconsin leaves a state with one of the lowest incarceration rates in the United States and enters a state with one of the highest, even though the crime rates of the two states are nearly the same. Going from Washington to Oregon or from Kansas to Oklahoma is a similar trip from one kind of corrections to another. Figure 8.2 shows the differences in incarceration rates and crime rates in these pairs of adjoining states.

The differences in style and philosophy of correctional programs in different communities reflect a very basic truth about law and order: Beliefs about right and wrong, and values about how to deal with wrongdoers, change from one community to the next. Throughout the years, the concept of community corrections has had many themes, but the core idea

Connecticut Halfway Houses, Inc.: A Nonprofit Corrections Agency

In 1962, Connecticut Halfway Houses, Inc. (CHHI), a private, nonprofit, community-based corrections agency, was founded by a group of concerned citizens with a grant from the Watkinson Foundation. Since 1966, CHHI has been delivering supervision, treatment, and comprehensive individualized services to sentenced offenders and those determined to be at risk of involvement with the criminal justice system, who have been referred under contract by agencies such as the Federal Bureau of Prisons, Federal Probation, Connecticut Department of Corrections, and Connecticut Office of Adult Probation. Outclient alternatives to incarceration as well as residential and aftercare services are provided to over 2,200 clients annually in fifteen programs and residential facilities located throughout the state. CHHI operates with an annual budget of over $3.5 million and a staff of 150.

Specialized services encompass case management, individual and group counseling, education, substance abuse services, AIDS education, relapse prevention, anger management, employment readiness training, literacy, life skills training, money management, and community service. A principal goal of the agency is to enhance the opportunities available to these individuals to become productive, contributing members of their families and communities.

Five residential programs serving a total of 126 adult males, adult females, and youthful offenders are operated by CHHI. Residential work release programs provide services to offenders who are either on pretrial status, on probation, approaching their sentence discharge date, or presently on supervised home release. Aftercare programs are offered as part of the discharge planning process and incorporate training in the use of community support services. Each residential

is that communities know best how to deal with their own crime problems.

At its broadest level, the concept of community corrections is best understood as a goal: to reduce reliance on traditional maximum security prisons in the punishment of offenders. In pursuit of this goal, community corrections embraces a wide spectrum of alternatives to incarceration among which judges and other officials may choose when offenders come before them.

Community Corrections Legislation

In the late 1960s and early 1970s, several states considered legislation that would establish financial and programmatic incentives for community corrections. In 1965 California passed the Probation Subsidy Act, which sought to reimburse counties for maintaining offenders in the local corrections system instead of sending them to state facilities. It was assumed that up to 25 percent of all correctional commitments represented offenders who could be kept at the local level. Therefore, the strategy undertaken was to develop a formula to determine

facility provides professional services and counseling to enhance the ex-offenders' rehabilitation and reintegration into the community.

Out-client substance abuse counseling programs are offered to clients who have been incarcerated or placed on probation because of behaviors affected by their drug use (committing crimes to support a habit, possession or distribution of drugs). Services include in-depth assessment and evaluation of their drug/alcohol status and history, supervision, urine screening, and case management.

As part of Connecticut's commitment to intermediate sanctions, alternative incarceration centers have been established. The programs accept predominantly court-referred clients as part of a pretrial diversion program in addition to probation and supervised home prerelease violators. Clients are required to have daily contact with the centers including providing an itinerary of their daily activities. Preapproved destinations, including places of employment, are spot-checked by telephone and with random site visits on an ongoing basis. Clients are required to submit to regular drug testing, participate in substance abuse counseling, and receive support services designed to meet their individual needs. Participation in community service work projects, designed to benefit the communities located near the centers, is viewed as an important program component and assists in developing community support. Supervised work crews provide labor to cities, towns, and charitable organizations.

While these projects have proved both a beneficial and cost-effective source of productive labor, more important they provide clients with an opportunity to give something back to their communities.

Now in its twenty-fifth year, Connecticut Halfway Houses, Inc. was awarded a certificate of merit for its community service projects by President George Bush in 1991. With the statewide growth in intermediate sanctions programs, the size of the annual budget and staff has tripled during the past three years. CHHI is currently investigating the development of new programs to serve the future needs of the criminal justice system.

the number of offenders that ordinarily would be sent to state institutions, and to pay the counties a specified sum for each offender not sent to prison. The counties could then use the money to strengthen probation and other local correctional services so that they could handle the additional offenders. In 1973 Minnesota passed the first Comprehensive Community Corrections Act, which provided for funding of local correctional systems with money saved by state corrections when individuals were not sentenced to state facilities. Colorado in 1976 and Oregon in 1978 passed legislation patterned after Minnesota's. The experience of these pioneering states in community correc-tions was so well regarded that by 1991, more than one-third of the states had passed community corrections legislation, as shown in Figure 8.3. Some of these more recent legislative acts allow the local government to contract with private, nonprofit agencies to manage offenders. In these states, halfway houses, drug treatment programs, and other forms of correctional strategies can be established by private individuals who enter into contracts with the local government to deal with selected offenders.

Community corrections legislation is based on the idea that local justice systems have little incentive to keep their own offenders in

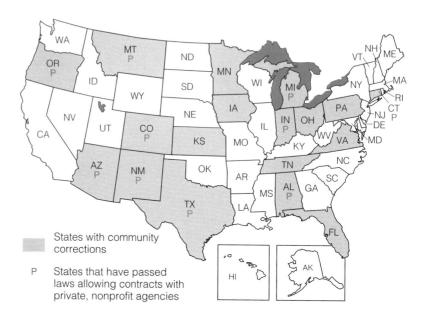

Figure 8.3 ■ States with Community Corrections Acts. Many states provide financial incentives for local governments to keep offenders in local corrections agencies instead of sending them to state prisons.

Source: Mary Shilton, *Community Corrections Acts for State and Local Policy Makers* (College Park, Md.: American Correctional Association, 1991).

local corrections. State-administered institutions are funded by statewide tax revenues, and it costs local taxpayers little to send a large number of offenders to state-administered institutions. The cost of keeping offenders in jail or on local probation is a much greater expense to local citizens, who must supply the tax revenues to pay for those services. Therefore, it is cost-efficient for local justice officials to send offenders to state facilities, where the cost of punishment will be spread across all the state's citizens.

Yet the cost of a year's incarceration in a state prison is substantially more than the cost of local incarceration or probation. Therefore, in the long run, centralized, state-administered punishments seem to be more expensive than local corrections. If one adds to this fact the assumption that many offenders are sentenced to state prison when this extreme punishment is not necessary, then it is easy to see that the financial incentives that favor imprisonment run contrary to good correctional policy.

The payback system has to establish some formula for determining what baseline prison commitment rates would be without the financial incentive provided by the legislation, and the same formula has to apply to all the state's

jurisdictions. There are problems with this idea, of course. Local corrections systems do not contribute equally to overincarceration of offenders; for example, urban and rural areas are bound to contribute differently. The funding formula, then, is likely to result in some serious inequities. California's formula did not adjust for counties that had traditionally restricted their use of incarceration; as a consequence, subsidies given to so-called progressive counties were unlikely to be equal to those given to more "conservative" counties. Further, California's original rate of payback ($4,000 per offender) was not adjusted for inflation, and by 1975 this amount was worth less than $2,500 per offender. In contrast, Minnesota's formula included an inflation factor and permitted adjustments for a locality's crime rate and the capacity of its corrections system. Yet it was criticized for providing lesser financial incentives to cities, which had more offenders and correspondingly larger corrections systems.

Ultimately, community corrections legislation has three aims:

1. to reduce the rate and number of persons sentenced to state correctional facilities

Most halfway houses are operated under government contract by nonprofit organizations. Good News Regeneration House is a place for offenders to live while they work in the community and receive drug counseling.

2. to reduce revenue dollars spent on corrections by transferring both the costs and the funding to less expensive local corrections facilities

3. to reduce prison populations

Have these aims been achieved? The answer is complicated.

Several evaluations of California's Probation Subsidy Act have been undertaken.[28] All agree on one point: The availability of probation subsidies resulted in several policy shifts and compensatory decisions on the part of local decision makers. Commitments to state facilities for adults and juvenile commitments decreased immediately following the enact-

ment of the probation subsidy. These early findings led supporters of the subsidy to conclude that it was extremely effective at reducing commitments.

Closer inspection raised questions as to whether the reduction in commitments reduced the overall level of control of offenders. In the local justice systems for both adults and juveniles, the general intrusiveness of corrections was increased. More offenders were given jail terms; more offenders received closer control through commitment to local drug treatment and mental health facilities. The overall effect of the subsidy was primarily to transfer the incarceration of offenders from state-funded prisons to state-subsidized local corrections—hardly a resounding victory for community corrections. An evaluation of Minnesota's system produced similar findings—at most a reduction of fifteen inmates from the state's previous average daily population.[29]

The community corrections movement has had limited impact on prison populations in most states that have enacted such legislation. Generally, their prisons remain extremely crowded. Parole decisions appear to have become more conservative in California and Minnesota, thus counterbalancing the modest reduction in commitments achieved by community corrections legislation.

Then has community corrections legislation failed? The results are not entirely conclusive. All studies of community corrections have found that some offenders were shifted to local corrections, and this is encouraging. The problem is to control local correctional programs to ensure that the penalties are actually reduced under the new policies as the legislation intended. The community corrections acts that allow the local government to contract with private, nonprofit businesses that provide services to offenders claim they create private jobs while reducing commitments to prison, and this aspect of community corrections acts may be a benefit to all concerned.

Certainly, it must be recognized that community corrections is no panacea. But the desire to reduce the penetration of offenders into the system must be supported by procedures to control the manner in which offenders are handled in local programs.

The Future of Intermediate Sanctions and Community Corrections

What does the future hold for intermediate sanctions and community corrections? Without a crystal ball it is impossible to tell, but certainly three recurrent problems must be addressed by all those who support these programs.

First, some way must be found to overcome the seemingly immutable tendency of the criminal justice system to resist placing offenders in less restrictive options and instead keep increasing the level of corrections. As we have seen, studies of nonprison alternatives find that even the most successful programs enroll only a minority of offenders who would otherwise have been incarcerated. The usual pattern is to place offenders in prison first, then release them to the community. New alternative programs are filled with persons who formerly would have been placed on regular probation. Nonprison programs, whether they be intermediate sanctions or community corrections programs, must improve their ability to attract the kinds of offenders for which they are intended.

Second, community support for these programs must become a central concern. Too often citizens fear the offenders in their midst. Active measures must be taken to allay those fears, to help citizens become comfortable with a corrections mission that recognizes a wide array of programs other than incarceration-based punishments.

Third, the purposes of these sanctions must be clarified. No program can operate successfully for long if its goals are not clearly defined. The goals espoused by most programs today are vague generalizations: reduction of overcrowding, rehabilitation, protecting the community, reintegration, cost-effectiveness, and so on. While no legitimate government operation can reject any of these considerations, some ordering of priorities must occur before these new forms of correctional functions can take their rightful place as core operations in the overall system.

Summary

Intermediate sanctions is a new movement that seeks to establish correctional programs falling between standard probation and prison. While a core argument for intermediate sanctions is that prisons are too overcrowded, a second reason for this strategy is to improve justice by increasing sentencing options. Many jurisdictions have tried to develop a continuum of sanctions as a way of responding to the need for greater sentencing options.

Some intermediate sanctions programs are operated by the courts; others are operated by probation and by corrections agencies. The main forms of intermediate sanctions are fines, community service, restitution, intensive supervision, house arrest, electronic monitoring, shock incarceration, and boot camps. These innovations have not been widely studied, and little can be said definitively about how well they work.

Community corrections may be viewed as the goal of diverting offenders from traditional prison to community-based correctional programs. Some states have enacted legislation to promote community corrections. The California Probation Subsidy Act was passed to encourage counties to maintain offenders in the community rather than send them to state correctional facilities. Colorado, Minnesota, and Oregon, among others, have passed similar legislation.

Some advocates of intermediate sanctions and community corrections have argued that they are cheaper than incarceration. This consideration has proved a powerful incentive to adopt this orientation. Community support for these programs is imperative if they are going to succeed.

For Discussion

1. Are intermediate sanctions better as a way to improve on probation or to avoid the negatives of imprisonment? Support your answers.

2. Should intermediate sanctions be run by traditional probation and prison systems, or by new agencies seeking to serve as alternatives to them?

3. What does the experience of the California probation subsidy program tell us about the interdependence of various elements of corrections?

4. Why do states with similar crime rates sometimes have different incarceration rates?

5. Do you think that intermediate sanctions are acceptable to the general public in the current political climate?

For Further Reading

Byrne, James M.; Lurigio, Arthur J.; and Petersilia, Joan. *Smart Sentencing: The Emergence of Intermediate Sanctions.* Newbury Park, Calif.: Sage, 1992. A collection of papers exploring various issues in the design and implementation of intermediate sanctions programs.

Irwin, John, and Austin, James. *It's About Time: Solving America's Prison Crowding Problem.* San Francisco: National Council on Crime and Delinquency, 1987. A description of the scope of the overcrowding problem and an analysis of strategies for resolving the crisis.

Lerman, Paul. *Community Treatment and Social Control.* Chicago: University of Chicago Press, 1975. A classic evaluation of the problems in community corrections strategies.

Morris, Norval, and Tonry, Michael. *Between Prison and Probation: Intermediate Punishments in a Rational Sentencing System.* Oxford: Oxford University Press, 1990. Urges development of a range of intermediate punishments that can be used to sanction offenders more severely than nominal probation but less severely than incarceration.

Petersilia, Joan. *Expanding Options for Criminal Sentencing.* Santa Monica, Calif.: Rand Corporation, 1987. A summary of the literature on the effectiveness of intermediate sanctions.

Notes

1. Adapted from David Howard, "Reform Is Key in Structuring Lives of Criminals," *Register Citizen* (Litchfield, Ct.), 17 August, 1991.

2. Norval Morris and Michael Tonry, *Between Prison and Probation: Intermediate Punishments in a Rational Sentencing System* (New York: Oxford University Press, 1990), p. 3.

3. Sally T. Hillsman, "Fines and Day Fines," in *Crime and Justice: A Review of Research,* vol. 12, ed. Michael Tonry and Norval Morris (Chicago: University of Chicago Press, 1990), pp. 49–98.

4. Ken Pease, "Community Service Orders," *Crime and Justice: A Review of Research,* vol. 6, ed. Michael Tonry and Norval Morris (Chicago: University of Chicago Press, 1985), pp. 36–80.

5. U.S. Department of Justice, Bureau of Justice Statistics, *National Corrections Reporting Program* (Washington, D.C.: Government Printing Office, January 1992), p. 40.

6. Joan Petersilia, Susan Turner, and James Kahan, *Prison vs. Probation in California: Public Choices and Alternatives* (Santa Monica, Calif.: Rand Corporation, 1987).

7. Don M. Gottfredson and Stephen D. Gottfredson, "Studies and Risk: Assessing the Potential for Criminal Violence," Report of the Justice Policy Research Corporation, Sacramento, August 1988.

8. James Austin and Barry Krisberg, "The Unmet Promise of Alternatives to Incarceration," *Crime and Delinquency* 28 (1982): 374–409.

9. Douglas McDonald, *Punishment Without Walls* (New Brunswick, N.J.: Rutgers University Press, 1986), p. 38.

10. Joe Hudson and Steven Chesney, "Research on Restitution: A Review and Assessment," in *Offender Restitution in Theory and Action,* ed. Burt Galaway and J. Hudson (Lexington, Mass.: Lexington Books, 1978), pp. 131–48; and K. Pease, S. Billingham, and I. Earnshaw, *Community Service Assessed in 1976* (London: Home Office Research Unit, 1977).

11. Jack McDevitt and Robyn Miliane, "Day Reporting Centers: An Innovative Concept in Intermediate Sanctions," in *Smart Sentencing: The Emergence of Intermediate Sanctions,* ed. James M. Byrne, Arthur J. Lurigio, and Joan Petersilia (Newbury Park, Calif.: Sage, 1992), p. 153.

12. Dale G. Parent, *Day Reporting Centers for Criminal Offenders: A Descriptive Analysis of Existing Programs* (Washington, D.C.: National Institute of Justice 1990), p. 1.

13. Peter Jones and Alan Harland, "Edgecombe: A Preliminary Analysis" (paper presented to the American Probation and Parole Association, St. Louis, Mo., September 1, 1992).

14. U.S. Department of Justice, *Bulletin: Probation and Parole, 1990* (Washington, D.C.: U.S. Department of Justice, 1991), p. 2.

15. Billie S. Erwin, *Evaluation of Intensive Probation Supervision in Georgia* (Atlanta: Georgia Department of Corrections, 1987).

16. Joan Petersilia and Susan Turner, *Intensive Supervision for High-Risk Offenders: Findings from Three California Experiments* (Santa Monica, Calif.: Rand Corporation, 1990).

17. Marc Renzema, "Home Confinement Programs, Development, Implementation, and Impact," in *Smart Sentencing: The Emergence of Intermediate Sanctions*, ed. James M. Byrne, Arthur J. Lurigio, and Joan Petersilia (Newbury Park, Calif.: Sage, 1992), p. 47.

18. Mark Renzema and D. T. Skelton, *Final Report: The Use of Electronic Monitoring by Criminal Justice Agencies, 1989* (Washington, D.C.: U.S. Department of Justice, 1990), p. 6.

19. Terry L. Baumer and Robert I. Mendelsohn, *The Electronic Monitoring of Non-Violent Convicted Felons: An Experiment in Home Detention*, Final Report of Grant No. 86-IJ-CX-0041 (Indianapolis: Indiana University School of Public and Environmental Affairs, 1990).

20. See A. Waldron and N. R. Angelino, "Shock Probation: A Natural Experiment on the Effect of a Short Period of Incarceration" (paper presented to National Conference on Criminal Justice Evaluation, Washington, D.C.: February 22, 1977); and James O. Finckenauer, *Scared Straight and the Panacea Phenomenon* (Englewood Cliffs, N.J.: Prentice-Hall, 1982).

21. Doris L. MacKenzie, "The Parole Performance of Offenders Released from Shock Incarceration (Boot Camp Prison): A Survival Analysis," *Journal of Quantitative Criminology* 7 (1991): 213–36.

22. Andrew von Hirsch, Martin Wasik, and Judith Greene, "Punishment in the Community and the Principles of Dessert," *Rutgers Law Journal* 20 (1989): 595–618.

23. Morris and Tonry, *Between Prison and Probation*, pp. 82–84.

24. Joan Petersilia and Susan Turner, "An Evaluation of Intensive Probation in California," *Journal of Criminal Law and Criminology* 82(3) (1991): 610–58.

25. Robin Robinson, "Intermediate Sanctions and the Female Offender," in *Smart Sentencing: The Emergence of Intermediate Sanctions*, ed. James Byrne, Arthur M. Lurigio, and Joan Petersilia (Newbury Park, Calif.: Sage, 1992), pp. 245–60.

26. James O. Finckenauer, *Scared Straight and the Panacea Phenomenon* (Englewood Cliffs, N.J.: Prentice-Hall, 1982).

27. *Annual Report of the Oregon Sentencing Commission* (Salem, Ore.: Oregon Sentencing Commission 1992), p. 23.

28. Paul Lerman, *Community Treatment and Social Control* (Chicago: University of Chicago Press, 1975).

29. Edwin Lemert and F. Dill, *Offenders in the Community* (Lexington, Mass.: Lexington Books, 1978); Lerman, *Community Treatment and Social Control*.

9

Incarceration

We have a system of justice
that provides each criminal
defendant the most elaborate
due process, free counsel, and
the most expensive trials
known anywhere, yet when
the trial is over, we simply
cast the guilty into nineteenth-century penal
institutions.

Former Chief Justice Warren Burger

Links to the Past
The Goals of Incarceration
Organization for Incarceration
Federal Bureau of Prisons
State Prison Systems
The Design and Classification of Prisons
Today's Designs
Location of Prisons
Classification of Prisons
Private Prisons
Correctional Facilities Today
Who Is in Prison?
Summary

*S*tainless-steel handcuffs snugly fastened around subdued wrists. Waiting at an outer gatehouse. Watching the uniformed reception officer dispassionately size me up. Then escorted past double fences, inner fences, through steel doors, electronic steel grilles into the inner sanctum of concrete and steel.

Fear. The kind that chews at the stomach and makes the fingers tremble. Fear of known and unknown hidden dangers.

The atmosphere is tense and strange. Still wearing street-side clothes, I am a curiosity. After a number of rights and lefts and double-locked stairways, we come to Admitting and Processing.

Catalogued, tagged, photographed, and deloused. Issued, not issued, acceptable, not acceptable, and then ordered into a cell slightly bigger than a walk-in closet. When that door slams shut, an ache of mental and emotional pain seizes the senses brutally and completely.

This description, written for this text by Wayne B. Alexander, now serving a life term for murder and other crimes, shows that entrance into prison is an emotional, depersonalizing, and jarring experience. Incarceration is something that no person would want to endure.

It should come as no surprise to criminal justice students that of the approximately 4.4 million adults under correctional supervision in the United States, only about 1.2 million are in jails and prisons. The general public thinks first of incarceration when the subject of the criminal sanction arises. And it is the prison that legislators and politicians have in mind when they consider changes in the penal code or the annual appropriation for corrections.

Since the early nineteenth century, when the penitentiary was invented, the sanction of imprisonment has been ascendant in the American criminal justice system. In many ways, it remains the core sanction of corrections, though some recent trends have made its function ambiguous. For example, although scholars dispute the efficacy of imprisonment, penal code reforms have tended to increase its

use and to add to the number of incarcerated adults in the United States. But at a time when governments are concerned about costs, we must recognize that the expense of maintaining prisoners in institutions normally runs eight to ten times that required for probation and parole.

In this chapter and four of the five that follow, we focus primarily on the incarceration of adult males, who make up almost 95 percent of the prison population. The discussion links the modern prison with the history of American corrections so that we can understand its antecedents. In Chapter 10 we look at the prison experience, the society of captives, the ways in which they cope with their incarceration, and some of the problems that result from imprisonment. The incarceration of women and the ways in which this differs from that of males is discussed in Chapter 11. But whether for men or women, a prison is unlike any other social institution. We must therefore look at the organizational framework and management practices of correctional institutions, as we do in Chapter 12. Chapter 13 describes the institutional programs—rehabilitative, industrial, maintenance, and recreational—that exist in all prisons but that have varying degrees of effectiveness. A discussion of the case law and the important issue of prisoner's rights under the Constitution is found in Chapter 14.

Links to the Past

*R*eformers are frustrated by the sheer durability of prisons. For example, the oldest prison in America, New Jersey's Trenton State Prison built in 1794, still holds offenders. Structures of stone and concrete are not easily redesigned when correctional goals change. Thus, elements of all the major reform movements of the past can be found within the walls. In line with the Quakers' belief that offenders could be redeemed only if they were removed from the distractions of the city, most

Prisons are built to last. Eastern Penitentiary opened in 1829 and was finally closed 150 years later in 1971. Today it stands as a historical relic as architects consider its restoration and reuse.

correctional facilities are still found in rural areas—Stateville, Illinois; Attica, New York; Walla Walla, Washington—far from most of the inmates' families and friends. Although many modern prisons are in "campus" settings, the stronghold remains the primary architectural style. The type of incarcerative sanction imposed varies with the type and locale of the institution and the characteristics of the inmates. Yet a prison is a prison, whatever it is called.

The image of Hollywood's "big house" is still imprinted on the minds of most citizens, though it has long ceased to be a realistic portrayal—if indeed it ever was. Of even more importance, a great deal of the social science literature about incarceration is based on studies conducted in big houses during the 1950s.

American correctional institutions have always been more varied than one might suspect from viewing films or reading some of the landmark prison studies. Yes, big houses were present in much of the country during the first half of this century, but some prisons, especially in the South, bore little resemblance to them. There racial segregation was maintained, prisoners were engaged in farm labor, and the forbidding structures were less common than they were in the industrial Northeast. In other states greater emphasis was placed on forest work camps. Until very recently, the correctional systems of still other parts of the country clung to the cruelty and corruption, hard labor, and corporal punishment that characterized the prisons of the late nineteenth century.

The typical big house of the 1930s and 1940s was made up of large, tiered cell blocks, a yard, shops, and industries. The prison society was essentially isolated, and access to visitors, mail, and other kinds of communication was restricted. Under a rigid daily routine, inmates and staff occupied strictly separate social spheres; rank was observed and discipline maintained. There was little in the way of treatment. Custody was the primary goal.

Since World War II prisons have undergone many changes. It is now far less common to find an old-style big house. During the 1950s and early 1960s most penologists accepted the rehabilitation model. Many states built new facilities and converted others into "correctional institutions." Although the new name was often the principal evidence of a change in philosophy, in some places treatment programs became a major part of institutional life. Indeterminate sentences, classification, treatment, and parole—the chief emphases of the rehabilitative approach—brought treatment personnel, such as counselors, educators, and psychologists, to the staff. Often disagreement erupted over the conflicting claims of treatment and custody.

The development of community corrections in the 1970s had an impact on prisons in that proponents argued that it was necessary to end the isolation of inmates from the world that they would reenter. They urged that outside groups, publications, and television be allowed to penetrate institutional walls. The ending of corrections' isolation from the wider community has had far-reaching influence.

The civil rights movement of the early 1960s had a profound effect on minority prisoners. Political activism erupted during this period as prisoners demanded their constitutional rights as citizens and a greater sensitivity to their needs. With a shift in judicial policy, the courts began to take notice of the legal rights of prisoners. Legal services were extended to corrections, and the judicial hands-off policy evaporated. Suddenly, administrators had to respond to the directions of the judiciary and run the institutions according to constitutional mandates. And, with the rise of public employee unions, correctional officers were no longer willing to work according to the paramilitary regime of the warden.

As the population of the United States changed, so did the inmate population. The proportion of African and Hispanic Americans grew, and inmates from urban areas became more numerous, as did persons convicted of drug-related and violent offenses. The average age was younger. In a number of states, former street gangs regrouped inside prison when their members were incarcerated. The gangs disrupted the existing inmate society and raised the levels of violence in many institutions.

There has also been a dramatic shift away from the treatment model of corrections during the past two decades. The rehabilitative programs so highly touted in the 1960s have been either abandoned or deemphasized; the determinate sentence has replaced the indeterminate sentence in about half the states, with the consequence that releasing mechanisms have been altered. As policymakers have assumed a model of crime control that emphasizes the importance of incarceration, there has been a great increase in the number of persons being held in prisons. The resultant overcrowding exacerbates tensions. Given all of these influences, humane incarceration seems to have become the contemporary goal of correctional administrators.

The Goals of Incarceration

As we saw in Chapter 4, the criminal sanction has had four broad goals: retribution, deterrence, incapacitation, and rehabilitation. When a judge sentences an offender to a prison term, one or several of these correctional goals lie behind the sanction. When we look at the prison, it is natural to believe that incapacitation, deterrence, or retribution is the goal being advanced, but we also know that the most sought-after goal of some institutions is the rehabilitation of the offender. Yet the prison's high walls, daunting fences, searches, checkpoints, and regular counts of inmates not only serve the security function of custody but, more important, set the tone and strongly color the daily operations of prisons. These measures also support the idea that deterrence requires extremes of deprivation, strict discipline, and punishment, all of which, together with the considerations of administrative efficiency, make prisons impersonal, quasi-military places. Questions remain as to the possibility of treatment within them.

Just as justifications for the criminal sanction have influenced sentencing decisions, correctional models have been developed to describe the purposes and approaches to be used in handling prisoners. Although models may provide a set of rationally linked criteria and aims, the extent to which a given model is implemented is a matter for empirical investigation. Like the stated purpose of the criminal sanction, a particular model may have little relation to the ongoing processes of corrections and the experience of the inmates under its jurisdiction.

Three models of incarceration have been prominent during the past five decades: the custodial, rehabilitation, and reintegration models.

The megaprison, often holding up to 3,500 offenders, may be cost-effective yet difficult to manage. Smaller institutions located closer to urban areas have been advocated by reformers.

Each may be viewed as an ideal type that summarizes the assumptions and characteristics associated with one style of institutional organization. The **custodial model** is based on the assumption that prisoners have been incarcerated for the protection of society and for the purposes of incapacitation, deterrence, and retribution. It emphasizes maintenance of security and order through the subordination of the prisoner to the authority of the warden. Discipline is strictly applied and most aspects of behavior are regulated. The model dominates most maximum security institutions today and was prevalent within corrections prior to World War II.

With the onset of the treatment orientation in corrections during the 1950s, the **rehabilitation model** of institutional organization was developed. In prisons of this sort, security and housekeeping activities are viewed primarily as a framework for rehabilitative efforts. Professional treatment specialists enjoy a higher status than other employees, in accordance with the idea that all aspects of the organization should be directed toward rehabilitation. During the 1980s, with the rethinking of the goal of rehabilitation, the number of institutions geared toward that end declined. Treatment programs still do exist in most institutions, but very few prisons can be said to conform to this model.

The **reintegration model** is linked to the structures and the goals of community corrections but has a direct impact on prison operations. Although an offender is confined in a prison, that experience is pointed toward rein-

---

custodial model A model of a correctional institution that emphasizes security, discipline, and order.

rehabilitation model A model of a correctional institution that emphasizes the provision of treatment programs designed to reform the offender.

---

reintegration model A model of a correctional institution that emphasizes maintenance of the offender's ties to family and the community as a method of reform, in recognition of the fact that the offender will be returning to the community.

tegration into society. Prisons that have adopted the reintegration model gradually give inmates greater freedom and responsibility during their confinement and move them to a halfway house, work release program, or community correctional center before releasing them to supervision. Consistent with the perspective of community corrections, the reintegration model is based on the assumption that it is important for the offender to maintain or develop ties with the free society. The entire focus of this approach is on resumption of a normal life.

It is possible to find correctional institutions in the United States that conform to each of these models, but most prisons for men fall much closer to the custodial than to the rehabilitation model. Treatment programs do exist in prisons but they generally take second place to the requirements of custody. Because almost all inmates return to society at some point, even the most custodial institution cannot neglect to prepare them for that move. In many correctional systems inmates spend the last portion of their sentence in a prerelease facility.

Charles Logan notes that we ask a lot of our prisons. "We ask them to correct the incorrigible, rehabilitate the wretched, deter the determined, restrain the dangerous, and punish the wicked."[1] Prisons are expected to pursue many different and often incompatible goals; hence, as institutions they are almost doomed to failure. Logan believes that the mission of prisons should focus on confinement. He argues that the essential purpose of imprisonment is to punish offenders fairly and justly through lengths of confinement proportionate to the gravity of their crimes. If the goal of incarceration is to do justice through confinement, then he summarizes the mission of the prison as "to keep prisoners—to keep them in, keep them safe, keep them in line, keep them healthy, and keep them busy—and to do it with fairness, without undue suffering, and as efficiently as possible."[2] Should this be the new goal for incarceration? Many correctional officials, researchers, and policymakers now believe so. If

the purpose of prisons is punishment through confinement under fair and just conditions, what are the implications for correctional managers? What measures should be used to evaluate prisons using these criteria?

Organization for Incarceration

Prisons are operated by all fifty states and by the federal government. Offenders are held in 1,037 confinement facilities, 94 percent of which are operated by the states with the remainder by the federal government.[3] Among these prisons, 889 (86 percent) are for men only, 71 (7 percent) are for women only, and 77 (8 percent) house both sexes. For the most part, prisons, as distinguished from jails, house convicted felons and those misdemeanants who have been sentenced to terms of more than one year. It is important to note that there are differences among the state governments and federal government as to the bureaucratic organization for incarceration, the number and types of institutions, staffing, and size of the offender populations. We will look at the federal and state systems in turn.

Federal Bureau of Prisons

Created by Congress in 1930, the Federal Bureau of Prisons, within the Department of Justice, was assigned the responsibility for "the safekeeping, care, protection, instruction, and discipline of all persons charged or convicted of offenses against the United States." Before that time, the administrators of the seven federal prisons then in operation functioned with relative freedom from control by Washington. Today the Bureau is highly centralized, a director is appointed by the president, and operations are carried out through six regional directors. The Bureau has a total staff of more than 20,000 who care for more than 70,000 prisoners.[4]

Figure 9.1 ■ **Institutions of the Federal Bureau of Prisons.** Prisons run by the Bureau are spread throughout the country and comprise a range of correctional institutions, detention centers, medical centers, prison camps, metropolitan correctional centers, and penitentiaries. Each is organized according to five security levels: minimum, low, medium, high, and administrative. Offenders are classified and assigned to an institution based on such factors as the severity of the offense, length of incarceration, type of prior commitments, and history of violence.

Source: U.S. Department of Justice, Federal Bureau of Prisons, *State of the Bureau 1990* (Washington, D.C.: Federal Bureau of Prisons, 1991).

To carry out its tasks, the Bureau of Prisons has a network of facilities ranging from penitentiaries to correctional institutions, detention centers, prison camps, and halfway houses. This array of correctional services, shown in Figure 9.1, is much broader than can be found in any single state.

The jurisdiction of the federal criminal law is unlike that of the states because it is restricted to crimes involving interstate commerce, certain serious felonies such as bank robbery, and violation of other federal laws and crimes committed on federal property. Histori-

cally, the federal prison has housed bank robbers, extortionists, persons who have committed mail fraud, and arsonists. Federal prisoners, over 70 percent of whom are white, are serious offenders. They are often a more sophisticated breed of criminal and of a higher socioeconomic class than the typical state prisoner, who is most often a burglar, robber, drug offender, or murderer.

In recent years, however, the characteristics of federal prisoners have changed. Not only is the total number of offenders greater, but now more than half are serving time for drug-related offenses. With the introduction of sentencing guidelines in 1987, there has been a substantial increase in the probability of imprisonment. Compared to the preguideline era, today's prisoners are incarcerated for longer periods.[5] With the increase in the number of drug offenders sent to federal prisons, much of the distinctive quality of the federal correctional population has been diminished. Interestingly, a quarter of federal inmates are foreign nationals.

Pretrial detention The national government does not have sufficient pretrial detention space to house most persons accused of violating the federal criminal law. Only a few centers are maintained, and about two-thirds of all persons being held are detained in state or local facilities on a contractual basis. The U.S. Marshals Service has responsibility for placing federal prisoners. Although all fifty states have laws requiring corrections to accept federal pretrial detainees, the marshals enter into intergovernmental service agreements with receptive jails. Because of crowding in recent times, the government has had increased difficulty finding state and local institutions that have room for federal prisoners. The unavailability of space seems to have developed also from the fear of local officials that sophisticated federal prisoners will bring lawsuits challenging the conditions of their confinement. They also tend to believe that federal officials expect higher standards to be maintained at local expense.

Incarceration The Bureau of Prisons currently operates eighty facilities, with new institutions under construction, spanning a range of security levels and physical types. Inmates and facilities are classified in a security-level system ranging from Level 1 (the least secure, camp-type settings) through Level 6 (the U.S. Penitentiary, Marion, Illinois). Between these extremes are Levels 2 through 5 federal correctional institutions—other U.S. penitentiaries, administrative institutions, medical facilities, and several specialized institutions. The Bureau is organized so that the wardens

report to one of the regional offices. In addition to the facilities administered by the Bureau of Prisons, fifty-one small federal detention centers and confinement facilities are operated by a branch of the military: Army (twenty-two), Air Force (one), Navy (twenty-one), and Marines (seven).[6]

The federal system is looked to for innovation in the field of corrections, and for many years, under the leadership of such directors as Sanford Bates, James Bennett, Myrle Alexander, Norman Carlson, and Michael Quinlan, the operations of the Federal Bureau of Prisons were the most advanced in the country, rivaled only by California's vast system. Today Director Kathleen M. Hawk, only the sixth individual to hold the position, has continued this tradition of excellence.

State Prison Systems

Although there is considerable variation among the states as to the organizational structure of corrections, the administration of prisons is a function of the executive branch of state government in all jurisdictions. This point should be emphasized since probation is often part of the judiciary, parole may be separate from corrections, and in most states jails are run by county government. Alaska, Connecticut, Delaware, Hawaii, Rhode Island, and Vermont operate combined jail-prison systems.

Commissioners of corrections normally are appointed by state governors, and they are responsible for the operation of prisons. As discussed in Chapter 12, each institution is administered by a warden (often called superintendent) who reports directly to the commissioner or a deputy commissioner for institutions. The number of correctional employees working in state prisons has risen dramatically during the past decade. Upwards of 300,000 individuals—administrators, officers, and program specialists—are today found in state institutions. In most jurisdictions these institutional employees constitute three quarters or more of all state correctional personnel.[7]

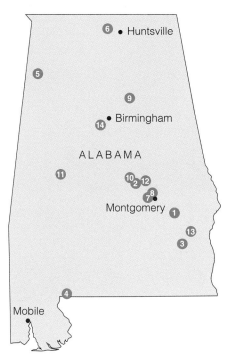

1. Bullock Correctional Facility, Union Springs
2. Draper Correctional Center, Elmore
   Elmore Correctional Center, Elmore
   Thomas F. Staton Correctional Center, Elmore
3. Easterling Correctional Facility, Clio
4. Escambia Correctional Center, Atmore
   G. K. Fountain Correctional Center, Atmore
   Holman Prison, Atmore
5. Hamilton A & I, Hamilton
6. Limestone Correctional Center, Capshaw
7. Red Eagle Honor Farm, Montgomery
8. Kilby Corrections Facility, Mt. Meigs
   Disciplinary Rehabilitation Unit (Kilby CC), Mt. Meigs
9. St. Clair Correctional Facility, Springville
10. Frank Lee Youth Center, Deatsville
11. State Cattle Ranch, Greensboro
12. Julia Tutwiler Prison for Women, Wetumpka
13. Ventress Correctional Facility, Clayton
14. West Jefferson Correctional Facility, Bessemer

Figure 9.2 ■ **Alabama Prison System.** The number and variety of institutions in Alabama is typical of most medium-sized states. What factors might influence the location of penal institutions?

Source: American Correctional Association, *Juvenile and Adult Correctional Facilities Directory* (College Park, Md.: American Correctional Association, 1991), pp. 4–6.

To a great extent, the total capacity of a state's prisons reflects the size of the state's population. Yet, as discussed in Chapter 17 on incarceration trends, the number of offenders in a state's institutions reflects something more than crime rates or social factors. States vary considerably in the number, size, type, and location of correctional facilities. Michigan's state prison at Jackson, for example, has a capacity of more than four thousand, while some specialized institutions house fewer than 100 inmates. Some states, such as New Hampshire, have centralized the incarceration of offenders in a few institutions, while other states (California, New York, Texas) have a wide mix of size and style of facilities—secure institutions, diagnostic units, work camps, for-

estry centers, and prerelease centers. As shown in Figure 9.2, Alabama has twelve correctional institutions (prisons), a disciplinary rehabilitation unit, an honor farm, the state cattle ranch, a prison for women, and a youth center for male felons under age twenty-five, in addition to eleven community-based facilities.[8]

The Design and Classification of Prisons

Since the era of John Howard in England and the Quakers in Philadelphia, attention has been given to the design of prisons. In all eras attempts have been made to design correctional institutions that would advance the current purpose of the criminal sanction. In this section, we discuss some of the changes and concepts in prison design.

A cardinal principle of architecture is that form follows function: The design of a structure should serve its purpose. Thus, during the era of the penitentiary, efforts were directed toward building institutions that would promote penance. When industry was added, a different style enhanced the efficiency of the workshops. When punishment through custody held sway, the emphasis was on the fortresslike edifice that ensures security. And during the 1950s and 1960s, new prisons were built in styles thought to promote treatment. At all times, however, the plans of the architects had to be "realistic" with regard to cost.

During the early nineteenth century, some of the greatest architects of England and the United States specialized in designing penitentiaries so that the space created would serve the purposes of contemplation, industry, and isolation, thought to be the necessary conditions for reform. The Boston Prison Discipline Society believed that to some degree the improvement of morals depended on the type of prison building that was constructed.[9]

As discussed in Chapter 3, Eastern Penitentiary in Philadelphia, designed by English emigré John Haviland, is probably the best example of a structure shaped by the commitment to moral uplift. The cell areas radiated from a central point like the spokes of a wheel from the hub. Each cell had its own exercise yard, with walls so arranged that other prisoners could not be seen. In many ways the prisons of Europe and the United States during the nineteenth century were designed, like the great cathedrals of an earlier era, to overwhelm the persons within them and impress upon them the need to mend their ways.

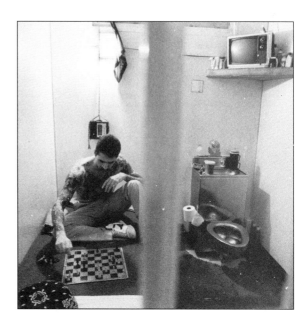

Even in the newest, best-designed prisons offenders are provided with only a minimum level of amenities, privacy, and space.

the functions required of them when new purposes of the criminal sanction are advanced, the inmate population swells, and the characteristics of prisoners change. Prisons are built to last. Four basic models can be found among America's prisons.

Radial design Prisons of the early nineteenth century tended to follow the **radial design** of Eastern Penitentiary (see Figure 9.3a). A control center at the hub makes it possible to monitor movement. From this central core, one or more "spokes" can be isolated from the rest of the institution during periods of trouble. Though Auburn Prison was organized to contrast with the separation and silence practiced at Eastern, it, too, was of the radial design. At

Today's Designs

The buildings constructed to suit the purposes of one era often cannot be adapted to perform

radial design   An architectural plan by which a prison is constructed in the form of a wheel, with "spokes" radiating from a central core.

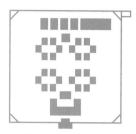

a Radial design   b Telephone-pole design   c Courtyard style   d Campus style

Figure 9.3 ■ **Prison Designs Used in the United States.** These four basic designs are used throughout the country for most prisons housing adult felons. Each style has certain features related to the goals of "keeping and serving" the prisoners. How does architecture influence the managing of these institutions?

other present-day locations, such as Leavenworth, Rahway, and Trenton, the old design persists, but few new prisons have been built to such specifications.[10]

Telephone-pole design In a prison based on the **telephone-pole design,** a long central corridor (the pole) serves as the means for prisoners to go from one part of the institution to another (Figure 9.3b). Jutting out from the corridor are cross-arms, each containing one of the functional areas of the institution: housing, shops, school, recreation area, and so on. Continuous surveillance is possible from the central axis, and access to each functional area may be controlled independently.

The telephone pole is undoubtedly the design most commonly used for maximum security prisons in the United States. Graterford, Pennsylvania; Marion, Illinois; Somers, Connecticut; and Jackson, Georgia, are designed in this fashion. Built for custody, the prison of this design can house prisoners according to classification levels: Certain housing areas may be designated for

inmates with special needs or for those whose conduct has merited extra privileges.

The telephone-pole prison can lead to what is called overdetermination: a situation in which everything—

> decisions, space, movement, and responsibility—is clearly and narrowly defined. All activities are scheduled. Social contacts are predetermined. The physical setting is limited and monotonous … It is a condition in which groups can be easily supervised, where authority can be maintained and one in which accountability for personal action lies beyond the individual.[11]

Another consequence can be that the prison population is cut off from the world they once knew and that daily and seasonal variations are lost. For these reasons, it can be argued that confinement "prepares only for confinement"; it does not prepare the inmate for reentry to the community.[12]

Courtyard style Some of the newer correctional facilities, including some maximum security prisons, are built in the **courtyard style** (Figure 9.3c). Movement along the endless corridors of the telephone-pole design from one part of the prison to another is replaced by movement across the courtyard. The housing

---

telephone-pole design An architectural plan for a prison calling for a long central corridor crossed at regular intervals by structures containing the prison's functional areas.

units and other functional areas surround the courtyard. In some facilities of this type, such functional units as the dining hall, gym, and school are located in the entry yard area.

Campus style A design long used for correctional facilities for juveniles or women, the **campus style** (Figure 9.3d), also appears among some of the newer institutions for men under maximum security. Relatively small housing units are scattered among the shops, school, dining hall, and other units of the facility. It is thought to be an important development not only because of the humane features of the design but also because individual buildings can be used more flexibly. As in prisons of the courtyard style, inmates and staff must go outdoors to get from one part of the facility to another. Although the campus style appears to provide less security than more conventional prison designs, Nagel and his team found that fences served the custody goal adequately. It must be emphasized, however, that most facilities of this type serve the medium and minimum security populations.[13]

Location of Prisons

As they were in the past, most prisons for adults are located in rural areas. Originally, the relative isolation was thought to help inmates repent because urban distractions and contacts with family would be missing. When more prisons were built later in the nineteenth century, the country setting was retained because the institutions were expected to maintain farms that would contribute to their self-sufficiency. At the present time, even though most prison inmates come from cities and reintegration has been emphasized as a correctional goal, new institutions are still being built in the countryside.

Part of the reasoning for this is related to land costs, but political factors also figure in the decision. Apparently, many people believe that serious offenders should be incarcerated but that prisons should not be built in their community. This attitude is often referred to as the NIMBY Syndrome (*Not In My Backyard*). Research has disputed the contention that the building of a correctional institution lowers property values, but these concerns and such others as community safety have the political impact of restricting the decisions of criminal justice planners to locate facilities in some areas. One result is that prisons tend to be welcomed only in the less economically developed parts of a state where it is believed that the institution will bring jobs and local spending to the community.

Classification of Prisons

Prisons for men are usually classified according to the level of security deemed necessary: maximum, medium, and minimum. Most states have so few women prisoners that they are all housed in one institution, and those who require higher levels of security are segregated. Male inmates are assigned to a specific type of facility, depending on such factors as the seriousness of the offense, the possibility of an attempt to escape, and the potential for violent behavior. Many states do not have an institution designed for each level of security, so a facility is often divided into sections for different categories of prisoners. There are no national design or classification standards, so a maximum security facility in one state may be run as a medium security facility in another. Yet some generalizations can be made.

Maximum security prison Usually an awesome edifice surrounded by high stone walls studded with guard towers, the **maximum**

---

courtyard style An architectural design by which the functional units of a prison are housed in separate buildings constructed on four sides of a hollow square.

campus style An architectural design by which the functional units of a prison are individually housed in a complex of buildings surrounded by a fence.

In the maximum security prison, control is a dominant goal. What are the problems of carrying out the other goals of incarceration in such an environment?

security prison (sometimes called the closed custody prison) is designed to prevent escapes and to deter prisoners from harming each other. Such facilities house 26 percent of all prisoners. Inmates live in cells, each with its own sanitary facilities. The barred doors may be operated electronically so that an officer can confine all prisoners to their cells with the flick of a switch. The purpose of the maximum security facility is custody and discipline; the approach to order is similar to that of the military. Groups of prisoners may be allowed to move from area to area only in the company of a guard. Prisoners march to meals and to work, wear uniforms, and follow a strict routine. Head counts are frequent, and surveillance of behavior—often through closed-circuit

television—eliminates privacy. Because these structures are built to last, many that went up at the turn of the century, when custody was the dominant model of incarceration, are still in use, even though their design makes it difficult to adapt many of them to the rehabilitation and reintegration models of contemporary corrections. The old prisons are not alone in their bad repute; a newer prison, Walpole State Prison in Massachusetts, built in the 1950s, has been described as the "concrete horror," one of the most dehumanizing facilities in the United States. Some of the most noted prisons, such as Stateville, Attica, Yuma, and Sing Sing, are maximum security facilities.

Medium security prison The **medium security prison** externally resembles the maximum security prison, but it is organized on a somewhat different basis and its atmosphere is less rigid and tense. In some states what is labeled a medium security prison seems much closer to a maximum security institution than to a minimum security institution. However, prisoners generally do have more privileges and contact with the outside world through visitors and mail, and access to radio and television is freer. Medium security prisons usually place greater emphasis on work and rehabilitative programs because the 49 percent of all inmates housed in them, although they may have committed serious crimes, are not perceived to be intractable, hardened criminals. Some of the newer facilities of this classification are constructed on the campus or courtyard model, though the barbed-wire fences, guard towers, and other security devices remain.

Minimum security prison The remaining 25 percent of inmates are housed in **minimum security prisons.** The architecture and secu-

---

maximum security prison A prison designed and organized to minimize the possibility of escapes and violence; to that end it imposes strict limitations on the freedom of inmates and visitors.

medium security prison A prison designed and organized to prevent escapes and violence but in which restrictions on inmates and visitors are less rigid than in facilities for more dangerous offenders.

rity measures of these facilities are quite different from those found at maximum security prisons. Housing the least difficult offenders, the minimum security prison does not have the guard towers and walls usually associated with correctional institutions. Often the buildings are surrounded by Cyclone fencing. Many of the newer institutions are built according to the campus model, with low, scattered buildings. Prisoners generally live dormitory style, or even in small private rooms, rather than in barred cells. There is a relatively high level of personal freedom: Inmates may have television sets, choose their own clothes, and move about casually within and among the buildings. Minimum security institutions rely more heavily on treatment programs and offer opportunities for education and work release. Some regions contain minimum security prison camps where the inmates work on forest conservation projects and perform firefighting duties. To the outsider, it may seem that little punishment is associated with a minimum security prison, but the inmates are segregated from society and their freedoms are restricted; it is still a prison.

Private Prisons

Corrections is a multibillion-dollar, government-funded enterprise that purchases supplies, materials, and services from the private sector. Many jurisdictions have long relied on private vendors to provide specific institutional services and to operate aftercare facilities and programs on a contractual basis. Businesses furnish food and medical services, education and vocational training, maintenance, security, and industrial programs. Health care and food services are two of the fastest growing sectors of the corrections enterprise with one corporation, Prison Health Services Incorporated, receiving $19 million in

It is sometimes difficult to recognize minimum security facilities as prisons. To the observer the Eagle River Correctional Center looks like a school or ski lodge.

1988, while prison food services are estimated to be a $1-billion-a-year business. The Campbell Soup Company reported that the fastest growing portion of the food service industry was with the nation's prisons.[14]

Especially since the rise of community corrections in the 1960s, there has been a great increase in the number and type of services purchased from nonprofit organizations operating halfway houses, group homes, juvenile care facilities, and work release programs. Now, with prisons and jails overcrowded and staff costs rising, private entrepreneurs have begun to build and run correctional facilities for adult offenders. They argue that they can operate such facilities as effectively, safely, and humanely as any level of government can, and that their efficiency can lower costs to taxpayers yet allow a profit for themselves.

The first secure correctional institution privately operated was the Intensive Treatment Unit, a twenty-bed, high-security, dormitory-style training school for delinquents opened in 1975 by RCA Corporation in Weaversville, Pennsylvania. A prison for youthful offenders near San Francisco, contracted by the U.S. Bureau of Prisons to Eclectic Communications, Inc., opened in 1983. Private facilities for aliens

minimum security prison A prison designed and organized to permit inmates and visitors as much freedom as is consistent with the concept of incarceration.

in Arizona, California, Colorado, and Texas are operated under contract from the U.S. Immigration and Naturalization Service (INS); some jails in Texas and Wyoming are run by Southwest Detention Facilities; and a 250-bed medium security facility in Chattanooga, Tennessee, is operated by Corrections Corporation of America. In January 1986, Kentucky's Marion Adjustment Center became the first privately owned and operated (by U.S. Corrections Corporation) facility for the incarceration of adult felons sentenced at a classification of at least minimum security. By mid-1992 Charles Thomas counted eighteen companies, such as Corrections Corporation of America, United States Corrections Corporation, and Wackenhut Corrections Corporation, running sixty adult confinement facilities totaling almost 20,000 beds in seventeen states. An additional seven facilities with a total of 5,000 beds are scheduled to be opened by mid-1993.[15] However, Charles Logan notes that it is difficult to be precise in this count because it is not always clear how to classify institutions and because contractual prisons and jails can spring so rapidly into and out of existence.[16]

The major advantages cited by advocates of privately operated prisons are that such prisons provide more cheaply and flexibly the same level of care now provided by the states. Logan's study of private prisons points to the difficulties of measuring the costs and quality of these institutions. One of the problems is that many of the "true costs" (fringe benefits, contracting supervision, federal grants) are not taken into consideration. The quoted rates of existing private facilities range greatly. A report for the National Institute of Corrections, for example, cites a cost of $30 per day at Okeechobee School for Boys in Florida and $110 a day at Weaversville. The INS facilities for illegal aliens operate on average daily rates of $23 to $28.[17]

As far as the issue of care is concerned, Logan's survey leads him to argue that until there are comparative private-public studies, reliance must be on anecdotal evidence, such as James Finckenauer's evaluation of the Weaversville facility. At the conclusion of his research Finckenauer expressed the opinion that the institution was "better staffed, organized, and equipped than any program of its size that I know."[18]

Political, fiscal, ethical, and administrative issues must be examined before corrections becomes too heavily committed to the private ownership and operation of prisons. The political issues, including ethical questions of the propriety of delegating social control functions to entities other than the state, may be the most difficult to overcome. Some people believe that the administration of justice is one of the basic functions of government and that it should not be delegated. They fear that correctional policy would be skewed because contractors would use their political influence to continue programs not in the public interest; would press for the maintenance of high occupancy levels, thus widening the net of social control; and would be interested only in skimming off the cream of the crop, leaving the most troublesome inmates to the public correctional system. As we have noted, it is not yet possible to demonstrate the economic value of private corrections, but labor unions have opposed these incursions into the public sector, pointing out that the salaries, benefits, and pensions of workers in such spheres as private security are inferior to those of their public counterparts. Finally, questions have been raised about the quality of services, the accountability of service providers to corrections officials, and problems related to contract supervision. Opponents cite the many instances of privately contracted services in group homes, day-care centers, hospitals, and schools that have been terminated after reports of corruption, brutality, or provision of only minimal services.

The idea of privately run correctional facilities has stimulated much interest among the general public and within the criminal justice community. The privatization of criminal justice services may expand, or it may become only a limited venture that was spawned at a time of prison crowding, fiscal constraints, and renewal of the free-enterprise ideology. The controversy has, however, forced corrections to rethink some strongly held beliefs. To this extent, the possibility of competition from the private sector may have positive results.

Correctional Facilities Today

The design and operational characteristics of correctional institutions for adult felons vary considerably from state to state, but most such institutions are old and large. More than half of the nation's inmates are in prisons with average daily populations of more than a thousand, and about 35 percent are in prisons built more than fifty years ago. More than 12 percent of inmates are held in facilities built before 1888.[19]

Some states and the federal government have created facilities that are small and are designed to meet individual correctional needs, but the rest of the states make do with antiquated megaprisons that have the maintenance and operational deficiencies associated with old, intensively used buildings.

With the national increase in the number of prisoners, the distinctions among the categories of facilities have been lost in some states. As prisons have come to be increasingly populated by persons who have committed serious violent crimes, security levels have risen. The line between maximum and medium security has disappeared in some correctional systems as crowding has forced administrators to house inmates requiring maximum security in medium security facilities. Some penologists believe that too great a share of the inmate population is housed in maximum security facilities, but others say that this level of security is necessary, given the nature of the inmates, and that prison space is so expensive that it must be used in a cost-effective manner.

Who Is in Prison?

The composition of the inmate population in terms of age, race, education, and criminal records has a determining impact on the operation of correctional institutions. What are the social characteristics of inmates in our nation's prisons? Do most offenders have long records of serious offenses or are there significant portions who have committed minor offenses and therefore do not "need" incarceration? These questions are crucial to an understanding of the policies and operations of America's prisons.

Although data on the social characteristics of prisoners are limited, there have been national surveys by the Bureau of Justice Statistics and interviews with individual prisoners by the Rand Corporation. On the basis of a national survey of state prisons, the Bureau of Justice Statistics (BJS) said in 1982, and later confirmed in 1991, that this population is predominantly made up of

> poor young adult males with less than a high school education. Prison is not a new experience for them; they have been incarcerated before, many first as juveniles. The offense that brought them to prison was a violent crime or burglary. On the average they have already served one and a half years on a maximum sentence of eight and a half years. Along with a criminal history, they have a history of drug abuse and are also likely to have a history of alcohol abuse.[20]

The summary characteristics described above are further illustrated by Figure 9.4. Note that most prisoners are in their late twenties to early thirties, have less than a high school education, and are disproportionately members of minority groups. In addition, more than half are incarcerated because of a violent crime.

Although many people may believe that many first-time offenders are incarcerated, such is not the case. A BJS survey has shown that more than 60 percent of inmates have been either incarcerated or on probation at least twice; 45 percent of them, three or more times; and nearly 20 percent, six or more times. In addition, almost half are incarcerated because of a violent crime or had previously been convicted of a violent crime. Thus, in the contemporary prison most offenders entering

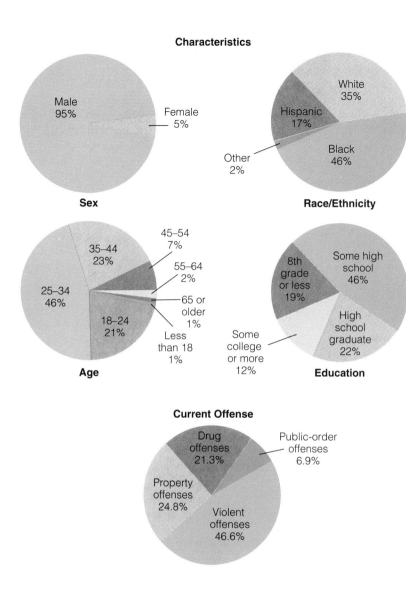

Characteristics

Sex

Male 95%

Female 5%

Race/Ethnicity

White 35%

Hispanic 17%

Black 46%

Other 2%

Age

45–54 7%

35–44 23%

55–64 2%

25–34 46%

65 or older 1%

18–24 21%

Less than 18 1%

Education

Some high school 46%

8th grade or less 19%

High school graduate 22%

Some college or more 12%

Current Offense

Drug offenses 21.3%

Public-order offenses 6.9%

Property offenses 24.8%

Violent offenses 46.6%

Figure 9.4 ■ Sociodemographic and Offense Characteristics of State Prison Inmates. These data tell us something about the types of people found in American state prisons. What do they indicate about the belief that many offenders do not "need" to be incarcerated? What do these characteristics tell us about the management of prisons?

Source: U.S. Department of Justice, Bureau of Justice Statistics, *Special Report* (Washington, D.C.: Government Printing Office, 1988), p. 3.

and most leaving have long, long records; they have histories of persistent criminality.[21]

Correctional officials have recently become aware of the increasing number of prison inmates who are older than fifty-five. As discussed in Chapter 5, that number is now more than 20,000, with about 400 over eighty-five years old. About half of these inmates are serving long sentences; the other half committed crimes late in life. Whereas older prisoners are still a small portion of the total inmate population, their numbers are doubling every four years. Elderly prisoners have security and medical needs that are different from the average inmate. In a number of states special sections of the institution have been designated for this older population so that they will not have to mix with the younger, tougher inmates. Costly medical needs are also a problem that corrections must address. For this aging group, chronic illnesses such as heart disease, stroke, and cancer may develop. The average yearly maintenance and medical costs for inmates over fifty-five is about $69,000, triple that of the norm. Will some prisons be renamed Centers for the Correctional Treatment of Old Folks?[22]

WORKPERSPECTIVE

Realization

Wayne B. Alexander

Hearing the cell door slam shut the first time, there is a gripping realization, almost spiritual for some, that the consequences of crime are terribly real. Every memory, all of the past, good and bad, returns to haunt. Every single indelible moment is etched upon the mind's eye at some point, and painful memories invade conscious thought. The act, the arrest, pretrial and trial, conviction and sentencing, and most of all the last three hours flood involuntarily into mind and heart.

I look around at the cool, unforgiving gray concrete walls and feel the hopelessness. The helplessness of my predicament. The accommodations are welded and brazed and anchored into the concrete to last for years of use.

The gnawing fear that has been building steadily since hearing the door slam shut prompts me to jump up and test the door to see if it's really locked. It is.

Coming to terms with this reality begins one of the many emotional storms raging inside me. The raw fear penetrates and subsides, and the fight to control myself from crying out or pleading like a small child is a constant struggle.

This sensation of being torn apart from within by conflicting emotions vying for control is the most frightening human experience known. Nothing compares to the realization that I am being confined and controlled so totally. "Oh, God, no," I cry to myself. "Please don't let this be!"

After two hours the door slides back and a shout—"Chow!"—is heard. Steel doors slam, keys clang, and there is the shuffling of hundreds of feet. The strange, listless, angry, and embittered faces of the others offer painful insight into this subculture.

With 68 percent of the adult inmate population under thirty-five, correctional officials have had to address such inmate-related issues as violence, boredom, drug use, and homosexual behavior. In addition, there is now the problem of AIDS and related health issues. It is precisely this age group, so heavily represented in prison, for which AIDS is expected to be the leading cause of death among males in the United States. As discussed in Chapter 5, officials have had to deal with a set of issues related to the segregation and treatment of AIDS victims.

Obviously, the characteristics of the prisoner population today differ markedly from that of even a quarter century ago. Compared with the "big house" era of the 1950s, today's inmate is more likely to be incarcerated for a violent offense and is more likely to be African or Hispanic American. The tensions of incarceration are heightened by the overcrowded facilities found in most states. Because prison space is an expensive resource, it can be expected—in the absence of expansion—that corrections will be working increasingly with the most serious offenders, while first-time and less violent criminals will be placed on probation or given intermediate sanctions in the community.

Lock in! 8:30 P.M. Until the morning meal, that door will be locked. Can I make it? The struggle rages again as I feel tears well up behind fatigued eyes. After two hours a uniformed arm pokes a flashlight into the cell for a moment and withdraws. Counted, and counted and counted again, I am among the best-monitored individuals outside an intensive care unit in the country. More than a half-dozen times a day I am counted to ensure that I still suffer. In addition, clothes, underwear, property, and every file about me bears the assigned number that was issued during the processing.

I didn't know until this day that it was possible to tag, count, and store human beings like merchandise in a warehouse. Yet in this modern maximum security "correctional institution," the insidiously antiseptic ritual of accepting an individual and transforming him into a number is as normal as sending youngsters on their way to school every morning on a yellow bus.

The consequences, again, become sparklingly clear and real. By committing a crime, I have plunged headlong into this nightmare of living death. I am condemned and I am so sorry; God, I'm sorry. I look around and realize there is no one to tell it to. In that moment I come to the realization that I have been forsaken. I have been cast out of a free society and branded with a number, never to achieve a position of trust or a level of responsibility that I might be capable of. I have come to the place of punishment and proved that the criminal justice system is alive and well in America.

I, the convicted, the incarcerated, come face to face with all these truths, only to sit mute upon my bunk, isolated by a society I so desperately want to apologize to.

Since 1974 Wayne B. Alexander has spent only a year and a half outside prison. Convicted of murder and other crimes, he is now serving a life term.

Source: Reprinted by permission.

Summary

Prisons today are very unlike the prisons of even the 1950s. The incarcerated population is larger, the convicts are different, and the goals are more ambitious. Unfortunately, most of the facilities were constructed in an earlier time when other goals were dominant and the population was of another sort.

Three models of incarceration have been prominent during the past two decades: custodial, rehabilitation, and reintegration. Each is linked closely to one of the goals of punishment, and its implementation requires a particular organizational emphasis with corresponding tasks.

The architectural design of prisons has been a concern of administrators since the construction of Eastern Penitentiary. Of the various plans that have been used, the telephone-pole design is most commonly found in maximum security prisons. The campus, courtyard, and radial designs are found in some areas.

Correctional institutions are classified as either maximum, medium, or minimum security prisons. This classification encompasses not only the physical aspects of the institution but also the internal organization of staff and the rules governing the prisoners. The higher the security level, the tighter the rules for prisoners and the more restricted their movements.

For Discussion

1. Although the custody model is the most popular for organizing a prison today, would any other model be appropriate?

2. What are the positive and negative aspects of the various prison designs? Do certain designs seem to correlate with certain goals of incarceration?

3. What ethical questions have been raised by the emergence of prisons run by private, profit-making organizations?

4. Which characteristics of the prison population may present major problems for the managers of institutions?

5. If you were a warden, what would be your policy with respect to prisoners with AIDS?

For Further Reading

Hawkins, Gordon. *The Prison.* Chicago: University of Chicago Press, 1976. A critical view of the American prison and its future, examining such policy issues as the role of correctional officers, prisoner's rights, and impediments to reform.

Jacobs, James B. *New Perspectives on Prisons and Imprisonment.* Ithaca, N.Y.: Cornell University Press, 1983. A collection of twelve essays written by the author depicting the socio-legal history of the American prison since 1960.

Johnson, Robert. *Hard Time: Understanding and Reforming the Prison.* Pacific Grove, Calif.: Brooks/Cole, 1987. A significant contribution to understanding the prison experience.

Keve, Paul W. *Prisons and the American Conscience.* Carbondale: Southern Illinois University Press, 1991. A history of U.S. federal corrections from 1776.

Logan, Charles. *Private Prisons: Cons and Pros.* New York: Oxford University Press, 1990. A definitive view of the issues surrounding the private prison question.

Nagel, William G. *The New Red Barn: A Critical Look at the Modern American Prison.* New York:

Walker, 1973. An argument for a greater focus on programs; written by an advocate of rehabilitation.

Notes

1. Charles H. Logan, "Criminal Justice Performance Measures for Prisons" (paper given at national conference of the Bureau of Justice Statistics and the Justice Research and Statistics Association, New Orleans, La., September 23–26, 1992), p. 6.

2. Ibid., p. 6.

3. U.S. Department of Justice, Bureau of Justice Statistics, *National Update* (Washington, D.C.: Government Printing Office, July 1992), p. 10.

4. U.S., Department of Justice, Bureau of Justice Statistics, *Bulletin* (Washington, D.C.: Government Printing Office, May 1992), p. 3.

5. U.S. Department of Justice, Bureau of Justice Statistics, *Special Report* (Washington, D.C.: Government Printing Office, June 1992), p. 6.

6. U.S. Department of Justice, Federal Bureau of Prisons, *State of the Bureau, 1991* (Washington, D.C.: Government Printing Office, 1992), p. 3.

7. U.S. Department of Justice, *Sourcebook of Criminal Justice Statistics—1990* (Washington, D.C.: Government Printing Office, 1991), p. 23.

8. American Correctional Association, *Juvenile and Adult Correctional Facilities Directory* (College Park, Md.: American Correctional Association, 1991), p. 4.

9. David B. Rothman, *Discovery of the Asylum* (Boston: Little, Brown, 1971), p. 83.

10. William G. Nagel, *The New Red Barn: A Critical Look at the Modern American Prison* (New York: Walker, 1973), p. 36.

11. Ibid., p. 40.

12. Ibid., p. 41.

13. Ibid., p. 36.

14. Paul Knepper, "A Brief History of Profiting from the Punishment of Crime" (paper presented at the annual meeting of the American Society of Criminology, San Francisco, November 20–24, 1991).

15. Charles Thomas, "Private Prisons Report," *Public Works Financing* (July/August 1992): 11–13.

16. Charles Logan, *Private Prisons: Cons and Pros* (New York: Oxford University Press, 1990), p. 16.

17. Camille G. Camp and George M. Camp, *Private Sector Involvement in Prison Services and Operations* (Washington, D.C.: National Institute of Corrections, 1984).

18. Cited in Kevin Krajick, "Punishment for Profit," *Across the Board* 21 (1984): 25.

19. U.S. Department of Justice, Bureau of Justice Statistics, *Report to the Nation on Crime and Justice* (Washington, D.C.: Government Printing Office, 1988), p. 107.

20. U.S. Department of Justice, Bureau of Justice Statistics, *Survey of State Prison Inmates* (Washington, D.C.: Government Printing Office, 1993), p. 3.

21. U.S. Department of Justice, Bureau of Justice Statistics, *Special Report* (Washington, D.C.: Government Printing Office, January 1988), p. 3.

22. Newsweek, 20 November 1989, p. 70.

10

The Prison Experience

I've wanted somehow to convey to you the sensations ... of what it is to be seriously a long-term prisoner in an American prison.... To be in prison so long, it's difficult to remember exactly what you did to get there.

John Henry Abbott, prisoner and author,
In the Belly of the Beast

Prison Society
Norms and Values
Indigenous or Imported?
Adaptive Roles
The Prison Economy
Prison Violence
Causes of Prison Violence
Prisoner-Prisoner Violence
Prisoner-Officer Violence
Officer-Prisoner Violence
Institutional Structure
What Can Be Done About Prison Violence?
Discipline of Prisoners
The Disciplinary Process
Summary

The gray bus with heavy wire mesh over the windows wends its way through the countryside. Inside, twelve passengers, the driver, and two uniformed guards sit quietly, each looking forward. The silence holds as the miles roll by. The riders do not seem to notice the stares of the curious in passing cars. There is tension in the air.

The twelve passengers are chained, one to another. It is the chain more than anything else that differentiates this bus and its passengers from those of Greyhound or Trailways. These are captives, prisoners being moved from the jail to the reception center of the state prison. The chain is justified for security reasons, to prevent the captives from taking over the bus or escaping. But the links also perform the function of symbolizing to those who are bound together that they are powerless and that the state will determine most aspects of the experience awaiting them in prison. The symbolism of the chain is so great that in the language of the captives, the bus in which they are riding is called "The Chain."

Even the most hardened criminal must be tense and nervous upon entering (or reentering) the prison. For the "fish," the newcomer, the first few hours and days must be a time of worry and anxiety. "What will it be like? Is it as bad as the stories told in the jail? How should I act? Will I be able to protect myself?" The new prisoner is apprehensive, just like the immigrant starting out in a country where the language is incomprehensible, the customs are strange, and the rules are unfamiliar. But unlike the immigrant, the prisoner has no freedom to choose where and with whom to live. It is this important factor that distinguishes the society of captives from other social groupings.

The experience of being incarcerated— What does it mean to the inmates, the guards, and the administrators? How do prisons function? Are the officers in charge or do the prisoners "rule the joint"? Because we will be examining the social and personal dimensions of prison life, assume that you are visiting a foreign land and attempting to learn about its culture and daily activities. The prison may be located in the United States, but the traditions, language, and relationships are unlike anything you are used to. This chapter will explore aspects of the prison experience so that as citizens we will have a better understanding of this portion of the criminal justice system, and so that as potential correctional administrators we may know some of the ways and problems of the society that constitutes a maximum security institution.

Prison Society

The 1934 publication of Joseph Fishman's *Sex in Prison* marked the beginning of the scientific study of inmate subcultures in maximum security institutions.[1] Since that time, social scientists have been fascinated by the prison as a functioning community with its own values, roles, language, and customs. By reviewing the major studies of prison society, we can learn about this "foreign" culture, appreciate the impact of incarceration on its subjects, see how inmates adapt to their environment, and trace changes in corrections over time.

All researchers recognize that the inmates of a maximum security prison do *not* serve their terms in isolation. Rather, prisoners form a society with traditions, norms, and a leadership structure. Some may choose to associate with only a few close friends, while others form cliques along racial or "professional" lines. Some are the politicians of the convict society: They attempt to represent the inmates' interests and distribute valued goods in return for support. Others assume different roles. Just as there is a social culture in the free world, there is a culture within the prison walls.

The concept of the prisoner subculture is useful for our purposes, but it should not be given undue importance. It is true that, like members of other groups who interact primarily among themselves and are physically separated from the larger world (the military, medical patients, monks), inmates develop their own myths, slang, customs, rewards, and sanctions. But in recent times, prisons have lost much of their isolation from the larger society, and the concept of the prisoner subculture as isolated, separate, and opposed to the dominant culture may be incorrect. Although prisons do create special conditions that compel inmates to adapt to their environment, most inmates are now incarcerated for less than three years, and the culture of the outside world enters the institution through television, magazines, newspapers, and visitors. In short, the prison is very much a product of institutional and political relationships between the prison and the larger society.

The appearance of Donald Clemmer's *Prison Community* in 1940 set the pattern for much of the subcultural analysis that followed. A staff member at the Menard Penitentiary in Illinois, Clemmer collected a wealth of data over a three-year period and described the institutional world with particular reference to language, distinctive roles, the group structure of the population, and sexual behavior. Clemmer developed the concept of **prisonization,** the adaptation of a new inmate to the customs of prison society.[2]

Gresham Sykes's study of the New Jersey State Maximum Security Prison, *The Society of Captives* (1958), built on Clemmer's foundation. Sykes argued that the new inmate is faced with five major pains of imprisonment to which each prisoner may respond in ways that are either alienative or cohesive. For Sykes, the major goal of the inmate system is cohesion, for inmate solidarity increases "the likelihood that the pains of imprisonment will be ren-

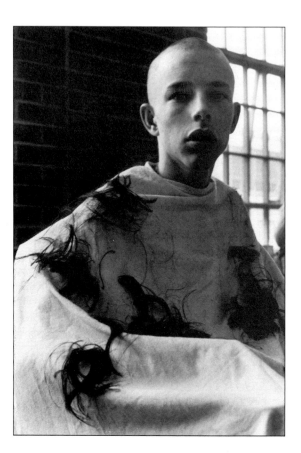

Entering prison society may be a depersonalizing experience.

dered less severe for the inmate population as a whole."[3]

Reflecting the new racial composition of the contemporary prison, Leo Carroll's *Hacks, Blacks, and Cons* (1974) was the first major subculture study to identify the emergence of race as a factor structuring inmate social relations during the politically explosive late 1960s.[4] This work was followed by Irwin's 1980 study of the division of the culture of California prisons into white, black, and Hispanic subgroups. Irwin documents the emergence of gangs in these institutions and further emphasizes the links of the prison community with the outside.[5]

Prisoner subcultures vary from institution to institution and change over time, reflecting

---

prisonization   The process by which a new inmate absorbs the customs of the prison society and learns to adapt to the environment.

shifts in the characteristics of the inmates, the administrator's style of management, and the influence of the outside world. The studies just discussed have made important contributions to our understanding of the convict world, and the concepts they propose are useful for the analysis of the way correctional institutions function. One must be cautious, however, in assuming that the culture that Clemmer found at Menard in the 1930s or that Sykes found in New Jersey in the 1950s is to be found at an institution today.

Norms and Values

Like any other society, the convict world has certain distinctive norms and values. The elements of the **inmate code** arise within the prison social system and help to define the convict's image of the model prisoner. The code also helps to differentiate the inmates and their values from the staff and staff values. The prisoner who follows the code can expect to enjoy a certain amount of admiration from other prisoners. Those who break the code can expect to be relegated to the bottom of the inmate social structure, alienated from the rest of the population and preyed upon.

The two primary rules of the inmate code are "do your own time" and "don't inform on another convict." As a result of his New Jersey study, Sykes refined the rules embodied in the code as follows:

1. Don't interfere with inmate interests: Never rat on a con, don't be nosy, don't have a loose lip, don't put a guy on the spot.

2. Don't quarrel with fellow inmates: Play it cool, don't lose your head, do your own time.

3. Don't exploit inmates: Don't break your word, don't steal from cons, don't sell favors, don't welsh on bets.

---

inmate code A set of rules of conduct that reflect the values and norms of the prison social system and help to define for inmates the image of the model prisoner.

4. Maintain yourself: Don't weaken, don't whine, don't cop out, be tough, be a man.

5. Don't trust the guards or the things they stand for: Don't be a sucker, guards are hacks and screws, the officials are wrong and the prisoners are right.[6]

How does the "fish," the newcomer, learn the norms and values of the prison society? In jail awaiting transfer to the prison, the fish hears from fellow inmates exaggerated descriptions of what lies ahead and anxiety mounts despite a possible show of bravado. The ride on "The Chain" and the reception center further initiate the novice. The actions of the reception center staff, folktales passed on by experienced cons, and the derisive shouts of the inmates on the inside all serve as elements of a degradation ceremony that shocks the new prisoner into readiness to begin the prisonization process. But not all prisoners complete this process; Clemmer suggests that such factors as a short sentence, continuation of contacts with the outside, a stable personality, and refusal to become part of the primary group can weaken the prisonization process.[7]

Because contemporary prison society has become increasingly heterogeneous, a single, overriding inmate code for a particular institution no longer seems to exist. A number of factors, among them the variety of cultural and subcultural (ethnic, class, and criminal) orientations, the variety of preprison experiences, and the intense, open hostility between segments of the prison population may work against the development of a code to which all inmates can subscribe. The lack of a single code accepted by the entire population makes administrators' tasks more difficult. They must be aware of the variations that exist among the groups, recognize the norms and rules differentially held and acknowledged, and deal with the leaders of many cliques rather than only a few inmates who have risen to top positions in the inmate society.

As the U.S. prison population has grown blacker, race has become a key variable dividing

Going In:
The Chain

Michael Knoll

We're crowded into the back of the police van, fifteen convicts en route to the state prison. I'm handcuffed to two other men, the chains gleaming dully at wrists and ankles. At intervals the man on my right lifts his hand to smoke, the red eye of his cigarette burning through the darkness in the van. When he exhales, the man at my left coughs, the sound in his lungs suggesting that he's old, maybe sick. I want to ask what he's in for. But I don't speak, restrained by my fear, a feeling that rises cold up the back of my spine. For a long time no one else speaks either, each man locked into his own thoughts. It's someone up front, a kid, his voice brittle with fear, who speaks first. "What's it like down there—in the joint? Is it as bad as they say?"

"Worse," someone answers. "Cell blocks are dirty. Overcrowded. Lousy chow. Harassment. Stabbings."

"How do you live there?"

"You don't exactly live. You go through the motions. Eat, sleep, mind your own business. Do drugs when you can get them. Forget the world you came from."

While the others ask the man questions, I let my mind wander back to a beach in Santa Monica, a girl's voice, perfume. When the van jerks and grinds sideways, the cuffs biting my wrist, I watch as the rear door swings open, hard sunlight flooding our faces.

"Everybody out. Slow."

Six khaki-suited guards surround the van, each man with a shotgun cradled over his arm. I examine their faces for compassion, find only contempt and indifference, and then strain to look past them into the compound. Within the perimeter are five gray stone buildings crowned with barbed wire. Encircling them is a high white stone wall, gun towers perched at intervals. My gut begins to knot as I realize I can see nothing beyond the high walls, that the walls for five years will fix the boundaries of my life. I feel my nerves tense and my legs go weak, the guard's voice floating toward me as if from a great distance. "Move it," the voice commands, and the column

convict society. Perhaps reflecting tensions in the broader community, many prisons are plagued by racially motivated violence, organizations based on racial symbolism, and the voluntary segregation of inmates by race in recreation areas and dining halls. Prisoners form small friendship groups and restrict interactions to these groups. For its members the groups afford protection from theft and physical assault, serve as the basis of wheeling and dealing activities, and provide a source of cultural identity.

The prisoner subculture designates inmates according to the roles they play in the society and the extent to which they conform to the code. Among the roles most frequently described in the literature are "right guy" or "real man" (upholder of prisoner values and interests), "square John" (an inmate with a noncriminal self-concept), "punk" (a passive homosexual), and "rat" (someone who squeals or sells out to the authorities).

Indigenous or Imported?

Where do the values of the prison subculture come from? How do they originate and become integrated into a code? Sykes argues that the

of prisoners moves reluctantly across the yard.

I walk behind the old man, noting that in the light he seems older, feebler, and somehow smaller. My attention shifts to the men gathering around us. Each is dressed in identical prison denim, each face showing the same predatory interest. Staring back, I understand slowly the source of their interest, sensing that for them we are the new meat. I wonder absently how I will live here.

The building into which we are taken is dimly lit, musty, and somehow archaic, as if built in another era. A red-faced guard unlocks our handcuffs, orders us to strip naked, spread our buttocks, hand over our clothes and personal property. "Donate the stuff or mail it home. Then line up to receive your numbers."

"What do you mean—numbers?" The old man's voice is frail but stiff with indignation. As if speaking to a child, the guard explains that the prison identifies inmates by number, that every man will have one.

I listen while the old prisoner and the guard argue, both their faces bright red, both their voices trembling. In the end the old man and all the rest of us accept a five-digit number, a bedroll, and a bundle of state-issue clothes. The room falls silent, the atmosphere one of restrained anger and muted frustration. The guard leads us out and down another dim corridor, emerging finally in a bright scorch of fluorescent light, a long high-ceilinged building. On two sides are stacked, six tiers high, cells as far as I can see. I flash back to the transport van, the man who'd advised: *Do drugs when you can. Forget the world you came from.* Looking down the shadowy tier, into the forest of green institutional iron, I think again of the Santa Monica beach, my girlfriend's face. The image clarifies vividly for one brief second. When I take my bedroll onto my shoulder, the memory vanishes. Walking slowly, I join the other prisoners, the old man, the red-faced guard who guides us purposefully toward our cells.

Source: Until his release in 1984, the author was a prisoner at the Arizona Correctional Training Center. Reprinted by permission of the author.

subculture arises within the prison in response to the pains of incarceration, which include the loss of liberty, personal autonomy, personal security, goods and services, and heterosexual relationships. These deprivations are an inescapable part of incarceration, and it is through full integration into the cohesive prison society that the captive is able to adapt to and compensate for them. Thus, this model emphasizes the deprivations of imprisonment as the basis for the emergence of the prisoner subculture; from Sykes's perspective the distinctive subculture of the prison emerged from within the institution.

An alternative to Sykes's theory of the indigenous prisoner subculture was first proposed by Clarence Schrag, who held that the values of the inmate community are also brought from outside the walls. He developed four major role configurations that he believed correspond to varying offense patterns, family and community experiences, and particular attitudes toward crime and society. These roles—"square John," "right guy," "con politician," and "outlaw"—are incubated outside and come with the prisoner to the institution, where they are further nurtured.[8] John Irwin and Donald Cressey refined Schrag's concepts.

Offenders do their time in a variety of ways. Some take advantage of prison programs while others do as little as possible. How would you do your time?

They argued that the prisoner subculture was really a combination of three subcultures: convict, thief, and "straight." The convict subculture, especially the subculture of the state-raised youth who makes a home of the prison, is indigenous; the other two subcultures are imported.[9]

Irwin and Cressey believe that the system of values, roles, and norms that exists in the adult prison results from the convergence of the convict and the thief subcultures. The convict subculture is found particularly among state-raised youth, those individuals who have been in and out of foster homes, detention centers, reform schools, and correctional institutions since puberty. They are used to living in a single-sex society, know the ways of institutional life, and in a sense make a home of prison. Thieves look upon crime as a lifework and are always preparing for the "big score." Irwin notes that thieves must exude a sense of "rightness" or "solidness" to be considered "all right" by their peers; the thief is a "right guy." "Straight" inmates ("square Johns") bring the culture of conventional society with them to the prison. They have been convicted for one-

time offenses and identify more with the staff than with the other inmates. They want to avoid trouble and get through their terms as quietly as possible.[10]

Adaptive Roles

On entering prison, the newcomer is confronted by the question "How am I going to do my time?" Some may decide to withdraw into their own world and isolate themselves from the other prisoners. Given the crowding of today's institutions, this strategy is probably a physical impossibility. Others may decide to become full participants in the convict social system, which "through its solidarity, regulation of activities, distribution of goods and prestige … helps the individual withstand the 'pains of imprisonment.'"[11] In other words, some inmates choose to identify mainly with the outside world while others orient themselves primarily toward the prison world. The choice of identity reflects the prisoner's values and strategies. Is the prisoner interested primarily in achieving prestige within the prison culture, or does the inmate want to maintain or realize the values of the free world?

Four concepts have been used to describe the lifestyles of inmates as they adapt to prison. "Doing time" and "gleaning" are the choices of inmates who try to maintain their links with and the perspective of the free world. "Jailing" is the style of those who cut themselves off from the outside and try to construct a world within the prison. The fourth category is the "disorganized criminal." Irwin believes the great majority of imprisoned felons may be classified according to these orientations.[12]

Doing time The "doing time" lifestyle is adopted by inmates who see the period in prison as a temporary break in their careers. They tend to be professional thieves—that is, criminals who look at their work as legitimate entrepreneurs look at theirs. A prison sentence to these inmates is one of the risks or overhead costs associated with their chosen profession. Such persons come to prison to "do time." They try to serve their terms with the least amount of suffering and the greatest amount of comfort. They avoid trouble by adhering to the inmate code, find activities to fill their days, form friendships with a few other convicts, and generally do what they think is necessary to get out as soon as possible.

Gleaning With rehabilitative programs available, some prisoners decide to spend their time "gleaning"—taking advantage of opportunities to change their lives by trying to acquire a skill, improve their minds, or "find themselves." They use every resource at hand: library, correspondence courses, vocational training programs, school. Some prisoners make a radical conversion to this prison lifestyle; those who do so are not usually committed to a life of crime.[13]

Jailing Convicts who have never had a commitment to the outside social world easily adopt a "jailing" lifestyle that makes a world of prison. They are likely to be state-raised youths. Because they know the institutional routine, have the skills required to "make it," and view prison as a familiar place, they often aspire to

leadership within the subculture. These are the inmates who seek positions that carry power and influence in the prison society. An assignment as a runner for a staff member enlarges the convict's freedom of movement within the institution and thus increases access to information. An inmate assigned to work in the kitchen storeroom can steal food and exchange it for cigarettes, the prison currency. By constantly dealing in goods that are valued—food, clothes, information, drugs—an inmate who is "jailing" can live more comfortably. This lifestyle has its rewards: the consumption itself and the increased prestige in the prison social system because of the display of opulence.

Disorganized criminal This category includes those who are unable to develop role orientations to prison life. Often of low intelligence or afflicted with psychological or physical disabilities, they have difficulty functioning within the prison society; they are the human putty that is manipulated by others.

Although we have touched on only four of the adaptive models chosen by inmates, we can see that prisoners are not members of an undifferentiated mass; individual members choose to play specific roles in the convict society. These models reflect the physical and social environment of the prison and contribute to the development of the system that maintains the institution's ongoing activities.

The Prison Economy

Incarceration has traditionally deprived inmates of more than liberty, for the belief has always been strong that prisoners should live a spartan existence; they should not be comfortable in confinement. The state feeds, clothes, and houses all prisoners, but amenities are scarce. Prison life is a kind of enforced destitution. The state has decreed that a life of extreme simplicity is part of the punishment of incarceration, and correctional

WORKPERSPECTIVE

My Husband Is in Prison

Tricia Hedin

Over the years, I've become quite resourceful in offering half-truths to those who ask about my marriage. "It is a commuter marriage," I say. Or, "My husband is an artist, working on a government grant." Sometimes, particularly when I'm tired, I try to change the subject. When my spirits and energy are high, though, I say the simple truth: "He is in prison."

The truth requires stamina, as any prison wife will explain. There are pitying smiles, silent reproaches, numerous questions, and shocked responses. I believe that few marriages come under such close scrutiny as those of inmates and their spouses. There are many reasons for the questions, usually founded on a lifetime of media images. But as with other marriages, there are no generalizations that hold true for all prison marriages. There are, however, experiences all prison wives share.

During the four years I have visited my husband in prison—he is serving a twenty-year sentence with a ten-year mandatory minimum for bank robbery—I have discovered an incredible support system among inmate wives. Some of the women have jobs; others receive public assistance. Many of them are single-handedly raising their children. Often it is the first time they have been on their own. One fifty-year-old woman waiting to visit her husband described to me the first time she changed a light bulb in her oven and completed her income-tax form. Another talked about taking the family cow to be slaughtered. Yet there is a camaraderie among us. We come from different ethnic backgrounds and economic classes, but we understand each other. We understand that we have had to become strong.

Wives of prisoners must adjust to arbitrary treatment by prison guards and administrators who treat us as if we were criminals like our husbands. We are subjected to reprimands, searches, and a multitude of bureaucratic requirements designed to discourage continued contact. ... Prison officials tend to discourage any type of networking among prisoners or their families. At the state penitentiary in Oregon, there is a rule against "cross-visiting": One inmate's visitor can't visit with another inmate. When we ask if the rule can be changed in order to promote a positive "community" atmosphere, we are told that there is no community among prison families nor does the prison wish to facilitate one.

Yet over and over again, women who are total strangers assist each other with advice about transportation and child care—and the techniques to fight bureaucratic battles. Our desire to keep our marriages and families intact

administrators believe that if discipline and security are to be maintained, rules must be enforced so that all prisoners are treated alike and none can gain higher position or status or comfort because of wealth or access to goods. Prisoners are deprived of everything but bare necessities; monotony reigns in diet and routine; uniformity of treatment takes away individual identity; rules are inescapable; recreational opportunities are few; and the sense of responsibility that is part of maturity cannot be exercised. As reflected in these and other ways

is a taxing one. Coping with the incarceration of a loved one is difficult and can often result in financial burdens, health problems, and social ostracism. Divorce is common; not all prisoners react positively when their wives begin to take control of their own lives. Some marriages break down when the prisoner is released and both parties have difficulty adjusting to the changes they have undergone.

There are only seven states that allow conjugal visits between prisoners and their wives. Therefore, prison wives must struggle with decisions about their sexual lives. Some base their decisions on individual moral and religious beliefs and remain celibate. Some work out detailed agreements with their husbands that may allow extramarital liaisons. Others base such decisions on the amount of time their husbands will be incarcerated. It is not sex with their husbands that most wives miss most of all; it is the intimacy and privacy. They long to be touched and held.

Organizations of prison wives are forming across the country, resulting in pressure for family-support groups, improved visitation conditions—including special playrooms where fathers can see their children—and better transition programs for released inmates. Studies show that inmates who maintain close family ties are less likely to commit crimes again.

But becoming involved in prison reform can be especially difficult for us. We must plan our actions carefully because we are always aware that our husbands are under the control of prison officials. Many small injustices must be ignored because prison guards have the power to harass and punish. Still, I believe that change is possible. Some prison officials have begun to recognize that family members are often forgotten victims in the criminal justice system and that we can assist in an inmate's rehabilitation. We know that prison is a destructive experience for those we care about, and we want to help lessen the negative impact. We also want to make sure they never return to prison.

I know the importance of love and trust in my relationship with my husband, of living in optimistic hope of a better future. I savor the time I spend in conversation with him, and I learn new ways of expressing intimacy in a crowded public area. I only hope that other prison wives will become proud of their special stamina. I hope that they, too, will cultivate connections with community leaders so they don't become isolated and that they will join to form the bridge from inside the prison walls to the outside world. For only we can help others understand that we are not crazy to love those who have made past mistakes. And we, who are strong enough to care, can really help keep our mates from going back to jail.

Tricia Hedin is a free-lance writer who resides in Eugene, Oregon.

Source: Newsweek, 15 December 1986, p. 14. Reprinted by permission of the author.

the prison is unique in having been deliberately designed as "an island of poverty in the midst of a society of relative abundance."[14]

Restrictions have eased a bit in recent years. Prisoners are still limited as to what they may have in their cells, but in some institutions, inmates now own television sets, civilian clothing, and hot plates.

How is this possible if possessions are taken from inmates when they enter the prison and if inmates are not permitted to hold money? Since the 1960s the items that prisoners in most institutions can acquire and possess through legitimate channels have greatly increased. Friends and relatives may send packages regularly as long as the gifts are prison-permitted items. Commissaries or "stores" run by the authorities sell a limited number of articles to the inmates, who use credits (scrip or coupons) drawn on the "bank accounts" (deposits from the outside or money earned from the sale of crafts or work in the prison industry).

Use of the commissary is a privilege that must be earned, however, and many inmates find that the usual stock does not satisfy their consumer needs. Prices are set to enable the store to break even or make not more than a modest profit, yet they are still too high for many inmates. As Susan Sheehan observed in her study of Green Haven Prison, New York, many things that the state does not provide are regarded by most prisoners as necessities simply because they are confined—"talcum powder and deodorant, because of the prisoner's more limited bathing facilities. Store-bought cigarettes, instant coffee, immersion coils for heating water and between-meal snacks—especially for the fifteen-hour period between supper and breakfast."[15] Offenders have difficulty adjusting to the lack of consumer goods. Sheehan notes that most of the men she studied were in prison "precisely because they were not willing to go without on the street. They are no more willing to go without in prison, so they hustle to obtain what they cannot afford to buy."[16]

As a consequence of the consumer needs and wants of prisoners, an informal, sub-rosa economy is a major element of the society of captives. It provides those things that are desired but unavailable through legitimate prison sources. The extent of the economy and its ability to produce desired goods and services—food, drugs, alcohol, sex, protection, preferred living conditions—vary in accordance with the nature of official surveillance, the demands of the consumers, and the opportunities for entrepreneurship. Whatever these

conditions may be, much inmate activity revolves around hustling.

Because inmates may not have currency or coins in their possession, cigarettes are the medium of exchange in the prison economy. Cigarettes are not contraband, are easily transferable, have a stable and well-known value, and come in denominations of singles, packs, and cartons. Further, they are in demand, and even inmates who do not smoke will keep them for trading purposes. If goods must be smuggled in from the outside, however, dollars are probably necessary. Smuggling is thus doubly dangerous: Importation of goods is against the rules, and so is money.

David Kalinich has documented the prison economy at the State Prison of Southern Michigan in Jackson.[17] He learned that a complete market economy provided goods (contraband) and services not available to the inmates through legitimate sources. Prison scrip, cigarettes, and "green" (real money) were the currencies used to buy and sell nine categories of goods and services: drugs, alcohol, gambling, appliances, clothing, institutional privileges, weapons, food, and prostitution. Through interviews he established the prices being charged. A pint of liquor smuggled in from the outside cost $15 or six cartons of cigarettes. "Spud juice," an alcoholic drink made on the grounds by the inmates, sold for $5 a quart or fifteen packs of cigarettes. Kalinich found that the prison economy, like a market on the outside, responded to the forces of supply and demand, and that risk of discovery replaced some of the risk associated with business in the free world. But also like a free economy, when it successfully provided desired goods and services, it contributed to the stability of interpersonal relationships within the institution.

What kind of person plays the role of merchant in the prison economy? Early studies of the inmate code seem to imply that the entrepreneur—especially one seen as an exploiter—is accorded a low status in the convict society. The "merchant" is given low prestige and the "real man" high status.[18] But the inmate leader

Doing Business Behind the Walls or Bartering in the Joint

Michael Knoll

There's something going on—a deal, I think—on the tier in front of my house, cell number A–15, maximum unit, Arizona State Prison.

Outside on the tier—a narrow iron sidewalk enclosed in layers of green wire mesh—two prisoners stand arguing. In the grainy hall light, their bodies are just shadows, their words punctuated with tense, emotional hand gestures. One of the men begins removing cigarettes from the lining of a slightly modified blue denim jacket. His movements are precise, fluid, lightning fast, emptying two packs at a time into the hands of the man standing beside him. Ten packages. Twenty. Thirty … As the cigarettes are being exchanged, the prisoners continue arguing, their words a jumble of language falling just short of where I'm standing.

Now the first man's coat is empty and both prisoners are silent. Forty packs of Camels have settled into the second man's denims. He arranges them to fit the contours of his body, while extracting from one pocket a small yellow plastic package. A balloon? He holds it briefly up to the light, runs one finger over its surface, then slips it into his mouth. The transaction complete, both traders hurry off.

Such exchanges are the basis for the prison economy. Had I followed the con with the cigarettes, I might have seen them traded for any of a dozen or so commodities necessary to a civilized existence. ("Civilized"—in a world that has been designed to be uncivilized—means not having to live on the bare essentials, the prison chow and the anonymous denim clothes, the institutional tobacco and the harsh state soap dispensed to inmates.) Each of the goods or services acquired in the initial transaction would be consumed, or more likely, traded again according to the tastes of the owner. None of those transactions involve paper money. No green stuff and no Master Charge. No paper and no plastic. Yet the exchanges would be performed efficiently and to the satisfaction of both parties, each of whom might think they received the best end of the deal.

There's a lot of reasons why cigarettes are the favored unit of exchange: The demand is constant and their small size makes them readily concealable in a setting where bartering is illegal (although deals must often occur under the noses of the guards).

Camel Regulars, the smallest available cigarette, are the most sought after, the most negotiable, and the most stable currency. They can be bartered for almost anything, from sex, drugs, and miscellaneous contraband, to televisions, jewelry, and a variety of services, including legal work performed by jailhouse lawyers.

Prices vary widely. A well-written appeal brief—suitable for submission to federal district courts—might bring anywhere from ten to twenty cartons of cigarettes depending on the competency of the prisoner lawyer, the amount of time and research involved, and the nature of the man's crime. Demand for legal services, which sometimes result in a retrial or reduction of sentence, remains very high. Sex is slightly cheaper, though the demand keeps abreast of the supply. A five-minute assignation with a prison drag queen might leave the john one carton poorer. The price could go higher though, according to how much he resembles a she. If he has recently received a hormone

Continued

injection (occasionally available through the barter system), it could jack the price up by another carton. Add another few packs if he arrives wearing panties, mesh stockings, perfume, eye shadow, or lipstick. It cost him to score these things, so he's going to hustle you for whatever he can. If you've been locked up for a few years, chances are you'll put up with it.

A steak sandwich, on the other hand, might retail for from four to six packs, while the purchase of a watch, always a good hedge against inflation, would run a little higher. Figure three to four cartons for the watch, more if it's a name brand. Drug prices fluctuate more erratically. When available, a matchbox of the killer weed might cost from two to ten cartons of smokes, the price varying according to the drug's purity and place of origin, the method used to bring it inside. When there's no dope around, other things get substituted. Catnip. Oregano. Parsley. To someone who hasn't had the real thing in a while, and doesn't have much chance of getting any, a little oregano can knock him out. Be careful about ripping people off here, though. There's only so far you can run....

Despite official restrictions, bartering flourishes. Most guards prefer simply to look

the other way—and avoid the confrontation associated with a bust. A few employees become actively involved: Manipulative prisoners con them into bringing contraband in, taking money out. With the aid of a guard, one fast-talking con was able to export the profits of his bartering operation outside the institution. Using the goods as security, he had his lawyer post an appeal bond and secure his release....

Under the barter system one of the great joys—and great frustrations—is the flexibility of prices. In any transaction the final price is never predetermined but evolves according to both the buyer's and seller's ability to negotiate. That ability is both a necessity as well as an acquired art, one requiring patience, tenacity, and imagination. In deals not involving cigarettes, the beauty of these virtues becomes more apparent....

I'm standing under the fifth tier, on a stairway crowded with prisoners, just after the evening meal. A little guy in a dirty blue cap—a convict renowned for his dealing skills—stands next to me holding a lamp. I have no idea where he got it. It's a large floor lamp with a shiny (and expensive-looking) brass stand, a bright yellow shade dotted with blue flowers. The thing seems totally incongruous here, where a small group of prisoners have con-

gregated out of boredom or curiosity. It's the little guy in the cap that's doing all the talking:

"Ya see this, don't ya? Only lamp like it in the joint. How many of ya' ever seen a lamp like this 'round here? Right. None of ya'. And ya' know what? I made this. I put this together with my own hands, hustled the parts from the Industrial Block. You believe that? It's like something ya'd see inna living room, onna television, someplace out in the real world. Now, what-a-you scumbags gimme for this fine lamp?"

A voice in back, muffled by the crowd of denim bodies, yells back. "I'll give ya' two cases of Pepsi. A half dozen watermelon."

A louder voice—this is a black guy—all but drowns him out. "I ain't goin' to give you nothin'. Somebody stole that lamp. It's hot-er-n a firecracker."

The guy in the cap looks past the black dude, pretending not to hear him. "What am I goin' to do with some damn watermelons? You crazy? Keep them, gimme the Pepsi and four cartons of smokes."

Black prisoner: "I saw that lamp out in front of the counselor's office. You bastard—you're trying to get somebody busted!"

Man in back: "I'll give ya' the Pepsi, two bags of instant coffee, and a dozen watermelon."

Guy in the cap: "I said no watermelons. Got that? I want cigarettes. Three, four cartons. Them, or some weed. Got any weed?"

Man in back, stepping forward now: "I don't have any weed for a hot lamp. Best I can do is the Pepsi, the instant coffee, and my old Playboy magazines. I got about a dozen of them."

"How old are the magazines?"

"Couple years. No pictures torn out and no pages stuck together. I got Bo Derek issue, and one with Brooke Shields."

"Still can't do business with ya' ... Hold it—you got Brooke Shields? Iz that the real young broad? Sweet little teenager? Throw in Brooke Shields and your inflatable rubber party doll—You still got that? The one I traded you? One with the soft vinyl boobs? Throw the doll in and the lamp is yours."

When doing business in this manner, it's helpful to maintain a running stock of high-demand items: jewelry, postage stamps, electric razors and calculators, stereo tapes and headphones as well as food products from the inmate store.

Entry into this economic system is not as difficult as it might seem, or as it might be under another system. Inside, those willing to work and acquire capital will share in the wealth. All others have a rough time. The motivated prisoner knows that almost any object, service, skill, or talent has potential value as a unit of trade.

"Fish inmates"—new arrivals at the prison—enter the economy by bartering their labor, muscle, or time. They run errands and perform services, including laundry and housekeeping, for prisoners who pay them in property....

Possibly the most positive result of this trade system has been its effect on the prison arts. Convicts with no money, no meaningful job or activity—but with an excess of time, emotion, and imagination—discover talents. They teach themselves to write, to paint, and to fashion jewelry, leather goods, wood carvings, macrame, and pottery. Their first art is at times passionately original, expressive—and human. Fashioning it provides an outlet for energies normally denied within the prison environment.

The Arizona Department of Corrections, which for years remained indifferent toward the arts, has now become an art patron. Under director Ellis MacDougall, art materials and tools have been made legitimately available to prisoners through the mail as well as the visiting rooms. Facilities for hobby and craft work have been set up at several of the state's penal institutions.

The items made in these facilities command top prices, at least within the walls. One convict may contract another to have a portrait or leather belt done. Staff members sometimes purchase inmate art work for their homes, placing the money on the prisoner's bunks.

Purchases by staff members, as well as the general public, are sanctioned by the MacDougall administration. Prison art of all kinds is currently on display at the Department of Corrections central office in Phoenix. Additional display areas will soon be opened in Tucson, and at the women's prison in Phoenix.

D.O.C. spokesperson Judy Burris, who oversees prison art programs, says all prices are determined by the Department after an appraisal by experts. Profits go directly to the prisoners and prices are nonarguable.

Should you desire to negotiate regarding price or method of payment, you'll have to commit a felony and hope there's a cell available at Florence. If you decide to do that, leave your Master Charge and Visa cards outside. Throw away your bank cards, traveler's checks, and passbooks. On this side of the walls, those things won't do you any good.

Source: Michael Knoll, "Doing Business Behind the Walls or Bartering in the Joint," *New Times Weekly,* 1–7 April 1982, pp. 11–12. Reprinted by permission.

may in fact be a more successful and subtle entrepreneur than the person labeled "merchant."[19] The status of the inmate leader is at least in part dependent on the ability to dispense goods and services to followers, and the profits may be shared with members of the clique.

As in the free world, the prison society has positions that provide some individuals with exceptional opportunities for entrepreneurship. Access to food, clothing, materials, and information allows inmates assigned to work in such places as the kitchen, warehouse, and administrative office to ply their trade. Virtually every job assignment allows access to something that can be exchanged or sold. Sheehan's description of Green Haven shows that possibilities for "swagging" (stealing from the state) abound.

George Malinow, the subject of Sheehan's study, is an entrepreneur who seems to have a finger in every opportunity that will improve prison life for him and his associates. The entries in the diary that Malinow kept for four days indicate that he seems to spend most of his time swagging, trading, and profiting. Whether his way of life is typical at Green Haven and whether he would be able to operate with comparable ease at another maximum security institution are not known. In the four days that were recorded, Malinow acquired about a hundred pounds of food from a friend in the kitchen in exchange for apparel stolen from his own workplace, the supply unit for inmates leaving the institution on parole. The food was then traded to others or consumed by Malinow and his friends. It became clear that the kitchen is a first-rate place to swag. Kitchen workers can take far more food than they can eat, and sell it or swap it. One of Malinow's friends, who receives five cartons of cigarettes a month from a crime partner he didn't rat on, doesn't smoke but loves to eat. His purchases from a kitchen worker included a dozen eggs (two packs of cigarettes), a pound of rice (one pack), a pound of coffee (one pack), and several steaks (three packs apiece). He also had a contract with his

friend in the kitchen for a daily loaf of soft bread (one carton a month). One gets the impression that members of this clique eat meals prepared by the kitchen staff only when victuals from other sources run out.[20]

It is important to recognize that while each "sale" in the prison economy is a one-to-one transaction, it is interrelated with other sub-rosa transactions that form a wider network. Thus, the exchange of a dozen eggs for two packs of cigarettes may result in the reselling of those eggs in the form of egg sandwiches made on a hot plate for five cigarettes each, while the kitchen worker who swagged the eggs may use the income to get a laundry worker to starch his shirts, to buy drugs from a hospital orderly, or to pay a punk for sexual favors. Economic transactions like these wind on and on.

Like other economies the prison economy may suffer occasional disruptions. Officials conduct periodic "lockdowns" and inspections, during which time contraband goods are confiscated and their owners disciplined. Such inspections initially result in temporary shortages in supplies and, just as in the free economy, subsequent price readjustments. When the heat is off, hustling returns, and the law of supply and demand is again in operation.

The prison economy could not survive without at least the tacit permission of some staff members. Although some guards are caught smuggling, many violate the rules primarily by looking the other way when they find contraband items in cells or on prisoners. Other officers bring in items that are labeled contraband but that they believe are harmless. In some instances, the officers' cooperation in the prison economy is repaid by inmates' willingness to work efficiently at assigned jobs or to not cause problems in the housing unit. In others, officers see the possibility of financial gain for themselves in providing goods for payment, and they may become enmeshed in the prison economy.

As on the outside, the prison economy is closely linked to the cultural and social values of the society it serves. The economy allocates goods and services, rewards and sanctions. If one party gives inferior goods or fails to pay the agreed price, these sub-rosa transactions can lead to violence.

The prison economy exists to meet the inmates' needs for good and services. It enables some inmates to live better than others and thus to assume power in the convict society.

Prison Violence

For most of us, the thought of being incarcerated raises images of the loss of freedom—and of the loss of personal security. The idea of living in close quarters among people who have engaged in violence and where we may be dependent on unsympathetic officials for protection is terrifying. Although collective violence in prisons has received considerable public attention—the riots in Attica in 1971, Santa Fe in 1980, and Atlanta in 1987 are cases in point—the mass media have had little to say about the interpersonal violence that occurs in correctional institutions.[21] In 1990, for instance, 98 prisoners committed suicide, 49 deaths were "caused by another," and 261 died of unknown causes that were apparently neither natural, self-inflicted, accidental, nor homicide.[22] Yet given the size of the incarcerated population, its death rate is probably no higher than that of some other segments of society; more than a hundred students, for example, are murdered in schools each year.

Causes of Prison Violence

Too often discussions of prison violence merely recite the deprivations and injustices of life in penal institutions. They usually mention the rules enforced by guards, the loss of freedom, and the boredom. Although such statements reflect concerns, they do little to explain why violence erupts where and when it does. Obviously, the causes of assaultive behavior in our penal institutions are more complex than simple answers suggest.

The absence of assaultive behavior may stem from a more effective prison management that provides few opportunities for attacks. The open character of European (especially Scandinavian) prisons is cited as a reason for the lower incidence of violence there, for imprisonment seems to be less stressful under such conditions. Yet many American penologists believe that additional freedoms may in fact raise the probability of violence because contacts with the outside world increase opportunities for the smuggling of contraband (weapons, drugs, food) that may spark conflict. Further, the contrast between freedom and regimentation may increase the frustrations of confinement.

Prisoner-Prisoner Violence

The number of deaths does not tell the entire story of prison violence, of course. Assaultive behavior is much more prevalent than those figures suggest. A study of four representative Virginia institutions registered a prisoner assault rate of 9.96 attacks per 100 inmates per year.[23] These levels of violence are not necessarily related to the size of the prisoner population in a particular facility. Some prisons are badly managed and violence is high. The sad fact is that countless inmates are injured by assaults. The need to always be on guard against victimization contributes to the pains of imprisonment. As Hans Toch has observed, the climate of violence in prison has no free-world counterpart. "Inmates are terrorized by other inmates, and spend years in fear of harm. Some inmates request segregation, others lock themselves in, and some are hermits by choice. Many inmates injure themselves."[24] Yet it might also be argued that most prisoners come from violent neighborhoods, and perhaps they are safer in prison than they would be if on the outside.

Although prison folklore may attribute violence to brutal guards, most of the violence is inmate to inmate. Not all prisons have the

Gangs organized along racial, ethnic, and geographic lines have become a major factor in many prisons.

same levels of violence, and some correctional systems have remained relatively safe for long periods. At times, however, violence has been a major problem in some institutions. During the 1970s, when prisons, particularly those in California, were infected with gang conflict and revolutionary zeal, an epidemic of violence erupted. But the government has both a legal and a moral responsibility to protect those it has decreed should be held in custody.

Inmate characteristics Incarceration is undoubtedly a harsh and painful experience, but it need not be intensified by physical assault or death at the hands of fellow inmates. Data from Western Europe indicate that incidents of prison violence are few there, a finding that may reflect lower rates of violent crime. Hence, the relative lack of prison violence may be explained by the character of the general population and the culture that inmates bring with them to the institution. Violent behavior in

prisons is undoubtedly related to the types of people who are incarcerated and the characteristics they bring with them. Among the characteristics that are thought to bear on the problem, four stand out: age, attitudes, relationships with the outside, and antagonism toward people not of one's own race.

Studies have shown that young people, both inside and outside prison, are more prone to violence than their elders. The group most likely to commit violent crimes consists of young men between the ages of sixteen and twenty-four. Not surprisingly, 96 percent of adult prisoners are men with an average age at the time of admission of twenty-seven years. The young not only have greater physical strength but also lack the commitments to career and family that tend to restrict antisocial behavior. In addition, many young men have difficulty defining their position in society; thus, many of their interactions with others are interpreted as challenges to their status.

"Machismo," the concept of male honor and the sacredness of one's reputation as a man, has great bearing on violence among the young, and threats of sexual assaults are likely to provoke retaliation. Some researchers and observers have argued that many homosexual rapes are nonsexual; rather, they are political— to impress on the victim the power of the aggressor and to define the target's role as passive or "feminine."[25] Some inmates adopt a preventive strategy of trying to impress their colleagues with their bravado, a ploy that may only result in counterchallenges and violence. Among this age group, a reputation for physical retaliation against those who make slurs on one's honor, sexual prowess, and manliness may be a sought-after goal. The potential for violence among prisoners with these characteristics is obvious.

One sociological theory advanced to explain crime is that certain economic, racial, and ethnic groups foster a "subculture of violence." Arguments are settled and decisions made by the fist rather than verbal persuasion. According to this theory, developed by Marvin Wolfgang and Franco Ferracuti, this subculture is found in the lower class, and in its value system violence is "tolerable, expected, or required."[26] They posit that persons reared in such a subculture are accustomed to violent behavior in their families and among their peers. The environment, then, has a direct bearing on the formation of attitudes that are brought into the prison.

Race has become the major factor that divides the contemporary prison population, reflecting tensions in the larger society. Racist attitudes seem to be acceptable in most institutions and have become part of the convict code. The fact of forced association, having to live with persons with whom one would not be likely to associate on the outside, exaggerates and amplifies racial conflict. Violence against members of another race may be the way that some inmates deal with the frustrations of their lives both inside and outside of prison. The presence of gangs organized along racial lines contributes to violence, and prisoners may be coerced to join the gang of their racial or ethnic group.

Prison gangs Organized along racial, ethnic, and geographic lines, prison gangs have developed in a number of systems since the early 1970s. Gangs are organized primarily with the intention of controlling an institution's narcotics, gambling, loansharking, prostitution, extortion, and debt-collection rackets. In addition, they provide protection for their members from other gangs and instill a sense of macho camaraderie. Members are often veterans of street gangs in their hometowns who have reconstituted their organization in prison. Intergang violence is often an extension of the street wars that dominated the young lives of members.

A national survey found that prison gangs existed in the institutions of thirty-two states and in the federal system (see Figure 10.1). The survey identified 114 individual gangs; overall gang membership totaled 12,634. The greatest numbers of prison gangs were reported by Pennsylvania (15) and Illinois (14). The greatest numbers of gang members were reported by Illinois (5,300), Pennsylvania (2,400), and California (2,050). Gang members are estimated to constitute about 6 percent of the total state and federal inmate population.[27] The number and composition of the prison gangs in the Texas system are outlined in Table 10.1.

The racial and ethnic basis of gang membership has been well documented in California. Beginning in the late 1960s, a Chicano gang whose members had known one another on the streets of Los Angeles and that in San Quentin was called the Mexican Mafia began to take over the rackets of that institution. In reaction, other gangs were formed, including a rival Mexican gang, La Nuestra Familia; CRIPS (Common Revolution in Progress); Texas Syndicate; the Black Guerrilla Family; and the Aryan Brotherhood. Gang conflict in California prisons became so serious in the 1970s that attempts were made to break up the gangs by dividing their memberships among a number of

KVCC KALAMAZOO VALLEY COMMUNITY COLLEGE LIBRARY

Figure 10.1 ■ Prison Gangs Are Reported to Exist in Most Jurisdictions. Racial and ethnic gangs have been prominent in Arizona, California, and Illinois, but why do they exist in other states, such as Nebraska and Oregon? What factors may account for the role of gangs in American prisons?

Source: U.S. Department of Justice, Office of Legal Policy, *Prison Gangs: Their Extent, Nature and Impact on Prisons* (Washington, D.C.: Government Printing Office, 1985), p. 4.

Prisons with gangs
Prisons without gangs

institutions. Contributing to prison violence is the fact that gang membership is often on a "blood-in, blood-out" basis: A would-be member must stab a gang's enemy to be admitted, and once in cannot drop out without putting his own life in danger. Given the racial and ethnic foundation of the gangs, violence between them can easily spill over into the general population.

Although many administrators say that prison gangs, like organized crime groups, tend to pursue their "business" interests without conflict, gangs in most institutions are viewed as a major source of inmate-inmate violence. In Texas, where the building-tender system of inmate "guards" was abolished following the case of *Ruiz* v. *Estelle* (discussed in Chapter 14), gangs soon emerged as racial and ethnic self-protection organizations.[28]

The amount of prison violence attributed to the gangs cannot be measured. Although many prison deaths may have resulted from the gang violence, intimidation and assaults are undoubtedly much more prevalent. To weaken the gangs, many correctional systems transfer known leaders to other institutions or move them out of state. Unfortunately, they often renew their membership in another "chapter" of the same gang in the new institution.

Protective custody For many victims of prison violence the only way to escape further abuse is to enter the protective custody unit. Most institutions have such a unit, along with units for disciplinary and administrative segregation. Often the physical conditions, programs, and recreational opportunities are little better for the inmates in protective custody than for those who have been moved out of the general prison population because of misbehavior. Inmates who seek protective custody are those who have been physically abused, have received homosexual threats, have reputations as snitches, or fear being assaulted by someone they crossed on the outside and who is now a fellow inmate. In state institutions where gang violence is a problem, large numbers of inmates want to serve their sentences in a protected environment.

Life is not pleasant for these inmates. In most institutions they remain in their cells almost twenty-four hours a day. They are let out briefly to exercise and to shower, but generally they must depend on books, radio, and televi-

Table 10.1 ■ **Prison Gangs in Texas.** Reflecting the racial and ethnic composition of the inmate population, the Texas prison gangs came to prominence during the period of conflict following the end of the building-tender system in the 1980s.

Name of gang	Racial composition	Size of membership	Year formed
Texas Syndicate	Predominantly Hispanic	296	1975
Texas Mafia	Predominantly white	110	1982
Aryan Brotherhood	All white	287	1983
Mexican Mafia	All Hispanic	351	1984
Nuestro Carneles	All Hispanic	47	1984
Mandingo Warriors	All black	66	1985
Self-Defense Family	Predominantly black	107	1985
Hermanos de Pistolero	All Hispanic	21	1985
Others		115	1985

Source: R. S. Fong, "The Organizational Structure of Prison Gangs: A Case Study," *Federal Probation* (March 1990):.36.

sion for stimulation. Inmates who ask to "lock up" have little chance of returning to the general prison population without repercussions. Anyone who has asked for protective custody has violated the inmate code and is considered a weakling—a snitch or a punk—to be preyed on. Even when administrators have transferred such inmates to another institution, their reputations follow them through the grapevine.

Prisoner-Officer Violence

The mass media have focused on riots in which guards are taken hostage, injured, and killed, but most violence in prisons is committed among the inmates; the violence that does take place against officers is situational and individual. Correctional officers do not carry weapons within the walls of the institution because a prisoner may seize them. Prisoners do manage to obtain lethal weapons and can use the element of surprise to inflict injury on an officer.

In the course of a workday an officer may encounter situations that require the use of physical force against an inmate—for instance, break-

ing up a fight or moving a prisoner to segregation. Such situations are known to be dangerous. With foreknowledge, an officer may gain the assistance of others so that the risk of violence is minimized. It is the unexpected attack against an individual officer that is of greatest concern: a missile thrown from an upper tier by a prisoner who wants to retaliate against an officer he thinks is out to get him, verbal threats and taunts, an "accidental" fall downstairs.

An injury received by an officer in the course of duty may not be the only damage incurred. The authority of an officer who has been victimized by a prisoner is greatly reduced, especially if the officer's response is less than forceful. After such an incident, administrators often have no alternative but to transfer the officer to tower duty.[29]

Officer-Prisoner Violence

Unauthorized physical violence against inmates by officers to enforce rules, uphold the officer-prisoner relationship, and maintain order is a fact of life in many institutions. Stories abound of guards giving individual prisoners "the treatment" outside of the notice of their superiors. Many guards view physical force as an everyday operating procedure and legitimize its use. In some institutions, authorized "goon squads" made up of physically powerful correctional officers use their muscle to maintain order and the status quo.[30]

It is sometimes difficult to distinguish the legitimate use of force from physically harsh violence used as punishment. Correctional officers are expected to follow departmental rules in their dealings with prisoners, yet supervisors are usually unable to directly observe staff-prisoner face-to-face confrontations. Prisoner complaints about officer brutality are often given little credence until an individual officer gains a reputation for harshness. Still, wardens may feel that they must uphold the actions of their officers if they are going to maintain their support.

Levels of violence by officers against inmates are undoubtedly lower today than in earlier periods. However, officers are expected to enforce prison rules and may use force to uphold discipline and prevent escapes. Questions as to what is *excessive* force for the handling of particular situations are usually unclear.

Institutional Structure

The social and physical environment of the institution helps to determine the level of violence. Lee Bowker lists five contributing factors: (1) inadequate supervision by staff members, (2) architectural design that promotes rather than inhibits victimization, (3) the easy availability of deadly weapons, (4) the housing of violence-prone prisoners near relatively defenseless persons, and (5) a general high level of tension produced by close quarters.[31] The physical size and condition of the prison, the pains of imprisonment, and the relationships between the inmates and staff also have a bearing on the level of violence.

The fortress prison certainly does not create an atmosphere conducive to normal interpersonal relationships. A large institution—some megaprisons hold up to three thousand inmates—can have problems of management. The massive scale of the megaprison provides opportunities for aggressive inmates to hide weapons, carry out private "justice," and engage more or less freely in other illicit activities. Size may also mean that some inmates "fall through the cracks," are misclassified with regard to their housing, and thus may be forced to live among more assaultive offenders.

The relationship between prison crowding and violence is unclear.[32] Some studies have shown that as personal space is reduced, the number of violent incidents rises. Prisons housing more offenders than a design capacity of sixty square feet per inmate are likely to have high assault rates. However, crowding can be measured in several ways (for example, number of people per area, amount of space per person, amount of unshared space per person, amount of time to oneself), and inmate perceptions of crowding seem to depend upon a number of relative factors such as prior experience. What is clear is that increased size of an institution's population puts a strain on such support facilities as dining halls, athletic areas, programs, and medical services. These strains must be offset by increased resources so that the quality of life can be maintained in the face of greater numbers. There are institutions where the population has more than doubled without increases in violence. Good management seems to be a major factor in keeping conditions from deteriorating.

The degree to which inmate leaders are allowed to take matters into their own hands can affect the level of violence among inmates. When administrators run a tight ship, security measures prevent sexual attacks in dark corners, the making of "shivs" (knives) in the metal shop, and open conflict among inmate groups. A prison must afford each inmate defensible space. Administrators should set as their goal the assurance that every inmate is secure from physical attack.

What Can Be Done About Prison Violence?

Prisons must be made safe for inmates. This is no easy task, for an emphasis on security and order may conflict with other correctional goals. If violence is to be eliminated, it may be necessary to limit the movement of inmates within the institution, cut off their contacts with the outside world, and prevent them from choosing their associates. Such measures seem to run counter to the goal of producing individuals who will be accountable when they return to society.

The measures that have been suggested to reduce violence are not always clear-cut or applicable to all situations. The following steps have been proposed:

- Improve classification so that violence-prone inmates will be separated from the general population.

- Create opportunities for inmates fearful of being victimized to seek assistance from staff.

- Increase the size and training of the custody force.

- Redesign facilities so that all areas can be put under surveillance; there should be no "blind spots."

- Install grievance mechanisms or an ombudsman to help resolve interpersonal or institutional problems.

- Augment the reward system as a way of reducing the pains of imprisonment.

These proposals may help to reduce violence, but strong administrative leadership—the quality of prison management—is probably the key factor.[33] There will always be some violence, given the type of people who are sent to prison, but that does not mean that violence and corruption should so dominate the institution that tension and fear reign. The quality of prison life must be a central concern of institutional administrators. Albert Cohen has stated the case well: "We must acknowledge that prisons contain a lot of people morally prepared and by experience equipped to take advantage of opportunities to dominate, oppress, and exploit others. The problem of the prison—to construct a system of governance that reconciles freedom with order and security—is also the problem of civil society."[34]

Discipline of Prisoners

The maintenance of order can be burdensome to prison administrators, given crowded conditions, the character of some inmates, the problems related to the correctional officer's role, and the limited rewards and punishments available. In an earlier era prisoners were kept in line with corporal punishment, and administrators did not hesitate to apply the lash. Today the withholding of privileges, recision of good time, and placement in "the hole" (the adjustment center or segregation) constitute the range of punishments available to discipline the unruly, and the Supreme Court has curbed administrators' exercise of discretion in the meting out of these punishments. Now some elements of procedural fairness must be included in the process by which inmates are sent to solitary confinement and the method by which good time credit may be lost because of misconduct.

Upon entering the reception center, the newcomer is given a manual, often running up to a hundred pages, that sets out in specific detail the rules that govern almost every aspect of prison life, from the type of clothing to be worn to dining room conduct and personal hygiene. Prominently listed are types of behavior that can result in disciplinary action: rioting, gambling, sexual activity, possession of currency, failure to obey an order, and so on. Prisoners are warned that some infractions of the rules are also violations of the state's criminal law and may be dealt with by the civil authority; most infractions, however, are the concern of an institutional disciplinary committee. The handbook for prisoners at the Connecticut Correctional Institution at Somers, for example, divides violations into three classes: Class A includes such offenses as arson, assault, and possession of drugs; Class B includes gambling, failure to obey a direct order, and loitering; Class C includes malingering, possession of contraband, and sanitary violations. The disciplinary committee may commit an inmate to punitive segregation for the number of days specified for each class of offense or apply other applicable sanctions. The state manuals vary; some merely list violations and give the disciplinary committee broad discretion as to the punishment.

A national survey of state prison inmates found that over half (53 percent) had been charged with violating prison rules at least once since entering the institution on their current sentence.[35] The study found that:

- Younger inmates and those with more extensive criminal careers or drug histories were the most likely to have violated prison rules.

- Inmates housed in larger prisons or maximum security prisons had higher percentages of rule violations than prisoners in other types of facilities.

- Whites and blacks committed infractions at the same rate—approximately 1.5 violations per inmate per year.

- More than 90 percent of the inmates charged with violating prison rules were found guilty in prison administrative proceedings.

The Disciplinary Process

Custodial officers act like the cop on the beat with regard to most violations of prison rules. For minor incidents a verbal reprimand or warning may be enough, but for more serious violations they may give the prisoner a "ticket." A ticket is a report describing the incident that is forwarded to higher authority for action.

Some correctional systems distinguish between major and minor violations: Major tickets go to the disciplinary committee; lesser tickets receive summary judgment by a hearing officer, whose decision may be appealed to a supervising captain, whose decision may in turn be appealed to the committee. In some systems all disciplinary reports go to a hearing officer, who investigates the charges, conducts the hearing, and determines the punishment. The decisions of the hearing officer may be reviewed by the commissioner of corrections, who can reduce the punishment but not increase it. Such procedures are relatively new.

Less than twenty years ago, formal codes of institutional conduct either did not exist or were ignored; punishment was at the full discretion of the warden, and inmates had no opportunity to challenge the charges. Then in 1970, in a case concerning welfare recipients (*Goldberg* v. *Kelly*), the Supreme Court ruled that all citizens have the right to due process of the law when a possibility exists that they may suffer loss through arbitrary or erroneous decisions by officials.[36] Four years later the Court ruled in *Wolff* v. *McDonnell* that inmates have certain (limited) procedural rights: to receive notice of a complaint, to have a fair hearing, to confront witnesses, to be assisted in preparing for the hearing, to be given a written statement of the decision.[37] The Court has not always been consistent, however, and has emphasized the need to balance the rights of the prisoner with the interest of the state. Two years after it guaranteed prisoners the fundamental rights of due process, it ruled that the assistance of counsel was not one of those rights.[38]

As a result of the Supreme Court decisions, most prisons promulgated rules that specify some elements of due process in disciplinary proceedings. In many institutions a disciplinary committee receives charges, conducts hearings, and determines guilt and punishment. Normally, disciplinary committees are composed of three to five members of the correctional staff, including representatives of custody, treatment, and classification, with a senior officer acting as chairperson. Sometimes inmates or citizens from the outside are included on these committees.

As part of the procedure, the inmate is read the charge, is given an opportunity to present his or her version of the incident, and may be allowed to present witnesses. In some institutions an inmate advocate may assist the prisoner. If the inmate is found guilty, a sanction is imposed. The inmate may usually appeal the decision to the warden and ultimately to the commissioner. Yet even with these protections, prisoners are still powerless and may fear further punishment if they too strongly challenge the disciplinary decisions of the warden.

Sanctions The loss of privileges, loss of good time, and confinement in punitive segregation are the sanctions most often imposed for violations of the institution's rules. The privileges that may be lost include visits, mail, access to the commissary, and recreation periods.

Confinement in punitive segregation is the most severe sanction that a disciplinary committee may give. The administrative rules of most institutions limit the amount of time that an inmate can spend in segregation and regulate the conditions of that confinement with respect to food, medical attention, and personal safety. Twenty days of continuous punitive segregation is the maximum in many prisons, but it is often possible to return an inmate to the hole after a token period outside.

Maintaining order among a group of offenders who live in close proximity to each other in conditions of deprivation is a major task for institutional administrators. In some prisons the nature of the population and the level of custody determine the extent to which rules of behavior must be specified and enforced to the letter. Officers must recognize that they have to walk a very narrow line between overrestrictiveness and permissiveness. They must recognize, too, that their objective is to encourage cooperation and behavior that conforms to the rules. But they must also understand that the rewards and punishments at hand are limited, and that

courts now insist that due process be observed in the enforcement of discipline and in proceedings against violators. These injunctions add up to a tall order, but with good management practices the objective can be reached. One index of a poorly run institution is a large number of violations of discipline, for they indicate that staff and prisoners are unable to prevent disruptive behavior or to function in an atmosphere of toleration, if not respect.

Summary

In our efforts to analyze contemporary prisons, we must rely on a limited number of descriptions of specific correctional institutions recorded at various points in time. We have the perspectives of such researchers as Clemmer, Sykes, Irwin, and Carroll, and more recently of journalists such as Bagdikian and Earley, but we still have to determine how useful their descriptions are for an analysis of the prison experience in a particular institution today.

Much as we must treat the research discussed in the literature with caution, we can use its findings and concepts for analysis of the current situation. We need not reinvent the wheel with each study. Such concepts as the prisoner subculture, the pains of imprisonment, argot roles, and adaptive behavior are useful and can serve as a foundation for new understanding. But the prison does not exist in isolation; it is part of a correctional subsystem within the criminal justice system. The political system and the wider society all influence corrections in many ways.

Although correctional facilities appear to have the characteristics of a total institution, they fall short of the model in many respects. The formal powers of administrators are limited by constitutional requirements, the need to gain the cooperation of inmates, the penetration of the outside world, and the system of rewards and punishments.

As in other situations in which people live together for extended periods, a system of norms and values develops. The contemporary prison society has been described as one of segmented order: The prison population is divided into hostile racial groups and violence-prone cliques and gangs. Criminologists argue about the origins of the values of the prison society. Some believe that they reflect the ways in which the prisoners adapt to the pains of imprisonment; others say that the values are brought into the institution from the outside.

One way in which prisoners adapt to their environment is by creating an economy in which desired services and goods are bartered. Prisons have canteens or stores in which some goods may be purchased, but their stocks are too limited to meet the inmates' needs. The resulting underground economy is a way of life for some inmates and a source of worry to administrators.

Violence is a major problem in correctional institutions. Violent behavior is related to the types of people who are incarcerated and the characteristics they bring with them, but institutional structure and administration also play their roles. Many victims of prison violence escape further abuse only by entering protective custody, but this is a drastic step to take because they can never go back into the general prison population.

Maintaining order in a prison can be a burdensome administrative task, given crowded conditions, violence, the character of some inmates, and the limited rewards and punishments available. Yet even in the most violent and fragmented institutions, such as San Quentin, a degree of order is still maintained. Today the withholding of good time, placement in administrative segregation, and restrictions on recreation time are the punishments that can be imposed to maintain discipline. The Supreme Court has ruled that some elements of procedural fairness be included in the process by which inmates are punished.

The American prison has changed. It no longer conforms to the image of the "big house"

depicted in much sociological literature. The prison population has a greater proportion of members of minority groups, and race seems to be the ingredient that is most important in the convict society. Prisoners are divided along racial lines and trust no one they do not know well. In an environment where personal safety is precarious, two strategies are employed: voluntary segregation and personalized relationships. Prisoners restrict their interactions to small friendship groups and other limited social units (gangs, for example) formed with members of their own race. Other than race, prisoners retreat into small orbits based on social characteristics such as (1) criminal orientation, (2) shared preprison experiences (coming from the same town or neighborhood or having been in other prisons together), (3) shared prison interests, and (4) forced proximity in cell assignment or work.[39]

The "right guy" was the model inmate leader of the 1950s and the "convict" was the acknowledged leader in the 1960s. In today's more violent prisons it seems that toughness, the ability to look after oneself, readiness to exploit the weak, and unwillingness to associate with more than a few close friends are the qualities that are admired. The solidarity of inmates against the administration described in the early literature has vanished. Prisons are crowded and, in an institution that seeks to promote reintegration with the community, inmates are moved from unit to unit. The population is in such flux that a stable prison society cannot be achieved.

For Discussion

1. You are a new prisoner. What are your immediate concerns? How will you handle them? What problems do you expect to face?

2. Some people say that the values of the prison culture are indigenous to the prison; others say that prisoners bring them from outside. Relate this controversy to the nature of today's prison in comparison to the nature of the prison of thirty years ago.

3. Studies of prison society have found that inmates play one of several adaptive roles. Which of these roles would you choose should you be incarcerated? Which role might someone with fewer advantages choose?

4. Social research of the 1950s described prison society as united against the guards. What factors may account for the fact that the culture of the contemporary institution is at odds with this view?

5. If you were the superintendent of a maximum security prison, what policies would you institute to end violence in the institution?

For Further Reading

Bagdikian, Ben H. *Caged: Eight Prisoners and Their Keepers.* New York: Harper & Row, 1976. Examines life in the United States Penitentiary at Lewisburg, Pennsylvania, focusing on eight prisoners. Written by a journalist who did not have full access to the institution yet was able to provide a very descriptive account of the prisoners and their keepers.

Carroll, Leo. *Hacks, Blacks, and Cons: Race Relations in a Maximum Security Prison.* Lexington, Mass.: Lexington Books, 1974. Discusses race relations in a small prison. Shows the segmentation of the inmate population along racial lines.

Colvin, Mark. *The Penitentiary in Crisis.* Albany: State University Press of New York, 1992. A case study of external as well as internal change and conflict that influenced the Penitentiary of New Mexico at Santa Fe prior to the 1980 riot.

Earley, Pete. *The Hot House: Life Inside Leavenworth Prison.* New York: Bantam Books, 1992. An eyewitness account of day-to-day life inside the United States Penitentiary in Leavenworth, Kansas, written by the first journalist given unlimited access to a maximum security institution of the Federal Bureau of Prisons.

Lockwood, Daniel. *Prison Sexual Violence.* New York: Elsevier, 1980. A study based on interviews with "targets" and "aggressors" in New York State prisons for males. Found that although many prisoners are targets of sexual aggression, the number of rapes is very low relative to other types of harm accompanying sexual incidents.

Rideau, Wilbert, and Wikberg, Ron. *Life Sentences: Rage and Survival Behind Bars.* New York: Times Books, 1992. Descriptions of life inside the Louisiana State Penitentiary by two former editors of *The Angolite,* the prison newspaper.

Sheehan, Susan. *A Prison and a Prisoner.* Boston: Houghton Mifflin, 1978. A fascinating description of life in Green Haven Prison and the way one prisoner "makes it" through "swagging," "hustling," and "doing time." It contains an excellent discussion of the inmate economy.

Useem, Bert, and Kimball, Peter. *States of Siege: U.S. Prison Riots, 1971–1986.* New York: Oxford University Press, 1989. A survey of prison riots with case studies of the upheavals at Attica, Joliet, Santa Fe, Jackson, and Moundsville. Summary chapters consider the nature and causes of prison riots.

Notes

1. Joseph Fulling Fishman, *Sex in Prison* (New York: National Liberty Press, 1934).

2. Donald Clemmer, *The Prison Community* (New York: Holt, Rinehart & Winston, 1940).

3. Gresham M. Sykes, *The Society of Captives: A Study of a Maximum Security Prison* (Princeton, N.J.: Princeton University Press, 1958), p. 107.

4. Leo Carroll, *Hacks, Blacks, and Cons: Race Relations in a Maximum Security Prison* (Lexington, Mass.: Lexington Books, 1974).

5. John Irwin, *Prisons in Turmoil* (Boston: Little, Brown, 1980).

6. Sykes, *Society of Captives,* pp. 63–108.

7. Clemmer, *Prison Community,* pp. 299–304.

8. Clarence Schrag, "Some Foundations for a Theory of Corrections," in *The Prison: Studies in Institutional Organization and Change,* ed. Donald R. Cressey (New York: Holt, Rinehart & Winston, 1961), pp. 30–35.

9. John Irwin and Donald R. Cressey, "Thieves, Convicts, and the Inmate Culture," Social Problems 10 (1962): 142–55.

10. Ibid.

11. Irwin, *Prisons in Turmoil,* p. 67.

12. Ibid.

13. Ibid., p. 78.

14. Virgil L. Williams and Mary Fish, *Convicts, Codes, and Contraband* (Cambridge, Mass.: Ballinger, 1974), p. 40.

15. Susan Sheehan, *A Prison and a Prisoner* (Boston: Houghton Mifflin, 1978), p. 90.

16. Ibid., p. 91.

17. David B. Kalinich, *Power, Stability, and Contraband* (Prospect Heights, Ill.: Waveland, 1980).

18. Gresham M. Sykes and Sheldon L. Messinger, "The Inmate Social System," in *Theoretical Studies in Social Organization of the Prison*, ed. Richard A. Cloward et al. (New York: Social Science Research Council, 1960), pp. 5–19.

19. Williams and Fish, *Convicts, Codes, and Contraband*, pp. 42–43.

20. Sheehan, *Prison and a Prisoner*, pp. 92–93.

21. There is an expanding literature on prison riots. See, for example, Mark Colvin, *The Penitentiary in Crisis* (Albany, N.Y.: State University of New York Press, 1992); Randy Martin and Sherwood Zimmerman, "A Typology of the Causes of Prison Riots and an Analytical Extension to the 1986 West Virginia Riot," *Justice Quarterly* 7 (December 1990): 711–21; Burt Useem and Peter Kimball, *States of Siege: U.S. Prison Riots, 1971–1986* (New York: Oxford University Press, 1989).

22. U.S. Department of Justice, *Sourcebook of Criminal Justice Statistics–1991* (Washington, D.C.: Government Printing Office, 1992), p. 701.

23. Lee H. Bowker, *Prison Victimization* (New York: Elsevier, 1980), p. 25.

24. Hans Toch, *Peacekeeping: Police, Prisons, and Violence* (Lexington, Mass.: Lexington Books, 1976), pp. 47–48.

25. Anthony M. Scacco, *Rape in Prison* (Springfield, Ill.: Thomas Publishers, 1975), p. 60; Wilbert Rideau and Ron Wikberg, *Life Sentences: Rage and Survival in Prison* (New York: Times Books, 1992), pp. 79–80. For an opposing view see David Lockwood, *Prison Sexual Violence* (New York: Elsevier, 1980), pp. 112–113.

26. Marvin E. Wolfgang and Franco Ferracuti, *The Subculture of Violence* (London: Tavistock, 1967), p. 263.

27. U.S. Department of Justice, Office of Legal Policy, *Prison Gangs: Their Extent, Nature, and Impact on Prisons* (Washington, D.C.: Government Printing Office, 1985); U.S. Department of Justice, Bureau of Justice Statistics, *Survey of State Arson Inmates, 1991* (Washington, D.C.: Government Printing Office, 1993) p. 20.

28. Robert S. Fong, "The Organizational Structure of Prison Gangs: A Texas Case Study," *Federal Probation* (March 1990): 36.

29. Stephen C. Light, "Assaults on Prison Officers: Interactional Themes," *Justice Quarterly* 8 (June 1991): 343–61.

30. Bowker, *Prison Victimization*, p. 103.

31. Lee H. Bowker, "Victimizers and Victims in American Correctional Institutions," in *Pains of Imprisonment*, ed. Robert Johnson and Hans Toch (Beverly Hills, Calif.: Sage, 1982), p. 64.

32. Gerald G. Gaes, "The Effects of Overcrowding in Prison," *Crime and Justice: An Annual Review of Research*, vol. 6, ed. Michael Tonry and Norval Morris (Chicago: University of Chicago Press, 1985); see also U.S. Department of Justice, Federal Bureau of Prisons, Gerald G. Gaes, "Prison Crowding Reexamined" (unpublished, 1990). Jeff Bleich, "The Politics of Prison Crowding," *California Law Review* 77 (October 1989): 1125–1180. Sheldon Ekland-Olson, "Crowding, Social Control and Prison Violence: Evidence from the Post-Ruiz Years in Texas," *Law and Society Review* 20 (1986): 389–421.

33. John J. DiIulio, Jr., *Governing Prisons* (New York: Free Press, 1987), p. 95.

34. Albert K. Cohen, "Prison Violence," in *Prison Violence*, ed. Albert K. Cohen, George F. Cole, and Robert G. Bailey (Lexington, Mass.: Lexington Books, 1975), p. 19.

35. U.S. Department of Justice, Bureau of Justice Statistics, *Special Report* (Washington, D.C.: Government Printing Office, December 1989), p. 1.

36. Goldberg v. Kelly, 398 U.S. 254 (1970).

37. Wolff v. McDonnell, 94 S. Ct. 2963 (1974).

38. Baxter v. Palmigiano 425 U.S. 308 (1976).

39. Irwin, *Prisons in Turmoil*, p. 182.

11

Incarceration of Women

When I came through the gate, I said to myself: "This is a prison?" All the trees and flowers—I couldn't believe it. It looked like a college with the buildings, the trees, and all the flowers. But after you're here a while—and it don't take long—you know it's a prison. Yeah, that's what it is—a prison.

Inmate, Federal Reformatory for Women, Alderson, West Virginia

Forgotten Offenders
Historical Perspective
The Incarceration of Women
    in the United States
The Reformatory Movement
The Past Sixty Years
Incarceration
Women in Prison
The Subculture of Women's Prisons
Male Versus Female Subcultures
Programs
Co-Corrections
Services
Mothers and Their Children
Release to the Community
Summary

As you approach New York's Bedford Hills Correctional Facility, you can have no question that it is a prison. You'll see guard towers, sliding gates of steel bars, and omnipresent television security cameras. However, once you are inside, you'll see things that are out of character for a prison: a nursery, a playroom, colorful wall murals, a baby crying. In the midst stands Sister Elaine Roulet, an energetic nun who believes that mothers must maintain close ties with their offspring, even in the impersonal world of the prison.

In Bedford Hills, as in other prisons for women, nearly 80 percent of the inmates have children. Sister Elaine has caused the Department of Correctional Services to develop a system of transportation, communication, and education to promote maternal bonding. Children born in the prison are cared for in the nursery for up to a year, and older children are brought to Bedford Hills for visits. In the summer there is a camp for longer stays. As Sister Elaine says, "We have women in here who might not have been good citizens, but they were wonderful mothers. The kids have done nothing wrong to cause this painful separation. We need to do all we can to strengthen these bonds so the kids don't come back to prison later in a different way." She continues, sounding resigned, "Prisons are here to stay. You don't change systems. You change people."[1] Clearly, Sister Elaine has set her sights on changing people.

Most states do not provide the level of services to women prisoners found in Bedford Hills. Because women make up such a small portion of the prison population, a greater portion of correctional budgets go to institutions for males. Yet female offenders have health, program, and security needs that are usually greater than the requirements for men.

Forgotten Offenders

Often referred to as the forgotten offenders, women have received little attention from criminal justice scholars, discriminatory treatment from judges, and few program resources from penal administrators. Various reasons have been given for the neglect of female criminals, including the facts that they make up such a small proportion of the correctional population, that their criminality is generally not serious, and that their place in the criminal justice system is merely a reflection of common societal attitudes that put all women in a subservient position.

The women's movement has focused attention on the condition of female offenders. Scholars have more actively sought to understand the basis of women's criminality, the nature of the subculture of women's institutions, and the problems that are faced by this small but significant portion of the offender population. In a period when equal opportunity has become public policy, decisions of judges, probation officers, wardens, and parole boards that continue to treat female offenders in a paternalistic and discriminatory manner have become the objects of criticism and litigation. Although the number of legal cases by women prisoners contesting the conditions of their confinement is not as extensive as those brought by men, the issue of equal protection has caused state and federal judges to intervene in a number of disputes.[2]

Only about 6 percent of the prison population in the United States is female; this figure has risen slightly during recent years as drug convictions have increased. Perhaps more important is that the rate of growth in the number of incarcerated women has exceeded that of men since 1981. Some have postulated that as women advance toward a position of equality with men in society, their behavior will become increasingly similar to men's, and so criminality among women may also increase. Others argue that inherent differences in the socialization of women and men make it unlikely the the criminality of women will ever approach that of men, especially for violent crimes. In fact, during the last decade the male population in state and federal prisons increased 112 percent while that of women increased by 202 percent.[3] The number of women now incarcerated in prisons and jails has reached 90,000.[4]

Females account for 22 percent of all arrests for the serious (index) crimes tabulated by the *Uniform Crime Reports,* yet women constitute about two-thirds of the persons arrested for prostitution and commercialized vice, 43 percent of those arrested for fraud, and 35 percent of persons arrested for forgery.[5] It is argued that because female offenders are so few and their crimes generally so much less serious than men's, it is rational public policy for correctional attention to be focused on the male offender.

Still, as shown in Figure 11.1 there has been a greater increase in arrests of women than of men during the past decade. This is particularly true for certain index offenses—larceny, robbery, aggravated assault, motor vehicle theft, and forcible rape.[6] Although it is impossible to show direct links between the status of women and their criminality, it can be argued that as they have moved into jobs from which they were formerly excluded, they have gained the opportunities and skills to commit criminal acts. As argued by Freda Adler, "When we did not permit women to swim at the beaches, the female drowning rate was quite low. When women were not permitted to work as bank tellers or presidents, the female embezzlement rate was low."[7] Others have challenged this view, pointing out that most property offenses committed by women consist of petty fraud and shoplifting, crimes that are not occupation-related.[8] However, as noted by Nichole Rafter the feminization of poverty over the past twenty years has meant that women and children make up 80 percent of the poor in the United States. She believes that it is the poverty of female single heads of households

that has contributed to the increase of crime, particularly of property offenses among women.[9] This is a controversial issue that is still to be clarified.

Throughout the criminal justice process, now and in the past, a **chivalry factor** has seemed to operate. "Criminological thought has been fraught with the sexism inherent in assuming that there exist only two distinct classes of women—those on pedestals and those in the gutter."[10] It has commonly been assumed that women are incapable of most criminal activity and that those who do commit crimes are "bad" or "fallen"—offenders against morality. Because women have been considered less capable than men in all spheres but the domestic, presumably they require greater legal protection than men and should be differentiated from them by the criminal justice system.

The chivalry factor seems to be at work from the time a crime is committed until the offender is paroled. Police often officially ignore women suspected of drug use or shoplifting, the offenses for which they are most frequently arrested.[11] Women are more likely than men to be released on bail, have their cases dismissed, and receive suspended sentences or probation.

Women who are convicted of crimes seem to receive lighter sentences than men for similar offenses. Judges have said that when they sentence women, they feel impelled to treat them differently from men, and not only because children are often involved. Analysts believe that this differential treatment arises from the fact that most jurists are men and have the attitudes typical of men: Women are weak and require gentle treatment; it is difficult for them to take women seriously. Perhaps they see their mothers or wives in front of them at the time of sentencing and just cannot imagine that women require severe punishment. But the

chivalry factor   The tendency of judicial and law enforcement personnel to view women as either frail creatures in need of protection or morally corrupt.

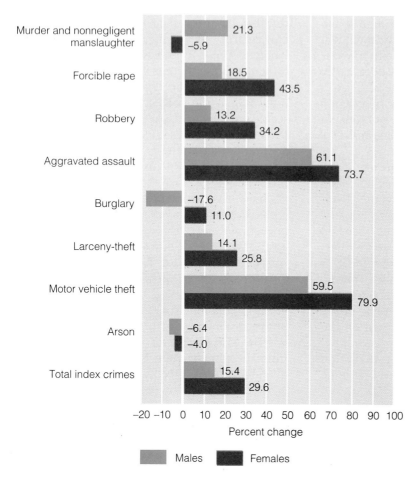

Figure 11.1 ■ **Index Crimes: Arrest Trends by Gender, Percentage Change, 1982–1991.** There has been a significant increase in the number of women arrested for certain offenses over the past decade. What explanations can you give for the apparent increased criminality of women?

Source: U.S. Department of Justice, *Crime in the United States* (Washington, D.C.: Government Printing Office, 1992), p. 218.

other side of the coin is that for some offenses, especially those involving sexual morality or drug abuse, women often receive much stiffer sentences than men. Judges, like other men, seem to believe that a woman's departure from the straight and narrow path is more to be condemned than a man's.

It is widely held that women suffer **benign neglect** in the postconviction process. Correctional officials have tended to minimize the female offender's special problems and needs. Although a greater proportion of women offenders than men offenders are placed on probation, those who are sent to prison find few opportunities for rehabilitation. One study

showed that women's prisons are less likely than men's prisons to have complete medical facilities, religious services, psychological counseling, and legal and recreational services.[12] These deficiencies are usually justified on the grounds of cost: Because of the small number of female inmates, the yearly cost of any service is higher for a woman than for a man. In addition, some states do not have correctional facilities for women; female offenders in those

benign neglect The slighting of female offenders' special problems and needs, particularly in the provision of programs and services.

states are sent under contract to institutions in other jurisdictions. Maintaining contact with their children and other relatives is thus made even more difficult.

Historical Perspective

It was not until the beginning of the nineteenth century that reformers started to press for separate correctional facilities and programs for female offenders. Until that time, all prisoners—men, women, children—in Europe and in the United States were housed together in jails and prisons. The available historical records seem to indicate that women were treated no differently than men when the criminal sanction was imposed; they too were lashed, transported, imprisoned, and hanged. Only with John Howard's exposé of prison conditions in England in 1777 and the development of the penitentiary in Philadelphia was the question of corrections for women addressed. The sexes were then segregated, but the conditions under which women prisoners lived were atrocious.

Elizabeth Gurney Fry, a middle-class Quaker, was the first person to press for changes in the treatment of sentenced women and children. When Fry and several fellow Quakers visited London's Newgate Prison in 1813, they were shocked by the conditions in which the female prisoners and their children lived.

Describing that first visit, Fry wrote, "The railing was crowded with half-naked women, struggling for the front situations with the most boisterous violence, and begging with the utmost vociferation." Fry had felt as if she were going into a den of wild beasts, and remembered "shuddering when the door was closed upon her and she was locked in with such a herd of novel and desperate companions."[13] She agitated for separate facilities for women, staffed by women, and with a domestic atmosphere. As a result of her efforts, a parliamentary committee in 1818 heard evidence about conditions in the prisons, and reforms were ordered.

The Incarceration of Women in the United States

News of Fry's efforts quickly traveled to the United States by way of the Quaker network. Although reformers were greatly excited about the development of the penitentiary, the question of corrections for women had not yet been broached. In 1844 the Women's Prison Association was formed in New York with the goal of improving the treatment of female prisoners and separating them from male prisoners. Elizabeth Farnham, head matron of the women's wing at Sing Sing from 1844 to 1848, sought to implement Fry's ideas but was thwarted by the male overseers and legislators and was forced to resign.

Few women were incarcerated in the nineteenth century. American judges, unlike their European counterparts, were unwilling to pronounce women guilty of crime unless they were habitual offenders. Thus the women who were convicted were, as inspectors at Sing Sing noted in 1844, "the most abandoned representatives of their sex." At this time prison in the United States was "the end of the road for women too far lost to virtue to offer much hope for redemption." Because it was then believed that only men had the ability to reason (women depended on feeling), women who committed crimes posed a much more serious threat to the established order: As they had gone against their "nature" and were not amenable to reason, how could they be reformed? "It seems to have been regarded as a sufficient performance of the object of punishment, to turn them loose within the pen of the prison and there leave them to feed upon and destroy each other."[14]

Until 1870 most women inmates were housed in the same prisons as men and were treated essentially the same as them.[15] Gradually

BIOGRAPHY

Elizabeth Fry (1780–1845)

Born in Norwich, England, Elizabeth Gurney Fry was second only to John Howard as a nineteenth-century advocate of prison reform in Europe. She came from an old Quaker family that had long been active in efforts to improve society.

Elizabeth Fry devoted much of her life to caring for the poor and neglected, and her most notable work was in prison reform. In April 1817 she helped organize the Association for the Improvement of Female Prisoners in Newgate, then the major prison in London. This group, made up of wives of Quaker businessmen, worked to establish prison discipline, separation of the sexes, classification of criminals, female supervision for women inmates, adequate religious and secular instruction, and the useful employment of prisoners. The positive results at Newgate were dramatic.

Largely through her personal efforts, methods similar to those employed at Newgate were rapidly extended to other prisons in England and abroad. Publication of the notes that she took while visiting the prisons of Scotland and northern England in 1818 brought her international recognition. Her treatise, *Observations in Visiting, Superintendence and Government of Female Prisons* (1827), was influential in the movement to reform American prisons for women. She made personal inspection tours of prisons throughout Europe: Ireland in 1827; France and Switzerland in 1838; Belgium, Holland, and Prussia in 1840; and Denmark in 1841. By the time of her death in 1845, her reform approaches had been widely accepted.

separate quarters were established for female convicts in prisons intended primarily for men. Most women who were incarcerated were held in jail for crimes against public order, especially for prostitution, alcoholism, and vagrancy. Quarters for the few women sentenced for more serious offenses were in out-of-the-way places where they had no access to exercise yards, visitors' rooms, or even fresh air and light. At Auburn in 1820, for example, "together, unattended, in a one-room attic, the windows sealed to prevent communication with men, the female prisoners were overcrowded, immobilized, and neglected."[16] The conditions of women imprisoned in other eastern and midwestern states before the Civil War have been similarly described. All such reports indicate that the offenders were disregarded, sexually exploited, forced to do the chores necessary to maintain the prison, and kept in facilities that were unsanitary.

The Reformatory Movement

As we saw in Chapter 3, the 1870 meeting of the National Prison Association in Cincinnati marked a turning point in American corrections. Although the Declaration of Principles did not address the problems of female offenders in any detail, it endorsed the creation of separate, treatment-oriented prisons for them. During the period immediately following the Civil War, the House of Shelter, a reformatory for women, opened in Detroit. Run by Zebu-

Ironing, laundry work, and cooking were the major job training programs available to female offenders until the 1960s.

lon Brockway, it became the model for reformatory treatment. The first independent female-run prison was established in Indianapolis in 1873.

As in the 1830s, the Quakers were active in prison reform. Sarah Smith and Rhoda M. Coffin were appointed in 1869 to make a tour of inspection of correctional facilities for women. They found "the state of morals in our southern prisons in such a deplorable condition that they felt constrained to seek some relief for the unfortunate women confined there."[17] Women volunteers in corrections, following the example of Elizabeth Fry, became very active in serving their fellow human beings; it was a way to act out their religious convictions. This missionary zeal was well expressed by Maud Booth, a leader of the Salvation Army: "We must work for regeneration, the cleansing of the evil mind, the quickening of the dead heart, the building up of fine ideals. In short, we must bring the poor sin-stained soul to feel the touch of the Divine hand."[18]

Three principles guided female prison reform during this period: (1) the separation of women prisoners from men; (2) the provision of differential, feminine care; and (3) control over women's prisons by female staff and management. "Operated by and for women, female reformatories were decidedly 'feminine' institutions, different from both custodial institutions for women and state prisons and reformatories for men."[19]

Like the reformers of the penitentiary movement, the advocates of women's reformatories were certain that correctional institutions should be placed in rural areas, away from the unwholesome conditions of the city. But the reformatory for women was not to emulate the fortress penitentiary; it was to consist of cottages grouped around an administration building. Many states adopted this plan in the expectation that housing that accommodated twenty to fifty women together would create a homelike atmosphere. At the Massachusetts Reformatory Prison for Women in Framingham, which opened in 1877, the

BIOGRAPHY

Mary Belle Harris (1874–1957)

Born in Pennsylvania in 1874, Mary Belle Harris is chiefly known as the first warden of the Federal Institution for Women that she opened in 1927 in Alderson, West Virginia. This pioneer woman penologist undertook a career in corrections in midlife after having been an archeologist, teacher, and social worker. Throughout her career in corrections she was known as an advocate of rehabilitation. She pursued that ideal as superintendent of the State Reformatory for Women at Clinton, New Jersey; as assistant director of the section on Reformatories and Detention Homes for the U.S. Department of War; as superintendent of the Federal Institution for Women; and as a member of the Pennsylvania Board of Parole.

Harris's work in corrections began in 1914. Through her friendship with Katherine Bennett Davis, New York City commissioner of corrections, she was offered the position of superintendent of the Women's Workhouse on Blackwell Island, at that time considered the worst of New York's twelve penal institutions. Faced with 700 inmates living in idleness in a facility built for 150, she created a library, introduced a classification system for inmates, built an exercise yard, and rescinded many of the petty rules that she believed were causing much staff-inmate conflict. As do most reformers, she had to battle opponents of change. She left the position after reform Mayor John Mitchell was defeated in the 1917 election.

Although Harris considered her work at the Blackwell Island workhouse only an interlude before returning to her scholarship, the experience there evidently ignited a passion that was to consume her entire life. She became an outspoken advocate of correctional reforms that were in keeping with the goal of offender rehabilitation. She worked to create classification systems geared to individual needs and talents, developed programs to educate and train her charges for their reentry into the community, and pushed for indeterminate sentences and release on parole. Viewing much of the criminality among women as resulting from their dependency upon men, she wanted her inmates to acquire skills that would break this bondage and give them self-respect. These aims were incorporated into the programs at Alderson, an institution that soon became a national model.

Retiring from Alderson in 1941 at the age of sixty-six, Harris returned to her native Pennsylvania, where she continued her dedication to correctional rehabilitation as a member of the state's parole board. Her experiences are chronicled in her autobiography, *I Knew Them in Prison* (1936), and in *The Pathway of Mattie Howard to and from Prison: The Story of the Regeneration of an Ex-Convict and Gangster Woman* (1937).

Mary Belle Harris died in 1957 at the age of eighty-two. She is remembered as an able correctional administrator and advocate of rehabilitation who succeeded in changing institutions to further that ideal.

inmates lived in private rooms rather than cells, had iron bedsteads and bed linen, and, if they behaved well, "could decorate their quarters, enjoy unbarred windows, and have wood slats instead of grating on their doors."[20] Opportunities would be provided for inmates to learn domestic skills suitable to their "true" female nature. It was expected that upon release they would use the skills they had acquired in domestic service or in maintaining their own homes and families.

The inmates of the reformatories were primarily women convicted of petty larceny, prostitution, or "being in danger of falling into vice." They tended to be viewed as errant or misguided women who needed help and protection within a female environment rather than as dangerous criminals who had to be isolated to safeguard society. The upper-middle-class Protestant women who were active in prison reform may have been able to remove from the offenders the stigma of "fallen women," but they developed correctional programs that treated the offenders as children. As Rafter points out, the women who lobbied state administrations for reformatories believed that they were being helpful, "but in the course of doing good…perpetuated the double standard that required women to conform to more difficult moral rules than men and punished them if they failed to do so."[21]

The reformatory movement was strongest in the East and Midwest; it gradually spread to parts of the South and West, but these other sections of the country were not so greatly influenced by the trend. In the South, corrections during this period was tied to the lease system of farm labor. When black women and children began to appear in large numbers before the criminal courts following the Civil War, officials had difficulty persuading lessees to accept these "dead hands," and the states were prompted to create separate asylum farms for them.[22]

As time passed, the original ideals of the reformers faltered, as such reform impulses so often did, overcome by societal change, admin-istrative orthodoxy, and legislative objections. By the 1930s, the accent on rural and domestic values, increases in the offender population, and shifts toward greater stress on custodial care made the reformatory seem out of touch with reality. The women's reformatory movement had by 1935 "run its course, having largely achieved its objective (establishment of separate prisons run by women) in those regions of the country most involved with Progressive reforms in general."[23]

The Past Sixty Years

It is difficult to discern a distinctive correctional model for women among the correctional approaches that have been tried since the 1930s. This situation may be due in part to the fact that recent theories about the causes and treatment of criminal behavior do not discriminate between the sexes.

The percentages of males and females arrested for serious (index) crimes are compared in Figure 11.2. As you can see, 32 percent of all persons arrested for larceny-theft during the time studied were women, yet women accounted for only 10 percent of auto thefts. During the period 1971–1985, the arrest rate for violent crime committed by women increased by 38 percent; the parallel increase for men during that same period was 4 percent. What effect are these changes having on corrections?

As women have been arrested for more serious crimes and as morals violations have become less prominent as reasons for punishment, custody has become a more important goal than reformation. Rehabilitative programs, many based on psychological or sociological premises, entered women's institutions in the 1940s and 1950s, as they had entered corrections for men. But it has been argued that attention and resources were devoted mainly to men's institutions and that the less serious offenders found in women's prisons were accorded lower priority. Educational and vocational programs for women have been geared

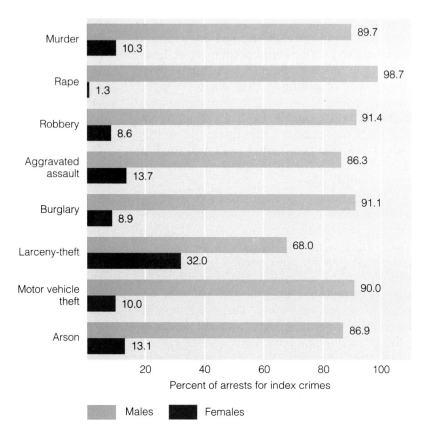

Figure 11.2 ■ **Percentage of Males and Females Arrested for Index Crimes.**
Although most arrests are of males, the proportion of arrests of females is highest for larceny-theft, while males are arrested at higher rates for other types of crime.

Source: U.S. Department of Justice, *Crime in the United States* (Washington, D.C.: Government Printing Office, 1992), p. 230.

toward traditionally "feminine" occupations that maintain gender stereotypes: hairdressing, food preparation, secretarial skills. With the de-emphasis of rehabilitation and the rise in prison populations during the 1970s and 1980s, corrections for women has been forced to defer to the rising concern about male offenders.

Differential treatment of men and women has characterized corrections in the United States since 1800. The original desire to separate women for their own protection yielded to the wish to restore the feminine virtues so that the offenders would return to the community and fulfill their duties as wives and mothers or as domestic servants. From the current perspective,

the history of corrections for women has been one of discrimination, not just differentiation. Although incarcerated women have generally lived in pleasanter surroundings than their male counterparts, they have been treated as girls. With the rise of the women's movement, new attention is being paid to the female offender, but the focus bears little resemblance to that of the Quaker women of the nineteenth century or of the Progressive reformers. Today there are increased demands that women be treated the same as men, yet as Nichole Rafter has pointed out, this seems to mean that "equal treatment usually means less adequate treatment."[24] She argues that inferior care is the rule today and that gender differences are not taken into account.

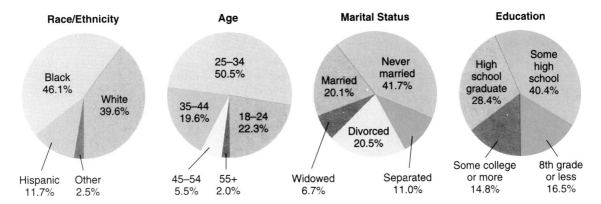

Figure 11.3 ▪ **Characteristics of Female Prisoners.** As with their male counterparts, female prisoners are young, have low education levels, are members of minority groups, and are incarcerated for a serious offense.

Source: Adapted from U.S. Bureau of Justice Statistics, *Special Report* (Washington, D.C.: Government Printing Office, March 1991), p. 2.

Incarceration

O f all adults incarcerated in the prisons of the United States, only 6 percent are women; of all offenders in local jails, only 9 percent are women.[25] As we mentioned earlier, the comparatively small numbers of female inmates in the nation's forty-seven institutions for women (forty-five state, two federal), the thirty-five coed facilities, and the approximately 3,500 local and county jails have a decided impact on the nature of incarceration for women. Life in women's prisons both resembles and differs from that in institutions for men. Women's facilities are smaller; security is not so tight; the relationships between inmates and staff are less structured; physical violence is less common; the sub-rosa economy is not so well developed; and female prisoners appear to be less committed to the convict code. Women serve shorter sentences than men do, so their prison society is more fluid as new members join and others leave.

Although these characteristics of correctional facilities for women may appear to be advantageous, some of the benefits tend to disappear when remoteness and heterogeneity are considered. Because only three states (Florida, Oklahoma, and Texas) operate more than one institution for women, inmates are generally far removed from their children, families, friends, and attorneys. In addition, because the numbers incarcerated in most states are small, there is less pressure to design programs for an individual offender's security and treatment needs. Classification categories are so broad that dangerous or mentally ill inmates are not effectively segregated from those who have committed minor offenses and have no psychological problems. The small numbers also limit the variety of vocational and educational opportunities available to women prisoners.

Women in Prison

In most respects, incarcerated women, like male prisoners, may be viewed as the disadvantaged losers in our complex and competitive society. Figure 11.3 summarizes some of the characteristics of female prisoners. A national survey of the backgrounds of women imprisoned found that almost 60 percent had not finished high school; about half had been unemployed or had

Excerpts from a Prison Journal

"The Rose"

This is an interview with myself. I've decided to write a book on things happening to me ... maybe someone else will read it and learn. I'm sitting in jail.

"Jail?" you say.

Sure. Haven't you ever seen one? That's the place you always believed, and were told, the bad people go. It's not true. They send good people there too. Look at me. I'm in a twelve-by-twenty-foot cell with two other "criminally oriented" females. They're O.K. One is here for not returning a car to the dealer she borrowed it from—known by some as Grand Theft Auto. The other is in here for writing too many checks on an account with no money.

The bunks are always too high, the mattresses are flimsy, and the pillows are falling apart. The window's got no glass in it; the cold north breeze blows in and freezes your ass off. So, if you ever plan on going to jail, hope it's in the summer.

The wind blows in, sending shivering chills up your spine. Oh! what you'd give to stand outside, with the sunshine beaming down, the birds singing, a tree to touch, a decent glass to drink out of, a proper plate to have your food on, a fork to eat with, a room without names all over the walls .... Hanging your towels over the heater to dry so you'll have a dry towel the next time you take a shower. The heater is a little portable thing that looks like someone took their frustration out on it. And you have to put everything up so it doesn't get wet, because the shower leaks and splatters all over everywhere .... Days of dripping shower, which is the worst sound in the world.

It's a sixty-eight-year-old building with steam heaters that whistle, jailers walking around with keys jingling, the elevator up and down all the time. They never come to get you. The phone rings from sunup to sundown. No calls for you. Calls only yours to be made when it's your turn. Knowing down inside no call will help you out of this mess.

The guys still flirt, no matter where—even through a little window in the door.... One of the girls is sitting under the sink having an obscene pipe conversation with Gary next door. He says it'll make him feel good, going down in history as an obscene pipe caller.

You'll never believe this. They're not trying to break out, just "escape to rape"— each other. I can hear the spoons digging now. Maybe they'll make it—by next year! The "escape to rape" fell through. We all knew it would, but it gave us something to do last night. We must've laughed for four hours straight. We got to do something. You can't just sit around and cry and find someone else to blame things on. A year is a long time when you live it in a box.

I made the news. Not like most of the people I went to school with. I'm going to write what it says so I'll never forget what Clovis, New Mexico, is really like.

———— [They spelled my name right!], convicted of issuing a worthless check and distribution of a controlled substance, is charged with being an habitual offender. District Judge ———— gave Ms. ———— a two-year state penitentiary sentence with one year suspended and to be served on parole probation. Ms.———— was originally given a suspended one-year sentence for issuing a worthless check. She was also previously given a five-year deferred penitentiary sentence for distribution of a controlled substance and was placed on probation.

Maybe someday I'll understand all this.

The worst feeling in the world was walking away and hearing my son scream for his mom. Knowing that I had to come back upstairs and be locked up. That's the hell in this hole—knowing people are close at hand and you can't touch or feel them.

I think what makes this so hard is that it's Christmastime. I'm almost crazy thinking I'm going to miss Santa Claus, Christmas carols, and my boys' smiling faces Christmas morning.

It's getting close to the time of my departure from a town I grew up in, learned to love. I feel a great loss as I'm going away knowing that returning may be a long ways away. Every passing moment brings thoughts I never conceived of having. I've never felt so alone. I've never felt so lost. I've never had so much taken from me in such a short time.

The strain of waiting for tomorrow has made me nervous, nauseous, and nuts. The three *n*'s. Sounds like a bad disease. I go to a fate that I have no concept of, praying and hoping that I can handle it.

(Later, from the State Penitentiary)

I came through the gate knowing very well that it will be many months before I will be able to leave. The Annex (for women) is a building separate from the Big House (for men). I've only been here thirty minutes and I'm already talking like a convict. They gave me a number and issued me two blankets, dark green; two sheets, white; two towels, white; soap; toothbrush and toothpaste. They gave me some books, paper, pen, and envelopes, brought me to this square box half the size of the county jail cell. It has one of the hardest beds I've ever seen, a toilet, a sink, a footlocker, two small bookcases, and a window. You can look out and see desert.

So far the women and matrons here seem very adaptable and willing to help. I've already had cookies, two glasses of milk, and two cups of hot chocolate brought to me before I sleep in my new box, sweet box. Don't get me wrong. I'll take all my days of working, bill collectors, children crying—and headaches, worries, and woes. I'll take my problems just not to hear that steel door slam shut and the key turn in the lock, a matron walk down the hall leaving me with an empty feeling, and a sound of clanking, jangling keys falling off in the distance.

Source: The twenty-four-year-old author of this journal chose the pen name "The Rose." Her identity has been disguised to protect her and her family, including two sons, ages two and six. These excerpts were written during the first five days following her conviction, while she was awaiting transfer from county jail to state prison. She served nine months in both maximum and minimum security facilities. Edited by Sue Mahan, from her interview notes. Reprinted by permission.

held unskilled jobs; and about 60 percent were Hispanic or African American. What most distinguished incarcerated women from men was the nature of their offenses, their drug use, and their correctional history.

Offenses Although it is commonly believed that most female inmates are incarcerated for such minor offenses as prostitution, sentences for such crimes are normally served in jails; prisons hold the more serious offenders, both male and female. The national survey found that 40.7 percent of the women prisoners were serving sentences for violent offenses (56.2 percent of male prisoners are convicted for such offenses), 41.2 percent for offenses against property (33.5 percent of men), 12.0 percent for drug-related offenses (7.1 percent of men), and 6.0 percent for public-order offenses (2.8 percent of men).[26] As we can see, the most significant difference between the sexes is in regard to violent offenses. This is not surprising in view of the fact that the *Uniform Crime Reports* arrest rate for violent crimes is so much higher for men than for women.

Drug use Although only 12.0 percent of women in the national survey were serving time for drug-related offenses, the study found that habitual use of drugs before incarceration is a much greater problem among female prisoners than this figure indicates. The researchers caution that the response rate was low to the drug questions, but almost 40 percent of women prisoners said that they used drugs on a daily basis in the month prior to their current offense.[27] Almost one-third said they had participated in at least one drug abuse treatment program other than any they may have been participating in at the time of the current offense. The extent of drug use has policy implications for correctional planners, for it indicates that a large percentage of female offenders need medical assistance as they go through withdrawal in jails and prisons.

Correctional history Almost 70 percent of the female prisoners have been on probation or

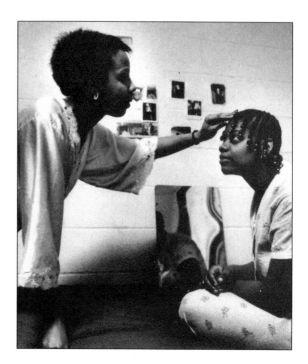

Compared with the convict society in prisons for males, many female prisoners form pseudofamilies, developing strong bonds with family members.

incarcerated in a correctional facility before their current sentence.[28] Differences between men and women on this variable seem to be related primarily to experiences as juveniles: More men reported having been on probation and incarcerated as youths.[29] Among the recidivists, men and women were similarly rated with regard to the type of prior offense; crimes against property occupied the highest rank for both sexes.

The Subculture of Women's Prisons

Studies of the subculture of women's prisons have been less extensive than those reported in Chapter 10 in regard to male convict society. Much of the early investigation of separate women's prisons focused on the types of social relationships female offenders maintained. As in all types of penal institutions, homosexual relationships were found, but unlike such relationships in male prisons, those among women appeared to be more voluntary than coerced. Perhaps more important, scholars reported that female inmates tended to form pseudofamilies in which they adopted various roles—father, mother, daughter, sister—and interacted as a unit. Women developed strong bonds with the other members of their groups rather than identifying with the total prisoner subculture. Esther Heffernan views these "play" families as a "direct, conscious substitution for the family relationships broken by imprisonment, or . . . the development of roles that perhaps were not fulfilled in the actual home environment." She also notes the economic aspect of the play families and the extent to which they are formed to provide for their members.[30] Such cooperative relationships help to relieve the tensions of prison life, to assist the socialization of the new inmate, and to permit individuals to act according to clearly defined roles and rules.

When David Ward and Gene Kassebaum studied sexual and family bonding at the California Institute for Women in Frontera, they identified homosexual roles but not the familiar roles found by other researchers in women's prisons. In the tradition of other studies of prisoner subcultures, Ward and Kassebaum examined adaptation to imprisonment through the development of roles expected of women in the larger society. The women in Frontera seemed to be less able to adapt to prison, and solidarity with one another did not develop as it had in the male institutions studied by Donald Clemmer and Gresham Sykes. Yet societal expectations in regard to the sex and social roles of women were important in the prisoner subculture.[31]

A more explicit attempt to compare the subculture of women's prisons with that of male institutions was made by Rose Giallombardo at the Federal Reformatory for Women in Alderson, West Virginia. Like John Irwin and Donald Cressey, Giallombardo hypothesizes that many of the subcultural features of

the institution are imported from the larger society.[32] She found that imprisoned women mitigate the pains of incarceration by developing marriage and kinship links with other inmates.

All societies have different expectations in regard to male and female roles. In the United States the woman's role is traditionally defined as that of wife and mother; the man is expected to play an occupational role, and his status depends on the status of his work. Thus "the family group in the female prison is singularly suited to meet the internalized cultural expectations of the female role. It serves the social, psychological, and physiological needs of the female inmates."[33] Through the prison homosexual marriage and the networks of kinship groupings, Giallombardo believes, female inmates express and fulfill their social needs during their incarceration. The cultural orientation of men, in contrast, precludes the formation of such groupings; prison punks and fags are looked down on, and the dominant males' entrance into homosexual relationships is explained as a temporary adjustment to sexual deprivation.

Giallombardo believes that in most respects the prison subcultures of men and women are similar, with one major exception: The informal social structure of the female prison helps inmates to "resist the destructive effects of imprisonment by creating a substitute universe—a world in which the inmates may preserve an identity which is relevant to life outside the prison." The orientation of female inmates is somewhat collectivist, with warmth and mutual aid being extended to family and kinship members; male prisoners adapt to prison life by stressing their self-sufficiency, developing a convict code, and showing solidarity with other inmates.[34]

Researchers do not seem to have arrived at a consensus in regard to the extent and nature of homosexual relationships in women's prisons. Imogene Moyer, for example, points out that the evidence must be analyzed within a framework that recognizes factors in each of the institutional settings. Thus policies designed to keep prisoners separate, average length of time served, distance from relatives, and level of regimentation must be assessed before generalized statements about social relationships can be made with any confidence.[35] Yet Robert Leger found that the lesbians he surveyed had longer sentences, were arrested at an earlier age, were more likely to have been previously confined, and had served more time than had the heterosexual women with whom they were imprisoned.[36]

The dispute over whether the subculture of prisoners is indigenous or imported led to some interesting findings in women's institutions. When Esther Heffernan began her study of the District of Columbia Women's Reformatory in Occoquan, Virginia, she expected to find a unitary inmate social structure arising from within the institution, as Clemmer and Sykes had done. But she found no "clear-cut pattern of acceptance or rejection of the inmate system, nor was there any relatively uniform perception of deprivations." Unlike the male maximum security institution, Occoquan, in line with most other prisons for women, has a heterogeneous population with the whole spectrum of offense types. Heffernan empirically demonstrates what Irwin and Cressey only suggest: that prisoners with similar orientations had developed "distinctive norms and values, a pattern of interrelationships and certain roles that served their own prison needs."[37] The typical offender types bring these orientations with them to the prison.

Adaptive roles Heffernan discovered three argot roles: "square," "the life," and "cool," corresponding to the noncriminal, habitual, and professional offenders in the institution. The term *square* is used in prison as it is used in the larger community; it describes a person who adheres to conventional norms and values. A square is a noncriminal who perhaps killed her husband in a moment of rage. She attempts to maintain a conventional life in prison, to gain the respect of officers and fellow inmates, and

to be a "good Christian woman." About 50 percent of the prison population are *in the life,* and they, too, act in prison as they did on the outside: They are antisocial. These are habitual offenders who have been involved in prostitution, drugs, numbers, and shoplifting. They have been in prison before and interact among others with similar experiences, finding community within the prison. Their adaptive role requires them to stand firm against authority. *Cool,* a term of general approbation in the world of jazz and among street gangs, is applied in the female prison to people who make a "controlled, pleasurable, manipulative response to a situation." They are the professionals who "keep busy, play around, stay out of trouble, and get out." They attempt to manipulate others and to do "easy time" by joining with like-minded inmates to gain as many amenities as they can without putting a short stay at risk.[38]

These three adaptations to incarceration correspond to criminal identities brought in from the outside. Prisoners who assume the various roles join together; thus three subsystems, each with its own perspective, exist within the society. Although divided, the inmates at Occoquan try to mitigate the deprivations of imprisonment through their informal social system.

Male Versus Female Subcultures

In looking at the research findings on the subcultures of male and female prisons, one discovers a great deal of correspondence but also major differences. Comparisons are complicated somewhat by the nature of the research, for most studies have been conducted in single-sex institutions, and theories and concepts first developed in male prisons have then been applied to female institutions. The concepts of argot roles, the inmate code, indigenous versus imported values, the prison economy, and so on have been central to this entire body of literature, and all have been found to have explanatory value in both types of institutions. Irwin, for example, describes the roles of "square John," "thief," and "convict" in a male prison; Heffernan uses the analogous terms "square," "cool," and "the life."[39] In both types of institutions, "making it" refers to the fact that by adapting to prison life, one can make the experience relatively painless. Inmates who cannot come to terms with incarceration can expect to do "hard time" and suffer.

A major difference between these two gender-specific societies lies in interpersonal relationships. In male prisons one gets a sense of individuals acting for themselves and being evaluated by others according to the way they live in relation to the norms of the subculture. As James Fox noted in his comparative study of one women's and four men's prisons, men feel they have to demonstrate physical strength and consciously avoid any manner that may imply homosexuality. To gain recognition and status within the convict community, the male prisoner must strictly adhere to these values. Men, too, form cliques, but not the networks of family relationships that have been found in prisons for women. Men are expected to do their *own* time. The norms emphasize autonomy, self-sufficiency, and the ability to cope with one's own problems. Fox found little sharing in the men's prisons.[40]

Women at the Bedford Hills Correctional Facility in New York placed less emphasis on the achievement of status or recognition within the prisoner community. Fox writes, "They were less likely to impose severe restrictions on the sexual (or emotional) conduct of other members."[41] In prisons for women, close ties seem to exist among small groups. Within one of these extended families, two individuals may be involved in a homosexual relationship; others play the roles of siblings, aunts, or cousins. The family networks provide emotional support and emphasize the sharing of resources. One inmate at Bedford Hills told an interviewer:

> The families sort of try to look out for their own. Like, I have a family here ———, she's kind of old and she has high blood pressure, and a lot of other things wrong

with her, so she's my mother. And if she thinks that I'm getting into something that she doesn't like, then we talk about it. I also have a brother, I have a sister, and we all sit and talk. But all the families aren't the same. Ours is sort of calm. ——— believes that we shouldn't get charge sheets, and if one of us gets a charge sheet, it's really something because we normally don't have any. So we try to stay on the cool side. When any of us gets a visit, we all cook together. When we go to the commissary, we put our sheets together and we buy food.[42]

The differences between male and female prisoner subcultures have been ascribed to the nurturing, maternal qualities of women. Some critics charge that such an analysis stereotypes female behavior and imputes a biological basis to personality where none exists. Of importance is the question of inmate-inmate violence in male and female institutions. The little data that exist indicate that women are less likely to engage in violent acts against their fellow inmates than are men.[43] It will be interesting to see whether such gender-specific differences continue to be found among prisoners as the feminist perspective gains in influence among researchers and as society comes to look at women and men as equals.

Programs

A major criticism of women's prisons is that they lack the variety of vocational and educational programs usually available in male institutions, and that existing programs tend to conform to stereotypes of "feminine" occupations—cosmetology, food service, housekeeping, sewing.[44] In one survey of fifteen institutions for women, among the vocational programs offered were clerical work, cosmetology, dental technician, floral design, food service, garment manufacture, housekeeping, IBM keypunch, and nurses' aide.[45] Such training does not correspond to the wider opportunities available to women in today's world. The programs are also

Formal training in the skills needed to be a beautician is among the vocational programs found in many prisons. Critics charge that training programs in women's prisons are for jobs that are stereotypically "feminine."

less ambitious than those in men's prisons, which often offer education at the secondary and college levels. The importance of vocational and educational opportunities during incarceration is underscored by the fact that upon release most women have to support themselves, and many are financially responsible for children.

Two studies conducted during the 1970s provide most of the information we have about educational and vocational programs in women's prisons. Ruth Glick and Virginia Neto surveyed sixteen prisons, forty-six jails, and thirty-six community-based programs in fourteen states.[46] The editors of the *Yale Law Journal* surveyed forty-seven male and fifteen female institutions that accounted for approximately 30 percent of the male and 50 percent of the female incarcerated populations.[47] Both studies confirm the general impression that fewer programs are offered in women's prisons than in men's institutions and that they lack variety. The Yale study discovered that, on average, male institutions had 10.2 vocational programs, female institutions, 2.7. The size of the inmate population is often cited to justify the number of programs offered, but it was found that although the smallest female population was 44 and the largest 739, every institution had at least one program and none had more than three.

The educational level of most female offenders is a factor that limits access to higher-paid occupations. In some institutions less than half of the inmates have completed high school. In some correctional systems these women are assigned to classes so that they may pursue the GED while others may pursue college work through correspondence study or courses offered in the institution. Employment opportunities in contemporary America are increasingly open only to those persons with the educational background necessary to meet the complexities of the work force.

Critics of corrections have pointed out that although the female work force in the broader community has greatly expanded since the 1960s and women now occupy positions formerly reserved for men, women prisoners are not being prepared for such jobs. Not all correctional administrators agree with the assessment. Martha Wheeler of the Ohio Department of Corrections, a past president of the American Correctional Association, asserts that some women "are not career-minded and they do not really have it in mind to go out and get a job and be self-supporting." She believes that many former inmates want the traditional roles of wife and mother. Wheeler asks, "Is it our responsibility to work with the woman on finding a whole new role, a whole new view of herself? Or is it our responsibility to meet her where she is and help her with programs which secure her where she is to deal more effectively, more productively, and hopefully more happily with the world that she is going to?"[48]

But is Wheeler's position realistic? The world that the released female offender is entering is unlikely to contain a man who is willing and able to support her and her children. Most women prisoners have no one to depend on but themselves. When they are released, they must be able to enter an occupation that will provide an income and some hope of advancement. Without a means of support, the released offender faces a life of welfare or illegal activity to gain access to the resources she and her children need. Programs to train offenders for postrelease vocations as well as incentives to pursue new roles are essential if offenders are to be successful in the community.

Co-Corrections

As we have seen, one of the major reforms of corrections introduced in the nineteenth century was separation of the sexes in penal institutions. Today, however, a few prisons are again housing felons of both sexes. Since the early 1960s, some juvenile homes and drug rehabilitation centers have been operated on a gender-free basis; in 1971 the Federal Correctional Institution at Fort Worth, Texas, was opened with both male and female inmates. Seventy-seven state and federal institutions are now being operated on this basis.[49]

This move toward co-corrections has been advocated for several reasons, among them the wish to reduce the disparity in programs available to male and female inmates. Aside from changes in programs, co-corrections has been advocated as a way to reduce the tensions and violence of single-sex institutions, to prepare prisoners for their return to a heterosexual so-

ciety, and to use facilities in a cost-effective manner.[50] It is the last reason that has done the most to make the idea of housing men and women together attractive to some correctional administrators. With the incarceration rate rising, co-corrections has been instituted in many states as a way of relieving pressure on male prisons. Although the wider variety of vocational programs and the greater resources of such institutions to meet the social needs of female offenders have attracted reform attention, the economical use of space seems to be the primary motive for co-corrections.

Co-corrections can mean different things in different contexts. In the federal system the term means more than merely putting male and female prisoners under the same roof. A determined effort is made to ensure that programs and social contacts are integrated in a minimum security setting. Restrictions are placed only on the presence of inmates of the opposite sex in the housing areas, and the rules limit physical contact to holding hands. By 1984, approximately 61 percent of federal adult female inmates were in co-correctional settings. In the states, however, while prisoners of both sexes may be housed in one facility, they may have contact with each other only in the dining room or the classroom. At the Albion Correctional Facility in New York the women and men are segregated except for work assignments, classes, and special programs. The women "are always escorted whenever they leave their housing block, which is surrounded by a chain link fence"; physical contact between members of the opposite sex can result in a transfer.[51]

As crowding continues to be a problem for most correctional systems, co-corrections can be expected to spread, but as a means to efficient use of space rather than for programmatic reasons. Some observers fear that even in a co-correctional institution the interests of female inmates will still be drowned in a sea of men. It has been suggested that rather than integrating the sexes, single-sex correctional institutions might coordinate their operations and

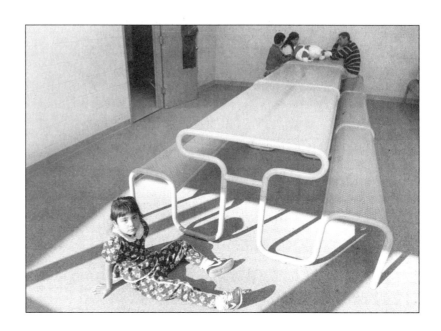

What is it like for a child to visit her mother in the sterile visiting room of a prison? Can bonds be maintained under such conditions?

share programs and services. In this way, each retains its identity and autonomy and stays within budgetary constraints.

Services

Women's prisons lack not only adequate vocational and educational programs but also proper nutritional and recreational services. The numbers game also affects the provision of medical services: Most women's institutions share physicians and hospital facilities with men's prisons, and most women prisoners have no access to a gynecologist. A situation at Bedford Hills Correctional Facility resulted in a lawsuit on behalf of the inmates because the institution provided no full-time physician or continuous medical care, and screening for medical problems was inadequate. The institution was found in violation of the Eighth Amendment's prohibition against cruel and unusual punishments because the state had deliberately been indifferent to known medical needs.[52]

Women should have additional medical and nutritional resources if they are pregnant. There are no data on the annual number of pregnancies in U.S. jails and prisons, but a study of female offenders in eight states found that 9 percent had given birth while behind bars.[53] Pregnancies raise numerous issues for correctional policy, including special diets, the right to an abortion, access to a delivery room and medical personnel, and the length of time that the newborn can remain with its incarcerated mother. Of special concern is the fact that a majority of pregnant inmates have factors (older than thirty-five years, history of drug abuse, prior multiple abortions, and sexually transmitted diseases) that indicate the potential for a high-risk pregnancy requiring special medical care.[54]

Prison conditions and treatment for pregnant inmates have sometimes aroused public outrage and led to lawsuits. Connecticut residents were shocked to learn that a prisoner in the Niantic Correctional Facility had been shackled to the obstetrical table until minutes before her child was delivered. In *Newman* v. *Alabama* female prisoners claimed that they had been deprived of proper and adequate medical treatment. The justices declared that conditions in the delivery room violated the Eighth Amendment:

While the more serious illnesses or injuries are treated outside the prison … an average of seven or eight babies are delivered at Tutwiler [prison] each year under conditions which endanger the lives of both mothers and infants. The delivery table has no restraints, paint is peeling from the ceiling above it, and large segments of the linoleum floor around the table are missing. There are no facilities to resuscitate the newborn or otherwise provide adequate care should any complications arise during delivery.[55]

Beyond the need for medical care, many people believe that the national policies of equal opportunity require that women be given the types and variety of programs and services offered to male inmates, and they cite the equal protection clause of the Fourteenth Amendment, the Civil Rights Act of 1964, and the proposed Equal Rights Amendment. Support for this view can be found in the 1979 case of *Glover* v. *Johnson,* in which the female inmates of the Detroit House of Correction charged that their educational and vocational programs were much poorer than those offered to male prisoners. The court ruled that prison officials had a responsibility to bring the level of services up to that of the services accorded men.[56] The decision was based in part on a New Mexico case, *Barefield* v. *Leach*, in which the judges said that the equal protection clause "requires parity of treatment, as contrasted with identity of treatment, between male and female inmates with respect to the conditions of their confinement and access to rehabilitation opportunities."[57]

Mothers and Their Children

Of greatest concern to incarcerated women is the fate of their children. The best available data indicate that about 75 percent of women inmates are mothers and that, on average, they have two dependent children. It is thus estimated that on any given day 167,000 children—two-thirds of whom are under ten years of age—in the United States have mothers who are in jail or in prison.[58] One recent study found that roughly half of these children do not see their mothers while they are in prisons.[59]

Because most incarcerated mothers do not have husbands or male partners who are able and willing to maintain a home for the children, the children are placed with other relatives or in state-funded foster care. In a study of 133 inmates and their children, Phyllis Jo Baunach found that children are most often taken care of by their maternal grandmothers. The knowledge that her children were with their grandmother gave the inmate peace of mind; she believed the youngsters were being well taken care of and that she would have no difficulty getting them back when she was released. Of particular interest is the fact that Baunach found that a higher proportion of the children of black inmates than of white inmates were being cared for by relatives.[60] When an inmate had no relative or friend who would take care of her children, they were often put up for adoption or placed in foster care. Having the fate of her children decided by a welfare worker was traumatic for the mother, and for the children as well.

Anxiety about the care of their children affects all imprisoned mothers, especially if their children are being cared for by strangers. In such cases, incarcerated mothers sometimes have difficulty retaining their parental rights. For example, in *Los Angeles County Department of Adoptions* v. *Hutchinson,* the court upheld an order terminating a mother's parental rights because she was incarcerated, even though she had objected and tried to make contact with her daughter. During the mother's four and a half years of confinement, the child had been shuttled among six foster homes. The judge said that he was ruling against the mother because she would not be released immediately, yet the case came to trial only six months before her release.[61]

Enforced separation of children from their mothers is bad for the children and the mothers. It is a heart-wrenching and stress-producing prison experience—and one that is not fully

The telephone is a prisoner's main link to family and friends. Women prisoners are often under stress because they worry about the life their children are leading.

shared by male inmates. Baunach found that regardless of race or age, women expressed guilt and shame that they had committed crimes that separated them from their children.[62] Those with drug problems may realize for the first time what their behavior has done to their children. Many are concerned about the eventual reunion, fearing that neither they nor the children will be able to readjust to each other after the long separation.

In most states, babies born in prison must be placed with a family member or a social agency within three weeks of birth. Yet great concern has been expressed about the early cessation of mother-infant bonding, thought to be so crucial for human development, and some innovative programs have provided for them to remain together longer. One example is the nursery operated at the Women's Correctional Institution at Bedford Hills, New York. Here, women move to the nursery for the last few months of pregnancy. They give birth at a nearby hospital and return to live in the nursery wing, caring for their infants for up to a year. Their primary responsibility is to care for their children and to learn parenting skills.[63]

Imprisoned mothers have difficulty maintaining contact with their children over the

miles that separate them. Visits are short and infrequent, phone calls are uncertain and irregular, and when the children come to the prison from time to time, the surroundings are strange and intimidating. Some correctional facilities make an effort to devise ways to help mothers maintain links to their children and nurture the relationships, but in others the children are required to conform to the rules governing adult visitation: no physical contact and strict limits. In their study of mothers in one institution, Susan Datesman and Gloria Cales found that 65 percent had visited with at least some of their children and that most kept in contact through phone calls and letters—70 percent at least once a week. The mothers emphasized the importance of visiting as a means of maintaining and strengthening the relationships with their children. One commented, "The main advantages of the visits are tightening up the relationships, watching your children grow, your children watching you grow, how you've changed, being able to love one another."[64]

Programs designed to address the needs of mothers and their children are being developed. In some states children may meet with their mothers at almost any time, for extended periods, and in playrooms or nurseries where contact is possible. Some states arrange transportation for children visiting their mothers. Some institutions even permit children to stay overnight with their mothers. In both South Dakota and Nebraska, children may stay with their mothers for up to five days a month. Four of the forty prisons that Virginia Neto and LaNelle Marie Bainer studied had family visiting programs that permitted the inmate, her legal husband, and her children to be together, often in a mobile home or apartment, for periods ranging up to seventy-two hours.[65]

The emphasis on community corrections as it developed in the 1970s gave rise to programs in which youngsters could live with their mothers in halfway houses. These programs have not expanded as much as they were expected to, however, in part because the presence of children upset the routine of the facility. Currently, however, many states have furlough programs that allow inmates to visit relatives and children in their homes during holiday periods and some weekends.

Release to the Community

The limited data available indicate that women are just as successful as men on parole. One study based on data from the *Uniform Parole Reports* indicated that after two years the same proportions of women and men were continued on parole but that, given similar characteristics, women have a greater probability of successful completion.[66] A California study found that two-thirds of the women returned to prison were sent back for violation of parole rules rather than for commission of a new crime.[67]

It is important to note, however, that upon release from prison women seem to have a greater variety of problems than men normally do, less confidence in their ability to cope with those problems—and less hesitation about admitting they need help. Because many are heads of households, they require extensive social services to help with the management of finances, work-related problems, child care, and household management; it is not enough for correctional workers to help them find employment and housing, as they do for men. In fact, parole officers have complained that female offenders in the community make many more demands on them than do male offenders.

Annette Brodsky has noted that women need more postrelease training and support services than men do—not only employment assistance but also, perhaps, counseling with regard to drug and alcohol abuse and help with reestablishing family relationships. Some women have the support of relatives, but many are on their own and have to care for young children. Even more burdensome to such a woman than these immediate needs is society's reaction to her as a criminal, a stigma that is very hard to lose.[68]

Summary

Without question, the treatment accorded the female offender by the criminal justice system is quite unlike that given to her male counterpart. The difference may be traced to the level and type of female criminality, society's perceptions of the role of women, the relatively small number of women in the offender population, and the special needs of women as a function of their responsibilities for young children and limits on their economic opportunities. At a time when the women's movement has focused national attention on the inequities to which women are subjected, the plight of the female offender has finally aroused the concern of correctional officials, legislators, and support groups. The fact that only 6 percent of the prison population is female has long been used to justify the allocation of only very limited resources to these offenders.

Early nineteenth-century reformers were appalled to find that women were not separated from men in penal institutions. With the establishment of separate institutions for women administered by women, the focus shifted to the creation of reformatories that would inculcate "feminine" habits by providing training in domestic skills. Today's reformers wish to see women offenders given vocational and other services on a par with those offered in men's institutions.

Research on the subcultures of male prisoners has been replicated in institutions for women. It has been determined that among women offenders, interpersonal relationships are often confined to a close group of friends in pseudofamilies. Because about 75 percent of incarcerated women are mothers, concerns about separation from their children are constant. Some institutions have devised ways to help women maintain contact with their children, but many prisons still make no such effort.

The gains made by women in the United States since the early 1970s might lead one to expect differences between prisons for men and women to have diminished. Co-correctional institutions have been established and some new resources have been provided for female prisons, but these gains have often been offset by the increase in the prison population and budgetary constraints. Female offenders may not be quite so overlooked as they were a generation ago, but they still receive far fewer services and attention than male prisoners receive.

For Discussion

1. How has the fragmentation of the corrections system affected the quality of services available to female offenders?

2. How might the unequal treatment of male and female offenders be justified? Should female offenders be given the same types of sentences that are given to men for similar crimes?

3. You are the administrator of a women's correctional center. What problems would you expect to encounter that are characteristic of the incarcera-

tion of women? How would you handle these problems?

4. How should the parental rights of prisoners be dealt with? Should children be allowed to live in correctional facilities with their mothers? What problems would this practice create?

5. Discuss the differences between the social structures of male and female correctional institutions. Why do you think they exist?

For Further Reading

Baunach, Phyllis Jo. *Mothers in Prison.* New Brunswick, N.J.: Transaction Publishers, 1985. One of the few studies to examine the relationship between female inmates and their children.

Freedman, Estelle B. *Their Sisters' Keepers.* Ann Arbor: University of Michigan Press, 1981. A history of the development of prisons for women in the United States.

Giallombardo, Rose. *Society of Women: A Study of a Women's Prison.* New York: Wiley, 1966. A study of the Federal Reformatory for Women in Alderson, West Virginia. Giallombardo found that in most respects the subcultures of prisons for men and women were similar.

Heffernan, Esther. *Making It in Prison.* New York: Wiley, 1972. Examines the argot roles of incarcerated women and their adaptation to prison life.

Rafter, Nicole Hahn. *Partial Justice: Women, Prisons and Social Control,* 2nd ed. New Brunswick, N.J.: Transaction Publishers, 1990. A history of prisons for women in the United States with two new chapters on the "parity movement" and responses to sex discrimination against the incarcerated.

Notes

1. Andrew H. Malcolm, "On Towns," *New York Times,* 13 September 1991, p. B2.

2. Nichole Hahn Rafter, "Gender and Justice: The Equal Protection Issue," *The American Prison,* ed. Lynne Goodstein and Doris Layton MacKenzie (New York: Plenum Press, 1989), p. 89.

3. U.S. Department of Justice, Bureau of Justice

Statistics, *Bulletin* (Washington, D.C.: Government Printing Office, March 1991), p. 2.

4. U.S. Department of Justice, Bureau of Justice Statistics, *Bulletin* (Washington, D.C.: Government Printing Office, May 1992) (update in May 1993), p. 4.

5. U.S. Department of Justice, *Crime in the United States* (Washington, D.C.: Government Printing Office, 1992), p. 230.

6. Ibid.

7. Freda Adler, "Crime, an Equal Opportunity Employer," *Trial Magazine* (January 1977): 31.

8. Peggy C. Giordano, Sandra Kerbel, and Sandra Dudley, "The Economics of Female Criminality: An Analysis of Police Blotters, 1890–1975," in *Women and Crime in America,* ed. Lee H. Bowker (New York: Macmillan, 1981), pp. 65–82; Darrell J. Steffensmeirer, "Sex Differences in Patterns of Adult Crime, 1965–1977," *Social Forces* 58 (1980): 344–57.

9. Nichole Rafter, *Partial Justice: Women, Prisons and Social Control* (New Brunswick, N.J.: Transaction Publishers, 1990), p. 178.

10. Ruth Diane Lown and Charlene Snow, "Women, the Forgotten Prisoners: *Glover* v. *Johnson,*" in *Legal Rights of Prisoners,* ed. Geoffrey P. Alpert (Newbury Park, Calif.: Sage, 1980), p. 195.

11. Meda Chesney-Lind, "Chivalry Reexamined: Women and the Criminal Justice System," in *Women, Crime and the Criminal,* ed. Lee H. Bowker (Lexington, Mass.: Lexington Books, 1978), cited in Sharon L. Fabian, "Women Prisoners: Challenge of the Future," in *Legal Rights of Prisoners,* ed. Geoffrey P. Alpert (Newbury Park, Calif.: Sage, 1980), p. 176.

12. Ralph R. Arditi, Frederick Goldbert, Jr., M. Martha Hartle, John H. Peters, and William R. Phelps, "The Sexual Segregation of American Prisons," *Yale Law Journal* 82 (1973): 1229.

13. E. R. Pitman, *Elizabeth Fry* (New York: Greenwood, [1884] 1969), p. 55.

14. W. David Lewis, *From Newgate to Dannemora: The Rise of the Penitentiary in New York, 1796–1888* (Ithaca, N.Y.: Cornell University Press, 1965), pp. 158–59.

15. Nichole Hahn Rafter, "Equality or Difference?" *Federal Prisons Journal* 3 (Spring 1992): 17.

16. Estelle B. Freedman, *Their Sisters' Keepers* (Ann Arbor: University of Michigan Press, 1981), p. 15.

17. Sara F. Keely, "The Organization and Discipline

of the Indiana Women's Prison" (proceedings of the Annual Congress of the National Prison Association, 1898), p. 275, quoted in Rose Giallombardo, *Society of Women* (New York: Wiley, 1966), p. 7.

18. Maud Ballington Booth, "The Shadow of Prison" (proceedings of the 58th Congress of the American Prison Association, 1898), p. 275, quoted in Rose Giallombardo, *Society of Women* (New York: Wiley, 1966), p. 46.

19. Nichole Hahn Rafter, "Prisons for Women, 1790–1980," in *Crime and Justice,* ed. Michael Tonry and Norval Morris, 5th ed. (Chicago: University of Chicago Press, 1983), p. 147.

20. Freedman, *Their Sisters' Keepers,* p. 69.

21. Rafter, "Prisons for Women," p. 165.

22. Lewis, *From Newgate to Dannemora,* p. 213.

23. Rafter, "Prisons for Women," p. 165.

24. Rafter, "Equality or Difference?" p. 19.

25. U.S. Department of Justice, Bureau of Justice Statistics, *Bulletin* (Washington, D.C.: Government Printing Office, May 1992).

26. U.S. Department of Justice, Bureau of Justice Statistics, *Special Report* (Washington, D.C.: Government Printing Office, March 1991), p. 2.

27. Ibid., p. 5.

28. Ibid.

29. Ann Goetting and Roy M. Howsen, "Women in Prison," *Prison Journal* 63 (Autumn/Winter 1983): 33.

30. Esther Heffernan, *Making It in Prison* (New York: Wiley, 1972), pp. 88, 91; Robert Culbertson and Ann L. Paddock, "The Self-Concept of Incarcerated Women and the Relationship to Argot Roles" (paper presented at annual meeting of Academy of Criminal Justice Sciences, Oklahoma City, Okla., March 1980).

31. David Ward and Gene G. Kassebaum, *Women's Prison: Sex and Social Structure* (Hawthorne, N.Y.: Aldine, 1965), p. 140.

32. Giallombardo, *Society of Women* (New York: Wiley, 1966), p. 6; John Irwin and Donald Cressey, "Thieves, Convicts, and the Inmate Culture," *Social Problems* 10 (Fall 1962): 145.

33. Giallombardo, *Society of Women,* p. 185.

34. Ibid., pp. 102, 103.

35. Imogene L. Moyer, "Differential Social Structures and Homosexuality among Women in Prison," *Virginia Social Science Journal* (April 1978): 13–14, 17–19.

36. Robert G. Leger, "Lesbianism Among Women Prisoners: Participants and Nonparticipants," *Criminal Justice and Behavior* 14 (December 1987): p. 463.

37. Heffernan, *Making It in Prison*, pp. 16, 17.

38. Ibid., pp. 41–42.

39. John Irwin, *The Felon* (Englewood Cliffs, N.J.: Prentice-Hall, 1970), pp. 67–80.

40. James G. Fox, *Organizational and Racial Conflict in Maximum-Security Prisons* (Lexington, Mass.: Lexington Books, 1982), pp. 100, 102.

41. Ibid., p. 100.

42. Ibid., pp. 100–101.

43. Candace Kruttschnitt and Sharon Krmpotich, "Aggressive Behavior Among Female Inmates: An Exploratory Study," *Justice Quarterly* 7 (June 1990): 371.

44. Clarice Feinman, "An Historical Overview of the Treatment of Incarcerated Women: Myths and Realities of Rehabilitation," *The Prison Journal* (Autumn/Winter 1983): 12–24.

45. U.S. Department of Justice, National Institute of Law Enforcement and Criminal Justice, Ruth M. Glick and Virginia V. Neto, *National Study of Women's Correctional Programs* (Washington, D.C.: Government Printing Office, 1977); Arditi et al. "Sexual Segregation," pp. 1243, 1271.

46. Ruth M. Glick and Virginia V. Neto, *National Study of Women's Correctional Programs* (Washington, D.C.: National Institute of Law Enforcement and Criminal Justice, 1977).

47. Arditi et al., "Sexual Segregation," pp. 1243, 1271.

48. Martha Wheeler, "The Current Status of Women in Prisons," in *The Female Offender*, ed. Annette M. Brodsky (Newbury Park, Calif.: Sage, 1975), p. 87.

49. U.S. Department of Justice, Bureau of Justice Statistics, *Prisons and Prisoners in the United States* (Washington, D.C.: Government Printing Office, 1992), p. xii.

50. John O. Smykla, *Coed Prisons* (New York: Human Sciences Press, 1980).

51. Claudine Scheber, "Beauty Marks and Blemishes: The Coed Prison as a Microcosm of Integrated Society," *Prison Journal* 64 (Spring/Summer 1984): 5.

52. Judith Resnik, "Should Prisoners Be Classified by Sex?" in *Criminal Corrections: Realities and Ideas*, ed. Jameson Doig (Lexington, Mass.: Lexington Books,

1983), p. 111. See Todaro v. Ward, 431 F. Supp. 1129 (S.D.N.Y., 1977).

53. Karen E. Holt, "Nine Months to Life: The Law and the Pregnant Inmate," *Journal of Family Law* 20 (1981–1982): 523; *New York Times,* 30 November 1992, p. A10.

54. U.S. Department of Justice, Federal Bureau of Prisons, Anita G. Huft, Lena Sue Fawkes, and W. Travis Lawson, Jr. "Care of the Pregnant Offender," *Federal Prisons Journal* (Spring 1992): 51.

55. Newman v. Alabama, 349 F. Supp. 282 (1981).

56. Glover v. Johnson, 478 F. Supp. 1075 (E.D. Mich., 1979).

57. Barfield v. Leach, Civ. No. 10282 (D.C. N.M., 1974).

58. *New York Times,* 30 November 1992, p. A10.

59. *New York Times,* 27 December 1992, p. D3.

60. Phyllis Jo Baunach, "You Can't Be a Mother and Be in Prison…Can You?: Impacts of the Mother-Child Separation," in *The Criminal Justice System and Women,* ed. Barbara Raffel Price and Natalie J. Sokoloff (New York: Clark Boardman, 1982), pp. 155–69.

61. Sharon L. Fabian, "Women Prisoners: Challenge of the Future," in *Legal Rights of Prisoners,* ed. Geoffrey P. Alpert (Beverly Hills, Calif.: Sage, 1980), p. 185.

62. Phyllis Jo Baunach, *Mothers in Prison* (New Brunswick, N.J.: Transaction Publishers, 1985), p. 75.

63. Ibid.

64. Susan K. Datesman and Gloria L. Cales, "'I'm Still the Same Mommy': Maintaining the Mother/Child Relationship in Prison," *Prison Journal* 63 (Autumn/Winter 1983): 147.

65. Virginia N. Neto and LaNelle Marie Bainer, "Mother and Wife Locked Up: A Day with the Family," *Prison Journal* 63 (Autumn/Winter 1983): 124.

66. William H. Moseley and Margaret H. Gerould, "Sex and Parole: A Comparison of Male and Female Parolees," *Journal of Crime and Justice* 3 (Spring 1975): 55.

67. J. E. Berecochea and C. Spencer, *Recidivism Among Women Parolees: A Long-Term Study* (Sacramento, Calif.: Department of Corrections, 1972), cited in Fabian, "Women Prisoners," p. 178.

68. Annette M. Brodsky, "Planning for the Female Offender," in *Female Offender*, ed. Annette M. Brodsky, p. 105.

12

Institutional Management

The prison, like other total institutions, is a place of residence and work where a large number of like-situated individuals, cut off from the wider society for an appreciable period of time, together lead an enclosed, formally administered routine of life.

Erving Goffman, sociologist, 1961

Formal Organization
Structure
The Impact of Structure
Governing Prisons
The Defects of Total Power
Rewards and Punishments
Co-Optation of Correctional Officers
Inmate Leadership
Leadership: The Crucial Element of Governance
**Correctional Officers: The Linchpin
     of Management**
Who Are the Officers?
Problems with the Officer's Role
Unionism
Summary

As Philip Carvalho and three of his fellow officers in the Massachusetts maximum security prison at Walpole eat lunch together, their conversation is devoted almost entirely to shop talk. It is the small talk of infantry GIs dissecting the foibles of the higher echelons back at division headquarters.

"If the people out front who make up the rules had to come in here and enforce them, they'd never make them up...."

"...Yeah, they ought to have an officer out there with 'em when they make up those damn things...."

"Yeah, yeah, yeah, but then they'd pick some guy who never worked in population... you want to bet on it... that's what they'd do...."

"If you run this institution by the book they give you, you'd have a riot. You can't do it. It's impossible. Hey, they tell you a guy can't go to another tier to see another guy even if that guy's his brother."[1]

How then should a prison be run? What rules should guide this institution, the only place in modern society where a group of people devote themselves to managing a group of captives? Prisoners do not come voluntarily to the prison nor do they stay voluntarily. They live according to the dictates of their keepers, and their movements are circumscribed. Prison administrators cannot select their clients and have little or no control over their release. Yet the administrators are expected to keep prisoners in custody, to use their labor to maintain the facilities or to produce goods for the state, and to provide treatment services that will allow the released offender to live a crime-free life in society. Obviously this is a tall order, one that requires skilled and dedicated managers.

Sociologist Erving Goffman developed the concept of the **total institution,** a place that completely encapsulates the lives of the people who work and live there.[2] A prison may be such an institution in the sense that whatever prisoners do or do not do begins and ends there; every minute behind bars must be lived according to the institution's rules as enforced by the staff. Adding to the totality of the prison is a basic split between the large group of persons (inmates) who have very limited contact with the outside world and the small group of persons (staff members) who supervise the inmates within the walls and yet are socially integrated into the outside world where they live. Each group sees the other in terms of stereotypes. Staff members view inmates as secretive and untrustworthy; inmates view staff members as condescending and mean. Staff members feel superior and righteous, inmates inferior and weak.

Although the maximum security custodial prison of the past may have conformed to the concept of the total institution, today's correctional facilities are permeated by outside influences. Contemporary inmates have greater access to communication with the nonprison world by way of television, radio, telephone, and visits. Community advocacy groups and the courts have intervened to shrink the power of institutional administrators. No longer are the warden and staff so isolated from public eyes that they can ignore the law. The mixture of racial and ethnic cliques among today's inmates discourages the development of a sense of solidarity in opposition to the staff. Where treatment programs are provided, the need for openness, caring, and a therapeutic environment has lessened the prevailing stereotypes of staff and inmate. In view of these changes, the concept of the total institution must be used with caution, yet the contemporary prison still differs so greatly from the free world that Goffman's concept remains useful for purposes of analysis.

It is important to remember that a wide range of institutions fall under the heading of

---

total institution An institution (such as a prison) that completely encapsulates the lives of the people who live and work within it. Behavior is governed by rules and the group is split into two parts, one of which controls all aspects of the lives of the other.

prison. Some are therapeutic communities serving a relatively small number of clients; others are sprawling agricultural complexes; still others are ranches or forest camps. But most prisons have comparable management structures and offender populations.

In this chapter we look at the ways in which institutional resources are organized to achieve certain goals. Since the prison is unlike any other social institution, we should expect its administration to be distinctive. At a minimum, prisoners must be clothed, fed, kept healthy, provided recreation, protected from one another, and maintained in custody. In addition, administrators may be charged with offering rehabilitative programs and using offender labor in agricultural or industrial pursuits. To do all these things in a community of free individuals would be taxing. To do them when the population consists of some of the most antisocial people in the society is surely a Herculean undertaking.

Formal Organization

The University of Texas, the General Motors Corporation, and the California State Prison at Folsom seem to be three disparate organizations, yet they have in common the fact that each was created in order to achieve certain goals. Because each exists to serve a specific purpose, differing structures of formal organization have been established so that the various parts of the university, auto manufacturer, and prison may be coordinated in the respective interests of scholarship, production, and corrections.

Unlike a family, a circle of friends, or a community, in which behavior develops as a result of networks of social relationships and a shared culture, the **formal organization** is deliberately established for particular ends. If accomplishing an objective requires collective effort, people set up an organization to help coordinate their activities and to provide incentives for others to join them. Thus, in a university, a business, and a correctional institution, the goals, the rules, and the status structure that define the relations between the members of the organization (the organization chart) have not emerged spontaneously but have been formally established: "They have been consciously designed a priori to anticipate and guide interaction and activities."[3]

Amitai Etzioni, a theorist of administration, has developed the concept of compliance as the basis for comparing types of organizations. **Compliance** refers to the way in which one person behaves in accordance with an order or directive given by another person. In compliance relationships, the order is backed up by one's ability to induce or influence another to carry out one's directives.[4] This concept helps us to recognize that people do what others ask of them because the superiors have at their disposal the means—remunerative, normative, or coercive—to get the subjects to comply. **Remunerative power** is based on material resources, such as wages, fringe benefits, or goods, that are exchanged for compliance. **Normative power** rests on symbolic rewards manipulated by leaders through ritual, allocation of honors, and social esteem. **Coercive power** depends on the application or threat of physical force to inflict pain, restrict movement, or control other aspects of a person's life.

Etzioni argues that all formal organizations employ all three types of power, but the degree to which any one is relied upon varies with the

formal organization A structure established for the purpose of influencing behavior in order to achieve particular ends.

compliance The act of obeying an order or request.

remunerative power The ability to obtain compliance in exchange for material resources.

normative power The ability to obtain compliance by manipulation of symbolic rewards.

coercive power The ability to obtain compliance by the application or threat of physical force.

desired goal. Thus, although the University of Texas probably relies mainly on normative power in its relationships with students and the public, remunerative power plays a role in its relationships with faculty and staff. And, although the General Motors Corporation is organized primarily for manufacturing purposes, it may appeal to "team spirit" or "Safety Employee of the Month" campaigns in efforts to meet its goals. The warden at Folsom may manage staff and employees on the basis of his remunerative power to increase their salaries and normatively to encourage all to make the institution the best correctional facility in the United States, but in working with the prisoners he relies primarily on coercive power. It is the presence in high-custody institutions of "highly alienated lower participants" (prisoners), Etzioni says, that makes the application or threat of force necessary in order to ensure compliance.[5]

We may agree that coercive power undergirds all prison relationships, but we should also recognize that correctional institutions vary in the extent to which physical force is used and in the degree to which the inmates are alienated. Correctional institutions may be placed on a continuum on the basis of goals of custody or treatment.[6] At one extreme is the highly authoritarian prison, where the movement of inmates is greatly restricted, relationships between staff and inmates are formally structured, and the greatest emphasis is on prevention of escapes. In such an institution treatment goals take a backseat. At the other end of the continuum is the institution whose dominant goal is treatment, which stresses the therapeutic aspect of every component of the physical and social environment. Here the staff is placed in a collaborative relationship with inmates so they may work together to overcome the inmates' problems. Between these ideal types of the high-custody authoritarian prison and the facility set up for therapy lie the great majority of correctional institutions.

However, to discuss prisons with reference to this treatment-custody continuum may neglect other aspects of the goal of imprisonment. As we saw in Chapter 9, the goal of the prison with respect to prisoners is to:

1. *Keep them in:* Maintain a secure facility that is impervious in either direction, outward or inward.

2. *Keep them safe:* Inmates and staff need to be kept safe, not only from each other but from various environmental hazards as well.

3. *Keep them in line:* Prisons run on rules, and the ability of prison administrators to enforce compliance is central to the quality of confinement.

4. *Keep them healthy:* Inmates are entitled to care of their medical needs.

5. *Keep them busy:* Constructive activity through work, recreation, education, and treatment programs are antidotes to idleness.[7]

All of these dimensions of prison work must be carried out with fairness, without undue suffering, and as efficiently as possible. This is a tall order, but should the state run correctional institutions with other goals? At lower or higher levels of quality?

Structure

For any organization to be effective, its leaders and staff must know the rules and procedures to be followed, the lines of authority, and the channels of communication. Organizations vary in hierarchical character, in the allocation of discretion, in the amount of effort expended on administrative problems, and in the nature of the top leadership.

The formal administrative structure of a prison is a hierarchy of staff positions, each with its own duties and responsibilities, each linked to the others in a logical chain of command. As shown in Figure 12.1, the warden (often called superintendent) is ultimately responsible for the operation of the institution. Deputy wardens oversee the functional divi-

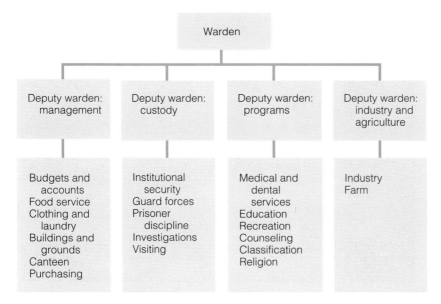

Figure 12.1 ■ **Formal Organization of a Prison for Adult Felons.** The formal organization of an institution may say little about the political and informal relationships among staff members that really depict how the prison operates.

sions of the prison: management, custody, programs, industry, agriculture. Under each deputy are middle managers and line staff who operate the departments. The extent to which functions are subdivided depends on the size and population of the prison.

Three concepts explain the functioning of hierarchically structured organizations: unity of command, chain of command, and span of control. **Unity of command** expresses the idea that it is most efficient for a subordinate to report to only one superior. If an individual in a work organization is expected to respond to orders from two or more superiors, chaos ensues. Unity of command is tied to the second concept, **chain of command.** Because the person at the top of the organization cannot over-

unity of command A management principle holding that a subordinate should report to only one supervisor.

chain of command A series of organizational positions in order of authority, each person receiving orders from the one immediately above and issuing orders to the one immediately below.

see all that is going on below, he or she must rely on those in lesser ranks to relay directions down the line. For example, the warden asks the deputy warden for custody to conduct a shakedown; the deputy warden passes along the directive to the captain of the guard; the captain then has the lieutenant in charge of a particular shift carry out the search. **Span of control** refers to the extent of the supervision by one person. If, for example, there are numerous educational and treatment programs in a correctional institution, the deputy warden for programs may not be able to oversee them all effectively. The deputy warden's span of control is stretched so far that a reorganization and division of responsibilities may be required.

Two other concepts clarify the organizations of the correctional institution: line and staff. **Line personnel** are directly concerned with furthering the institution's goals. They are

span of control A management principle holding that a supervisor can effectively oversee only a limited number of subordinates.

Leadership is the crucial element of governance. Wardens find that "management by walking around" is an effective way of learning what concerns inmates and staff.

the people who have direct contact with the prisoners—the custody force, industry and supervisors, counselors, medical technicians. **Staff personnel** provide services in support of the line personnel. They are usually found in offices concerned with accounting, training, purchasing, and so on. Staff personnel usually work under the deputy warden for management.

The custodial employees, who make up over 60 percent of the personnel, normally are organized in a military-style hierarchy, from deputy warden to captain down to correctional officer. The professional personnel associated with the management, program, and industry functions (about 25 percent of the personnel), such as clinicians, teachers, and industry supervisors, are not part of the regular custodial organizational structure and have little in com-

---

line personnel   Employees who are directly concerned with furthering the institution's goals; persons in direct contact with clients.

staff personnel   Employees who provide services in support of line personnel (for example, training officer, accountant).

mon with the custodial employees. All employees are responsible to the warden, but the treatment personnel and the civilian supervisors of the workshops have their own salary scales and titles. Their responsibilities do not extend to providing special services to the custodial employees. The top medical and educational personnel may formally report to the warden but in fact look to the central office of the department of corrections for leadership.

The multiple goals and separate employee lines of command often cause contention and ambiguity. In the larger prisons a subbureaucracy develops for each functional division, and the various divisions compete with each other for resources, scheduling of inmate's activities, and use of their labor.

Warden   As Thomas Mott Osborne aptly demonstrated, the attitude that a warden brings to the job has an enormous effect. In the not too distant past the prison warden was an autocrat who ran the institution without direction from the department of corrections or intrusion of courts, labor unions, or prisoner support groups. The legendary administration of Warden Joseph E. Ragen of Stateville Penitentiary

BIOGRAPHY

Thomas Mott Osborne

(1859–1926)

In 1914, following a series of fires and riots at Sing Sing and the subsequent resignation of the warden, Thomas Mott Osborne was named warden. Born in 1859, in Auburn, New York, Osborne was a successful businessman who in 1903 became active in politics, serving as mayor of his hometown and as a member of the New York Public Service Commission. Appointed chairman of the New York State Commission on Prison Reform in 1913, he had himself incarcerated at Sing Sing under the alias Tom Brown as a means of self-education.

Osborne was warden of Sing Sing for only two years (1914–1916), yet during his short tenure violence abated and industrial production increased as he invited the prisoners to participate in making decisions concerning the institution. Osborne fought against the political influences that dominated the prison's administration, and he resigned under political pressure.

Osborne was wedded to the idea that the purpose of imprisonment was to reform rather than to punish. He believed that inmates could be reformed only if they were involved in meaningful decision making within the prison. He introduced the Mutual Welfare League, a form of prisoner self-government, to further his objective at Sing Sing. All inmates automatically were members, and elections were held for membership on the Board of Delegates. A judiciary committee handled inmate grievances and additional committees dealt with other aspects of prison life. This exercise in self-government was designed to educate prisoners in their societal responsibilities.

Osborne was warden of the U.S. Naval Prison at Portsmouth, New Hampshire, from 1917 to 1920. Before his death in 1926, he investigated prison reform in England and Greece. Osborne was the author of three books: *Within Prison Walls* (1914), a description of his own incarcerative experience; *Society and Prisons* (1916), a description of prison systems and the Mutual Welfare League; and *Prisons and Common Sense,* a rebuttal to the critics of his methods.

(see Focus box, pages 321–323) is a classic example of this type of correctional leadership.

Today's warden is the institution's main contact with the outside world. Responsible for the operation of the prison, the superintendent normally reports to the deputy commissioner for institutions in the central office of the department of corrections. With the superintendent's attention and energy directed outward, daily operation of the prison is delegated to a deputy, usually the person in charge of custody. In recent years wardens in most states have lost much of their autonomy to managers in the central office who handle such matters as budgets, research and program development, public information, and legislative relations. The warden's job security, however, still rests on his or her ability to run the institution efficiently. At the first sign of trouble, the warden may be looking for a new job. In some states it seems that top management of corrections is constantly in flux.

Warden—An Impossible Job

George D. Bronson

A few years ago, an entrepreneur introduced the perfect coffee mug for prison wardens. Every surface symbolized authority with titles such as boss, commander-in-chief, honcho, and numero uno emblazoned into the porcelain. The discretion and authority of a prison's chief executive officer has always been perceived to be even more than that mug's morning wakeup call. Add mystique and deference with a modicum of media drama, and that CEO becomes bigger than life; it is the *PRISON WARDEN*. Do prison wardens have such broad discretion and dictatorial powers? Is this image consistent with contemporary reality? Let us examine these legendary mammoths through a modern lens.

Wardens are charged with the responsibility of administering prisons. They are the chief executive officers whose management responsibilities are compounded by the complex nature of the prison as entity. Beyond the phenomena of the prison, there are other external and internal forces that challenge and compete for the warden's authority; these forces are seemingly ubiquitous, and currently affect all wardens in the United States.

The warden has what can be termed an impossible job. Public ambivalence with regard to morality, punishment, and rehabilitation has promoted a "damned if you do, and damned if you don't" environment. This has not, however, always been the case. Only when there were newspaper outcries over issues of corruption, mismanagement, or brutality did the public and their representatives raise questions about the warden's conduct. Beginning in the 1960s, however, many structural changes took place, especially the creation of state departments of correction with a commissioner and professional staff.

With the advent of such departments, the warden's level of control, communication patterns, and other administrative functions caused the role and responsibilities of the position to change. This change lies within the heart of communications and chain of command patterns. For example, wardens used to enjoy a very strong and often personal relationship with the governor of their respective state. This 1935 conversation between Warden Joseph Ragen of Stateville (Illinois) prison and Governor Henry Horner is illustrative:

> Once the warden made up his mind that this was the place to start, he picked up the phone and called the governor. "I'm going to start reorganizing the guard force, Governor," he said. "I'm going to fire the incompetents and look around for men who can do this job right."
>
> "That's fine, Joe," the governor said. "If I can be of any help, just say so."[a]

Another vivid example of the warden's control is by James B. Jacobs in *Stateville*. His description of Warden Ragen offers substantial insight into the dominance, authority, and discretion of wardens in the early twentieth century:

> Joe Ragen's thirty year "rule" of Stateville was based upon the patriarchal authority that he achieved. In the vocabulary of both employees and inmates, "he ran it." The "old boss" devoted his life to perfecting the world's most orderly prison regime. He exercised personal control over every detail, no matter how insignificant.

He tolerated challenge neither by inmates nor by employees nor by outside interest groups. He cultivated an image which made him seem invincible to his subordinates as well as to the prisoners.[b]

Although these descriptions illustrate that Ragen had a free hand in running his prison and wide support from his governor, his situation was not unusual. Most prison wardens had the same degree of freedom in managing their facilities. Running a prison without interference and away from the public eye was the norm. What has happened during the past quarter century? What led to the reduction of the discretionary authority of the warden? Ten forces are offered as important in directing this change.

1. Structural change

With the establishment of hierarchically organized departments of correction, the warden is no longer able to communicate directly with the governor—the commissioner is in between. This change from one of simple control to a bureaucratic structure curtailed the warden's authority. The making of decisions unencumbered by chain of command was lost. Control of budgets, hiring, firing, classification, and inmate discipline was no longer unilateral.

2. Rehabilitation and reform

Organizational reform may be directly linked to loss of the warden's discretionary powers. In the early twentieth century, prison reform movements enhanced the discretion of wardens, giving them increased authority to treat inmates on a case by case basis. Reform later inhibited the warden's discretion through claims that prisoners were being coerced into participating in rehabilitative programs. The coercion ostensibly took the form of punishments for prisoners who refused to participate in treatment programs. During this same period, many existing programs were challenged on the basis of their

efficacy and ethics. These reforms caused the warden's role to be redefined.

3. Judicial intervention

Prior to 1970, judges displayed a hands-off approach to correctional matters. Since then there has been a radical shift in the posture of federal and state courts. The result has been a host of litigation involving correctional practices. Called into question was the warden's authority, discretion, and expertise. Such challenges have had the effect of eroding the warden's autonomy and power. Matters of discipline, mail review, use of segregation, transfers, and the general conditions of confinement became major issues before the courts.

4. Inmate grievance procedures

The force of petition for redress has been legitimized and formalized. Administrative mechanisms that outline and mandate appeal authority above the warden are now commonplace. As noted by Singer and Keating:

> The essential and unassailable fact is that the era of *unlimited* administrative discretion is coming to an end. Whether the limits are set by judicial fiat, by inmate violence, by unionization, or by the administrators themselves, limits inevitably will be set.[c]

5. Inmate self-government

Experiments with inmate self-government date back to 1793 at the Walnut Street Jail. These experiments did not affect the warden's discretionary authority to any great degree. However, in the mid 1970s politicization of prisoners and the idea of inmate self-government became a force that impacted on the warden's discretion. According to sociologist John Irwin, an advocate of inmate self-government:

> The criticism emanating from prisoners, the prison movement organizations, and

Continued

WORKPERSPECTIVE, *Continued*

the public inspired criminologists and sociologists to rethink their ideas on prisons and prisoners and quickly to devise new solutions to the prison crisis. Prison administrators and guards, the primary recipients of the criticisms, fumed and then finally responded with vengeance.[d]

Prisoners' rights movements through publicity exaggerated the prisoners' role and caused a disequilibrium in the system.

John DiIulio, in his book *Governing Prisons*, points out that there was little evidence to support the claim that prisons with inmate self-government were better than those with less or no self-government. As he says, "where inmates come to participate in the formulation and administration of prison policy, prisons change little or become worse."[e]

In reality, the polarization between the advocates of prison democracy and prison administrators contributed to the limitation of the warden's discretion.

6. Labor unions

The unionization of correctional officers and other employees has had a dramatic impact on warden-staff relationships. Compared to Warden Ragen at Stateville, the authority of the modern warden to hire and fire, offer job incentives, and promote and direct human resources has been greatly reduced. Wardens are no longer on a pedestal; they have lost power and often respect. This may be a result

of what has been called administrative succession. It suggests that conflicts with the officers may be caused by new wardens who assume their chair without rite of passage.

Correctional officers often conceive the warden as being "drunk with power." Thus the new administrator is often met with subtle resistance by those who feel that the warden has not "paid his dues." This, in turn, is exacerbated by unionization that again compromises the warden's authority.

7. Politics

Corrections is no longer an issue discussed behind closed doors. It has become politicized. How often have we heard that "inmates have too many privileges"? Politicians have focused attention on prisoner-related privileges, and the reactions of both the public and the politicians have often been impassioned. A major reason for this focus is that corrections has been taking a bigger and bigger part of the budgetary pie. It is "big business" at the state and federal levels.

Wardens have always understood that they must be prepared to "pack their trailer" as a result of a notorious administrative failure. However, the increased frequency of politicizing incidents and embarrassing governors has made some wardens "gun-shy." Realizing that they may be replaced as a result of such issues may cause them to demure.

8. Media

A media that publicizes only the highly charged issues can undermine a prison war-

Management Bureaucracies tend to increase the personnel and resources devoted to maintaining and managing the organization. Some people believe that this tendency is especially strong in public bureaucracies, where great stress is placed on financial accountability and report-

ing to higher agencies of government. Correctional institutions demonstrate this phenomenon. The deputy warden for management is responsible for housekeeping tasks: purchase of supplies, upkeep of buildings and grounds, provision of food, maintenance of financial records,

den. When a warden becomes hesitant because of potential bad press, effectiveness will very likely deteriorate. Thus wardens are less willing to exercise their discretionary authority if every time it is used, it becomes front page news.

9. Desk work versus MBWA

The warden who sits behind the desk and concentrates on paperwork, not people work, will eventually find discretion to be circumscribed. By neither seeing firsthand nor getting a feel for how the prison is running, in effect, authority is limited de facto. Most seasoned wardens understand the power game between inmates, supervisors, unions, volunteers, and any other group looking for control. Too much empowerment or not regularly touring will handicap the warden's discretion. Management by Walking Around (MBWA) is a powerful deterrent to this force, however, if used as a management style.

10. Burnout

The conflict created by the impingement of all these forces may have such a devastating impact that the warden stops exercising discretion as a protest to these impositions. This burnout has another dimension. Sometimes the warden will take the safe alternative because of fear created by this condition. Even when they are right, some wardens will hedge decision making by checking with higher authorities. This internal force can cripple the warden's position.

Conclusion

These ten forces are both external and internal to the organization. Some are pragmatic, others sociopsychological. Each has worked to limit the warden's discretion over the last fifty years. In effect, they combine to give a Sisyphean quality to the warden's exercise of discretion. And although Sisyphus might like to drink from the warden's coffee mug, he, like the warden, doesn't have the time.

George D. Bronson was warden of the Connecticut Correctional Institution-Somers, a maximum security facility for 1500 males, from 1984 to 1989, and of Connecticut's Carl Robinson Institution, a minimum security facility for 1300 males, from 1989 to 1991. He is now a Ph.D. candidate in sociology at the University of Connecticut and Deputy Commissioner of Corrections for the State of Rhode Island.

Source: This is the first publication of "Warden: An Impossible Job." Used by permission.

[a]Gladys A. Erickson, *Warden Ragen of Joliet* (New York: E. P. Dutton, Inc., 1957), p. 51.

[b]James B. Jacobs, *Stateville* (Chicago: University of Chicago Press, 1977), p. 29.

[c]Linda R. Singer and J. Michael Keating, "Prisoner Grievance Mechanisms," *Crime and Delinquency*, 19 (1973): 367–377 (italics added).

[d]John Irwin, *Prisons in Turmoil* (Boston: Little, Brown, 1980), pp. 87–88.

[e]John J. DiIulio, Jr., *Governing Prisons* (New York: Free Press, 1987), p. 38.

and the like. In some states many of these tasks have been centralized in the office of the commissioner in order to promote accountability and coordination among the constituent institutions. Computers have made it possible to collect and analyze budgetary data on a statewide basis. The purchase of supplies from one warehouse serving all state agencies has decreased the discretion of prison management to contract locally for provisions.

Most personnel assigned to manage the service component of the correctional institution have very little contact with the prisoners; in some facilities they conduct their business in buildings separate from the main plant. Only personnel directly involved with the provision of services to the institution, such as the head of food services, have direct contact with the prisoners.

Custody Later in this chapter, we provide a full discussion of the role of the correctional officer. Here it is important to note that the custodial force comprises graded ranks, each with accompanying differentials and job titles following the chain of command.

Unlike the factory or the military, which has separate groups of supervisors and workers or officers and enlisted personnel, the prison requires its employee with the lowest status, the correctional officer, to be both a supervisor and a worker. The officer is seen as a worker by the warden but as a supervisor by the inmates. This is a major cause of role conflict and makes officers vulnerable to corruption by the inmates. Officers know that the warden is judging their performance by the way they manage the prisoners, and they can seldom manage them without at least some measure of cooperation by the prisoners. Therefore the officers ease up on some rules so that the prisoners will become more willing to go along with other rules and to comply with requests.

Programs The modern correctional institution is concerned not only with punishment through incarceration but also with encouraging the participation of prisoners in educational, vocational, and treatment programs that will improve their chances of living crime-free after their release. Such programs have been a part of corrections since the reform period that began in the late nineteenth century, but the enthusiasm for rehabilitation that swept corrections following World War II brought a wider variety into being. This array of programs will be the subject of Chapter 13. Here we need only mention that rehabilitative and educational personnel have difficulty achieving their goals in an institution whose primary goal is custody.

Industry and agriculture From the invention of the penitentiary and its development at Auburn, New York, inmate labor has been used for industrial or agricultural production. As we shall see in Chapter 13, the importance accorded these functions has varied over time and among regions. In some southern prisons most of the inmates' time is spent tending crops. In the Northeast, prison farms have disappeared because they are uneconomical and ill matched to the urban backgrounds of most inmates.

From an organizational standpoint, industrial and farm production, like other programs, is usually administered outside of the strict hierarchical structure of the custody function. But unlike educational or treatment programs, work in the factory or on the farm customarily requires assignment of supervisors. Administrators often find themselves in disputes over the competing needs for correctional officers in the guard towers or housing units, for example, and in the field or factory.

The Impact of Structure

The organizational structure of correctional institutions has changed over time. The traditional prison had custody and perhaps industry or agriculture as its goals. Given this orientation, it was run as an autocracy, with the warden dominating the guard force. Discipline of employees was often as unbending as that imposed on the inmates. With the coming of rehabilitation as a goal of the criminal sanction, treatment and educational programs were incorporated into the organization, and a separate structure for programs, often headed by a deputy warden, was added. Its employees were professionals, trained in the social and behavioral sciences. Their perspective on the purpose of the institution resulted in frequent clashes with the warden over the dominance of custody.

Stateville: A Penitentiary Through Fifty Years

The administration of the Stateville Penitentiary, a maximum security prison in Illinois, underwent several changes during the period from 1925 to 1975 as its leadership responded to shifts in political power, correctional reforms, and the composition of the inmate population. Stateville passed through four distinct stages—anarchy, charismatic dominance, drift, and crisis—before beginning in 1975 to integrate the reforms of the earlier decades with elements of authoritarian control. By examining the Stateville case study undertaken by James B. Jacobs, we can see how politics, the leadership styles of wardens and commissioners, the provision of resources, and societal factors influence the operations of a penitentiary. It is essential that we understand the roles of these informal forces, for they structure the leadership and administration of all prisons.

Anarchy (1925–1936)

When it opened in 1925 Stateville Penitentiary repre-sented the response of Progressive era reformers to the overcrowded, dilapidated, and scandal-ridden Joliet prison. Yet the new facility, like other manifestations of the reformers' efforts, had its faults: Partisan politics pene-trated the institution, and the warden and most of the staff owed their positions to patronage. Without experi-ence or a long-term commit-ment to correctional work, the staff were unable or unwilling to exercise author-ity. Authority passed from the hands of correctional officials to the hands of pow-erful gang leaders. Favoritism, lack of uniform standards and rules, and pref-erential relationships charac-terized the organization.

Thus no consistent organi-zational or correctional goals were pursued and no stable internal equilibrium devel-oped. The prison and its inmates were beyond the concern of society, and it was isolated from the institutions and value systems of the larger community.

Charismatic dominance (1936–1961)

The appointment in 1936 of Joseph E. Ragen as warden by a reform governor marked a turning point in the leader-ship of Stateville. Ragen cre-ated an "authoritarian system of personal dominance," an independent political base, and a "mystique about his own invincibility and omni-science." Ragen's was a form of highly personalized leader-ship. He inspected the prison grounds and talked to in-mates and guards daily. He demanded absolute loyalty from his staff, and he was a master at cultivating political ties outside state government to support his administration.

During Ragen's tenure the inmate social system of Stateville conformed to scholarly descriptions of the big house. A status system among the inmates was based on criminal identities brought from the street. Sentences were long, rewards for good behavior were few, punishment was severe, and the natural inmate leaders "were co-opted by good jobs and the legitimate and illegitimate opportunities which were attached." The convict world remained stable, permitting the warden to handle prison-ers' problems through the informal leadership of the inmates.

Ragen ruled as a totalitar-ian patriarch whose charis-matic leadership left no doubt as to who was in charge and how the peniten-tiary was to be run. "To the Illinois public, press, and politicians, Joe Ragen was 'Mr. Prison' in Illinois."

Drift (1961–1970)

Ragen left Stateville in 1961 to become director of public

Continued

safety of Illinois, yet until his retirement from public life in 1965, he continued to act as if he were still running the institution. His successor, Frank Pate, had moved up the ladder from guard to serve under Ragen as assistant warden. Pate was unable to exercise the charismatic authority, "and the administration of the prison drifted into collegial rule." The new warden's leadership was further eroded by the loss of autonomy, for formal authority had been shifted to the office of Director Ragen in the capital. With Ragen's retirement in 1965, Ross Randolph, a professional correctional administrator, was appointed director of public safety.

During the remainder of the decade, policies in regard to the operation of Stateville continued to be centered in the Department of Public Safety. Programs instituted by Randolph were designed to liberalize aspects of Stateville's environment. The inmate dress code was relaxed, prisoners were allowed to talk in the dining room, civilian educators were hired, the guards' union was recognized, and outside

groups were brought in to run recreational and rehabilitative programs.

Other pressures from the outside further reduced Pate's effectiveness. The civil rights movement of the 1960s greatly affected the prison minority-group population, now a majority of the inmates. The Black Muslims challenged the authority of the patriarchal system. Pate responded with a policy of massive resistance, only to face the Warren Court's extension of substantive and procedural rights to prisoners. Reform of the Illinois penal code brought changes in sentencing and parole policies that resulted in the early release of more than three hundred old-timers serving long terms. As a consequence, the old-con power structure was destabilized. "By 1970 the forces of bureaucratization, politicization, and the penetration of juridical norms had undermined the traditional system of authority to the extent that control itself had become problematic." In the fall of 1970, Pate resigned.

Crisis (1970–1975)
Following a year-long study, a task force appointed by Governor Richard Ogilvie

recommended a department of corrections separate from the Department of Public Safety. The new department was created in 1970 and Peter Bensinger, a Yale-educated businessman, was appointed the first director. Over the next few years Bensinger forged a powerful, active, and centralized administration for the Department of Corrections in Springfield and virtually eliminated the autonomy of wardens in the correctional facilities, including Stateville. In addition, Bensinger and his associates looked to such professional organizations as the American Correctional Association and academic experts for advice.

The two wardens who succeeded Pate at Stateville, John Twomey (1970–1973) and Joseph Cannon (1973–1975), adhered to the rehabilitative ideal and human relations model of management. They attempted to replace the authoritarian system with a regime based upon consensual authority. Trained in sociology (Twomey) and social work (Cannon), the two men were viewed as civilians by the custodial staff. To those who had served under

Ragen, the new wardens were "permissive" and were giving the place away to the inmates.

Professionalization of the Stateville administration, introduction of the rehabilitation approach, intrusion of the legal system, and penetration of the street gangs contributed to a crisis in control that lasted until 1975. The courts raised the prisoners' hopes, yet the physical conditions at the prison deteriorated. By 1970 the inmate population began to be dominated by four Chicago-based gangs. The gang leaders brought with them to the prison a set of high expectations about the kinds of deference they could demand of institutional authorities. The staff found it impossible to maintain order.

As confrontations between guards and gang members grew more frequent, the custodial staff became more and more demoralized and finally stopped trying to discipline inmates. During the years from 1970 to 1975, the greatest percentage of inmates in Stateville's history were placed in isolation and segregation. The level of violence and destruction reached levels beyond anything previously seen in Illinois.

Restoration (1975–)

In December 1974 David Brierton, assistant director of the Department of Corrections, assumed direction of Stateville. Brierton had risen through the Department of Corrections from guard at the Cook County Jail to serve as a troubleshooter at several juvenile institutions before assuming the assistant directorship.

During his initial period as warden, Brierton shook up the staff of the prison, and six of nine department heads resigned or were fired. He introduced management techniques that were task-oriented, keyed to identifying problems and finding solutions. He began a complete reorganization of the facility, changed the disciplinary process, increased the number of civilian employees, and worked to strengthen security and to improve services to the inmates. "He rejected the rehabilitation ideal and the human relations model of management in favor of a highly rational, problem-oriented 'corporate' model of management which is characterized as professional, detached, and cost-conscious."

Unfortunately, Jacobs's study ended before he had time to assess the new management style, but he does point to some of the limits of the corporate bureaucracy that was implanted:

- The reluctance of the legislature to appropriate the resources necessary to run the institution as Brierton envisioned;

- The ability of this style of administration to respond to prisoners' problems, needs, and expectations of substantive justice;

- The potential for conflict with the media, private interest groups, and reformers; and

- the question of the ability of top administrators to shape the existing staff to the new orientation.

In recording the shift from an autocratic, charismatic, individualistic regime to a corporate bureaucratic approach, Jacobs's study shows the impact of changes in the larger society on the prison community.

Source: Adapted from James B. Jacobs, *Stateville* (Chicago: University of Chicago Press, 1977).

Although it is theoretically possible to run a prison in an authoritarian manner backed up by force of arms, that is neither effective nor efficient.

As some institutions gave preference to rehabilitation, correctional planners and scholars frequently contrasted the traditional prison organization with that of a collaborative administration. Most of the 1967 President's Commission on Law Enforcement and Administration of Justice report, for example, speaks promisingly of the future correctional institution in which a professionally trained and dedicated staff will work with other administrators and with prisoners to identify the problems of each prisoner and to strive for rehabilitation.[8] Such an institution would require structural changes to de-emphasize the rigid control of the traditional style, enlarge the role of treatment personnel in overall decision making, and allow input from the prisoners in regard to the operation of the facility. By the 1980s it was hard to find either any prisons being run in this fashion or correctional leaders advocating that they be so run. Some observers say that the collaborative organizational style was never really followed in more than a few institutions.

Although a prison run solely along rehabilitative lines was not realized, correctional institutions are today more humanely administered than they were in the past. This change is in part a response to the presence of reha-bilitative personnel and programs, the increased training and professionalism of correctional personnel, the intrusion of the courts, and citizen-observer groups that monitor operations. Change has come about also because society will no longer tolerate the conditions that were prevalent earlier. The deplorable situation at the Cummins Farm Unit at Arkansas State Prison that was discovered by Warden Tom Murton and depicted in the film *Brubaker* could probably not now exist for long without exposure in the media. Rehabilitation may not have fulfilled the hopes of its supporters in the sixties, but the values that brought it to prominence still have force in corrections.

A formal organization chart does not convey the whole story of a prison's organization; no chart can show how the people who occupy the positions actually perform. As theorists tell us, an informal network of behaviors exists alongside the formal structure with its rules and procedures, chain of command, and channels of communication. Every organization has individuals who find it in their interest to ignore the directives of superiors, bypass the chain of command in their communications to the top, and negotiate with others who perform parallel or associated functions.

How, then, do prisons function? What are the means by which the prisoners and staff attempt to meet their own goals? In view of the conflicting purposes and complex set of role relationships within the prison society, it is amazing that prisons are not places of social chaos. Although the U.S. prison may not conform to the ideal goals of corrections and although the formal organization may have little resemblance to the ongoing reality of the informal relations, order is kept and a routine is followed.

Governing Prisons

Surprisingly little has been written about the management of prisons. Most of the scholarly writing is by sociologists who have looked at prisons as social systems rather than institutions to be governed. As political scientist John DiIulio points out, sociologists have written about the effects on inmates of life in prison, racial and ethnic cleavages within prisons, consequences of rehabilitative programs, inmate argot and roles, and informal distribution of authority in prisons.[9] The literature helps us understand prison society but does not supply policy recommendations that will assist correctional officials in managing inmates and staff. In fact, most sociological research seems to say that little can be done by administrators to govern prisons because—despite formal rules and regulations (see the Focus box for one set of rules of conduct)—institutions are run mainly through the informal social networks among the keepers and the kept. What DiIulio finds shocking is the extent to which correctional officials seem to have accepted sociological explanations for institutional conditions rather than pointing to faulty management practices.

What distinguishes a well-run prison from a substandard prison? DiIulio argues that the crucial variable is not the ethnic or racial distribution of the population, the criminal records of the inmates, the size of the institution, levels of crowding, or the level of funding. What is important is *governance:* the sound and firm management of inmates and staff.

What quality of life should be maintained in a prison? DiIulio says that a good prison is one that "provides as much order, amenity, and service as possible given the human and financial resources."[10] *Order* is here defined as the absence of individual or group misconduct that threatens the safety of others, for example, assaults, rapes, and other forms of violence or insult. A basic assumption should be that because the state sends offenders to prison, it has the responsibility of ensuring their safety there. *Amenity* is anything that enhances the comfort of the inmates, such as good food, clean cells, recreational opportunities, and the like. This does not mean that prisons are to function as hotels, but contemporary standards stipulate that correctional facilities should not be deleterious to inmates' mental and physical health. Finally, *service* includes programs designed to improve the life prospects of inmates: vocational training, remedial education, and work opportunities. Here, too, we expect inmates to be engaged in activities during incarceration that will make them better persons and enhance their ability to lead crime-free lives upon release.

If we accept the premise that well-run prisons are important for the inmates, staff, and society, what are some of the problems that must be faced and solved by correctional administrators? The sociological literature points to four factors that make the governing of prisons different from the administration of other public institutions: (1) the defects of total power; (2) the limited rewards and punishments that can be used by officials; (3) the cooptation of the correctional officers; and (4) the strength of inmate leadership. After we review each of these research findings, we will then ask what kind of administrative systems and leadership styles can be used by administrators and corrections managers to ensure that prisons are governed in ways that will make them safe, humane, and able to serve the needs of the inmates.

Rules of General Conduct, Michigan Department of Corrections

1. All residents are expected to obey directions and instructions of members of the staff. If a resident feels he/she has been dealt with unfairly, or that he/she has received improper instructions, he/she should first comply with the order and then follow the established grievance procedures outlined later in this booklet.

2. Any behavior considered a felony or a misdemeanor in this state also is a violation of institutional rules. Such acts may result in disciplinary action and/or loss of earned good time in addition to possible criminal prosecution.

3. Any escape, attempt to escape, walk away, or failure to return from a furlough may result in loss of good time and/or a new sentence through prosecution under the escape statute. At one time or another, most persons in medium or minimum custody have felt restless and

uneasy. When this happens, we urge you to see your counselor or the official in charge for guidance and advice. Occasionally, the department has asked that those who have walked away impulsively not be prosecuted when they have turned themselves in immediately after the act, realizing their mistake.

4. Any resident may, if they feel they have no further recourse in the institution, appeal to the Director of Corrections, Deputy Director, the Attorney General, state and federal courts, Michigan Civil Rights Commission or the Governor in the form of sealed and uncensored mail.

5. Reasonable courtesy, orderly conduct, and good personal hygiene are expected of all residents. Standards for haircuts, beards, and general appearance are listed later in this rule book.

6. Residents cannot hold any group meetings in the yard. Meetings for all legitimate purposes require staff approval; facilities, if available, will be scheduled for this purpose and necessary supervision provided.

7. While residents are permitted to play cards and other games, gambling is not allowed. In card-playing areas there shall be no more than four persons at a table. Visible tokens or other items

of value will be sufficient evidence of gambling. Games are prohibited during working hours on institutional assignments.

8. All typewriters, calculators, radios, TVs, electric razors, and other appliances, including musical instruments, must be registered with the institutional officials by make, model, and serial number.

9. Items under Paragraph 8 cannot be traded, sold, or given away without written approval of the Deputy Warden or Superintendent.

10. Residents cannot operate concessions, sell services, rent goods, or act as loan sharks or pawnbrokers.

11. All items of contraband are subject to confiscation.

12. When a resident desires to go from one place to another for a specific and legitimate reason, he/she should obtain a pass from the official to whom they are responsible, such as the housing unit supervisor, work foreman, teacher, etc.

13. No resident is allowed to go into another resident's cell or room unless specifically authorized.

Source: Michigan Department of Corrections, *Resident Guide Book* (Lansing: Michigan Department of Corrections, n.d.).

The Defects of Total Power

In his path-breaking investigation of the New Jersey State Prison, Gresham Sykes emphasizes that although in formal terms the correctional institution is in an unparalleled position with respect to the men "it rules and from which it is supposed to extract compliance," the officials' ability to exercise power is limited and they are in many ways dependent on the cooperation of the captives.[11] This perspective is at odds with the public's view of the way prisons are run. Most citizens assume that the captives live according to an authoritarian regime: Officers give orders; inmates follow orders. Rules specify what the captives may and may not do, and they are strictly enforced. The officers have a monopoly on the legal means of coercion and can be backed up by the state police and the National Guard if necessary. Members of the staff have the right to grant rewards and to inflict punishment. In theory, any inmate who does not fall into line should end up in solitary confinement. Why, then, should questions arise about how the prisons are run?

We could imagine a prison society made up of hostile and uncooperative captives ruled by force. Prisoners can be legally isolated from one another, physically abused until they cooperate, and put under continuous surveillance. While all these things are possible, of course, such practices would probably not be countenanced for long because the public expects correctional institutions to be run humanely.

It must also be understood that prisoners, unlike members of other authoritarian organizations such as the military, do not recognize the legitimacy of their keepers and therefore are not moved to cooperate. No sense of duty propels prisoners to unquestioning compliance. This is an important distinction since a sense of duty supplies the secret strength of most social organizations. With it, rules will be followed—and need not be explained first.

The notion that correctional officers have total power over the captives has a number of other flaws. "The ability of the officials to phys-

Although the fortress prison backed up by the power of the state is the popular image of the way inmates are managed, there are defects in this reliance on total power.

ically coerce their captives into the paths of compliance is something of an illusion as far as the day-to-day activities of the prison are concerned and may be of doubtful value in moments of crisis."[12] Forcing people to follow commands is basically an inefficient method to make them carry out complex tasks; efficiency is further diminished by the realities of the ratio of officers to inmates (typically 1:40) and the potential danger of the situation.

One should not get the idea that physical coercion is not used as a means of controlling prisoners. The tactics may be in violation of the criminal law and administrative procedures, but they have long been known to occur in prisons throughout the United States—and cannot be considered to be idiosyncratic or sporadic. In a study of the use of force in a Texas prison, it was found that physical punishment was used against inmates by a small but significant percentage of the officers. The use of force controlled the prison population and induced cohesion among the officers, maintaining a status differential between officers and inmates, and helping officers to win promotions.[13]

Rewards and Punishments

Correctional officers often rely on a system of rewards and punishments to induce cooperation. In an effort to maintain security and order among a large population living in a confined space, they impose extensive rules of conduct. Rather than use physical measures to ensure obedience, they reward compliance with privileges and punish refractory behavior with loss of privileges.

Several policies may be followed to promote control. One is to offer prisoners who cooperate rewards such as choice job assignments, residence in the honor unit, and favorable parole reports. Time off for good behavior—good time—is given to inmates at a rate prescribed by regulations. Informers may also be rewarded, and administrators may purposely ignore conflict among inmates on the assumption that it prevents the prisoners from uniting and working together against the authorities.

The system of rewards and punishments has some deficiencies. One is that the punishments for rule breaking do not represent a great departure from the prisoners' usual circumstances. Because they are already deprived of many freedoms and valued goods—heterosexual relations, money, choice of clothing, and so on—not being allowed to attend, say, a recreational period does not carry much weight. In addition, the inmate code in force in a particular prison may dictate that the convict gains standing among the other prisoners by defiance. Another deficiency is that the authorized privileges are given to the inmate at the start of the sentence and are to be taken away only if rules are broken; few further rewards are authorized for progress or exceptional behavior, although a desired work assignment or transfer to the honor block will induce some rule-conforming behavior. As time passes and the inmate approaches the time when reintegration with society becomes possible, opportunities for furloughs, work release, or transfer to a halfway house will perhaps serve as incentives to obey the rules.

Co-optation of Correctional Officers

One way that correctional officers obtain inmate cooperation is by tolerating minor rule infractions in exchange for compliance with major aspects of the custodial regime. The correctional officer is the key person in the interpersonal relationships among the prisoners and the link with the custodial bureaucracy. The correctional officer

> must supervise and control the inmate population in concrete and detailed terms ... must see to the translation of the custodial regime from blueprint to reality and engage in the specific battles for conformity. Counting prisoners, periodically reporting to the center of communications, signing passes, checking groups of inmates as they come and go, searching for contraband or signs of attempts to escape—these make up the minutiae of [the officer's] eight-hour shift.[14]

The officers and prisoners are in close association throughout the day and night: in the cell block, workshop, recreation area. The formal rules stipulate that a social distance be maintained between the two groups and that they speak and act toward one another accordingly, but both groups recognize that they are in many ways dependent on each other. The officers need the cooperation of the prisoners so they will look good to their superiors, and the inmates depend on the officers to relax the rules or occasionally look the other way.

Even though officers are backed by the state and have the formal authority to punish any prisoner who does not follow orders, they often discover that the best path of action is to make "deals" or "trades" with the captives in their power. As a result, officers buy compliance or obedience in some areas by tolerating rule breaking elsewhere. The officers are expected to maintain "surface order": the "inmates are conforming voluntarily to the institution's most important rules, and custody is running smoothly; it is required only that there be no visible trouble and no cause for alarm."[15] Because officers' job performance is judged on ability to maintain surface order, bargaining goes on and both sides have a tacit understanding.

Correctional officers must be careful not to pay too high a price for the cooperation of their charges. Sub-rosa relationships that turn into manipulation of the officers by the prisoners may result in the smuggling of contraband or other illegal acts. Officers are under pressure to work effectively with prisoners and may be blackmailed into doing illegitimate favors for them to gain cooperation. When leadership is thus abdicated, authority passes to the inmates.

Inmate Leadership

In the traditional prison of the big-house era, administrators enlisted the leaders of the inmate social system in the work of maintaining order. In 1954, Richard Korn and Lloyd W. McCorkle wrote:

> Far from systematically attempting to undermine the inmate hierarchy, the institution generally gives it covert support and recognition by assigning better jobs and quarters to its high-status members provided they are "good inmates." In this and other ways the institution buys peace with the system by avoiding battle with it.[16]

Descriptions of the contemporary maximum security prison raise questions about administrators' ability to run institutions according to the older technique. When the racial, offense, and political characteristics of the inmate populations of many prisons began to change in the mid-1960s, the former leadership structure of the convicts was replaced by multiple centers of power. Some institutions became violent, unsafe places as official authority broke down.

It now appears that prisons are being run more effectively than they were in the recent past. Although they are more crowded than ever, the incidents of riots and reports of violence have declined. It may be that in many prisons the inmate social system has undergone

reorganization and now correctional officers are again able to work through prisoners who have the respect of their fellow inmates. Yet some observers contend that when wardens maintain order in this way, they enhance the positions of some prisoners at the expense of others. The leaders profit by receiving illicit privileges and favors, and they enhance their influence among inmates by distributing their benefits to others.

Leadership: The Crucial Element of Governance

One of the amazing facts about prisons is that most of the time they work: Order is maintained and activities are carried out. Any prison is made up of

> synchronized actions of hundreds of people, some of whom hate and distrust each other, love each other, fight each other physically and psychologically, think of each other as stupid or mentally disturbed, "manage" and "control" each other, and vie with each other for favors, prestige, power and money.[17]

Still, most prisons do not fall into disarray, although at times conditions in certain institutions have approached near chaos: for example, Soledad in California, during a period of racial and political unrest in the 1960s; Walla Walla in Washington in the 1970s, when an experiment with inmate self-government was being tried; and the Eastham Unit and some other Texas prisons during court-ordered reform in the 1980s. And many correctional facilities are nationally recognized as being well governed. What are the elements that seem to affect the quality of life in American prisons? What is the role of management?

Organization structures of most prisons exhibit a similar bureaucratic form, yet management styles vary. While studying the management of selected prisons in California, Michigan, and Texas, DiIulio found differences in the leadership philosophy, political environment, and administrative style of individual wardens. DiIulio argues that the quality of prison life as measured by levels of order, amenity, and service is mainly a function of the quality of management. Prisons can be governed, violence can be minimized, and services can be provided to the inmates if correctional executives and wardens exhibit leadership. He argues, "Prison managers must effect a government strong enough to control a community of persons who are most decidedly not angels. At the same time, however, prison managers must be subject to a vigorous system of internal and external controls on their behavior, including judicial and legislative oversight, media scrutiny, occupational norms and standards."[18]

Prison systems perform well if leaders work competently with the political and other pressures that make for administrative uncertainty and instability. In particular, management is successful when prison directors:

■ Are in office long enough to learn the job, make plans, and implement them;

■ Project an appealing image to a wide range of people both inside and outside of the organization;

■ Are dedicated and loyal to the department, seeing themselves as engaged in a noble and challenging profession; and

■ Are highly hands-on and proactive, paying close attention to details and not waiting for problems to arise. They must know what is going on inside, yet also recognize the need for outside support. In short, they are strangers neither in the cell blocks nor in the aisles of the state legislature.[19]

From this perspective, making prisons work is a function of administrative leadership and the application of management principles. Governing prisons is an extraordinary challenge, but it is a task that can be and has been accomplished. DiIulio's research challenges

the common assumption of many correctional administrators that "the cons run the joint." Rather, the success as such legendary administrators as George Beto of Texas, New Jersey's William Fauver, Anna Kross of New York's Riker's Island, and William Leeke of North Carolina demonstrate, prisons can be well managed so that inmates are able to serve their time in a safe, healthy, and productive environment.[20]

Correctional Officers: The Linchpin of Management

 1968 survey of American teenagers by pollster Louis Harris revealed that only 1 percent had considered a career as a correctional officer in a prison.[21] More than a quarter century later, results of a similar survey might well be the same, for the occupation is not accompanied by great prestige in the public's mind. The correctional officer's occupational prestige is tarnished by the company he or (increasingly) she must keep—the adult felon. The prisoner, of course, is not pleased by being kept in custody, and the community, the benefactor of the correctional officer's activities, seems not to care except when a riot or escape occurs.

Since Harris's survey, the role of the correctional officer has changed greatly. The officer is now the crucial professional in the correctional institution because he or she has the closest contact with the prisoners and is expected to perform a variety of tasks. Correctional officers are no longer responsible merely for "guarding." Instead, as we see in Philip Carvalho's Workperspective on the following page, they are expected to counsel, supervise, protect, and process the inmates under their care. In many jurisdictions their hours are long, their pay is low, entry requirements are minimal, and turnover is high. Given these conditions, why would someone want to enter this field?

WORKPERSPECTIVE

A Day on the Job— in Prison

Philip Carvalho

The buzzer of the white clock radio drones through the bedroom. The hands of the luminous dial point to 5:20 A.M.

For Philip Martin Carvalho, the jarring sound is the same prelude to the morning ritual that millions of Americans call "going to work." But unlike most other job-bound early risers, his workplace is different: It's behind eight steel, barred doors within the walls of the Massachusetts maximum security prison at Walpole.

Phil Carvalho holds the rank of senior correctional officer. He has covered virtually every custody assignment in the eight years he has been in a prison that has been jarred by inmate riots and strikes by its personnel. Since last January, his post has been Ten Block, the segregation unit where Massachusetts houses up to sixty of its toughest and most incorrigible inmates....

For Phil Carvalho and thousands like him, reporting for the seven-to-three shift in America's maximum security prisons, the workday begins with the small ironies that sometimes blur the distinctions between the guard and the guarded.

"All persons entering the lobby," the sign on the prison doorway says, "must have their packages, pocketbooks, etc. inspected. Failure to do so, the officer on duty will refuse entry to the lobby. This applies to employees of the institution also."

Phil Carvalho punches the time clock, moves through the first of the electronically controlled steel doors, opens his lunch bag for inspection by another officer, empties his pockets of keys and small change, and removes his buckled belt before stepping through the archway of the metal detector. The unseen electronic eye doesn't flicker any alarm....

Ten Block is a steel, barred island within the walled continent of the prison...insulated and isolated for those who live there and those who work there. It is an island cut off from the institutional mainland by more than the click, bang of steel. Because it confines or segregates those who have assaulted guards and inmates, it is often territory that is ostracized by other guards and inmates.

"Nobody is going to be in a hurry to do anybody any favors down here," Carvalho says.

Ten Block also is an island marked by the paraphernalia of violence. Handcuffs dangling from a pegboard...a trio of fire extinguishers within easy reach on the floor...a convex Plexiglas riot shield resting in the corner. Its sixty cells are divided between two floors, fifteen to a corridor. Some of the cells on the first floor have solid steel doors, in front of the bars, that are clanged shut when an inmate does punitive isolation time.

When Carvalho arrives, nine young officers already are beginning to fill cardboard trays with muffins, cereal, and paper cups of coffee from the kitchen wagon. Like Carvalho, all are volunteers for Ten Block.

"Yeah, you gotta be crazy to work here," one of them says, "but it's got good days off." Most of the officers have been spit at by some of their charges. Some have been hit by urine and excrement.

Before Carvalho has a chance to move through the door of the cubicle that serves as

Continued

WORKPERSPECTIVE, *Continued*

an office, one of the three phones inside rings.

"Ten. Carvalho."

The phone is sandwiched between the cheek and the shoulder of the 220-pound, six-foot two-inch Carvalho. For the next eight hours, it will ring incessantly, with rare moments of silence. For Carvalho, the telephone is something more than an electronic instrument.

He growls at it, purrs into it, persuades, cajoles, allowing the cadence of his voice to vary with the purpose of his message. "Yeah, right. Hey, sweetheart, do me a favor...."

Carvalho shares the responsibilities of running Ten Block with Arthur Latessa, the most recently promoted supervisor of the Walpole Prison. Ten Block is the lowest rung of desirable supervisory assignments and the newest man usually is in the job. When Latessa is absent, Carvalho runs the block by himself.

For his efforts, Carvalho takes home $199 a week, some $17 more than the younger officers.

"Guard House, Guard House..." the inmate's voice comes from midway down the corridor. "Hey, Phil...Phil...Phil Carvalho."

One of the other officers unlocks the corridor's steel entry gate. He never lets his eyes wander from Carvalho's back as he moves down the hallway....

The conversations are always on a first-name basis, sometimes flecked by touches of jailhouse humor that softens the harshness of where they take place. There is a subconscious line between Carvalho and the inmates that marks the perimeter between levity and insolence, between what is permitted and what is not. Since he arrived in Ten Block, Phil Carvalho never has been spit at or assaulted by anything more than a barrage of four letter words.

In the office, the phones are ringing again.

"Ten. Carvalho."

"Yeah, O.K. Sullivan's visit cancelled. O.K. Thanks."

"Ten. Carvalho."

"No. I can't do it. I don't have a place to put him. Look, sweetheart, he can have a legal aid visit. Yeah, but not today. I got visits at 11, at 11:30, at 1:30, and a disciplinary board. Yeah, try tomorrow. Sorry. You're doing a great job...a great job."

Carvalho recalls that a few weeks earlier a lawyer had to interview his client in the elevator that is used to transport the food cart between the two floors of the block.

"It's confined, this block. It's too small a place. After a while, even the officers start arguing with themselves. It happens every day. Any old thing sets the officers off. Out in [the general prison] population, at least you're walkin' around, you got space out there. Or you may have the yard duty or you go on transportation, or hospital detail or something. But down at Ten. Where you goin'? Upstairs, downstairs, that's it. We're bangin' into one another."

An officer comes into the cubicle with a handful of small brown envelopes. Carvalho counts them, records the total and the time in the dog-eared logbook in front of him.

"Medication," he says. "O.K., give 'em out."

Ten Block distributes medication more frequently than meals. Four times a day, inmates may receive prescriptions that include sedatives, tranquilizers, and sleeping pills. During the morning distribution, fourteen of twenty-eight inmates on the first floor receive pills. Five milligrams of Valium four times a day plus a sleeping pill at night is not unusual.

"I can't understand it," says Carvalho. "These guys when they're on the street can't be gettin' that medication. Impossible. Some of 'em need it for their nerves. Being in this situation they need something to calm them down. But the pain pills they put out, the depressants … it's unbelievable. In the street, these guys don't go, 'Hey, wait a minute, I got to take my pill. I'll be right back to help you rob the bank or somethin.' Everyday they've got to get their pills. Now they're dependent on it. They need it or they're goin' to crash. In a way, we're making pill addicts out of 'em. Yeah, and I've heard a medic say that, too."

"Yeah, Charlie?"

"Listen, Phil, you gotta get that son-of-a-bitch out of here…." The voice in the dimly lighted cell details a complaint against an officer on the three-to-eleven shift.

Other inmates shout their own litany of complaints. Hands holding mirrors protrude from the other fourteen cells in the section, giving their owners a glass-reflected picture of the officer and the visitor.

"The only thing I can tell you," Carvalho responds, "is that I've got to get McLaughlin down here."

Thomas McLaughlin is deputy superintendent at Walpole. He is one of the key reasons why Phil Carvalho volunteered for Ten Block. "He backs you up. And he's there when you need him.… All these guys," Carvalho says, pointing to the young officers, "they're there when you need 'em.…"

The office in its clutter and congestion offers another reminder of the similarities between the guard and the guarded. Like the cells, it too is cramped. It is only an hour into the shift and the half empty coffee cups are beginning to accumulate. Cigarette butts are piling up in the ashtray, and some from days and weeks before are in the corners. A calendar with a picture of a nude girl dangles from a pegboard holding twenty-one keys.

When McLaughlin arrives, Carvalho takes him through the corridor where the inmates are complaining about the officer. They move from cell to cell like army medics making rounds in a crowded hospital. The deputy superintendent is a listener. Occasionally, he asks a question, sometimes he nods, but his face shows neither a flicker of sympathetic agreement nor cynical disbelief. Later, he tells Carvalho there will be a meeting with the night officer at the end of the shift.

"Hey, Phil … Phil…." Another voice from the cell in the corridor. Carvalho again moves into the narrow hallway.

"Hey, Phil, I need a legal visit. My case comes up on the fourteenth."

"O.K. I'll take care of it."

From a hall phone, Carvalho dials an extension, "Yeah, Phil Carvalho. I need a legal visit for …"

The demands made on Carvalho are not phrased in convoluted euphemisms. They are direct. They deal with basic wants in the limited, cramped world of the segregation unit … an appointment for a visitor, a phone call to a relative … some writing paper. Sometimes the demands attempt to stretch the narrow boundaries of Ten Block. Either way, the answers are equally direct. Carvalho's booming voice, intoning, "I'll try," or "Yes," or "No," leaves little room for doubt.

Why this job?

The pressure is momentarily off. Carvalho lights another cigarette and tilts back in his chair. Why did you become a correctional officer? he is asked.

"One word: security. That's what I was looking for. Not in two years, five years, but overall. In twenty years when you are ready to retire. The benefits are there. The job has its bad points and its good points."

What are those good points? What do you get out of this job besides security?

"Well, I try to accomplish something … personal satisfaction. If I've done somethin' to help 'em. Me, I can go home and use the phone, watch TV, go out to my neighbor's

Continued

house, buy a drink if I want to … these guys can't. Their only line of communication is through me. So if they want to use the phone I'll say, 'I'll see what I can do.'

"It's somethin' like that that makes you feel good—that would be the word for it. Especially when a guy is having trouble. His wife hasn't written him or come up to see him and you let him make a phone call and he goes back and he thanks you. Things are cooled down.

"You can't do it to them all because some of them don't even let you get near 'em. They're just cold. You don't make waves there either. You don't go out of your way to gaff this guy or stick him. Hey, you can't. It's impossible to go in there with that attitude. You're not going to last. I don't care if it's Ten Block or the rest of the institution. You're not going to last. Because one of 'em will definitely get you. A pipe, a knife or somethin' like that, but they'll definitely get you. Or if they don't do it that way, they'll make it miserable for you.

"Even though they're the toughest, hey, they're human beings, you know. I don't care what they did. Well, I shouldn't say that because we know what they did on the outside or what they did to other corrections officers, but when he comes into Ten Block,

I'm not going to mess with a guy's meals or throw letters away. You've got to communicate. These guys are livin' with you. It's going to be an easy day or it's going to be a tough day."

The noon food wagon arrives, and the officers dish out the meal into the paper trays. After the inmates are served, the officers grab a tray and bring it into the office, a few at a time. Some have brought their lunch and eat it piecemeal between running upstairs or into the cell corridors. Elsewhere in the prison, most corrections officers eat in the staff mess hall. In Ten Block, there is no formal sit-down dining.

Carvalho, between bites, dials the phone again. "Yeah, Russ.… He's back in Block Three. Yeah, he's back. My count is fifty-eight." The count of inmates is reported to control at the beginning of the shift, at noon, or whenever any inmate leaves or returns to Ten Block.

. . .

A young officer comes in and hands Carvalho another packet of brown envelopes. Medication. Second distribution. Carvalho registers them in the log.

The logbook is something of a barometer for the shift. It records the traffic like a counter at a busy intersection. And it offers some distinctions between the shifts.

Who Are the Officers?

The early literature of criminal justice either ignored the prison officer or painted a picture of an individual with a "lock psychosis" resulting from the routine of numbering, counting, checking, and locking. Some of the prison studies of the 1940s and 1950s give the impression that officers were incompetent and psychologically inferior, performing the only job to which they could gain access. Custodial officers were viewed as the primary opponents of rehabilitation, at loggerheads with both the inmates and the administrators. The report of the commission that investigated the Attica riots labeled the guards as racists. Some observers have referred to them as "frightened, hostile people."[22] Who are the correctional officers? Have they been accurately

The preceding three-to-eleven P.M. shift had seven entries for its entire eight-hour segment. The eleven-to-seven A.M. shift showed three entries. By noon, Carvalho had written twenty-one separate items into his log.

The clock on the office wall ticks the shift slowly to an end.

Carvalho leaves a little early to attend the "front office" meeting with the administration and the officer of the incoming shift about whom the inmates complained. The decision: Keep him at his post.

Fifty minutes and twenty-seven traffic-congested miles later, Carvalho is back in his private world on the outer fringes of suburbia. He is greeted by his wife and his fourteen-year-old daughter, Cheryl. A miniature poodle and a tiny Yorkshire terrier come bounding across the lawn as the advance contingent of the welcome. Supper is on the table a half hour later. The small talk is about an afternoon shopping trip in search of parochial school uniforms for Cheryl. There is no small talk about Ten Block.

"He doesn't talk about the job," his wife, Shirley, says. "He tells his father about the job and his father tells his mother and she tells me some things. That's how I get information about the prison. If he comes home and he's in a good mood, I'll know he had a fine day. If he comes home a little bit aggravated, then I

know he had a bad day and I'll just go about my business.

"But I worry about him all the time. The last time there was a riot, it was on the late news. I didn't know a thing about it. I was lying on the couch, watching the news, and that came on in a big way. I thought I'd die. I tried calling the prison, but all the lines were tied up. He finally called me about an hour after and said that he would be home early in the morning. But, oh, my God. Who could sleep?"

When Shirley is out of earshot, Carvalho acknowledges her worrying. "I know it affects my wife. I'll tell her, 'I'm not going in today,' and she'll say, 'Oh, good. Call in sick.' And then I tell her I'm only kidding. And I trudge in there. But I must like it because I keep goin' back."

"It has its good days and its bad. Today was a good day," he says.

The Plexiglas protective shield remained unused. No inmate had refused to return to his cell. None of the young officers had urine or excrement thrown at them. The fire extinguishers remained in their places.

Shirley nods in agreement. Today Phil Carvalho came home in a good mood.

Source: From Edgar May, "A Day on the Job—In Prison," *Corrections Magazine* (December 1976): 6–11. Reprinted by permission of the Edna McConnell Clark Foundation.

---

depicted? What kind of person accepts a job that offers low pay and little hope of advancement?

Studies have shown that one of the primary incentives for becoming a correctional officer is the security that civil service provides. In addition, since most correctional facilities are located in rural areas, work at the prison is often better than other available employment options, and the salary can often be supple-

mented by part-time farming. The officers studied at New York's Auburn Correctional Facility "came to prison in search of security and financial rewards *after* employment in the outside economy"; correctional officers at Stateville took their jobs "after periods of unemployment, layoffs or because an injury prevented them from pursuing their former occupations."[23] In a sense, many correctional officers are pushed into prison work by circumstances. As one officer at Auburn said: "I flunked out of college and was in the dumps. I just played around for three years, worked in a factory, and got married. I hated the factory: not much money, hot, and rotten. They were hiring guards in 1972–1973, and the pay was good: $12,000 per year and overtime. I took the test, sat around for a year, and got called."[24]

Since correctional officers are recruited locally, they have been overwhelmingly rural and white. In 1972 the Attica Commission found that only 2 percent of the five hundred employees were members of minority groups; in contrast, 63.5 percent of the inmates were black and 9.5 percent were Puerto Rican.[25] Over the past quarter century, however, through the prodding of the federal courts, the 1964 Civil Rights Act, and affirmative action programs, the racial and gender composition of the correctional officer force has changed dramatically. Today, approximately 31 percent of correctional officers are members of minority groups and 16 percent are women; Figure 12.2 shows the racial/ethnic composition of correctional officers in adult systems.

Research has shown that the role orientation of correctional officers is "diverse, multidimensional, and complex."[26] A survey of officers in one southern system found that they define their work as being a correctional "officer" rather than "guard" and are supportive of the concept of rehabilitation. The officers were found to adopt a human service approach to dealing with inmates and "see prisons as places in which the reformation of offenders should, and can, take place."[27]

Since 1970 most states have developed training programs for new correctional officers. Modeled on police academies, the programs give recruits at least a rudimentary knowledge of their work and familiarity with the rules governing corrections. The classroom work, however, bears little resemblance to the problems that will be confronted in the cell block or on the yard. Therefore, upon completion of the course, the new officer is placed under the supervision of an experienced officer. There, on

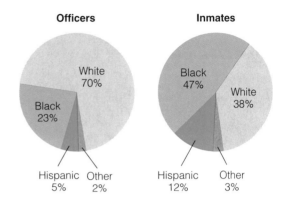

Figure 12.2 ■ **Racial/Ethnic Composition of Correctional Officers and Inmates, Adult Systems Nationwide.** Although the racial/ethnic composition of correctional officers does not equal the racial/ethnic composition of the inmate population, great strides have been taken during the past quarter century.

Source: U.S. Department of Justice, Bureau of Justice Statistics, *Sourcebook of Criminal Justice Statistics, 1991* (Washington, D.C.: Government Printing Office, 1991), p. 108; *Prisons and Prisoners in the United States* (Washington, D.C.: Government Printing Office, April 1992), p. 13.

the job, the new correctional officer experiences real situations and learns the techniques and procedures necessary. The need for correctional workers has increased during the past decade, and in most states recruitment of good personnel has been given high priority. Salaries have been increased so that the average yearly pay now runs from about $15,000 in some southern and rural states to $30,000 in places such as New York, California, and Minnesota. The annual turnover among officers seems to be inversely proportional to the level of compensation with some low pay states losing 30 percent of their force annually.[28]

Women are no longer confined to work with female prisoners. In states such as Alabama where one-third of correctional officers are women, fully 89 percent work in male institutions. In the Federal Bureau of Prisons 11 percent of the staff are women and 59 percent of them work among male inmates.[29]

An increasing number of women officers work in male institutions. As has been true in other formerly all-male domains, female officers reported initial difficulties in being accepted by their male counterparts.

Just as female police officers have often found themselves excluded from certain assignments and from being fully a part of the social group that constitutes the force, women in corrections feel discriminated against. In a study of women officers in two prisons for men, Lynn Zimmer found that their male counterparts were opposed to sexual integration of the guard force.[30] Male officers argued that women could not handle the violence and confrontations with inmates that occur in prisons. In reality, however, women officers had less trouble with the inmates than their male counterparts had, although there was harassment when they first appeared on the job. In some states male prisoners raised the issue of privacy when female officers were assigned to cell block duty; courts have upheld objections with regard to women's supervising inmate shower and toilet facilities.

For most correctional workers a position as a custody officer is a dead-end job. Though officers who perform well may be promoted to higher ranks within the custodial staff, very few ever move into administrative positions. Yet in some states and in the Federal Bureau of Prisons, there are career paths for persons with college degrees to move up the ladder to management positions. Increasingly it is possible to achieve these positions without having to advance up through the ranks of the custodial force.

The job Lucien Lombardo has used the concepts of "people worker" and "bureaucrat" to analyze the role of the correctional officer. These concepts may be used in a fashion similar to Lipsky's street-level bureaucrat discussed in Chapter 1. As a people worker, the officer must cope "with the human problems of inmates on a personal level."[31] But the worker also functions as a member of a complex bureaucratic organization and is thus expected to treat clients impersonally and to follow formally prescribed procedures. To fulfill these contradictory role expectations is difficult in itself, and the difficulty is exacerbated by the physical closeness of the officer and the inmate over long periods of time.[32]

Although most prison work is widely perceived to be routine, guarding is not an undifferentiated occupation: Guards supervise the cell houses, dining areas, and shops, transport prisoners to hospitals and courts; take turns serving on the disciplinary board; sit perched with rifles in the towers on top of the wall; and protect the gates leading into and out of the interior. Unscheduled activities range from informal counseling to breaking up fights to escorting prisoners on family visits in the community.[33]

The custodial staff of correctional institutions is organized along paramilitary lines, with ranks of officer, sergeant, lieutenant, and captain. The sergeant supervises a complement of officers in one area of the prison—housing unit, hospital, and so on. The lieutenants are the main disciplinarians of the institution, conducting shakedowns, breaking up fights, and supervising the removal of inmates to segregation. The few captains on a staff have primarily administrative responsibilities and serve as the links between the custody personnel and the warden and other top management officials.

The military nomenclature and organization extend to the relationships among staff members. Officers are subject to inspections; in some institutions they may be given "tickets" (disciplinary reports) by their superiors; and when they are housed in quarters attached to the facility, rules govern their off-duty behavior. To guard against the possibility that officers may bring contraband into the institution, the staff is kept under rigorous discipline. The fact that the rules and organization of the officers parallel those that govern the inmates is not lost on the correctional staff. "We're all doing time here," they say, "except that we're doing it in eight-hour shifts."

Lombardo found seven types of job assignments at Auburn Correctional Facility, New York, which we may classify according to their location within the institution, the duties required, and the nature of the contact with the inmate population: (1) block officers, (2) work detail supervisors, (3) industrial shop and school officers, (4) yard officers, (5) administration building assignments, (6) wall posts, and (7) relief officers.[34]

Block officers Of all the correctional staff, the officers in the cell blocks have the closest contact with the prisoners and, one may assume, the greatest potential for inducing behavior change in them. Work in the housing units is dangerous because the officers are without weapons, are greatly outnumbered, and can be easily overwhelmed by the prisoners.

In units housing between three and four hundred inmates, the five to eight block officers are responsible for the movement of their charges to meals, work, hospital, and the like. They must see to maintenance of the unit, watch for potential breaches of security, handle the personal problems and questions of individual prisoners, enforce the rules, ensure the safety of the inmates, and carry out the orders of the warden. Given the breadth of these responsibilities, the cell block officer is a key individual who must possess essential management and leadership skills.

Work detail supervisors Inmates provide the labor for feeding, cleaning, and maintaining the institution and its population. A portion of the custody staff must supervise various work details connected with these tasks. The work area is a more relaxed place than the cell block. The work groups are small, and officer and prisoners may engage in conversation. Esprit may develop as they collectively try to complete their assignments. This is especially true when the same persons are assigned to a particular duty over an extended period of time. In the kitchen, clothing room, welding shop, or hospital, for example, the relationship between inmate and officer is analogous to that between worker and foreman in a factory. Yet the correctional officer has no counterpart in the business or industrial world.

In a study of field operations at a plantation-style southern prison, Ben M. Crouch found that officers focused on two goals: "completing the agriculture task at hand and returning to the building the same number of inmates 'turned out' at the beginning of the day."[35] Officers in the field displayed little interest in the rules of dress and demeanor that so concerned building personnel. Though most fights between inmates

Correctional officers are the linchpins of management because they are in constant contact with inmates. They must enforce the rules yet gain the cooperation of the prisoners. A difficult job!

were stopped immediately, on some occasions the two antagonists were allowed to "duke it out," an unheard-of occurrence in the cell block. Crouch found that officers in the field adopted a paternalistic style that evoked the unequal relationship of parent to child. Social distance between inmate and supervisor in the field was not as great as it was inside, so officers came to know their men and there was a resulting informality between them.

Industrial shop and school officers In industrial shops and in the prison school, officers primarily have maintenance and security responsibilities. They work alongside civilians, such as shop supervisors, teachers, and counselors. Here the correctional officers act principally to ensure that the inmates who are supposed to be in the shops or school are there at the appointed time. The officers keep atten-

dance, ascertain the whereabouts of absentees, attempt to prevent pilfering, and handle inmate problems and complaints.

Yard officers "In the blocks inmates are at home; in the school, shops, and on work details they are at work; but in the yard inmates are 'on the street.'" The yard is probably the most unstructured environment in the prison. Officers are a presence in the area but have no specific duties other than "supervising" the inmates. They are expected to maintain order and to be concerned about security. "In the yard it's mainly the observation of key individuals—the supposed troublemakers. You keep an eye on them so they're not causing any trouble that the prison doesn't need."[36]

Administration building assignments Officers on assignment in the administration building are generally removed from contact with the inmates and interact mainly with institutional administrators, correctional officials from the commissioner's office, and civilians. They are responsible for security at the gates to the institution, supervise the visitors' room, and escort outsiders to administrative offices. Because the appearance and behavior of these officers is thought to color the general public's impression of the correctional institution, care is taken in their selection for these assignments.

Wall posts Officers assigned to the towers or along the walls are almost completely removed from contact with the inmates. Alone with telephone and weapon, the guard on tower duty has a solitary and boring existence. Traditionally the assignments have been reserved for new recruits and partially incapacitated veterans, or those who have difficulty getting along with the inmates. In recent years, with increases in prison violence, some correctional officers have sought to flee the inmates by transferring from the cell blocks or dormitories to the safety of the towers. This is seen as one way to avoid the frustration and troubles of the cell blocks and yard.

Relief officers Relief officers are assigned to a variety of tasks, depending on vacancies in the staff due to vacations and sick days. Because they work for only short periods in any particular area of the institution, they do not develop close contacts with the inmates. Relief officers are experienced workers who can step into any assignment where their presence is required.

Problems with the Officer's Role

During recent decades most correctional systems have had to contend with the fact that the role officers are expected to play is not clear, especially when both custodial and treatment goals are set. Officers are held responsible for preventing escapes, maintaining order, and ensuring the smooth functioning of the institution. At the same time, they are expected to cooperate with treatment personnel by counseling inmates and demonstrating an understanding attitude. Beyond the incompatibility of those roles lies the rehabilitative ideal, which stresses attempts to treat each person as a unique being, a task that seems impossible in a large people-processing institution. Officers are to use discretion yet somehow behave both custodially and therapeutically. As Cressey notes, "If they enforce the rules, they risk being diagnosed as 'rigid'; if their failure to enforce rules creates a threat to institutional security, orderliness or maintenance, they are not 'doing their job.'"[37]

Officers complain that the rules are constantly changing, and neither they nor the inmates know where they stand. Many look back nostalgically to the days when their purpose was clear, their authority unchallenged, and they were respected by the inmates.

The jobs of correctional officers are complicated not only by treatment programs but also by racial tensions and legal restrictions on the disciplining of inmates. The officer is both a manager and a worker—a manager to the inmates, a low-status worker to the supervisors. Required to interact almost exclusively with prisoners during the work shift, the officer is nevertheless expected to maintain a formal distance from them. As the person at the lowest level of the correctional staff, the officer is constantly under the scrutiny of supervisors in the same way that the inmate is under surveillance. Because of the fear of trafficking in contraband, officers are often shaken down, just as inmates are. As officers write disciplinary reports on inmates, lieutenants write down rule infractions of the officers. Even the disciplinary board for officers is quite similar to the tribunal that hears inmate cases.

The correctional officer is undoubtedly the key figure in the penal equation, the one on whom the whole edifice of the prison system depends. And given the current emphasis on humane custody, the officer must be able to have a positive influence on inmates. Yet despite these demands, the corrections officer has "either been ignored or traduced or idealized but almost never considered seriously."[38] Correctional officers are asked to do an almost unperformable task without proper training, for low pay, and at great risk.

Unionism

Collective bargaining for prison workers is a fairly recent phenomenon. The first unions for prison employees with collective bargaining rights were established in 1956 in Washington, D.C., and New York City, but the movement did not register major gains until the 1970s, when many states passed laws permitting unionization by public employees. By 1981 correctional employees in twenty-nine of fifty-two jurisdictions (state, federal, and District of Columbia) were unionized.[39] The unions that represent correctional officers include two national public employee associations, American Federation of State, County, and Municipal Employees (AFSCME), a part of the AFL-CIO, and Service Employees International Union (SEIU); the International Brotherhood of Teamsters; and locally based state employee organizations. The fact that custody and program staff may be in separate unions has resulted in intraorganizational conflict in some states; in others the different perspectives on correctional goals cause conflict between union groups as each seeks to advance the interests of its members.

Like other labor organizations, unions representing prison employees seek to improve wages and working conditions for their members. Because the members are public employees, most are prohibited by law from engaging in strikes, but some work stoppages and "sickouts" have occurred all the same. In 1979 the 7,000 officers of the New York State system went on strike for seventeen days, and Governor Hugh Carey was forced to call up more than 12,000 members of the National Guard to maintain order.[40] In Connecticut, 800 officers were on strike for three days, and 100 officers called in sick at the New Jersey State Prison in 1976. Although all of these work stoppages were settled within a short time (the New York strike was the largest and longest), they had an impact beyond the specific issues in dispute.

In addition to bargaining with management on questions of wages and working conditions, unions representing correctional workers are active in the political process.[41] Like other public employee organizations, they attempt to persuade legislators to pass laws and budgets that will benefit their members. Their lobbying has often worked to the advantage of corrections as a whole. Improvements in the prison system usually enhance the conditions in which officers work. This fact has not been lost on commissioners and other correctional administrators, for they can often gain the assistance of organized labor at budget time. Unlike other recipients of government services, prisoners are not interested in promoting the needs of the department with which they are associated. Given the absence of supportive clients, commissioners may depend on correctional employees and their unions to help advance the legislative goals of the department.

With the rise of prison employee unions, relationships between employees and administration are now more formalized: When the rights and obligations of each side are stipulated by a labor contract, an old-style warden can no longer dictate working conditions. Unionization has brought officers not only better pay and job security but also greater control over their work. Seniority now determines assignments and officers have an increased role in setting institutional policies. Nonetheless, many people fear that unions and pro-inmate groups may become allies on certain issues against the administration.

Summary

Management of a correctional institution is an exacting and complex task. The formal structure of a coercive organization does not begin to describe the actual management of the prison. Although the warden, administrators, clinicians, and officers have the formal authority of the state behind their actions, the idea that they have total power is wide of the mark. The relationship between the managers and the prisoners is much more fragile than the organization chart in the front office indicates.

Successful management depends on the leadership abilities of the top administrators. As the experience at Stateville shows, effective styles of leadership change over time with shifts in the nature of the inmate community, decisions emanating from the commissioner's office, and political pressures from the outside.

As the largest employee group in correctional institutions, custodial officers play a crucial role: They are the line personnel in constant contact with the prisoners. The officer is both a manager and a worker—a manager to the inmates, a low-status worker to the supervisors. Placed in an environment where most interactions are with prisoners, the officer is nevertheless expected to maintain a formal distance from them.

For Discussion

1. Is it useful to describe the contemporary maximum security prison as a total institution?

2. You are the superintendent of a prison. What sort of management problems must you face? What people can help you solve them?

3. In what way is the idea of total power in the institutional setting defective?

4. What would you expect Stateville to be like today? What types of concerns might its administrators have?

5. Would you like to be a correctional officer? What aspects of the job make it attractive? What aspects make it unattractive?

For Further Reading

Crouch, Ben M. (ed.). *The Keepers: Prison Guards and Contemporary Corrections.* Springfield, Ill.: Charles C. Thomas, 1980. An excellent collection of articles about the role of correctional officers and the changes in that work that have taken place over time.

DiIulio, John J., Jr. *Governing Prisons.* New York: Free Press, 1987. A major critique of the sociological view of prisons. DiIulio argues that governance by correctional officials is the key to the maintenance of good prisons and jails.

Irwin, John. *Prisons in Turmoil.* Boston: Little, Brown, 1980. A sociological perspective of the changes that took place in the American prison during the 1970s and their implication on the life of the inmates and officers.

Jacobs, James B. *Stateville.* Chicago: University of Chicago Press, 1977. Analysis of changes in a large prison over a half century.

Lombardo, Lucien X. *Guards Imprisoned.* New York: Elsevier, 1981. An in-depth look at the working life of correctional officers as they perceive and experience it.

Zimmer, Lynn. *Women Guarding Men.* Chicago: University of Chicago Press, 1986. Exploration of the innovative policy of employing women as correctional officers in prisons for men.

Notes

1. From Edgar May, "A Day on the Job—In Prison," *Corrections Magazine* (December 1976): 6.

See Officer Carvalho's Workperspective on pages 331–335 in this chapter.

2. Erving Goffman, *Asylums* (Garden City, N.Y.: Anchor, 1961).

3. Peter M. Blau and W. Richard Scott, *Formal Organizations* (San Francisco: Chandler, 1962), p. 5.

4. Amitai Etzioni, *A Comparative Analysis of Complex Organizations* (New York: Free Press, 1961), p. 3.

5. Ibid., pp. 5–7, 27.

6. Donald R. Cressey, "Prison Organizations," in *Handbook of Organizations,* ed. James G. March (Chicago: Rand McNally, 1965), pp. 1023–70.

7. Charles Logan, "Well Kept: Comparing Quality of Confinement in Public and Private Prisons," *Journal of Criminal Law and Criminology* 83 (1992): 207.

8. President's Commission on Law Enforcement and Administration of Justice, *Task Force Report: Corrections* (Washington, D.C.: Government Printing Office, 1967), ch. 5.

9. John J. DiIulio, Jr., *Governing Prisons* (New York: Free Press, 1987), p. 13.

10. Ibid., p. 12.

11. Gresham Sykes, *The Society of Captives* (Princeton, N.J.: Princeton University Press, 1958), p. 41.

12. Ibid., p. 49.

13. James Marquart, "Prison Guards and the Use of Physical Coercion as a Mechanism of Prisoner Control" (paper presented to the American Sociological Association, San Antonio, Texas, August 1984).

14. Sykes, *The Society of Captives,* p. 53.

15. Robert B. Reich, "Bargaining in Correctional Institutions: Restructuring the Relationship Between the Inmate and the Prison Authority," *Yale Law Journal* 81 (March 1972): 726.

16. Richard Korn and Lloyd W. McCorkle, "Resocialization Within Walls," *Annals* 293 (1954): 191.

17. Edwin H. Sutherland and Donald R. Cressey, *Criminology* (Philadelphia: Lippincott, 1970), p. 536.

18. DiIulio, *Governing Prisons,* p. 235.

19. Ibid., p. 242.

20. John J. DiIulio, Jr., *No Escape: The Future of American Corrections* (New York: Basic Books, 1991), ch. 1.

21. Joint Commission on Correctional Manpower and Training, *Corrections 1968: A Climate for Change* (Washington, D.C.: Government Printing Office, 1968).

22. James B. Jacobs and Norma Crotty, *Guard Unions and the Future of Prisons* (Ithaca: New York State School of Industrial and Labor Relations, 1978), p. 2.

23. Lucien X. Lombardo, *Guards Imprisoned* (New York: Elsevier, 1981), p. 21; James B. Jacobs and Harold G. Retsky, "Prison Guard," *Urban Life* 4 (1975): 6.

24. Lombardo, *Guards Imprisoned*, p. 21.

25. Leo Carroll, "Race Ethnicity and the Social Order of the Prison," in *The Pains of Imprisonment*, ed. Robert Johnson and Hans Toch (Newbury Park, Calif.: Sage, 1982), p. 185.

26. Francis T. Cullen, Faith E. Lutze, Bruce G. Link, and Nancy Travis Wolfe, "The Correctional Orientation of Prison Guards: Do Officers Support Rehabilitation?" *Federal Probation* (March 1989): 40.

27. Ibid. See also James B. Jacobs and Norma Crotty, *Guard Unions and the Future of Prisons* (Ithaca: New York State School of Industrial and Labor Relations, 1978), p. 134; Robert Johnson, *Hard Time* (Monterey, Calif.: Brooks/Cole, 1987), p. 120.

28. U.S. Department of Justice, *Sourcebook of Criminal Justice Statistics* (Washington, D.C.: Government Printing Office, 1992), p. 112.

29. Ibid.

30. Lynn E. Zimmer, *Women Guarding Men* (Chicago: University of Chicago Press, 1986).

31. Lombardo, *Guards Imprisoned*, p. 6.

32. Ben M. Crouch, "Guard Work in Transition," *The Dilemmas of Corrections*, 2nd ed. Kenneth C. Haas and Geoffrey P. Alpert (Prospect Heights, Ill: Waveland Press, 1991), p. 164.

33. Jacobs and Crotty, *Guard Unions*, p. 3.

34. Ibid., p. 39.

35. Ben M. Crouch, "The Book vs. the Boot: Two Styles of Guarding in a Southern Prison," in *The Keepers*, ed. Ben M. Crouch (Springfield, Ill: Charles C. Thomas, 1980), pp. 207–24.

36. Lombardo, *Guards Imprisoned*, p. 42.

37. Cressey, "Prison Organizations," p. 1025.

38. Gordon Hawkins, *The Prison* (Chicago: University of Chicago Press, 1976), p. 106.

39. David Duffee, "Careers in Criminal Justice: Corrections," in *Encyclopedia of Crime and Justice*, ed. Sanford H. Kadish (New York: Free Press, 1983), p. 1232.

40. Jacobs and Crotty, *Guard Unions*, p. 3.

41. James Jacobs and Lynn Zimmer, "Collective Bargaining and Labor Unrest," in James Jacobs, *New Perspectives on Prison and Imprisonment* (Ithaca, N.Y.: Cornell University Press, 1983), pp. 145–59.

Institutional Programs

13

Program, program. If you want to get out, you've gotta have a program.

San Quentin inmate

Managing Time
Time and Security
The Principle of Least Eligibility
Classification
The Classification Process
Objective Classification Systems
Classification and the Inmate
Rehabilitative Programs
Psychological Programs
Behavior Therapy
Social Therapy
Vocational Rehabilitation
Religious Programs
**The Rediscovery of Correctional
　　Rehabilitation**
Prison Industry
The Contract Labor, Piece-Price, and Lease Systems
The Public Account System
The State Use System
The Public Works and Ways System
Prison Industry Today
Prison Maintenance Programs
Prison Recreation Programs
Prison Programming Reconsidered
Summary

The median time served in most U.S. prisons is about two years. Imagine where you were two years ago. What were you doing? Now imagine every day, every hour since that time lived in a prison. Think of the experiences you would have missed. Think, too, of how long the prison term would seem to have lasted—decades, an eternity.

The pervasive theme in prison is time. It is the one thread that links the experiences of all prisoners. Much of the small talk among prisoners relates to time: "time in the joint," "doing time," "good time," "time left," "straight time." Questions frequently asked by staff and by prisoners alike are "How much time did you get?" "When do you come up for parole?" "What's your maximum release date?" Calendars are prominent in the cells, and some inmates carefully mark the passing of each day. Time, counted in months and years, is the common denominator of the prison society.

Institutional programs mitigate the oppressiveness of time in prison. They also provide opportunities for prisoners to improve their lives, whether the programs involve counseling, education, or merely recreation. When rehabilitation is a dominant correctional goal, the parole board sees participation in a treatment program as an indication of readiness for supervision in the community. But perhaps the major merit of programs is the fact that they keep prison time from becoming dead time. When minutes seem to crawl, the soul grows bitter.

Managing Time

Prison administrators use institutional programs to help manage the problem of time. Work assignments occupy the middle hours of the day; treatment and recreational hours are held before and after work assignments; and special programs (Junior Chamber of Commerce meetings, Bible study, Alcoholics Anonymous sessions) take up the remaining hours. Experienced administrators know that the more programs they offer, the less likely it is that the inmates' boredom will turn into hostility toward the staff. The less cell time, the fewer tensions.

Prison programs also provide the administrator with privileges to use as incentives for discipline. Inmates know that when they break the prison rules, they will be denied access to prison programs, and this will make their time in prison go slower.

We use the broadest possible definition of **prison program** in this chapter. A program is any formal, structured activity that takes prisoners out of their cells and sets them to instrumental tasks. Thus prison programs range from group therapy sessions to chair-making factories, from baseball teams to reading groups. Some prison programs are designed to rehabilitate, others use inmate labor to reduce the cost of running the facility. The fundamental need that all prison programs serve is the management of time.

There are three general types of programs. The most controversial are those that serve rehabilitative purposes. Many such programs attempt to improve the offender's job skills or educational achievement. Still others are meant to alter the offender's propensity for criminal behavior through psychological or social treatment. A second type of program is industrial; in these programs, prisoners are employed in operations that turn out products or goods for consumption by others. The third type involves the daily maintenance of the institution—janitorial and kitchen tasks, laundry, and the like. Maintenance programs are all but universal because every prison needs them to get its work done.

prison program   Any formal, structured activity that takes prisoners out of their cells and sets them to instrumental tasks.

Time and Security

Prison programs are constrained by security. No matter how beneficial a program may be, it must not conflict with the institution's security requirements. Criminologist Donald J. Newman has pointed out that even if a thousand evaluations showed that pole vaulting was a valuable skill for prisoners to learn, it still would never be taught in prison.

Security requirements impinge on programs in a variety of ways. Whenever a program requires the use of sharp tools or materials that could be fashioned into tools, heavy security prevails. This is a particular problem for maintenance programs, but it affects many types of industrial programs too. Plumbing and electrical operations use knives, pipes, hammers, and wrenches, any one of which could be used as a weapon. Such common prison industries as woodworking, welding, and auto repair likewise involve the use of potentially lethal objects.

Security requires repeated counts of tools, searches of inmates as they leave work areas, and detailed accounting of raw materials. In a typical shop, inmates are searched as often as twice a shift and material inventories are taken three or more times a day. The heavy emphasis on security has two important consequences. First, the unceasing surveillance adds to the degradation of the inmates and sharpens their sense of captivity. Prisoners are lined up and checked out so often that their consciousness of their status as security risks is constantly reinforced. The most rudimentary tasks of prison labor call for a level of control that exacerbates the effects of an already dehumanizing environment.

Security requirements also make maintenance and industrial programs inefficient. Every time a tool is used it must be signed out and signed in; each time material is obtained for a task, paperwork must be done; even coffee breaks are circumscribed by security measures. Captives are seldom the most industrious of workers, and prison security measures do nothing to improve their efficiency.

Despite the negative effects of security, most authorities strenuously support tight control of potentially dangerous items. They recognize that even one handcrafted knife or bludgeon can constitute a serious physical risk to inmates and staff. Stabbings and other instrument-aided mayhem are far too frequent. Yet cynics question the utility of overly intrusive security, pointing out that even in the most closely monitored prisons periodic shakedowns uncover hundreds of contrived weapons and other contraband. Prisoners are ingenious at creating weapons out of anything that comes to hand; even such seemingly harmless items as spoons and ballpoint pens can be turned into tools of violence. The only remedy—and a weak one at that—is unremitting vigilance. And some kinds of programs are simply impractical in the prison, because the equipment and materials are too easily misused by inmates.

Institutional security affects rehabilitative programs in a different way. When inmates are engaged in classwork or counseling, they know their interactions with other prisoners are being observed closely for possible violations of security. Even in a therapy session a prisoner is aware that any remark made to a staff member touching on a possible violation is likely to have unpleasant consequences. Security concerns make it difficult to bridge the gap between the keepers and the kept.

The effect of that gap on rehabilitative programs can be very serious. The relationship between the therapist and the client is generally considered to be of central importance to the success of treatment. Many writers have analyzed this matter in some detail; one of the most vivid descriptions is provided by Thomas Harris in his popular book *I'm OK, You're OK*.[1] Harris points out that patients in therapy find it difficult to solve their problems as long as they are made to feel what he calls "not OK": dependent, untrustworthy, incompetent. Yet these are precisely the feelings aroused in prisoners by security practices. Hence prison therapists are in the position of fighting the effects of the environment in which they work: It's not easy to make a prisoner feel OK.

In sum, although the stated objectives of a program—to improve the prisoners' sense of themselves or to make them more vocationally competitive— may be laudable, it is not easy to achieve such objectives in a total institution. The need for tight security dilutes the effectiveness of prison programs, except as a means to fill time.

The Principle of Least Eligibility

Institutional programs are also affected by society's expectation that prisoners will not receive for free any extra services for which law-abiding citizens have to pay. This expectation is often referred to as the **principle of least eligibility.** The argument is that prisoners, because of their proved wrongful behavior, are the least eligible of all citizens for social benefits beyond the bare minimum required by law. Taken to its extreme, the principle seemingly would prohibit numerous institutional benefits for offenders, such as free college courses and surgical procedures for cosmetic purposes. Indeed, many programs now available in prisons are not available without cost outside the walls. The disparity has sometimes had significant effects on corrections.

Administrators find it difficult to justify the practice of offering services to prisoners that may exceed in quality those available to law-abiding citizens. Public reaction is often quite hostile to creative programming for inmates, and this factor affects correctional planning of virtually all programs. The story is told that a miniature golf course built on the grounds of a Connecticut prison by inmate labor in off-hours with the inmates' own funds was left unused after a newspaper reporter exposed it in a series of stories on the "country-club prison."

The principle of least eligibility reflects a strong public ambivalence about correctional programming. Citizens want prisoners to have opportunities for rehabilitation; but they do not want programs that seem to reward criminal conduct. Hence prison programs are seldom the most desirable of innovative social services; often they are only weak versions of free-society programs. If the prison offers job training, it is not to prepare inmates for positions in the most prestigious or financially advantageous occupations. If the prison offers psychological services, they frequently take the form of group or individual counseling sessions rather than intensive therapy. If the prison offers education, it tends to be very basic, barely remedial.

Consider the public reaction to a recent suit brought by an Oregon prisoner who forced the state to pay $17,000 for a sex-change operation. The surgery is considered a legitimate (if unusual) procedure in free society, but its free provision to a member of the least eligible class is interpreted by many observers as unwarranted exploitation of the public by the offender. Yet such an operation is often justified in terms of the psychological or social well-being of the prisoner and its positive effects on future behavior.

All prison programs are constrained by the forces of time management, security, and the principle of least eligibility. The inmates who wish to participate in them face a further constraint: the procedures used to classify prisoners with respect to security and programs.

Classification

At Elmira Reformatory in the 1800s, Zebulon Brockway initiated a process of **classification** so that inmates could be grouped according to custody requirements and program needs. In the modern institution, prisoners are still being classified, and

principle of least eligibility The doctrine that prisoners ought to receive no goods or services in excess of those available to persons who live within the law.

their housing, work assignment, treatment program, and readiness for release are determined by their classification.

Classification was an important activity during the rehabilitation era because the treatment model is predicated on a clinical assessment of the inmate's needs. According to that model, clinical personnel—psychologists, physicians, and counselors—interviewed prisoners, tested them, and examined case files in order to determine appropriate courses of treatment and levels of custody. The 1963 *Inmate Classification Manual* of the California Department of Corrections defined classification as "a systematic study of the individual inmate" that was to include "a complete evaluation of the inmate's past development, present needs and behavior, and potential for the future." The information developed by this study was to be used to further understanding of the inmate, to prepare the individual for rehabilitation, and to design "a realistic integrated program of custody, treatment, training, institutional assignments and housing."[2]

Although rehabilitation services receive less emphasis today, classification is still an important tool of prison management. Modern systems of classification are ongoing processes. Instead of treatment programs, contemporary prison classification systems focus on the offender's potential for escape, violent behavior, or becoming a victim of other inmates.

During their incarceration prisoners may be reclassified as they encounter problems or finish treatment programs. Classification status also changes if inmates transfer to another institution and as they prepare for release to the community. The National Advisory Commission on Criminal Justice Standards and Goals describes classification as "a grouping process based on needs and problems. From an administrative standpoint, classification systems

Classification is the process of evaluating an offender's needs and developing custody and treatment programs.

can provide for more orderly processing and handling of individuals. From a financial standpoint, classification schemes can enable administrators to make more efficient use of limited resources and to avoid providing resources for offenders who do not require them."[3]

The Classification Process

In most correctional systems all new prison-bound offenders pass through a reception and orientation center where, for a period that usually lasts three to six weeks, they are evaluated and classified. In some states the center is a separate facility, but in most states each institution has its own reception center. Social scientists have likened reception and classification to a process of mortification. As the recruit is socialized to the army by basic training, the college student to a fraternity by pledge week, and the monastic brother to a religious order through the novitiate, the sentenced felon is introduced to the new status of prison inmate by the reception process, a deliberately exaggerated degradation ceremony that seeks to depersonalize the inductee. Newcomers are stripped of their personal effects and given a

---

classification A process by which prisoners are assigned to types of custody and treatment appropriate to their individual needs.

uniform, rulebook, medical examination, and shower. This underscores the fact that they are prisoners now and no longer citizens of the free community.

In some correctional systems, classification consists merely of sorting prisoners on the basis of age, severity of offense, record of prior incarceration, and institutional conduct. Such approaches are designed mainly as a management tool to ensure that inmates are assigned to housing units appropriate to their custody level (low, medium, high, segregation), are separated from those who are likely to victimize them (for example, the young, slight, and timid from the "gorillas"), and are grouped with members of their work assignment (for example, kitchen duty).

At institutions where rehabilitation is taken seriously, batteries of tests, psychiatric evaluations, and counseling sessions are administered so that each prisoner can be assessed for purposes of treatment as well as custody. Among the tools used in this kind of classification process is the Minnesota Multiphasic Personality Inventory (MMPI), which differentiates ten types of offenders and assists in development of their programs.[4] Since treatment resources are limited in most prisons, they must be allocated in ways that will benefit the inmates most in need of them. The diagnostic process serves this purpose.

The classification decision is often made by a committee that usually consists of the deputy warden and the heads of departments for security, treatment, education, industry, and the like. In some correctional systems a separate classification committee makes decisions about an inmate's program and custody status. At the hearing, caseworkers or counselors present information gathered from presentence reports, police records, and the reception process. The inmate appears before the committee, personal needs and assignments are discussed, and decisions are made. Because it is difficult to assemble so many top administrators for classification hearings, some institutions delegate the task to two or three staff members who are part of the reception team. They make assignments according to procedures prescribed by the department of corrections and the institution's needs.

The classification staff of adjustment centers in four California prisons were found to talk a great deal about the individual program needs of inmates, but in committee sessions they tended to categorize the inmates according to stereotypes rather than diagnostic criteria. The categories used in practice were:

■ *Inmates whose orientation was racial:* Inmates who held strong commitments to the various militant racial and ethnic gangs then common in California prisons.

■ *Pressure artists:* Predators who roamed the prison demanding everything from sex to cigarettes from other prisoners.

■ *The weak and pressured:* Those who because of their youthful appearance were the targets of the pressure artists.

■ *Prison rats:* Informers who were known to the general population and had to seek protection in the adjustment center.

■ *Others:* Those who did not fit any other category and were not seen as tough cases; usually they had been sent to the adjustment center for minor infractions of the rules.[5]

Researchers found that inmates contributed to the stereotyping process by their behavior before the classification committee: Many were uncommunicative and appeared to be cynical about the meeting. By fitting each inmate to one of the stereotypes, the staff was able to routinize the classification process, thus serving the personal needs of the staff and the organizational needs of the institution.

It must be recognized that in practice, classification decisions are often made on the basis of the institution's needs rather than those of the inmate. Enrollment in certain programs of treatment and training is limited, and the demand is great. Thus inmates may find that the few places in, for example, the electrician course are filled and there is a long waiting list. Because the institution's housekeeping must be done by the inmates, large numbers of inmates must be assigned to these tasks.

Objective Classification Systems

The prison crowding crisis and litigation challenging existing procedures have forced many correctional systems to reexamine their classification procedures. As space becomes a scarcer and more valuable resource, administrators feel pressured to ensure that it is used as efficiently as possible: that levels of custody are appropriate and that inmates are not held in "oversecure" facilities. From the standpoint of the courts, a system of classification "must be clearly understandable, consistently applied and conceptually complete. Methods of validation must be implemented and means of redress for irregularity must be provided."[6]

New predictive and equity-based classification models have been developed that use the point totals from check-off instruments to determine inmates' classification. Predictive models are designed to distinguish inmates in respect to the risk of escape, misconduct in the institution, and future criminal behavior. Clinical, socioeconomic, and criminal factors (such as previous prison escapes, for example) are given point values, and the resultant total point score determines an appropriate security level. Models of classification based on the equity principle use only a few explicitly defined legal variables reflecting current and previous criminal characteristics. Such variables as race, employment, and education are not used, for it is argued that it is unfair to manage inmates on the basis of these characteristics. As James Austin has noted, in reality the two models frequently use similar variables to classify inmates, but the "predictive models use empirical validation methodologies to determine appropriate factor weights and cutting points, whereas equity models use so-called consensus building processes among practitioners and classification 'experts' which ultimately may be as subjective as traditional classification approaches."[7]

Objective models are more efficient and less costly to use because line staff can be trained to administer and score the instrument, and clinicians and other senior administrators need not be involved. A staff member can determine the appropriate level of custody by entering the relevant data, adding up the total points for factor scores, then applying numerical criteria to indicate the classification. Inmates who score 25 or above, for example, might be sent to maximum security, those who score less than 15 to minimum security, and the remainder to medium security. The factors used in three different prison classification systems are illustrated in Table 13.1.

Classification and the Inmate

Classification serves the program and custody goals of the institution, but the process also places a label on each prisoner. The inmate may take from the classification process a new identity and a knowledge of the official evaluation that has been made. When prisoners become aware of the labels given them by correctional evaluators, they interpret those labels as the viewpoint that those who have almost unlimited power over their lives have of them.

Hans Toch has described the crude realities of prison classification: "With some exceptions, prison systems assign inmates on the basis of space available.... Security/custody classification is system oriented rather than person oriented, and carries few psychological implications. A state with 75 percent maximum security spaces will tend to classify 75 percent of its intake population as maximum security."[8] Indeed, most states overclassify inmates, placing them in higher custody levels than appears necessary simply because there is more high-security space available than all other types of facilities.[9] As a result, treatment assignments for which prisoners in maximum security are not eligible (such as work release) are simply unavailable to the vast majority of inmates.

This classification policy can have severe implications for the prisoner, since many privileges are linked to classification level. In

Table 13.1 ■ **Various Factors Used in Prison Classification Systems.** In order to classify inmates, various factors are considered. The NIC model was developed by the staff of the National Institute of Corrections in Washington, D.C. The Correctional Classification Profile was developed by a private team of consultants. The Federal Bureau of Classifications system was developed by its research division.

Factor	National Institute of Corrections model	Federal Bureau of Prisons model	Correctional Classification Profile
Severity of current offense	x	x	
Degree of violence in current offense			x
Use of weapon in current offense			x
Nature of sexual offense			x
Length of sentence			x
Expected length of incarceration		x	
Type of detainer	x	x	x
Severity of prior commitments		x	
Number of prior commitments			x
Number of prior felony convictions	x		
History of violence	x	x	x
History of institutional violence	x		
History of escape	x	x	x
History of prior supervision			x
Precommitment status[a]		x	
Substance abuse	x		x
Age	x		
Education	x		x
History of employment	x		x
Program/service needs	x	x	x
Other[b]			

Source: Robert Buchanan and Karen Whitlow *Guidelines for Developing, Implementing, and Revising an Objective Classification System* (Washington, D.C.: National Institute of Justice, 1987), p. 12.

[a]i.e., own recognizance, voluntary surrender, not applicable.

[b]Includes types of sentence requiring a management designation (e.g., misdemeanor, narcotic addict, split sentence, psychiatric) and considerations such as medical health, aggressive sexual behavior, and involvement in disruptive group.

Colorado, for example, early release from prison is restricted to inmates classified as minimum security. In many states the amount of good time that can be earned is tied to security classification. Further, release on parole often depends on a good record of participation in treatment or educational programs. Prisoners often have difficulty explaining to the parole board that they really did want to learn a skill but were given no opportunity to do so.

Rehabilitative Programs

Rehabilitative programs have as their aim the reformation of the offenders' behavior. Some people argue that imprisonment is so painful that it is itself reformative: Offenders change their ways to avoid a repetition of the experience. The reformative power of prison, its ability to convince offenders that a life of crime is undesirable, is often called its special deterrence effect.

Many scholars believe that simply undergoing imprisonment is not reformative enough, that the inmate's prison activities must also be reformative. These people advocate for rehabilitative programs in the prison setting. There is little dispute about the desirability of providing for the rehabilitative needs of offenders, but there is much dispute—as we discussed in Chapter 4—about the emphasis that should be given to rehabilitative programs and the types that ought to be offered.

Rehabilitative programs can be grouped roughly in five categories, depending on the assumptions made about the offender's needs and the best means to approach those needs: psychological, behavioral, social, vocational, and religious programs.

Psychological Programs

The treatment most commonly available in free society is in some ways the most controversial in the prison setting. Psychological treatment in its various forms—psychotherapy, counseling, and so on—is routinely sought by millions of Americans to help them weather various crises in their lives. In prison, psychotherapy is used to treat the underlying emotional or psychological problems that led inmates to criminality.

This requires a significant assumption: that emotional problems are indeed the primary cause of most offenders' criminality—or even more basically, that the concept of mental illness makes sense. These were mainstay ideas underlying the medical model, discussed in Chapter 3. A significant body of opinion questions this model. In his famous critique of the mental illness model, psychiatrist Thomas S. Szasz flatly states: "I submit that mental illness is a myth. Bodies are physical objects; minds, whatever they may be, are not physical objects. Accordingly, mental diseases (such as depression or schizophrenia) cannot exist in the same sense in which bodily diseases (such as broken noses or ulcerated skins) exist."[10]

Szasz questions the applicability of the medical model used in connection with physical ailments to the human "problems in living" that are commonly called mental illness. The notions of diagnosis, prognosis, and treatment not only are irrelevant to these problems but also mislead us when we attempt to deal with the perplexing predicament we mistakenly call mental illness.

Others who have been critical of mental health treatment in prisons do so from a much less radical posture. They assert that the notion of mental illness is an inadequate explanation of criminal behavior. Many additional factors enter into an offender's decision to behave criminally: opportunity, rational motivation, skill, acquaintances, anger. To demonstrate convincingly that some mental problem underlies all or even most of such decisions is not possible.

The lack of consensus regarding diagnoses of mental illness points to some of the drawbacks in the general concept that mental illness is at the base of much criminal behavior. Trained psychiatrists, for example, disagree on the diagnosis of patients' mental problems as often as half the time. If the experts cannot see eye to eye on the nature of an "illness," then it seems reasonable to question whether the idea of the "illness" itself has merit.

The poor reliability of the methods of diagnosing mental illness may be one reason that the treatments have been so ineffective. Robert Martinson's review of more than two hundred evaluations of treatment programs, discussed in Chapter 3, provides perhaps the most stark conclusion: that, with few exceptions, rehabilitative efforts reported up to that point were having no appreciable effect on recidivism.[11] Martinson was referring to a wide variety of programs, but his conclusion was particularly applicable to programs designed to improve the emotional or psychological functioning of the offender. That these programs do little for criminal offenders should not be surprising. A similar review of psychiatric methods used in connection with all types of patients found "that psychotherapy, as practiced over the last forty years, has had an average effect that is modestly positive. It is clear, however, that the averaged group data on which this conclusion is based obscure the existence of a multiplicity of processes occurring in therapy, some of which are known to be either nonproductive or harmful."[12]

Psychotherapy, the generic term used to refer to all forms of "treatment of the mind," takes on a revised meaning when it is applied in the prison setting. The most common arrangement in psychotherapy is entrepreneurial: The individual enters into a voluntary, financial contract with the therapist for help; either party is free to terminate the agreement at any time. Because the client is the purchaser, it is easy to see why the therapist keeps the client's interest foremost during the treatment process.

In prison, however, it is not the offender but society that purchases the therapist's services. The interests of the purchasers—society—assume more importance to the therapist than those of the offender. This, says Szasz, turns the accepted practices of most of the field upside down. The client is not the centerpiece; instead, society's desire that the client develop a crime-free lifestyle becomes the virtually nonnegotiable theme. This is why so many offenders have complained that prison psychotherapy gets into aspects of their lives with which they do not need help.

When a third party to the patient-therapist relationship (society, in the case of prisoners) establishes both the need for and the goals of therapy, it is called **coercive therapy.** Under coercive therapy, the patient finds it hard to resist the imperative of getting help, even though psychotherapeutic treatment may be inappropriate. Indeed, coercive therapy has a Catch-22 aspect: Any reluctance on the offender's part to agree that help is needed is interpreted as "resistance," a sure sign that the prisoner does indeed need the therapy.

Despite these problems, programs intended to change the offender's emotional or psychological orientation remain quite popular. Such programs emphasize either individual therapy (the psychologist sees the offender alone) or group therapy (the professional sees several offenders together).

Individual psychotherapy It is at once easy and difficult to describe individual psychotherapy in the correctional setting. It is easy because the actual behavior engaged in is mere talking: conversation between the offender and the therapist. It is difficult because underlying the simple, seemingly social behavior of the therapist-client relationship is a panoply of possible theories, methods, and approaches that the therapist may be using to treat the client.

The therapist may be convinced that the client is confused by illogical or irrational thinking; or is mired in self-damaging behavior

---

coercive therapy   Treatments in which the therapist determines the need for and the goals of treatment processes that are required, whether or not the client agrees.

Group counseling where inmates discuss their problems, hopes, and fears is one of the major rehabilitative techniques used in prisons.

in relationships with others; or is unable or unwilling to face up to the significance of alienation; or is reacting to failure to achieve a satisfying level of personal potential. These interpretations reflect the thinking of some schools of psychotherapeutic thought, of which there are many. The most usual therapies in the prison setting, however, are reality therapy and transactional analysis.

Reality therapy has a very simple tenet: A person's problems will be reduced when the person begins to behave more responsibly. Reality therapy holds that things get difficult for people when their behavior bucks the realities of their lives. The therapist's role is to return the client consistently and firmly to an analysis of the real consequences of his or her behavior, with particular attention to the troubles that follow inappropriate behavior. Reality

therapy is popular in corrections for three reasons. First, it takes as a given that the rules that society sets for its members are inescapable. Second, its techniques are such that the staff can quickly become proficient in them. Third, the method is short term and thus is highly adaptable to prison circumstances.

Transactional analysis focuses on the points of view (called ego states) taken by persons in their interactions with others. Three general ego states are involved: Parent, Adult, and Child. The Parent is judging and controlling; the Adult is mature, realistic, and ethical; the Child is playful, dependent, and sometimes naughty. The aim of transactional analysis is to lead people to a realization that their problems commonly result from approaching the world as an angry Parent or weak Child rather than

reality therapy   Treatment that emphasizes personal responsibility for actions and their consequences.

transactional analysis   Treatment that focuses on how a person interacts with others, especially on patterns of interaction that indicate personal problems.

as an Adult. The life stance of many prisoners has been that of naughty Child: "Try to catch me." The therapist's role is largely that of teacher; he or she spends substantial time explaining the concepts of transactional analysis and demonstrating to the client how to use them in analyzing his or her own life. Transactional analysis is considered well suited to the correctional context for some of the same reasons that reality therapy is popular: It is simple, straightforward, and short-term. Moreover, the use of a formal therapy "contract" between the client and the therapist helps to eliminate some of the insidious aspects of coercive therapy.

Group psychotherapy Offenders engaged in group psychotherapy come together to discuss problems they share. A professional therapist structures the interaction to help change the participants' orientations toward living.

Group treatment is considered important because people are social animals; most of their behavior occurs in groups. It is in groups that we learn to define ourselves and to interpret our experiences. This idea is particularly appropriate to criminology, because a large proportion of crime is committed by groups or in groups, and much criminal behavior is reinforced by group norms, by manipulation, and by elaborate rationalizations. Hence prison treatment groups are often highly confrontational. Group members are asked to "call" the manipulations and rationalizations others are using to justify their deviant behavior, and they are encouraged to participate wholeheartedly in the process. It is believed that in this way they come to understand their own versions of those manipulations and rationalizations.

Typically, an adaptation of an individual therapy, such as reality therapy or transactional analysis, is used as the primary group method. Perhaps the most common group therapy technique in the prison setting is guided group interaction, a variant of reality therapy. Its primary aim is to help the assembled clients to understand how problems arise from failure to acknowledge reality and to behave responsibly.

Instead of pursuing that aim directly, however, the therapist seeks input from group members about their own self-destructive behavior. Because those who question any particular offender's motives and honesty are also offenders, guided group interaction is thought to be particularly effective in conveying the message that these offenders need to change their ways if they are ever to accommodate to reality better than they have been doing.

Group treatment in prison has been somewhat controversial. An evaluation of a major program of guided group interaction in a California prison for adults found that it produced no lasting effect. Was this due to inadequacies of the method, poor management of the program, or something else? A reevaluation of the program found that offenders had little motivation to attend the sessions, that prison security needs had undermined the integrity of the process (members were asked to report to the warden statements made by others in the group), and that the leaders lacked professional competence.

Behavior Therapy

Much recent work in the field of psychotherapy has focused on treating behavior rather than the mind. In **behavior therapy,** the approach to correctional rehabilitation postulates that the differences between persons labeled deviant and nondeviant lie not within the individual but in how the person responds to problems in the environment. According to this idea, what needs reformation is not the offender's mind or emotions but his or her behavior. The method seeks behavior change directly, by attempting to identify the environmental conditions that promote problem behavior and then to alter those conditions.

---

behavior therapy Treatment that induces new behaviors through reinforcements (rewards and punishments), role modeling, and other active forms of teaching.

The underlying concept is that behavior is learned, and it is learned because it has some positive payoff. Behavior can be unlearned if that payoff is eliminated and a more rewarding payoff is offered for a different kind of behavior.

Behavior therapy, then, is concerned with direct manipulation of the behaviors that lead offenders into criminal lifestyles. Ordinarily the target of the behavior-change effort is not criminality per se but the variety of problem behaviors that surround a criminal lifestyle: verbal manipulation and rationalization; deficiency in social skills, such as conversational ability; the ability to control anger and frustration; and so on. Obviously, such problem behaviors can lead to trouble in keeping jobs, avoiding conflict, and handling disappointment. It is believed that criminal behavior typically is related to such crucial personal experiences.

One variant of behavior therapy is called **cognitive restructuring.** Advocates of this approach argue that offenders develop antisocial patterns of reasoning that make them believe criminal behavior makes sense. This is similar to the basis for reality therapy, but the treatment method is different. Cognitive restructuring uses group and individual training methods to teach offenders new ways to think about themselves and their actions.[13]

The **token economy** is a systematic behavior therapy in which any benefits the offender wants—television or recreation time, library privileges, and so forth—must be purchased with tokens. The tokens can be earned only by completion of certain approved tasks, such as attendance at a work assignment or achievement of good grades in the classroom. Thus the inmate gradually develops behavior patterns that mirror the values held in the larger society: People must earn what they get; it is important to save up for things that one wants; postponement of gratification is often the best way to obtain greater gratification.

Experience with token economies suggests that they can often be powerful techniques for managing the time the prisoner is spending in the prison. In some token economies, virtually everything has a price—choice of menu, furloughs to visit family, availability of night reading—and prisoners quickly learn that if they want reasonably comfortable time, they had better earn the currency to buy it.

The token economy, then, is a behavior-oriented version of reality therapy. Like reality therapy, behavior therapy claims that those who behave responsibly reap the benefits—except that behavior therapy goes on to create a world in which that precise formula is universally true. But does real life, life on the streets, actually mirror the behavior-reward pattern so carefully constructed in the prison setting? Follow-up studies of token economies provide inconclusive evidence that what is learned is transferable. The problem may lie less in the prison than in the streets. It is questionable whether responsible behavior there always pays off in the direct manner of the token economy. In fact, the departing prisoner may rejoin friends and acquaintances who promote a very different idea: The way to the good life is to take it. Very often strong peer pressure moves the former offender back into a criminal lifestyle in which the law-abiding reinforcement patterns of the token economy count for next to nothing.

Critics of behavior therapy raise two points: first, that the technique is often successful with the target behaviors but fails to alter criminality; second, that the methods of therapy often lead to serious abuses of coercive power in corrections.

The first criticism is easy to understand. Behavior therapy programs in institutions for juveniles, for example, often focus on modifying social behaviors (interactions with peers), academic performance, and conformance to institutional regulations. It is unclear how these

---

cognitive restructuring   A form of behavior therapy that focuses on changing the thinking and reasoning patterns that accompany criminal behavior.

token economy   A type of behavior therapy that uses payments (such as tokens) to reinforce desirable behaviors in an institutional environment.

behaviors are related to overall compliance with the law. Indeed, the general assumption appears to be a bit naive—that "good" kids (those who comply with adult expectations) do not commit crimes. Hence the concern arises that behavior programs may alter the target behaviors without affecting subsequent criminality. Such appears to be the case with at least some of the programs, although recent studies have shown that these treatments, particularly for juveniles, can reduce recidivism as well as alter target behaviors.[14]

The idea that behavior therapy is abusive has been highly controversial and relates primarily to its more extreme versions, particularly the more dramatic aversive behavior treatments that have been used recently for certain serious offenders. Aversive conditioning involves an attempt to link the offender's problem with some unpleasant reaction or feeling. In some programs, for example, male child molesters were shown pictures of nude children, and their genitals were subjected to electric shocks whenever monitoring instruments showed they had experienced arousal. The intentional infliction of pain by the use of nauseating drugs or electric shocks is repulsive to many people, though some of the same people are not noticeably upset by the intentional pain of imprisonment.

What makes some behavior therapy upsetting is its potentially coercive nature: The therapist takes advantage of the inmate's powerlessness to force alterations in behavior. To many observers such manipulation is a frightful misuse of government power.

Social Therapy

The weaknesses of behavior and psychological programs have led some authorities to develop therapy systems that attempt to recreate healthy social patterns of support among offenders. We use the broad term **social therapy** to denote these programs because they attempt to develop a prosocial environment within the prison to help the offender develop

noncriminal ways of coping outside. These programs are often referred to as *milieu therapy, therapeutic community,* or *positive peer culture.* They are based on the idea that people learn lawbreaking values and behaviors in social settings from peers to whom they attach importance. If these values (and resultant behaviors) are ever to be permanently altered, it is argued, the peer relationships and interaction patterns have to be changed.

Since the idea of social treatment was introduced by Maxwell Jones under the name *therapeutic community* in 1956, the concept has grown dramatically and has been extended to a large number of settings, particularly for juveniles. The primary aim of this model is to change the institution into a more democratic operation in which all inmates have a say in what goes on. In its most developed form, the therapeutic community is governed by three principles:

1. Productive work and rapid return to the community are emphasized. Every form of activity within the institution is used to help the inmate get ready for early release to the outside community as a responsible citizen.

2. Inmates are reoriented through educational techniques and there is liberal use of group dynamics and group pressures for constructive purposes. Inherent in such an approach is the belief that for some purposes group treatment is more effective than individual treatment.

3. Authority is widely diffused among personnel and inmate clients. The authority that in custodial prisons rests on rank or position is supplemented by authority based on treatment competence, including inmates. The system is strongly democratic rather than authoritarian.[15]

---

social therapy   Treatment that attempts to make the institutional environment supportive of prosocial attitudes and behaviors.

The approach assumes that true change occurs when offenders begin to take responsibility for creating and maintaining the social climate within which they must live. All actions are directed toward developing an inmate culture that promotes a law-abiding lifestyle with appropriate social attitudes. Such a program requires significant shifts in institutional policy, all of which are supportive of a prosocial institutional climate:

■ *Institutional practices must be democratic rather than bureaucratic.* It is easy for inmates to rationalize anti-institutional behavior when they perceive themselves as having little or no influence on the rules and their enforcement. The therapeutic community attempts to place responsibility for adherence to rules and maintenance of institutional order at least partly in the hands of the prisoners.

■ *The program must focus on treatment rather than custody.* All prisoners and all staff are equally charged to be responsive to the emotional and personal needs of their peers. Every transaction in the institution is designed to promote the inmates' growth and emotional maturity.

■ *Humanitarian purposes have priority over institutional routines.* The inmates' needs for vocational and educational development are central to programming, and the likely responses of the prisoners to various policies is an important factor in determining how the prison is run.

■ *Flexibility is valued over rigidity.* Schedules are subject to wide individualization, and the fixed routines that predominate in most prisons are kept to a minimum. Inmates are given considerable leeway in deciding where they will go in the institution and when.

It is exceedingly difficult to turn a prison into a therapeutic community. Three strategies are used to do so.

First, efforts are made to recruit staff and inmates whose personal orientations toward the work are consistent with the therapeutic community ideal. All correctional staff, including guards and professionals, are trained in the techniques of social treatment. Inmates must have normal intelligence and willingness to verbalize their feelings.

Second, the prison architecture has to fit the therapeutic aims. Thus the facility must be "open," with few locked doors, cells, and bars; it must be suitable for dormitory-style living and must have freely available space.

Third and most significant, small inmate groups are convened daily to discuss prison management, staff-offender interaction, and offender behavior. The functioning of a group is both democratic, in that many of the policy decisions are discussed fully before they are adopted, and therapeutic, in that each member of a group (whether staff or inmate) agrees to take responsibility for the emotional well-being of all other members. Sometimes a group will confront individual members with the negative aspects of their behavior; at other times the group will assist an individual who is trying to work out a particular problem. It is through this regularly scheduled social interaction that the aims of the therapeutic community are most fully realized.

The therapeutic community has come under widespread criticism. Some critics consider the idea impractical, and many studies suggest that the method is of limited effectiveness in reducing crime. The impracticality of the idea is apparent from a description of its intent. How can a prison, intentionally established as a setting for degradation, pain, intrusion, and hardship, be transformed into a caring, supportive environment? How can the keepers, trained in control and ever vulnerable to the threats of the kept, who outnumber them, ever give up meaningful institutional authority to groups of inmates without harm to their own security and that of the institution?

These criticisms have significant experiential support. For example, as we saw in Chapter 12, chaos resulted in Stateville Prison when a new, liberal administration lost control while trying

Learning new skills can help prepare offenders for their return to the outside. Unlike this machine tool training program, prison programs often are not geared to the job market.

to adopt the principles of total social treatment. Similarly, when Jerome Miller, then commissioner of the Massachusetts Youth Authority, tried to reform the juvenile institutions into social treatment communities, he was met with so much staff resistance that he eventually chose to close the institutions rather than face staff hostility to the notion of democratic treatment.[16] For such reasons, attempts to build social treatment into the institutional setting are frequently aborted after a brief period of experimentation.

The programs that have lasted long enough to be evaluated have yielded ambiguous results. Most reviews found that parolees from therapeutic milieus did no better or worse than parolees from traditional prisons.[17] Interestingly, early evaluations of social treatment settings for juveniles showed positive results, but more recent reanalyses cast doubt on those findings. In short, evaluations of the major attempts to reform the correctional environment in order to reform offenders turn up limited evidence of success, even for juvenile offenders.

Belief in the potential of these programs to rehabilitate offenders, especially drug-dependent offenders, has recently undergone something of a renaissance. For carefully selected groups of offenders, certain social treatment programs, properly run, have been shown to be effective.[18]

Vocational Rehabilitation

One of the oldest ideas in prison programming is to give the prisoner a skill that can help him or her get a job. This idea has much to recommend it because offenders constitute one of the most undereducated and underemployed groups in the U.S. population. One survey found that only about a third of all prison and jail inmates have completed high school, compared to an 85 percent completion rate for twenty- to twenty-nine-year-old non-prisoners,[19] and the unemployment rate of former offenders is more than three times that of nonoffenders.[20] Certainly, then, offenders possess limited capability to perform successfully as producers and wage earners. Many people believe that criminal behavior stems from this kind of economic incapacity, and they urge the wide use of educational and vocational programs to counter it.

Educational programs Many prisoners' ability to learn is hampered by lack of basic reading and computational skills. Moreover, research has increasingly shown a link between learning disabilities and delinquency; many incarcerated offenders have experienced disciplinary as well as academic failure in school. Thus the prison education program must cope with inmates who have neither academic skills nor attitudes appropriate for learning.

The problems of prison education are exacerbated by other factors. Inmates are normally well beyond the age associated with their current educational attainment. It is not unusual for a twenty-nine-year-old prisoner to be performing at the sixth-grade level, for example. Very few available texts are appropriate for such adults. Imagine a thirty-two-year-old two-time robber with self-inflicted tattoos struggling through a passage in a fifth-grade reader about Johnnie and Susie learning how to bake cookies. The sheer inappropriateness of the material to the age and interests of inmates drives them away from remedial schooling.

Similarly, the needs of adult prisoners differ from those of youthful students. Their attention span is different, their life experience much broader, their sophistication greater. Adult learning curricula are unlike typical school curricula, but prison budgets seldom have the flexibility to permit the purchase of specialized educational aids, so the education programs often have to make do with inadequate, outdated, largely ill-suited materials.

A handful of prisons offer college courses, but the ordinary correctional education program is directed toward the general equivalency degree (GED). Applicants for the GED take a written examination that assesses general comprehension and ability in the basic academic areas—reading, writing, science, and mathematics. The GED is considered equivalent to a high school diploma, and many prisoners seek it because it can satisfy the minimum educational requirement of most nonprofessional jobs in the United States.

How successful is prison education as a rehabilitative program? Only a handful of studies have been done on the subject. Most, like Daniel Glaser's original study of prison education conducted in 1961, find that prisoners who complete education programs do no better than other prisoners upon release.[21] A further analysis led Glaser to conclude that even though education achievers in prison do well on parole, their success may be due to the fact that it is the better-risk prisoners who are the education achievers. He also speculated that those who complete GEDs in prison may have unrealistic hopes for postprison success and be greatly disappointed if the GED does little to improve their prospects in the job market.[22]

Vocational programs Vocational programs attempt to give offenders a job skill that will enhance their ability to compete in the job market. Vocational programs suffer from the principle of least eligibility, however: The types of training provided are often directed toward less desirable jobs in industries that already have access to large labor pools—barbering, printing, welding, and the like. It is all but impossible to arrange a program that will prepare offenders for desirable and sought-after jobs because free citizens often resent the special advantage being given to prisoners.

Other problems plague prison vocational programs. For one thing, students are often trained on obsolete or inadequate equipment, because prison budgets generally cannot afford contemporary technology. A story is told about a very popular print-shop apprenticeship program at one large state reformatory in which inmates were trained on presses donated by the local newspaper. Upon parole, the inmates discovered that their acquired skill was unsalable because the machinery they knew how to operate was so inefficient it had gone out of use (which is why it had been donated). Prisoners who emerge from vocational programs rarely have skills that are up-to-date.

Another problem is that the behaviors and attitudes necessary to obtain and keep a job— punctuality, cordiality to supervisors and fellow workers, accountability—are often foreign to offenders, as is the ability to locate a job opening and survive an interview. So a skill is not the only thing a prisoner needs to be taught; most prisoners need help with the entire vocational lifestyle. But the prison regimen, which tells the prisoner what to do and where to be each moment from morning to night, can do little to develop responsible job attitudes needed outside the walls.

Yet another problem is perhaps the most resistant of all to solution. The **civil disabilities** that attach to the former offender, discussed in more detail in Chapter 16, severely limit job mobility and flexibility. Occupational

---

civil disabilities Legal restrictions that prevent released felons from voting and holding elective office, engaging in certain professions and occupations, and associating with known offenders.

All prisons have chaplains and religious services. There is increasing evidence that these programs are very important to some offenders as they try to come to grips with their situations.

restrictions force offenders into menial jobs at low pay, which may lead them back to crime. In one state or another, barred occupations include nurse, beautician, barber, real estate salesperson, chauffeur, worker where alcoholic beverages are sold, cashier, stenographer, and insurance salesperson. Nearly six thousand occupations are licensed in one or more states; convicted offenders may find the presumption against them either difficult or impossible to overcome.[23] The fact that some prison vocational programs promoted for rehabilitative purposes lead to restricted occupations seems to have been ignored.

Despite their detractors, prison vocational programs receive considerable support from many experts because poor job skills seem to be so closely tied to the problems inmates face upon release into the community. The additional income and taxes produced by vocationally trained inmates may actually offset the cost of their training programs and may also have reduced the rates of recidivism among participants.

Religious Programs

Religious programs do not fit easily into any of the programming categories discussed thus far. Yet religion does fit our definition of prison programs: Inmates become involved in religious programs as a way to make the burdens of time in prison less difficult. Because the First Amendment guarantees everyone's right to religious belief and practice, religious programs are available to all prisoners.

The two main religions in prison are Christianity and Islam, but prisons around the United States are host to the same array of faiths existing in free society. In the West and Southwest, Native Americans practice their faith by spending meditative time in fasting and in "sweat lodges," which are small steam rooms where the devotee will spend up to a day in quiet contemplation. In the Northeast and Southwest, Catholic masses are frequently a daily occurrence in larger prisons. In the South, called the Bible Belt, religious programs in prisons tend to be heavily evangelical Christian.

Few studies have been conducted of religion in prison. A recent national study found that religious activity plays a role in helping inmates to adjust to prison, and participation in religion can reduce disciplinary infractions in prisons.[24] Interviews with religious inmates indicated a number of reasons why religion is helpful in the prison environment: Involvement in religion often provided both a psychological and even physical "safe haven" away from the harsh realities of prison life, and it enabled inmates to maintain ties with their families and with outsiders who were religious volunteers. Many administrators believe that having strong religious inmate groups—even nontraditional religions such as Islam—makes a prison easier to run, because the influence of these inmates stabilizes the prison culture.

Religious programming in prison can be controversial. Because the practice of religion is a legal right, some inmates try to use claims of religion to force certain benefits out of the prison authorities. A few years ago, for example, a group of inmates formed "The Church of the New Song" and claimed that religious rites required certain dietary and clothing benefits not usually provided within the prison. Though they based their case on successful legal claims earlier made by Muslims (who sought dietary and dress allowances dictated by their faith), courts refused to recognize the new group as a legitimate religion.

There is also the problem of "jailhouse religion"—inmates who pretend to "get religion" in order to look good for correctional authorities, particularly the parole board. This may not really be a significant problem, however, since research has shown generally that parole boards do not consider an inmate's religiousness in their release decisions, and no hard empirical basis exists to support the claim that "religious" inmates do better than anyone else upon release.

The Rediscovery of Correctional Rehabilitation

After Martinson's 1975 study showed that prison rehabilitation programs were ineffective, prison treatment programs began to decline. They were replaced with a new vision of the prison as a place that should provide safe and secure custody while punishing offenders.

Even though some correctional officials abandoned the rehabilitation ideal, many remained who believed the eradication of rehabilitation from prisons was unwise. In recent years, these penologists have become a strong minority voice calling for a renewed emphasis upon rehabilitation programs in corrections. In a book aptly titled *Reaffirming Rehabilitation*, Francis Cullen and Karen Gilbert have argued that correctional treatment is more humane than mere custody and punishment, and these programs can be effective when appropriately designed and implemented.[25]

Following their lead, a team of Canadian researchers analyzed a large number of recent evaluations of correctional treatment and found that there are six conditions under which treatment programs will be effective:

1. They are directed toward high-risk clients;

2. They respond to the offenders' problems that caused the criminal behavior;

3. The treatment takes into account the offender's psychological maturity;

4. The treatment providers are allowed professional discretion on how to manage the offender's progress in treatment;

5. The program is fully provided as intended; and

6. There is follow-up support for the offender after the treatment program has ended.[26]

Studies such as these have sparked a new interest in rehabilitation among influential penologists. The National Institute of Corrections, a division of the Federal Bureau of Prisons, has funded a series of demonstration programs designed to show how treatment programs can be effectively implemented in corrections. Whether this new emphasis on treatment will become as popular among policymakers as it once was remains to be seen. Although the research basis in support of rehabilitation is growing, some scholars have argued the new studies are misleading and overstate their results.[27]

Prison Industry

American prisoners have always worked, and making them work was seen as a way to accomplish numerous correctional objectives. "'Hard labor' is punishment meted out by the court; but work in the prison is also a reward for the restless. Idleness is seen as a vice of the prison, but it is also used as individual punishment or reward.

Meaningful, productive work, especially for payment, is personally satisfying, especially in an institution where time must be 'filled.' Back-breaking slave labor, backed by force or threat of force, adds 'time' to the punishment of the body."[28] Even in the earliest prisons—the Pennsylvania system of solitary confinement—prisoners worked. Labor was viewed as part of the reformative process. It was also believed that prisoners' labor was legally forfeited as a result of their criminality, and that the state could reasonably expect to profit from their incarceration. To a great extent, the debate between adherents of the Pennsylvania system and the Auburn system was about economics: The latter point to the economic advantages of congregate (though silent) labor.

Some scholars have recently declared that historians have focused too heavily on the humanitarian and reformist basis for the rise of the penitentiary and reformatory. The traditional analysis, they say, does not adequately reflect the influence of economic forces in the emergence of the prison. John Conley expresses this perspective well: "The thesis is that prison industries were a central feature of penal development in the United States, and that production and profit were the cornerstones of penal policy. Changes in the physical structure, administrative processes, and disciplinary methods were directly related to the desire among state officials and private businessmen to exploit inmate labor for profit."[29]

Conley and others show that the industrial prison played an important economic role during various eras. They analyze the operation of nineteenth-century institutions in three industrial states (Massachusetts, New Jersey, and New York) and the industrial model of prisons in the Midwest and South during the early twentieth century (Kansas, Louisiana, and Oklahoma) to support their insights.[30]

The theme of labor for profit is accompanied by a concern about idleness. Much of the history of prison industry revolves around the search for suitable ways to occupy inmates' time while also meeting the financial interests of forces outside the walls. Four trends in that history can be identified: (1) the contract labor, piece-price, and lease systems; (2) the public account system; (3) the state use system; and (4) the public works and ways system.

The Contract Labor, Piece-Price, and Lease Systems

In the earliest days, inmates' labor was sold to private employers, who provided the machinery and raw materials for the work they would do. The products made by this **contract labor system** were then sold on the open market. Alternatively, in the **piece-price system,** the contractor established a purchase price for goods that inmates produced with raw materials provided by the contractor. These arrangements exploited inmates in extreme ways. They worked in sweatshops and the fees for their labor were paid to the prisons; "free" during the day, they returned to the prison at night. In the **lease system,** a variation of the piece-price system, the contractor maintained the prisoners, working them for twelve to sixteen hours at a stretch. These systems enabled many prisons in the later nineteenth century—even the vaunted Auburn—to operate in the black. Cheap wages increased the contractors' profit margins. The prisoners, of course, worked for nothing and gained nothing.

---

contract labor system A system under which inmates' labor was sold on a contractual basis to private employers, who provided the machinery and raw materials with which they made salable products in the institution.

piece-price system A labor system under which a contractor provided raw materials and agreed to purchase goods made by prison inmates at a set price.

lease system A variation on the piece-price system in which the contractor provided prisoners with food and clothing as well as raw materials. In some southern states, under this system prisoners were leased to agricultural producers to perform field labor.

The arrangements led to extreme corruption. The sizable contracts were fought for, and kickbacks and bribes were among the weapons used. Wardens took advantage of easy opportunities to line their pockets—and caused predictable public scandals when they were caught.

It was not long before organized labor began to attack the prison labor arrangements. In fact, a coalition of humanitarian reformers and labor leaders led to laws against contract inmate labor late in the nineteenth century. States began then to experiment with alternative forms of free-market inmate labor.

The Public Account System

Oklahoma turned to the **public account system** when contract labor was outlawed. Instead of selling inmate labor to private entrepreneurs, the prison itself began in 1909 to make twine, buying raw materials and using inmate labor to turn out the product. Similar twine-making factories existed in Minnesota and Wisconsin. At first the reform was enormously successful, reducing costs of twine to Oklahoma farmers and producing profits that defrayed two-thirds of the costs of prison operations, but ultimately the experiment failed. The financial pressure that wardens had felt earlier did not die with the contract labor system, and they often succumbed to it by padding budgets and altering records. In any case, it was impossible to sustain full employment of inmates by means of an industry that had such a narrow market. And when prisons began to turn a profit on goods that the private sector also produced, cooperation from private industry and labor ceased.

The State Use System

In response to the problems associated with the use of inmate labor to produce goods for the competitive market, many states turned to a **state use system** in which prisoners were employed in the production of goods and services used only in state institutions and agencies. Many experts consider this arrangement reasonable and beneficial, and many states mandate that their agencies must purchase goods produced by inmate labor when they are available. This requirement creates something of a state monopoly on certain products. Today the state use system is the most common form of prison industry.

The state use system has several advantages. Prison labor, which by many accounts is cheaper than free labor, is not allowed to compete with other labor pools in the open market, and the saving in labor costs permits state agencies to make some purchases more cheaply. Under this system it is not unusual for state agencies to buy a great variety of prison-made items—school chairs and desks, soap and paper towels, milk and eggs, and so on.

The state use system has drawbacks as well. Even when prison products are reserved exclusively for government use, the system certainly restricts the available free-labor market. Moreover, many of the goods produced within the system—license plates are a good example—have no close equivalents outside the walls, so the skills inmates acquire in prison often have little transferability to outside industry upon the inmates' release. And even when an analogous outside industry exists, prison industry is so inefficient and its methods so outmoded that prisoners often must shed what they learned there before they can be successful in private industry. Farming, a very common prison

public account system A labor system under which a prison bought machinery and raw materials with which inmates manufactured a salable product.

state use system A labor system under which goods produced by prison industries are purchased by state institutions and agencies exclusively and never enter the free market.

Most prisons are located in rural areas and agriculture is a major activity. This is particularly true in the South where prisons have always been run in a plantation manner.

industry, is an example. It has been estimated that over 250,000 acres are devoted to prison farms, and the products are consumed in the prisons and other public institutions. Yet the enterprise typically teaches little in the way of advanced agricultural methods; prisoners usually engage in manual chores, despite the fact that farmhand positions are drying up across the country. The prison farm may be good economics, but it is a poor school.

The Public Works and Ways System

In a version of the state use system called the **public works and ways system,** inmates work on public construction and maintenance projects. Road crews fill potholes. Other crews construct or repair buildings and bridges. It is not a coincidence that this approach was introduced in the 1920s, when the automobile was gaining popularity and surfaced roads were needed.

The use of inmate labor in this manner has aroused some controversy. Advocates praise the tremendous economic advantages of the system and point out that prisoners learn new skills while producing goods and services use-

public works and ways system A labor system under which prison inmates work on public construction and maintenance projects.

ful to society. One such project is the College Inn on the campus of Sam Houston State University in Texas, a complex of offices, classrooms, and hotel rooms that houses the university's criminal justice education and training functions and attracts meetings of justice system groups. The building was constructed almost entirely by inmate labor at great saving to the state.

Public works systems seldom teach much; prisoners do the more arduous jobs on a project and then free craftworkers are hired to perform the tasks that demand skill. Some of the system's detractors say that it amounts to exploitation; the state receives a benefit but does not fairly compensate prisoners for their contributions to it.

Prison Industry Today

Until very recently the trend has been away from free-market use of prison labor and toward state monopolies. From 1885 to 1940 the private use of inmate labor, once the most popular form of prison industry, vanished. There are several reasons for what happened. First, the public became increasingly aware of the exploitive character of prison industry. Southern prison systems expanded dramatically after the Civil War, and former slaves accounted for much of the growth. The labor of most of these prisoners was contracted out in one way or another, leading some critics to say that industrial capitalists had replaced plantation owners as exploiters of the former slaves.

Labor union consciousness began to grow during this period as well. With the rise of the labor movement, state legislatures passed laws restricting the sale of prisoner-made goods so that such goods would not compete with those made by free workers. As early as 1801 New York had required that boots and shoes produced at Auburn be labeled "State Prison." In another application of the principle of least eligibility, whenever unemployment became extensive, political pressures mounted to prevent prisons from engaging in enterprises that might otherwise be conducted by private business and free labor.

In 1900 the United States Industrial Commission endorsed the state use plan and in 1929 Congress passed the Hawes-Cooper Act, followed by additional legislation in 1935 and 1940, which banned prison-made goods from interstate commerce. In an excess of zeal, by 1940 every state had passed laws banning the importation of prison-made goods from other states. These restrictions crippled prison production and forced the abandonment of the open-market system of employing prisoners. With the outbreak of World War II, President Franklin Roosevelt issued an executive order permitting the federal government to procure goods for the military effort from state and federal prisons. Under labor pressure, the wartime order was revoked in 1947 by President Harry Truman, and prisoners returned to idleness. By 1973 the National Advisory Commission found that throughout the correctional system "only a few offenders in institutions have productive work."[31]

The past decade has seen a renewal of interest in channeling prison labor into revived industrial programs that would relieve idleness, allow inmates to earn wages that they could save until release, and reduce the costs of incarceration to the state. In 1979 Congress lifted restrictions on the interstate sale of products made in state prisons and urged correc-

tional administrators to explore with the private sector means to improve prison industry programs. In the same year the Free Venture program of the Law Enforcement Assistance Administration made funds available to seven states to develop industries that would operate according to six principles: a full workweek for inmate employees; wages based on productivity; private-sector productivity standards; responsibility for hiring or firing inmate workers vested in industry staff; self-sufficient or profitable shop operations; and a postrelease job-placement mechanism. Once again inmate labor would compete with free labor. The Prison Industries Enhancement (PIE) program started in seven states in 1982 and requires the actual involvement of private business in the prison industries. Prisoners employed by Zephyr Products, Inc., for example, receive the wage prevailing in the private sector. Table 13.2 lists some of the types of products and services these industries provide.

The change in attitude toward prison industries may be related to the fact that many large U.S. firms have moved their operations to the Third World in search of cheap labor. Because of increased shipping costs and problems related to the running of plants overseas, some manufacturers may be seeing in the prison labor pool an attractive alternative to foreign-based production. Union opposition may weaken if it can be shown that the prisoner is not taking a job away from a taxpaying free worker.

These new developments—the decline of treatment programs, the high costs of incarceration, and changing public attitudes with regard to the role of private enterprise—portend a reinvigoration of prison industries. Indeed, the federal government seems to be moving in this direction. In February 1985 the National Institute of Justice sponsored a national conference on the privatization of corrections, and funding efforts have encouraged experimentation with private corrections of all types, from prison industries to the entire operation of prisons.

Table 13.2 ■ Sample List of Prison Industries Today. In some states the private sector is involved in different types of prison industries operated by the department of corrections. In other states prison industries are privately managed.

State	Industrial activity
Arizona	Computer terminals have been installed by Best Western in a women's facility; 30 inmates make reservations for the hotel chain.
Florida	Pride, Inc. (a nonprofit corporation) operates 50 percent of all state prison industries and plans to take over the balance.
Iowa, Kansas, Nevada, Utah	Private-sector firms employ inmates in a variety of small enterprises.
Kansas	A unique privately managed prison industry operates outside the walls of the state penitentiary. Staffed almost entirely by prison inmates who are bused to and from work, Zephyr Products, Inc. is a sheet metal company developed specifically to reduce prisoner idleness.
Michigan	City Ventures Corporation is building a model industries program for the Huron Valley Correctional Facility.
Minnesota	Disk drives for Control Data Corporation are manufactured by 45 inmates; another 140 inmates manufacture light metal products for a private firm. Stillwater Data Processing Systems Inc. employs 10 inmates as computer programmers in its independently managed company at Stillwater Prison.
Mississippi	Condensing units for Koolmist are manufactured by 20 inmates.
Oregon	Senate Bill 780 creates a privately managed prison industry arrangement similar to Florida's.

Source: Adapted from U.S. Department of Justice, *The Privatization of Corrections* (Washington, D.C.: Government Printing Office, 1985), p. 3.

Early indications are that the supposed efficiencies of private industry in corrections are less dramatic than they were expected to be. It is true that inmate labor is cheaper than free labor, but recent reforms include higher wages for prisoners than those formerly paid by private contractors, and security requirements drive up the costs of prison industry. The cost to private industry of supervising workers and controlling materials is only a fraction of the cost of security in a prison operation—a cost that enters into the balance sheet.

The future of prison industry is unclear because we find ourselves in a period of change. Inadequate work assignments, poor preparation for the job market, and forced idleness are not considered acceptable and are potentially disastrous in a crowded prison. At the same time, mechanisms for more productive use of inmate labor to provide goods and services that are competitive in the free market are not proven successes.

Prison Maintenance Programs

Running a prison is like running a town. The typical prison must provide every major service that is available in a community and more: a fire department, electrical and plumbing services, janitorial maintenance, mail delivery, restaurant, drugstore, administrative record keeping, and so on. All aspects of these operations have to be coordinated. If only to keep the costs of these services manageable, prisoners do the bulk of the work.

Prison Industries Enter the Space Age

Forget all those movie cliches about convicts' making license plates. Prison industry is a multimillion-dollar business making products for the space shuttle and Trident missiles.

It is exacting work. Soldering is done in a special room where heat and humidity must be controlled to prevent dust from contaminating hot metal. Each piece of work is inspected and tested.

"If you're going to solder two pieces of metal together that are going on the space shuttle, you want to be damned sure it works," said Robert W. Cross, superintendent of prison industries at the Federal Correctional Institution in Danbury.

"We're still trying to live down the stigma of all you can do is make license plates."

The Federal Prison Industries Corporation, known as UNICOR, began in 1934 under an executive order and an act of Congress. It is completely self-sustaining, using its own profits to pay prisoners' salaries, buy supplies, and provide some vocational training programs. Cross said the money also is used to buy a Christmas present for each prisoner in the federal system. Any surplus money is returned to the U.S. Treasury.

Sales totaled more than $153 million in the 1983 fiscal year. Danbury's cable assembly plant contributed $16.1 million in sales during fiscal 1984 and showed a net profit of more than $4 million.

Cross said the corporation serves a dual purpose: providing products for the federal government and employing prisoners. Work passes the time and reduces the idleness for the 213 inmates working in the cable

factory. There are 1,062 inmates at the federal prison.

The plant looks and smells like any other assembly factory. Work stations are set up throughout the 20,000-square-foot room, and long sections of black cable housings snake along the floor. The air smells of burning rubber and solder.

For the first time in their lives, many prisoners have become part of the work world. They learn a skill, earn some money, and regain some of the self-esteem lost when they entered the prison system.

"One of the things about getting locked up is a man loses all his pride and dignity. That's one of the most serious consequences," said Joseph Guerriero, manager of the electronics factory. "I enjoy seeing the time come when an inmate has to leave, because he at least has something for the basis of making a living."

Pride in workmanship is one thing Andrell Prysock will take with him when he

---

The one thing that is abundant in a prison is human resources, and perhaps the most frequent type of job in any given prison has to do with its day-to-day maintenance.

In most prisons the maintenance jobs constitute an elaborate pecking order of assignments and tell something about prestige and influence within the prison. The choice jobs are those involving access to sources of power.

A clerical job in the records room (which contains inmates' files) provides the inmate with a corner on one of the most sought-after commodities in the closed setting of the prison: information. The records room inmate can learn who is doing time for what, who is eligible for privileges (such as reclassification, reassignment, and parole), and what decisions are being made about whom. The contents of

leaves the cable assembly plant. The thirty-two-year-old native of Washington, D.C., is a lead man in the "potting" section, where molten plastic is molded onto cable ends. He and several other inmates are working on cables for the Trident missile....

Turning out the best possible product is something of a crusade for Cross, who retires next month after twenty years with the federal prison system. It is an attitude derived from his years with Firestone Tire & Rubber and B. F. Goodrich. Throughout the plant, signs carry his motto: "Good Enough Is Not Good Enough."

"Perfect is good enough," Cross said.

This approach is one reason UNICOR is able to assemble cables formerly made by Bendix and General Dynamics. Quality control checks are made for soldering, assembly, and molding on each cable. Any cable that does not meet the exact specifications of the Defense Department or has the appearance of shoddy workmanship is not shipped.

"It's important to us that it is a quality product," Cross said.

This desire for perfection is also apparent in the prison's new textile factory, where prisoners make tee-shirts for the U.S. Army. The plant opened in November and produces about 2,400 shirts a day.

Larry E. Terry, age forty, who worked in banking and finance before going to the federal prison, sews sleeves onto the shirts. Around him prisoners busy themselves with various tasks. Some cut the pattern or sew shirt bodies, while others check the final product.

Here and there an inmate wears a small mask to keep from inhaling dust. Somewhere a radio plays an old Simon and Garfunkel song, "Homeward Bound."

"There are people who come here with no training at all," Terry said as he worked the sewing machine.

"It's a myth that because we're in prison we don't want to do a good job. The men in here take a lot of pride in their work."

Terry, who is serving an eighteen-month sentence for embezzlement, said another benefit of working for prison industries is better pay. Terry makes the top salary—$1.12 an hour.

Guerriero said many prisoners send money home to their families or save it for their release. Terry uses some of his pay to offset the cost of calling home to Waldorf, Maryland.

Prisoners volunteer for the industries program, and some wait months for one of the well-paying jobs. Once they arrive, these outcasts from society become part of a nationwide business.

Source: From M. D. Thompson, "Prison Industries Enter the Space Age," *Hartford Courant,* 16 January 1985, p. B1. Reprinted by permission.

inmates' files are confidential, but it is hard to prevent the records room clerk from sneaking a look—and trading the information for money or a favor.

Clerical jobs in support of prison administrators are similarly prestigious. Desk assignments permit access to authority figures (and very likely to such favors as flexibility in scheduling, better food, and sometimes information) and make inmates who get them the first contributors to the institutional rumor mill. Often inmates must qualify as trusties before they are given clerical assignments.

Among the most desirable jobs are those that allow access to goods or services that can be sold within the prison economy. For example, an inmate who works in the laundry can charge two packs of cigarettes as insurance that another inmate's clothing will all be returned neatly folded and without rips or tears.

Also desirable are jobs that provide access to contraband goods. Kitchen details enable inmates to purloin extra food to trade or sell. Library assignments allow prisoners to make liberal use of law books and other popular reading matter. Assignments to the dispensary, even with its very tight security on drugs and other medical items, and the stockroom can pay off in various ways.

Different benefits, not so obvious perhaps, can be derived from other assignments. The electrician's aide and the message runner, for instance, usually have flexible schedules and relatively varied work that make the time go faster.

The least desirable jobs are the most plentiful: janitorial services. Mop details are frequently the initial job assignments given to inmates who must prove themselves for later reassignment; they are also given as disciplinary measures. Mopping halls and cleaning latrines is not particularly interesting; repeated three or more times a day in the same areas, the tasks become painfully monotonous. Although janitorial assignments certainly eliminate idleness, they prevent many inmates from making as great a contribution as they otherwise might.

Prison maintenance jobs are essential to the day-to-day management of the prison in two ways. First, they lower the cost of operations by eliminating the need to hire staff members to do the work. Second, the job hierarchy provides a system of rewards and punishments to enforce prison discipline. Prisoners who cooperate with the administration receive the choice assignments; those who do not get the dirty work.

Many inmates spend their time doing physical fitness training and body building.

Prison Recreation Programs

When prisoners are not working, in treatment, or in their cells, they are probably engaging in some form of recreation. Organized recreation is one of the prisoners' favorite pastimes—and it is often central to their prison experience. Most men's prisons have teams—baseball, basketball, even football—and they often compete with outside teams on a regular basis. Many prisons also provide such leisure-time activities as table tennis, weight training, music, drama, and journalism clubs. Often the recreation and leisure time become central to a prisoner's experience.

Recreation programs have two primary functions in addition to filling time. First, they are integral to the social life of the prison. Prisoners vary in their intellectual and physical capacities; a variety of programs enables inmates to meet with others who share their interests and abilities, and to form positive social contacts around those interests. Second, prison recreation and leisure-time pursuits can be rehabilitative in several ways. They can teach such social skills as cooperation and teamwork, they provide a means for prisoners to grow in experience and enhance their self-image, and they serve as a productive backdrop to the general alienation of the prison environment.

Recreation programs humanize the prison, but they also present opportunities for custody and security risks to develop. Whenever prisoners congregate, they have a chance to plan disruptive activities. Especially in the recreational context, where prisoners compete with one another, tempers may flare. And so, although prisons without leisure activities would be torturous, recreation programs require careful management.

Prison Programming Reconsidered

Our discussion of prison programs has focused on the types of activities used to occupy the time of prisoners. Underlying this discussion is an unstated question: Is this prison time useful? The answer is equivocal.

Offenders are often sent to prison with the expectation that they will engage in treatment and rehabilitative programs that will prepare them to adjust to society when they are released. We have seen that this ideal is at best ephemeral, because most rehabilitative programs have serious shortcomings and limited effectiveness. At the same time, the degree to which a prison can focus on rehabilitation is open to question. Surprisingly, a large number of inmates are considered to be in no appreciable need of treatment in the areas of education, vocational training, and drug or alcohol rehabilitation. Of those considered to need help in these areas, frequently less than half actually participate in available programs.

The nonrehabilitative programs—prison industry and maintenance assignments—raise their own problems for the successful administration of the prison. Weighing down the impact of all correctional programs is the albatross of the need for security, which places severe constraints on prison practices.

Yet a programless prison is unthinkable. Time is burden enough for prisoners to manage; to provide no opportunity to fill the time with positive pursuits is out of the question. Structured activity must be available. More-

over, it is not realistic to suppose that people would come in from outside to perform the daily chores of keeping a prison operating—for low wages and at some personal risk.

Some experts have said that prison programs ought to be voluntary. Their philosophical arguments in favor of free choice and against coercion and exploitation are attractive and sound reasonable. But in the face of the realities of prison life—the need to run the prison, the need to occupy time, and the need to give both staff and prisoners hope that life will be better for the inmates after they leave—it is unlikely that prison programs will change in any dramatic way.

Summary

Managing the time of prisoners is one of the major problems of institutional managers. The plain fact is that there are just not enough activities available to keep inmates busy. Idle time allows inmates to behave in ways that are detrimental to the goals of the institution. Rehabilitative, industrial, and maintenance programs are found in all institutions.

Programs are run within the constraints imposed by the need for security and according to the principle of least eligibility. The requirements of custody make certain activities unsuitable in prisons and dictate that tools and other objects that might be used as weapons must be controlled and that programs must be interrupted at intervals for head counts. The principle of least eligibility, according to which people who have violated society's rules should receive no goods or services in excess of those available to persons who live within the law, makes many prison programs controversial. Many goods and services that the state provides to prisoners in the name of rehabilitation are not generally provided without charge to the law-abiding. Should they then be withheld from prisoners?

Classification is a process by which prisoners are grouped according to such considerations as security level, program and housing needs, and reassessment schedule. Classification originated as a diagnostic process to help correctional officers understand the behavioral problems that led an offender to commit a criminal act and as a means to determine which institutional resources could best assist the offender. Unfortunately, studies have shown that organizational needs too often take precedence over the needs of individuals when classification decisions are made.

Rehabilitative programs are designed to help offenders and to act as special deterrents so that the offenders will not return to crime. These programs are psychological, behavioral, vocational, and social in orientation.

Prison industries have always been a part of American corrections; however, organized labor and legislation restricting the sale of prisoner-made products have been serious impediments to their success. Federal efforts have given new life to prison industries in some states and in the U.S. Bureau of Prisons.

Maintenance programs provide the institution with labor and reduce idleness among prisoners. As in other program areas, most institutions find that they have more hands than uses for them.

The role of programs in prisons changes with the nature of the prison population, management goals, and outside influences. As rehabilitation has declined as a goal of corrections, emphasis on programs—with the exception of prison industries—has declined as well.

For Discussion

1. How strictly should the principle of least eligibility be applied? Support your viewpoint.

2. What factors limit the possibility of running prison industries as profit-making ventures? What could be done to improve the profitability of prison industries?

3. Correctional technologies have been said to be of uncertain value. Evaluate rehabilitative programs and determine if some seem to be more effective than others. What reasons might you point to?

4. Should prisoners be forced to participate in programs? What would you do if an inmate did not want to leave the cell?

5. Is a programless prison a possibility?

For Further Reading

Clements, Carl B. *Offender Needs Assessments*. College Park, Md.: American Corrections Association, 1986. A presentation of approaches to assessing and documenting the offenders' needs for services.

Cullen, Francis, and Gilbert, Karen. *Reaffirming Rehabilitation*. Cincinnati, Ohio: Anderson, 1983. A defense of the effectiveness of rehabilitation.

Palmer, Ted. *The Re-emergence of Correctional Intervention*. Newbury Park, Calif.: Sage, 1992. A description and analysis of the most effective strategies for offender treatment.

Ross, Robert, and Fabiano, Elizabeth. *Time to Think: A Cognitive Model of Delinquency Prevention and Offender Rehabilitation*. Johnson City, Tenn.: Institute of Social Science and Art, 1985. A description of the "cognitive restructuring" approach to rehabilitation.

Sechrest, Lee; White, Susan O.; and Brown, Elizabeth, eds. *The Rehabilitation of Offenders: Problems and Prospects*. Washington, D.C.: National Academy of Sciences, 1979. The most comprehensive review of correctional treatment and its effects.

Notes

1. Thomas Harris, *I'm OK, You're OK* (New York: Harper & Rowe, 1960).

2. John Irwin, *The Felon* (Englewood Cliffs, N.J.: Prentice-Hall, 1970), p. 43.

3. National Advisory Commission on Criminal Justice Standards and Goals, *Corrections* (Washington, D.C.: Government Printing Office, 1973), p. 201.

4. Edwin I. Megargee and Martin J. Bohn, Jr., *Classifying Criminal Offenders* (Newbury Park, Calif.: Sage, 1979).

5. Robert E. Doran, "Organizational Stereotyping: The Case of the Adjustment Center Classification

Committee," in *Corrections and Punishment,* ed. David F. Greenberg (Newbury Park, Calif.: Sage, 1977), pp. 41–68.

6. Ramos v. Lamm, 458 F. Supp. 128 (1979).

7. James Austin, "Assessing the New Generation of Prison Classification Models," *Crime and Delinquency* 29 (October 1983): 563.

8. Hans Toch, "Inmate Classification as a Transaction," *Criminal Justice and Behavior* 8 (March 1981): p. 4.

9. James Austin, *Evaluation of Utah Correctional Classification* (San Francisco, Calif.: National Council on Crime and Delinquency, 1981), p. 7.

10. Thomas S. Szasz, *The Myth of Mental Illness* (New York: Harper & Row, 1969), p. 30.

11. Robert Martinson, "What Works? Questions and Answers about Prison Reform," *Public Interest* (Spring 1974): 25.

12. A. E. Bergen, "The Evaluation of Therapeutic Outcomes," in *Handbook of Psychotherapy and Behavior Change,* ed. A. E. Bergen and S. L. Garfield (New York: Wiley, 1971), p. 263.

13. Paul Gendreau and Robert R. Ross, "Revivification of Rehabilitation: Evidence from the 1980s," *Justice Quarterly* 4 (1987): 349–408.

14. Paul Gendreau and Bob Ross, *Effective Correctional Treatment* (Toronto: Butterworths, 1980).

15. Hassim Solomon, *Community Corrections* (Boston: Holbrook, 1976), p. 51.

16. Lloyd Ohlin, Alden O. Miller, and Robert B. Coates, *Juvenile Correctional Reform in Massachusetts* (Washington, D.C.: National Institute for Juvenile Justice and Delinquency Prevention, 1975), p. 36.

17. Douglas Lipton, Robert Martinson, and Judith Wilkes, *The Effectiveness of Correctional Treatment: A Survey of Treatment Evaluation Studies* (New York: Praeger, 1975).

18. Ted Palmer, *The Re-emergence of Correctional Intervention* (Newbury Park, Calif.: Sage, 1992).

19. National Institute of Justice, *Report to the Nation on Crime and Justice* (Washington, D.C.: U.S. Department of Justice, 1988), p. 32.

20. James B. Jacobs, Richard McGavey, and Robert Merio, "Ex-Offender Employment, Recidivism, and Manpower Policy: CETA, TUJTC, and Future Initiatives," *Crime and Delinquency* 30 (October 1984): 487.

21. Daniel Glaser, *The Effectiveness of a Prison and Parole System* (Indianapolis: Bobbs-Merrill, 1961).

22. Ibid., p. 22.

23. L. L. Riskin, "Remaining Impediments to Employment of Work-Release Prisoners," *Criminal Law Bulletin* 8 (1972): 761–64.

24. Todd R. Clear, Bruce D. Stout, Harry S. Dammer, Linda L. Kelly, Patricia L. Hardyman, and Carol A. Shapiro, *Prisoners, Prisons, and Religion* (Final Report, Rutgers University, Newark, N.J., November 1992).

25. Francis Cullen and Karen Gilbert, *Reaffirming Rehabilitation* (Cincinnati, Ohio: Anderson, 1982).

26. Don A. Andrews, Ivan Zinger, Robert D. Hodge, James Bonta, Paule Gendreau, and Francis Cullen, "Does Correctional Treatment Work? A Clinically Relevant and Psychologically Informed Meta-Analysis," *Criminology* 28(3) (1990): 369–429.

27. John T. Whitehead and Steven Lab, "A Meta-Analysis of Juvenile Correctional Treatment," *Journal of Research on Crime and Delinquency* 26 (1989): 276–95.

28. Martin B. Miller, "At Hard Labor: Rediscovering the Nineteenth-Century Prison," *Issues in Criminology* 9 (Spring 1974): 91.

29. John A. Conley, "Prisons, Production, and Profit: Reconsidering the Importance of Prison Industries," *Journal of Social History* 14 (1980): 257.

30. See, for example, John A. Conley, "Revising Conceptions About the Origin of Prisons: The Importance of Economic Considerations," *Journal of Social History* 22 (1980): 257.

31. Gordon Hawkins, "Prison Labor and Prison Industries," in *Crime and Justice,* ed. Michael Tonry and Norval Morris (Chicago: University of Chicago Press, 1983), p. 91.

14

Prisoners' Rights

*There is no iron curtain
drawn between the
Constitution and the prisons
of this country.*

Wolff v. *McDonnell,* 1974

The End of the Hands-Off Policy
The Foundations of Prisoners' Rights
The Constitution of the United States
State Constitutions
State Statutes
Federal Statutes
Constitutional Rights
First Amendment
Fourth Amendment
Eighth Amendment
Fourteenth Amendment
A Slowing of the Pace?
The Problem of Compliance
Prisoner Litigation: The Best Route?
Alternatives to Litigation
Inmate Grievance Procedures
The Ombudsman
Mediation
Legal Assistance
The Impact of the Prisoners' Rights Movement
Summary

During the early morning hours of October 30, 1983, Keith Hudson, an inmate at the State Penitentiary, Angola, Louisiana, was washing clothes in his cell toilet. Jack McMillian, a correctional officer, came to the cell, used racially abusive language, and told Hudson to stop flushing the toilet and go to sleep. Believing that he was doing nothing wrong, Hudson kept doing his laundry. An argument ensued. McMillian, assisted by officers Marvin Woods and Arthur Mezo, seized Hudson, placed him in handcuffs and shackles, and walked him toward the penitentiary's administrative lockdown area known as the "dungeon." Hudson later testified that on the way McMillian pushed him up against the wall and punched him in the mouth, eyes, chest, and stomach while Woods held him in place and kicked and punched him from behind.

"Hold him," McMillian told Woods. "Let me knock his gold teeth out."

As Hudson was being assaulted, Officer Mezo, the supervisor on duty, is alleged to have said, "Don't have too much fun!" The pummeling split Hudson's lip, broke his dental plate, and left him "bleeding and swelling about the body."

Keith Hudson sued the three corrections officers in the federal district court alleging that his rights under the Eighth Amendment's prohibition of cruel and unusual punishments had been violated. A magistrate found for Hudson and awarded him $800. However, the U.S. Court of Appeals for the Fifth Circuit reversed this decision, holding the Eighth Amendment did not apply since Hudson's injuries were minor and no medical attention was required.

With the persistence of a jailhouse lawyer devoted to his cause, Hudson appealed that decision to the U.S. Supreme Court; in a seven-to-two decision, the Court agreed with the inmate. Writing for the majority, Justice Sandra Day O'Connor said, "When prison officials maliciously and sadistically use force to cause harm, contemporary standards of decency always are violated. This is true whether or not significant injury is evident."[1]

The fact that the U.S. Supreme Court heard an inmate's case and intervened in the operation of a state prison is fairly new to American corrections. Only since the 1960s have federal courts reviewed prisoner civil rights claims. Traditionally, the separation of powers among the executive, legislative, and judicial branches of government has been presumed to prevent the courts from intervening in the operations of any executive agency. Thus judges accepted the notion that because they were not penologists, their intervention in the internal administration of prisons would be disruptive of prison discipline. They also accepted the view that prisoners do not have the same rights as free citizens under the Constitution. This belief was well stated by a Virginia judge in *Ruffin* v. *Commonwealth* (1871): "The prisoner has, as a consequence of his crime, not only forfeited his liberty, but all his personal rights except those which the law in its humanity accords to him. He is for the time being the slave of the state."[2]

Since the late 1960s the courts have become increasingly involved in prison matters. Not only have judges responded to claims by inmates that their rights have been violated, but judges have gone so far as to declare entire correctional systems to be operating in ways that violate the Constitution. In part, the courts' increased involvement must be credited to the civil rights movement of the 1960s and the efforts since the end of World War II to bring about a fundamental democratization of American society. Like the movements to bring nonwhite minorities, women, children, gays, the handicapped, the aged, and mental patients into the societal mainstream, the pressure for policies to advance the rights of inmates was an "effort to redefine the status (moral, political, as well as legal) of prisoners in a democratic society."[3]

The End of the Hands-Off Policy

The 1964 decision of the U.S. Supreme Court in *Cooper* v. *Pate,* stating that prisoners in state and local institutions are entitled to the protections of the Civil Rights Act of 1871, signaled the end of the traditional **hands-off policy.**[4] In that case the justices ruled that a prisoner could sue a warden or other official under Title 42 of the United States Code, section 1983 (42 U.S.C. 1983), which imposes **civil liability** on any person who deprives another of constitutional rights.

As a result of this ruling, the Court now recognized that prisoners are *persons* whose rights are protected by the Constitution, and prisoners could use the federal courts to challenge the conditions of their confinement in both state and federal institutions. As Jacobs points out, "Just by opening a forum in which prisoners' grievances could be heard, the federal courts destroyed the custodian's absolute power and the prisoners' isolation from the larger society. And the litigation in itself heightened prisoners' consciousness and politicized them."[5]

The amount of prisoner-inspired litigation in the courts skyrocketed after *Cooper* v. *Pate.* The number of suits brought by state prisoners and pending in federal courts rose from 218 in 1966 to a high of 20,346 in 1987.[6] Additional cases, of course, are filed in state courts arguing infringement of rights guaranteed by the constitutions and laws of the various states; but prisoners, like other marginal groups, have generally looked to the federal courts to protect their rights.

The Supreme Court has ruled that inmates must have access to information about the law. Much of the increase in prisoner suits under 42 U.S.C. 1983 may be attributed to this ruling.

The first successful cases concerning prisoners' rights involved the most excessive of prison abuses: brutality and inhuman physical conditions. In 1967, for example, the Supreme Court invalidated the confession of a Florida inmate who had been thrown naked into a "barren cage," filthy with human excrement, and kept there for thirty-five days.[7] Gradually, prisoner litigation has come to focus more directly on the daily activities of the institution, especially on the administrative rules governing inmates' conduct.

In 1969 the Supreme Court ruled in *Johnson* v. *Avery* that prison officials could not prohibit one inmate from acting as a jailhouse lawyer for another inmate unless the state provided the inmate with free counsel to pursue a claim that rights had been denied.[8] This was followed in 1977 by *Bounds* v. *Smith* in which the court required that inmates have access to law libraries or the help of persons trained in the law.[9] Such organizations as the American Civil Liberties Union's National Prison Project and the National Association for the Advancement of

hands-off policy A judicial policy of noninterference in the internal administration of prisons.

civil liability Responsibility for the provision of monetary or other compensation awarded to a plaintiff in a civil action.

Colored People's Legal Defense Fund became concerned about prisoners' rights as an issue. These forces not only expanded the legal protections of inmates but created a climate conducive to lawsuits. It was no longer unheard-of for prisoners to sue wardens or commissioners of corrections.[10]

The Civil Rights Act has been a tool for protecting and enforcing the constitutional rights of prisoners and those detained to await trial. By bringing actions in the federal courts, primarily under 42 U.S.C. 1983, state and local prisoners have sought relief from such abuses as brutality by guards, inadequate nutrition and medical care, theft of personal property, victimization by other inmates, and restrictions on religious freedom, among many others. The sheer volume of these filings places heavy burdens on the federal judiciary, state attorneys general, and correctional administrators. However, recent Supreme Court decisions suggest that the courts' willingness to intervene in such cases may not be limitless. Beginning in 1981 the Court announced a series of decisions that have considerably weakened the provisions of 42 U.S.C. 1983.[11]

The Foundations of Prisoners' Rights

T he legal rights of persons confined in correctional institutions rest on four basic foundations: (1) the U.S. Constitution, (2) the constitution of the state in which the institution is located, (3) state statutes and regulations, and (4) federal statutes and regulations. Most correctional litigation has involved rights claimed under the U.S. Constitution. Most state constitutions generally parallel the U.S. Constitution but sometimes confer other rights. Over and above these constitutional minimums, legislatures are of course free to grant additional rights to inmates and to authorize corrections departments to promulgate regulations that give the rights sub-

stance. Federal law generally affects only federal correctional institutions, although certain statutes, such as the Civil Rights Act of 1871, give state inmates the right to bring suits in the federal courts.

The Constitution of the United States

The constitutional rights of persons living in the United States are not completely lost when they are convicted of a crime or sentenced to prison. However, the courts have emphasized that some rights may be abridged when they are outweighed by legitimate governmental interests and when the restriction imposed is no greater than necessary to accomplish those limited objectives. The three specific interests that the courts have recognized as justifying some abridgment of the constitutional rights of prisoners are (1) the maintenance of institutional order, (2) the maintenance of institutional security, and (3) the rehabilitation of inmates. *Order* refers to calm and discipline within the institution; *security* refers to the control of individuals and objects entering or leaving the institution; and *rehabilitation* refers to practices necessary for the health, well-being, and treatment of inmates. Whether or not these interests are implicated in a given situation and whether or not the proposed restriction is greater than necessary to preserve them are questions of fact that must be determined on a case-by-case basis. Thus the development of a body of correctional law has essentially been based on efforts to balance these legitimate interests against the specific rights enumerated in the Constitution.

State Constitutions

The courts of each state are empowered to declare correctional conditions and practices in violation of either the state or the federal constitution, but most inmates choose to file their claims in federal courts. Inmates generally seem to perceive that federal judges are more

The first amendment to the Constitution provides for the free exercise of religious practices. The Black Muslims have been a major factor in forcing correctional administrators to recognize that right.

attentive to such petitions, and the procedures for filing such claims are usually easier to follow. While most state constitutions do not give inmates any greater rights than those granted by the U.S. Constitution, others may. Provisions of the California and Oregon constitutions are increasingly cited as the bases for state court claims challenging conditions of confinement. A California court, for example, has ruled that electronic surveillance of prisoners violates the privacy guarantees of state statutes; in Oregon it has been ruled that the state constitutional guarantee against "unnecessary rigor" in correctional practices provides grounds to enjoin certain genital searches.[12]

State Statutes

State legislatures are free to grant specific rights to inmates beyond those conferred by the state constitutions or the U.S. Constitution. Some state statutes have been held to create "liberty interests" that cannot be denied without due process of law. Some states have also enacted "right to treatment" legislation and other statutes that charge correctional officials with particular duties. Prisoners may bring state tort claims against officials who fail to fulfill their statutory duties and obligations. If such claims

are upheld, inmates may be entitled to collect monetary damages from the responsible officials and/or to receive injunctive relief.

Federal Statutes

Just as state statutes and regulations may create a "liberty interest" for state prisoners, federal laws and regulations may create similar interests for federal prisoners. In addition, some statutes passed by Congress have a direct bearing on prisoners held by the states. As noted earlier in this chapter, *Cooper* v. *Pate* (1964) established that inmates have protections under the Civil Rights Act of 1871. This act allows state prisoners to challenge conditions of their confinement in the federal rather than the state courts. Most suits brought under this act have involved allegations of the deprivation of one or more rights guaranteed by the U.S. Constitution.

Constitutional Rights

A multitude of constitutional claims are filed by prisoners, yet the constitutional rights applicable to inmates are essentially summarized in a handful of phrases in just four of the amendments to the Constitution. Three of these—the First, Fourth, and Eighth Amendments—are contained within the Bill of Rights (the first ten amendments to the Constitution) and became effective on December 15, 1791. The fourth, the Fourteenth Amendment, became effective on July 28, 1868. In this section, we'll present the text of those amendments and discuss rights under them in some detail.

First Amendment

Amendment I: Congress shall make no law respecting an establishment of religion, or prohibiting the free exercise thereof; or abridging the freedom of speech, or of the press; or the right of the people peaceably to assemble, and to petition the government for a redress of grievances.

Beginning with a group of cases decided in the 1940s, the Supreme Court has maintained that the First Amendment holds a special position in the Bill of Rights. The First Amendment guarantees freedom of speech, press, assembly, petition, and religion, all deemed essential to our democracy. Given the preferred position of this amendment, it is not surprising that some of the early prisoners' rights decisions concerned rights protected by it: access to reading materials, censorship of mail, and religious practices. Some of the more significant cases decided under this amendment are shown in Table 14.1.

Since the 1970s the federal and state courts have extended the rights of freedom of speech and expression to prisoners and have required correctional administrators to show why restrictions on these rights must be imposed. For example, in 1974 the Court said that censorship of mail could be allowed only when there is a substantial governmental interest in maintaining security. The result has been markedly increased communications between inmates and the outside world.

The courts have held that the concepts of **least restrictive methods, compelling state interest,** and **clear and present danger** set the boundaries between speech that is protected and speech that is not. Thus when officials have proved that an inmate poses a threat to himself or herself, other inmates, or the staff, courts have supported institutional rules that restrict the rights enumerated in the First and other amendments. A rule prohibiting the receiving of nude photographs of wives and girlfriends, for example, has been found unconstitutional. The court ruled that the right to receive such photographs was protected; since, however, other inmates might be aroused by the sight of them, a rule against their display would have been proper.[13] Similarly, a court has also struck down the practice of punishing inmates for writing inflammatory political tracts because officials could merely have confiscated the material.[14] However, in the recent case of *Turner* v. *Safley,* the Court upheld a Missouri ban on correspondence between inmates. Justice O'Connor, writing for a five-to-four majority, said that such a prison regulation was valid if it was "reasonably related to legitimate penological interests."[15]

The First Amendment also prevents Congress from making laws respecting the establishment of religion or prohibiting its free exercise. The history of the Supreme Court's interpretation of this clause has been long and complex. Although religion has been described as an important tool for rehabilitation, the courts have been cautious in applying the clause to the prison setting. Although freedom of belief has not been challenged, claims concerning the free exercise of religion have caused

---

least restrictive methods   Means of ensuring a legitimate state interest (such as security) that impose fewer limits to prisoners' First Amendment rights than alternative means of securing that end.

compelling state interest   An interest of the state that must take precedence over rights guaranteed by the First Amendment.

clear and present danger   Any threat to security or to the safety of individuals that is so obvious and compelling that the need to counter it overrides the guarantees of the First Amendment.

Table 14.1 ■ Selected Interpretations of the First Amendment as Applied to Prisoners. The Supreme Court has made numerous decisions affecting prisoners' rights to freedom of speech and expression and freedom of religion.

Case	Decision
Procunier v. *Martinez* (1974)	Censorship of mail is permitted only to the extent necessary to maintain prison security.
Turner v. *Safley* (1987)	Inmates do not have a right to receive mail from one another, and this mail can be banned if "reasonably related to legitimate penological interests."
Saxbe v. *Washington Post* (1974)	Rules prohibiting individual interviews with members of the press are justified to prevent some inmates from enhancing their reputations.
Theriault v. *Carlson* (1977)	The First Amendment does not protect so-called religions that are obvious shams, that tend to mock established institutions, and whose members lack religious sincerity.
Gittlemacker v. *Prasse* (1970)	The state must give inmates the opportunity to practice their religion but is not required to provide a member of the clergy.
O'Lone v. *Estate of Shabazz* (1987)	The rights of Muslim prisoners are not violated when work assignments make it impossible for them to attend religious services if no alternative exists.
Kahane v. *Carlson* (1975)	An orthodox Jewish inmate has the right to a diet consistent with his religious beliefs unless the government can show cause why it cannot be provided.
Fulwood v. *Clemmer* (1962)	The Muslim faith must be recognized as a religion and officials may not restrict members from holding services.
Cruz v. *Beto* (1972)	Prisoners who adhere to other than conventional beliefs may not be denied the opportunity to practice their religion.

the judiciary some problems, especially when the practice in question may interfere with institutional routine. In addition, the Court has ruled that administrators must first ascertain whether inmates are sincere in the beliefs they profess and whether the purported religion, with its associated practices, is in fact a religion at all.

The growth of the Black Muslim religion in prisons set the stage for suits demanding that this group be granted the same privileges as those extended to adherents of other faiths: special diets, access to clergy and religious publications, opportunities for group worship. In the 1970s many prison administrators believed that the Muslims were primarily a radical political group posing as a religion, and they denied them the benefits extended to prisoners who practiced conventional religions.

In an early case (*Fulwood* v. *Clemmer*, 1962), the U.S. District Court for the District of Columbia ruled that correctional officials must recognize the Muslim faith as a religion and not restrict members' rights to hold services. It did not accept the view of the commissioner of corrections that the Muslims were a "clear and present danger."[16] In another prisoner religion case, *Cruz* v. *Beto* (1972), the justices declared that it was discriminatory and a violation of the Constitution to deny a Buddhist prisoner opportunities to practice his faith comparable to those given to fellow prisoners who belonged to religions more commonly practiced in the United States.[17]

Muslims and other prisoners have succeeded in gaining some of the rights they consider necessary for the practice of their religions. No widely accepted judicial doctrine exists in this area, however, and courts have varied in their willingness to order institutional policies changed to meet Muslim requests. Court deci-

The Supreme Court has not extended the right against unreasonable searches and seizures to prisoners.

sions have upheld the right to be served meals consistent with religious dietary laws, to correspond with religious leaders and possess religious literature, to wear a beard if one's religious belief requires it, and to assemble for religious services. This one religious minority has broken new legal ground in matters related to both the First Amendment and other constitutional issues.

Fourth Amendment

Amendment IV: The right of the people to be secure in their persons, houses, papers, and effects, against unreasonable searches and seizures, shall not be violated, and no warrants shall issue but upon probable cause, supported by oath or affirmation, and particularly describing the place to be searched, and the persons or things to be seized.

Upon entering a correctional institution, prisoners surrender most of their rights under the Fourth Amendment. The amendment prohibits only *unreasonable* searches and seizures, not all such practices that are required to maintain an institution's security and order. The courts have not been active in extending Fourth Amendment protections to prisoners; the decision in *Hudson* v. *Palmer* (1984) sanctioned the right of officials to search cells and confiscate any materials found there.[18]

As in the cases of other constitutional protections, the Supreme Court's Fourth Amendment opinions, some of which are outlined in Table 14.2, reveal the fine balance between the right to privacy and institutional need. Body searches have been harder for administrators to justify than cell searches, for example, but they have been upheld when they have been part of a clear policy demonstrably related to an identifiable legitimate institutional need and not conducted with the intent to humiliate or degrade.[19] Courts have ruled that staff members of one sex may not supervise inmates of the opposite sex during bathing, use of the toilet, or strip searches.[20] Here the inconvenience of ensuring that the supervisor is of the same sex as the inmate does not justify the intrusion. Yet the right of female guards to "pat down" male prisoners, excluding the genital area, has been upheld.[21] These cases illustrate the lack of clear-cut constitutional principles in regard to the right to privacy when institutional need is at stake.

Eighth Amendment

Amendment VIII: Excessive bail shall not be required, nor excessive fines imposed, nor cruel and unusual punishments inflicted.

The Constitution's prohibition of cruel and unusual punishments has been tied to prisoners' need for decent treatment and minimal health

Table 14.2 ■ **Selected Interpretations of the Fourth Amendment as Applied to Prisoners.** The Supreme Court has often considered the question of unreasonable searches and seizures.

Case	Decision
Bell v. *Wolfish* (1979)	Strip searches, including searches of body cavities after contact visits, may be carried out when the need for such searches outweighs the personal rights invaded.
Lee v. *Downs* (1981)	Staff members of one sex may not supervise inmates of the opposite sex in toilet and shower areas even if provision of a staff member of the same sex is inconvenient to the administration.
United States v. *Hitchcock* (1972)	A warrantless search of a cell is not unreasonable, and documentary evidence found there is not subject to suppression in court. It is not reasonable to expect a prison cell to be accorded the same level of privacy as a home or automobile.
Hudson v. *Palmer* (1984)	Officials may search cells without a warrant and seize materials found there.

standards during their confinement. Three principal tests have been applied by the courts under the Eighth Amendment to determine whether conditions are unconstitutional: whether the punishment shocks the general conscience of a civilized society; whether the punishment is unnecessarily cruel; and whether the punishment goes beyond legitimate penal aims.

These are rather vague guidelines, but they have been used to designate as unconstitutional such practices as corporal punishment, physical abuse by guards, inadequate diet, and overcrowding. More typical, however, has been the courts' use of the concept of **totality of conditions** to declare an institution to be in violation of the Eighth Amendment. This concept developed with the 1976 decision in *Pugh* v. *Locke*, in which Federal District Court Judge Frank M. Johnson, Jr., found that "the evidence … establishes that prison conditions [in Alabama] are so debilitating that they neces-

---

totality of conditions The aggregate of circumstances in a correctional facility that, when considered as a whole, may violate the protections guaranteed by the Eighth Amendment, even though such guarantees are not violated by any single condition in the institution.

sarily deprive inmates of any opportunity to rehabilitate themselves or even maintain skills already possessed."[22]

In an earlier suit a federal court cited the notorious Cummins Farm Unit of the Arkansas State Penitentiary as being in violation of the Eighth Amendment. This case was the basis for the 1980 film *Brubaker,* in which Robert Redford played the role of the reform warden Tom Murton. The federal court found that brutal punishments were administered for minor offenses. The court also cited the use of inmates as prison guards and said that prisoners had a constitutional right of protection by the state while they were incarcerated. As the judges noted, a system that relies on trusties for security and that houses inmates in barracks, leaving them open to "frequent assaults, murder, rape, and homosexual conduct," is unconstitutional.[23] Judicial supervision of the Texas prison system as a result of this case lasted for a decade and ended on March 31, 1990.

In *Hutto* v. *Finney* (1978) the Supreme Court upheld a lower court's decision that confinement in Arkansas's segregation cells for more than thirty days was cruel and unusual. In that decision the Court also summarized three principles with regard to the Eighth Amendment:

Table 14.3 ■ **Selected Interpretations of the Eighth Amendment as Applied to Prisoners.** The Supreme Court is called on to determine whether corrections' actions constitute cruel and unusual punishments.

Case	Decision
Estelle v. *Gamble* (1976)	Deliberate indifference to serious medical needs of prisoners constitutes the unnecessary and wanton infliction of pain, and thus violates the Eighth Amendment.
Rhodes v. *Chapman* (1981)	Double celling and crowding do not necessarily constitute cruel and unusual punishment. It must be shown that the conditions involve "wanton and unnecessary infliction of pain" and are "grossly disproportionate" to the severity of the crime warranting imprisonment.
Whitley v. *Albers* (1986)	A prisoner shot in the leg during a riot does not suffer cruel and unusual punishment if the action was taken in good faith to maintain discipline rather than for the mere purpose of causing harm.
Ruiz v. *Estelle* (1975)	Conditions of confinement in the Texas prison system were unconstitutional.

1. Courts should consider the totality of conditions of confinement.

2. Courts should specify in remedial orders each factor that contributed to the violation and that required a change in order to remove the unconstitutionality.

3. Where appropriate, courts should enunciate specific minimum standards that if met would remedy the total constitutional violation.[24]

The Court has also indicated, however, that unless certain conditions are found, the courts must defer to correctional officials and legislators. Yet the Court has intervened in many states where the general conditions of the institutions or specific aspects of their operation have been found to be in violation of the Eighth Amendment; some examples are outlined in Table 14.3.

Of particular concern to correctional officials have been court orders requiring an end to overcrowding in violation of the Eighth Amendment. Among the conditions that the courts have found to violate the Constitution is the crowding of inmates into cells that afford each person less than sixty square feet of floor space (see Figure 14.1). However, the Supreme Court upheld double celling (housing two inmates in a cell) in Ohio as not constituting a condition of cruel and unusual punishment.[25] In other cases, courts have ruled overcrowded conditions to be unconstitutional and have issued orders requiring that space be increased or prison population decreased. These orders have come at a time when the size of prison populations has skyrocketed in most states.

Many conditions that violate the rights of prisoners may be remedied by administrative action, training programs, or a minimal expenditure of funds, but overcrowding requires an expansion of facilities or a dropping of the intake rate. Prison officials have no control over the sizes of their institutions or the numbers of offenders sent to them by the courts. New facilities are expensive, take time to build, require appropriations by legislatures, and often must be approved by voters in bond referendums. In some states a reduction in prison overcrowding has only increased the size of jail populations. In states that have undertaken building programs, the number of new cells has been outpaced by the number of new prisoners.

Fourteenth Amendment

Amendment XIV: All persons born or naturalized in the United States, and subject to

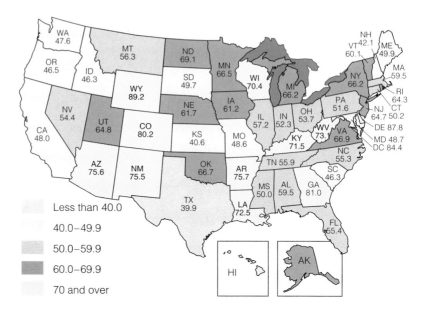

Figure 14.1 ■ **Average Square Footage Allotted to State Prison Inmates Shown by State.** The amount of space allotted to each inmate varies by state. Can you imagine living in a space that is less than sixty square feet?

Source: U.S. Department of Justice, Bureau of Justice Statistics, *Report to the Nation on Crime and Justice*, 2nd ed. (Washington, D.C.: Government Printing Office, 1988), p. 108.

the jurisdiction thereof, are citizens of the United States and of the state wherein they reside. No state shall make or enforce any law which shall abridge the privileges or immunities of citizens of the United States; nor shall any state deprive any person of life, liberty, or property without due process of law, nor deny to any person within its jurisdiction the equal protection of the laws.

Two clauses of the Fourteenth Amendment are relevant to the question of prisoners' rights: those requiring **(procedural) due process** and **equal protection.** This area of the law produced a great amount of litigation in the 1970s. The statutes of many states provide inmates with certain protections with regard to

due process (procedural) The constitutional guarantee that no agent or instrumentality of government will use any procedures to arrest, prosecute, try, or punish any person other than those procedures prescribed by law.

equal protection The constitutional guarantee that the law will be applied equally to all persons, without regard for such individual characteristics as gender, race, and religion.

parole release, intraprison transfers, transfers to administrative segregation, and disciplinary hearings. With regard to due process, however, the Supreme Court has been more cautious in recent years.

Due process in prison discipline Administrative discretion in determining disciplinary procedures can usually be exercised within the prison walls without challenge. The prisoner is physically confined, lacks communication with the outside, and is legally in the hands of the state. Further, either formal codes stating the rules of prison conduct do not exist, or the rules are written vaguely. Disrespect toward a correctional officer, for example, may be called an infraction of the rules but not be defined. Normally, disciplinary action is taken on the word of the correctional officer, and the inmate has little opportunity to challenge the charges.

In a series of decisions made in the 1970s, the Supreme Court began to insist that procedural fairness be part of the most sensitive of institutional decisions: the processes by which inmates are sent to solitary confinement and the methods by which good time credit may be lost because of misconduct.

Table 14.4 ■ **Selected Interpretations of the Fourteenth Amendment as Applied to Prisoners.** The Supreme Court has ruled concerning procedural due process and equal protection.

Case	Decision
Baxter v. *Palmigiano* (1976)	Although due process must be accorded, an inmate has no right to counsel in a disciplinary hearing.
United States v. *Bailey* (1980)	An inmate who seeks to justify an escape from prison on the grounds of duress or necessity for self-protection must show having attempted to surrender to an authority.
Wolff v. *McDonnell* (1974)	The basic elements of procedural due process must be present when decisions are made concerning the disciplining of an inmate.

In the 1974 case of *Wolff* v. *McDonnell,* certain due process rights were extended to prisoners.[26] The Supreme Court specified that when a prisoner faces serious disciplinary action that may result in the withdrawal of good time or in segregation, the state must follow certain minimal procedures that conform to the guarantee of due process:

■ The prisoner must be given twenty-four-hour written notice of the charges.

■ The prisoner has the right to present witnesses and documentary evidence in defense against the charges.

■ The prisoner has the right to a hearing before an impartial body.

■ The prisoner has the right to receive a written statement from that body concerning the outcome of the hearing.

The Court did, however, recognize the special conditions of incarceration and said that prisoners do not have the right to cross-examine witnesses and that the evidence presented by the offender may not be unduly hazardous to institutional safety or correctional goals. It noted the special problems associated with the prison environment, "where tension is unremitting [and] frustration, resentment, and despair are commonplace."[27]

As a result of the Supreme Court's decisions, some of which are outlined in Table 14.4, most prisons have established rules that provide some elements of due process in disciplinary proceedings. In many institutions, a disciplinary committee receives charges, conducts hearings, and decides guilt and punishment. Such committees are usually made up of administrative personnel, but sometimes inmates or citizens from the outside are included. Even with these protections, prisoners are still powerless and may risk further punishment if they challenge the warden's disciplinary decisions too vigorously.

Equal protection Institutional practices or conditions that discriminate against prisoners on the basis of race or religion have been held unconstitutional. In 1968 the Supreme Court firmly established that racial discrimination may not be official policy within prison walls.[28] Racial segregation is justifiable only as a temporary expedient during periods when violence between the races is demonstrably imminent. Equal protection claims have also been upheld in relation to religious freedoms and access to reading materials of interest to blacks.

A Slowing of the Pace?

During the early years of the prisoners' rights movement, noteworthy victories were won primarily in federal district and circuit courts. As noted earlier in this chapter, the Supreme Court did issue a significant decision in *Cooper* v.

Pate (1964), which allowed prisoners to sue state officials under the Civil Rights Act, but it was not until 1974, in *Wolff* v. *McDonnell,* that the Court "finally provided the kind of clarion statement that could serve as a rallying call for prisoners' rights advocates."[29] In that case Justice Byron White, speaking for the court, said:

> [The State of Nebraska] asserts that the procedure for disciplining prison inmates for serious misconduct is a matter of policy raising no constitutional issue. If the position implies that prisoners in state institutions are wholly without the protection of the Constitution and the Due Process Clause, it is plainly untenable. Lawful imprisonment necessarily makes unavailable many rights and privileges of the ordinary citizen, a retraction justified by the considerations underlying our penal system.... But though his rights may be diminished by the needs and exigencies of the institutional environment, a prisoner is not wholly stripped of constitutional protections when he is imprisoned for crime.[30]

This language and the language contained in the Court's decisions in several cases that followed gave a symbolic lift to the movement. It gave prisoners' rights advocates the feeling that the Supreme Court was backing their efforts.

Close examination of the opinions, however, reveals that the justices did not want to impose strict restrictions on prison officials. In *Wolff,* for example, they concluded that procedural safeguards did not apply even when inmates were placed in solitary confinement and lost good time. They limited the procedural rights to receiving written notice of the alleged violation, calling witnesses and presenting evidence, and receiving a written statement justifying the actions taken. The Court emphasized that prisons are a dangerous environment and that it would defer to officials' expertise in running them and pursuing correctional goals.

Beginning in 1979 with *Bell* v. *Wolfish* and followed by *Rhodes* v. *Chapman* (1981), the Court, under the leadership of Chief Justice Rehnquist, has indicated that it wishes to slow the expansion of rights, if not to return to the hands-off policy. In *Bell,* detainees held for the federal government in the newly constructed Metropolitan Correctional Center in New York City objected to double celling, restrictions against receiving hardcover books from publishers and bookstores, and strip searches. In their six-to-three decision, the justices not only addressed the issues presented but went further by rejecting the "compelling necessity" test; they said that the question was whether the particular restrictions were intended as punishment or as an "incident of some other legitimate governmental purpose." In addition, the Court seems to have taken great pains to communicate its belief in the need for judicial deference to prison officials: "Prison administrators ... should be accorded wide-ranging deference in the adoption and executing of policies."[31]

In *Rhodes* v. *Chapman,* prisoners challenged the double celling at the Ohio maximum security prison on the grounds that it constituted cruel and unusual punishment, in violation of the Eighth Amendment. They argued that the celling policy was especially bad because it involved long-term prisoners, the population size was beyond capacity, and prisoners had to stay in their cells most of the time. Although the lower courts ruled in favor of the prisoners, the Supreme Court reversed the ruling, holding that the conditions fell short of those that constitute cruel and unusual punishment. To prove violation of the Eighth Amendment, it must be shown that the punishment either "inflicts unnecessary or wanton pain" or is "grossly disproportionate to the severity of the crime warranting punishment." The Court said that in the Ohio situation these conditions did not exist because the prisoners were not being deprived of such essentials as food and medical care. Unless the conditions were "deplorable" or "sordid," the Court declared, the courts should defer to correctional authorities.[32]

The opinions in several cases that limit the ability of prisoners to sue correctional officials indicate that the present members of the Supreme Court are less sympathetic to civil rights claims than earlier justices. In particular, the Court ruled in 1986 that prisoners could sue for damages in federal court only if officials had inflicted injury intentionally or deliberately.[33] The chief justice wrote for the majority that "the due process clause is simply not implicated by a negligent act of an official causing unintended loss or injury to life, liberty, or property." He said that the due process clause was put into the Constitution only to prevent an "abuse of power" by public officials and that "lack of due care" or carelessness is not included. This reasoning was extended in the 1991 case of *Wilson* v. *Seiter* when the court said that the standard for the review of official conduct is whether the state policies or actions by correctional officers constitute "deliberate indifference" to constitutional rights.[34] Many scholars believe that this indicates a switch in the court from the use of objective criteria (i.e., totality of conditions) to subjective criteria (i.e., the state of mind of correctional officials) to decide if prison conditions are unconstitutional. This may result in prisons not fit for human habitation being able to avoid judicial intervention.[35]

In addition, the emergence of the doctrine that "due deference" must be given to penologists to run their prisons has struck some observers as a return to the hands-off doctrine dropped by the court in the 1960s.[36] Yet the justices seem to distinguish the two doctrines, expressing a willingness to hear cases involving substantive rights issues but being unwilling to intervene in problems of administration. This distinction is explained in a 1985 federal circuit opinion: "In the great majority of cases it would be sheer folly for society to deny prison officials discretion to act in accordance with their professional judgment. At the same time it would be abrogation of our responsibility as judges to assume such judgments (or, more precisely, to reassume) a 'hands-off' posture, requiring categorical acquiescence in such judgments."[37]

That the pace of prisoners' rights cases may be slowed even further is indicated by *McCleskey* v. *Zant* (1991) limiting access to the federal courts. Here, the Court ruled that all habeas claims must be raised in the initial petition.[38] Also in *Coleman* v. *Thompson* the Court said that a prisoner's appeal should not be granted even when there were violations of state procedural rules committed through attorney error.[39] Thus, although prisoners have a right to access to the courts via law libraries and the assistance of fellow inmates, the reality is that access has been diminished, especially for those prisoners who lack counsel and are likely to be tripped up by the stricter procedural rules.

The pace of civil rights litigation as experienced under the Warren and Burger Courts has definitely been slowed. Litigation by prisoners continues, but victories are less frequent. It would seem that the justices have carved out a portion of the Bill of Rights that is applicable to prisoners and, having done that, are not interested in expanding that area.

Although the Supreme Court may be cooler toward prisoners' rights claims, the lower federal courts and many state courts continue to support judicial intervention to uphold civil rights. A return to the hands-off policy does not seem possible, yet greater deference is being given to prison administrators.

The Problem of Compliance

From the beginning of the United States it has been recognized that the courts, including the Supreme Court, are in a difficult political position because they possess the power of neither the "purse nor the sword." In our system of separation of powers and of federalism, the courts, in the final analysis, depend on the legislative and executive bodies of the state and national governments to implement their decisions. As a result, these political bodies can compromise or defy judicial orders for years, so that the Court's intention is often thwarted.

In the field of corrections, the courts are in a dilemma. They are charged with upholding the Constitution, yet they are unable to appropriate funds to carry out remedial actions or to manage the day-to-day operations of correctional facilities. Although some states have resisted judicial orders, the courts have managed to close institutions, release inmates, place entire correctional systems in receivership, and appoint special masters to monitor compliance with their orders. These actions have led critics to charge that an "imperial judiciary" has intervened in the rightful prerogatives of the executive and legislative branches in this important area of public policy.

The cost of implementing guaranteed rights as a result of court orders can range from as little as $5 million for some county governments to as much as $1 billion or more for some state governments.[40] As a result, correctional officials are caught between legislators who do not want to increase taxes, the political unpopularity of prison reform, and judicial pressures to make institutional conditions conform to the Constitution. Yet judges have not accepted financial constraints as an excuse for failure to comply with their order: "Shortage of funds is not a justification for continuing to deny citizens their constitutional rights."[41]

The greatest difficulty in complying with judicial orders is overcrowding. Some courts have ruled double celling to be unconstitutional; others have ordered the minimum size of cells to be increased. Many states are engaged in an institutional building boom. Construction takes time, however, and as we noted earlier, the intake of new prisoners has often outrun the number of new cells. The situation has also produced a conflict for many advocates of prison reform, such as the American Civil Liberties Union, who want improvements in prison conditions but also favor a moratorium on new construction in the belief that new cells will only expand the size of the incarcerated population.

Given the politics of corrections, it comes as no surprise that some correctional officials appear to be secretly pleased by judicial intervention and look upon the judges as their allies in the struggle for increased budgets. As noted by Harriman and Straussman, courts *have* affected state spending for corrections in that there have been increases in budgets following judicial decisions.[42]

The state budgetary process is not simply a rational allocation of resources to meet needs; it is a political scramble by competing groups for what they consider their fair share of the fiscal pie. Administrators in the areas of education, law enforcement, and most other public services can look to some groups in the community for support and can expect certain legislators to vote for their interests. Corrections unfortunately cannot create groups that will lobby for its interest—there is no "prison vote." Religious and other humanitarian groups may periodically support prison reform, but former prisoners seldom form alliances with corrections, and tax increases to pay for better prisons are not popular. But judicial intervention has been the catalyst for increased funding in many states. Governors and legislators are able to provide new funds and at the same time to save themselves politically with the voters by saying that court orders and the need to uphold the Constitution leave them no choice.

Prisoner Litigation: The Best Route?

Although the U.S. Supreme Court's decisions make headlines, they are only the very tip of the iceberg of prisoner litigation. In more than twenty thousand suits filed annually, state prisoners request the lower federal courts to order certain practices stopped as well as money damages because of such abuses as brutality by guards, inadequate nutrition and medical care, theft of personal property, and violence by other inmates. A very large number of these suits are deemed frivolous and are dismissed for failure to state legitimate claims. Among the remainder, only a few are decided in ways that affect anyone but the individual litigants.

It is generally recognized that many prisoners have legitimate claims that must be heard, yet correctional specialists, judges, and even litigators are questioning the suitability of litigation as the means of resolving them. Litigation is a cumbersome, costly, and often ineffective way to handle such claims because, except for class action and isolated individual grievances, most resemble matters settled in small claims courts. As former Chief Justice Burger has said, "Federal judges should not be dealing with prisoner complaints which, although important to a prisoner, are so minor that any well-run institution should be able to resolve them fairly without resort to federal judges."[43]

Although most suits filed by prisoners under the Civil Rights Act are dismissed before trial, the remaining cases force correctional officials to expend time and resources in litigation, to face the possibility of being sued personally, and to risk the erosion of their leadership. Complaints that survive the initial scrutiny of a judge often require defendants and other staff members to put in long hours conferring with counsel and providing the depositions demanded during the discovery process. Many nonfrivolous suits concern small monetary sums, and the time devoted to them by administrators is disproportionate to the amounts involved. More complicated suits, particularly those filed as class actions, require attorneys general to expend considerable resources. Even if correctional officials are able to win the suits against them, leadership may be hurt when wardens, rather than the responsible line staff members, are placed on trial. In the adversarial process, plaintiff and defendant—prisoner and warden—are legally and symbolically equal, a fact that does not go unnoticed by the people the warden must supervise.

Most prisoner actions tend to be filed *pro se* (without assistance of counsel) and are therefore subject to screening by judges and clerks to determine if they are frivolous or malicious. Inmates may well become disillusioned with the judicial system and turn into a problem in correctional administration when they learn that their complaints—in which they have invested considerable emotional resources—have been dismissed as being without merit. Perhaps most important, meritorious claims and grievous wrongs may go unnoticed because they never have an effective airing in court.

Most cases filed under Section 1983 (the Civil Rights Act) charge that the individual prisoner has received unconstitutional treatment by a correctional official and ask for money damages. However, the constitutional standards in such cases are elusive because in many areas conduct that is illegal has been ambiguously defined; such wrongful conduct as "willful negligence" or "deliberate indifference" is hard to prove. In medical malpractice cases, for example, when the state presents records that show a history of treatment for the plaintiff's health problem, as it usually can do, the plaintiff's case fails to satisfy the Supreme Court's basic criteria, and thus no remedy is available under 42 U.S.C. 1983.

Although the prisoners' rights movement has achieved court-ordered reforms in some state correctional systems, successful suits under Section 1983 often have little effect on the individual plaintiff. Given the backlog in most U.S. district courts, inmates whose cases survive screening and motions to dismiss have often been transferred to other institutions or released on parole by the time the cases come to trial. When a case is successful, the court's decree may have to run the bureaucratic gauntlet before any action is taken, or the services of a special master may be necessary to force the institution to comply with it.

Correctional administrators are naturally not happy when an outside master is appointed to oversee their work, and the intervention may cause tensions within the staff. Because court decrees are not always models of clarity, administrators and the master may disagree as to the court's requirements. Further, masters often find that implementing the decree is impeded because the parties disagree over what specific changes the order requires and whether those changes can be accomplished by the defendants. Rather than give the correctional officials discretion to implement changes to fit the special conditions of the institution, the master may go back to the court for further instructions. The implementation process can thus be so time-consuming and vexatious that significant improvements may never be made.

Most observers agree that prisoners have grievances that must be addressed. Yet the ability of prisoners to sue under Section 1983 has produced myriad cases that have taken up the resources of the judiciary, state attorneys general, and correctional administrators without noticeably changing prison conditions, policies, and practices.

Officials have also become concerned about the effect of the adversarial system on the correctional environment. An institution whose prisoners have successfully sued administrators may find its staff members reluctant to exercise discretion to resolve festering and potentially serious situations because they fear being named in a suit. In an institution where prisoner litigation is in progress, problems may go uncorrected until the suit is adjudicated, a process that may take years. The emotional costs that litigation has on both the staff and the inmates may significantly increase tensions and so produce new management and security problems.

From the perspective of the prisoner, litigation in the federal courts may be neither effective nor satisfying. Most prisoners who complain about the unconstitutionality of the conditions of their confinement face three problems: (1) They generally lack legal representation, (2) constitutional standards are difficult to meet, and (3) even if a suit succeeds, changes in policies or compensation may be slow in coming. In addition, when meritorious claims go unnoticed in the crush of litigation, the inmates' faith in the law and social institutions is further eroded. In view of these problems, most correctional systems provide alternatives to litigation.

Alternatives to Litigation

Given the drawbacks of litigation as a means to resolve prisoners' grievances equitably and effectively, the need for noncourt mechanisms to resolve the group of cases that may be called administrative is apparent. These are the nonfrivolous, non–class action complaints filed by state prisoners under the provisions of Section 1983. They are the cases that may be meritorious yet that under current conditions are being screened out by judicial clerks or that are unable to withstand motions for summary judgment. Examples include cases brought in quest of prosthetics, changes in mail or visiting procedures, compensation for lost personal property, the transfer of a guard, a special diet, restoration of good time, or any of the multiple measures of relief that prisoners typically seek.

Scholars and practitioners in various fields have encouraged the development of techniques for resolving disputes without resort to litigation. No-fault automobile insurance, mediation of marital disputes, arbitration in labor relations, landlord-tenant negotiations, and consumer-merchant settlement processes are all useful alternatives to the courts. As prisoners have only recently won the right to assert claims in court, however, the development of alternative mechanisms to resolve their disputes is still in its infancy.

Though alternative mechanisms for the resolution of prisoners' complaints do save judicial and correctional resources, their primary importance lies in other advantages they offer over litigation. Four factors have been emphasized.

1. The informality of the mechanisms makes them a more effective means of responding to the kinds of complaints raised by prisoners than the complex and often cumbersome judicial process.

2. Concrete issues underlying seemingly abstract complaints may be more thor-

oughly explored through an informal dispute-resolution mechanism. It has often been said that administrative problems require administrative solutions.

3. As nonadjudicatory processes are often less time-consuming than litigation, inmates' problems can be handled before they become magnified.

4. The mutual agreement produced by some of the informal mechanisms is believed to be more meaningful to the inmate than a solution imposed by a court.

People concerned with the prisoners' rights issue are virtually unanimous that every effort should be made to resolve inmates' disputes outside the judicial arena. Four mechanisms of dispute resolution have been incorporated in the correctional systems of various states: inmate grievance procedures, an ombudsman, mediation, and legal assistance. All are designed to solve problems before they reach the point where the inmate feels compelled to file suit, but mediation and legal assistance may also be invoked after a suit has been initiated.

Inmate Grievance Procedures

Although informal procedures for hearing inmates' complaints have existed for many years, it is only since the mid 1970s that formal grievance mechanisms have been widely used. All states and the U.S. Bureau of Prisons now have grievance procedures.

In the usual procedure, complaints are submitted to a designated staff member within the institution, often called a grievance coordinator. An inmate who is dissatisfied with the response may usually appeal to a higher authority. In some institutions, appeals follow the chain of command; in more innovative institutions, inmates, line staff, and outsiders are frequently involved in making or reviewing decisions.

Inmate grievance programs vary in the prominence they accord to such procedural

elements as (1) inmate participation, (2) informal resolution at an early stage, (3) time limits for the steps of the process, and (4) exclusion of certain types of cases.

Inmate participation Inmate participation in grievance procedures is controversial in that many corrections officials resist the idea that an inmate should be in a position to decide another's fate. Yet in many states inmates do sit on grievance boards. In New York, for example, the Inmate Grievance Resolution Committee, the basic decision-making body in each institution, consists of two inmate representatives elected for six-month terms and two staff members appointed for five-month terms. They receive cases, investigate them, and make recommendations to the institution's head. In most correctional systems, however, administrators have been skeptical of inmate participation, arguing that the prisoners selected would use their positions to enhance their own influence with staff and other inmates.

Informal resolution The view that prisoners should attempt to resolve their problems informally before filing complaints is widely held. Some grievance procedures specifically require a good-faith effort to resolve the issue. Many complaints originate in misunderstandings, which often can be cleared up if the prisoner discusses the problems with a case counselor, staff member, or fellow inmate. When no good-faith effort is required, decisions tend not to be made and cases not to be resolved because it is easier for staff members to pass the issues on to higher authority than to assume responsibility for a solution.

Time limits Most grievance procedures set time limits for the actions taken at each level of decision making. Most observers believe that the period for investigation and decision should be as short as possible in the early stages. Many grievances can be easily resolved through informal processes, and the prisoner should not be kept in a state of agitation if the problem can be resolved quickly. If the problem is complex, requiring actions by officials at higher levels, the time limits for decisions at later stages may be longer.

Exclusion of cases Systems vary as to the nature of the complaints that may be submitted to the inmate grievance procedure. Some institutions have separate processes for complaints concerning discipline and property claims. Other systems exclude questions about an inmate's sentence or release on parole, as such matters lie outside the jurisdiction of correctional administrators.

Structure and process A three-step process for the resolution of grievances is typical in most correctional systems. A staff person or committee in each institution usually receives complaints, investigates them, and makes decisions. If the prisoner is dissatisfied with the outcome, the case may then be appealed to the warden and ultimately to the commissioner of corrections.

Most systems require or encourage prisoners to bring grievances to the attention of a staff member so that informal resolution may be attempted, and most report that up to 70 percent of complaints are resolved at this level. An inmate who believes that a grievance should go forward submits the proper form and the complaint is formally investigated by a staff member. The staff member then communicates the decision reached to the inmate and states the reasons for the action. If the inmate is dissatisfied, the decision can be appealed to the second and ultimately the third level of review.

Reports indicate that some grievances are more easily resolved than others. Many inmates complain that they are not receiving proper medical treatment, for example, but because medical personnel can usually document the treatment they have provided, such complaints normally subside. Complaints of lost personal property are another matter. Many such complaints are made, most involving items deposited at the reception/release

centers at the time of arrival or not transferred with the prisoner to another institution. Staff members often cannot account for missing property, and the process for receiving compensation for property lost or damaged as a result of staff neglect can be complicated. Probably the most difficult situation for a grievance process to resolve is alleged brutality by a guard. Such a complaint virtually always comes down to the inmate's word against the guard's. It takes quick action to get other staff members to come forward, and even then it is an unusual staff member who will report a fellow officer.

The inmate grievance procedure is a useful device for defusing tensions in correctional facilities. It has also been found useful as a management tool. By attentive monitoring of the complaint process, a warden or commissioner is able to discern patterns of inmate discontent that may warrant actions to prevent the development of more serious problems.

The Ombudsman

Ombudsman programs now constitute the second most frequently found dispute-resolution mechanism in corrections. The institution of the **ombudsman,** originally a Swedish public official with full authority to investigate citizens' complaints against government officials, has been successfully used in correctional settings throughout the United States for more than a decade.

Generally, the ombudsman is empowered to receive complaints, to investigate them, to report findings and make recommendations to the proper authority, and to make findings public. As ombudsmen can only recommend, their success in resolving conflicts and ensuring compliance with the agreed-upon decisions rests on their reputations for impartiality and

---

ombudsman A public official who investigates complaints against government officials and recommends corrective measures.

their ability to persuade. Given full access to records and the authority to conduct investigations, the prison ombudsman may be effective in resolving disputes and averting litigation.

Independence, impartiality, and expertise have traditionally been cited as the requirements for successful ombudsmen. Their independence from both domination by correctional officials and partisanship for inmates has been the focus of much discussion. The appointment and funding of ombudsmen by sources outside of departments of corrections enhance their independence and thus bolster their legitimacy, especially in the eyes of prisoners. Several ombudsmen report directly to the commissioner of corrections and oversee the department's administrative grievance process. In some correctional systems, however, staff members perform the function, but such appointments seem to be at odds with the usual conception of the office. In fact, several ombudsmen report directly to the commissioner of corrections and oversee the department's administrative grievance process.

The ombudsman's ability to handle complaints before they are filed in the federal courts may help to avert litigation under Section 1983, particularly if inmates have quick and easy access to the office. When ombudsmen are respected by inmates, their advice as to the merits of grievances may help to reduce the number of frivolous claims; when they see merit in claims, they can try to convince authorities that attention must be paid and that it would be in their interest to resolve the matters out of court.

Mediation

Mediation is a distinctive approach to conflict resolution in that both parties must agree to submit the complaint to arbitration and to abide by the terms of any resolution that is proposed. This is thus a consensual and voluntary process in which a neutral third party assists the contestants to reconcile their differences. Mediation has been advanced as an appropri-

ate means to settle disputes because the informality of the process stands in contrast to the complex, cumbersome procedures of the courtroom. Proponents point out that in the mediation setting straightforward questions may be asked so that underlying issues may be explored. This feature is of special advantage to prisoners, most of whom would not have the assistance of counsel if they were to take their cases to court. Mediation is particularly effective when the essence of a complaint is not a conflict of abstract principles but an administrative problem requiring an administrative solution. The adversarial nature of litigation, in contrast, tends to transform nonfrivolous but not necessarily clearly constitutional questions about administrative policy into hardened positions. The mediator's ability to uncover the real nature of the problem and to help in the search for meaningful solutions agreeable to all makes the system seem attractive, and certainly a mediator's services are far less costly than court proceedings.

In the abstract, mediation is appealing. It has, however, had only a limited trial in the correctional setting and has yet to live up to its potential since neither party seems willing to be bound by the decision.

Legal Assistance

As noted earlier, the Supreme Court has emphasized that prisoners must have access to legal resources so that they may seek postconviction relief.[44] Since the early 1970s several legal assistance mechanisms have been instituted in state correctional institutions, including staff attorneys paid by the state to assist inmates with their legal problems, inmate ("jailhouse") lawyers, and law school clinical programs.

----

mediation Intervention in a dispute by a third party to whom the parties in conflict submit their differences for resolution and whose decision (in the correctional setting) is binding on both parties.

Litigation assistance may seem counterproductive if the goal of correctional administrators is to avoid Section 1983 cases, but lawyers do more than simply help prisoners file suits. They also advise their clients as to the legal merits of their complaints, and thus are in a position to discourage frivolous suits. Counsel is also helpful in determining the underlying issues of a complaint and therefore is able to frame questions in terms that will be understood by other legally trained persons.

The Impact of the Prisoners' Rights Movement

One result of the prisoners' rights movement is that conditions reflected in this 1967 photograph no longer exist in most American correctional institutions.

The impact of the prisoners' rights movement is difficult to measure accurately. There are problems in identifying the influence of specific cases and in defining success or failure in many instances. How can one show that any action of a correctional bureaucracy was taken in response to litigation? Individual cases may make only a dent in such organizations, but over time basic shifts may occur.

Some general changes in American corrections during the past decade can probably be credited to the prisoners' rights movement. The most obvious are improvements in institutional living conditions and administrative practices. Prisoners in solitary confinement undoubtedly suffer less neglect than previously. Although overcrowding is now a major problem in many institutions, many conditions are much improved. This is not to say that prison life has become a bed of roses, but conditions are better and the more brutalizing features have been diminished. Further, law libraries and legal assistance are now generally available; communication with the outside is easier; religious practices are protected; inmate complaint procedures have been developed; and elements of due process are observed.

But in several prison systems the impact of judicial orders has led to periods of instability with increases in violence. For example, as explained in the Focus box, the rulings in *Ruiz* v. *Estelle* (1980) dictated the end of the building-tender system in Texas prisons. Until that time, correctional administrators had used selected inmates to handle the rank-and-file prisoners. Abolition of the system created a vacuum that led to the disruption of social patterns. Individual and gang-led violence took an upturn, and it was only with time, the addition of trained correctional officers, and implementation of other reforms that stability returned to the system.

The effects of the prisoners' rights movement have also been felt by correctional officials. Surely the threat of suit and public exposure has placed many in the correctional bureaucracy on guard. It can be argued that the result has been merely the increased bureaucratization of corrections as staff members take care to document their actions in order to protect themselves against suits. At the same time, judicial intervention has forced corrections officials to rethink many of their procedures and organizational structures.

The Impact of *Ruiz* v. *Estelle*

In December 1980 William W. Justice, federal judge for the Eastern District of Texas, issued a sweeping decree against the Texas Department of Corrections. He ordered prison officials to address a host of unconstitutional conditions, including overcrowding, unnecessary use of force by personnel, inadequate numbers of guards, poor health care practices, and a building-tender system that allowed some inmates to control other inmates. The abolition of the building-tender system caused a major disruption in the social patterns that served to maintain control of the inmates in the Eastham Unit of the Texas penal system.

Eastham is a large maximum security institution housing recidivists over the age of twenty-five who have been in prison three or more times. It is tightly managed and has been the depository for troublemakers from other Texas prisons. To help with these hard-core criminals, the staff relied upon a select group of inmates known as building tenders (BTs). By co-opting the BTs with special privileges, officials were able to use them and their assistants, the turnkeys, to handle the rank-and-file inmates.

Officially, the building-tender system was an information network. Because the staff were at the fringe of the inmate society, the BTs could help officials penetrate and divide that society. In turn, the BTs and turnkeys had snitches working for them. Information about troublesome inmates, guards, and conditions was passed along by the BTs to officials. With this information, the staff were able to exercise enormous power over the inmates' daily activities. The BTs and turnkeys were rewarded, enjoying power and status far exceeding those of ordinary inmates and even of lower-ranking guards. Unofficially, the BTs kept order in the cell blocks through intimidation and the physical disciplining of those who broke the rules.

In May 1982, Texas signed a consent decree, agreeing to dismantle the building-tender system by January 1983. BTs were reassigned to ordinary prison jobs; stripped of their power, status, and duties; and moved to separate cell blocks for their protection. At the same time Eastham received 141 new officers, almost doubling the guard force, to help pick up the slack. These reforms were substantial and set off a series of shifts that fundamentally altered the guard and inmate societies.

With the removal of the BTs and turnkeys, with restrictions on the unofficial use of force by guards, and with institution of a prisoner discipline system emphasizing due process, fairness, and rights, the traditional social structure of Eastham came under severe strain. The reforms brought about three major changes within the prison community: changes having to do with interpersonal relations between the guards and inmates, reorganization within the inmate society, and the guard subculture and work role.

Guards and inmates

Formerly, ordinary inmates had been subject to an all-encompassing, totalitarian system in which they were "dictated to, exploited, and kept in submission." But with the new relationship between the keepers and the kept, inmates challenge the authority of correctional officers and are more confrontational and hostile. In response to the verbal and other assaults on their authority, the guards have cited inmates for infractions of the rules. The changes in the relationship between guards and inmates result from a number of factors,

Continued

including the fact that there are more guards, the restrictions on the guards mean that physical reprisals are not feared, the guards no longer have the BTs to act as intermediaries, and the social distance between guards and prisoners has diminished. The last factor is important because one result of the civil rights movement is that prisoners are no longer viewed as "nonpersons." Inmates have rights and may invoke due process rules to challenge decisions of guards and other officials. "Although the guards ultimately control the prison, they must now negotiate, compromise, or overlook many difficulties with inmates within the everyday control system."

Reorganization within the inmate society

The purging of the BT-turnkey system created a power vacuum characterized by uncertainty. One outcome was a rise in the amount of inmate-inmate violence. Whereas in the past the BTs had helped to settle disputes among inmates, during the postreform period these conflicts more often led to violence in which weapons were used. Violent self-help became a social necessity. As personal violence escalated, so did the development of inmate gangs. Gang members

know that they will have the assistance of others if they are threatened, assaulted, or robbed. For nongang prisoners, heightened levels of personal insecurity mean that they must rely upon themselves and avoid contact with inmates known for their toughness.

Guard subculture and work role

The court-imposed reforms have upset the foundations of the guard subculture and work role. The guards' world of work is no longer well ordered, predictable, or rewarding. One aspect of the change is increased fear of the inmates among rank-and-file guards. Upon removal of the BTs, guards were assigned to cell block duty for the first time; this placed them in close contact with inmates. The fact that most of the guards were new to prison work meant that they were hesitant to enforce order. Many officers believe that because they cannot physically punish inmates and their supervisors do not back them up, it is better not to enforce the rules at all. They think that their authority has been undermined and that the new disciplinary process is frustrating. Many would rather look the other way.

The court-ordered reforms brought Eastham's operations more in line with constitutional requirements of

fairness and due process but disrupted an ongoing social system. Before the *Ruiz* decision, the prison had been run on the basis of paternalism, coercion, dominance, and fear. Guards exercised much discretion over inmates, and they used the building tenders to help maintain order and as a source of information. During the transition to a new bureaucratic-legal order, levels of violence and personal insecurity increased. Authority was eroded, combative relations between inmates and officers materialized, and inmate gangs developed to provide security and autonomy for members.

Judicial supervision of the Texas prison system as a result of this case lasted for a decade and ended on March 31, 1990. And an overriding question still remains: Can a prison be administered in ways that conform to the requirements of fairness and due process yet maintain security for the inmates and staff?

Source: Adapted from James W. Marquart and Ben M. Crouch, "Judicial Reform and Prisoner Control: The Impact of *Ruiz* v. *Estelle* on a Texas Penitentiary," *Law and Society Review* 19 (1985): 557–86.

Well-managed institutions are probably the best means to avert litigation. When prisoners do voice complaints, however, correctional administrators must be able to distinguish the frivolous from the potentially meritorious. When this determination has been made, they should then have mechanisms to solve problems quickly, in a manner that satisfies the disputants and avoids the cost of litigation. By using the alternatives best suited to the individual correctional environment, administrators may resolve a significant number of cases, thus freeing judicial and legal resources to cope with those controversies that can be settled only by the courts. Despite their limitations, alternative dispute-resolution processes offer a promising means to handle a serious problem that affects the judiciary, correctional administrators, and prisoners alike.

Although the federal courts have been sympathetic to prisoner litigation during the past decade, the caseload crunch and a subsequent rethinking of the judicial role may result in some retrenchment in cases that contest conditions of confinement in state and local institutions. All the same, inmates may be expected to keep trying to improve their conditions, which may worsen with expected future overcrowding. Even in the face of efforts to develop alternative dispute mechanisms, some prisoners may see the courts as their only recourse, and others, less interested in the ultimate merits of their own cases, may pursue litigation simply to harass institutional administrators. At the same time, public opinion, finances, and increased demands for other services may place corrections in a weakened position in the competition for resources. Innovation in this atmosphere will be difficult, even if the alternatives can be shown to lead to the desired result.

In sum, after more than two hundred years of judicial neglect of the conditions under which prisoners are held, courts have recently abandoned their hands-off doctrine and begun to look more closely at the situation. Building on some of the decisions of the Warren Court in the civil rights field, the Supreme Court under Chief Justice Burger took a particular interest in the field of corrections. To date, the Court under Chief Justice Rehnquist has not been as supportive of prisoners' rights.

Summary

U ntil the 1960s the courts held to a hands-off policy with regard to the internal administration of prisons and the rights of inmates. With the civil rights movement and the extension of due process rights by the Supreme Court, prisoner groups and their supporters pushed to secure rights for inmates. After initial successes with regard to portions of the First Amendment to the U.S. Constitution, prisoners' rights advocates have seen additional amendments linked to prison conditions by the courts.

The Supreme Court's 1964 decision in *Cooper* v. *Pate* set the stage for a flood of cases brought by prisoners to challenge the conditions of their confinement. In that opinion the Court ruled that prisoners could sue correctional officials under Title 42 of the United States Code, Section 1983. This portion of the law imposes civil liability on any person who deprives another of constitutional rights.

The foundations of prisoners' rights are the U.S. Constitution, the constitution of the state in which the institution is located, state statutes, and federal statutes and regulations. In particular, the First, Fourth, Eighth, and Fourteenth Amendments to the U.S. Constitution have been important bases for the extension of prisoners' rights.

Litigation is not always the best way to secure the rights of prisoners and to correct institutional conditions. Many suits brought by prisoners have been dismissed as improperly drafted, outside the court's jurisdiction, and filed in quest of solutions that are difficult to implement. Alternatives to litigation, including inmate grievance procedures, ombudsmen, mediation, and legal assistance now have a place in most correctional systems.

Although the past two decades have often been turbulent as basic rights have been extended to inmates, the overall result must be viewed as positive. The courts have insisted that fundamentally unfair practices end and judges have exerted their influence to change correctional systems. Many correctional officials have opposed some of these moves yet most now agree that the impact has generally been positive.

For Discussion

1. When the courts abandoned the hands-off policy, what problems did correctional administrators then encounter?

2. What difficulties might you, as a correctional officer, foresee in attempting to run your unit of the institution while at the same time upholding the legal rights of the prisoners?

3. The standards set by the U.S. attorney general stipulate that inmates should participate in the operation of grievance procedures. Why have many prison superintendents resisted this idea? Is their view justified?

4. A group of prisoners in the institution you manage call themselves the "Sons of the Purple Flower" and claim that their association is a religious organization. They have asked for a special diet and for permission to chant when the moon is full. They insist that these practices are necessary for the full exercise of their rights under the First Amendment. How would you determine whether you must grant these requests?

5. What can an administrator do to reduce the potential for lawsuits contesting conditions of confinement?

For Further Reading

Crouch, Ben M., and Marquart, James W. *An Appeal to Justice.* Austin: University of Texas Press, 1989. Analysis of the reform of the Texas prison system brought about by the actions of the federal courts.

DiIulio, John J., Jr., ed. *Courts, Corrections, and the Constitution.* New York: Oxford University Press, 1990. A collection of essays that examine the capacity of judges to intervene in ways that improve the quality of life behind bars.

Knight, Barbara B., and Early, Stephen T., Jr. *Prisoners' Rights in America.* Chicago: Nelson-Hall, 1986. An excellent overview of the law with reference to the incarcerated.

Martin, Steve J., and Ekland-Olson, Sheldon. *Texas Prisons: The Walls Came Tumbling Down.* Austin: Texas Monthly Press, 1987. A history of the Texas prison system focusing on the rise of the writ-writers, the case of *Ruiz* v. *Estelle,* and the impact of Judge William Justice's decision.

Murton, Tom, and Hyams, Joseph. *Accomplices to the Crime: The Arkansas Prison Scandal.* New York: Grove Press, 1970. A history of the Arkansas prison system and the scandal that led to *Holt* v. *Sarver.*

Notes

1. *New York Times,* 26 February 1992, p. 1.

2. Ruffin v. Commonwealth, 62 Va. 790 (1871).

3. James B. Jacobs, *New Perspectives on Prisons and Imprisonment* (Ithaca, N.Y.: Cornell University Press, 1983), p. 35.

4. Cooper v. Pate, 378 U.S. 546 (1964).

5. Jacobs, *New Perspectives,* p. 37.

6. U.S. Administrative Office of the Courts, *Annual Report* (Washington, D.C.: Government Printing Office, 1988), p. 116.

7. Brooks v. Florida, 389 U.S. 413 (1967).

8. Johnson v. Avery, 393 U.S. 483 (1969).

9. Bounds v. Smith, 430 U.S. 817 (1977).

10. Kenneth C. Haas and Geoffrey P. Alpert, "American Prisoners and the Right of Access to the Courts: A Vanishing Concept of Protection," *The Dilemmas of Corrections,* 2nd ed. ed. Kenneth C. Haas and Geoffrey P. Alpert (Prospect Heights, Ill.: Waveland Press, 1992), p. 203.

11. Haas and Alpert, p. 216.

12. Sterling v. Cupp, 290 Ore. 611, 625 P. 2d 123 (1981); DeLancie v. Superior Court of San Mateo County, 31 Cal. 3d 865 (1982).

13. Pepperling v. Crist, 678 F.2d 787 (9th Cir., 1982).

14. Sostre v. McGinnis, 442 F.2d 178 (1971).

15. Turner v. Safley, 107 S.Ct. 2261 (1987).

16. Fulwood v. Clemmer, 206 F.Supp. 370 (1962).

17. Cruz v. Beto, 92 S.Ct. 1079 (1972).

18. Hudson v. Palmer, 52 L.W. 5052 (1984).

19. Smith v. Fairman, 678 F.2d 52 (7th Cir., 1982).

20. Lee F. Downs, 641 F.2d 1117 (4th Cir., 1981).

21. Smith v. Fairman, 678 F.2d 52 (7th Cir., 1982).

22. Pugh v. Locke, 406 F.Supp 318 (1976).

23. Holt v. Sarver, 442 F.2d 308 (8th Cir., 1971).

24. Hutto v. Finney, 98 S.Ct. 2565 (1978).

25. Rhodes v. Chapman, 452 U.S. 337 (1981).

26. Wolff v. McDonnell, 418 U.S. 539 (1974).

27. Ibid.

28. Lee v. Washington, 390 U.S. 333 (1968).

29. Cooper v. Pate, 378 U.S. 546 (1976); James B. Jacobs, *New Perspectives on Prisons and Imprisonment* (Ithaca, N.Y.: Cornell University Press, 1983), p. 42.

30. Wolff v. McDonnell, 418 U.S. 539 (1974)

31. Bell v. Wolfish, 441 U.S. 520 (1979).

32. Rhodes v. Chapman, 452 U.S. 337 (1981).

33. Daniels v. Williams 474 U.S. 327 (1986).

34. Wilson v. Seiter, 111 S.Ct. 2321 (1991).

35. Christopher E. Smith, "Justice Antonin Scalia and Criminal Justice Cases," *Kentucky Law Journal* 81 (1992–93): 207.

36. Charles H. Jones, "Recent Trends in Corrections and Prisoners' Rights Law," *Correctional Theory and Practice,* ed. Clayton A. Hartjen and Edward E. Rhine (Chicago: Nelson Hall, 1992), p. 119.

37. Abdul Wali v. Coughlin, 754 F.2d 1015 (2nd Cir., 1985), as quoted in Jones, "Recent Trends," p. 122.

38. McCleskey v. Zant, 111 S.Ct. 1454 (1991).

39. Coleman v. Thompson, 111 S.Ct. 2546 (1991).

40. Linda Harriman and Jeffrey D. Straussman, "Do Judges Determine Budget Decisions? Federal Court Decisions in Prison Reform and State Spending for Corrections," *Public Administration Review* (July/August 1983): pp. 343–51.

41. Two cases relevant to this issue—Gates v. Collier and Holt v. Sarver—are discussed in Harriman and Straussman, "Do Judges Determine," pp. 343–51.

42. Ibid.

43. Warren E. Burger, "Chief Justice Burger Issues Year-End Report," *American Bar Association Journal* 62 (1976): 189, 190.

44. Johnson v. Avery, 393 U.S. 499 (1969).

15

Release from Incarceration

My thoughts seem to be focusing on that day when I'll be walking into that room full of strangers who really don't know me, and pray that I have done whatever they expected me to do here.

Inmate, maximum security prison

Release: From One Part of the System to Another
Contemporary Methods of Release
Origins of Parole
The Decision to Release
Discretionary Release
Mandatory Release
The Consequences of the Release Decision
The Effect on Sentencing
The Organization of Releasing Authorities
Autonomous Versus Consolidated
Field Services
Full-Time Versus Part-Time
Appointment
Release to the Community
Summary

A black minister active in party politics, a retired corporate executive, a man who owns a small business, and a woman interested in civic affairs sit as a parole board to consider the lengths of the sentences of Maurice Williams and nineteen other inmates. Williams, convicted of first-degree robbery, is serving his first major sentence, five to ten years. As he enters the hearing room at the maximum security prison, he is outwardly relaxed and confident, seemingly more sure of himself than most inmates at parole hearings. His time in prison has been productive: He has earned a high school equivalency certificate; he has received a good report from the director of the drug treatment program and a supporting report from the prison psychiatrist; and his brother has written that he will give him a job in his grocery store in the old neighborhood. Still, he is a bit nervous. He has never been before the parole board before, and he wonders about the people he is facing. Who are they? What do they know about him? How will they react to his file?

The minister asks Williams about his plans for the future. He answers that he will live with his brother and work in the store. The woman wants to know if he will be hanging out with his old buddies. Williams tries to assure her that although many still live nearby, he will avoid them. "I've learned my lesson. I'm gonna keep away from those guys." After a few more minutes during which the members shuffle through the papers in his file, Williams is told that he can return to his cell and that he will learn the board's decision by evening.

In the discussion that follows Williams's departure, several panel members express skepticism about his prison performance and wonder if he is merely a good con artist who will do anything to earn early release. The businessman predicts that Williams will fall back into trouble soon after he hits the streets: "I know that neighborhood. It will be impossible for him to stay away from those influences." In the next few minutes they all ponder the Williams case, compromise, and decide to grant an extended parole—that is, he will be paroled, but not on the date he first becomes eligible. One member has already started to study another of the files stacked before him. It is 9:20 A.M.—one down on a typical hearing day and nineteen to go before the four citizens can return to their own worlds.[1]

Release: From One Part of the System to Another

Until the recent advent of determinate sentencing and release guidelines, almost 85 percent of prisoners were returned to society by the grace of parole boards. Throughout the era when rehabilitation was the dominant goal, the parole release drama as just described was played out daily across the country. The parole board used its discretion to fix the release date somewhere between the minimum and maximum terms of the offender's sentence, taking into account such factors as participation in treatment programs, job prospects, and the individual's criminal history.

During most of the twentieth century the term **parole** referred to both a release mechanism and a method of community supervision. It is still used in this general sense, but since the adoption of the deserved punishment model of the criminal sanction (as discussed in Chapter 4), the dual usage is no longer appropriate in most states. Now we must distinguish between a releasing mechanism and supervision. However, it must be underscored that although releasing mechanisms have changed in many states during the past decade, most former prisoners are still required to serve a period of time under parole supervision. Only

parole The conditional release of an inmate from incarceration under supervision after a portion of the prison sentence has been served.

Release is what all inmates await, but merely leaving the confines of a prison does not end correctional supervision. What lies ahead for this parolee?

felons are released on parole; adult misdemeanants are usually released directly from local institutions on expiration of their sentences. This chapter focuses on the methods and context of the decision to release felons from incarceration. Supervision of the approximately 550,000 ex-inmates on parole and their adjustment to the community will be discussed in Chapter 16.

Before examining the decision to release, we should place this aspect of corrections in its proper context. Although it is possible to describe release procedures according to the concepts that we have used to define the corrections system in Chapter 1, two factors stand out: (1) The process is carried out by various levels of government, and (2) complex and competing goals influence the decision.

Release to the community is an activity of state and federal (but not local) governments. A variety of organizational structures have been developed to effect the release of prisoners. In many states the parole board is part of the department of corrections; in others it is an autonomous body whose members are appointed by the governor.

Like so many other activities of corrections, the decision to release is made in the context of complex and competing goals. Traditionally, parole has been justified in terms of rehabilitation. Along with the indeterminate sentence and treatment programs, early release is logically linked to that goal. In theory, parole board members are called upon to evaluate the offender's progress toward rehabilitation and readiness to be law-abiding. In practice, they consider other factors as well. Even where determinate sentencing or parole guidelines are in effect, correctional officials have some influence on release; the decision is not as cut and dried as proponents have claimed. Numerous questions bear on the release decision no matter what procedures are followed. What will the public's reaction be? Who will be blamed if the offender commits another crime? Is the prison so crowded that an early release is necessary to open up space for the newly sentenced? What effect will the offender's release have on judges and prosecutors? Clearly, a mixture of goals, some conflicting and some unrelated to the formally stated goals of the criminal sanction, may enter into the decision.

Contemporary Methods of Release

Parole has customarily been defined as the conditional release of a prisoner from incarceration but not from the legal custody and supervision of the state. Thus offenders who comply with the conditions of parole and do not come into further conflict with the law receive an absolute discharge from supervision at the end of their sentences. If parolees break a rule, parole may be revoked and they must return to a correctional facility. Parole, then, rests on three concepts.

1. *Grace or privilege:* The prisoner could be kept incarcerated but the government extends the privilege of release.

2. *Contract of consent:* The government enters into an agreement with the prisoner whereby the prisoner promises to abide by certain conditions in exchange for being released.

3. *Custody:* Even though the offender is released from prison, he or she is still a responsibility of the government. Parole is an extension of correctional programs into the community.

During the past decade a major change has occurred in the manner in which offenders are released from prison. The passage of determinate sentencing laws and the establishment of parole guidelines have removed most of the discretionary aspects of the release decision in some jurisdictions. These new sentencing laws are based on the assumption that it is the judge who gives the offender a specific amount of time to serve. In about half the states and in the federal system, felons are now released to community supervision as the law stipulates, not at the discretion of the parole board. In these states the mechanisms for leaving prison may be referred to as **mandatory release** because correctional authorities have little leeway to consider whether an offender is ready for community supervision.

In Maine the determinate sentencing law formally abolished parole supervision. As a consequence, inmates are given what are called **expiration releases:** unconditional releases from incarceration when their terms expire, minus good time. Some prisoners in other states are also released unconditionally upon expiration of their full sentence or after reductions for good time. No further supervision of them in the community is required.

The remaining states continue to follow **discretionary release** procedures, by which the parole board (or its equivalent) determines the exact date for an inmate to enter the community (see Table 15.1). Discretionary release on parole is usually justified as a means of providing early release from incarceration consistent with the goal of rehabilitation. It is designed to work in conjunction with the indeterminate sentence so that parole boards may determine the most appropriate time for release on the basis of a diagnosis provided by correctional personnel. Parole boards, then, are faced with a dilemma: On their decision depend both the offender's release and society's protection. Often these two goals seem to be incompatible.

mandatory release The required release to community supervision of an inmate from incarceration upon the expiration of a certain time period, as stipulated by a determinate sentencing law or parole guidelines.

expiration release The release of an inmate from incarceration after full service of a sentence or after reduction earned good time credits. Supervision in the community is not required.

discretionary release The release of an inmate to community supervision from incarceration at the discretion of the parole board within the boundaries set by the sentence and the penal law.

Table 15.1 ■ **Ten Release Mechanisms in South Carolina.** Until a task force on overcrowding consolidated some of the provisions, South Carolina recognized more than ten ways to leave a prison (beside escape or death). All of the following types of release have been specified in the state statutes or administrative procedures.

Type of release	Eligibility	Calculation
Discretionary parole	All felons	"Life," eligible at 20 years Less than 10 years, eligible at ¼ of sentence 10 years or more, eligible at ⅓ of sentence
Good time	All felons	Lifers earn 15 days off maximum term for every 30 days in prison; others can earn 20 days for every 30 days in prison
Earned work credits	All felons on special work assignments	1 day off maximum term for every 2 days in work assignment up to 180 days per year
Extended work release	All felons with no more than 1 prior conviction	Placed on work release status 2 months before parole eligibility
Supervised furlough I	All felons with: clean disciplinary record less than 5-year sentence less than 2 prior convictions	Released 6 months before parole eligibility
Supervised furlough II	All felons with 6 months' clean record	Released 6 months before parole eligibility
First-day-of-month rule	All felons	Released on first day of month in which eligibility is reached (after other reductions)
Emergency release provision	Felons within 90 days of eligibility for parole	When prison reaches state of crisis because of crowding, governor may roll back sentences to reduce numbers
Provisional parole	All felons	Released 90 days before eligibility at discretion of parole board
Christmas parole	All felons	If parole eligibility is reached between 18 December and 30 January, released on 18 December at discretion of parole board

The impact of the change in release mechanisms that have occurred since the mid 1970s is evident in Figure 15.1. Whereas 71.8 percent of state prisoners left prison in 1977 through the discretionary decision of a parole board, by 1990 this portion had dropped to 40.5 percent. Conversely, the mandatory releases from state prisons grew from about 6 percent of all releasees in 1977 to 29.6 percent in 1990.

Origins of Parole

Parole in the United States evolved during the nineteenth century out of such English, Australian, and Irish practices as conditional pardon, apprenticeship by indenture, and "tickets-of-leave" or licenses. These methods have as their common denom-

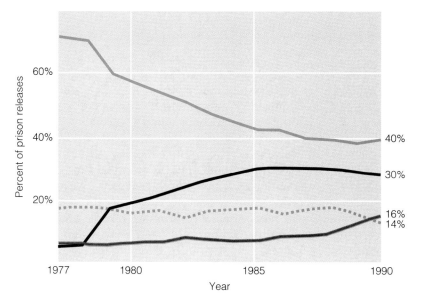

Legend:
— Discretionary parole releases
— Mandatory releases
···· Expiration releases
— Other conditional releases

Figure 15.1 ■ **Percentage of State Prisoners Released by Various Methods, 1977–1990.** With determinate sentences and mandatory release gaining momentum, fewer prisoners are released by parole boards.

Source: U.S. Department of Justice, Bureau of Justice Statistics, *Bulletin* (Washington, D.C.: Government Printing Office, November 1991), p. 5.

inator the movement of criminals out of prison (usually in response to overcrowding), the need for labor, and the cost of incarceration rather than any reason linked to the goal of the criminal sanction.

As we mentioned in Chapter 2, England relied on transportation as one of the major sanctions until the middle of the nineteenth century. With the independence of the United States, Australia and other Pacific colonies became the outlets for England's overcrowded prisons; offenders were given conditional pardons known as tickets-of-leave and sent to those outposts of the empire.

In the development of parole, two individuals stand out: Captain Alexander Maconochie and Sir Walter Crofton. Maconochie criticized definite terms and developed a system of rewards for good conduct, labor, and study. Through a classification procedure he called a mark system, prisoners could enter upon stages of increasing responsibility that led to freedom. These stages were (1) strict imprisonment, (2) labor on government chain gangs, (3) freedom within a limited area, (4) a ticket-of-leave or parole resulting in a conditional pardon, and (5) full restoration of liberty. He reasoned,

"When a man keeps the key of his own prison, he is soon persuaded to fit it to the lock."[2] Maconochie's ideas did not, however, sit well with the colonists in Australia, where the discharged felons would be released.

It was in Ireland that Maconochie's mark system was realized and linked to a ticket-of-leave, thanks to Crofton, who developed what became known as the Irish or intermediate system. After a period of strict imprisonment, offenders were transferred to an intermediate prison where they could accumulate marks based on work performance, behavior, and educational improvement. Eventually they would be given tickets-of-leave and released under supervision. Parolees were required to submit monthly reports to the police, and an inspector helped them find jobs and generally oversaw their activities. One study of 559 prisoners showed that only seventeen licenses had to be revoked. The concepts of the intermediate prison, assistance, and supervision were Crofton's contributions to the modern system of parole.

The effects of the English and Irish developments were felt across the Atlantic. Conditional pardons and reductions for good time

BIOGRAPHY

Alexander Maconochie

(1787–1860)

A naval officer, geographer, and penal reformer, Alexander Maconochie was born in Edinburgh, Scotland, in 1787. He entered the Royal Navy in 1803 and served in the Napoleonic Wars. A founder of the Royal Geographic Society (1813), Maconochie became private secretary to the lieutenant governor of the colony of Van Diemen's Land (now Tasmania) in 1836. This appointment was to lead to a more important post in the colony's administration, but after completing a report condemning the condition of discipline in the island's penal colony, he was removed from his position.

Maconochie held two views in regard to penology: (1) Punishment should be aimed at reform, not at vengeance, and (2) a sentence should be indeterminate, with release depending on the prisoner's industriousness and effort, not on time served. In 1840 he was given an opportunity to apply these principles as superintendent of the Norfolk Island penal settlement in the South Pacific. Under his direction, task accomplishment, not time served, was the criterion for release. Marks of commendation were given to prisoners who performed their tasks well, and they were released from the penal colony as they demonstrated willingness to accept society's rules.

Returning to England in 1844 to campaign for penal reform, Maconochie was appointed governor of the new Birmingham Borough Prison in 1849. But he was unable to institute his reforms there because he was dismissed from his position in 1851 on the grounds that his methods were too lenient. He died in 1860.

had been a part of American corrections since the beginning of the nineteenth century, but offenders whose terms were shortened in this manner were released without supervision. During a visit to Ireland in 1863, Gaylord Hubbell, warden of Sing Sing, was impressed by Crofton's innovations and urged that graded institutions and the mark system be made a part of New York's correctional arrangements. Franklin Sanborn, secretary of the State Board of Charities for Massachusetts, championed the Irish system. At the Cincinnati meeting of the National Prison Association in 1870, specific references to the Irish system were incorporated into the Declaration of Principles, along with such other reforms as the indeterminate sentence and classification based on a mark system.[3]

With New York's adoption of an indeterminate sentence law in 1876, Zebulon Brockway, superintendent of Elmira Reformatory, began to release prisoners on parole when he believed they were ready to return to society. Initially, the New York system did not require supervision by the police, as in Ireland, because parolees were placed in the care of private reform groups. As their numbers increased, the state replaced the volunteer supervisors with correctional employees.

The extension of the parole idea in the United States was linked to the indeterminate sentence. As states adopted indeterminate sentencing, parole followed. By 1900 twenty states had parole systems, but it was not until the 1920s that parole really caught on. From 1910, each federal prison had its own board made up

What adjustment problems face a "lifer" such as Israel Karp, released after spending 51 years of a life sentence in prison? Karp was convicted of second-degree murder and entered prison at the age of 17.

Parole has been controversial throughout its history. When an offender who has committed a particularly heinous crime, such as Charles Manson, becomes eligible for parole or when someone on parole has again raped, robbed, or murdered, the public is outraged. During the recent debate on rehabilitation, both parole and the indeterminate sentence were criticized on the grounds that release was tied to treatment success, that parole boards were abusing their discretion, and that inmates were being held in suspended animation—one more pain of imprisonment. It must be remembered, however, that while parole may be justified in terms of rehabilitation, deterrence, or the need to protect society, it performs other functions as well. As it reduces time spent in prison, it affects plea bargaining, the size of prison populations, and the level of discipline in correctional facilities.

The Decision to Release

An inmate's eligibility for release on parole depends on the requirements set by law and the sentence imposed by the court. During the shift away from the goal of rehabilitation since 1975 and the accompanying move to determinate sentences and mandatory release on parole, many states and the federal government have restructured the releasing mechanism. The release processes instituted by some states are so new that even now adjustments are being made in them. In some states prison crowding has required an easing of release criteria so that the size of the population can be reduced.

Although the mechanisms vary, in jurisdictions that have determinate sentences or parole guidelines, release from prison to community supervision is mandatory once the offender has served the required amount of time. Mandatory release becomes a matter of bookkeeping to ensure that the correct amount of good time and other credits have been allocated and that

of the warden, the medical officer, and the superintendent of prisons of the Department of Justice. The boards made release suggestions to the attorney general. The U.S. Board of Parole was created by Congress in 1930. Thus by 1932, forty-four states and the federal government had put this release mechanism in place. Today all jurisdictions have some mechanism for release of felons into the community under supervision. As we noted earlier, however, the shift to determinate sentencing has severed the connection between release on parole and performance in prison treatment programs. In states that have the determinate sentence, inmates must be released at the completion of their terms minus good time and other reductions. They nevertheless must remain under supervision for a time.

In most states a prisoner is released at the discretion of the parole board. What would you tell these people that would increase the probability of your being released?

the court's sentence has been accurately interpreted so that the offender moves automatically into the community at the expiration of the period. Where parole guidelines are in force, the releasing authority's discretion is formally restricted, but some discretion can be exercised informally. In the majority of states, however, the decision itself is discretionary, and the parole board has the authority to establish a date on the basis of an inmate's rehabilitation and characteristics.

Discretionary Release

In 1933 the American Prison Association asserted that the prisoner's fitness for reentry into the community should determine the release time. The decision to release a prisoner, it said, should depend on the answers to the following questions:

■ Has the institution accomplished all that it can for the offender?

■ Is the offender's state of mind and attitude toward the offender's own difficulties and problems such that further residence will be harmful or beneficial?

■ Does a suitable environment await the offender on the outside?

■ Can the beneficial effect already accomplished be retained if the offender is held longer to allow a more suitable environment to be developed?[4]

These and other questions that parole boards ask are, by their very nature, subjective interpretations.

Since the 1930s some boards have attempted to use prediction tables containing data specifying inmate characteristics that have been shown over time to correlate with parole success. Like actuarial tables used in the insurance industry, the tables attempt to predict behavior. They are based on the assumption that there is a "right" time to grant parole. An offender who is released too soon is likely to recidivate; an offender who is held in prison too long becomes bitter and is also likely to return to crime. Prediction tables were once thought to be useful devices to counter the tendency of parole boards to bow to pressures from correctional officials and the community, and so to hold inmates longer than necessary. Studies have shown that by and large these

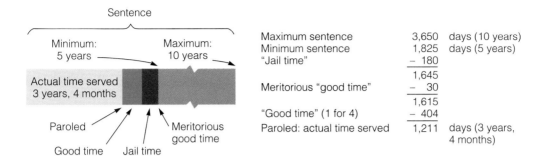

Maximum sentence	3,650	days (10 years)
Minimum sentence	1,825	days (5 years)
"Jail time"	− 180	
	1,645	
Meritorious "good time"	− 30	
	1,615	
"Good time" (1 for 4)	− 404	
Paroled: actual time served	1,211	days (3 years, 4 months)

Figure 15.2 ■ Computing Parole Eligibility: Discretionary Release.
Parole boards take into account a variety of factors when calculating parole eligibility, as shown in these calculations for Maurice Williams, discussed in this chapter's opening.

attempts at prediction have been unsuccessful. The tables have also been criticized on the grounds that they make no allowance for individual differences.

Procedure During the past decade the procedures used by discretionary release boards have undergone major changes. Most states have taken measures to ensure due process at the release hearing; about half the states now allow counsel to be present and witnesses to be called, and keep verbatim transcripts. In addition, most parole authorities now provide the inmate with both a written and an oral explanation of the decision immediately after action is taken. This is a far cry from the process as it was carried out in earlier years, when the inmate went alone into the "room full of strangers," was given about five minutes before the board, and later was told in writing only "granted" or "denied." Yet most inmates do not have access to their files even now and so are unable to determine the primary reason for denial or approval. And although the Supreme Court has issued due process rules for revocation hearings, it has not extended these procedures to the release interview.

Eligibility for a release hearing in discretionary states varies greatly. In prison films and novels, one regularly hears inmates say that they are going to "apply" for parole. In fact, one does not apply. Appearance before the parole board is a function of the individual sentence, statutory criteria, and the inmate's conduct during incarceration. Often the offender is eligible to be considered for release at the expiration of the minimum sentence minus good-time credits. In other states eligibility is at the discretion of the parole board or is calculated at one-third or one-half of the maximum sentence.

Figure 15.2 shows the calculations involved in computing parole eligibility for Maurice Williams, who was given a sentence of a minimum of five years and a maximum of ten years for the crime of first-degree robbery. At the time of sentencing he had been held in jail for six months awaiting trial and disposition of his case. Williams did well in the maximum security prison to which he was sent. He did not get into trouble and was thus able to amass good-time credit at the rate of one day for every four that he spent on good behavior. In addition, he was given thirty days' meritorious credit when he completed his high school equivalency test after attending the prison school for two years. After serving three years and four months of his sentence, he appeared before the Board of Parole and was granted extended parole. He will be released into the community after having served a total of three years and four months. Although the formal release decision is granted by the board acting as a whole, in most states this power is delegated to panels of two or three members sitting at the parole-granting hearings. In some other states the responsibility is further delegated to a hearing examiner, usually a staff member, who conducts the actual interview with the inmate and makes a recommendation to the full board. A survey of parole practices in 1976 found that regardless of the composition of the boards, most heard an average of between twenty and thirty cases a day.[5]

Release criteria What criteria do board members use to determine whether an inmate can be released? Parole boards provide inmates with a formal statement of the factors that are considered in making the release decision. These standards normally include:

- The nature and circumstances of the inmate's offense and the inmate's current attitude toward it

- The inmate's prior criminal record

- The inmate's attitude toward family members, the victim, and authority in general

- The inmate's institutional adjustment, participation, and progress in institutional programs for the inmate's self improvement

- The inmate's history of community adjustment

- The inmate's physical, mental, and emotional health

- The inmate's insight into the causes of the inmate's past criminal conduct

- The adequacy of the inmate's parole plan

Although the published criteria may help inmates know the board's expectations, the actual decision is a discretionary matter and is probably based on a combination of information and moral judgment. It is frequently said that parole boards release only good risks. However, one member counters, "There are no good-risk men in prison. Parole is really a deci-

sion of when to release bad-risk persons." Other considerations, such as internal prison control and morale, public sentiment, and the political implications of their decisions, weigh heavily on board members. Maurice Sigler, a former chairman of the Federal Parole Board, observed, "We have this terrible power; we sit up here playing God."[6]

In one study of parole decision making, Susette Talarico found that because about half of the variance among cases could be explained by seven of the specified criteria listed in the board's guidelines, the process was not completely arbitrary. The fact that the unexplained portion was so large, however, "implies that the decisional process is not the detailed, clinical assessment of treatment effects that the parole theory and model are based on."[7] Although inmates tend to think that their behavior in prison is the crucial factor in parole decisions, in fact it is of secondary importance to the parole board. Instead, the board seems to place great reliance on the background characteristics of the inmate (including family stability) and the inmate's parole plans (offers of a job, plans for a residence). This is not made clear and inmates may be misled by the reasons they are given when release is denied: They are often told to try harder to solve their personal problems through therapy, job training, or educational programs.

Talarico found significant variation among board members and among the three-person panels that sat to make the decisions. Some members responded more demonstrably to some offenses than to others. One member was very concerned about releasing sex offenders. Another questioned inmates very closely about attendance at religious services. Participation in treatment programs was also of special interest to some members. The variations in board members' attitudes and in the composition of the panels contributed to the seemingly whimsical nature of some of the decisions.

How to win release "If you want to get paroled, you've got to be in a program." This statement reflects one of the most controversial aspects of discretionary release: the link between treatment and release. Although penal authorities emphasize the voluntary nature of most treatment services and although clinicians will argue that therapy cannot be successful in a coercive atmosphere, the fact remains that inmates believe they must "play the game." Most parole boards stipulate that an inmate's progress in self-improvement programs is one of the criteria to be considered in a release decision. Accommodation to the perceived desires of the board may be the dominant motivation of many inmates; if they participate in certain rehabilitative programs their records will look good, the board will be impressed, and they will be released: "When I go to my therapy group, I can just play the game.... We sit there and talk about our problems so that the counselor will give us a good report. It is a lot better than making hay at the farm out in the hot sun."[8]

Many offenders come up for parole only to find that either they have not done enough to satisfy the board or they have been in the wrong program. The mismatch may result from the changing composition of the board (especially where a hearing examiner or a three-person panel is used). In addition, the availability of educational and rehabilitative services in most American prisons is limited, so that many offenders must wait long periods before they can be accepted into a program that fits their needs or that impresses the board. As we have seen, offenders' assignments to work, education, and treatment programs often have more to do with the institution's needs than with their own.

Consequences of discretionary parole

During the 1972 riot at New Jersey's Rahway Prison, inmates held aloft a banner that boldly proclaimed: "Abolish parole!" Why? Though inmates criticize the somewhat capricious actions of some parole boards, they also point out that indeterminate sentences and discretionary release leave them constantly in limbo—the uncertainty is demoralizing.

When release is discretionary, the parole board's power is much like that of the sen-

tencing judge. Detractors emphasize that unlike the judge, the board makes its decisions outside the spotlight of public attention. As Sol Rubin, a lawyer long critical of parole procedures, has pointed out, "In the face of similar responsibilities, a marked contrast prevails in the procedures used by parole boards and judges. Whereas the sentencing procedure must be surrounded by a fair amount of due process of law, the parole hearing is entirely devoid of either substantive or procedural due process requirements."[9]

Supporters of discretionary release maintain that parole boards are able to make their decision without community pressure and that they can rectify judicial sentencing errors. It can be said that legislatures, responding to public pressure, often prescribe maximum sentences that are unreasonable—thirty, fifty, a hundred years. But most penal codes also prescribe minimum sentences that are closer to the actual times served; the parole board is able to grant release after a period of incarceration that is "reasonable."

Mandatory Release

In response to the criticism that parole boards' release decisions are arbitrary and that rehabilitation should not be the primary criterion for returning inmates to the community, the discretionary power of parole boards in many states has been curtailed by the institution of guidelines designed to structure the release decision. In states where determinate sentences have been legislated, inmates are released when their sentences have been served, with adjustments made for good time.

A major charge against discretionary release is that being kept in limbo in regard to length of stay adds to the pains of imprisonment. Even longer incarceration would be more bearable, inmates say, if they could be told early in the sentence when they would be released. In some mandatory release states inmates receive a statement from the prison records office soon after they enter prison giving the expiration date of their incarceration and explaining how good-time provisions can reduce the sentence. Some jurisdictions that use parole guidelines also follow this procedure; in others, the inmate is told the release date at a hearing shortly before the minimum sentence is due to expire.

Parole guidelines Because of the wide discretion previously held by parole boards, guidelines have been developed primarily to reduce the disparities among the times served by offenders who have committed the same or similar crimes. A national survey conducted in 1986 found that eighteen jurisdictions used formal guidelines in making parole release decisions.[10]

Guidelines have been designed as a flexible way to structure the decision-making process to provide equity among groups of similar offenders, while still considering individual case factors.

Release is usually granted to those prisoners who have served the amount of time stipulated by the guidelines and who meet the following criteria:

■ An eligible prisoner has substantially observed the rules of the institution in which he or she has been confined.

■ The prisoner's release will not depreciate the seriousness of the offense or promote disrespect for the law.

■ The prisoner's release will not jeopardize the public welfare.[11]

In most jurisdictions in which parole guidelines are used prisoners are eligible for a release hearing within 120 days after incarceration; at that time a presumptive date of release is set on the basis of the guidelines. As indicated in Table 15.2, the Oregon Parole Guidelines include a "severity scale" that ranks crimes according to seriousness and a "criminal history/risk assessment" score that is based on offenders' characteristics as they are thought to relate to successful completion of community supervision.[12] When the offender's history/risk

score is placed next to the relevant offense on the severity scale, the board, the inmate, and correctional officials are able to know the average total time that will be served before release.

The criminal history/risk assessment scoring mechanism, shown in Table 15.3, is based on research indicating that certain kinds of inmates—first offenders, for example—have a greater probability of remaining free of crime than other sorts of inmates, such as drug addicts. This aspect of the guidelines may be opposed by civil libertarians and others who believe that to deny freedom on the basis of characteristics over which a person may have no control is at odds with the concepts of equal protection and due process. Others argue that the guidelines result in fixed and mechanical decisions that do not allow for the influence of rehabilitative programs or institutional behavior.

The presumptive release date may be modified at regularly scheduled parole review hearings (usually every eighteen months) and six months before the previously set date. The presumptive release date may be postponed because of disciplinary infractions, failure to establish a suitable community supervision plan, or new adverse information that comes to the attention of the board. Alternatively, the presumptive release date may be advanced because of good conduct, superior achievement in institutional programs, and other exceptional circumstances.

Determinate sentencing As we have discussed, determinate or fixed sentences have been adopted in response to criticisms of the rehabilitation model, with its emphasis on indeterminate sentences and discretionary parole release. Emerging from the deserved punishment model of the criminal sanction, determinate sentencing is based on the assumption that judges should give offenders a specific amount of time to serve rather than a minimum and a maximum. States vary somewhat in the discretion they permit the judge in choosing a term of incarceration from a range of years. But all convicted offenders who

Table 15.2 ■ **Number of Months to Be Served Before Release Under the Oregon Guidelines for Adult Offenders.** The amount of time to be served is related to the severity of the offense and the criminal history/risk assessment of the inmate. In this table, offenses are grouped according to severity; examples are included.

Offense severity	Criminal history/risk assessment score			
	11–9 Excellent	8–6 Good	5–3 Fair	2–0 Poor
Category 1: Bigamy, criminal mischief I, dogfighting, incest, possession of stolen vehicle	6	6	6–10	12–18
Category 2: Abandonment of a child, bribing a witness, criminal homicide, perjury, possession of controlled substance	6	6–10	10–14	16–24
Category 3: Assault III, forgery I, sexual abuse, trafficking in stolen vehicles	6–10	10–14	14–20	22–32
Category 4: Aggravated theft, assault II, coercion, criminally negligent homicide, robbery II	10–16	16–22	22–30	32–44
Category 5: Burglary I, escape I, manslaughter II, racketeering, rape I	16–24	24–36	40–52	56–72
Category 6: Arson I, kidnapping I, rape II, sodomy I	30–40	44–56	60–80	90–130
Category 7: Aggravated murder, treason	96–120	120–156	156–192	192–240
Category 8: Aggravated murder (stranger–stranger, cruelty to victim, prior murder conviction)	120–168	168–228	228–288	288–life

Source: Adapted from State of Oregon, Board of Parole, ORS Chapter 144, Rule 255-75-026 and Rule 255-75-035.

receive determinate sentences know, before they leave the courtroom, how much time they must serve. Under this model, release is not tied to participation in treatment programs. Instead, at the end of the term, less credited good time, the prisoner is automatically released to community supervision.

One effect of the determinate sentencing laws has been to shift the power to set the actual amount of time served from the parole board to the judge, but most of the new laws also provide for generous amounts of good time to be allocated by correctional officials. The rate at which good time can be accumulated, provisions for its vesting, and the amount that can be taken away for an offense are usually set by law. Institutional officials have, however, had a great deal of leeway in interpreting these rules, in devising the procedures

for revocation of good time, and in structuring the provisions so that good time can be used to enforce discipline. In some states, good-time provisions have been adjusted in response to the problem of prison crowding. In others, release to the community due to overcrowding has been formalized through legislation.

Some observers believe that in practice the discretionary releasing power lost by parole boards has been shifted to wardens and other correctional executives. In some states that have abolished discretionary release, good time can reach 55 percent of the term. In one such state, Connecticut, inmates may apply a year in advance of their discharge date for transfer to a halfway house or work release. A committee within the Department of Correction decides which prisoners may move to the community under a supervised

Table 15.3 ■ **Oregon Parole Guidelines: Criminal History/Risk Assessment Scoring Factors.** Determine the score by adding the points assigned to each factor.

Factor	Points	Score
A. No prior felony convictions as an adult or juvenile:	3	
One prior felony conviction:	2	
Two or three prior felony convictions:	1	
Four or more prior felony convictions:	0	_____
B. No prior felony or misdemeanor incarcerations (that is, executed sentences of ninety days or more) as an adult or juvenile:	2	
One or two prior incarcerations	1	
Three or more prior incarcerations:	0	_____
C. Verified period of three years conviction-free in the community prior to the present commitment:	1	
Otherwise:	0	_____
D. Age at commencement of behavior leading to this incarceration was _____; D.O.B. was _____/_____/_____.		
Twenty-six or older and at least one point received in Items A, B, or C:	2	
Twenty-six or older and no points received in A, B, or C:	1	
Twenty-one to under twenty-six and at least one point received in A, B, or C:	1	
Twenty-one to under twenty-six and no points received in A, B, or C:	0	
Under twenty-one:	0	_____
E. Present commitment does not include parole, probation, failure to appear, release agreement, escape, or custody violation:	2	
Present commitment involves probation, release, agreement, or failure to appear violation:	1	
Present commitment involves parole, escape, or custody violation:	0	_____
F. Has no admitted or documented substance abuse problem within a three-year period in the community immediately preceding the commission of the crime conviction:	1	
Otherwise:	0	_____
Total History/Risk Assessment Score:		_____

Source: Adapted from State of Oregon, Board of Parole, ORS Chapter 144, Rule 255-35-015.

home release program before the expiration of their sentences.

Some states have already informally developed mechanisms that have blunted the effect of determinate sentences. With prison populations at an all-time high, corrections departments are reinventing procedures akin to discretionary parole release so as to regain flexibility at times when the number of prisoners meets capacity ceilings. Since 1980 twenty-one state legislatures have enacted emergency powers acts (EPA) designed to provide authorization for either the governor or commissioner of corrections to declare that crowded conditions require that parole eligibility or mandatory release dates be advanced so that prison numbers can be reduced.[13]

The Consequences of the Release Decision

The actions of parole boards and sentencing judges directly affect the size and composition of the body of offenders in prison and in the community. Policy decisions that affect the size of one group may well affect the other. An increase in prison commitments, for example, eventually leads to a rise in the number under community supervision. A tightening of parole board policies slows releases and may increase the number of revocations, thus adding to the institutional population. Shifts in sentencing or good-time policies affect the length of the period between incarceration and consideration for discretionary or mandatory release. The rate of return of parole violators, the rate of parole release, and the prison time served are controlled, within statutory constraints, by the paroling authority. But the attitudes of judges and the actions of institutional officials also enter into the mix.

National data show that over ten thousand more offenders are now entering prison each year than the number that leave, but it is difficult to determine the role of parole release in this situation.[14] States with higher parole release rates tend to have smaller than expected prison populations when compared to states with lower parole release rates. Yet in the states where parole was granted at a lesser rate, prisoners did not necessarily serve longer average terms. As a result of shorter sentences, more generous good-time rates, and greater exercise of executive clemency, time served was often relatively short, even when parole was granted less frequently. These data impress upon us the complexity of the interrelationships of the correctional subsystems and the extent to which changes in one portion may be offset by changes in another portion. They show that many factors may serve to shorten the prison term.

With the numbers incarcerated continuing to rise and with states under increased fiscal restraints, the 1990s will undoubtedly see a rebirth of discretionary release and far greater numbers of offenders on parole.

The Effect on Sentencing

Although U.S. judges are often said to give the longest prison sentences in the Western world, little attention has been paid to the amount of time that offenders actually serve. One of the important features of parole is that it allows an administrative body to alter a judge's pronouncement significantly. In states that have moved to determinate sentencing or to the use of parole guidelines, this is no longer so, but various reductions are built into the sentence so that full time is still rarely served.

To understand the effect of parole on criminal justice, one needs to compare the amounts of time actually served in prison with the sentences specified by judges. In some jurisdictions up to 80 percent of felons sentenced to prison are paroled after their first appearance before the board. In most states the minimum term of the sentence, minus good time and jail time, ordinarily determines eligibility for parole consideration.

While there is considerable variation among the states, it is estimated that, on a national basis, first-time felony inmates serve an average of two years before release. As shown in Figure 15.3, the amount of time served in prison varies with the nature of the offense. Indeterminate sentences, good time, and parole release shorten the amount of time that inmates spend in prison. Note that although offenders who received longer terms did remain in prison for longer periods, the proportion of the sentence actually served dropped rapidly as the length of sentence increased. For example, the robbery offenders who were sentenced to terms of 12 to 60 months actually served 76 percent of their terms; those sentenced to terms of 181 to 240 months actually served only 38 percent. Most members of the general public would probably be shocked to learn that the actual time served is so much less than the sentences announced in court and published in the newspapers.

Because the defendant is primarily concerned about when he or she will be freed, and because the prosecutor is concerned about a sentence that the public will view as appropriate to the crime but that will still encourage a plea bargain, parole's impact on the time actually served is in the interests of both sides.

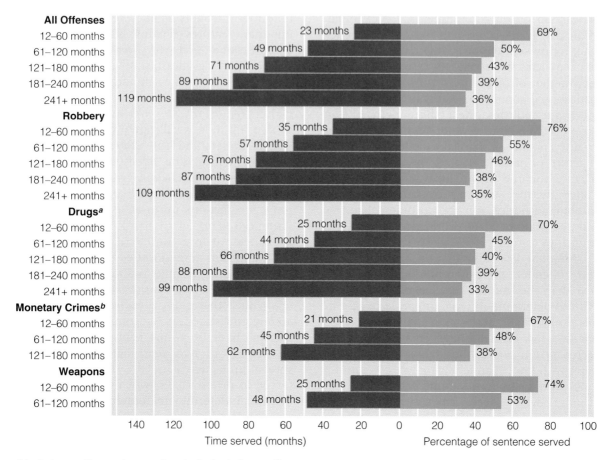

All Offenses
12–60 months — 23 months / 69%
61–120 months — 49 months / 50%
121–180 months — 71 months / 43%
181–240 months — 89 months / 39%
241+ months — 119 months / 36%

Robbery
12–60 months — 35 months / 76%
61–120 months — 57 months / 55%
121–180 months — 76 months / 46%
181–240 months — 87 months / 38%
241+ months — 109 months / 35%

Drugs[a]
12–60 months — 25 months / 70%
61–120 months — 44 months / 45%
121–180 months — 66 months / 40%
181–240 months — 88 months / 39%
241+ months — 99 months / 33%

Monetary Crimes[b]
12–60 months — 21 months / 67%
61–120 months — 45 months / 48%
121–180 months — 62 months / 38%

Weapons
12–60 months — 25 months / 74%
61–120 months — 48 months / 53%

Time served (months)   Percentage of sentence served

[a] Includes marijuana, drug, and controlled substance offenses.

[b] Includes counterfeiting, forgery, fraud, mail theft, embezzlement, interstate transportation of stolen securities, and receiving stolen property with intent to sell. Excludes burglary and theft.

Figure 15.3 ■ **Average Time Served by Adults Convicted of Selected Federal Offenses.** Note that the longer the sentence, the smaller is the percentage of time actually served. What accounts for this anomaly?

Source: U.S. Department of Justice, Bureau of Justice Statistics, *Special Report* (Washington, D.C.: Government Printing Office, June 1987), p. 4.

From the standpoint of prison administrators, good time and parole release help to maintain inmate discipline and reduce crowding.

Supporters of discretion for the paroling authority argue that the courts do not adequately dispense justice and that the availability of parole has invaluable benefits for the system. Parole mitigates the harshness of the penal code, it equalizes disparities in-

evitable in sentencing behavior, and prison administrators need it to maintain order. Supporters also contend that postponing sentence determination to the parole stage affords an opportunity for a more detached evaluation than is possible in the atmosphere of a trial, and that early release is economically sensible because the cost of incarceration is considerable.

The Organization of Releasing Authorities

By the statutes they enact, legislatures either grant authority to parole boards to release prisoners or stipulate the conditions for mandatory release from a determinate sentence. Historically, such power was in the hands of the governor, and even up to 1939 the chief executive remained the only paroling authority in sixteen states. The chief executive no longer has that power, though in most states the governor appoints the members of the parole board.

Clusters of questions surround the choice of organizational structure for the releasing authority:

- Should the board be autonomous or consolidated with the corrections authority?

- How are field services to be administered?

- Should the board sit full- or part-time?

- How are board members to be appointed?

During the past decade the answers to these questions have tended to forge strong links between the paroling authority and the department of corrections, with an emphasis on professionalization of parole board personnel.

Autonomous Versus Consolidated

A board may be either independent from the correctional institutions (autonomous model) or an independent decision-making body within the department of corrections (consolidation model). The states are about equally divided in their choice of model. Proponents of the autonomous model argue that independence from correctional personnel makes for more objective parole decisions. The board should not be influenced, they say, by such considerations as the institution's wish to reduce the size of its population or to punish inmates who do not conform to the rules. But others say that the autonomous parole board can become unresponsive to the needs and programs of corrections and is too far removed from the daily activities of the institutions to appreciate the subtleties of each case.

This problem is exacerbated by the fact that autonomous boards depend on others for the information on which they base their decisions. When the decision-making process is fragmented, the institutional staff and the parole board may work at cross-purposes. Parole boards have often been critical of the information they are given to help them make crucial decisions. Frequently, the facts are fitted into a stereotyped format and the individual aspects of a given case are lost, with the result that the decision may be arbitrary and unfair as well as undesirable from a correctional standpoint. Many prisoners would rather have the releasing decision made by institutional personnel who know them personally than by an outside board. Other critics say that persons with little knowledge of or experience with the correctional process are often appointed to autonomous boards.

In response to these criticisms, parole activities have tended recently to be located within the department of corrections or in a multifunctional department of human services. Under this model the board retains its independent decision-making authority but is organizationally close enough to the department to be sensitive to institutional and correctional needs. When parole decisions are made by people who are closely connected with corrections, it is thought they are more likely to be based on the individual offenders' suitability for release.

But we must remember that no matter what the formal organizational structure, the paroling authority does not exist in a vacuum, immune to political and organizational influences. The autonomous parole board may develop conflicts with correctional authorities so that the information needed for decision making may be "unavailable" or biased. The board that is closely tied to corrections runs the risk of being viewed by prisoners and the general public as merely a rubber stamp for the department.

WORKPERSPECTIVE

The Mix of Backgrounds and Perspective of the Alabama Parole Board

Joel Barfoot, State of Alabama
Board of Pardons and Paroles

 With my background as a police officer and my conservative political viewpoint, you might presume that I would be the most conservative board member, but that distinction belongs to the Reverend John Nettles, a civil rights activist. My lock-em-up-and-throw-away-the-key mentality began to shift when I saw people being locked up who could just as well have been handled through alternative means. This only makes victims out of every tax-paying citizen.

As parole board members, we focus on three areas: (1) public protection, (2) rehabilitation, and (3) punishment. Public protection is our key concern—we must be reasonably sure that the release of an inmate won't endanger the public.

We review files approximately sixty days in advance of the parole hearing to determine suitability for parole. We look at the crime itself, time served, disciplinary record while in prison, program participation in prison, prior record, protest letters, letters in favor of the inmate, warden reports, institutional parole officer's reports, and any other miscellaneous information. At the parole hearing itself we review the file and listen to anyone who wishes to speak in behalf of or against the inmate. At this time we can either grant or deny parole.

One factor that causes prison overcrowding and puts pressure on the parole board in Alabama is the Habitual Offender Act. Another problem is disparity in sentencing.

Because of these problems, someone who walks away from the work release program or steals a small amount of property, for example, can receive a life sentence while someone who sets his or her child on fire may get only ten years. In cases such as these the board makes an effort to adjust and equalize the sentences in order that offenders serve approximately the same time for the same offense.

Which offenders make the best candidates for parole? Let's examine a few types.

- **Murderers.** Surprisingly, convicted murderers generally make the best parolees. Predatory and multiple murderers should be kept in prison, but persons who murder in the heat of the moment can usually be rehabilitated.

- **Sex offenders.** Because recidivism rates for these offenders are high, they are poor candidates for parole. If sex offenders are paroled, it is usually after they have completed an intensive treatment program, and they are placed under strict supervision with a strong aftercare program.

- **Drug offenders.** Although these offenders have a high parole revocation rate, we try to get them into treatment programs to work out their problems rather then simply return them to prison. And if we do revoke parole, we do so for only a few months to get the parolee some help inside.

- **Property offenders.** Most of these offenders are also substance abusers and if they can get this problem under control, they usually succeed on parole. An exception is some female offenders, who don't consider the consequences of these crimes or are kleptomaniacs.

- **Assaulters.** After participating in mental health workshops and intensive programs in anger management and anger-induced acting-out, these offenders become better candidates for parole. Ongoing counseling upon being paroled is important, however.

Because we are really playing God with inmates' lives as well as the general public, we take our responsibilities seriously—a bad decision can have a catastrophic effect on so many people.

Judith C. O'Connor, State of Alabama
Board of Pardons and Paroles

I have always dreamed about and worked toward serving on the Alabama parole board. However, my dreams never included the nightmarish situations we are constantly confronted with.

The most difficult and stressful decisions revolve around trying to balance the department's interests with those of individual employees. I have observed a number of personnel incidents in which what seemed best for the individual employee was in direct conflict with what seemed best for the agency, especially considering that the manner in which you treat one employee sets a precedent for future treatment of other employees.

A similar conflict comes into play in decisions to parole or not to parole in trying to balance society's interests with those of victims and their families. In some cases the best interests of society conflict with the best interests of individual victims. For example, in the case of first-time offenses with victim injury or death where all factors strongly indicate parole as an appropriate course, this decision might be emotionally anguishing to the victim. Moreover, prison overcrowding forces parole board members to choose between attempting to prevent future victimization and ignoring the feelings of the victim.

No matter how difficult and stressful my current position is, however, field parole and probation officers have it worse. These officers have equally difficult, though different, responsibilities and liabilities but have less authority. Responsibility without equal authority to make the final decisions places these people in a tough situation. As a board member, I do take into consideration the supervisability of a parole candidate because I remember what it was like to be the field officer.

Another factor that makes being a parole and probation officer more stressful has to do with the length of time a case must be dealt with. Once parole board members make their decision, their task is complete. By contrast, the parole officer maintains long-term, on-going, working relationships with parolees and probationers. To illustrate, picture an enormous boulder on an incline with two workers, each with a chisel and hammer, chipping away at the boulder—one worker, the parole board member, on the upper side of the incline, and the other worker, the field parole and probation officer, on the lower side. As a parole board member, even though my ultimate task is the same as that of the field parole and probation officer, I do not have the added stress of fearing that the boulder will roll over me. One of my main objectives as a board member is to reduce the incline, provide a jackhammer instead of hammer and chisel, and hire an army of workers.

If any offender changes for the better as a result of contact with this agency, that change is primarily a result of the ongoing contact with the field officer. The better the working conditions and the tools, and the smaller the ratio of staff to offender, the better the chances of positive change on behalf of the offender.

John S. Nettles, State of Alabama
Board of Pardons and Paroles

About four years ago, when I was appointed to the parole board, I assumed I was being placed in a prestigious position that would demand little and please many. That assumption was short-lived.

In addition to my current responsibilities as a member of the Alabama Pardons & Paroles Board, I also serve as a State President of the Alabama Southern Christian Leadership Conference and Southeastern Regional Vice President.

Despite being an activist in the Civil Rights Movement for more than thirty-five years, I have become the most conservative member of the board as it related to violent crimes! One might wonder whether I am just another black man who has been placed in a position of authority and has developed amnesia. This could not be further from the truth! I am constantly seeking to create positive change for African Americans on the front end of the social and economic spectrum. In other words, this "outsider" who has now become an "insider" maintains an unwavering pledge to uphold the laws of Alabama and the Constitution of the United States.

Moreover, while racism and discrimination still exist in Alabama and across America, the African-American community must also deal with its self-imposed impediments. Not everything that happens to African Americans is the fault of white America. We must assume part of the blame for our own shame. Though we comprise only 25 percent of Alabama's population, we make up more than 70 percent of its prison population.

As a Board member, I see more than victims and their relatives; I also see the relatives of inmates. And I feel the pain, the disappointments, the victimizations of the parents of inmates. But unequivocally, I also see another entity too often overlooked. I see the victims. I see individuals who have labored and sacrificed to achieve a certain level of living, only to have someone take it away. I feel the pain of the victims who have been robbed, injured, and raped, and those whose loved ones have been murdered. Although I do not believe in capital punishment I do think murderers, rapists, and other Class A felons should receive harsh sentences if punishment is to be a deterrent.

During the process of one revocation hearing, an African-American man said, "Reverend, I know that you are going to let me out. You are a true brother!" His record reflected a history of assaultive behavior, including several assaults, an attempted murder, and a murder. All of the victims had been African Americans. My response to him was, "You have wounded and killed my brothers." His parole was revoked based on the testimony at the hearing. As a minister, I will temper mercy with justice, but I will do all within the realms of my responsibility to ensure equitable punishment and the protection of every Alabamian.

Joel Barfoot, a former sheriff, is chairman of the Alabama Parole Board. Judith O'Connor is a former parole officer. John Nettles is a full-time minister.

Family and community relations have to be reforged when a prisoner is released.

cational release. Hence, it is argued that the institutional staff and the parole board must be coordinated—an objective more easily attained if they are in the same department.

Full-Time Versus Part-Time

A third set of questions concerns the matter of a full-time board versus a part-time board. Because of the increased complexity of corrections, many people, both in discretionary and in mandatory release states, hold that administration of parole should be a full-time enterprise. The type of person who is able to serve full time on a parole board differs considerably from one who serves on a part-time basis. Membership on a board that meets full time requires one to devote all of one's energies to the job; such positions attract correctional professionals. Part-time boards receive more input from the community because their members have other careers and devote only a portion of their energies to parole.

Appointment

Members of the paroling authority may be appointed by the governor or by the head of the corrections department. Some people believe that gubernatorial selection insulates the members from the department, provides "better" members, and permits greater responsiveness to public concerns. Others believe that the parole mechanism should be apolitical and that it should be operated by people who really know something about corrections.

Selection of members of parole boards is often based on the assumption that people with training in the behavioral sciences are able to discern which candidates have been rehabilitated and are ready to return to society. The statutory qualifications for parole board membership in five states are listed in Table 15.4. However, in many states political considerations dictate that members should include representatives of specific racial groups

Boards of both types have to operate under the pressure of public opinion. Parole board members understand that they have to be very cautious in releasing prisoners because if parolees become involved in further offenses, the news media always point to the board as having let them out.

Field Services

Questions similar to those concerning the organization of the releasing authority surround the organization of field services. Should community supervision be administered by the paroling authority, or should it be part of the department of corrections? When the board administers field services, proponents of this model say, consistent policies can be developed with regard to parole, release, and supervision. During the past decade, however, there has been a movement to make the transition from incarceration to the community more gradual, and most departments have instituted such preparole programs as work release and edu-

Table 15.4 ■ Statutory Qualifications for Parole Board Membership in Selected States. Although many states require that board members meet certain educational criteria, political considerations are important in other states.

Jurisdiction	Statutory qualifications for membership
Montana	Academic training that qualifies board member for professional practice in a field such as criminology, education, psychiatry, psychology, law, social work, sociology, or guidance counseling. Related work experience in these areas listed may be substituted for these educational requirements. One board member must have particular knowledge of Indian culture and problems.
New York	Each member of the board shall have graduated from an accredited four-year college or university with a degree in the field of criminology, administration of criminal justice, law enforcement, sociology, law, social work, corrections, psychology, psychiatry, or medicine, and shall have had at least five years of experience in one or more of such fields.
Ohio	No person shall be appointed a member of the board who is not qualified by education or experience in correctional work, including law enforcement, probation, parole, in law, in social work, or in a combination of the three categories.
Pennsylvania	An individual shall have at least six years of professional experience in parole, including one year in supervisory or administrative capacity, and a bachelor's degree. Any equivalent combination of experience and training shall be acceptable.
West Virginia	Each member of the board shall have had experience in the field of social science or administration of penal institutions and shall be familiar with the principles, practices, and problems thereof and shall be otherwise competent to perform the duties of his office.

Source: Edward E. Rhine, William R. Smith, and Ronald W. Jackson, *Paroling Authorities: Recent History and Current Practice* (Laurel, Md.: American Correctional Association, 1991), p. 36.

or geographical areas. The Mississippi board recently consisted of a contractor, a businessman, a farmer, and a clerk; the Florida board included a newspaperman, an attorney, and a man with experience in both business and probation; the state of Washington's board had persons with training and experience in sociology, government and law, the ministry, and juvenile rehabilitation. As you might imagine, boards as disparate as these turn out widely varied release decisions.

Release to the Community

The development of community corrections has had a great impact on the operation of most aspects of the corrections system. Some of the most striking effects have been on the nature of incarceration and on decisions concerning release.

Out of the philosophy of community corrections came the reintegration model of prison

Table 15.5 ■ Characteristics of Prerelease Programs in Various Jurisdictions. Correctional systems have developed programs to help ease the inmates' transition to the community. Note the variety of organizations prepared to assist the offender upon release.

State	Eligibility	Role of outside agencies and/or volunteers
Arkansas	Inmate must have a projected release date of not more than 120 days at time of transfer; must not have pending felony detainers; has not been convicted of a sex offense or exhibited a history of abnormal sexual behavior while incarcerated; does not have a pending prior disciplinary charge; and does not require special medical consideration which cannot be handled by the unit/center.	The Arkansas Employment Security Division (outside agency) assists in obtaining employment for prerelease inmates and assists with transportation for them to and from job interviews. Outside community volunteers provide religious activities and some counseling.
Florida	Before release from community correctional centers, immediately prior to participation in community work release.	Citizen volunteers are utilized as well as other community, private, and state agencies.
Maryland	Twelve months from next parole hearing or expiration date; maintain an infraction-free adjustment for a minimum of six months; first- and second-degree sex offenses are precluded along with those convicted of three serious offenses with at least one prior commitment.	Provide various services, including employment readiness, drug and alcohol therapy, vocational training, and some psychological services.
Oregon	Inmate must be within six months of an established release date and must be minimum custody.	Utilize practicums and volunteers for counseling inmate club activities, and religious services. Also present a release services seminar twice a month which relies almost solely on volunteer instruction.
South Carolina	No detainers; participation is during final 30 days of incarceration, prior to good-time release. Parole board may specify participation prior to effecting parole.	Approximately 75 percent of all prerelease programming is conducted by other agencies and volunteers. They are the primary providers of all such services.

Source: Adapted from *Corrections Compendium* 5–8 (8 March 1984): Copyright ©1984 Contact Center, Inc. Reprinted by permission.

life. The goal of this model is to prepare the offender for reentry into society through the gradual allocation of freedoms and responsibilities during the period of incarceration. Where this model has been adopted, prisoners are placed at a high level of custody when they enter the institution and are periodically evaluated. As they progress, the level of custody is lowered so they can reestablish family ties and begin to heal the damage done by their crime and subsequent incarceration. Furloughs and increased visitation privileges are often arranged. Toward the latter part of the sentence, the offender may be placed on work release, transferred to a halfway house, or given other opportunities to live in the community. The characteristics of selected prerelease programs are shown in Table 15.5.

In most states, prison programs have been designed to prepare the offender for release to community supervision. Prerelease counseling is provided so that the offender understands the conditions of supervision, and assistance is given in the search for employment and a place to live. In some correctional systems these activities begin as much as a year in advance of the targeted release date; in others they begin only after the parole board has set that date.

California, for example, provides a three-week, full-time training program for inmates who are within fifteen to forty-five days of release. Inmates are given training in the attitudes needed to get and keep a job, communication skills, family roles, money management, and community and parole resources. The prisoners and their needs are evaluated. Each prisoner is then given a list of five objectives to be achieved within thirty days of being paroled, and the names and addresses of five public or private agencies that can be called upon for assistance. During the training program each prisoner participates in at least one mock job interview and acquires a California driver's license.

A similar program in North Carolina includes transfer of the participating inmates to a housing unit reserved for prereleases. One week of the four-week period is devoted to family readjustment training. With the emphasis on reintegration and community supervision, offenders are no longer confined to one cell in one institution for the duration of their terms; they move about a great deal from one security level to another and from one institution to another as they prepare for the day when they will be released.

Knowledge of the date of an offender's release exerts a powerful influence on all aspects of incarceration. With release to community supervision, the final phase of the offender's ties to corrections begins. At least it is hoped that this will be the final phase, and that the inmate will not reenter the criminal justice system.

Summary

During most of the twentieth century the parole board decided when most prisoners were released to the community. With the coming of determinate sentencing and guidelines, releasing power has essentially been taken from the board in many states. It is now necessary to distinguish between discretionary release and mandatory release. The word *parole* has remained as a general term for release and supervision in the community.

Parole in the United States evolved in the nineteenth century from practices in England, Ireland, and Australia. Alexander Maconochie and Walter Crofton made significant contributions to the development of parole.

Discretionary release is influenced by the rehabilitation model. Parole boards consider such factors as participation in treatment programs, readiness for the community, the seriousness of the offense, and the availability of suitable employment.

Mandatory release is determined on the basis of a determinate sentence or the use of parole guidelines. These mechanisms limit the discretion of correctional officials.

The release decision affects the size of the prison population, plea bargaining, and the lengths of sentences. One criticism of discretionary release is that it shifts responsibility from the judge to the parole board.

Releasing authorities are organized in a variety of ways. Questions about organization concern the method by which members are appointed to the board, whether the board meets full time or part-time, whether it is independent of the department of corrections, and whether it administers field services.

Increased reliance on the reintegration model of institutional operation has affected the way prisons are run. Where this model has been implemented, inmates are placed in housing units of decreasing security levels as their release dates approach. Furloughs, work and educational release, halfway houses, and pre-release training are elements of the reintegration model. One result of this orientation is that prison populations are more transient than they were in the days of the big house, and close ties among inmates have less chance to develop.

For Discussion

1. Mandatory release has been developed as a means of harnessing the discretion of the parole board and judge. What are the implications of mandatory release for the corrections system? How will corrections adjust to this new factor?

2. What factors should a parole board consider when it evaluates a prisoner for release?

3. As a parole board member, you are confronted by a man who has served six years of a ten-to-twenty-year sentence for murder. He has a good institutional record, and you do not believe him to be a threat to community safety. Explain the reasons behind your decision regarding whether to release him to parole supervision at this time.

4. You have been asked to decide whether the department of corrections or an independent agency should have authority over release decisions. Where would you place that authority? Explain your reasoning.

5. Given the current attitudes of the public toward criminals, what do you see as the likely future of parole release?

For Further Reading

Glaser, Daniel. *The Effectiveness of a Prison and Parole System.* New York: Bobbs-Merrill, 1964. A classic study of the links between incarceration and parole.

Goodstein, Lynne, and Hepburn, J. R. *Determinate Sentencing and Imprisonment: A Failure of Reform.* Cincinnati, Ohio: Anderson, 1985. Examination of the impact of the determinate sentencing reforms on incarceration and parole.

Rhine, Edward E.; Smith, William R.; and Jackson, Ronald W. *Paroling Authorities: Recent History and Current Practice.* Laurel, Md.: American Correctional Association, 1991. A national survey conducted by the ACA Task Force on Parole.

Stanley, David T. *Prisoners Among Us.* Washington, D.C.: Brookings Institution, 1976. Still the only major published account of parole release decision making. Emphasis upon parole board discretion.

Von Hirsch, Andrew, and Hanrahan, Kathleen J. *The Question of Parole.* Cambridge, Mass.: Ballinger, 1979. Examines parole from the "just deserts" perspective and urges its reform.

Notes

1. Adapted from Susette Talarico, "The Dilemma of Parole Decision Making," in *Criminal Justice: Law and Politics,* 5th ed., ed. George F. Cole (Pacific Grove, Calif.: Brooks/Cole, 1988), p. 442.

2. David T. Stanley, *Prisoners Among Us* (Washington, D.C.: Brookings Institution, 1976), p. 2.

3. Harry Elmer Barnes and Nedgley K. Teeters, *New Horizons in Criminology* (Englewood Cliffs, N.J.: Prentice-Hall, 1944), pp. 550, 553.

4. Quoted in Edwin H. Sutherland and Donald R. Cressey, *Criminology* (Philadelphia: Lippincott, 1970), p. 587.

5. Vincent O'Leary and Kathleen J. Hanrahan, "Law and Practice in Parole Proceedings: A National Survey," *Criminal Law Bulletin* 13 (May-June 1977): 182.

6. Quoted in Robert Wool, "The New Parole and the Case of Mr. Simms," *New York Times Magazine,* 29 July 1973, p. 21.

7. Susette M. Talarico, "Patterns of Decision Making in the Judicial Process: The Special Case of Probation and Parole" (Ph.D. dissertation, University of Connecticut, 1975), p. 136. For a report of parole decision making in Pennsylvania see John S. Carroll, Richard L. Wiener, Dan Coates, Jolene Galegher, and James J. Albirio, "Evaluation, Diagnosis, and Prediction in Parole Decision Making," *Law and Society* 17 (1982): 199–228.

8. George F. Cole and Charles H. Logan, "Parole: The Consumer's Perspective," *Criminal Justice Review* 1 (Fall 1977): 71.

9. Quoted in Ronald L. Goldfarb and Linda R. Singer, *After Conviction* (New York: Simon & Schuster, 1973), p. 282.

10. S. Christopher Baird and Donna Lerner, *A Survey of the Use of Guidelines and Risk Assessments by State Parole Boards* (Washington, D.C.: Government Printing Office, 1986).

11. Barbara Stone-Meierhoefer and Peter B. Hoffman, "Presumptive Parole Dates: The Federal Approach," *Federal Probation* 46 (June 1982): 41.

12. Oregon's Parole Guidelines do not apply to offenders sentenced under the state's new presumptive sentencing system, but they are still in effect for inmates serving long sentences under the previous code.

13. Edward E. Rhine, William R. Smith, and Ronald W. Jackson, *Paroling Authorities: Recent History and Current Practice* (Laurel, Md.: American Correctional Association, 1991), p. 28.

14. U.S. Department of Justice, Bureau of Justice Statistics, *Bulletin* (Washington, D.C.: Government Printing Office, May 1992), p. 4.

16

Making It: Supervision in the Community

When I get out, I'm going to get a steak, a bottle, and a blonde.

Inmate, Stateville

Overview of the Postrelease Function
Community Supervision
Revocation
The Structure of Community Supervision
Agents of Community Supervision
The Community Supervision Bureaucracy
Residential Programs
The Offender's Experience of Postrelease Life
The Strangeness of Reentry
The Problem of Unmet Personal Needs
Barriers to Success
Making It As a Game
Postrelease Supervision
How Effective Is it?
What Are Its Prospects?
Summary

Returning to the streets after years behind bars is a shock; the most normal, unremarkable events seem to take on overwhelming significance. Max, an inmate who was in prison for six years, recently described his experience to a team of researchers.

> The first few days out were a flash. That's all I can say, man. There's cars and dogs and trees and people, you know, and you walk down the street and there's mailboxes and there's houses and screen doors. And it all comes back to you. Things that you'd wanted to do, places that you'd wanted to go, things you wanted to see. It's all there, and you try to get them all at once. That's one reason why a lot of people are going back, man, because they're trying to do everything at once. I'm still flashing. Sometimes I think I'm back in the joint, man. I say, "Wow, where am I? I'm free. I'm here. I'm doing fine."[1]

The popular notion is that once offenders have completed their prison sentences, they have paid their "debt" and are ready to start life anew. The reality is that the vast majority of offenders released from prison remain subject to correctional authority for some time. For many offenders, this authority is represented by the parole officer; for others, it is the staff of a halfway house or work release center. The "freedom" of release is constrained: The whereabouts of offenders are monitored and their associations and daily activities are checked.

The freedom of offenders who are released outright—either because they have completed their maximum term (the maximum sentence minus good time) or, in the case of Maine, because there is no parole supervision—is also less complete than it may seem. The former inmate still has many serious handicaps to face: long absence from family and friends, legal and practical limitations on employment possibilities, the suspicion and uneasiness of acquaintances, even the strangeness of everyday living. The outside can seem alien and unpredictable after even a short time in the artificial environment behind bars.

No matter what the intentions of others, the former inmate always faces the cold fact that no truly "clean start" is possible. The change in status is from convict to former convict; the new status is nearly as stigmatizing as the old, and in many ways is more frustrating. In the former convict's mind, he or she is "free." Yes, the crime was a big mistake, but the prison time has paid for it and now there is a chance to turn over a new leaf. Yet most people look at the parolee askance and treat him or her as though there is still something to prove. The experience can be more than disappointing: It can be embittering.

This chapter is about "making it," the struggle of the former inmate not to return to prison. Many fail; about half of all released offenders return to prison within six years. From another perspective, though, the number of offenders who succeed is impressive. Most are under the scrutiny of agents of the state; all are faced with significant legal, familial, and social strains. How many of us would be vulnerable to misconduct under such pressures? Released offenders are playing with what seems to be a stacked deck; that so many make it is testimony to their perseverance.

Overview of the Postrelease Function

Parolees are released from prison on condition that they remain within the law and that they live in accordance with rules designed both to aid their readjustment to society and to control their movement. The parolee may be required to abstain from alcohol, to keep away from undesirable associates, to follow good work habits, and not to leave the community without permission. These requirements, called **conditions of release,** serve to regulate conduct that in itself is not criminal but that is thought to be linked to the possibility of future criminality. Specific conditions of release are set forth in Figure 16.1, a parole contract that New Jersey parolees are required to sign.

Community Supervision

The restrictions placed on parolees are justified on the grounds that people who have been incarcerated must readjust to the community gradually, so that they will not simply fall back into their preconviction habits and associations. Some people hold that the attempt to impose on parolees standards of conduct that are not imposed on others is wrong and likely to lead to failure. It is further argued that new parolees find themselves in such daunting circumstances that it is very hard for them to live according to the rulebook.

When releasees first come out of prison, their personal and material problems are staggering. In most states they are given only clothes, a token amount of money, a copy of the rules governing their release, and the name and address of the parole officer to whom they must report within twenty-four hours. Although a promised job is often a condition of release, an actual job may be another matter. Most former convicts are unskilled or semiskilled, and parole stipulations may keep them from moving to areas where they could find work. If they are black and under thirty, they join the largest group of unemployed in the country, with the added handicap of former convict status.

Reentry problems help explain the fact that most parole failures occur relatively soon after release—nearly one-quarter during the first six months. With little preparation, offenders move from the highly structured, authoritarian life of the institution into a life filled with temptations and complicated problems. They are expected to summon up extraordinary cop-

---

conditions of release   Restrictions on the parolees' conduct that must be obeyed as a legally binding requirement of being released.

ing abilities. Not surprisingly, the social, psychological, and material overload sends many parolees back. For return rates for parolees of various characteristics, see Table 16.1.

Revocation

When people fail on parole, their parolee status is revoked and they return to prison to continue serving their sentences. Parole can be revoked for two reasons: commission of a new crime and violation of the conditions of parole (a "technical violation"). Technical violations are controversial because they involve conduct that is not criminal, such as failure to report an address change to the parole officer.

Critics of parole argue that it is improper to reimprison a parolee for misbehavior of such a minor nature. In practice, revocations seldom result from a single rules violation—prisons are far too crowded to make this kind of strictness a reasonable practice. To be returned to prison on a technical violation, a parolee usually has to demonstrate a persistent pattern of noncompliance or else give his parole officer reason to believe he has returned to crime. Observers believe that most revocations occur only after arrest on a serious charge or when the parolee cannot be located by the officer.

Perspectives on the parolee's status in the community have changed over the years. Early reformers saw parole decisions as *grace* dispensed out of the goodwill of the correctional authority. According to this notion, parole can be revoked at any time and for any reason. Later reformers began to think of parole as a *privilege*, earned through good behavior in prison and retained as long as the parolee abides by the conditions of parole. More recently some commentators have begun to describe parole as a *right* of prisoners who have served enough time in prison, and they urge that technical violations be eliminated as a basis for return to prison. The "rights" view does not now prevail officially in any parole system, although the state of Washington places strict limits on the penalty that may be imposed upon technical violators.

State of New Jersey
STATE PAROLE BOARD

Certificate of Parole

Page 1 of 4

The State Parole Board, by virtue of the authority conferred upon it by the provisions of P.L. 1979, c.441 (C.30:4-123.45, et seq.) and under the rules and regulations promulgated pursuant thereto, does hereby grant a parole to **XXXX XXXXXX, SP#XXXXX**, who was convicted of the crime(s) and sentenced as indicated below:

Date of Sentence and Offense	County and Term	Relation and Assessment(s)
XXX XX, XXXX	XXXXX	XX.XX
XXXXXX XXXXXXX	XXX	

TOTAL TERM: XXX

Said inmate is now confined in the XXXXXXX XXXXXXX XXXX by virtue of the sentence(s) imposed for the said conviction of the crime(s) aforesaid. This parole is applicable solely to said aforesaid sentence(s) and to no other, limited by and subject to the conditions annexed hereto and made a part hereof, and is effective on XXXXXXX XXXXXX or as soon thereafter as a suitable parole plan has been approved by the State Parole Board, and upon the further condition that the said inmate accepts the conditions contained herein and annexed hereto, as evidenced by his/her signature affixed hereto and to a copy hereof retained as a part of the record of the parolee.

This parole is subject to revocation for violation of the conditions annexed hereto and forming a part hereof.

IN TESTIMONY WHEREOF, I have hereunto set my hand, and caused our Seal to be affixed this XXXXXX day of XXX in the year of our Lord one thousand nine hundred and NINETY-THREE.

STATE PAROLE BOARD

Certifying Member(s): XXXXXXXXXX XXXXXXX   XXXXXX XXXXXX

GENERAL CONDITIONS OF PAROLE:

From the date of your release on parole until the expiration of your maximum sentence(s) or until you are discharged from parole, you shall continue to be under the supervision of the Bureau of Parole. A warrant for your arrest may be filed and this parole may be revoked for serious or persistent violations of the conditions of parole. You shall not be credited for time served on parole from the date a parole warrant is issued for your arrest if you are in violation of parole to the date that you are arrested and placed in confinement for violation of parole.

1. You are required to obey all laws and ordinances.
2. You are not to act as an informer for any agency which requires you to violate any conditions of your parole.
3. You are to report in person to your District Parole Supervisor or his/her designated representative immediately after you are released on parole from the institution, unless you have been given other written instructions by the institutional parole office, and you are to report thereafter as instructed by the District Parole Supervisor or his or her designated representative.
4. You are to notify your Parole Officer immediately after any arrest and after accepting any pre-trial release, including bail.
5. You are to obtain approval of your Parole Officer:
   a. For any change in your residence or employment location.

Witness _____   Dated _____ 19____   _____ Signature

SPB-130

State of New Jersey
STATE PAROLE BOARD

Certificate of Parole

Page 2 of 4

XXXXXX XXXXXX, SP#XXXXX

b. Before leaving the state of your approved residence for longer than 24 hours, except as otherwise directed for good cause by the Parole Officer.
6. You are required not to own or possess any firearm, as defined in N.J.S.2C:39-1f, for any purpose.
7. You are required not to own or possess any weapon enumerated in N.J.S.2C:39-1r.
8. You are required to refrain from the use, possession or distribution of a controlled dangerous substance, controlled substance analog or imitation controlled dangerous substance as defined In N.J.S.2C:35-2 and N.J.S.2C:35-11.
9. You are required to make payment to the Bureau of Parole of any assessment, fine, restitution, D.E.D.R. penalty and Lab Fee imposed by the sentencing court and/or the New Jersey State Parole Board.

Total Fine(s)/Penalty(s):
Total VCCB Assessment(s):
Total Restitution:

SPECIAL CONDITION(S):

You will be paroled to any outstanding detainer(s) only initially; thence upon resolution of said detainer(s), you will be released to a parole plan acceptable to the New Jersey Bureau of Parole with the following Special Conditions:

You are to participate in random urine monitoring acceptable to the District Parole Office until discharge is approved by the District Parole Supervisor. You are to refrain from the use of any controlled dangerous substance.

You are to participate in and comply with the regulations of an out-patient drug counseling program acceptable to the District Parole Office until discharge is approved by the District Parole Supervisor. You are to refrain from the use of any controlled dangerous substance.

You are to participate in a Narcotics Anonymous Program with a community sponsor acceptable to the District Parole Office until discharge is approved by the District Parole Supervisor. You are to refrain from the use of any controlled dangerous substance.

You are to participate in and comply with the regulations of an out-patient alcohol counseling program acceptable to the District Parole Office until discharge from such is approved by the District Parole Supervisor. You are to refrain from alcohol usage.

You are to participate in an Alcoholics Anonymous Program with a community sponsor acceptable to the District Parole Office until discharge is approved by the District Parole Supervisor. You are to refrain from alcohol usage.

You are to participate in mental health counseling acceptable to the District Parole Office.

I HEREBY ACKNOWLEDGE THE IMPOSITION OF THE SPECIAL CONDITION OF PAROLE THAT I ENROLL AND PARTICIPATE IN A MENTAL HEALTH COUNSELING PROGRAM. I ACKNOWLEDGE MY NEED TO PARTICIPATE IN A MENTAL HEALTH COUNSELING PROGRAM AND ACKNOWLEDGE THAT I MUST FULLY COOPERATE WITH THE TREATMENT STAFF OF THE DESIGNATED PROGRAM. I HEREBY AUTHORIZE THE DESIGNATED REPRESENTATIVES OF THE DEPARTMENT OF CORRECTIONS AND THE STATE PAROLE BOARD TO RELEASE EITHER VERBALLY OR IN WRITING ALL DIAGNOSTIC PROGNOSTIC AND TREATMENT RECORDS PERTAINING TO MY MEDICAL AND MENTAL HEALTH TO THE STAFF OF ANY MENTAL HEALTH AGENCY REQUESTED TO PROVIDE OR PROVIDING SERVICES TO ME. I ACKNOWLEDGE THAT I UNDERSTAND THAT THIS AUTHORIZATION TO RELEASE INFORMATION MAY NOT BE

Witness _____   Dated _____ 19____   _____ Signature

SPB-130

Figure 16.1 ■ **Conditions of Release, New Jersey.** Newly released offenders must comply with specific conditions in order to remain in good standing on parole.

Table 16.1 ■ **Recidivism Rates of Young Parolees (Aged 17–22) by Personal Characteristics and by Offense.** Women do better on parole, as do drug offenders and those with more education. Nevertheless, failure rates for parolees are high regardless of their backgrounds.

	Percent of young parolees who within six years of release from prison were		
	Rearrested	Reconvicted	Reincarcerated
All parolees	69%	53	49
Sex			
Men	70	54	50
Women	52	40	36
Race/Ethnicity			
White	64	49	45
Black	76	60	56
Hispanic	71	50	44
Other	75	65	63
Education			
Less than twelve years	71	55	51
High school graduate	61	46	43
Some college	48	44	31
Paroling offense			
Violent offenses	64	43	39
Murder	70	25	22
Robbery	64	45	40
Assault	72	51	47
Property offenses	73	60	56
Burglary	73	60	56
Forgery/Fraud	74	59	56
Larceny	71	61	55
Drug offenses	49	30	25

Source: U.S. Department of Justice, Bureau of Justice Statistics, *Report to the Nation on Crime and Justice* (Washington, D.C.: Government Printing Office, 1988), p. 111.

If parole is a privilege, as many people argue, its revocation is not subject to due process or rules of evidence. In some states liberal parole policies have been justified on the grounds that revocation is swift and can be imposed whenever the offender violates the parole rules. The New York statute, for example, provides that if a parole officer has reason to believe that a parolee has lapsed or is probably about to lapse into criminal conduct or into the company of criminals, or has violated any important condition of parole, the officer may rearrest the parolee. The officer's power to recommend revocation because the parolee is "slipping" seems to hang over the parolee like the sword of Damocles, suspended by a hair.

When the parole officer alleges that a technical violation of parole has occurred, a two-stage revocation proceeding is held. The U.S. Supreme Court has exempted such a proceeding from the normal requirements of a criminal trial but has held that many due process rights must be accorded the parolee.[2] In the first phase of the two-step hearing process required by the Court, the parole board determines whether there is probable cause that a violation has occurred. The parolee then has the right to be notified of the charges, to be informed of evidence, to be heard, to present witnesses, and to confront the parole board's witnesses (providing no witness would be endangered by such a confrontation). In the second phase of the revocation process, the parole board determines if the violation is sufficiently severe to warrant returning the parolee to prison.

The number of parole revocations is difficult to determine. A combined revocation and recommitment rate of approximately 25 percent in three years has been reported for years; these data, however, do not distinguish between persons returned to prison for technical violations and those returned for new criminal offenses. Recent studies using standard definitions of revocation rates have put this figure a bit higher in some jurisdictions (see Table 16.1) but have also disclosed that the total failure rate varies dramatically, from 23 percent to 40 percent. The degree to which these rates reflect technical rules violations varies among states as well (see Table 16.2). As we shall see, these variations can result more from differences in policy and parole officers' attitudes than from differences in parolees' behavior.

It is also true that parole failures tend to occur early in the release period but also continue throughout supervision. Arrests accumulate through the first six years of release; fur-

Adjusting to the free world is more complicated than most ex-offenders believe. What are the immediate problems that confront persons upon their release to the community?

ther, as shown in Table 16.3, the pattern is more pronounced for younger parolees. A study completed several years ago showed that federal parolees born in the same year (a cohort) continued to be arrested up to thirty years after release.[3] For parolees, failure is an ominous probability.

Table 16.2 ■ Parolees and Unconditional Releasees Returned to Prison Within Three Years After Release for Technical Violations and New Offenses, 1976–1981, in Four States. The reason for a releasee's return to prison depends on the strictness of enforcement of parole conditions.

| State and year of release | All returns | Parolees | | Unconditional releases |
		Technical violation	New sentence with or without technical violation	
California, 1977	100%	24%	74%	2%
Minnesota, 1981	100	43	46	11
Nebraska, 1980	100	37	34	29
New York, 1976	100	51	43	6

Source: Adapted from James F. Wallerstedt, *Returning to Prison,* Special Report, U.S. Department of Justice, Bureau of Justice Statistics (Washington, D.C.: Government Printing Office, November 1984), p. 3.

Table 16.3 ■ Cumulative Rates of Return to Prison as Exhibited by Releasees. Nearly two-thirds of all offenders succeed on parole, but only half of the young parolees make it.

| Age at time of prison release | Years after release from prison | | | | | | |
	1	2	3	4	5	6	7
18–24 years old	21%	34%	41%	45%	48%	49%	50%
25–34	12	21	28	33	37	41	43
35–44	7	14	18	22	26	30	34
45+	2	4	6	8	10	11	12
All ages	14	23	29	34	37	40	42
Median age of those returning (in years)	23.5	25.5	26.3	27.2	27.8	28.6	32.4

Source: U.S. Department of Justice, Bureau of Justice Statistics, *Report to the Nation on Crime and Justice* (Washington, D.C.: Government Printing Office, 1988), p. 111.

Information on the typical length of reconfinement for a technical parole violation is even more elusive than the number of revocations. The guidelines of the Federal Parole Commission recommend up to eight months for revoked parolees who do not have a history of violations and a longer period (eight to sixteen months) for persistent violators, those whose violations occur less than eight months after release, and those found to have a negative employment/school record during supervision. Most states do not have such guidelines. Potentially, the offender whose parole is revoked may be required to serve the remainder of the unexpired sentence.

Parolees Are People

The general public tends to think of parolees, people who have been in prison, as probably dangerous, certainly as strange and different from "us." When parole agents talk informally among themselves, they tend to describe parolees in catch phrases that emphasize their inadequacies and proneness to wrongdoing—for example, "They were failures before we got them—they proved that or they wouldn't be here." Even in more formal statements, the official assumptions about parolees as a group seldom emphasize their potentialities, strengths, and capacities for independent action. In general, parolees tend to be seen as weak persons with multiple problems, who are either extremely resistant to help or largely dependent on others for direction and prodding in "taking care of business."

...However, parolees are people, as diverse in capacities and problems as any other segment of the population. It is true, because of the nature of selection for criminal conviction in the United States, that the parole population is heavily weighted with persons from socially disadvantaged, economically deprived, and ethnic minority groups. Nevertheless, one finds among them men from all walks of life, with a wide range of educational and economic backgrounds. Only a few are as socially dangerous as the stereotype suggests, while many of them perform minor miracles of human survival in daily coping under handicaps.

The diversity and range of life patterns evident among parolees is suggested by the following word pictures....

■ A sullen, bleary-eyed, battered hulk of a man, an Indian and an alcoholic, who was interrupted while he was preparing his solitary meal in a hot, smelly tenement room where the bed, bureau, two-burner gas plate, and one chair left only standing room.

■ A university researcher in a paneled, book-lined home study overlooking the city below his windows, whose need to talk of his ten years on parole led to seven two- to three-hour interviews.

■ A one-armed Mexican parolee, who was moving his family back to a small town in Mexico, now that his son at age three was an American citizen and had received all his immunizations. He was happy, eager to talk of his plans to use the agricultural and construction skills he had learned in prison to modernize the village, proudly displaying the modern toilet and the reading and arithmetic primers he was

The Structure of Community Supervision

Three forces influence the newly released offender's adjustment: the parole officer, the parole bureaucracy, and the experiences of the offender. Carl B. Klockars has pointed out that this structure of relationships can determine the results of supervision. Klockars described the supervision process as a series of stages in which attachments develop among those forces (see Figure 16.2). In the initial stages of supervision the strongest attachment is between the officer and the bureaucracy, with a minor attachment between the parolee and the offi-

packing on his truck as equipment for his family's future life.

- A bearded, hippie youth surrounded by his wood carvings, who spoke of his parole agent with real affection as "a beautiful man," while describing the way he managed to live his wandering and unemployed life without "worrying the agent."

- A sixty-year-old black man, who might have played the part of "de Lawd God" in *Green Pastures*, who owned his own home, lived on a pension, was deacon of his church, and whose only regret was that the rules against association among parolees interfered with his ability to befriend and guide some of the younger men whom he had known in prison.

- A vital, large-built factory foreman, who welcomed the agent and the observer into the tiny living room in the home he had recently purchased, where he and his wife with the five children were eating dinner before the TV. He and the agent embarked on a familiar joking game about the parolee's imminent discharge and the favors he was doing the agent in hiring other parolees, while the others became absorbed in the hour-long thrust-and-parry between the two men much as they might have watched a hard-fought tennis match.

- A scrawny black youth, in severe pain from a back injury, standing in handcuffs with tears running down his cheeks, who had just learned he was being returned to prison; he had been arrested some weeks before for drinking and his parole rules forbade the use of any liquor.

…Like any other subpopulation, parolees have certain attributes in common, most of which stem from the fact that they have shared certain special experiences. All have been through the drastic process of being turned into outcasts from the community, a social demotion that marks each of them in some way for the rest of their lives. Each has, for some important period of personal time, been subjected to the abnormal, often deforming, life of the prison. They share a supervised role in the parole agency. And each, in one way or another, has dealt with the difficult problems of moving from prison life to the quite different demands of life in the community. Because of this set of shared experiences, parolees constitute the primary source of expert knowledge on the tasks and problems of "doing a parole."

Source: Elliot Studt, U.S. Department of Justice, *Surveillance and Service in Parole* (Washington, D.C.: Government Printing Office, 1973), pp. 13–15.

cer and a negative attachment between the parolee and the bureaucracy. The parolee's negative attachment to the bureaucracy, compounded of suspicion of its rules and fear of its policies, never changes during supervision. As the parolee and officer get to know each other better, however, the officer's strongest attachment gradually shifts from the bureaucracy to the parolee. Finally, the two develop rapport, the ability to communicate positively and with mutual trust.[4]

This characterization of the supervision process explains why parolees' rule violations are often overlooked: The parole officer identifies more closely with the offender than with the bureaucracy that promulgates the rules. But the process does not always follow that pattern. Often rapport never develops and the

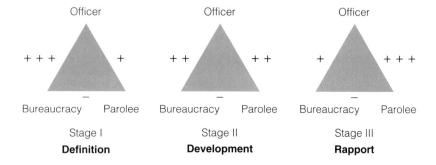

Figure 16.2 ■ **Positive and Negative Attachments at Three Stages of the Supervision Process.** Parolees and their parole officers tend to develop a positive attachment as the supervision proceeds.

Source: Adapted from Carl B. Klockars, "A Theory of Probation Supervision," *Journal of Criminal Law, Criminology, and Police Science* 63 (1972): 556. Copyright © by Northwestern University School of Law. Reprinted by special permission.

attachment between the parolee and the officer sours. When strain develops between the parolee and the other forces, it is very difficult for the offender to succeed.

What determines the outcome of the supervision process? What factors lead to its success or failure? The answer lies in a complex of attitudes, situations, policies, and random events. To better understand the situation of the offender attempting to make it upon release from incarceration, we must first consider in detail two major forces: the parole officer and the bureaucracy.

Agents of Community Supervision

The parolee's principal contact with the criminal justice system is through the parole officer, many of whom are asked to play two roles: cop and social worker. As police officers, they are given the power to restrict many aspects of the parolee's life, to enforce the conditions of release, and to initiate revocation proceedings if violations occur. In states that subscribe to the concept of parole as grace, officers have the power to search the parolee's living quarters without warning, to arrest him or her for suspected violations without the possibility of bail, and to suspend parole pending a hearing before the board. One common practice when parolees misbehave is to "hold" them in jail for a day or two to persuade them not to challenge the officer's authority in the future. Like other street-level bureaucrats in the criminal justice system, officers have extensive discretion that may be used in low-visibility situations. The officer's relationship with the offender thus has an authoritative component that can be expected to produce in the offender a sense of insecurity that can stand in the way of the development of rapport and mutual trust.

Parole officers are responsible for assisting parolees' adjustment to the community as well as for policing their actions. They must act as social workers by helping parolees find jobs and restore family ties. They must be prepared to serve as agent mediators or advocates between the parolees and the organizations with which the parolees deal, and to channel them to such human service agencies as psychiatric clinics. As caseworkers, officers must be able to develop a relationship that fosters trust and confidence; such a relationship is not likely to develop if parolees are made constantly aware of the officers' ability to send them back to prison.

How can parole officers reconcile these conflicting role demands? It has been suggested that the responsibilities be divided, so that the officer carries out the supervisory aspects of the posi-

Emphasis on control

	High	Low
High	Paternal officer	Welfare worker
Low	Punitive officer	Passive agent

Emphasis on assistance

Figure 16.3 ■ **Differing Role Orientations of Parole Officers.** Daniel Glaser has identified four different types of parole officers based on their attitudes toward the job.

Source: Adapted from Daniel Glaser, *The Effectiveness of a Prison and Parole System,* abridged edition. Copyright ©1969 by Macmillan Publishing Company. Reprinted by permission.

tion and other persons perform its casework functions. Alternatively, the officer could be charged solely with the casework functions and local police could check for violations. Recently, Georgia experimented with having a team of two supervisors handle a caseload jointly. One person (often a former police officer) was designated the surveillance officer; the other was the probation officer, providing assistance. An evaluation of the system found that the conceptual distinction often became vague in practice: Clients often looked to surveillance officers for help and saw probation officers as enforcing the conditions of supervision.[5] Despite the conflict between the roles of enforcer and helper, the job seems to require that both roles be performed by any person having supervisory contact with the offender. Criteria for those providing parole services have been summarized as follows:

■ *Be known.* Parolee must know where to go, or where to find out where to go.

■ *Be open for business.* Problems arise at 4:00 A.M., and guidance or temporary remedies must be available around the clock.

■ *Be reachable.* Located near clients or with provision for transportation.

■ *Be comprehensive.* Whatever the difficulty—money, drugs, or alcohol, family problems—a remedial service should exist.

■ *Be trusted.* Parolees must feel that they will not be punished or threatened when they reveal a problem.

■ *Be voluntary.* Offenders have been coerced and told what to do for long enough: Forced treatment is unlikely to be effective treatment. In the free community they must make their own choices, and compelling their participation will delay their rehabilitation.[6]

Daniel Glaser has attempted to understand the various ways in which parole officers play their roles and adapt their personal styles and orientations to their tasks.[7] Officer role orientations may be divided along the two dimensions of assistance and control, yielding four conceptions of parole work (see Figure 16.3).

Paternal officers protect both the offender and the community by means of assistance, lectures, praise, and blame. They have ambivalent emotional involvement with offenders and with others in the community, taking first one side and then the other. Paternal officers tend to have little formal training but much dedication and experience.

Punitive officers are guardians of middle-class morality and attempt to bring the offender into conformity by threats and punishment. They stress control and protection of the public against offenders, and they are suspicious of the people they supervise.

Welfare workers want the greater good of their clients, and they help the clients' individual adjustment toward that end. They believe that the community's protection lies in that personal adjustment. Emotionally neutral, they have diagnostic and treatment skills that take into account the situation, needs, and capacities of their clients.

Passive agents see their jobs as sinecures and expend only minimal energy on them. Often political appointees, they have little

For some ex-offenders, such as writer Jack Henry Abbott, life on the outside is evidently too much of a challenge. After being lionized by the New York literary establishment for his book about prison life, In the Belly of the Beast, *Abbott was returned to prison on charges of stabbing to death an aspiring young actor.*

interest in the parolees but like the pay, independence, and opportunities to pursue their own interests.

There is some dispute about the ways officers balance concern for assistance and concern for control. Some people believe that the roles are incompatible and that effectiveness requires making a choice in emphasis between the two. Others argue that the effective officer needs to be able to shift from role to role. A recent study of role adoption in supervision approaches suggested that an officer's emphasis on control was largely a product of personal preferences, but the degree of emphasis on assistance will depend on the overall philosophy of the organization.[8]

Parole officers will influence supervision by the way they approach the offender. The officer's style has been referred to as the hidden condition of supervision. An officer's expectation of the client's response is manifested in two ways. First, the officer's attitude toward the client is expressed in his or her style of supervision. Glaser's paternal officers like to take a parental approach; welfare workers approach the job as professional caseworkers; punitive officers see themselves as community

protection agents; passive agents are bureaucrats. Each approach leads to a style of interaction with clients—gruff, distant, or friendly—that is an informal determinant of the supervision process. Style can be so significant that it can overwhelm other aspects of the work. For instance, a famous study of parole officers in California revealed that their individual styles were so varied that each one could be thought of as almost a separate agency.[9]

The second manifestation of the hidden condition of supervision is the supervision plan. In most agencies each officer and parolee develop a supervision plan (or treatment plan) that states what the parolee is going to do about the problems (unemployment, drug abuse, marital conflict, and so on) that make adjustment to the community troublesome. The officer has a great deal of discretion in developing this plan and may choose to put a lot of energy into it or very little. This latitude may explain why officers who are oriented toward providing assistance tend to write significantly more supervision objectives for their clients and get involved in more areas of parolees' lives.[10]

As street-level bureaucrats, officers are affected by organizational demands unrelated to either assistance or control. Richard McCleary's study of parole officers in Cook County (Chicago) disclosed that decisions about individual parolees are influenced by the organization's definition of the situation, the officer's own perception of the client, and the officer's professional reputation. Members of the parole bureaucracy strive to maintain desirable professional conditions: a good working atmosphere, independence from supervisory oversight, and the use of discretion. Certain parolees are viewed as threatening to the status quo because they make trouble for their officers and for the officers' superiors, and they therefore elicit special responses from their officers.

McCleary believes that by typing each parolee from the start, the officer neutralizes potential trouble. On the basis of parolees' dossiers, initial interviews, and home visits, the officer categorizes those clients who seem sincere, criminally inclined, and dangerous. "Dangerous" refers not to parolees who are potentially violent but rather to those few the officer believes may act irrationally or unpredictably, those who don't respond to warnings and who go out of their way to make trouble.[11] The "dangerous" parolees are the most worrisome, for it is hard for an officer to maintain control over them. McCleary found that, surprisingly, one way was to bargain with them:

> All right, Johnny, this is how it is. I've got you on paper for the next seven years, but I'll make a deal with you. You give me two years of good behavior and I'll recommend you for early discharge. When I say "good behavior," though, I mean *cooperation*. When I tell you to do something, you do it. You don't argue with me about whether I'm right or wrong or whether it's fair or not, or even whether I have the right to tell you to do it. You just do it. If you give me two years of cooperation like that, I'll give you an early discharge.[12]

Thus parole officers represent one set of forces that affect a parolee's chance of making it. Officers may be supportive of clients or may hinder their adjustment to the community. Parole officers "read" clients and then decide how they will treat them. They have the formal power to revoke parole on the basis of violations, but they have even greater informal power—to make life for their clients difficult or easy, depending on the way they approach their jobs.

The Community Supervision Bureaucracy

Parole officers do not work in a vacuum. Although the job is often attractive to persons who like flexible schedules and substantial latitude, every officer works in an organizational context, and mostly in close contact with other officers. Parole officers therefore face limits on the approaches they can take to cases. The limits vary from the specific need to manage a work load that exceeds available time to the general need to respond to organizational philosophies and policies.

Work load In his award-winning essay on human services, Michael Lipsky made the point that the difficulties faced by many clients of human services are so complex that "the job… is in a sense impossible to do in ideal terms."[13] In practical terms, then, the organization must structure the relationship between the officer and the client by means of a classification system. The system allows the parole bureaucracy to prescribe rules for the allocation of officers' time, and priority is given to the parolees most in need because the time available is not enough to permit an ideal level of supervision to be devoted to all. The system used in New York (see Table 16.4) is typical. In general, officers spend more time with the newly released than with those who have been in the community for some time. The level of supervision is later adjusted to "active" or "reduced" surveillance, depending on how the releasee functions in the

Table 16.4 ■ Varying Levels of Supervision Provided to Releasees in New York. Most parole systems vary the amount of supervision they provide based on the risk posed by the offender, length of time on parole, and response to the supervision.

Type of contact	Intensive supervision	Active supervision	Reduced supervision
Reporting to parole office	Weekly or semi-monthly	Monthly or up to but not exceeding every two months	Quarterly, or less frequently up to and including annually
Employment check	Monthly	Every two months	Same as reporting
Employment visit	Every three months	Every three months	At least as frequently as reporting
Home visit	Every three months	Monthly	Not mentioned
Other and collateral visits	More frequently than active or reduced	Not mentioned	Not mentioned

Source: David T. Stanley, *Prisoners Among Us* (Washington, D.C.: Brookings Institution, 1976), p. 96.

community. As the officer gains confidence in the parolee, only periodic check-ins may be required. Finally, at the end of the maximum length of the sentence or at the time specified by the parole board, the former convict is discharged from supervision.

The report of the President's Commission in 1967 recommended that caseloads be no more than thirty-six per officer. In reality, caseloads vary dramatically, but the average number of parolees per officer is about eighty. This is smaller than the probation caseload, but the services required by parolees are greater.

The caseload influences the number of contacts made with parolees and the amount of assistance that can be given each one. Some states structure low-number, specialized caseloads for officers who supervise certain types of parolees, but a study of federal parole reported that each offender could expect no more than "7.7 hours of supervision per year—or thirty-eight minutes a month or nine minutes a week."[14]

One reason for the small amount of time spent in contact with parolees is that officers have organizational responsibilities to fulfill. Some part of the day may be spent in the field

helping clients to deal with other service agencies—medical, employment, educational—but a great portion is spent in the office meeting the paperwork and administrative requirements of the bureaucracy. One study of federal parole officers found that they spent 80 percent of their time at nonsupervisory work.[15]

Philosophy and policy Originally parole officers worked directly for parole boards, but in recent decades parole staffs have increasingly become part of departments of corrections. Some parole boards argue that they should also be responsible for the supervision of field services, but the counterargument has prevailed in most places. With the emphasis on parole as an aspect of community corrections and the growing use of prerelease programs, halfway houses, and other community-based services, it is thought that there needs to be a coordination of institution and field activities months before an inmate's release on parole. The long view requires that the policies governing institutional programs, work release, and parole supervision must be coordinated—a situation

Purpose dimension

Figure 16.4 ■ Various Approaches to Case Management in Correctional Field Services. The approach depends on the agency's goals and service delivery structure.

Source: Adapted from T. R. Clear and P. K. Benoit, "Case Management in Probation and Parole Supervision," in *Probation and Parole,* ed. John O. Smykla (New York: Macmillan, 1984), p. 234.

that calls for parole services to be part of the department of corrections.

In many states probation and parole staffs are combined because they perform similar functions. As we have pointed out, however, probation officers have ties to judges, and parole is seen as part of corrections. Parole has a greater law enforcement orientation: Parole agents in some states carry guns, and all are sworn officers. It appears that individuals with social work orientations are more likely to gravitate toward positions in probation departments.

The organizational structure of a parole agency also influences its philosophy and its policies. Research shows that two dimensions of organization policy differentiate all correctional field service operations. The *purpose dimension* is the degree to which the system emphasizes offender control (surveillance and monitoring of offenders' actions) over offender change (providing assistance to clients). This distinction is similar to that made by individual parole officers, but here it operates at the organizational level and represents organizational philosophy. The *structure dimension* reflects the degree to which staff are assigned general work loads (a cross-section of clients) or specialized work loads (subgroups of clients sharing a sim-

ilar characteristic, such as drug abuse). The structure dimension is related to organizational resource policy. Extreme emphases on these dimensions create four stereotypical case management approaches in field services (see Figure 16.4).[16]

Agencies that stress offender control rely primarily on the skills and abilities of their own staffs. The referral of parolees to other agencies (such as public welfare) for assistance is ordinarily considered tangential to parole supervision and direct contact with the offender. Change-oriented agencies make more extensive referrals to external agencies, and the officer's main function is seen as helping offenders to become involved with social service agencies whose programs are relevant to their needs. Of course, all parole agencies must support both the control and change functions of supervision, but agencies differ in the priorities they attach to control and change.

The traditional case management agencies are control-oriented and distribute clients more or less randomly to parole officers in order to keep caseloads of equal size. In such agencies, which are the most common across the United States, officers are fairly well isolated from their peers and supervisors. Because an officer's work ordinarily draws little attention unless a client creates a problem (perhaps by a new arrest), the case management structure gives officers an incentive to monitor cases closely in order to avoid surprises. Officers have significant latitude, and the understood message is that they will be left alone until a client's behavior draws a superior's attention. The high potential for second-guessing reinforces the typical staff injunction to "cover your bases."

Program agencies are also control-oriented, but parole officers are assigned specialized caseloads so they can concentrate on particular kinds of problems. Thus one officer may have a special caseload of drug users, another may supervise unemployed offenders, and so on. The argument for specialization is that the more homogeneous work load makes better use of

Many offenders are released to halfway houses and other residential settings while they adjust to the community. Counseling, job placement, and re-entry programs are available to help these offenders.

staff expertise, and officers are better able to understand and respond to clients whose situations are similar. Yet the program strategy breeds discontent among officers because the specialties often come in conflict. For one thing, it is difficult to equalize work loads. Who can tell, for instance, whether it takes more or less effort to supervise thirty drug users than to supervise forty sex offenders? Moreover, because officers want to think of their jobs as important, they often clash over whose work (and special clientele) is the most central to the agency's mission. Staff members devote substantial effort to showing how they are trying to prevent the commission of new offenses, because recidivism is the common denominator that allows all specialties to be compared. The underlying value of offender control thus emerges, because workers with special assignments are normally judged on how well they manage the potential criminality of their clients.

In the broker agency, by contrast, the primary emphasis is on offender change: helping offenders cope with factors in their lives that may lead to criminality by referring them to agencies that can offer assistance. The main role of the corrections worker is to determine the client's most serious problems, to locate agencies that handle such problems, and to help the client make use of the agencies' services. Only in unusual cases does the worker provide direct counseling or delivery of services. Staff members specialize in different service areas—one person may specialize in employment agencies, for instance, another in substance abuse agencies. Once a client's needs are diagnosed, he or she meets with staff members whose specialties cover those needs. The meetings eventuate in referrals to other agencies. Although many people are impressed by the way the broker approach involves clients with the community, some believe that the small amount of direct contact between worker and offenders leads to a lack of accountability and control over offenders.

Accountability is increased in the advocacy agency, in which corrections staff work more closely with offenders in conjunction with parole agencies. Rather than referring offenders to other agencies, advocacy staff accompany offenders to the agencies and involve themselves supportively in the treatment. To facilitate community work, caseloads are usually organized by geographical region.

The advocacy approach provides the most intensive level of assistance and control, and also requires the most extensive commitment of staff resources. It is not realistic to expect this approach to be followed by most correctional field service units because their resources are limited. Moreover, some people think it is inappropriate for workers to be so heavily involved in the lives of offenders.

Each of the case management models has advantages and disadvantages; none is uniformly to be preferred over the others. Decisions that determine organizational structure in field services also influence the manner in which staff members perform their work. The decision to specialize staff according to client characteristics focuses staff expertise more directly on client needs; the decision to emphasize use of outside agencies increases staff concern for client change as opposed to control.

Other constraints Parole officers are often portrayed as having absolute authority over their clients, as being able to manage offenders in any way they see fit. Although there is a grain of truth in that statement, it is more accurate to say that officers balance many constraints in the use of discretion.

The bureaucratic context exerts pressures on parole officers to "go along with the system," just as police officers are pressured to cover for their partners. In this respect, parole is like other corrections functions: Line workers are isolated from administration and dependent on one another for support. They feel constrained to behave in ways that are supportive and to let well enough alone. As one parole supervisor said:

> I won't stand for one of my parole officers (POs) second-guessing another. If I tolerated that, I'd have grudges going on here. Pretty soon I'd have an office full of snitches. A few years ago, I had a PO who couldn't keep his nose out of the other caseloads. I spoke to him about it but that didn't do any good. He thought he was the conscience of the Department of Corrections. I finally got fed up with his meddling and I gave him a taste of his own medicine. I went over to his files and found unfinished work for him to do.[17]

Parole officers must learn how to perform their jobs in ways that maintain office norms without threatening their co-workers. The knowledge serves to reduce their discretion, however, because often they are forced to take certain actions in regard to problems that in the absence of organizational pressures they would have handled another way. In recent times, for example, jails and prisons have become so overcrowded that officers have felt informal (but very clear) pressures not to crowd the institutions further with revocations for "nonserious" violations. Officers learn that they would be wise to act only on the most serious misbehaviors of their clients and ignore the rest.

The bureaucracy of parole, then, is a force in the offender's postrelease experience in several ways:

- It structures the activities of parole officers according to philosophical orientations that have become traditional.

- It provides rules and policies for managing work loads that would otherwise be unbearable for most officers.

- It provides a context of unwritten and informal norms that define appropriate and inappropriate officer conduct.

Residential Programs

R esidential programs serve offenders when they are first released from prison. Most house a limited number of offenders at any one time (usually no more than ten to twenty-five), are medium or minimum security facilities, have treatment staff who help offenders work out plans to address their problems, and place heavy emphasis on involving the offenders in regular community functions.

Residential programs are often referred to as **community correctional centers.** Most require that offenders live on the premises while working in the community. They usually provide counseling and drug treatment, and have strict curfews for residents when they are not working. Many of these facilities are renovated from private homes or small hotels, since this permits a less institutional atmosphere. Individual rooms with group dining and recreation areas help to promote a homelike character to these facilities. Often residents can earn greater freedom to move in the community by passing through security "phases." By obeying the rules and maintaining good behavior in the facility, the resident gradually achieves a reduction in restriction—for instance, the ability to have limited free time within the community. The idea is to provide treatment support to the offender, while helping the step-by-step adjustment to community life.

Residential centers face problems, however. With very high staff-resident ratios, they are relatively expensive to operate; they represent a real cost saving only when they enable a jurisdiction to avoid construction of a new prison. Studies also demonstrate that some of these centers have high failure rates—one-third or more of the clients may be arrested in a year.

The main problems of these centers are political. Their vulnerability to misbehavior by its clients makes them unpopular with local community residents. A facility may be relatively successful with its clients, but if only one client commits a serious offense, the result can be a strong public sentiment against the center. The syndrome is so common that it has been given an acronym: NIMBY, which stands for "not in my back yard." Citizens do not want groups of offenders to be living in their midst.

Finding and holding a job is one of the major problems faced by those released from prison. How would you discuss your incarceration with an interviewer?

The most common type of community correctional center is the halfway house, or **work release center.** The idea of work release originated in Wisconsin in 1913. The passage of the Huber Law in that year enabled prisoners to work in gainful occupations outside the prison as long as they returned to their cells at night.

Two kinds of work release programs are available today. In the more secure of the two,

community correctional center A small group living facility for offenders, especially those who recently have been released from prison.

work release center A facility that allows offenders to work in the community during the day, while residing in the center during nonwork hours.

prisoners work during the day (often in groups), then return at night to a group housing unit. In the other version, sometimes called work furlough, offenders work and live at home during the week and return to the prison over the weekend.

The idea underlying the halfway house is straightforward: Return to the community after institutionalization requires an adjustment, and a relatively controlled environment improves adjustment. Because studies indicate that the highest failure rates of parolees occur in the early months of parole, this idea seems plausible. Recently, halfway houses have become more than stopping points for prisoners released from custody; they employ direct treatment methods (such as therapeutic community techniques) to help offenders confront the problems they face when they return to the community. By these standards, how have the release programs fared?

The earliest studies of residential release programs tended to find their offenders performed slightly worse on parole than those given regular parole supervision and had higher rates of return to prison. Gordon Waldo and Ted G. Chirico's experimental evaluation of work release found no difference in the arrest rates of work release and other prisoners but still speculated that work release may be justifiable on humanitarian or economic grounds.[18] In general, no strong scientific basis exists to support these centers, though the research certainly indicates that remaining in prison is not preferable to work release.

One problem is the schizophrenic environment within which the programs operate. The pressures of institutional crowding establish a premium for these programs; without them many correctional systems would be unable to manage their ballooning populations. Yet reliance on release programs makes leaders of corrections systems vulnerable to instances of highly publicized failures. The most extreme example was Willie Horton, the Massachusetts inmate who absconded and committed serious and violent crimes while on furlough. By widely advertising the incident during the 1988 presidential campaign, George Bush was able to portray his opponent, Michael Dukakis, as "soft on crime."

Certainly release programs do not inevitably lead to reintegration of offenders. Perhaps their approach is faulty: Prisoners do not necessarily benefit from more supportive assistance at the release stage. Or, more likely, the problem with contemporary release programs is more fundamental: The negative impact of the prison on offenders is not easily eradicated by the simple mechanism of graduated release. The only thing we know is that the effectiveness of programs designed to handle offenders who are being released from incarceration has been disappointing.

The Offender's Experience of Postrelease Life

O ffenders' experiences following their release have a powerful influence on their adjustment to life in the community. As illustrated in the Focus section entitled "Coming Out—The Man Who Fell to Earth," a new releasee faces three realities: the strangeness of reentry, unmet personal needs, and barriers to success. Each must be dealt with separately; each poses a challenge to the newly released offender.

The Strangeness of Reentry

Although release can be euphoric, it can also be a letdown, particularly for parolees who return after two, three, or more years away. In their minds, families and friends have been snapshots in time, but now everyone is changed (and the parolee has changed): moved, taken a new job, or, perhaps most disturbing, become almost a stranger. The first attempts to restore old ties can be threatening experiences and can deeply disappoint. How many relationships—with spouses, children,

Coming Out— The Man Who Fell to Earth

Michael Knoll

In the gray light of the prerelease unit, in a prison dormitory modified to accommodate prisoners awaiting release, I stand with a group of twelve convicts. Each of us is uncomfortable with the idea of freedom, as nervous as if we were about to pull a robbery. I've been waiting for this day for five years, a few of the others have been waiting longer. In those years, I've become accustomed to waiting—it's the nature of doing time. Today it's particularly agonizing, and a line of sweat begins to seep through my almost-new shirt. As the wait becomes longer, begins to seem interminable, brief conversation flares up around me, dies, flares up again, returning each time to the topic of freedom: life in the mythic "free world" to which we're returning.

One man, incarcerated four years, mentions lobster, his voice bright with anticipation. "I'm gonna eat lobster in a *restaurant*. I'm gonna be *waited* on. A four-course meal. After I've finished with the food, I'm going home with the waitress."

"I think that the woman should come *before* the meal," argues a twentyish B&E artist. "The woman, then the food. It's not like we haven't eaten here inside the walls."

A narcotics dealer down five years for heroin sales has another point of view. He says that drugs should take precedence. "Junk is the best thing on the streets. And I hear it's cheaper these days. Better quality than a few years ago."

"The dope'll send you back here, though," counters another man. "Stick with women, money, cars. Pick an easy hustle. Or, what the hell, you could even go to college."

The discussion continues as each man identifies what he wants most on the outside. Most of the talk is spiced with fantasy: chic women and fast cars. Listening, I juxtapose the fantasy and the grim visible landscape. What lies beyond the coils of barbed wire has become wholly abstract and vague, an imagined place only a little more tangible than the surface of Mars. Acknowledging this, I feel a slow tension move up my back, something quite like the tension I brought in through the gates with me. I don't pause to consider the irony of this, that the fear I came in with was merely another form of the fear I'm experiencing today. To admit that would be to admit I've become institutionalized, and

that isn't easy to think about. I dwell instead on the talk around me in the dorm. "Freedom, man," one voice says, and the others repeat it. "Freedom." The word sounds so good. Sounds glorious. Sounds so damned easy.

The "free world" address to which we're delivered later is the Department of Corrections halfway house in Tucson. For us, this is the last stop of a release process that began with a parole board or work furlough hearing. This phase involves a final fingerprinting, a fast series of mug shots, and the filling out of various forms. We do the paperwork quickly, then listen as a parole officer rattles off the rules: "No illegal drugs or alcohol. No association with ex-felons.... You will be gainfully employed at all times and report all income to the Parole Department."

As the litany continues, I tell myself I can do it, that I'll do anything to avoid coming back. As I'm thinking this, I hear the same vow spoken out loud by another man, a kind of desperation in his voice: "No more of this. No more of this madness."

I lived for the first week at the home of a friend, Jay, an instructor who taught a writing class in the institution. When he offered me a place to stay several months back, neither of us had imagined I'd actually make it out, that I'd be deposited eventually in his living room, would sit across from him at his coffee table. Jay and his wife greeted me casually at the front door, but at that point, free just two hours, I was almost too uptight to speak. Their living room and its conventional furnishings appeared infinitely different from the furnishings I was used to, the bile-green concrete and rusted iron decor of the cell block.

Their initial questions concerned the nature of my experience inside, and they seemed hopelessly difficult to answer. I tried, though, describing for them the banalities of the prison routine, the extortion activities of gangs, and a dining room incident in which I'd been forced to watch as a friend's throat was slashed. They listened and nodded politely, but their faces implied incomprehension, that they understood only a little of what I was saying. I wondered then if anyone, anyone who hadn't walked a prison yard or shuddered as a cell door slammed tight against his back, could understand what I was feeling. I talked to them another twenty minutes before I gave up, asking tentatively if I might go outside. Jay reminded me I didn't need a movement pass out here, and I realized abruptly where I was. There were no bars on these windows, and the door locked from the inside.

I spent an hour that night walking the streets of Tucson, checking things out and exploring the world I'd stumbled into. I felt at first a sense of excitement, a euphoria that faded gradually into anxiety as I realized that I knew no one out here, that I had no place to go and exactly nothing to do. I felt like a guest—an uninvited guest—from some other world. Something like the protagonist in *Brother from Another Planet* or *The Man Who Fell to Earth*. When I arrived finally at the strangest place of all, a McDonald's, I ordered a cheeseburger and decided it was delicious. "This is better than lobster," I told another customer, and watched, embarrassed, as he stared back at me in silence. Stared as if I really had arrived from another planet, had come two million miles through space to eat a cheeseburger in this chrome and glass high-tech restaurant.

The biggest problem initially, bigger than my considerable sense of alienation, was where to get a job and some income. My fifty dollars in gate money, the check I'd received from the state on the day of my release, I'd donated to Jay as a down payment on my room and board. I hadn't anticipated any major problems in finding work; after all, I had exactly three-fourths of a college education. I discov-

ered that securing a job with a prison record is not easy and that my years of college were of substantially less interest to prospective employers than my FBI rap sheet.

Most of the interviews went like this: I'd arrive early at the office where I was to be interviewed. Wearing a meticulously laundered prison-industries shirt, I'd inform the receptionist that I was interested in applying for a job. She'd stare at me, examine my clothes and inside-the-walls haircut, and then shove an application in my face. That application, at first glance, seemed simple. I'd sail through the "Education History," stumble only a little on the "Employment History"—where had I worked for the last five years?— but then stop dead at the box asking "Have you ever been convicted of a felony?"

My parole officer had warned me of the felony question, stating that I must be totally honest about my criminal history. If I had to be honest about that, I wanted to do so in person, and so I wrote in the threatening box, "I will explain in person." During the interviews, those times when I actually got that far, I wasn't able to explain away five years of incarceration.

The job for which I was hired a week later was with an apartment painting crew,

Continued

working for fifty cents less than the minimum wage. The employer justified the low wage by saying that no money would be deducted for taxes, that I'd be paid "under the table." I told him that was fine. I got along pretty well with my co-workers, Hispanics from Cuba and Central America, most of them in the country illegally. In my ragged Spanish I told them I felt somewhat as they must have felt: like an alien, someone who'd jumped a border and now lived precariously in a foreign country.

I kept the painting job two weeks before I was accepted as a senior at the University of Arizona in its program in creative writing. In preparing for school, I decided I needed some clothes. My subsequent trip to a shopping mall was one of my strangest postrelease experiences.

In prison I'd lived in a cell with just one other occupant, isolated, when the doors closed, from the rest of the population. On the yard I'd kept a safe distance from other cons, allowing no one to come very close and never letting anyone get behind me. To allow another con to get behind you in maximum was to risk a shank in the back or a possible assault. At the Tucson mall there were suddenly hundreds of people on all sides, front and back, shoving, crowding. Intel-

lectually I understood that I was in no danger, but the old alarms went off anyway, the joint-induced paranoia. I ran out of the mall without buying anything, too nervous even to notice the girls, swarms of them, dressed up and perfumed. I thought of them later in my apartment. Afterward I went shopping only in smaller stores. Never again in a mall.

My experience at the university had emotional parallels to the experience at the Tucson mall: the same paranoia, alienation, and sense of confusion. I was certain, even in my free-world clothes, that every student I passed could identify me as an ex-felon, not a real student but a kind of impostor. To counter that fear I went out of my way to act like a student. I wore student clothes and used student language, picking up the slang of the university just as I'd picked up prison slang my first days in the joint. I told myself that the university was only another institution, and no more difficult than the one I'd just been released from.

I did well academically, but socially I was never comfortable. I never felt as though I totally belonged. The few people I talked to regularly were students or teachers in the writing program, and I never told them everything—about how it really felt to walk down a university hall four weeks

out of prison, for instance, in a mixture of terror and dread. I never talked at all about my distrust of people, which prison had reinforced so well. To trust another man in prison was to risk my life. Outside it was different. Outside it was just as deadly not to trust, to remain apart. Because I didn't understand that, I stayed apart from other students and after a while I felt as if I were doing fine. I was free, but I acted like I was doing time.

Other habits were equally difficult to change. Before my incarceration as an addict, I'd shoplifted regularly to finance my habit. I didn't use drugs my first months free, but I occasionally boosted small things from stores, not big things and not things I needed. Once in the university bookstore I slipped a copy of *War and Peace* inside my shirt. I was sure no one had seen me, that I'd been fast enough. On my way out I found myself blocked by a security cop, his badge flashing notice of my pending arrest.

I thought that incident— petty larceny, a misdemeanor —would send me back to prison, but the bookstore didn't press charges. My parole officer only gave me a warning. With a weariness that implied a countless number of previous such warnings, he told me that the next time I'd go back to the walls so fast my head would swim. When I told him there wouldn't be another slip, I meant it, yet I wondered to myself if I could ever live out here. My life was becoming a kind of treadmill, and I could feel myself tiring.

At that time I'd been out of prison seven months. I still felt only a little more at home in the free world than I had my first days out of the joint. When I formed relationships, they tended to be superficial and brief. I still couldn't talk about feelings, how it felt to awaken and make simple decisions, like what to have for breakfast, what clothes to put on, how to structure my day. In prison all of these choices had been made by someone else, a guard or administrator. Then I could move through my days and make no decisions at all. Any freedom I had was mental, and it was nothing like what confronted me outside: total freedom to administer my own life. The weight of that responsibility became a source of fear and anxiety, something I needed to talk about and didn't, something that eventually helped lead me back to narcotics.

When I returned to drugs, I did so cautiously, still hoping to complete my degree and to enter graduate school the following year. The only drugs I let myself use were prescription narcotics, substances provided by a doctor. To compensate for using them—the guilt I felt in get-

ting high—I began to work harder in school, adding more courses and taking a part-time job as a tutor. I wanted to finish my B.A. as quickly as possible and my grades had to be high enough for a graduate scholarship. That scholarship had already been dangled in front of me. I just needed another point or two on my average.

Before the academic year ended, my drug use had become an addiction, something I wasn't able to control. Because my relationships were all so tenuous, I told no one what was happening. I considered informing my parole officer and requesting placement in a drug treatment program, but I realized that doing so would be admitting to a violation of parole: no use of illegal drugs or narcotics.

When I was eventually arrested, I'd been out of prison a year and was only a few months from graduation. The new charges, two of them—obtaining narcotics by fraud—came after I accepted prescriptions for Percodan under a false name. I left my apartment, which was littered with textbooks, term papers, and my student clothes, on the arms of two detectives. On the way to the county jail I took a long look at the city I was leaving, a world I never really got to know, and wondered what it might have been like actually to live there.

The transport bus that carried me back was a duplicate of the bus that had carried me to freedom a year before. The other passengers, about a dozen returning convicts, seemed almost identical to the group that had left prison with me. The talk was flat, resigned, bitter. When a man asked why I was going back, I didn't say anything and just stared at him in silence, my mind glazed with anger and despair. When we reached the walls, a guard waved us out of the bus and I watched as a group of departing cons was ushered into our places. Their faces were hopeful, nervous, a little bit fearful. Like my own face a year earlier. One man I'd known inside recognized me and yelled an insult, scornful at seeing me come back. I was incapable of returning that insult. Later that night, housed again in a six-by-ten cell, I thought of him and his fellow riders. I knew what they'd be going through, and I wished them all the best.

Source: Michael Knoll, author of several pieces in this book, was incarcerated from 1976 to 1980 in Arizona. This piece describes his first period of release to the community and his subsequent return to prison. After a further period of incarceration (1982–1984), Mr. Knoll was released on parole. His period of supervision is now over, and he has earned a master's degree at Boston University. Reprinted by permission of the author.

Some ex-offenders are assisted on the outside by social service organizations. Delancy Street Foundation runs a successful bakery employing ex-offenders.

and even dear friends—can survive the strain of long separation unscarred?

As if reestablishing old relationships were not difficult enough, it has to be done in an unfamiliar environment. In the prison every aspect of life is programmed: waking, eating, relaxing, talking, sleeping. One effect of institutionalization is that routine decision-making skills atrophy.

The decisions about one's daily life are made by others. There are plenty of sad-funny stories of parolees looking at a menu for the first time in years and panicking at the prospect of choosing a meal and ordering it. Compare this simple task to the more important tasks of finding a job and finding housing. The rule of prison is dependence. The rule on the outside is independence, and this takes a shifting of mental gears.

The Problem of Unmet Personal Needs

Parolees are aware that they have critical needs, problems they must face if they are to make it on the streets. As one parolee has said,

> The first few days I was out were about the roughest days of this entire period … no money, no transportation, no job, and no

place to live. Now these things have a way of working themselves out in time, but you have to contact the right people, and sometimes it's hard to find the right people. I was lucky enough to make a contact with a fellow at the Service Center and he gave me enough money to tide me over out of a fund that they had. I'd say the first week was rough.[19]

When asked to name their needs, parolees have very practical concerns: education, money, and job tend to top the list. Yet they are not always realistic in their thinking about how to meet their needs. Many parolees are unable to identify the specific things to avoid doing in order to stay out of trouble.

Barriers to Success

Soon after release, offenders learn that they have achieved an in-between status: They are back in society but not totally free. They face restrictions on opportunities beyond the close monitoring of the parole officer. Many restrictions are statutory, stemming from a common-law tradition that persons who are incarcerated are "civilly dead" and have lost all civil rights.

Civil disabilities The right to vote and to hold public office are two civil rights that are generally limited upon conviction. Three-fourths of the states return the right to vote after varying lengths of time; the remainder keep felons off the voting lists until pardoned or restored to citizenship. Twenty-one states return the right to hold public office to felony offenders following discharge from probation, parole, or prison; nineteen states permanently restrict that right except for pardoned felons. Other civil rights, such as serving on juries, holding public office, and holding positions of public trust (such as most government jobs), are denied felons in many states.

Employment Barriers to employment are both formal and informal. Employers hesitate to hire parolees because they view a conviction as evidence of untrustworthiness. To the cumulative effect of statutory and informal discrimination must be added many offenders' unrealistic expectations for employment.

> Contrary to my prison expectations, finding employment was not an easy task. In fact, it took me over six weeks to find my first job, even though, at least for the first month, I made a conscientious and continuing effort to find employment. I quickly found that I had no marketable skills. My three years' experience working for a railroad before I was imprisoned provided me with no work skills transferable to other forms of employment. Nor did my prison assignments in the tag shop (making license plates and street signs), in the soap shop (making soap), or as a cellhouse worker prove to be of any assistance. The only job openings available to me were nonskilled factory work and employment in service-oriented businesses. Finally, after six weeks, I found employment mixing chemicals in vats for placement later in spray cans. After two weeks the personnel manager told me that he had to discharge me because I had lied about my criminal history (I had). Even though my foreman spoke up for me, supposedly company policy had to be followed.[20]

The legal barriers to employment are perhaps the most frustrating because they constitute an insurmountable wall between the offender and job opportunities. Three major studies of such statutes have been done. One found 307 occupations that required licenses in one or more states, licenses that were denied to former offenders merely on the basis of a prior conviction. Some statutes were very specific, barring people convicted of certain offenses from particular jobs (convicted child molesters from employment in day-care centers, for instance). Other statutes were much broader, barring from employment in some fields any person who gave evidence of moral turpitude or a lack of good moral character—characteristics that many people attribute to persons convicted of crimes.[21]

Such statutes bar employment in some job areas that are most important to former offenders. All of the states, for instance, restrict former offenders from employment as barbers (even though many prisons provide training programs in barbering), beauticians, and nurses. Jobs that pay well tend to be reserved for people with no criminal records.[22] It is not unusual for newly released offenders to find themselves legally barred from jobs they held before they were incarcerated.

A study of restrictions on government positions found that most states bar or restrict the employment of former offenders through either civil service regulations or special statutes. Even a prior arrest for a felony without a conviction can lead to rejection. Cities and counties have more restrictions than state governments. A prior arrest, even as a juvenile, is an absolute bar to employment in a criminal justice occupation in a fifth of the jurisdictions studied, though criminal justice agencies that have hired former convicts rate their job performance equal to, or better than, that of the average employee.[23]

Legal restrictions on the hiring of former offenders appear to be loosening. States are recognizing that such restrictions often work at cross-purposes to efforts to reintegrate offenders into the community. Some of the changes are dramatic.

The result is that in many states ex-offenders have now penetrated professions that have been closed to them for centuries. Perhaps the most inspiring success story is that of Robert Young. Young served several years in state and federal prisons in California in the mid-1960s after convictions for mail theft, carrying a deadly weapon, and other offenses. After his last release, he got not only a college degree but also a law degree. After practicing law for several years, he ran for election to a judgeship. He won. While a few years ago Young spent his days behind bars, he now spends them wrapped in black robes.[24]

The options for most offenders, however, remain severely limited. They have lost certain legal rights; some jobs are not open to them; and many opportunities are closed off. The quandary is real: Should offenders tell prospective employers about their criminal records and risk being denied a chance to prove themselves? Or should they lie and risk being fired if their criminal records come to light?

The only real solution for offenders is **expungement** of their criminal records. Formally, expungement means the removal of a conviction from state records. In practice, while offenders whose records have been expunged may legally say that they have never been convicted, records of the convictions are kept and can be made available upon inquiry. Moreover, the practicalities of expungement legislation are generally both cumbersome and inadequate. Although expungement is often thought to overcome the deleterious personal effect of a criminal record, it really provides little true relief from the consequences of imprisonment.

What is true of expungement is true of **pardons,** which are executive acts of clemency that in effect excuse the offender from suffering all the consequences of conviction for a

criminal act. Contemporary pardons serve three main purposes: (1) to remedy a miscarriage of justice, (2) to remove the stigma of a conviction, and (3) to mitigate a penalty. Full pardons for miscarriages of justice are rare but do occur. For example, you may have read of an individual released from prison after the discovery that the crime had been committed by someone else. Pardons are most commonly given to expunge the criminal records of first-time offenders. But in most states pardons are given infrequently, only a handful each year.

Thus offenders must have certain misgivings about reentry: adjustment to a strange environment; the unavoidable need for job training, employment, money, and support; limitations on opportunity. The stigma of conviction stays with the former felon. The general social condemnation of ex-cons adds to the pressures of continuing correctional authority, personified by the parole officer or work release counselor. If offenders believe that the cards are stacked against them, they have reason for thinking so.

Making It As a Game

One way to think about the postrelease situation is as a game with three players: the parolee, the parole officer, and the parole bureaucracy. The game consists of a series of moves and countermoves. Each participant has certain objectives and certain strategies for attaining them.

The parole bureaucracy seeks to maximize its stability in a turbulent environment. Parole has always been subject to attack because its failures are highly visible (new crimes, sometimes extravagantly publicized in the media)

---

expungement   A legal process that results in the removal of a conviction from official records.

pardon   An action of the executive branch of state or federal government excusing an offense and absolving the offender from the consequences of the crime.

Increasingly, parole officers are expected to visit offenders in neighborhoods that are not safe. What problems might this parole officer encounter as he makes home visits?

and it is perceived as institutionalized leniency. It has recently been disparaged by advocates of determinate sentencing and mandatory sentencing. As a consequence, most parole agencies seek to avoid controversy and negative public attention. Policies based on accountability and crime prevention are parole agencies' strategies to avoid being seen to fail by their detractors.

In the organizational context of the parole bureaucracy, a well-intended action can bring on untoward consequences. Officers learn to cover all the bases, but the need to do so often conflicts with a very real desire to help offenders. Job satisfaction comes largely from seeing clients make it, and so parole officers perform their roles with ambivalence. On the one hand, they are painfully aware of the agency's vulnerability to public reaction and the leadership's concern that proper procedures be followed. On the other hand, they are in daily contact with the limitations of their clientele. They cannot speak with certainty about everyone in their caseloads, nor can they realistically enforce all of the rules against their clients. So they balance these pressures, sometimes choos-

ing to go to bat for their clients and at other times coming down hard on them to protect the bureaucracy.

It is safe to say that all but truly deviant offenders seek primarily to avoid returning to prison. But they seek to advance a wide variety of individual aims as well. Some want to live the good life, with well-paying jobs, families, and mainstream lifestyles. Others want a different kind of good life: money, thrills, fast times. Every lifestyle in between is also represented. The task of the newly released offender is to try to achieve his or her personal ends, often against the weight of the bureaucracy and the orientation of the parole officer. Offenders seem to be disadvantaged in comparison to the other two players in the postrelease game because they have little formal power and stand to lose the most.

Parole officers and the bureaucracy have substantial interests at stake in the game and face significant limitations as well. In some respects, the officers are in the most vulnerable position. The bureaucracy expects caseloads to be managed effectively, yet caseloads are usually far too large to permit supervision unless some corners are cut. Offenders see officers as potential adversaries who may eventually take away their freedom. Parole workers thus have to balance their interests. Without information and (at least surface) cooperation from parolees, the officers' job is nearly impossible. In their efforts to avoid problems with the agency, officers are in a position of informal dependence on the conduct of offenders, and so they select strategies designed to elicit cooperation. The last thing they want is to be forced to revoke a client's parole, and they do so only in the most extreme and well-documented cases.

Parole officers function with serious technical uncertainty. It is never clear what supervision approach will work best or how the parolee will respond to any approach. Officers choose among strategies in the knowledge that they may not work. Thus officers are aware that:

- There is not enough time to do all that should be done with clients.

- What is about to be done may not turn out satisfactorily.

- A case action will be reviewed only if it fails. For the officers, the situation has a constant potential for negative feedback.

The bureaucracy, for its part, operates in a volatile sociopolitical environment. Parole failures are serious events and can lead to public disenchantment with parole practices. Every parole administrator can tell a story about a heinous crime committed by a parolee that brought down public wrath. On such occasions the bureaucracy needs to show that its actions were reasonable; it needs records that demonstrate the extent of supervision and justify its handling of the case.

One of the key elements of bureaucratic correctional services is paperwork—the records kept about parole cases. Paperwork performs two vital functions for the bureaucracy. First, it forces all parole officers to consider a uniform set of criteria in making decisions about classification and supervision. Thus the use of forms promotes the

regularity in procedure and policy that is a fundamental need of the bureaucracy under conditions of uncertainty. Second, paperwork ultimately forms the foundation on which the agency builds its defense against potentially damaging outside scrutiny. When courts review a parole officer's decisions or when the media express an interest in a case, the best response is that "proper procedures were followed." Paperwork alerts the officers to the procedures and to policy.

Paperwork, then, plays a big part in the game. Because of the volume of paperwork and the frequency of minor violations, it is virtually impossible for parole officers to write up every incident that occurs. They therefore often use informal means (such as increased parolee reporting or heavier surveillance) to respond to misbehaviors rather than the formal route of warrants for violations. Said one officer: "If the cops catch one of my men shooting up, I go through the motions of requesting a warrant. But if I catch the man myself, I handle it my own way. My way accomplishes the same thing and only takes one tenth of the time. If I went by the book, they'd have me down here six days a week writing reports."[25]

From the parole officers' point of view, the game involves picking and choosing among the actions that may be taken on the wide variety of incidents that regularly occur. Sometimes an officer uses the fact that no written record is being made of a problem to persuade a parolee to be more cooperative; at other times, the filing of a form may serve more effectively to persuade a parolee to "come around." In either case, the officer is using informal discretion to decide which information to record as a means of moving the supervision relationship toward the ultimate stage referred to as rapport. The officer's primary need is for the offender to play the game appropriately—to report as directed, communicate productively, and stay clean.

The parolee's essential strategy is to follow the parole officer's lead. If the officer wants a client to play it straight, the parolee must make a convincing show of doing so. If the officer wants minimal interaction, the parolee must accede to the officer's terms. Most parolees have an inflated view of the officer's power, derived from their recognition that the officer regularly decides whether or not to record officially all manner of incriminating information. Therefore it behooves the parolee to convince the officer that the information does not portend larger subsequent problems. In the absence of true rapport, parolees must rely on their ability to give the officers confidence that they are trying to do well.

The parole bureaucracy is removed from the daily interactions of the parole officers and offenders but can be thought of as the playing field where they come together. Pressures to revoke (or to ignore minor violations), a history of recriminations against officers whose clients have had major problems, a tradition of close supervision of officers' actions—such organizational characteristics are the backdrop of the officer-client interaction. When the bureaucracy's need to protect itself against potential criticism conflicts with an officer's desire to handle a client's misbehavior informally, the strength of the bureaucratic norms is likely to determine whether the officer will follow the book or take a chance with the client.

The game ends when supervision is terminated, and the manner of termination determines who won. It is possible for both parties to win: Offenders can be terminated in a "positive adjustment status," essentially a success. But there are many ways in which one or both parties can lose. Obviously, offenders lose if they are returned to prison, for any reason. But officers lose a great deal in such situations as well. Aside from the knowledge that the approach chosen did not work, officers always stand to be second-guessed. Supervisors can review files and ask why some action was or was not taken. When supervision has clearly failed, it is difficult to defend subjective decisions to a third party who was not involved. So when a parolee loses, the officer also loses—unless that bulky file of paperwork can justify the actions that were taken. When an officer

processes a technical violation, the decision-making authority may refuse to revoke the client's parole, and then the officer is forced to try to supervise the victor-client—not the best of situations. Finally, the agency stands to lose when an offender fails because a high return rate leads the public to question the agency's overall effectiveness. And so it is that revocation is a last resort, invoked only for the more dangerous offenders. This fact is known to experienced parolees, and the knowledge gives them some leeway to maneuver as they play the supervision game.

Postrelease Supervision

We've seen that postrelease supervision can be viewed as a game. But how effective is that game? How do we determine that effectiveness? What might the game be like in the future? Will its rules change?

How Effective Is It?

The effectiveness of corrections is usually measured by rates of recidivism, the percentage of former offenders who return to criminal behavior after release. The rates reported vary from 5 percent to 50 percent, depending on how one does the counting. One of the problems with statistics on recidivism is that the concept means different things to different people. The recidivism rate depends on how one counts three things: the event (arrest, conviction, parole revocation), the duration of the period in which the measurement is made, and the seriousness of the behavior counted. A common analysis of recidivism is based on reimprisonment within one or two years for either another felony conviction or a parole violation.

Although for decades criminology texts repeated the assertion that 50 to 75 percent of former convicts recidivated, recent evidence suggests that these figures vary depending on the time period, the group being studied, and the definition of recidivism being employed. A study by Robert Martinson and Judith Wilkes of the histories of about 100,000 criminals found that the three-year recidivism rate—as measured by returns to prison—for the 1970s was slightly below 25 percent, and was lower for parolees than for mandatory releases.[26] A somewhat different story was found by research on a natural experiment occasioned by the court-ordered release (without supervision) of a group of Class D felons (who have committed less serious offenses) from Connecticut prisons. When Howard Sacks and Charles Logan compared this group with a similar group under parole supervision, they found that those discharged without supervision recidivated—as measured by having a new conviction for any crime—at a faster rate, especially during their first year of freedom. By the third year 77 percent of the parole group had recidivated, compared with 85 percent of those discharged directly to the street.[27]

The effectiveness of traditional parole work has also been questioned as a result of studies of small parole caseloads. These studies find that the assumptions underlying attempts to reduce caseload size are incorrect. When parole caseloads are reduced to thirty to thirty-five clients per officer, the officers do not spend more total time with clients (instead, they improve on the quality of paperwork), nor do the offenders become more likely to succeed.[28] Officers may well be overburdened with cases, but the evidence is scant that simply unburdening them is the answer.

On the other hand, evidence is growing that parole supervision can be effective if it is structured to achieve certain aims. A study of close surveillance and sporadic urine testing for drug addicts on parole found that this technique reduced rates of new addiction, new crime, and drug-related death.[29] Similarly, a project in Wisconsin that oriented close supervision toward the offenders of the highest risk was able to reduce their rearrest rate.[30] One of the most important new strategies for improving supervision effectiveness is to increase the structure placed on the discretion of parole officers and to focus that structure on approaches that are likely to be successful. In a recent Texas parole study, traditional supervision methods were compared to a structured strategy including a standardized intake interview, a carefully monitored classification and case planning system, and a systematic program of officer performance appraisal. Parolees supervised under the new, more structured approach fared better in terms of criminal behavior and social adjustment (as measured by such factors as employment).[31]

The effectiveness of parole supervision has earned mixed reviews. Yet, because it is known that parolees who are crime-free after two years often succeed thereafter, correctional administrators continue to seek to revise parole practice in ways that will help offenders make it.

What Are Its Prospects?

Many changes have been made in the way offenders are released from prison, as we saw in Chapter 15, but these changes are not reflected in the practices of postrelease supervision. Even states that have altered their release laws or policies seem to recognize that offenders need some form of help or control in the months following release, and research suggests that parole does help them stay crime-free, at least during the early months after prison. It is likely that postrelease supervision, whether in the form of parole, work release, or some other program, will be part of the experience of most offenders who undergo incarceration.

The nature of supervision, however, is likely to be altered significantly over the next few years. Increasing evidence suggests that it is not appropriate for all offenders but should be oriented toward those who are most likely to fail and should be very close. The broad discretionary power of the parole officer is disappearing. In its place a much more restrictive effort is becoming popular, one in which limited special conditions are imposed and stringently enforced. The helping role of the officer—counselor, referral agent, and so forth—is being freed from the coercive role, and the help offered is increasingly seen as an opportunity that offenders may choose not to take. Postrelease supervision is likely to be streamlined in years to come as the courts continue to review officers' decisions and their agencies' policies.

What is not likely to change is the situation of the released offender. Poor training and poor education lead to poor job prospects; public distrust of offenders leads to discrimination. These conditions will continue to be the realities of the postrelease experience. Offenders will need to hone their strategies if they are to succeed in the community.

Summary

The postrelease function has three main participants: the offender, the community supervision agent, and the bureaucracy. The goals of postrelease supervision—assistance and control—do not mix well, and both clients and officers must struggle with the resulting inconsistencies. A parole officer is expected to develop a relationship with a client, and the pair come to depend on each other as they work toward a successful outcome to their joint endeavor. Technical uncertainty permeates the entire system and makes actions taken by officers and clients always risky. The operation is carried out in a bureaucratic context that limits both participants' ability to choose among courses of action.

As a result, postrelease supervision is much like a game. Offenders seek ways to convince parole officers that they are adjusting well to the community in order to avoid reimprisonment; officers seek ways to avoid accusations that their decisions have been inappropriate; the bureaucracy seeks to maintain an image of effectiveness with the general public. Each participant has

substantial ability to influence the others' capacity to get what they desire out of the postrelease relationship. They are in a classic pattern of exchange: They try to support one another's needs as long as their own are being met.

Research has shown that postrelease supervision is of limited effectiveness unless it is structured to deal individually with particular offenders and their particular problems. It is by this means that the parole officer can do the most to help the offender make it.

For Discussion

1. Imagine that you have just been released from prison after a five-year term. What are the first things you will do? What problems can you expect to face?

2. Why is it said that probation officers tend to take a social work approach and parole officers tend to take a law enforcement approach? How might these differences in approach be explained?

3. Research shows that some parole officers are reluctant to ask that a client's parole be revoked for technical violations. Why? What organizational pressures may be involved?

4. Many occupations are closed to ex-felons. Why?

5. What policy changes might be made to lessen the recidivism rate of parolees?

For Further Reading

Clear, Todd R. *Prediction in Corrections.* Report of the Kutak Series on Correctional Research. Washington, D.C.: National Institute of Corrections, 1988. A review of methods for classification and prediction of release success.

Erickson, Rosemary J.; Crow, Wayman J.; Zurcher, Louis A.; and Connett, Archie V. *Paroled But Not Free.* New York: Human Sciences Press, 1973. A study of the perceptions of offenders of their parole needs and problems.

McCleary, Richard. *Dangerous Men: The Sociology of Parole,* 2nd ed. Albany, N.Y.: Harrow and Heston, 1992. A study of the bureaucracy of parole supervision.

Sacks, Howard R., and Logan, Charles H. *Does Parole Make a (Lasting) Difference?* West Hart ford: University of Connecticut School of Law Press, 1979. A study of the impact of parole supervision on parole success.

Studt, Elliot. *Surveillance and Service in Parole Supervision* Washington, D.C.: Government Printing Office, 1973. A classic study of parole officers and parolees.

Notes

1. Rosemary J. Erickson, Wayman J. Crow, Louis A. Zurcher, and Archie V. Connett, *Paroled but Not Free* (New York: Human Sciences Press, 1973), p. 15.

2. Morrissey v. Brewer, 408 U.S. 471 (1972).

3. Daniel Glaser, "The Recidivism of Parolees: A Thirty-Year Follow-Up," *Federal Probation* 40 (August 1976): 14–20.

4. Carl B. Klockars, "A Theory of Probation Supervision," *Journal of Criminal Law, Criminology, and Police Science* 63 (1972): 550–57.

5. Billie S. Erwin, *Evaluation of Intensive Probation Supervision in Georgia* (Atlanta: Georgia Department of Offender Rehabilitation, February 1985), p. 16.

6. David T. Stanley, *Prisoners Among Us* (Washington, D.C.: Brookings Institution, 1986), p. 170.

7. Daniel Glaser, *The Effectiveness of a Prison and Parole System* (New York: Bobbs-Merrill, 1969), pp. 292–93.

8. Todd R. Clear and Edward E. Latessa, "Surveillance vs. Control: Probation Officers Roles in Intensive Supervision," *Justice Quarterly* 10:3 (1993): 441–462.

9. Elliott Studt, *Surveillance and Service in Parole* (Washington, D.C.: Government Printing Office, 1973).

10. Todd R. Clear and Vincent O'Leary, *Controlling the Offender in the Community* (Lexington, Mass.: Lexington Books, 1982), p. 120.

11. Richard McCleary, *Dangerous Men: The Sociology of Parole*, 2nd ed. (Albany, N.Y.: Harrow and Heston), 1992.

12. Ibid., p. 113.

13. Michael Lipsky, *Street-Level Bureaucracy* (New York: Russell Sage Foundation, 1980), p. 82.

14. Andrew von Hirsch and Kathleen J. Hanrahan, *The Question of Parole* (Cambridge, Mass.: Ballinger, 1979).

15. Stanley, *Prisoners Among Us*, pp. 125–26.

16. Todd R. Clear and P. Kevin Benoit, "Case Management in Probation and Parole Supervision," in *Probation and Parole*, ed. John O. Smykla (New York: Macmillan, 1984), p. 234.

17. McCleary, *Dangerous Men*, p. 63.

18. Gordon Waldo and T. G. Chirico, "Work Release and Recidivism: An Empirical Evaluation of Social Policy," *Evaluation Quarterly* 1 (1986): 87–108.

19. Ibid., pp. 17–18.

20. Robert M. Grooms, "Recidivist," *Crime and Delinquency* 28 (October 1982): 542–43.

21. James W. Hunt, James E. Bower, and Neal Miller, *Laws, Licenses, and the Offender's Right to Work* (Washington, D.C.: National Clearinghouse of Offender Employment Restrictions for the American Bar Association, 1973), p. 16.

22. James W. Robinson, "Occupational Licensing, the Ex-Offender, and Society," *Journal of Criminal Justice* 1 (September 1975): 69–77.

23. Herbert S. Miller, *The Closed Door* (Washington, D.C.: Georgetown University Law Center, 1972), pp. 95–99.

24. Andrew D. Gilman, "Legal Barriers to Jobs Are Slowly Disappearing," *Corrections Magazine* 5 (December 1979): 68–72.

25. McCleary, *Dangerous Men*, p. 133.

26. As cited in Selwyn Raab, "U.S. Study Finds Recidivism Rate of Convicts Lower than Expected," *New York Times*, 7 November 1976, p. 61.

27. Howard R. Sacks and Charles H. Logan, "Does Parole Make a (Lasting) Difference?" in *Criminal Justice: Law and Politics*, 4th ed., ed. George F. Cole (Pacific Grove, Calif.: Brooks/Cole, 1984) pp. 362–78.

28. Daniel Glaser, "Supervising Offenders Outside of Prison," in *Crime and Public Policy*, ed. James Q. Wilson (San Francisco: ICS Press, 1983), pp. 207–27.

29. William H. McGlothlin, M. Douglas Anglin, and Bruce O. Wilson, *An Evaluation of the California Civil Addict Program*, publication of U.S. Department of Health, Education, and Welfare (Washington, D.C.: Government Printing Office, 1977).

30. S. Christopher Baird, Richard C. Heinz, and Brian J. Bemus, *Wisconsin Case Classification/Staff Deployment Project: Two-Year Follow-Up* (Madison: Wisconsin Department of Health and Social Services, 1979).

31. Greg Markley and Michael Eisenberg, *Follow-Up Study of Texas Parole Case Management Project* (Austin: Texas Board of Pardons and Paroles, 1987).

As we approach the beginning of the twenty-first century, American corrections is confronted by a number of issues concerning current practices and future trends. In Part III we examine several of these issues, describe various career opportunities in corrections, and look at new developments as the correctional system faces the future.

CHAPTER 17

Incarceration Trends

CHAPTER 18

Death Penalty

CHAPTER 19

Surveillance and Control in the Community

CHAPTER 20

American Corrections Today and Tomorrow

17

Incarceration Trends

While there is little question that the United States has a high rate of crime, there is much evidence that the increase in the number of people behind bars ... is a consequence of harsher criminal justice policies ... rather than ... rising crime.

Marc Mauer, The Sentencing Project

Explaining Prison Population Trends
Regional Factors
Demographic Changes
Better Police and Prosecution
Tougher Sentencing Practices
Construction
War on Drugs
Dealing with the Population Crisis
The Null Strategy
The Selective Incapacitation Strategy
The Population-Reduction Strategy
The Population-Sensitive Flow-Control Strategy
The Construction Strategy
The Impact of Prison Crowding
Does Incarceration Pay?
Summary

Every American who is at all attentive to public issues knows that we have a serious problem of prison crowding. The media has given much coverage to the increased number of Americans in prison. Attention has been given to research revealing that incarceration rates in the United States are higher than other developed countries, including South Africa and the former Soviet Union.[1] And politicians continue to call for tougher sentences as a way of combating crime.

Over the last decade, the incarceration rate has more than *doubled* and the trend seems to be ever upward. One response has been to build more institutions, resulting in a prison construction boom and increased employment of correctional officers across the nation. Budgets have climbed 13 percent annually since 1986, and many states have diverted money from education and health programs to meet the soaring needs of corrections. The cost of building and operating prisons is now more than $20 billion per year.

The increase in the prison population has led to calls for a moratorium on further construction and the development of intermediate punishments to remove from prisons those who "don't belong" there. Supporters of current policies argue that the prison population is high because the level of violent crime in the United States is itself high. Some researchers have even argued that the costs to society of incarcerating some types of criminals is less than if they were on the streets. In this chapter we want to explore these issues by:

- Trying to explain the recent rise in incarceration

- Considering ways to deal with the crowding crisis

- Examining the impact of crowding on prison systems

- Evaluating the argument that incarceration is cost-effective

Explaining Prison Population Trends

For most of the last fifty years the numbers of persons incarcerated in the United States remained fairly stable. The rate of incarceration throughout the 1940s, 1950s, and 1960s remained at a near constant 110 inmates per 100,000 of the population. However, during the period of rising crime rates in the late 1960s, the incarceration rate surprisingly dropped; but since 1973, when the amount of crime started to level off, the number of persons in prison has been increasing (see Figure 17.1). Planners point to the emphasis on rehabilitation and community corrections to explain the low incarceration rate from 1965 to 1973. Others have noted that historically we have incarcerated fewer people during periods of war since the crime-prone age groups of males is under military supervision or overseas. The drop in the prison population during the Vietnam War was similar to the drop during World War II, but unlike other periods, crime rose even with the "troops" away.

The skyrocketing prisoner population has created a crisis in American corrections highlighted by overcrowded prisons and greatly increased costs. With the influx of new adult inmates, the prisons in most states have been stretched to capacity. This has meant that some offenders have had to be held in county jails until prison space became available. Others have been housed in temporary buildings, converted gymnasiums, corridors, and basements. In most states prison construction has become a growth industry even in a time of economic recession, with massive public appropriations for new facilities. Today, many states spend more to incarcerate offenders than they spend on higher education.

The upward trend began in 1973 when the incarceration rate was 98 per 100,000 and has steadily risen so that by 1993 it was 329 per 100,000. Every year the Bureau of Justice

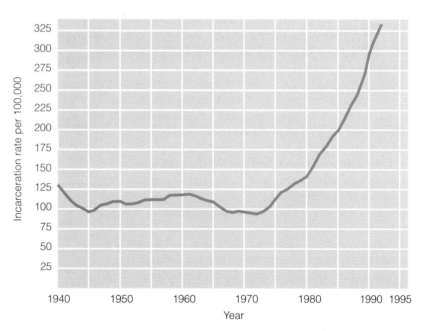

Figure 17.1 ■ Incarceration per 100,000 Population, 1940–1992. For most of the past fifty years the incarceration rate has been steady. It has only been since 1973 that there has been a continuing increase. Today the incarceration rate is about double what it was in 1982.

Source: U.S. Department of Justice, Bureau of Justice Statistics, *Sourcebook of Criminal Justice Statistics, 1991* (Washington, D.C.: Government Printing Office, 1992), Table 6.71; *Bulletin* (May 1992), p. 2; *Bulletin* (May 1993), p. 2.

Statistics announces that a new high has been reached. At this writing their most recent count (December 31, 1992) showed that 883,593 men and women were incarcerated in state and federal prisons. During the decade from 1982 to 1992, the number of persons incarcerated more than doubled.[2]

Why this increase? One might think that the growth in the correctional population over the past decade was related to crime rates. Research has shown that this logical relationship explains little. During the 1980s there was only a marginal increase in crime rates, yet a major surge in the size of the incarcerative population. Here, we will explore six often-cited reasons to account for the recent growth of the American prison population: (l) regional factors, (2) demographic change, (3) better police and prosecution, (4) tougher sentencing practices, (5) prison construction, (6) war on drugs. No one of these reasons should be viewed as a single, explanatory variable. Each contributes to the equation, with some having a greater impact than others.

Regional Factors

Some people declare that regional attitudes toward crime and punishment account for much of the increase. As shown in Figure 17.2, the highest ratio of prisoners to the civilian population is in the South. That region incarcerated at the rate of 355 persons for each 100,000 inhabitants, a higher ratio than the national average of 329.[3] The penal codes in many southern states provide for the longest sentences, and inmates there spend extended periods in institutions. Those favoring this regional perspective also point to high levels of violence in the South and to a long history of racial conflict. It is suggested that African-American men are prime candidates for incarceration in the South. But there are exceptions to the regional hypothesis: As revealed in Figure 17.2, Alaska, Arizona, the District of Columbia, and Nevada all have high incarceration rates.

Demographic Changes

The size of the prison population is influenced

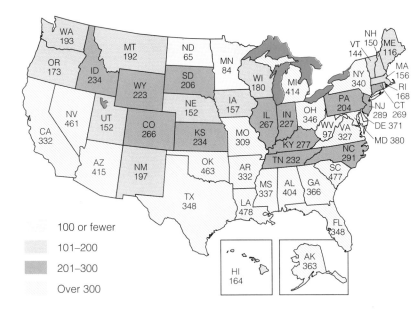

Figure 17.2 ■ **Sentenced Prisoners in State Institutions per 100,000 Civilian Population at Year's End 1992.** What can be said about these differences with respect to incarceration among the states? There are regional differences but differences also exist between contiguous states that would seem to have similar socioeconomic and crime characteristics.

Source: U.S. Department of Justice, Bureau of Justice Statistics, *Bulletin* (Washington, D.C.: Government Printing Office, May 1993), p. 2.

by the number of persons "at risk"—that is, those who are most likely to commit crimes and be sent to prison. Criminologists have long pointed to lower economic status males between the ages of sixteen and twenty-four as being in the crime-prone group. Much of the rise in crime during the latter part of the 1960s was attributed to the fact that the "baby boomers," the large cohort of persons born in the years immediately after World War II, were reaching their crime-prone years by 1968.

Whereas arrest rates begin to peak around age eighteen, rates of imprisonment do not begin to peak until the mid-twenties. Only after successive periods of probation or of incarceration in youth facilities or in jail does the average youthful offender graduate to state or federal prison. Analysts in the mid-1970s attributed the rise in incarceration to the fact that members of the baby boom cohort were now entering correctional institutions. At that time many criminal justice planners argued that the rise in prison populations during the early 1980s was only temporary, as the "boomers" would move through their life cycle.

If states could weather this temporary increase, prison populations would return to "normal" levels. This has not been the case.

Males, blacks, and persons in their twenties are overrepresented in prisons compared to their portions in the general population. Males constitute 48 percent of the population, yet are 94 percent of all prisoners. African-Americans are 11 percent of the U.S. population, but 48 percent of inmates. Persons in their twenties are 24 percent of the population, but 50 percent of those incarcerated. Research by Patrick Langan has shown that by 1986 the numbers of persons ages twenty to twenty-nine, both black and white, climbed to a record high (42 million), and the largest cohort from the baby boom, those born in 1961, reached the peak age of imprisonment, age twenty-five.[4] However, his analysis indicates that demographic shifts account for only a portion of the prison population explosion. As he notes, "The number of whites in their twenties grew by 16 percent but the highest prison-prone segment, blacks in their twenties, grew by 40 percent."[5] These and other population shifts explained 20 percent of admissions growth.

The homogeneity of race and ethnicity among prisoners, as shown in this image from the 1947 movie Brute Force, *has changed greatly since World War II. Blacks and Hispanics now compose a disproportionate share of low-income Americans and also of the prison population.*

Better Police and Prosecution

Some have argued that the billions spent by federal, state, and local governments on the crime problem may be paying off. When the crime rate began to rise dramatically in the 1960s, the incarceration rate was proportionally low. Crime rates for serious offenses have steadied, but arrest and prosecution rates have gone up. Accordingly, it is argued, the impact of the success of the police and prosecution is being felt by the corrections subsystem.

The logic of this analysis has come under scrutiny. When we compare the rates of reported crime in 1974 and 1986, the latter are somewhat higher. However, this has been offset by lower arrest rates for most offenses. For example, Langan found that the reported robbery rate increased by 10 percent but there was a 7 percent drop in the arrest rate for that crime. He found that only 9 percent of the growth of prison admissions could be accounted for by changes in crime and arrest rates.[6]

Tougher Sentencing Practices

It is held by some that a hardening public attitude toward criminals is reflected in longer sentences, in a smaller proportion of those convicted being granted probation, and in fewer inmates being released at the time of their first parole hearing. John J. DiIulio, Jr., has pointed to legislative decisions calculated to increase the total number of persons under correctional supervision as a major reason for the growth in prison populations.[7]

As discussed in Chapter 4, the past decade has seen many states passing penal codes that greatly limit the discretion of judges with regard to probation and sentences for offenders who have committed certain types of crimes. The shift to determinate sentences has also removed the safety valve of parole release, so important to corrections administrators when prison populations rise.

Incarceration rates can be affected by changes in penal codes, but the sentencing behavior of judges is a crucial factor. Judges

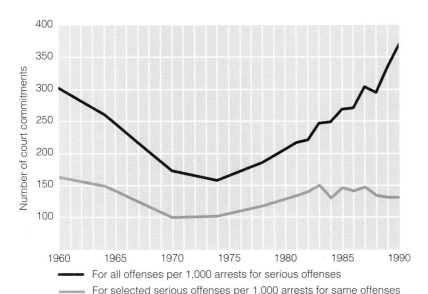

Figure 17.3 ■ **Commitments to State Prison Relative to Offenses and Arrests, 1960–1990.** Although the number of serious offenses reported to the police that result in a commitment to prison has not changed much over time, there has been a sharp increase among those arrested who are sent to prison.

Source: Data from U.S. Department of Justice, Bureau of Justice Statistics, *Bulletin* (Washington, D.C.: Government Printing Office, May 1992), p. 8.

For all offenses per 1,000 arrests for serious offenses

For selected serious offenses per 1,000 arrests for same offenses

Note: Selected serious offenses include murder, nonnegligent manslaughter, forcible rape, robbery, aggravated assault, and burglary.

must impose the law. Have judges sent a greater number of offenders to prison than in the past? Again, Langan's research helps us look at this question. He found that imprisonment rates (the number of prison admissions divided by adult arrests) increased for every offense category except fraud during the period 1974 to 1986. For example, a person arrested for sexual assault had a 9 percent chance of going to prison in 1974 but a 16 percent chance in 1986.[8] As shown in Figure 17.3, since 1980 the number of adults arrested for serious offenses who have been sent to prison has climbed dramatically.

Construction

Organization theorists contend that available public resources will be used: In other words, beds will be filled; once built, prisons will stay filled. After new cells are constructed, judges may feel little hesitation in sentencing offenders to prison. Yet when space was short, the same judges reserved incarceration for only the most violent convicts.

So the increased rate of incarceration may be related to the creation of additional space in the nation's prisons. Prison construction has been a growth industry, with an estimated $30 billion invested in new prisons from 1980 to 1990. One result is that capacity has doubled. For health and safety reasons, crowded conditions in existing facilities could not be tolerated: Many states attempted to build their way out of these problems. Also, public attitudes in favor of more punitive sentencing policies may have influenced legislators to build more prisons.

But construction is slow, and economies and political winds can change quickly. Many states found that the new institutions they had planned in the mid-1980s were ready to "go on line" by 1990, a time of economic recession and state budget deficits. For example, between 1980 and 1990 Florida added 25,000 beds at a cost of $389 million. It now has an additional 3,100 beds, but the state does not have the funds to operate them. This comes at a time when public opinion surveys indicate that less than 10 percent of those surveyed favor increased fund-

The doubling of the incarceration rate has created a boom in the prison construction industry. Many people now wonder if it is possible for a state to build itself out of the crowding crisis.

ing for the criminal justice system. Perhaps the construction option is no longer viable.

War on Drugs

Crusades against the use of marijuana, heroin, cocaine, and other drugs have been a recurring theme of American politics since the late nineteenth century. The latest manifestation began in 1982 when President Ronald Reagan officially declared another war on drugs and requested that Congress appropriate more money for drug enforcement personnel and for prison space. The war was continued during the Bush administration when in 1989 the president appointed America's first "drug czar" to coordinate enforcement efforts and urged Congress to appropriate almost $8 billion for an all out effort against drugs.

With additional resources and pressures for enforcement, arrests for drug offenses increased steadily throughout the 1980s. As a result, nationally, drug offenders now make up an increasing portion of the prison population. Langan attributes 8 percent of the 1973 to 1986 growth of the incarcerated population to the war on drugs.[9]

There may, however, be a future decline of offenders sent to prison for drug violations and a reduction in the number of drug-related arrests.[10] Data from the FBI and a National Council on Crime and Delinquency study of drug offense commitments to prison in sixteen states has confirmed this lowering of the arrest rate. It is suggested that state and local fiscal problems have reduced police drug efforts. In addition, increased use of forfeiture laws, allowing the police to retain the assets of arrested drug offenders, may mean that law enforcement officials are more selective in their choice of targets, focusing more on the big operators rather than on street dealers. In some states there has already been a noticeable decline in prison commitments for drug offenses. As noted by Connecticut's Commissioner of Corrections, Larry Meachum, "Prison population is not driven by crime. It is driven by public policy. Crimes come and go in public policy. And whenever a crime is in vogue, the prison population goes up."[11]

· · ·

It is difficult to point to one factor as the major cause of the doubling of the incarceration rate during the past decade. As we've seen, there are a number of plausible hypotheses. Research by Langan and others point to a toughening of public attitudes and official policies toward offenders.[12] It is argued that public support of current incarceration policies is reflected by the actions of Congress and the state legislatures. This tougher stance is also reflected in the actions of prosecutors, judges, probation officers, and parole boards. As a result, offenders arrested for serious offenses have a greater likelihood of being sent to prison than during the more rehabilitative era of the 1960s and 1970s. The 1980s and 1990s have seen not only more convictions but also more prison sentences as a percentage of punishments imposed.[13]

Given current public attitudes on crime and punishment, continued high crime rates, and the expansion of prison space, it is likely that incarceration rates will remain high. Perhaps it is only when the costs of this form of punishment have a direct impact on the pockets of taxpayers will there be a shift in policies. At some point there may again be a change in the attitudes about corrections, with a greater emphasis being placed on alternatives to incarceration.

Dealing with the Population Crisis

The increase in the prison population comes at a time when the public seems to be urging a more punitive approach to crime, yet seems reluctant to provide the money to carry out such a policy. Further, given the lag time of up to seven years from authorization of a public construction project until completion, the immediate need for space cannot be satisfied.

Blumstein suggests five possible approaches that states may take to address the crowding crisis.[14] Each approach has economic, social, and political costs, and each entails a different amount of time for implementation and impact.

The Null Strategy

Proponents of the **null strategy** say that nothing should be done, that prisons should be allowed to become increasingly congested. This, of course, may be the most politically acceptable approach in the short run; taxpayers need not dig into their pockets for new construction. In the long run, however, the approach may lead to riots as prisoners take control and staff members become demoralized. It may ultimately result in the courts declaring conditions in the facilities unconstitutional and taking over their administration. Advocates of the null strategy assert that demographic studies point up the temporary nature of crowding and predict falling incarceration rates by mid-1990, especially as funds for the War on Drugs decrease. Philosophical opponents of incarceration may support this approach because they fear that other strategies will only result in greater numbers of persons imprisoned. They may also reason that with the prisons filled, lesser, nonviolent offenders will be placed on probation or diverted from the system. This reasoning reflects the reality that society does, in effect, let off minor offenders when serious crime has become endemic. When violent offenses are common, proposals to decriminalize such "victimless crimes" as prostitution and gambling arise. On the other hand, when serious crime is not viewed as a problem, society penalizes less serious offenses. Thus, if murder is relatively uncommon, more criminal justice resources are devoted to shoplifters, drug users, or prostitutes.

The Selective Incapacitation Strategy

Proponents of the **selective incapacitation strategy** argue that expensive and limited prison

null strategy The strategy of doing nothing to relieve crowding in prisons on the assumption that the problem is temporary and will disappear in time.

space should be used more effectively by target-ing the individuals whose incarceration will do the most to reduce crime. Studies of selective incapacitation, as we pointed out in Chapter 4, show that the incarceration of some career crim-inals has a payoff in the prevention of multiple serious offenses. The point about time lags and the cost of new construction supports the selec-tive incapacitation strategy in the eyes of its par-tisans. Opponents see serious ethical and legal problems related to the incarceration of individ-uals on the basis of predicted criminal behavior because no available prediction techniques can make the selection process reliable. Some also argue that today's prisons are, in fact, filled with serious offenders and it is only mythology that space is being used for those convicted of minor crimes who "don't belong there."

The Population-Reduction Strategy

The **population-reduction strategy** incor-porates front-door and back-door approaches. Front-door strategies divert offenders to intermediate sanctions, among them commu-nity service, restitution, fines, house arrest, and intensive probation supervision. Some critics contend that even if such alternatives were fully incorporated, they would affect only first-time, marginal offenders, as they are not appropriate for serious criminals if crime control is a goal. They also assert that front-door strategies widen the net so that a

greater number of citizens come under cor-rectional supervision.

Back-door strategies—parole, work release, good time—are devices to get offenders out of prison before the end of their terms in order to free space for newcomers. Blumstein points to research that suggests that certainty of punish-ment is more important than severity. Given this perspective, the longer the time that indi-viduals serve in prison, the more likely it is that they would have terminated criminal activity had they been on the street. Research has shown that criminal careers are relatively short, with 10 to 20 percent of offenders "retir-ing" from crime annually. Thus it is thought that a long period of incarceration at the end of a criminal career is wasted.[15] Proponents also point to studies that say that incapacitation has its primary effect during the periods immedi-ately following conviction. From these per-spectives, shorter sentences may be more effec-tive than longer ones.

The Population-Sensitive Flow-Control Strategy

Corrections has little or no control over the intake of its raw material—offenders—so the **population-sensitive flow-control strategy** urges that sentencing be linked to the avail-ability of prison space, that policies be devel-oped allowing for the release of prisoners when facilities become crowded, and that each court be allotted a certain amount of prison space so that judges and prosecutors will make their decisions accordingly.

Linking sentences to penal space can be achieved by providing judges with sentencing guidelines. For example, Minnesota's sentenc-ing guidelines (see Chapter 4) are updated by a

---

selective incapacitation strategy   The strategy of making optimum use of expensive and limited prison space by targeting for incarceration those individuals whose incapacitation will do the most to reduce crime.

population-reduction strategy   A strategy to reduce or at least hold constant the prison popula-tion by reducing new admissions to prisons through alternatives to incarceration and by releasing inmates to parole and community corrections before the expiration of their terms.

population-sensitive flow-control strategy   A strategy of linking sentencing to the availability of prison space, releasing prisoners when facilities become crowded, and allocating specific amounts of space to judges and prosecutors.

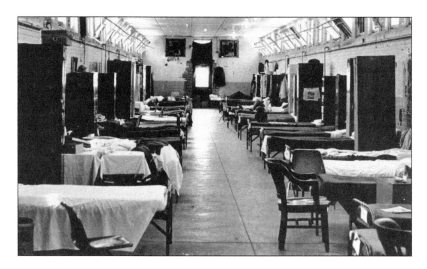

In many states prison crowding has forced the creation of "temporary" housing units. What are some of the problems to be expected under these conditions?

commission charged with taking prison capacity into account. During 1990, while the U.S. prison population increased by 8.2 percent, Minnesota's grew by only 2.4 percent. During the decade of growth, 1980 to 1990, the U.S. incarceration rate increased by 111 percent while Minnesota's grew by only 47 percent.

A second approach to the population-sensitive flow-control strategy is illustrated by Connecticut, Michigan, and some other states that have passed emergency legislation that allows corrections to grant early release or parole as a means of reducing the incarcerated population. This approach depends on a number of factors, including strict definition of institutional capacity. It also depends on the political will to release prisoners when capacity is breached even in the face of public protest.

Finally, it has been suggested that admissions policies be used to regulate the number of offenders entering prison. It is argued that because there are no "costs" for a county judge to send an offender to state prison, incarceration space should be allocated to each court. Under such an arrangement, if a jurisdiction exhausted its allocation, it would have to identify an occupant of one of its cells to be released in order to obtain the needed space for the new inmate.[16]

This approach has been tried in Texas, which, beginning in 1987, began allocating prison bed space according to historical admissions for each county. For example, since Harris County was historically responsible for 24 percent of prison admissions, that jurisdiction was allowed to send up to 182 offenders per week (equal to 24 percent of annual admissions) to the Texas Department of Corrections. In 1990, this policy was changed through the development of a county "shipping" formula based on such factors as that jurisdiction's prior admissions, crime factors, population, and unemployment level.[17] Under this model, the state prison supplies bed space, while the counties demand space based primarily on felony convictions.

The Construction Strategy

The approach that usually comes to mind when legislators or correctional officials confront prison crowding is to expand the size and number of facilities. But given contemporary financial restrictions on state budgets and the recent unwillingness of voters in some states to authorize bond issues for new prisons, the **construction strategy** may not be as feasible as it seems.

Typically, legislatures discuss new construction costs in terms of $50,000 to $75,000 per cell, but analyses by economists have shown that these figures are very low. One study computed the true cost of constructing and operating a hypothetical 500-bed medium security prison as $82,246 per bed ($41 million for the facility) when such costs as architects' fees, furnishings, and site preparation expenses are added to the base cost of $61,015 per bed, or approximately $30 million for the facility. If operating cost is conservatively estimated as $14,000 per inmate per year, the annual cost would be $7 million per year. Thus the thirty-year bill to the taxpayers for construction and operation would be $350 million—for what would be considered a $30 million prison.[18]

Opponents of new construction believe that given the nature of bureaucracy, prison cells will always be filled. This belief, as well as concern about conditions in prisons and the detrimental effect of incarceration on offenders, provoked the National Council on Crime and Delinquency to call in 1972 for a moratorium on further construction until alternatives to incarceration could be fully realized.[19] Out of this debate the National Moratorium on Prison Construction was formed to lobby against expansion. Opponents of new construction argue that prisons are not suitable for many purposes other than holding offenders. Prisons are solidly built to be secure, and they last for decades—as witness twenty-five facilities now in use were built before 1875. New prisons could soon become white elephants. This perspective lost political ground during the 1980s as a tougher crime control stance became dominant across the nation.

· · ·

States are adopting a variety of strategies to manage prison crowding. The problem exists in all states and has a definite impact on corrections nationally. A mixture of approaches may best suit the needs of a particular correctional system.

---

construction strategy   A strategy of building new facilities to meet the demand for prison space.

In the current political and social climate, support for continued high levels of incarceration seems to remain firm, yet the great expense of building and operating new prisons may limit expansion. What is not talked about is the extent to which incarceration influences crime rates. Analysts have thrown into serious doubt the common assumption "that states build prisons in response to crime and that their reliance on imprisonment in turn reduces crime."[20] Yet there are also those who argue that stability of the crime rate since the mid-1970s is a result of increased incarceration.

The Impact of Prison Crowding

T he size of the inmate population directly affects the ability of correctional officials to do their work because crowding means proportionately fewer offenders in rehabilitative programs, increases the potential for violence, and greatly strains staff morale. In addition, the makeup of the inmate community in terms of age, race, and criminal record determines the way institutions are operated. Because prison space is an expensive resource, it can be expected—in the absence of expansion—that corrections will be working increasingly with the most serious offenders as first-time and less violent criminals are placed on probation for lack of cells.

As discussed above and in Chapter 9, surveys of state correctional institutions indicate that inmates who are recidivists and those convicted of a violent crime make up an overwhelming portion of the population. A Bureau of Justice Statistics study showed that more than 60 percent of inmates have been either incarcerated or on probation at least twice; 45 percent of them, three or more times; and nearly 20 percent, six or more times. Two-thirds of the inmates were serving a sentence for a violent crime or had previously been convicted of a violent crime.[21] These are major

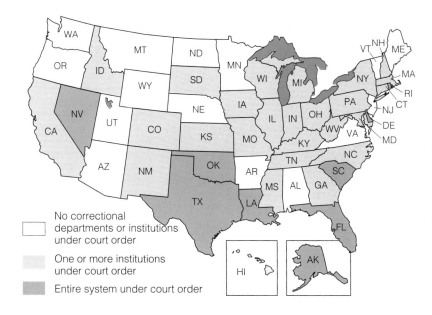

Figure 17.4 ■ **Correctional Departments Under Court Order to Rectify Prison Conditions.** Judges have the obligation to uphold the Constitution and ensure that rights have not been violated. One or more conditions of confinement have been found to violate prisoners' rights and the states have been ordered to bring their institutions into compliance.

Source: Data from American Correctional Association, *Juvenile and Adult Correctional Directory* (College Park, Md.: American Correctional Association, 1992), p. xvi.

shifts from the prison populations of earlier decades, when only about 40 percent of all inmates had committed such offenses.

As a direct consequence of the higher incarceration rate, courts have cited a number of states for maintaining prisons so populous that they are in violation of the Eighth Amendment protection against cruel and unusual punishments.[22] Courts have imposed population ceilings, specified the number of offenders who may occupy a cell, specified a minimum floor space per person, and ordered the removal of prisoners from overcrowded prisons and jails. As shown by Figure 17.4, the entire prison systems of nine states and one or more facilities in thirty-two states are under court order to rectify crowded conditions.

Does crowding cause inmate ill health, misconduct, violent behavior, and postrelease recidivism? Crowding as an influence on behavior cannot be measured merely by the number of inmates housed in a prison designed for a certain capacity. The architecture of the building, whether living units are cells or dormitories, characteristics of the inmates, management practices, and the past experience of prisoners with regard to social density are all

variables that seem to impinge on the problem. Most researchers agree on the following points:

■ Prisoners housed in large, open-bay dormitories are more likely to visit clinics and to have high blood pressure than are prisoners in other housing arrangements (single-bunked cells, double-bunked cells, small dormitories, large partitioned dormitories).

■ Prisons that contain dormitories have somewhat higher assault rates than do other prisons.

■ Prisons housing significantly more inmates than a design capacity based on sixty square feet per inmate are likely to have high assault rates.[23]

In overcrowded facilities the contemporary inmate population presents correctional workers with a challenge. With resources unavailable to provide rehabilitative programs for most inmates, the goal of maintaining a safe and healthy environment may tax the ability of the staff. Corrections is faced with a different type of inmate, one who is more given to violence, in a prison society where racial tensions are great. The need to house these individuals in crowded, out-of-date facilities exacerbates the problem. How well this correctional challenge is met will have an important impact on crime in American society.

Does Incarceration Pay?

An announcement by The Sentencing Project, an organization that promotes alternatives to prison, that the United States has the highest incarceration rate in the world has provoked a renewed discussion on the use of incarceration as a goal of the criminal sanction. To be stigmatized as being more repressive than South Africa or the former Soviet Union strikes many Americans as inconsistent with the freedom we so highly prize. Opponents of contemporary penal policies believe that they have resulted in a misuse of incarceration. They argue that offenders whose crimes do not warrant the severe deprivation of prison are nonetheless being sent to prison. Others say that most inmates have committed serious crimes, often with violence, and that they are repeat offenders. Supporters of incarceration believe that current policies have succeeded in lowering the crime rate. To not incarcerate repeat offenders they say is costly to society.

Is incarceration misused in the United States? One explanation of why we incarcerate more people is because crime is greater in the United States than in such countries as England, Germany, and Japan. More than 150 countries, both developed and undeveloped, have lower murder rates than the United States. This point is buttressed by research comparing the likelihood of imprisonment for robbery, burglary, or theft in the United States, Canada, England, or West Germany. The research showed that there was little difference among the countries as shown in Figure 17.5.[24]

Although there is a long reform tradition that is critical of incarceration, it has only been recently that proponents of the current penal policies have argued that there is value to prisons.[25] A major debate among researchers and

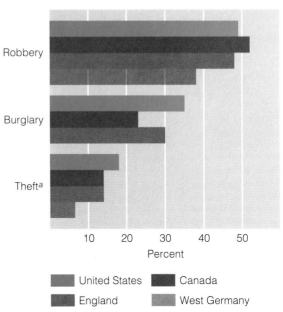

a West Germany includes burglary and auto theft in the theft category; therefore there is no separate figure for burglary.

Figure 17.5 ■ Percentage of Arrested Adults Who Are Incarcerated After a Conviction for Selected Offenses. Comparison of the incarceration rates among these four countries shows that there is little difference.

Source: U.S. Department of Justice, Bureau of Justice Statistics, *Special Report* (Washington, D.C.: Government Printing Office, February 1987), p. 2.

policymakers concerns the cost-effectiveness of imprisonment. This debate was touched off in 1987 by a report by Edwin Zedlewski, an economist at the National Institute of Justice.[26] Zedlewski estimated that the annual per prisoner cost of incarceration was $25,000. Using national crime data and the findings of victimization surveys, he estimated that the typical offender commits 187 crimes a year when on the street at a "social cost" of $430,000. By comparing the costs of incarceration with the costs of allowing a felon to remain on the street, he argued that incarceration has a benefit-cost ratio of just over 17. In other words, to put 1,000 felons behind bars costs $25 million a year. But allowing these same felons to remain at large costs society about $430 million a year from additional crimes.

Zedlewski's report brought an immediate retort from critics like Franklin Zimring and Gordon Howkins who charged that the work was flawed in that it overstated the number of crimes committed per offender and the social costs per crime.[27] These critics pointed out that if Zimring's statistics were accurate, the huge increase in prison population since 1973 should have saved enough money to almost cancel out the national debt and should have reduced crime to a *negative* number by 1992.[28] Obviously, this didn't happen.

However, DiIulio used a similar approach to estimate the cost-effectiveness of imprisonment in Wisconsin. He came to the conclusion that imprisoning a typical felon costs Wisconsin $14,000 per year, but letting him freely roam the streets in search of victims costs society $28,000 per year.[29] Still, crime in Wisconsin has increased despite the growth in prison populations.

Does incarceration pay? Until a number of crucial methodological problems are solved it will be impossible to give a definitive answer to this question. In particular, we need a more accurate estimate of the amount of crime each felon commits, a better method of calculating the social costs of crime, and a way of determining costs so they include capital and indirect costs, not merely operating costs. Even if we should be able to refine the method and have a more accurate view of the cost-benefit differential, there are political and moral issues that must be addressed before a rational incarceration policy can be designed. Perhaps as Norval Morris has said, "We have an exaggerated belief in the efficacy of imprisonment. We make life really terrible for some people and then blame them when they become dangerous."[30]

Summary

After decades of stability, the incarcerated population in the United States has doubled in the past decade. The states and federal government have responded with a massive program of prison construction. In this chapter we have examined some of the reasons for this growth and looked at various ways to deal with the crowding of prisons. Corrections is in the position of being unable to control the inputs to its portion of the criminal justice system and must rely on legislatures to appropriate the funds to finance construction and operations. After a period during which prison budgets seemed ever upward, states are now having to face the reality that incarceration is expensive. There are analysts, however, who argue that to incarcerate is more cost-effective than to allow felons to live in the community.

The incarceration policies of the past decade are now under scrutiny. Have they served to decrease crime? Can they decrease crime in the future? Or are they a means of controlling that portion of the population who do not have the education and training to function in today's high-tech world?

For Discussion

1. A number of hypotheses have been given to explain the doubling of the incarceration rate. Which of these seem most plausible to you? What other reasons might be added?

2. Which of the strategies for dealing with crowded prisons seems most viable to you?

3. Imagine that you are incarcerated in a double-celled prison that is over capacity. What are some of the factors that will influence the way you serve your time?

4. Some critics believe that the American prison is becoming a place where the urban poor receive better housing, health care, education, and job training than they do on the outside. What do you think of this argument?

5. The incarceration rate has become a political issue. Summarize the position of the two sides.

For Further Reading

Morris, Norval. *The Future of Imprisonment*. Chicago: University of Chicago Press, 1974. An early critique of imprisonment with recommendations for future correctional policies.

Sherman, Michael, and Hawkins, Gordon. *Imprisonment in America*. Chicago: University of Chicago Press, 1981. Addresses the question of building more prisons at a time when the recent surge of incarceration was only beginning.

Zimring, Franklin E., and Hawkins, Gordon. *The Scale of Imprisonment*. Chicago: University of Chicago Press, 1991. Questions the scale of society's prison enterprise compared to other criminal sanctions and to the general population. The authors call for a political economy of imprisonment.

Notes

1. Marc Mauer, *Americans Behind Bars: A Comparison of International Rates of Incarceration* (Washington, D.C.: The Sentencing Project, 1991), p. 2; *Washington Post*, 6 January 1991, p. 3.

2. U.S. Department of Justice, Bureau of Justice Statistics, *Sourcebook of Criminal Justice Statistics, 1991* (Washington, D.C.: Government Printing Office, 1992), Table 6.71; *Bulletin* (May 1992), p. 2; *Bulletin* (May 1993), p. 2.

3. Ibid.

4. Patrick A. Langan, "America's Soaring Prison Population," *Science* 251 (29 March 1991), p. 1569.

5. Ibid., p. l572.

6. Ibid.

7. John J. DiIulio, Jr., "Crime and Punishment in Wisconsin," *Wisconsin Policy Research Institute Report* 3 (December 1990): 2.

8. Ibid.

9. Ibid.

10. James Austin, *Overcrowded Times* 3 (April 1992): 7.

11. *Hartford Courant* 28 January 1992, p. A6.

12. John J. DiIulio, Jr., "The Value of Prisons," *Wall Street Journal*, 13 May 1992.

13. Ibid.

14. Alfred Blumstein, "Prisons: Population, Capacity, and Alternatives," in *Crime and Public Policy*, ed. James Q. Wilson (San Francisco: ICS Press, 1983), pp. 254–57.

15. Alfred Blumstein, "Prison Populations: A System Out of Control?" in *Crime and Justice: A Review of Research*, vol. 10, ed. Michael Tonry and Norval Morris (Chicago: University of Chicago Press, 1988), p. 246.

16. Peter F. Nardulli, "The Misalignment of Penal Responsibilities and the Prison Crisis: Costs, Consequences, and Corrective Actions," *University of Illinois Law Review* (1984): 365.

17. James W. Marquart, Steven Jay Cuvelier, Madhu Bodapati, and Shihlung Huang, "Testing the Prison Allocation Formula Over Time," *Criminal Justice Research Bulletin* 7(2) (1992): 4.

18. Edna McConnell Clark Foundation, *Time to Build?* (New York: Author, 1984), pp. 18–19.

19. William G. Nagel, "On Behalf of a Moratorium on Prison Construction," *Crime and Delinquency* 23 (April 1977): 154.

20. Jack H. Nagel, "Crime and Incarceration Across American States," *Criminal Corrections: Ideals and Realities*, ed. Jameson W. Doig (Lexington, Mass.: Lexington Books, 1983), p. 47.

21. U.S. Department of Justice, Bureau of Justice Statistics, *Special Report* (Washington, D.C.: Government Printing Office, 1988), p. 2.

22. Richard B. Cole and Jack E. Call, "When Courts Find Jail and Prison Overcrowding Unconstitutional," *Federal Probation* (March 1992): 29–39.

23. Gerald G. Gaes, "The Effects of Overcrowding in Prison," in *Crime and Justice: A Review of Research*, vol. 6, ed. Michael Tonry and Norval Morris (Chicago: University of Chicago Press, 1985), p. 95.

24. U.S. Department of Justice, Bureau of Justice Statistics, *Special Report: Imprisonment in Four Countries* (Washington, D.C.: Government Printing Office, 1987), p. 2.

25. See, for example, John J. DiIulio, Jr., "The Value of Prisons," *Wall Street Journal*, 13 May 1992.

26. Edwin W. Zedlewski, "Making Confinement Decisions," *Research in Brief* (Washington, D.C.: National Institute of Justice, 1987).

27. Franklin E. Zimring and Gordon Hawkins, "The New Mathematics of Imprisonment," *Crime and Delinquency* (October 1988): 425–36.

28. Ibid. See also Franklin Zimring's letter to the editor, *New York Times* 19 July 1992.

29. John J. DiIulio, Jr., "Crime and Punishment in Wisconsin," *Wisconsin Policy Research Institute Report*, 3 (December 1990): 53. See also John J. DiIulio, Jr., and Anne Morrison Piehl, "Does Prison Pay?" *Brookings Review* (Fall 1991): 28–35.

30. *New York Times*, 19 July 1992, p. E4.

18

Death Penalty

Our system has always been haunted by the ghost of the innocent man convicted. It is an unreal dream.

Judge Learned Hand

Justification for the Death Penalty
The Death Penalty in America
The Death Penalty and the Constitution
Continuing Legal Issues
Who Is on Death Row?
A Continuing Debate?
Summary

The electrocution of Roger Keith Coleman by the Commonwealth of Virginia in May 1992 once again focused the attention of the American public on a host of questions surrounding the death penalty. At the time of the murder and rape of Wanda McCoy in the small Appalachian coal mining town of Grundy, Roger Coleman, then twenty-two, was married to Wanda's younger sister. Police arrested Coleman and he was convicted for the crime following a four-day trial. His conviction seemed to be largely based on the fact that he had previously served time for attempted rape, lacked a convincing alibi for his whereabouts the night of the murder, and on the testimony of a jail-house snitch who said that while sharing a cell, Coleman confessed that he and another man had raped Wanda and that the other person killed her. The snitch was released from serving the remainder of his four-year prison term after Coleman's trial.

Roger Coleman maintained his innocence until his death. Over the ten years from his conviction to his electrocution, supporters argued that Coleman was poorly represented by his court-appointed attorney, that evidence to vindicate the defendant was not presented in court, and that there was insufficient proof of Coleman's guilt. The conviction was appealed through the state and federal courts, to Governor L. Douglas Wilder, and finally to the U.S. Supreme Court, which refused to hear the case on the grounds that Coleman's lawyer had missed the filing deadline by one day. In the period leading up to the execution, Coleman's supporters mounted a media campaign citing the many questions that had arisen since the trial and maintaining that an innocent man was about to die. Critics of this last-minute push pointed to facts that substantiated guilt. In the end, Governor Wilder announced that Coleman had failed a lie detector test. Still proclaiming his innocence, Roger Coleman died in the Virginia electric chair on May 19, 1992. His death added to the continuing debate over capital punishment.

Justification for the Death Penalty

Among the goals of the criminal sanction, retribution, deterrence, and incapacitation are usually cited as the basis for the death penalty: retribution because of the belief that one who takes another's life deserves a punishment equal to the victim's; deterrence because of the impact of the execution on others; and incapacitation for the obvious reason that the dead offender will no longer be able to commit future crimes.

Ernst van den Haag, a supporter of capital punishment, notes that arguments for and against the death penalty are either moral or utilitarian. From the standpoint of the moral position of retribution, van den Haag says, "Anyone who takes another's life should not be encouraged to expect that he will outlive his victim at public expense. Murder must forfeit the murderer's life, if there is to be justice."[1] Abolitionists, however, argue that only God has a right to take a life, not instruments of society. Opponents also emphasize that mistakes can and have been made, and that administration of the death penalty is discriminatory in that poor and racial minorities are disproportionately given this sentence. Van den Haag counters by arguing that abolitionists would continue to oppose capital punishment even if they could be certain that "none but the guilty are executed, and without discrimination or capriciousness."[2]

The utilitarian argument is based on the belief that executions of wrongdoers serve to deter others from committing the crime. As noted in Chapter 4, the impact of general deterrence sounds reasonable to most people, yet the scientific basis does not exist to help us understand if knowledge of the death penalty plays any role in persuading some people to not commit murder. Research published during the past half century comparing murder rates in states with capital punishment with

Supporters of capital punishment argue that justice demands that offenders pay for their crimes. The families of some victims believe that the only way they can feel that society cares about their loss is to punish the murderer in this way.

Many opponents of the death penalty argue on humanitarian grounds that it is wrong for the state to kill people. What other arguments are made in opposition?

similar localities without the penalty has been much disputed. The work of Isaac Ehrlich arguing that each execution in the United States from 1933 to 1969 prevented seven or eight murders because of the deterrent effect was much criticized on methodological grounds. Others have been unable to replicate his findings.[3]

In 1991 a San Francisco television station sued the state for permission to provide live coverage of California executions. The suit and the publicity it generated contributed to the ongoing debate over the death penalty in this country. Arguments in support of and opposed to capital punishment may be summarized as follows:

Support

■ The death penalty deters criminals from committing violent acts. If criminals know that they face execution for murder, they will be less likely to commit the act.

■ The death penalty achieves justice by paying back killers for their horrible crimes.

Society exacts an appropriate measure of revenge: "an eye for an eye." Victims' families can be reassured, knowing their relatives' murderers received a just punishment and will not kill others. By executing murderers society emphasizes the high value placed on life.

■ The death penalty prevents criminals from doing further harm upon their release from prison. Offenders not eligible for release pose a threat to corrections officers and fellow inmates.

■ The death penalty is less expensive than holding violent criminals in prison for decades or for life. By executing these serious offenders, the state can save up to a million dollars of incarceration costs over the lifetime of each murderer.

Opposition

■ There is no evidence that the death penalty deters violent crime. Many people who kill are drunk, under the influence of drugs, psychologically disturbed, in an emotional rage, or otherwise unable to control themselves. Thus, the threat of capital punishment never enters their minds when they commit violent crimes.

■ It is wrong for a government to participate in the intentional killing of its citizens. State-sponsored executions convey the harmful message that life is cheap and that violence is an appropriate response to violence.

■ The death penalty is applied in a discriminatory fashion. Historically, racial and ethnic group members convicted of murder have been significantly more likely to receive the death penalty than members of the majority group. Moreover, poor defendants who cannot obtain pretrial release on bail and who are represented by public defenders are more likely to receive the death penalty than are other convicted murderers.

■ Innocent people have been executed.

The Death Penalty in America

From the colonial period to the present, the death penalty has been an issue of controversy. As discussed in Chapter 2, until the middle of the eighteenth century, the focus of criminal punishment in Europe and in the American colonies was on the body of the offender. Along with mutilation, whipping, and dismemberment, death was a common punishment for a range of felonies—from premeditated murder to striking one's mother or father (New York) to witchcraft and adultery (Massachusetts).[4] Executions were carried out in public until the 1830s, when most were transferred to behind prison walls.[5] In some regions, particularly in the West and South, public executions continued into

the twentieth century. The last public execution in the United States took place in Owensboro, Kentucky, on August 14, 1936, when an estimated 20,000 spectators converged on this small town.[6] The death penalty has strong historical roots in American culture.

Yet even though capital punishment was extensively used, as early as the seventeenth century critics argued that the death penalty was immoral, an ineffective deterrent, "a violation of the ideal of proportionality in sentencing, and a breach of the increasingly widespread belief that the criminal could be reformed."[7]

Between 1930 and 1967, when the Supreme Court ordered a stay of executions pending a hearing on the issue, 3,859 men and women were executed by state and federal authorities, as shown in Figure 18.1. In 1935, 199 people were put to death; after that, the number of executions began to fall steadily. An average of 128 per year were executed during the 1940s, 72 during the 1950s, and 19 during the 1960s. This decline in number of deaths led many abolitionists to believe that the United States, like the countries of Europe, would end the death penalty either by law or de facto through lack of use.[8] This was not to be the case. Since the Supreme Court reaffirmed the constitutionality of the death penalty in 1976, executions have resumed.

In a democracy public opinion is generally viewed as having an important impact on public policy. Although there was majority support for capital punishment until 1960, it declined, reaching a low of 40 percent in 1965. With the rise in crime in the late 1960s, public opinion shifted to a tougher stance toward law enforcement and punishment.[9] Legislators, always ready to respond to public concerns, began to press for changes in sentencing laws and urged that the death penalty be reestablished. By 1989 there had been a major reversal of public opinion, with 80 percent of Americans supporting the death penalty. Yet a number of populous states, such as New York, Michigan, and Massachusetts, still reject capital punishment in favor of life sentences for murders.

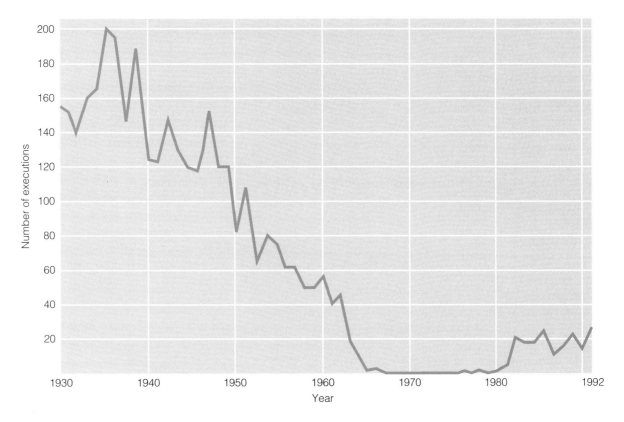

Figure 18.1 ■ **Persons Executed in the United States, 1930–1992.**
The steady decline of executions after 1940 gave abolitionists the impression that, like Europe, the death penalty would eventually end. The belief was shattered after executions resumed in 1977.

Source: U.S. Department of Justice, Bureau of Justice Statistics, *Bulletin* (Washington, D.C.: Government Printing Office, October 1992), p. 12; NAACP Legal Defense and Educational Fund, *Death Row, USA* (Winter 1992): 3.

Figure 18.2 shows the change in public support for the death penalty.

Some analysts, however, have argued that the public's opinion on the death penalty is somewhat confusing; it is difficult to determine if the public is supporting capital punishment in general, the application of the penalty to murderers, or whether people are merely supporting the right of the government to take a life under specific circumstances. Much depends upon the wording of the question.[10]

The reality of the death penalty versus the abstract concept of the punishment may have had an impact on Louisiana jurors. During the summer of 1987, that state executed eight men in eleven weeks, causing newspapers to proclaim Louisiana "Death Mill, USA." Since that time there has been a sharp decline in both death sentences and executions, even though there was an increase in murder arrests, rising from 225 in 1987 to 425 in 1989. Opponents of the death penalty say that the spate of executions in 1987 may have had

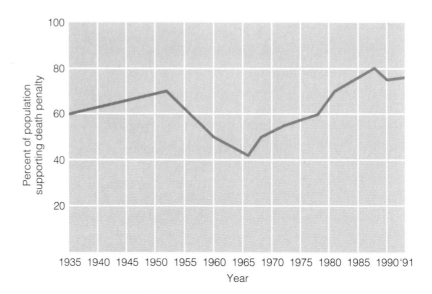

Figure 18.2 ■ **Attitudes Toward the Death Penalty for Persons Convicted of Murder—Selected Years, 1936–1991.** There has been a major reversal of public attitudes toward the death penalty since 1966. Now about 75 percent of Americans support capital punishment for those convicted of murder. What factors may have brought about this change?

Source: U.S. Department of Justice, *Sourcebook of Criminal Justice Statistics* (Washington, D.C.: Government Printing Office, 1991), Table 2.1.

subtle psychological effects not only on jurors but also on judges, prosecutors, defense attorneys, and defendants. Judges may have been more lenient in pretrial rulings, prosecutors may have been less forceful in asking for the death penalty, and defendants may have been more willing to plead guilty in exchange for a life sentence. Supporters of the death penalty have scoffed at these statements.[11]

After the Supreme Court reauthorized use of the penalty in 1976, state legislatures were quick to enact new laws providing for executions of convicted murderers under some circumstances. With thirty-six states and the federal government now authorizing capital punishment, more than 250 death sentences are given out each year, and the number of people on death row has risen to more than 2,600. However, as of this writing, the number of executions since 1976 has never exceeded thirty-one in any one year (1992). Capital punishment remains a controversial issue, one that the courts, correctional professionals, researchers, and the public seem to be unable to resolve.

The Death Penalty and the Constitution

The fact that death is different from other punishments has been invoked by courts in examining questions of due process in capital punishment cases.[12] This orientation has led to constitutional rulings concerning every phase of the proceedings, from jury selection to sentencing instructions. Because life is in the balance and mistakes have been made, capital cases must be conducted according to a higher standard of fairness, if the state is to impose the ultimate punishment. Judicial decisions about the constitutionality of the death penalty and the procedures in capital cases are many. Here we will examine three major cases—*Furman* v. *Georgia*, *Gregg* v. *Georgia*, and *McCleskey* v. *Kemp*—that challenged the constitutionality of the sanction.

In the 1972 case of *Furman* v. *Georgia*, the Supreme Court ruled for the first time that the death penalty, as administered, constituted cruel and unusual punishment, thereby voiding the

The gas chamber, such as this one at San Quentin, California, is being used less frequently as lethal injection has taken its place as an execution method. What does the shift from public hanging to lethal injection say about society's attitudes toward capital punishment?

laws of thirty-nine states and the District of Columbia.[13] Every member of the Court wrote an opinion, for even the majority could not agree on the legal reasons to support the ban on the death penalty. Only two of the justices argued that capital punishment per se was cruel and unusual, in violation of the Eighth Amendment.

Although headlines declared that the Court had banned the death penalty, many legal scholars believed that state legislators could write capital punishment laws that would remove the arbitrariness from the procedure and thus pass the test of constitutionality. By 1976 thirty-five states had enacted new legislation designed to meet the faults cited in *Furman* v. *Georgia*. In many states the new laws expanded the methods of execution. Many leg-

islators thought that lethal injection would be a "cleaner" way of bringing about death (see Figure 18.3).

One of the new laws was tested before the Supreme Court in June 1976 in the case of *Gregg* v. *Georgia*.[14] The Court upheld the new Georgia law requiring the sentencing judge or jury to take into account specific aggravating and mitigating factors in deciding which convicted murderers should be sentenced to death. Many state legislatures quickly revised their laws to accord with those of Georgia.

Opponents of the death penalty received a critical blow to their hopes in April 1987. In the case of *McCleskey* v. *Kemp* the U.S. Supreme Court rejected a constitutional challenge to administration of the death penalty in Georgia.[15] Warren McCleskey, a black man, had been convicted of two counts of armed robbery and one count of murder following the robbery of an Atlanta furniture store and the killing of a white police officer during the incident. After his sentencing to death, McCleskey's appeals were taken over by the NAACP Legal Defense and Education Fund. It argued that the death penalty in Georgia was being unconstitutionally administered in a racially discriminatory manner.

After McCleskey lost two appeals in lower federal courts, his case was presented before the U.S. Supreme Court. McCleskey's attorneys cited research that showed a disparity in the imposition of the death sentence in Georgia based on the race of the murder victim and, to a lesser extent, the race of the defendant.[16]

By a five-to-four vote the justices rejected McCleskey's assertion. Justice Lewis Powell, for the majority, said that the appeal challenged the discretionary aspects of the criminal justice system, especially with regard to prosecutors, judges, and juries. He wrote that discretion would certainly lead to disparities but that to show the Georgia law was being administered in an unconstitutional manner, McCleskey would have to prove that the decision makers in his case had acted with a discriminatory purpose by producing evidence specific to the case. McCleskey was executed in 1991.

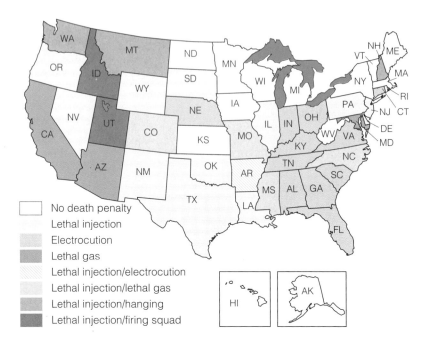

Figure 18.3 ■ **Methods of Execution Authorized by State.** Some states authorize more than one method of execution. An increasing number of states authorize the use of lethal injections. What reasons might be given for the acceptance of this execution method?

Source: U.S. Department of Justice, Bureau of Justice Statistics, *Bulletin* (Washington, D.C.: Government Printing Office, October 1992), p. 7.

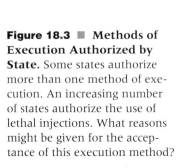

After *McCleskey*, opponents of the death penalty are likely to bring challenges to the courts on a case-by-case basis rather than through litigation that seeks to overturn the laws of a particular state. It can be expected that in the future death sentences will be appealed on the grounds that counsel was ineffective, that fair-trial rights were violated, that the defendant was under eighteen when the act was committed, or that the circumstances of the crime did not warrant execution.

Continuing Legal Issues

In recent years there has been a shift in the challenges to capital punishment. Although the case law since Furman would indicate that capital punishment is legal so long as it is imposed fairly, some opponents now argue that it is cruel and unusual per se to uniformly execute *all* those receiving the sentence of death. It is claimed that certain classes of death row inmates should not be executed because they are insane, were underage at the time they committed the crime, or are mentally retarded. According to this argument, it is morally wrong to execute a person who does not have the mental capacity of an adult.[17]

Execution of the insane Insanity is a recognized defense for commission of a crime because *mens rea*, criminal intent, is not present. But should people who become mentally disabled after they are sentenced to death be executed? The Supreme Court answered this question in 1986 in the case of *Ford* v. *Wainwright*.[18] Ford was convicted of murder in 1974 and sentenced to death. There was no suggestion at his trial or sentencing that he was incompetent. Only after he was incarcerated did he begin to have delusions, believing that the Ku Klux Klan was part of an elaborate conspiracy to force him to commit suicide and that his women relatives were being tortured and sexually abused somewhere in the prison.

With evidence of these delusions, Ford's counsel invoked the procedures of the Florida law governing the determination of competency of a condemned inmate. Three psychiatrists examined the offender for thirty minutes in the presence of others, including counsel and correctional officials. Each psychiatrist filed a separate and conflicting report with the governor who subsequently signed a death warrant.

Justice Thurgood Marshall delivered the opinion for the Court and concluded that the Eighth Amendment prohibited the state from inflicting the death penalty on the insane—the accused must comprehend that he had been sentenced to death and second, must be able to comprehend why. Marshall cited the common law that questioned the retributive and deterrence value of executing a mentally disabled person. In addition, he argued, the idea is offensive to humanity. The justices also found the Florida procedures defective because they did not provide for a full and fair hearing on the competence of the offender.

Although one might think that the Ford decision would end questions about competency to be executed, the issue arose again in 1991 during the height of Governor Bill Clinton's campaign for the Democratic nomination for president.[19] Rickey Ray Rector killed two men, one of whom was a police officer, and then put a pistol to his own head. He shot himself in the temple, lifting three inches off the front of his brain, a de facto frontal lobotomy, leaving him with the understanding of a small child. He was convicted at trial and given the death sentence. In prison he howled throughout the day and night, jumped around, exhibited other aspects of abnormal behavior, and seemed to have no idea that he was to be executed.

The U.S. Supreme Court turned down his appeal. The Arkansas Parole and Community Rehabilitation Board held a clemency hearing but unanimously turned down a recommendation that Governor Clinton commute the death sentence to imprisonment for life without parole. Clinton did not stop the execution and Rector died on January 24, 1991, through a lethal injection.

Execution of minors The laws of thirteen states do not specify an age below which offenders cannot be given capital punishment. In 1642, the Plymouth Colony, Massachusetts, hanged a teenage boy for bestiality. Since then, 281 people who committed their crime when they were juveniles have been executed.[20] Opponents of the death penalty have focused their position on the long-held recognition that the turmoil of the adolescent psyche puts it in a kind of diminished capacity, thus exempting juveniles from execution.

The Supreme Court has been divided on the issue of the death penalty for juveniles. In *Thompson* v. *Oklahoma* (1988) the court narrowly decided that William Wayne Thompson, who was fifteen years old when he committed murder, should not be executed.[21] A plurality of four justices held that executing juveniles did not comport with the "evolving standards of decency that mark the progress of a maturing society." The dissenters said that Thompson had been correctly sentenced under Oklahoma law. Within a year the Court again considered the issue and this time upheld the death sentence. In two cases, *Stanford* v. *Kentucky* (1989) and *Wilkins* v. *Missouri* (1989), by a five-to-four majority the justices upheld the convictions of offenders who were sixteen and seventeen years old at the time of their crime.[22] All of the justices agreed that interpretation of the cruel and unusual punishment clause rests on the "evolving standards of decency that mark the progress of a maturing society." However, the justices disagreed as to the factors that should be used to make that determination. The majority said that the Court should look only to the evidence of state legislative enactments and the decisions of sentencing juries. The minority argued that other indicators such as the views of those with expertise, public opinion polls, and governmental policies in other parts of the world should be used in determining whether death is a punishment acceptable in a civilized society.[23]

With the Supreme Court evidently sanctioning executions of juveniles under some circumstances, Louisiana put to death Dalton Prejean, who was a minor at the time of the offense, on May 18, 1990. There are currently thirty-four males on death rows who were under the age of eighteen at the time their offense occurred, yet since Prejean there have not been additional executions of juveniles.[24]

Execution of the retarded An estimated 250 offenders on the nation's death rows are classified as retarded. It is argued that retarded people have difficulty defending themselves in court since they have problems remembering details, locating witnesses, and testifying credibly in their own behalf. It is also asserted that executing the retarded serves no deterrent purpose since the general public may believe that it was the fact of the mental disability that caused the offender to commit the crime. Others note that it is only minimally retributive because of the diminished responsibility of the mentally impaired.[25] In 1989 the Supreme Court upheld the Texas death penalty statute and said that the Eighth Amendment does not prohibit execution of the mentally retarded. The case involved Johnny Paul Penry, a convicted killer with an IQ of about 70 and the mental capacity of a seven-year-old. The majority said that a national consensus is lacking against executing mentally retarded people so as to conclude that it is categorically prohibited by the Eighth Amendment.[26] The Court noted that only Georgia and Maryland prohibited execution of the mentally retarded. Now, years after the Supreme Court decision, Penry is still on death row in Texas, in part because of the appeals process.

Appeals One aspect of the modern dilemma over capital punishment is the long appeals process. The average length of time between imposition of the sentence by a trial court and the date that the sentence is carried out is between seven and eight years. During this time, sentences are reviewed by the state courts and, through the writ of habeas corpus, by the federal courts. Chief Justice Rehnquist has been particularly active in pushing to limit the

The case of Randall Dale Adams, who lived under the sentence of death for twelve years before his exoneration, is a prime example of the fact that "death is different." The film The Thin Blue Line *presented the circumstances surrounding Adams's conviction and helped win his release.*

appeals process in death penalty cases. A committee he set up, headed by retired Justice Lewis Powell, recommended that only one habeas corpus appeal to the federal courts be allowed. This proposal was not endorsed by the Judicial Conference, the top policymaking body for the federal judiciary, yet the chief justice recommended its passage by Congress.

Appellate review is a time-consuming and expensive process, but it also has an impact. From the beginning of January 1973 to the end of December 1992, 4,291 persons were sentenced to death and 189 people were executed. Of the remainder, 2,676 were still on death row at the end of December 1992; however, 1,426 had been removed from death row as a result of appeal, commutation by a governor, or death while awaiting execution.[27] Figure 18.4 shows the disposition of prisoners removed from death row. Would these death sentences have been overturned with the expedited appeals process advocated by the chief justice?

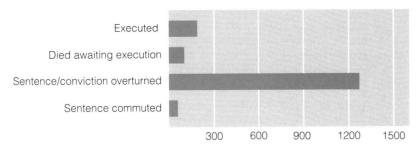

Figure 18.4 ■ **Disposition of 1,426 Sentenced Prisoners Removed from Death Row, 1973–1992.** A great portion of those given the death sentence are never executed.

Source: NAACP Legal Defense and Educational Fund, *Death Row, USA* (Winter 1992): 3.

The writ of habeas corpus is the only means by which the federal courts can hear challenges by state inmates of their convictions and sentences. A long time is required to exhaust state appeals before filing a habeas corpus petition in the federal courts. Frequently, intervening court decisions have changed the law to help the offender's case. Yet in two 1990 decisions the Court limited the ability of death row inmates to base appeals on new favorable rulings issued after their convictions. Chief Justice Rehnquist said that the refusal to allow state prisoners to benefit from later decisions validated the "good faith interpretations of existing precedents made by state courts though they are shown to be contrary to later decisions."[28]

In a major ruling affecting death penalty appeals, the Court sharply curtailed the ability of offenders to file multiple challenges to the constitutionality of their sentences. In *McCleskey* v. *Zant*, the Court said that, except in exceptional circumstances, the lower federal courts must dismiss a prisoner's second and subsequent habeas corpus petitions. By filing multiple petitions that raise different constitutional claims, death row inmates have attempted to have their case overturned before the execution date. Observers believe that the impact of this ruling will mean that the states will carry out death sentences more quickly.[29]

Appeals to the federal courts were further restricted by the Supreme Court in 1993 when a majority of the justices said that an offender who presents belated evidence of his innocence is not ordinarily entitled to a new hearing in a federal court before execution. Leonel

Herrera was convicted in Texas and sentenced to death for the 1982 murder of two police officers. Ten years later Herrera's nephew asserted in an affidavit that before he died in 1984, his father, Raul Herrera, Sr., told him that it was he and not his brother, Leonel, who had shot the officers. Statements from three other people who had earlier named Raul as the murderer were presented to the court. Texas law provides only thirty days for filing a motion for a new trial based on undiscovered evidence. The Supreme Court rejected Herrera's argument that his case should be reopened because of the new evidence. The Chief Justice, writing for the majority, said that only in "truly persuasive" cases should a hearing be held.[30] Herrera was executed on May 12, 1993. His last words were "I am innocent; I am innocent. God bless you all."

Who Is on Death Row?

Death row inmates tend to be male, poorly educated, and of low-income backgrounds. The number of minority group members is far out of proportion to their composition in the general population (see Figure 18.5, p. 490). The criminal history of these offenders shows that 70 percent have a prior felony conviction, over 8 percent have a prior homicide conviction, and about 40 percent were on probation, parole, or in prison at the time of the capital offense.[31]

Only forty-three women are currently on death row. Only one woman, Thelma Barfield

Awaiting Execution

Stephen Gettinger

At 10 A.M. Wednesday, I found it too easy to visualize what Robert Austin Sullivan was going through as he awaited his execution at the Florida State Prison at Starke.

He had described his fears to me dozens of times, in letters and in person: choking down his last meal, feeling the razor as it shaved his head and leg, feeling the leather belts cinch him into the big oak chair that inmates call "Old Sparky."

Several years ago, I sat in that same chair, for a few minutes, and tried to imagine what it would be like: gagged and bound, drinking in one last vision before they dropped the hood over my eyes. Would there be one caring face in that crowd of witnesses, or only eyes hardened against me?

Mr. Sullivan slept with that vision for ten years, longer than anyone else on death row. Doing research for a book, I first met him in June 1976. College-educated and middle-class, he was more like me than most of those who populate death rows across the country. Mr. Sullivan didn't blink at my questions: What do you imagine it will feel like? Do you dream about it? Will you fight the guards when they come to get you? His direct answers, delivered with a slight stutter, and his wide eyes told me he thought about these things all too often.

A week later, I was back on death row taking photographs. In response to questions from Mr. Sullivan, I told him gently that the Supreme Court had rejected his appeal the day before. He said his lawyer hadn't bothered to call him. Mr. Sullivan's photograph shows him behind bars of his cage, a portly young man standing in his underwear, looking wistful.

In May 1979, Mr. Sullivan peered across the prison yard at the dim movements in the death house as John Spenkelink was executed. Later, he wrote a long reconstruction of the incident filled with disturbing detail: "A special lubricant solution was applied to his shaved head and leg to increase the conductivity and to reduce burning."

A few weeks later, the governor signed Mr. Sullivan's first death warrant. I edited the diary he kept during that week of tension. It showed what a hell he had been through: dreaming of his childhood, of running through the summer evening after dinner to play baseball — only to wake in a sweat wondering how much time was left. A judge gave him a reprieve thirty-eight hours before the execution.

(executed in 1984 by North Carolina), has had the sentence carried out.[32] Although one of seven arrestees for murder is a woman, judges and jurors seem reluctant to sentence them to death. What some might call a double standard may end as public attitudes toward women change.

Of particular interest is the distribution of death row inmates among the states (see Figure 18.6, p. 491). About 60 percent of those under sentence of death are in the South, an additional 21 percent are in the West, and 15 percent are in the Midwest. Less than 6 percent are in the Northeastern death penalty states of Connecticut, New Jersey, and Pennsylvania. It is also revealing to note that of the 189 executions since January 1973, 170 have been carried out by eleven states, most of

In 1981, I visited him. He was in pain from an abscessed tooth and from back problems, but he was full of plans for his appeals. He seemed more mature; the stutter was gone.

This year his letters were less optimistic. "Quite frankly, my status has grown much worse," he wrote in January. "Needless to say, many thoughts are racing through my mind. Death is among them. I am compelled to face the possibility of a horrible death, one that boggles the mind." In the spring, he was alarmed by the execution of John Evans in Alabama, particularly by the malfunctioning electric chair that took thirteen minutes to kill him. The smiling happy face Mr. Sullivan always drew next to his signature disappeared.

When he wrote to tell me of his second and final death warrant, he projected an air of strength. "This warrant is a very serious matter. Because I view my friends and my supporters as my family, I must honestly tell you that this friendship has helped me more than words alone can express. Because of my friends I have never walked alone, nor do I now."

News reports said that Mr. Sullivan was calm during the night before his execution but that he broke down and cried several times in the death chamber. His last words, according to one witness, were: "I hold malice to none. May God bless you all."

I have tried to blot out the scene with images of the murder of which Mr. Sullivan was convicted: Donald Schmidt, assistant manager of a restaurant, kidnapped from his office at midnight, driven out to a deserted spot in the woods, kneeling blindfolded while a shotgun blew his head open. But there is a nagging chance that Mr. Sullivan may not have done it: His evidence that he was not involved, while questionable, was never given a full examination in court. Aside from that, the firm belief grows that one nightmare does not cancel out another. The horror inflicted on thirty-six-year-old Robert Sullivan diminishes us all: executioners, observers, those who ignored it.

Albert Camus wrote: "The devastating, degrading fear that is imposed on the condemned for months or years is a punishment more terrible than death. For there to be equivalence, the death penalty would have to punish a criminal who had warned his victim of the date at which he would inflict a horrible death on him and who, from that moment onward, had confined him at his mercy for months. Such a monster is not encountered in private life."

Source: Adapted from S. Gettinger, "Awaiting Execution," *New York Times*, 5 December 1983. Copyright © 1983 by The New York Times Company. Reprinted by permission.

which (Texas, Florida, Louisiana, Virginia, Georgia, Alabama, North Carolina, South Carolina, Mississippi) are southern states.

These data give credence to the research by David Baldus and others that found that imposition of the death penalty in Georgia was influenced by the race of the murder victim and, to a lesser extent, the race of the offender.[33] Of over 2,000 Georgia murder cases, defendants charged with killing white persons had received the death penalty eleven times more often than had those charged with killing black victims. Even after compensating for 230 factors, the death sentence was four times more likely to be imposed when the victim was white. Although 60 percent of Georgia homicide victims are black, all seven people put to

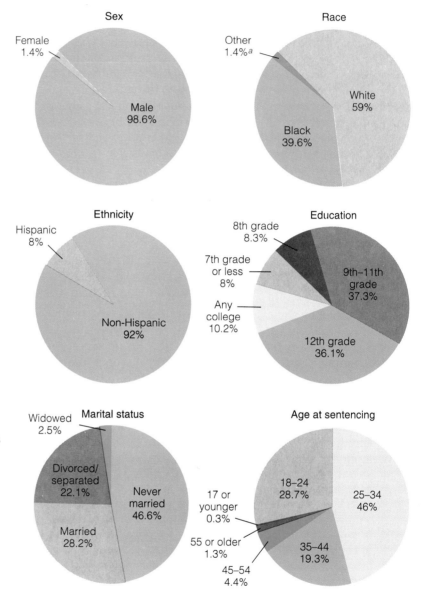

Figure 18.5 ■ Characteristics of Death Row Inmates.
Like other prisoners death row inmates tend to be younger males with less than a high school education. Members of minority groups are proportionally greater than in the U.S. population as a whole.

Source: U.S. Department of Justice, Bureau of Justice Statistics, *Bulletin* (Washington, D.C.: Government Printing Office, 1992), p. 3.

a 23 American Indians, 13 Asians

death in that state since 1976 had been convicted of killing white people; six of the seven murderers were black.

It would seem that a defendant with certain characteristics who commits a murder in certain states has a higher probability of being given the death penalty than if the offense was committed in another part of the United States.[34] The fact that there are approximately 20,000 murders in the United States each year yet only 250 death sentences gives credence to this view.

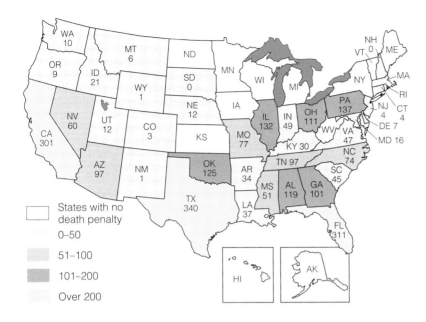

Figure 18.6 ■ **Prisoners Under Sentence of Death by State.** Why is there such variation among the states as to use of the death penalty?

Source: U.S. Department of Justice, Bureau of Justice Statistics, *Bulletin* (Washington, D.C.: Government Printing Office, October 1992), p. 4.

A Continuing Debate?

Although public opinion polls show high support for the death penalty and about 250 offenders per year are given this sentence, the number of executions remains low. Does this tell us something about capital punishment in American society in the 1990s?

Debate on this important public policy issue has gone on for more than a hundred years, yet there is still not a consensus. Present-day opponents of the death penalty argue that poor people and members of racial minority groups receive a disproportionate number of death sentences. The finality of death in light of the number of acknowledged mistakes that have taken place in the past is also given as a reason to oppose capital punishment.[35] Opponents also note that there is no hard evidence proving that execution deters crime. In addition, they argue that in most developed countries it is viewed as barbaric to execute fellow humans.

Proponents of the death penalty say that it deters criminals from committing violent acts and that justice demands that retribution be accorded murderers. Supporters say that given the high levels of violent crimes in the United States, we must retain the severest penalties. To give someone a life sentence of incarceration for murder diminishes the worth of the victim, is costly to society, and does not lessen the possibility that the offender will do further harm either while incarcerated or upon release on parole.

Amidst the controversy is the fact that one or more death row prisoners are released each year because of perjured testimony, withheld evidence, or mistakes of identification. Additional numbers have their sentences converted to life imprisonment without the possibility of parole. Will the United States increase the pace of executions, allow the number of capital offenders in prison to grow, or provide some alternatives such as life imprisonment without parole for convicted murderers? These are seemingly enduring questions.

WORKPERSPECTIVE

The Deathman

Sam Jones, State Executioner of Louisiana,
1983–1991

When Louisiana reinstated the death penalty in 1976, it also revived the need for official executioners. But many of the men who possessed the expertise, former professional executioners, had died or had grown old and retired from the killing business without having trained another generation to replace them. While other states simply assigned the responsibility to their corrections officials, Louisiana wanted its own public executioner, not a member of any law enforcement or correctional agency. Grady Jarratt had died during the moratorium and there were no professional executioners to be found, but Louisiana's problem was quickly solved when a Baton Rouge electrician volunteered his services. "I heard that the executioner they had here died in Texas," Sam Jones explained to *The Angolite* (the newspaper of the Louisiana State Penitentiary). "Somebody told me. So I took a regular civil service application and filled it out, put my phone number on it, and they contacted me." Then-warden Frank Blackburn hired him, giving him the alias "Sam Jones," after the governor who oversaw Louisiana's switch from hanging to electrocution decades before.

Why be an executioner? "I believed in it," Jones explained. "I never was the kind of person to say so-and-so ought to do something. If I felt that strong about it, I'd do it myself." He emphasized that the money he's paid has little to do with his being an executioner. On the contrary, he said that it actually costs him money. "I go in the hole on

these executions," he said. "Sometimes it costs me $800 to fly and I only get $400. I usually hand that to my kids and they use it in their church, or whatever."

· · ·

Sam had no professional expertise as an executioner when he was hired, but it didn't matter. Louisiana was willing to allow him to learn the art of execution through on-the-job training, trial and error. In 1984 he recalled his first execution, that of Robert Wayne Williams in 1983, for Baton Rouge's *Morning Advocate* reporter Melinda Shelton: "Everybody has their doubts when they do something for the first time and, sure, I had mine. The first time I was nervous because it was the first time. I didn't doubt I could do it, but I didn't know what to expect. I had no previous experience, and I'd never seen one [an execution] before."

Jones has since acquired definite opinions about execution, one being that the condemned feels no pain. "I've been shocked before," he told *Playboy* in 1986, "but I didn't feel any pain. Been hit with 480 and I didn't feel anything. I never experienced no pain getting shocked. Neither do they....There're two phases. It comes in through the head and out the leg, just like an element in a toaster."

The Angolite showed Sam several color post-execution photos of Robert Wayne Williams, asking if he had seen the burns on Williams's body before....There was a long pause while he studied the pictures. "No, I've never seen that," he said, shaking his head. "That's the first time I've seen that. I didn't see that on him when they had him in the chair. It may have come up later. I don't know what happens to 'em, what procedure the body goes through after they're electrocuted."

Asked if he had seen similar burns on any of the other eighteen men he has executed, he answered: "No. I don't remember seeing it on 'em. As soon as they take 'em out of the chair, they put 'em in a body bag and they're gone....I don't remember seeing it on Wayne."

. . .

During his first several years as executioner, Sam insisted on working under his alias and not being photographed. More recently, he has started allowing himself to be photographed and has even appeared on television.

He was asked how allowing his face to be photographed protected his anonymity. "People don't recognize you," he explained. "I've been sitting in a lounge before and be on TV and the barmaid served me a drink and not even know who she's serving a drink to. And I've never had nobody walk up to me and say, 'You're so-and-so.'"

Sam differs greatly from past executioners not only in his readiness to court fame but also in his role as executioner. In the past, executioners were generally responsible for the entire execution scenario. For instance, Grady Jarratt would check out the execution site a couple of days early to make sure that everything was in proper working order. He greeted witnesses and officials and dealt with the condemned face-to-face, executing him in full view of everyone.

Sam, on the other hand, avoids all contact with the witnesses and others present. He discretely arrives at the death house shortly before the execution and waits behind the wall adjacent to the electric chair while the shackled prisoner enters the death chamber and is strapped into the chair by prison security officers. Through a small rectangular window in the wall, he observes the ritual and waits for the warden's nod—the signal for him to push the button that sends thousands of volts of electricity burning through the con-

demned. He departs just as secretly as he arrived....Unlike most executioners throughout history, Sam is not asked to do very much. His sole duty has been reduced to pushing a button, something a child, an animal, or even a machine could do—though Louisiana's requirement that the executioner be a certified electrician implies a larger responsibility.

Sam Jones performed his last electrocution in Louisiana on July 22, 1991. Corrections authorities informed The Angolite *editors that, regardless of how executions are conducted in the future, the services of "Sam Jones" would no longer be needed, bringing his tenure as official state executioner to an end.*

Source: Wilbert Rideau and Ron Wikberg, *Life Sentences: Rage and Survival Behind Bars* (New York: Times Books, 1992), pp. 313–18.

Summary

Capital punishment continues to be a most controversial sanction. Issues of morality, utility, and equity dominate the debate. This has been the case in the United States for almost two hundred years.

With the numbers on death row rising each year yet the number of executions remaining low, questions have been raised about the future of this punishment. Following the 1976 Supreme Court decision in *Gregg* v. *Georgia*, thirty-six states rewrote their statutes so as to provide for the death penalty. Since that time, the Court has dealt with continuing questions about the death penalty including the execution of the mentally ill, juveniles, and the retarded. Of late, Chief Justice Rehnquist has urged the judiciary to limit opportunities for appeals so as to ensure that the penalty is carried out.

The characteristics of those on death row show that compared to the general population they are more likely to be low-income males who are members of minority groups. The data show that the greatest use of the death penalty is in the South and that the race of the victim is an important factor.

Although public opinion is seemingly supportive of the death penalty, some argue that this support is shallow. It is also argued that life imprisonment without parole might be an acceptable alternative to the death penalty.

For Discussion

1. What are the major arguments in favor of and opposed to capital punishment? Which one seems to you to be the most important?

2. Should the death penalty be imposed on a person whose crime was committed as a juvenile? Do you believe that the "evolving standards of decency" of our society support such an execution?

3. Why is there support for the death penalty in the United States when it has been abolished in the countries of Europe?

4. Are there alternatives to death that could achieve the retributive, deterrent, and incapacitative goals of capital punishment? Describe any alternatives that meet these criteria.

5. What does the future hold for the death penalty?

For Further Reading

Baldus, David C.; Woodworth, George G.; and Pulaski, Charles A., Jr. *Equal Justice and the Death Penalty: A Legal and Empirical Analysis*. Boston: Northeastern University Press, 1990. A statistical study of Georgia's capital sentencing system that explores the degree of arbitrariness and racial discrimination. The authors call for modification of trial-level guidelines and state supreme court review.

Bedau, Hugo Adam. *Death Is Different*. Boston: Northeastern University Press, 1987. The author, a major opponent of the death penalty, argues that the death penalty is different from other punishments in its morality, its politics, and its symbolism.

Johnson, Robert. *Death Work*. Pacific Grove, Calif.: Brooks/Cole, 1989. A study of those on death row—prisoners and correctional officers—and the impact of capital punishment on their lives.

Radelet, Michael L. (ed.). *Facing the Death Penalty: Essays on Cruel and Unusual Punishment*. Philadelphia: Temple University Press, 1989. A collection of sixteen essays written by criminologists, theologians, philosophers, and prisoners. The authors offer various justifications for their conclusion that the death penalty is inherently cruel and unusual.

White, Welsh S. *The Death Penalty in the Nineties*. Ann Arbor: University of Michigan Press, 1991. An examination of capital punishment in the context of criminal justice decision making, racial discrimination, and defendants who elect execution.

Notes

1. Ernst van den Haag, "For the Death Penalty," *New York Times*, 17 October 1983.

2. Ibid.

3. Isaac Ehrlich, "The Deterrent Effect of Capital Punishment: A Question of Life and Death," *American Economic Review* 65 (1975): 397–417. But see also William J. Bowers and Glenn L. Pierce, "The Illusion of Deterrence in Isaac Ehrlich's Research on Capital Punishment," *Yale Law Journal* 85 (1975): 187–208.

4. *Voices Against Death*, ed. Philip English Mackey (New York: Burt Franklin & Co., 1976), p. xi.

5. Louis P. Masur, *Rites of Execution: Capital Punishment and the Transformation of American Culture, 1776–1865* (New York: Oxford University Press, 1989).

6. Harry Elmer Barnes and Negley K. Teeter, *New Horizons in Criminology*, 3rd ed. (Englewood Cliffs, N.J.: Prentice-Hall, 1959), p. 308.

7. Ibid., p. 4.

8. Franklin Zimring and Gordon Hawkins, *Capital Punishment and the American Agenda* (New York: Cambridge University Press, 1986).

9. Thomas J. Keil and Gennaro F. Vito, "Fear of Crime and Attitudes Toward Capital Punishment: A Structural Equations Model," *Justice Quarterly* 8 (December 1991): 447. The authors find a link between fear of crime in the neighborhood and a greater willingness to endorse the death penalty.

10. Frank P. Williams, III, Dennis R. Longmire, and David B. Gulick, "The Public and the Death Penalty: Opinion as an Artifact of Question Type," *Criminal Justice Research Bulletin* 3 (1988): 3.

11. *New York Times*, 25 June 1991.

12. Hugo Adam Bedau, *Death Is Different* (Boston: Northeastern University Press, 1987).

13. Furman v. Georgia, 408 U.S. 238 (1972).

14. Gregg v. Georgia, 428 U.S. 155 (1976). Three other cases were decided by the Court with Gregg. Florida's death penalty law was upheld, being similar to Georgia's—Profitt v. Florida, 428 U.S. 242 (1976)—while the laws of Texas and North Carolina were struck down—Jurek v. Texas, 428 U.S. 262 (1976) and Woodson v. North Carolina, 428 U.S. 280 (1976).

15. McCleskey v. Kemp, 478 U.S. 1019 (1976).

16. David C. Baldus, George F. Woodworth, and Charles A. Pulaski, Jr., *Equal Justice and the Death Penalty: A Legal and Empirical Analysis* (Boston: Northeastern University Press, 1990).

17. Mark A. Small, "A Review of Death Penalty Caselaw: Future Directions for Program Evaluation," *Criminal Justice Policy Review* 5 (June 1991): 117. Candace McCoy, "The Death Penalty Continued," *Federal Probation* (March 1990): 77.

18. Ford v. Wainwright, 477 U.S. 399 (1985).

19. Marshall Frady, "Death in Arkansas," *New Yorker* (February 23, 1993): 105.

20. Ron Rosenbaum, "Too Young to Die?" *New York Times Magazine* (March 12, 1989).

21. Thompson v. Oklahoma, 108 S.Ct., 2687 (1988).

22. 45 Cr.L.Rptr. 3203 (1989).

23. Mark C. Seis and Kenneth L. Elbe, "The Death Penalty for Juveniles: Bridging the Gap Between an Evolving Standard of Decency and Legislative Policy," *Justice Quarterly* 8 (December 1991): 464.

24. NAACP Legal Defense and Educational Fund, Inc. *Death Row, USA* (Winter 1992): 2.

25. Philip L. Fetzer, "Execution of the Mentally Retarded: A Punishment Without Justification," *South Carolina Law Review* 40 (1989): 419.

26. Penry v. Lynaugh, 45 Cr.L.Rptr. 3188 (1989).

27. *Death Row, USA*, NAACP Legal Defense, p. 4.

28. *New York Times*, 6 March 1990, p. A20.

29. David M. O'Brien, *Supreme Court Watch—1992* (New York: W.W. Norton, 1992), p. 188.

30. *New York Times*, 26 January 1993, p. 1.

31. U.S. Department of Justice, Bureau of Justice Statistics, *Bulletin* (Washington, D.C.: Government Printing Office, October 1992), p. 2.

32. NAACP Legal Defense, *Death Row, USA*, p. 4.

33. David Baldus, Charles Pulaski, and George Woodworth, "Comparative Review of Death Sentences: An Empirical Study of the Georgia Experience," *Journal of Criminal Law and Criminology* 74 (1983): 661–85.

34. Raymond Paternoster, "Race of the Victim and Location of the Crime: The Decision to Seek the Death Penalty in South Carolina," *Journal of Criminal Law and Criminology* 74 (1983): 754–85.

35. Hugo Adam Bedau and Michael L. Radelet, "Miscarriages of Justice in Potentially Capital Cases," *Stanford Law Review* 40 (November 1987): 21–179.

Surveillance and Control in the Community

19

The real master shift about to take place is toward the control of whole groups, populations, and environments—not community control, but the control of communities.

Stanley Cohen, *Visions of Social Control*

The Growth of Surveillance
The Techniques of Surveillance and Control
Drug Controls
Electronic Controls
Human Surveillance
Programmatic Controls
The Goals of Surveillance
Communities and Community Protection
Control: A Double-Edged Sword
The Politics of Surveillance and Community Protection
The Limits of Control
Technology
Human Responses
Moral and Ethical Limits
Toward an Acceptable Community Control
Summary

Y ou awaken in the early morning to the sound of your phone ringing. The alarm clock next to your bed tells you it is 3:45 A.M. The loud phone startles you awake, but oddly, it does not surprise you. This happens every third or fourth day, at irregular intervals in the nighttime.

Taking the receiver to your ear, you mutter a slight obscenity.

The voice on the other end of the line is not a human voice; it is one of those robot-voiced machines. It says, "This is the Madison County Community Control Department. Please enter your offender code."

You type into the phone the first five digits of your social security number.

"Thank you," says the heartless voice. "Please verify your identity by placing your index finger on the Veri-Pad."

Next to the phone is a heat-sensing pad. You put your right index finger on it and wait for three seconds while it registers the information it is receiving from your skin.

The voice: "Mr. Juan Agostino, have you committed any crimes since your last observation?"

You are not unnerved by the question—it is a part of the routine for these nighttime calls. And you know the Veri-Pad is also a lie detector.

You answer, "No."

There is a slight pause.

Then the voice, again: "Thank you, Mr. Agostino. You have tested negative for drugs, for alcohol, and for new crimes, and you are in residence as required. You are approved to remain in the community until the next contact." The voice clicks off.

You hang up the phone, with a funny sense of annoyance but also relief. Nine months ago, you were convicted of burglary—your second conviction. If you can put up with the intrusion for another year, you will not have to go to prison.

You hang up the phone. Next to it, the alarm clock reads: March 15, 2001 … 3:50 A.M.

At 6:30 the alarm will go off, and you will have to get up and go to work....

This scenario may sound farfetched, but it is not. The technologies it describes either exist now and are being used, or are nearly perfected. They are the technologies of control, and they are especially designed to be applied to offenders in the community.

Perhaps you do not find the story particularly dismaying; if so, it is a sign of how far our society has come in the normalization of community surveillance. Thirty years ago, the description would have provoked outraged objection from liberals and conservatives alike. Today, the techniques of community control surround us and we are no longer amazed or alarmed by them.

In this chapter we explore one aspect of corrections that has grown more rapidly than perhaps any other in the last twenty years— the existence of surveillance in the community. The chapter argues neither for nor against this trend, but it does begin with an assumption: Personal liberty is the precious ability to live freely within our homes, families, and communities, not being subjected to inordinate controls over our autonomy. Any correctional trend that touches on this aspect of liberty raises profound questions.

The Growth of Surveillance

T he impetus for community surveillance comes from prison and jail overcrowding. With limited space for new prisoners, officials have been looking for alternative ways to handle the growing number of offenders. Most of these officials believe that without some capacity for controlling offenders' behavior, alternatives to prison leave the community at too much of a risk.

The intermediate sanctions movement, discussed in Chapter 8, is an expression of this concern. It is based on the argument that for many offenders, probation is not stringent enough, but prisons are too expensive and destructive. This has led to the creation of a range of community sanctions whose severity falls between prisons and probation. Each of these sanctions calls for some degree of surveillance and control.

Surveillance itself is very common in modern society—and is not necessarily a bad thing. Parents put listening devices in infants' rooms so they can hear when the baby wakes up; banks put monitors in their money machines to take photos of the people who withdraw money; airports check all carry-on bags with X-rays; credit cards are checked before a purchase to be certain they are valid. The advent of the information age has meant that surveillance is a more likely option for preventing problems than ever before in history.

As we shall see, along with surveillance technologies, systems of control have also grown. These are technical ways to limit behavior, through either physical constraints or other means. The total impact of the advent of technical surveillance has been a change in the orientation of corrections. Instead of merely punishing or promoting rehabilitation, the corrections system is called upon to establish *control* over the offender's behavior in ways that prevent misconduct.

The Techniques of Surveillance and Control

T echnologies of correctional surveillance and control have multiplied in recent years. There are four general types of control strategies used by corrections: drugs, electronics, human surveillance, and control programs. They may be used separately or in combination.

Drug Controls

It is perhaps ironic that in a society so concerned about drug abuse, one of the main strategies for controlling human behavior is the use of chemicals. Yet the use of drugs is one of the more common ways to control behavior, and a long tradition of prescribing drugs for these purposes exists in the United States. Here, we describe only a few such drugs, but the extent of their use underscores the importance of chemical controls.

Antabuse is frequently given to alcohol abusers. When combined with alcohol, it makes a person become violently nauseated, and it therefore suppresses the desire for alcohol. But Antabuse also has the side effect of seriously reducing sexual response. The drug is controversial because it is seldom taken voluntarily, and its side effects are so undesirable. For example, imagine the predicament of a prisoner who wants to have the right to go home to visit his spouse on a furlough but is required to take Antabuse as a condition of the furlough.

Sometimes called "chemical castration," the drug **Depo-Provera** has the main effect of constraining male sexual response. It is used to reduce or eliminate the drive of men convicted of certain sex offenses. The drug is fairly effective in eliminating the capacity for males to sustain an erection, but critics do not find this a persuasive argument in behalf of its use. They say that the aggression inherent in sex offenses, which involves fondling children or violence against women, is not inhibited by reduced sexual performance. Moreover, the causes of sexual deviance are not altered by the drug's use.

The drug **Thorazine** has long been prescribed for persons suffering from certain psychiatric problems that lead to violent behavior. Thorazine is a very strong drug that creates a lethargic mood within its users and, by diminishing the capacity for excitement and expres-

Antabuse   A drug that, when combined with alcohol, causes violent nausea; it is used to control a person's drinking.

Depo-Provera   A "chemical castration" drug that eliminates sexual response among males.

Thorazine   A drug used to control violent or aggressive behavior caused by psychiatric problems.

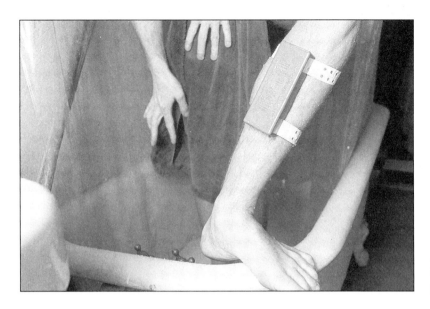

Advances in electronic technology have increased the effectiveness of surveillance in the community.

sive emotions, reduces the likelihood of violence. It is precisely this lowering of the person's affect that leads many to criticize its use.

For offenders who suffer from depression, the drug **Prozac** is often prescribed. Widely used among nonoffenders, this drug decreases the low, sad feelings that accompany depression. While few offenders commit crimes as the direct result of depression, it can be a contributing factor to some criminality, in that people who are unmotivated to get a job or improve their lifestyle may be undeterred by the threat of punishment for crime.

This is certainly not an exhaustive list, but these are some of the drugs more commonly used to control criminal behavior. The few drugs we've touched on illustrate the range of problems addressed through drugs and the variety of physical, biological, and emotional responses these drugs produce. These examples also show the controversial nature of chemical controls—they often have side effects, and they are never 100 percent effective.

Prozac   A drug that reduces depression.

Electronic Controls

Perhaps the dominant penal innovation of the 1980s has been electronic monitoring. As we saw in our discussion of it in Chapter 8, the idea of electronic monitoring has much to make it popular: It is "high-tech" corrections, and it costs less than prison. Since its earliest beginnings in the 1980s, electronic monitoring has grown to become a major industry, and thousands of offenders are now under monitoring each day.

The electronic age has made possible a quantum leap in surveillance possibilities. In this chapter, we speculate about the future of the various technologies. As one example, the technology already exists to have visual monitoring via telephone wires. It would be possible to use video screens to be certain the offender is actually present at home during the phone call. The probation officer would dial the offender up on the phone and then carry on a face-to-face interview without ever leaving the office.

An argument could also be made for routine, random video surveillance without the telephone hookup. Under this system the probation officer could activate the video camera into the offender's home at any time and obtain direct, unbiased information about the offender's behavior and compliance with the law.

As another level of surveillance, consider the technology of the "electric fence" that is now used to confine some dogs. It establishes a perimeter (usually the yard) outside of which the dog may not venture without triggering an electronic shock. It is easy to see how this kind of technology might be adapted to keep certain offenders away from schools, taverns, or other areas. In theory, at least, it could allow extensive freedom within the necessary restrictions.

But Americans have a tradition of respect for individual privacy—and there is no question that these devices invade privacy. We are especially suspicious of any invasion of the home, no matter what its benefits might be. Yet the arguments in favor of such surveillance are twofold: First, they are almost always less restrictive than prison (suggesting that convicted criminals' rights to privacy are not strong); and second, the right to privacy might be deemed less important than the need to prevent crime.

Human Surveillance

The technological advances of electronics and drugs are more systematic than mere human interaction; however, personal contact allows the correctional worker to process an array of subtle information—body language, attitudes, odors, and so forth—that these other systems cannot provide. When it comes to surveillance, there is no approach that fully supplants the basic strategy of increasing the offender's contact with the experienced correctional worker.

Intensive supervision systems have been used to increase this surveillance contact, in both frequency and diversity. The frequency is increased by reduced caseloads and minimum contact requirements for every offender under supervision. Typically, these offenders are seen at least weekly, sometimes more often than that. What makes the surveillance effective is not just the amount of contact, but where and when it

occurs: Offenders are seen at the office, in their homes, and at work; they are seen at regular intervals and in "surprise" visits, without prior notification. The effect is an aura of surveillance, in which no aspect of the offender's life is totally free of potential observation.

By routine, random contacts, the officer is able to see a wider range of the offender's behavior and the observations occur in a broader array of situations. This means that the official understanding of the offender's compliance with the law is spread to more situations.

Programmatic Controls

The most widely used techniques of surveillance and control are established elements of treatment programs. Drug testing is a good example. In these programs, urine samples are taken routinely to test for an offender's drug use. The normal approach is to require the offender to submit a urine sample (watching as it is "produced," to be certain it is truly the offender's urine and not a substitute), then label the sample, and send it off to a lab for testing.

Not only is this procedure awkward and invasive, it is also untimely—the delay separates the time of surveillance (the actual urine evaluation) from the time of action (arrest and revocation, in the case of a "dirty" urine). Recently, on-the-spot tests have been developed, usually involving a drug-sensitive strip of paper. Some are used with urine samples; new tests are being performed on saliva samples. Finally, since the traces of some drugs leave the urine and saliva within hours of drug use, some programs have adopted the expensive alternative of hair testing. Traces of an illegal drug can be found in human hair for a year or more after the drug's ingestion.

Programs also sometimes provide for systems of surveillance and control. The most famous example is Vermont's "Relapse Prevention Program" for sex offenders. This program trains the offender to be aware of signals of potential for reverting to sexual offenses. These signals take the form of sudden changes in mood, renewed drinking, loss of a job, depression, and so forth. What makes this program unusual, however, is that selected persons living in the offender's community—family, friends, therapists, and co-workers—are also taught to look for the same signals. In effect, these persons become additional eyes and ears for the corrections worker, who contacts them on a regular basis to see if there has been any evidence of a behavior change on the part of the offender that should concern the authorities. The community augments the system, providing additional surveillance.[1]

The Goals of Surveillance

Community surveillance of offenders has multiple goals. The main goal might seem to be community protection: We keep offenders under surveillance in order to remain safe from them. Certainly, the rationale for most surveillance programs and the way they are described to the public fits this goal. The rhetoric of "tough" supervision is designed to help a doubting public have confidence in the idea that offenders are living in the community. The reasons for having these offenders live in the community indicates the other goals of surveillance.

Communities and Community Protection

Most offenders are not "dangerous." This is true for two reasons. First, many offenders, once caught and processed by the system, will not become reinvolved in crime. Second, even when offenders continue their criminal behavior, most of their crimes are petty behavior that causes loss to their victims but really does not endanger them. To provide surveillance to these offenders suggests that the aim of "protection" is not necessarily the most important reason for surveillance.

One of the motivations for developing these programs is the insidious problem of institutional overcrowding. Because of overcrowding, a majority of offenders must reside in the community. Yet the "get tough" movement has created an atmosphere in which tolerance for offenders in the community is very limited. Policymakers find themselves in a bind. The electoral politics of the 1980s required politicians to promise zero tolerance for crime. Yet the cost of incarceration is such that to increase prison capacity requires increases in public spending—and taxes—certainly a difficult political choice.

By building correctional programs in the community around themes of surveillance, it is possible to get out of the serious bind by presenting the programs to be as "safe as prison." It is debatable whether these programs are as safe as they claim. The point is that the "tough surveillance" demeanor of the new community programs serves a latent goal—it allows the system to retain numerous offenders in the community, without having to address the problem of public fear of crime. Thus, surveillance acts like a program assurance—the public can have confidence in the correctional system keeping so many offenders on the streets because they are being watched so closely.

There are other goals to surveillance. Treatment providers point out that without some degree of surveillance, it is not possible to know for sure if the treatment is having an effect. They argue that some form of drug testing, for instance, is essential to any drug treatment program. The law enforcement–minded argue that tough surveillance deters crime in two ways. It makes offenders less willing to decide to commit a crime because they are being watched so closely; and it catches active criminals earlier in their recidivism.[2]

Control: A Double-Edged Sword

For most of us, a first reaction to the idea of tighter surveillance is that it is a good thing to have. Even if the main intention is to increase public confidence in corrections, it can be argued that this is much needed. But the other aims of community protection, more effective treatment, and better deterrence of crime, are all desirable on their face.

The increase in community surveillance comes at a price, however. The main cost is civil liberty. Just as studies have shown that families suffer from incarceration, they also indicate that house arrest, electronic monitoring, and intensive supervision place stress on the family and sometimes infringe directly on the privacy of innocent people. For instance, return for a moment to the story that started this chapter. Can you imagine the annoyance of Juan Agostino's wife whenever the phone rings in the middle of the night? Or think of the intrusion of surreptitious video monitoring of the home.

Critics of the new community surveillance argue that history has always shown that when government is allowed to intervene into citizen's lives without restraint, tyranny results. Unless we jealously protect civil liberty against intrusion by the state, there will be an inevitable and continuing loss of freedom. In behalf of their case, these critics point out that airport metal detectors were supposed to be temporary when they were first developed and that the social security number was supposed to have no official use other than keeping track of social security benefits.

The advocates of control respond by saying, "Yes, perhaps this is true. But airplane hijackings have decreased in frequency, and life is more convenient now that we have social security numbers." The debate about freedom and control is a very old one, and one that cannot be resolved in a few pages.

We must admit, however, that when new technologies are developed for corrections, it is difficult to stop them from spreading, for they become quite popular very quickly. Who can argue against electronic fences for criminals if it can be shown they work? Already, some city streets are blocked off to prevent drug sales. The image of a future society in which whole

Surveillance technology has become almost commonplace in our society. Its potential uses for observing and tracking offenders in the community are only now being realized.

sections of town are cordoned off from certain people for legal reasons may not be farfetched.

Thus the new surveillance and control emphasis of corrections is a major change, not just for the field but also for the community in which the field operates. We must recognize that the advocacy of technological surveillance and control changes our communities, perhaps in some ways we would not choose.

The Politics of Surveillance and Community Protection

Community surveillance and control occupy a controversial position in modern American politics. To better understand this controversy, we can compare traditional conservative and liberal views about the role of government in the community and then assess how the problem of crime shifts those views.

Traditionally, conservatives have been those who argue against government intrusion into personal affairs. They seek as much autonomy as possible for individual citizens and want the government to be conservative (reluctant) in taking action—the basic idea is to allow interpersonal relations to be unencumbered by government oversight. Yet when it comes to the problem of crime, this position is reversed. The traditional conservative view calls for broad and extensive government action and control. Thus the existence of crime in the community serves to refract the ordinary conservative idea of government restraint into a modern view of government as protector of the private citizen. The primary conservative spokespersons turn out to be advocates for all sorts of electronic, chemical, and human control over fellow citizens.

Liberals also shift their traditional stance. Ordinarily, the liberal view calls for the use of government power to advance equal access of citizens to the benefits of society. Thus liberals will seek programs that alleviate social inequalities, and this will often mean a fairly extensive level of government involvement in communities, especially in the form of ameliorative social programs. Yet when it comes to crime, liberals are suspicious of the expansion of government surveillance and control, and they seek to place firm limits on the development of these approaches. Instead of concern about the way the crime reduces the victim's access to social benefits, liberals often express their concern about potential overinvolvement in the offender's life, through government control.

Why this shift? Much has to do with the ways the traditional political positions contrast the value of social order and personal liberty. Conservatives place a strong emphasis upon the social order. They take the existence of crime as a serious threat to normal private relations, throwing off-center the ordinary processes of human commerce. To prevent the distortions of society caused by crime, conservatives are willing to sacrifice the offender's interest in being free of undue government control. While the conservative ordinarily wants the individual to look out for his or her

own interests, crime is seen as a situation into which the government must intervene to manage the interests of the private citizens.

Liberals, because they value liberty, tend to be alarmed by the deep intrusion of government into the freedom of offenders. They treat government control of citizens as inherently dangerous, and regardless of its potential benefits in controlling crime, liberals feel the price of extending government power into homes as far outweighing them. While the liberal wants government to guarantee equal access of all citizens to the social arena, crime is seen as a situation in which government action reduces human liberty, rather than advancing it.

There is a further, more practical, issue in the politics of community surveillance and control: Which communities get controlled? In the United States, crime is much more pervasive in our inner cities, where minorities and the poor live in great concentration. It is these communities that are targeted for control, and the practical politics of community crime control is the expanded intrusion of government power into the lives of poor and minority citizens. This is probably another reason why the traditional viewpoints of conservatives and liberals are altered by the problem of crime. Liberals, more than conservatives, are troubled by the image of massive, government-run surveillance programs applied to minority, inner-city residents.

The Limits of Control

A few years ago, when the first stirrings of the "get tough" movement were afoot, Nils Christie wrote an essay against punishment, entitled *Limits to Pain*.[3] His argument, which has become a classic criticism of penal reform, was that the focus of liberals on punishment might backfire and result in an expansion of the penal system and more people under government control.

His predictions turned out to be correct—though as we'll see in Chapter 20, not everyone would argue this has been bad for society. Imprisonment has grown in scope and cost. At the same time, community correctional programs have become tougher, more oriented toward control and surveillance, and quicker to revoke offenders who fail to comply with the strict requirements of the system. We might well ask, "What are the limits of this trend?"

Technology

The most direct limit on this trend is technical. All technologies have the capacity to fail, and offenders who wish to can often figure out a way to defeat even the most ingenious technical apparatus. The growing list of crimes committed by people who are on electronic monitoring attests to this fact.

Technologies are also limited in terms of capacity. Even though marvelous things are done with computers these days, anyone with some contact with computers will have experienced the "bugs" that can develop in these systems. Large companies, such as IBM or AT&T, can afford to spend hundreds of thousands of dollars in constant upgrading of information capability, but corrections systems need reliable computers that do not require extensive management. Thus the correctional version of an information system is usually not the state-of-the-art. When advances in surveillance and control technologies require sophistication in technical support, this is often lacking for corrections.

Human Responses

A second form of limitation is human. Those who work in corrections often come to this field because they like working with people. Many resent the intrusion of technical surveillance into their work. Others take exception to the shift in goals from helping to controlling, and they undermine the change by being resistant to its policies. It is always possible to find some staff who enjoy the surveillance part of the job, but in most agencies they are a minority.

Although electronic surveillance gets the public's attention, private security officers are being used in increasing numbers. What influence might this have on the behavior of ex-offenders?

Offenders also resent the surveillance and control aspect of their sentence. Although there is often little they can do about it directly, there are indirect ways to resist. The unenthusiastic offender comes to the office late, sulks during interviews, is sullen when the probation officer visits the home, and generally lets it be known that the close control is unwanted.

Offenders are also, like all of us, relatively unpredictable. Any system of control is based partly upon prediction—how the offender will respond to the system and what the offender will and will not be able to do about it. When we recognize that offenders are not completely predictable, we say in yet another way that there is no foolproof way to control them.

Moral and Ethical Limits

Some of the scenarios about community control are downright distasteful. They remind us of totalitarian strategies in which mind control is used by the powerful to squelch all dissent. There is, of course, a difference between dissent and crime. But when we recognize that the correctional population of the United States is made up of disproportionate numbers of young African-American and Hispanic males, especially from city slums, it should make us pause in developing whole systems of control and surveillance to surround them. After a while, it begins to appear almost as though the homes, streets, schools, and families of a whole ethnic group are being subjected to official control and invaded by penological technologies of surveillance. The image is not an attractive one.

At some point the trade-off between safety and freedom becomes a concern. In terms of crime, some of the safest societies in history have been the totalitarian regimes of Nazi Germany and Stalinist Russia. There are worse ways to live than with crime in the streets.

Toward an Acceptable Community Control

How do we resolve this dilemma? Stanley Cohen has written eloquently about this problem. He takes the position that there is nothing inherently wrong with "control."[4] The issue is who benefits from it. If the sole purpose of correctional control is to strengthen the capacity of government to rule citizens' lives and to reduce the degree of autonomy among us, then the control is a net negative, and it is anticommunity. If, on the other hand, the surveillance and control are designed to *maintain* communities by allowing offenders to find ways to continue to live there, despite their offense, then the approach is inclusive, and helps to build community.

The distinction is not an obvious one, and few of the modern correctional forms of surveillance and control can be easily classified and truly "inclusive" or ultimately anticommunity. We can, however, begin to get an idea of the value of the correctional method by asking these questions:

- Is the surveillance/control truly being used in lieu of imprisonment? That is, without this control, would the offender actually be in jail or prison?

- Is the offender's risk to the community such that without this control, there is a very high likelihood the offender would engage in crime? In other words, is the surveillance/control really necessary, or is it being used to mollify public sentiment that is basically erroneous?

- Could some other method that is less intrusive achieve about the same result? That is, is the technology being used because it is high-tech and not because it succeeds better than other alternatives?

- Are steps taken to eliminate the indirect intrusions of the surveillance on the lives of innocents who live with or work with the offender?

- Is the offender allowed opportunities to demonstrate self-control, so that the surveillance/control system can be gradually reduced?

To the degree there are positive answers to these questions, we might think of the correctional system as being necessary, limited, and offender-focused.

Summary

A s more and more offenders reside in the community, there has been a growth in technologies of surveillance and control. These technologies include drug controls, electronic controls, program controls, and human actions, which are all designed to watch offenders more effectively and exert more control over their actions.

This shift in community corrections has resulted in a change in the goals of corrections. It has also served the latent goal of increased public confidence in corrections. But the increase in surveillance and control comes at a cost in terms of civil liberties. If we are careful in the way we design and implement these programs, we can minimize the cost.

For Discussion

1. Would "electronic fences" be a good thing for some offenders? If so, which offenders? How would you use the fences?

2. Discuss the trade-off between liberty and community safety, when it comes to mandating that some offenders comply with drug controls such as Antabuse or Depo-Provera.

3. Analyze the value of electronic-monitored house arrest for pretrial detainees. In performing your analysis, use the questions posed just before this chapter's summary section.

4. Do offenders' family members have a right to have their privacy protected from correctional surveillance? Why or why not?

5. Should high school students be tested regularly for illegal drug use? Why or why not?

For Further Reading

Cohen, Fred. *Deprivation of Liberty*. Raleigh, N.C.: Carolina Academic Press, 1992. A legal and historical analysis of social control in community and institutional settings.

Cohen, Stanley. *Visions of Social Control*. Cambridge: Polity, 1985. A critical assessment of community-based correctional surveillance and control.

Cohen, Stanley. *Against Criminology*. New Brunswick, N.J.: Transaction, 1988. A description of the recent history of thinking about crime control strategies, with a special emphasis on penology.

Sherman, Lawrence. *Ethics in Criminal Justice Education*. Hastings-on-Hudson, N.Y.: Institute for Social Ethics, 1982. A review of problems in criminal justice education, with suggested standards.

Notes

1. G. A. Marlatt and J. R. Gordon, *Relapse Prevention* (New York: Guilford Press, 1985); see also L. Bays, R. Freeman-Congo, and D. D. Hiedebran, *How Can I Stop? Breaking My Deviant Cycle* (Orwell, Vt.: Safer Society Press, 1990).

2. Joan Petersilia and Susan Turner, *Intensive Supervision for High-Risk Probationers* (Santa Monica: Rand Corporation, 1990).

3. Nils Christie. *Limits to Pain* (Oxford, England: Martin Robinson, 1981).

4. Stanley Cohen, *Against Criminology* (New Brunswick, N.J.: Transaction, 1988), pp. 104–24.

American Corrections Today and Tomorrow

If the only tool you have is a hammer, you tend to see every problem as a nail.

Abraham Maslow

Five Correctional Dilemmas
Mission
Methods
Structure
Personnel
Costs
Issues in the Profession
Education
Training and Continuing Education
Civil Service Versus Professionalism
Career Opportunities for Women
Insider Versus Outsider Promotions
Technology
Directions and Counterdirections
De-Escalation
Demystification
Devaluation
Development
Changing Corrections: A Summary

L ooking back on the last quarter of the twentieth century—since the mid-1970s—the American corrections system appears to have embarked upon something of a social experiment. The main tenet of the experiment has been described in Chapter 17: the inexorable increase in the reach of the corrections system.

By every measure the penal system has grown in unprecedented ways. Since 1973 the incarceration rate has grown from under 100 persons per 100,000 citizens to nearly 400 per 100,000 citizens. Including probation, parole, and jails, the number of people under correctional control has quadrupled in that same time, from under a million to over four million.

This pattern is disproportionately spread among our citizens. Over one in four African-American males, aged eighteen to twenty-four, is currently under correctional control—more than are in colleges and universities. Some have estimated that in Los Angeles this year, where the police were videotaped while repeatedly beating Rodney King, about one in three African-American youths will be arrested, though far fewer will be prosecuted. It is not hard to see why many in these communities feel the criminal justice system is designed to afflict them and the corrections system is intended to remove males from their neighborhoods. Consider the situation in New York State. Of the nearly 58,000 inmates in the state's prison system, it has been estimated that about three-fourths come from just seven neighborhoods in New York City—all of them minority neighborhoods.[1]

It is hard to imagine that in the last twenty years, we have deliberately created the corrections system we most want. To the contrary, most of those in charge of today's corrections system would argue that what we are doing today is self-destructive and that an overhaul of the corrections system is long overdue. But finding agreement about the fitting aims of such an overhaul is difficult.

The lack of agreement about the aims of correctional reform is one of the reasons why it is not really accurate to refer to the unprecedented growth in corrections since the early 1970s as an "experiment." To conduct an experiment, planning is needed, and some hypotheses about the value of the experiment—why it should work—must be established. The surge in corrections has not been strategic; rather, it has been the result of disjointed, incremental policy shifts in sentencing and law enforcement. For example, the population of drug offenders in U.S. prisons has increased by 650 percent since 1980, more than *five times* the rate of increase in other offenders, and this was largely the result of the "drug war" of the 1980s.

If we had conducted a deliberate experiment, we would also expect to see some "results." In the case of the twenty-year spiraling of correctional growth, the results are unclear. Depending on the type of offense and the way it is measured, crime rates have either grown, remained about the same, or fallen slightly over that period—though some claim they would have been even higher had we not expanded the corrections system.[2] State correctional budgets have nearly doubled in the last decade, while other state budget items such as education or transportation have declined.

If we could go back to the year 1970 and begin working over again to build a corrections system with an eye toward the year 2000, would we envision the costly, cumbersome behemoth we have today?

Of course, we cannot go back and re-create history. But we can examine today's corrections system in light of what we want it to become over the next twenty years. We can identify—and begin to confront—the dilemmas and issues that must be faced if we are to create a corrections system that reflects our nation's most cherished values.

Five Correctional Dilemmas

A dilemma is a situation that forces one to choose among unsatisfactory alternatives. Corrections faces many dilemmas, a fact to which any worker in the field will attest; we are selecting only a few for extended comment. Unlike much of what we have presented in previous chapters, our description of the dilemmas is not an objective restatement of facts and studies; rather, it is a subjective interpretation of many facts, studies, and observations. We have selected five dilemmas as particularly important because they are what we considered orienting dilemmas for corrections. That is, not only must each corrections system confront them as it moves into the 1990s, but the resolution of most other issues—from daily problems in offender management to larger considerations—will be profoundly influenced by the manner in which these dilemmas are faced. Indeed, today's difficulties and potential are very much tied to the manner in which these five dilemmas were faced in the past. Thus we have identified five concerns: mission, methods, structure, personnel, and costs.

Mission

Corrections lacks a clear mission, and one of the reasons is that it has so many different kinds of clients; corrections serves offenders, the general public, and other government agencies alike. Each has a different expectation of corrections. Viewing the matter simplistically, we recognize that offenders want fairness, leniency, and assistance; the public wants protection from and punishment of criminals; government agencies want cooperation and coordination. Obviously, the expectations often come into conflict. Ultimately, a goal of corrections must be to disentangle the expectations and establish a set of priorities for handling them.

It is also easy to see that none of these competing expectations can be ignored. How do courts respond when corrections fails to provide rehabilitative services to offenders? How does the public respond to instances of brutal recidivism? How do government agencies manage balky corrections officials?

One of the common solutions in corrections is to attempt to meet all expectations: provide the services that are requested, take actions to protect the public when danger becomes an issue, cooperate with agencies when asked to do so. The advantage of this approach appears to be that corrections can avoid the strains that accompany goal conflict because it is easier not to make hard choices about priorities. Of course, this supposed advantage does not really materialize. The conflicts between attempts to serve clients and protect the community, to coordinate government practices and provide assistance or protection are real. When corrections attempts to meet all of these competing expectations equally, the conflicts have to be resolved informally by corrections workers.

It is important for corrections to confront the problems created by ambiguity of mission. Doing so requires that choices be made. In the early 1960s most people agreed that the primary mission of corrections was the rehabilitation of offenders, but the devaluation of treatment and the recent movement toward determinate sentencing leave a void in this area. Some writers have suggested that corrections must take on the role of offender management; others have argued that the role of corrections is risk control; still others have suggested punishment as corrections' mission. Whatever the choice of mission, there is a critical need for leaders to take control over the philosophy of corrections and establish a clearer policy to guide its work. Both staff members and persons outside the system must be able to know what it is that corrections does and what they may appropriately expect from its efforts.

Methods

It seems obvious that if the correctional mission is unclear, there must be ambivalence about the best correctional strategies and techniques. When goals are in conflict, staff members have difficulty choosing among the competing methods they may use to perform their work: surveillance or service, custody or treatment. But this is not the only problem with correctional methods; much more significant is the fact that correctional techniques seem so often to be unsuccessful.

We have discussed technical uncertainty and its implications for corrections; chronic uncertainty brings with it other results as well. First, a debilitating lack of confidence occurs when apparently promising strategies, upon evaluation, turn out to lack merit. The list of failed correctional methods includes small case-loads, offender counseling, family counseling, group treatment, restitution, and classification. All these and many more have been promoted as *the* answer to a given pressing problem. Each time another correctional strategy proves ineffective, the failure feeds an already pervasive feeling among workers that corrections is incapable of performing its basic functions well.

This is one reason that the short-term history of corrections seems to be dominated by fads. As each new technique or program arrives and is implemented, corrections is confronted by the method's limited ability to solve the technical problems it was intended to solve, and so it is replaced by something newer still.

The consequences of these frequent changes are largely negative. No firm, central technical process is allowed to develop and mature. Because corrections works with people, it seems that the central technologies should involve communication and influence, but the parade of new programs subtly shifts the emphasis from process to procedures. The dynamic work of corrections is stalled by the static and routinized activities that ebb and flow with each new program. Bureaucratic approaches to offender management and warehousing come to dominate the technical approach to the job. Workers become cynical about changes and about the potential of the work itself. Who can blame them? Those who are most experienced in the job have seen many highly praised programs come and go, having failed to produce the results expected of them.

Another issue is raised by correctional methods: fairness. In recent years the concept of just deserts has dominated the definition of fairness, and much thought has been devoted to ways to achieve it. Although the just deserts model of criminal justice is quite elaborate, it boils down to a single generalization: Offenders should be punished equally in accordance with the severity of their offenses. This seems to be a straightforward assignment.

Yet something is wanting in the doctrine of just deserts. The fact is that the power and coercion of correctional methods apply in practice almost exclusively to the poor and predominately to minorities. One is left with the feeling that merely to be "equal" in our use of state power under these circumstances is not to be really fair in the broadest sense of the term. Real fairness must enhance the lives and the life potential of those we bring under correctional control. But if the history of good intentions in corrections has taught us anything, it is that we often injure the people we try to help. We know very little about how to assist offenders effectively, but it is certainly not sufficient to punish them equally and be done with it. The dilemma of methods is complex. Can we overcome the tradition of faddism in corrections without becoming stodgily bureaucratic in method? Can we improve the life chances of correctional clients without injuring them further by our good intentions?

Structure

Corrections is simply not in a position to influence its own fate deeply, and much of its inability to do so has to do with its internal and external structure. Internally, corrections is a process divided against itself. Jails, prisons, probation, and parole all struggle with one another; the practices of each become contingencies for the others. Externally, corrections is the conclusion of the criminal justice process, and it has little formal capacity to control the demand for its services. Thus correctional leaders are faced with two structural dilemmas. First, their colleagues are often the ones who put the most immediate obstacles in the way of their attempts to manage their operations effectively. Second, the correctional system is dependent on significant factors outside of its control.

The results of corrections' structural dilemma are sometimes quite startling. In many jurisdictions, for example, large amounts of money have been spent to renovate or build new jails because the old jails are substandard, overcrowded, or both. Too often the new version is soon just as overcrowded as the old one was or is found to be legally substandard. The fault lies with the inability of corrections to coordinate architectural planning with programmatic needs of such nonjail agencies as the courts and probation. What seemed at first to be a problem of space is really a problem of how space is used, and the way jail space is used is influenced by persons other than jail administrators. The courts (through sentencing and pretrial release), law enforcement (through arrest), and probation/parole (through revocation) all use jail space for their own purposes. The lack of programs in these external agencies to buttress the effects of new construction can eliminate the advantages of this expensive option. This is only one of the deficiencies that occurs again and again in correctional planning.

Formally, we refer to the problem of structure in corrections as one of interdependence and coordination. The ability of corrections to work well is in some ways dependent on processes that it must either respond to, influence, or at least understand. If it is to do so, its processes must be better coordinated with those of the external agencies that produce the dependence and the dissension.

The problem is that there is really no easy way to coordinate them. Separation of powers is both a constitutional and a traditional bulwark of our government. Each agency is jealous of its own power and reluctant to reduce it by coordination or planning. Thus, when a new jail is being designed, the approval of the municipal engineering bureau is seen as a hurdle to be jumped rather than a potential source of assistance in planning. Each time an interagency control is put into place, it becomes an obstacle rather than a coordinating mechanism.

Most correctional administrators find that their greatest frustrations lie in getting other agencies to avoid actions that severely constrain their ability to function. Recently there has been a trend toward high-level commissions and task forces composed of heads of correctional, justice system, judicial, and executive branch agencies whose job it is to improve coordination. This is a promising step, but a small one.

Personnel

Because corrections is a people-processing operation, its personnel are its major resource. The two essential goals in regard to staff are to find ways to motivate the right kinds of people to work in corrections and, once they are employed, to motivate them to remain. Corrections traditionally has not done well in either area.

The initial recruitment problem stems frequently from the low starting salaries provided. Salaries vary widely from place to place, but corrections employees' salaries are often lower than those paid for comparable positions elsewhere. Corrections officers frequently begin at wages lower than those of local law enforcement officers. The starting salaries of probation and parole officers, who normally are required to have a college degree, are often not competitive with those offered to social workers and teachers.

For this reason, corrections positions are often regarded as good entry positions. A person new to the job market can obtain stable employment for a year or two while seeking alternative employment. The most qualified individuals find it relatively easy to move on to other occupations; less qualified people often stay longer, some for their entire careers.

Monetary rewards bring further problems. As a result of collective bargaining, most correctional employees receive equal pay raises regardless of performance. Inevitably, a system of equality becomes a disincentive to employees whose work efforts surpass those of others. Very often significant personnel decisions, such as promotion, salary levels, and other incentives, are completely out of the hands of the correctional administrator.

In times of fiscal plenty, salary is not so great a problem, but a decade of salary crunch in government employment combined with a constricted job market makes for many bitter correctional employees. The organizational culture of many correctional operations is dominated by animosity toward management and cynicism toward the job. Too often correctional employees see themselves as unappreciated, manipulated, and alienated. Under these conditions it is exceedingly difficult for a corrections system to perform its people-work function effectively because its most valued resource—the staff—is demoralized.

On the surface, the solution to the personnel problem seems simple: measure the performance of staff, reward those who are productive, get rid of those who are not. This kind of solution does not work in government employment (and may not work very well in the private sector either). For one thing, correctional performance is exceedingly difficult to measure. While the overall yardsticks of recidivism, institutional security, and so forth provide useful assessments of corrections' performance, it is not appropriate to use them as indicators of an individual's performance. Who can say that a parolee's failure was the parole officer's fault? Indeed, a case can be made that it represents the officer's success at surveillance. Too often secondary performance measures, such as con-

tacts with clients, paperwork, and training, are substituted for primary measures of job success. These secondary measures are fairer because they fall within the staff's control. But for a secondary measure of performance to be useful, it must be clearly related to organizational success. In this respect, most secondary measures in corrections are inadequate. In another vein, government employment is often sought because of its purported job security; altering the personnel picture to overcome lethargy is likely to cause extreme strain among the staff.

The correctional leader's choices in the personnel area, unhappily, involve no short-term solutions. The answer, if there is one, lies in long-term staff development: A sound staff is built by innovative selection and promotion methods; professional growth on the job is encouraged by education and training incentives; and "human resource" management approaches are taken to involve staff in the operations of the organization. Turnover at the top of the corrections hierarchy is often so great that the administrator who undertakes to address personnel issues may not be on the job to reap the rewards of the efforts.

Costs

One of the most notable lessons learned about corrections is that it is costly. The cost of a prison is upwards of $100,000 per cell, before financing. Each personnel position represents expenditures equal to twice the total annual salary when fringe benefits, retirement costs, and office supplies are taken into consideration. The processing of an offender through the correctional system can go as high as $20,000 in direct costs and nearly half that much again in indirect costs (such as defaulted debts, welfare to families, and lost wages and taxes). The decision to punish an offender is a decision to allocate precious public resources, often irretrievably. Corrections administrators understand this now more than ever before. The attempt to use correctional resources wisely is a real challenge.

Institutional crowding, combined with fiscal restraint, has produced an unprecedented concern about correctional costs. The public is beginning to question the advisability of correctional growth. One might say the public is practicing a form of political schizophrenia: The desire for criminals to be punished is not backed up by a willingness to pay for the punishment.

The ambivalence about punishment and money has left correctional leadership in a bind. The arguments for expansion of large, secure facilities must be contrasted with equally strong arguments for increased emphasis on community-based corrections. The former arguments are in some ways simple to understand. Crime continues to be a matter of great public concern, and prisons may never have been so crowded as they are today.

Most correctional officials recognize that a concentration on prisons is regressive rather than progressive. Many of our existing secure facilities are decrepit and need to be replaced, but the evidence is very strong that (1) simply building prisons does not do away with crowding and (2) the prospects of an incapacitation strategy for crime control are limited, and in any event such a strategy is highly prone to error. The officials also know that once a prison is built, it represents a continuing management focus for as long as it is used—in contrast to field services, which are much more responsive to change and innovation. The dilemma for the administrator is that the public seems to want more prisons but does not want to pay for them.

To this puzzle must be added the recent trend toward privatization of corrections. Time will tell if this trend will become a lasting force; meanwhile, privatization is a potential threat to the administrator's ability to manage the system. Most privatization plans call for skimming off the best of the worst—the nonserious offenders who can be efficiently processed. Thus the government-run part of the correctional system faces the possibility of having to manage only the most costly, most intractable offenders on a reduced budget, and with the worsened fiscal and personnel situations that would result from such a development.

Issues in the Profession

As our discussion of correctional dilemmas revealed, the corrections profession has been and is still confronted with a number of controversies. A significant part of these controversies has to do with the degree to which corrections work is truly professional. To understand this issue, we must first examine seven elements of a profession and consider whether correctional work meets these criteria.

1. *A professional philosophy.* The Hippocratic oath is an example of the unifying philosophy of medicine. There is no accepted philosophy of corrections, though many philosophers would argue that the functions of punishment are controversial.

2. *An accepted body of knowledge.* Most professions teach a core of knowledge as the basis for joining the profession—lawyers learn case law, physicians learn anatomy, and so forth. There is controversy over the correct body of knowledge for corrections workers to receive.

3. *A science of new knowledge.* The principles of science are applied to the main disciplines of learning, both in such physical sciences as biology, and in such human sciences as sociology. There is a long tradition of science in penology, although most of it is borrowed from established disciplines of study.

4. *Licensing procedures.* Professions establish requirements of educational attainment for admission to the profession, usually a postgraduate degree from an accredited school. Many also require separate performance tests; for example, many states

license psychologists after written and oral examinations, and lawyers have to pass a bar exam to be able to practice. No equivalent requirements exist for correctional workers.

5. *A tradition of continuing education.* All professions require that practitioners keep up-to-date with new knowledge, usually through a process of continuing education courses. These are new for corrections workers and have been received by many corrections professionals with ambivalence.

6. *Professional associations.* Like most professions, correctional workers are represented by associations. Instead of national and regional associations, however, corrections work tends to be represented by multiple groups: The American Correctional Association and the American Probation and Parole Association are just two examples. At the local level these groups often act more as traditional workers' unions interested in advancing wages and benefits than professional associations interested in advancing the profession itself.

7. *Established ethical standards.* The ethical requirements of lawyers and doctors is well established and filters through a strong professional-client privilege. Whether an equivalent privilege exists for corrections workers is not clear; certainly, ethical standards tend to be established by the courts through litigation, rather than through official statements by professional associations.

Education

Since by definition, education is a critical part of professionalism, let us first ask what the appropriate educational background is for corrections workers.

For many years it was assumed that the core educational requirement for corrections ought to be the various types of schooling in

In most states correctional officers must graduate from a training academy before they can take their places on the line.

human behavior: social work, counseling, psychology, and so forth. It was thought that the material covered in these fields would best prepare the correctional worker for the kinds of problems to be encountered in dealing with offenders.

In part, this emphasis on education in human behavior was based on the idea of rehabilitation: To meet the goals of rehabilitation, correctional personnel should be effective in helping offenders change their behavior. As the rehabilitative ideal came under increasing criticism, views began to change about the best educational grounding for corrections. A more managerial type of preparation was desired, making certain that new employees were knowledgeable about the criminal justice system and the criminal law.

The growth of criminal justice undergraduate education since the 1960s has reflected this change. In 1960 there were but a handful of criminal justice undergraduate programs and almost no true graduate programs in the area. By 1993, barely a generation later, there are over five hundred undergraduate programs offering degrees or concentrations in criminal justice, and scores of programs offering advanced degrees, including over twenty doctoral programs. By any measure, the criminal justice-educated practitioner is the new generation for the field.

Not everyone finds this emphasis on law and "the system" to be appropriate. Critics argue that recent graduates, trained in these areas, often lack critical interpersonal skills needed to work effectively with offenders. It is argued that instead of viewing corrections as a communications profession, they tend to see it more as a matter of formal policy management with offenders. The concern is that those educated in criminal justice are less creative with offenders and are prone to an unimaginative, *pro forma* kind of interaction with them.

Whether this is the case is a matter for research. But it is unlikely that these criticisms will turn undergraduate criminal justice majors from corrections. In many universities the criminal justice major is one of the most popular among students, and the program is seen as a feeder for entry-level careers in corrections. And, according to the *New York Times*, the jobs in corrections are multiplying. In fact, the job "correction officer" is one of the ten fastest-growing job titles in the United States—the only job listed in the top ten that is not in the health professions.

How much education ought to be required of corrections workers? When correctional work was seen as a counseling profession, it was argued that a graduate degree in a human behavior field ought to be required. A few states instituted such requirements (or preferences), and the result was that in states such as Wisconsin, California, and Alabama, most correctional workers (other than corrections officers) had graduate degrees.

The emphasis on advanced education has waned in recent years, however. One of the reasons for this change is the de-emphasis on human behavior approaches to correctional work. Another is that close inspection of the work itself has indicated that many correctional workers make minimal use of a sophisticated education in interpersonal skills. For example, a government study of the work of probation officers in Michigan in the 1980s, including observation of them working in the field and direct interviews, concluded that a college degree was not needed to perform the functions. As a result, the title "probation officer" was opened up to persons whose formal education ended with a high school diploma.

There are those who would not find this alarming. They argue that there is a dramatic difference between education and common sense—and the presence of one does not necessarily mean the presence of the other. From this point of view, it is argued that common sense is what makes a good corrections worker. In searching for effective workers, life experience and problem-solving skills should count more than anything. This is the kind of argument some people have made in behalf of hiring reformed ex-offenders—they understand the problems of offenders and make credible role models.

Training and Continuing Education

Some people maintain that the educational background of a corrections worker before hiring is far less important than the training provided after work has started. A case can be made that the experiences in corrections work are not easily translated to the classroom, and that a much more effective way to prepare corrections workers is to provide them with structured training experiences that enable them to better understand the work and its challenges. This may be especially important while workers are in the early stages of their careers, before they become cynical or jaundiced.

Most corrections agencies require a level of orientation training for all staff within the first months of their employment. Typically, for example, a corrections officer will attend an "academy" for a period ranging from two to four weeks, often staying in a dorm. The academy will cover a wide range of topics, from physical training to agency policy. By the time the new recruit graduates, it is assumed that he or she is ready to perform adequately on the job.

Many agencies require a certain level of continuing education of their staff as well. Continuing education has two functions. The manifest function is to allow staff to be aware of the latest developments in the field. A secondary function is motivation—staff who receive training in areas of continuing interest will be able to sustain their interest in the job more easily.

Typically, the continuing education requirement is expressed in terms of "hours" of course work. For instance, Pennsylvania probation and parole officers are required to take forty hours of continuing education every two years; they select from a long list of programs offered by the agency, or they attend programs offered by local educational institutions.

Continuing education has been facilitated by the expanded use of the **continuing education unit** (CEU). The CEU represents the equivalent of an hour of professional training, and it is usually offered in a preapproved program whose curriculum has been reviewed by a professional association and determined to be of value. Correctional workers who attend a three-hour workshop entitled, for example, "Overcoming Stress on the Job" could receive three CEUs.

One of the problems with the training aspect of the professional role is that there are too few providers of training, and many are of suspect quality. Even if professional bodies are able to review a curriculum and approve it, there is no simple, inexpensive mechanism for evaluating the actual training to see that it was delivered in an effective and professionally relevant manner. Some people are concerned that inadequate training may be widespread and that staff may care more about getting their CEUs than learning how to improve on the job.

Civil Service Versus Professionalism

When government is a major employer, a tension exists between the natural desire of elected officials to reward their supporters and friends by offering them jobs and the taxpayer expectation that jobs will go to the best-qualified person seeking the job. There is no obvious solution to this problem.

Advocates of political appointments argue that crime and justice are political issues, and so correctional policy needs to be responsive to the leadership of elected officials. This is an argument for the political accountability of administrators, but it is hard to see how the politics of corrections can justify the political appointment of line staff. Moreover, it is pretty obvious that when governments change, a spoils system for correctional employees would be disruptive and make effective offender management in prisons and community corrections nearly impossible.

For this reason, most nonadministrative posts are classified as **civil service** positions, filled on the basis of a competitive examination of qualified applicants. The Civil Service Authority determines the minimum qualifications for a position, in terms of education and experience. It then advertises for vacant positions and announces an examination. The examination is normally objective, using mul-

---

continuing education unit (CEU) The equivalent of one hour of training in a professional area of responsibility that is used to meet requirements for regular education of professional staff.

---

civil service The use of an objective system for evaluating government employees for hiring and promotion.

Prison expansion during the last decade has provided opportunities for more women and minorities to gain professional positions in corrections.

But there are criticisms of the civil service system. The strongest objection is that multiple-choice questions are an inadequate way to select employees whose main responsibility will be to communicate with offenders. Paper-and-pencil tests are like IQ tests in that they measure intelligence but not ability. Critics of civil service also say that corrections will never be a profession unless it professionalizes its hiring procedures—no one would ever select their physician on the basis of a multiple-choice exam.

Instead, it is argued, communication skills are better gauged by interviews and observations in work test situations. This has led to the development of **assessment center** methods for selecting staff. In assessment centers, applicants are brought together and put through a series of simulated job situations. For example, they may be asked to pretend they encounter a client who is high on drugs, and then they are asked to show how they would handle the situation. Their performance in these simulated tests is evaluated, and job readiness is determined from how they deal with the situations.

Assessment center strategies have become popular among government reformers, but they are far from widespread. For one thing, they are much more expensive to administer than mere paper-and-pencil examinations. For another, the construction of appropriate job simulation activities and objective ways to assess performance on them is not easy.

Career Opportunities for Women

Women have always worked in corrections, but until the last thirty years, their roles have often been limited to supervising other women offenders or working with juveniles in nurturing mother-substitute roles. In modern corrections, however, women can take on any job assignment that does not require privacy for

tiple-choice questions. Applicants are ranked on the basis of their correct answers to the questions, and the hiring authority is usually restricted to hiring from among the highest-scoring individuals, who are usually interviewed before being hired.

There are several advantages to the civil service model. The use of objective tests allows people who are not politically connected to apply for and compete for jobs. The hiring decision is restricted to those who have demonstrated knowledge about the job, but the use of the interview helps to prevent the hiring of obviously inappropriate individuals.

assessment centers   A way to evaluate prospective employees by putting them in simulated job situations and seeing how well they perform.

the male offender. That is not to say that women are equally represented in the profession. Women still tend to be overrepresented in line staff roles in juvenile corrections and in assignments managing female offenders.

In supervisory and administrative positions, the problem of underrepresentation is even greater. While women are more and more being promoted to administrative positions, at this writing only five states employ women as top administrators of their corrections agency.[3] Fears that many men do not want to be supervised by a woman have led some to believe that women are not allowed to compete fairly for promotions to supervisory positions.

Insider Versus Outsider Promotions

Corrections is inherently conservative. It deals with people who represent a risk to the community, and there is the constant potential that a decision about an offender may backfire— sometimes with drastic political consequences.

One of the manifestations of correctional conservatism is that correctional leaders tend to promote from within: When supervisory and administrative positions open up, they tend to be filled from the ranks within the agency. There are many advantages to this practice: It breeds a sense among staff that good performance will be rewarded, it promotes agency continuity, and it allows leaders to know the strengths and weaknesses of their subordinates. Like any conservative practice, however, promotion from within tends to reduce creativity and innovation in managerial positions. It also sometimes results in making new managers supervise former peers, a practice that may lead to resentment.

Some people argue that the best way to help corrections combat its conservative posture is to bring in "new blood" by recruiting outside for leadership positions. In recent years, for example, it has become normal to replace top administrators with outsiders. The top position often becomes vacant when the political

leaders believe the corrections system is in need of a change in direction or philosophy. Filling the position with an outsider is seen as the best way to help change the agency in these ways.

The same kind of argument can be made for filling lower leadership positions with outsiders. Doing so helps to bring in new ideas and stimulate new thinking among staff. It is especially valuable to bring in outsiders who have designed or run special programs that the agency wants to import, such as new treatment strategies or unique technical systems. One of the ways to disseminate innovations is through the job mobility of the people who have designed them.

Technology

The information age is influencing corrections just as it is workers in every occupation. The main change has been in records keeping. Lengthy, narrative-style records used to be kept on offenders: Probation and parole officers maintained detailed chronological case notes; prison and jail officials kept elaborate case folders. This information was kept in bulky files, stored for years in dusty records rooms.

The theory behind the old-style information, if there was one, was a kind of the-more-the-better approach. Chronological records recorded the daily activities of an offender, including descriptions of adjustment to the community and response to supervision. Often there would even be pay stubs and receipts for bills paid, as evidence of the offender's performance. Prison folders kept lists of visitors, correspondence, tests and evaluations, and counselors' observations. These records also always contained the criminal history information, including previous presentence reports.

Staff often resent the paperwork time these manual records require. Whenever a staff member takes an action regarding a case, there is a need to record it to keep an adequate paper trail in case questions later arise about the offender's supervision. Time studies of correctional workers have found that paperwork was a major component of staff activity. Studies also found that there was very little consistency in the way many records were kept, and gaps in information were common.

In the future, correctional practice will become increasingly systematic. This will partly be a natural result of the influence of computers, which require operational systems. Computerized records systems are designed to streamline and systematize paperwork. Time is saved by establishing predetermined categories of information to be collected on offenders, often through checklists. Systematic coverage is ensured by programming computers to require answers to a standard set of questions, whenever information is entered about a case.

Of course, this has meant that corrections staff have to become computer-literate. For the new generation of professionals, this has not been a problem, but old-timers often resist the change. Computerization has also meant a greater focus exists on the information that is retained, and this may reduce the creativity and flexibility staff feel they have in responding to clients.

Directions and Counterdirections

How will corrections respond to these dilemmas and issues? There are many possible answers. We have chosen to identify four themes we believe should (and we hope will) become more significant as corrections enters the 1990s. We see each as a direction in which corrections could (and should) move, and we point out the consequences that may attend a move in the opposite direction.

De-escalation

Regardless of its many failures, corrections in the United States is a high-powered, if sputtering, machine. A common public perception is that criminal offenders are punished less than they should be, even though opinion studies reveal that citizens overestimate the amount of punishment actually given to offenders.

Yet a move to meet public demands for punitiveness detracts in the long run from public confidence in corrections. Punishments increase, prisons are filled to overflowing, and still there is crime in the streets. This is a cycle that is nearly impossible to break: The experience of crime leads to a public outcry for punishment as a means to prevent crime, but because the increased punishment has little direct effect on the amount of crime, the cry for more punishment continues unabated. We Americans have become so convinced that punishment is beneficial to society that we have inflicted it on criminals in numbers far beyond our capacity to pay in terms of bricks and mortar. And still we believe that it is not enough.

The time has come to recognize two crucial facts:

1. The United States hands out punitive sanctions far in excess of those imposed by most other Western democracies.

2. We have under correctional supervision a far larger proportion of our citizenry than any other comparable nation.[4]

We have escalated the correctional sanction so far that punishments that are clearly severe (and in many other countries are employed with reluctance) are considered to be ludicrously lenient. For instance, when the U.S. Sentencing Commission recently recommended capping drug possession sentences at thirteen years instead of the current thirty-year sentence provisions, some prosecutors complained this would be too lenient—even though drug offenders now serve terms longer than many violent offenders, and they are beginning to clog up our prisons. We have increased the going rate of punishment for crime until it is no longer within our reach or our national interest.

The problem is one of scale. When the penal code's normal punishment for an offense is incarceration, then such sanctions as fines, restitution, and community service seem pallid by comparison and are imposed only as a "second chance" rather than as a direct punishment for a crime. When everyone placed on probation is given a community service sentence and a fine as well, each of these sanctions loses some of its punitive impact and symbolic value.

We are suggesting that, for all but those who commit multiple and heinous crimes, the scales of justice need to be scaled down. Loss of freedom is significant in itself, and some months in custody can normally accomplish the same purpose as much longer sentences for most offenders. Community service and fines should be used sparingly so that they can make a statement about the reprehensibility of misconduct instead of being window dressing for the standard probation sentence. In general, corrections must spend its limited resources of staff and facilities with greater circumspection.

In order to de-escalate correctional punishment, there must be a revision in our thinking about the driving force for the penalties we impose. Judicial and legislative decision makers often are inclined to use imprisonment whenever it is felt that this sanction *might* result in greater deterrence or incapacitation. Yet existing research demonstrates that under most conditions, the deterrent and incapacitative effects of imprisonment are negligible. A considerable shift would occur in the use of correctional resources if use of incarceration were limited only to circumstances in which a clear evidentiary basis demonstrated that significant gains *would* result from its imposition. This would counteract years of punitive escalation that have produced little or no benefit, and it would bolster the meaningfulness of nonincarcerative sanctions. Moreover, it is a move that would be supported by a new series of public-opinion studies showing the public very supportive of rehabilitation for offenders, which would suggest that it is time for such a move.

Of course, corrections has virtually no direct control over any potential de-escalation; the form and extent of punishment are largely in the hands of the courts and legislatures, which seem now to be moving toward greater and greater severity. The result of this counterdirection is apparent to us all: extreme crowding, chaos in release mechanisms, "public relations" sentencing in which the actual terms or conditions served bear no relationship to the announced punishment. Yet the public still has no greater consideration for the plight of corrections.

Demystification

For far too long corrections officials have screened the public from the realities of the correctional system on the grounds that their work is unusual and difficult to understand. On the one hand, corrections workers have claimed a special expertise that should enable them to make their informed judgments in regard to offenders without external meddling. On the other hand, they argue that offenders, as a class, are such an antisocial and uncontrollable lot that no one can realistically blame the corrections system for its failures. Though the two arguments seem logically inconsistent, both point to the same conclusion: Corrections work is special and difficult (and some would say mysterious), and corrections officials should be left alone to do it.

We agree that corrections work is special and difficult, but we also think that the mystification of corrections is counterproductive to its larger aims. There need be nothing secretive about the work of corrections. People in positions of authority make judgments about those in their charge. The judgments are informed by experience, behavioral science, and sometimes intuition. They are sometimes wrong, and when they are, the consequences can be disastrous. An offender may be released as a good parole risk only to commit a new crime. Likewise, an offender may be denied parole as a bad risk even though the offender would have adjusted very well to community supervision. The constant need to make judgments and the inevitability of error are inescapable themes in corrections.

The frank realities of judgment and error need to be faced more squarely than they commonly are today. Corrections basically consists of human beings working with human beings; no perfected science exists for predicting human behavior or repairing human emotions. Judgments will be made, and some of them will be errors. The responsibility of corrections is to minimize error wherever possible, to eliminate avoidable error, and to study itself so as to learn from error. But there is no way to prevent all new crimes without wholesale incarceration of "safe" offenders; there is no way to prevent unneeded incarcerations without releasing some people who will commit new crimes. Further, there is no way to erase the pains suffered by the victims of crime, no matter the amount of victim compensation or the severity of punishment of the offender.

We are calling for a greater openness about what corrections can and cannot do. It can manage its own resources efficiently, given the authority. It cannot prevent all (or even a great deal) of crime. It can behave in a humane manner with respect to the needs and problems of its clients; it cannot rehabilitate all (or even most) of those assigned to its supervision. It can articulate and monitor the bases for its decisions; it cannot guarantee the outcomes of those decisions. It cannot undo the effects of crime on individuals or communities.

The counterdirection is, in our view, potentially disastrous. Corrections can continue to claim to prevent new crime, rehabilitate offenders, and punish criminals. It can continue to demand autonomous control over the processes that it operates. Ultimately, corrections becomes accountable for its actions, and broad claims of expertise and effectiveness will be tough to justify with facts.

Devaluation

As a society, we simply expect too much of corrections: We expect it to prevent crime. The amount and type of punishment meted out to individual offenders is believed to be closely related in some way to the amount of crime that is committed in society. It should be clear by now that the relationship is a weak one at best. For one thing, most crimes go unpunished because the criminals who commit them are not caught and convicted. For another, minor fluctuations in the severity of punishment given to offenders generally cannot be expected to exert a heavy influence on the amount of crime they or others commit, and major fluctuations in the severity of punishment are unthinkable, given current correctional resources. More to the point, crime is so much more a response to societal pressures and conditions than to correctional practices that it seems preposterous to focus on punishment as the fulcrum of its prevention.

When we call for the devaluation of corrections, we do not mean to imply that corrections is overbudgeted. We know of no state or locality where this is so. But the value attached to those dollars ought to be more realistically understood than it is today. Dollars spent on corrections should not be considered crime-prevention dollars, for their value in that regard is limited. Instead, corrections must be thought of as having symbolic value over and above its value as a crime-prevention device. The practices of corrections tell us how well we as a society treat our misbehaving members. By what we do in corrections, we describe ourselves as a nation: humane or vicious, tolerant or intolerant, just or inequitable. These are great symbolic values indeed, and they deserve our close attention and our public funds.

But as a social utility, corrections must be devalued. In our view, the utilities derived from schools, improvements in living, health care, transportation, and opportunity exceed those gained from prisons. We should recognize that the public good is further advanced with these functions than with prisons. The counterforces signal that we should continue to place our confidence in the correctional system as the primary means for crime control. It should be clear to the reader by now that it is a mistake to do so. Further, we should be careful about claiming that corrections serves as one of many means of crime control. While this claim is true, its overemphasis will lead to what we believe are mistaken priorities for a society bent on maximizing the public good.

The evidence that we have overstated the value of corrections to society is all around us. Prisons are one of the most rapidly growing industries in our nation. Legislation to increase the level of punishment imposed on offenders is routine and no longer unusual. Jail, prison, or probation are common life experiences for our poor and minority citizens. Is this the society we wish to portray through our social priorities?

Development

These three proposals for de-escalation, demystification, and devaluation may seem to reflect pessimism, but we are far from pessimistic. Of course, one person's pessimism is another person's realism, but it seems to us that unbridled enthusiasm has been the source of many of corrections' greatest failures. That observation must not leave the impression that we believe there is little to be done. Every indication exists that corrections work will continue to grow as we enter the coming century. Indeed, corrections, we hope, stands at the threshold of a period of development unprecedented in its history.

The development of corrections is linked to contemporary processes. First, we have a larger legacy of knowledge on which to base correctional policy than ever before. Research practices begun in the 1960s positively blossomed in the 1980s. While the legacy tells us more about what cannot be accomplished than about what can, it has begun to affect significantly our daily correctional practice, grounding corrections work in data. Second, the field is growing as a profession. The skills and abilities of the people in line and staff roles have increased tremendously. Corrections' management and administrative techniques still lag

behind those of other public and private enterprises, but they are catching up. Training and education have slowly expanded the capacity of the field.

Development is a long-term proposition, as we view it. We can expect few dramatic or immediate positive results. But we can expect a fundamental commitment to growth in a qualitative rather than a quantitative sense. From the top of the organization down, there will be a steadily increasing emphasis on principles of management. At the line level, this will apply to the decisions made about the offender: The strategy of "managing the offender through the system" will become ever more important. At supervisory and administrative levels, technical management skills will be seen as the core of effective performance.

The emphasis on management will not replace the "human behavior" tradition of the field, but it will focus this tradition. Instead of merely understanding the behavior of offenders, the management model will increasingly require the kind of knowledge that promotes effective action.

We believe that, over time, teams will become more common at the line level. Offenders—especially serious offenders—exhibit complicated problems that require special expertise, and it is not reasonable to expect one person to possess all the expertise in the problem areas of a single offender's life. Expert teams will be used to be certain that the maximum level of skill is being applied to the most serious offenders in corrections. Use of these teams will have the secondary benefit of increasing workers' job satisfaction. By increasing the rewards for workers, not just in money but also in job flexibility and involvement, we can recruit and retain personnel of greater ability and commitment. Development requires a continuing emphasis on the fundamentals of research, planning, innovation, and evaluation, even in the face of crisis. It requires a stable correctional leadership with vision.

The counterdirection to development is both unthinkable and unlikely. Emphasis can be given to short-term aims instead of long-term goals, to temporary shifts in the sociopolitical context rather than to basic improvement in the field. The history of corrections is adequate commentary on what we can expect if we fail to develop the field.

Changing Corrections: A Summary

Throughout this book we have portrayed the correctional system as buffeted by its environment, changing yet unchanging. External pressures arise to move correctional leadership in one direction, only to be replaced by counterpressures in the opposite direction. One state abolishes parole release; another reinstates early release mechanisms. One prison reduces its treatment programs; another adds professional counseling staff. The image is one of an unplanned, reactive style rather than a planned, forthright attempt to lead corrections down a path of gradual improvement.

To a great extent, the image is accurate, but it too is changing. It is changing partly because the field is in fact developing. Several forces contribute to this change, but predominant among them are the professional associations and governmental agencies that are serving to stimulate it.

Perhaps the greatest influence is exercised by the National Institute of Corrections (NIC), a division of the Federal Bureau of Prisons in the Department of Justice. The NIC has served as (1) a national clearinghouse of information about correctional practices, (2) a source of technical assistance to local and state correctional agencies that wish to upgrade their practices, and (3) a training operation on both basic and advanced levels open to any correctional employee. The NIC has become to corrections what the FBI is to law enforcement: a strong force for professional standards, policy and procedural improvement, and general development of the field.

Similarly, the American Correctional Association (ACA) has become an active lobbyist for the field. Over a decade ago it promulgated a set of national standards for correctional practices in jails, prisons, and field services. Correctional agencies that meet these standards may be accredited, much as universities are accredited by outside observers. While the ACA has not gone uncriticized, its work is indicative of the kind of ground-level upgrading that is going on in corrections today.

The American Probation and Parole Association (APPA) serves a function similar to that of the ACA but is focused on field services. It has only recently begun a high-visibility national campaign to organize the profession and to develop an improved professional consciousness of the importance of field services in probation and parole.

As important as these forces for change are, a new force for steady correctional growth and development is likely to outstrip all of them. That force is represented by the person who is holding this book: you, the student of corrections. For most of its history, the field has been the domain of amateurs, part-time reformers who were moved by zeal for helping prisoners, and local workers who took the jobs because nothing else was available. In recent years corrections has become a field of study for persons interested in long-term professional careers, perhaps persons like you. This is a dramatic change because it indicates a growing employee constituency with an interest in corrections to sustain the field's growth and development. This, more than any other influence, may be a stabilizing force for corrections in the years to come.

For Discussion

1. Should the main educational basis for most correctional workers be communication skills? Why or why not?

2. Is corrections work a profession? How is its status as a profession changing?

3. What kind of job satisfaction would come from a probation officer making an arrest of one of his clients? What does this tell you about the profession?

4. What limits, if any, should be made in hiring women for jobs dealing with male offenders? Why or why not?

5. How does the promotion to a supervisory role change the corrections worker's job perspective? What about the effect on job satisfaction?

For Further Reading

Box, Stephen. *Recession, Crime, and Punishment.* Totowa, N.J.: Barnes & Noble, 1987. An empirical assessment of the relationship between unemployment, crime rates, and punishment.

Duffee, David E. *Explaining Criminal Justice: Community Theory and Criminal Justice Reform.* Cambridge, Mass.: Oelgeschlager, Gunn, & Hain, 1980. An award-winning description of the way in which community characteristics influence justice system processing.

Wilkins, Leslie T. *Punishment, Crime, and Market Forces.* Brookfield, Vt.: Dartmouth, 1991. An analysis of the economics of policy and ethical choices in punishment systems.

Notes

1. Francis X. Clines, "Ex-Inmates Urge Return to Areas of Crime to Help," *New York Times*, 23 December 1992, pp. A1, B2.

2. John DiIulio, "Crime and Punishment in Wisconsin," *Policy Research Institute Report* 3(7) (December 1990): 1–56.

3. Those women are Sally Halford, Iowa; Dora Schriro, Missouri; Elaine Little, North Dakota; Lynne DeLano, South Dakota; and Judith Uphoff, Wyoming. In addition, Catherine Abate is commissioner of New York City's corrections department, which is larger than most state systems.

4. National Council on Crime and Delinquency, *Policy Statement on Sentencing* (San Francisco: National Council on Crime and Delinquency, 1992), pp. 1–5.

APPENDIX
Career Opportunities in Corrections

The correctional job market is expanding. In the last twenty-five years, the correctional system has *quadrupled* in size. Since 1971, according to the Bureau of Justice Statistics, correctional budgets have grown 990 percent. In addition to the traditional functions of probation, prisons, and parole, the corrections system operates an array of programs, mostly intermediate sanctions but also diversionary programs. This appendix provides a brief description of some of the more common titles in the correctional system.

Institutional Corrections

Corrections officer

Job description: The term *corrections officer* is relatively new in the field; for most of the history of corrections, the term was *guards*. This reflects a change in thinking about the functions of the role. The older term gives the impression that the job's main duties are watching inmates to prevent escapes and fights. The new title depicts the worker as more integral to the corrective functions of the system. It recognizes that the corrections officer has responsibility for overseeing the offender's adjustment to the prison or jail, and for assisting offenders in finding ways to turn away from crime.

Duties: The institution requires security twenty-four hours a day. The typical corrections officer works an eight-hour shift and has an assignment that pertains to a cell-range or housing unit within the facility. Normally, the shifts rotate, so that the corrections officer works days sometimes, then nights.

Requirements: The basic educational requirement is a high school degree, but more and more, recent college graduates are recruited to the job.

Pay: Starting pay averages $18,000–$20,000.

Corrections counselor

Description: The professional responsibilities are threefold: (1) to support the inmate's adjustment to incarceration, (2) to determine the best work and program assignments for the inmate during the incarceration, and (3) to help the inmate prepare for release.

Duties: Corrections counselors are given a caseload to manage. They meet with these inmates when they first arrive in the facility to learn about their special needs, and they see them on a regular basis during their incarceration to monitor their progress. Corrections counselor also serve as a contact between the inmate and the outside family.

Requirements: Almost always a college degree is required, and frequently additional training in counseling psychology.

Pay: Starting pay averages $23,000–$33,000.

Correctional teacher

Description: A correctional teacher provides classroom education to inmates who want to complete their high school education. The institutional school can be a challenging environment in which to work. Inmate motivation is often not very strong, and teaching is frequently made more difficult by inmate learning problems and histories of school failure.

Duties: The correctional teacher evaluates student progress in the same way as any schoolteacher.

Requirements: The correctional teacher is required to have the same credentials as a regular schoolteacher.

Pay: Starting pay averages $23,000–$29,000.

Vocational program staff

Description: Vocational program staff are involved in the facility's rehabilitation process. They teach inmates job skills and basic job disciplines, such as punctuality, teamwork, and responsible behavior.

Duties: Setting up and running a vocational training program, (woodworking, furniture repair, auto repair, and so on) and evaluating inmate progress in learning the vocational skill.

Requirements: Vocational program staff are required to have a license and demonstrated skill in a vocational area, and experience in vocational training.

Pay: Starting pay averages $24,000–$34,000.

Community Corrections

Probation/parole officer

Description: Probation and parole officers supervise offenders who are living in the community. They help offenders become successful citizens in the community, but they also have an obligation to be concerned about community safety. This balancing of "help" and "control" gives the probation/parole officer job satisfaction but is also the source of the greatest job stress. To balance the needs of the offender and the interests of the community is not easy.

Duties: Probation officers routinely carry one hundred cases or more, parole officers almost that many. The officer monitors community adjustment by meeting with these offenders in the office and in their homes. Because it is difficult to have meaningful contact with the entire caseload, officer must choose the cases on which they concentrate their efforts.

Requirements: Probation/parole officers usually are required to have a college degree; some states require more advanced education.

Pay: Starting pay averages $21,000–$32,000.

Intensive supervision officers

Description: Intensive supervision officers provide much more comprehensive supervision of offenders than regular probation/parole officers are able to provide. They work closely with the offender in employment and family matters in order to help ensure a better adjustment to the community.

Duties: The intensive model calls for an emphasis on surveillance, and it augments that responsibility by providing much smaller caseloads than ordinary—usually thirty or fewer clients.

Requirements: Intensive supervision officers are normally the elite of their peers. They are specially selected from among regular probation/parole officers and represent the best of their profession.

Pay: Intensive officers are usually paid somewhat in excess of regular probation/parole officers.

Residential workers

Description: Residential staff work in facilities that provide residential placements for offenders: halfway houses, group homes, work release centers, and day treatment centers.

Duties: Residential workers are somewhat like corrections officers, with responsibility for the security of the residential facility. But they are also like probation or parole officers, helping offenders learn how to adjust to the community, and supporting treatment, education, and vocational efforts of their clients.

Requirements: Educational requirements vary widely, ranging from a minumum of a high school degree for basic positions, to college and even advanced degrees for positions that include counseling responsibility.

Pay: Starting pay averages $24,000–$30,000.

Treatment specialists

Description: Three main typres of this specialized treatment are offered: substance abuse treatment, sex offender treatment, and anger control. These treatments are the cornerstone of many correctional programs, since they deal with problems that are central to the criminality of many correctional clients.

Duties: Treatment personnel use a variety of techniques—group and individual counseling, structured intervention—to reduce the chances of return to substance abuse.

Requirements: Advanced education and training in the area of treatment specialty is required for these positions.

Pay: Starting pay averages $30,000–$45,000.

Management and Administration

Supervisors

Description: The supervisor's primary role is to facilitate staff creativity and effectiveness by providing support in the form of advice and consultation. A secondary function of staff control, which is carried out by ensuring that the standard organizational policies and procedures are followed by line staff.

Duties: Supervisors review and evaluate the effectiveness of line staff. They serve as conduits of information between line staff and administration, and they conduct audits of staff performance.

Requirements: In addition to the education requirements placed on line staff, supervisors are required to have a minimum number of years of experience in the line staff position.

Pay: Starting pay averages $29,000–$41,000.

Administrator

Description: Administrators manage the organization and determine its mission and policy. In large organizations, there are often several administrators, some of whom manage divisions and report to a chief executive officer.

Duties: The professional life expectancy of the administrator is based on how well he or she keeps the political sources of support pleased with the management of the agency. The result is a natural tendency to be conservative in setting organization policy and procedure.

Requirements: A person becomes an administrator after years of service in various roles in the organization. The top administrator is appointed by some outside authority.

Pay: Starting pay averages $55,000–$75,000.

Glossary

Age of Reason *See* **Enlightenment.**

alcohol abuser A person whose use of alcohol is difficult to control, disrupting normal living patterns. Such persons frequently violate the law while under the influence of alcohol or in attempts to secure it.

Antabuse A drug that, when combined with alcohol, causes violent nausea; it is used to control a person's drinking.

assessment centers A way to evaluate prospective employees by putting them in simulated job situations and seeing how well they perform.

bail An amount of money specified by a judge to be posted as a condition for pretrial release for the purpose of ensuring the appearance of the accused in court as required.

behavior therapy Treatment that induces new behaviors through reinforcements (rewards and punishments), role modeling, and other active forms of teaching.

benefit of clergy The right to be tried in an ecclesiastical court, where punishments were less severe than those meted out by civil courts, given the religious focus on penance and salvation.

benign neglect The slighting of female offenders' special problems and needs, particularly in the provision of programs and services.

bondsman An independent business person who provides bail money for a fee, usually 5 to 10 percent of the total.

boot camp A physically rigorous, disciplined, and demanding regimen emphasizing conditioning, education, and job training. Designed for young offenders.

campus style An architectural design by which the functional units of a prison are individually housed in a complex of buildings surrounded by a fence.

capital punishment Punishment of the convicted offender by death.

career criminal A person for whom crime is a way of earning a living. Over time the career criminal has numerous contacts with the justice system and may come to look upon the criminal sanction as a normal business expense.

chain of command A series of organizational positions in order of authority, each person receiving orders from the one immediately above and issuing orders to the one immediately below.

chivalry factor The tendency of judicial and law enforcement personnel to view women as either frail creatures in need of protection or morally corrupt.

civil disabilities Legal restrictions that prevent released felons from voting and holding elective office, engaging in certain professions and occupations, and associating with known offenders.

civil liability Responsibility for the provision of monetary or other compensation awarded to a plaintiff in a civil action.

civil service The use of an objective system for evaluating government employees for hiring and promotion.

classification A process by which prisoners are assigned to types of custody and treatment appropriate to their individual needs.

clear and present danger Any threat to security or to the safety of individuals that is so obvious and compelling that the need to counter it overrides the guarantees of the First Amendment.

coercive power The ability to obtain compliance by the application or threat of physical force.

coercive therapy Treatments in which the therapist determines the need for and the goals of treatment processes which are required, whether or not the client agrees.

cognitive restructuring A form of behavior therapy that focuses on changing the thinking and reasoning patterns that accompany criminal behavior.

community correctional center A small group living facility for offenders, especially those who recently have been released from prison.

community corrections A model of corrections based on the assumption that the reintegration of the offender into the community should be the goal of the criminal justice system.

community service Compensation for injury to society by the performance of service to the community.

compelling state interest An interest of the state that must take precedence over rights guaranteed by the First Amendment.

compliance The act of obeying an order or request.

conditions of release Restrictions on the parolees' conduct that must be obeyed as a legally binding requirement of being released.

congregate system A penitentiary system developed in Auburn, New York, where each inmate was held in isolation during the night but worked with fellow prisoners during the day under a rule of silence.

construction strategy A strategy of building new facilities to meet the demand for prison space.

continuing education unit (CEU) The equivalent of one hour of training in a professional area of responsibility that is used to meet requirements for regular education of professional staff.

continuum of sanctions A range of correctional management strategies based on degree of intrusiveness and control over the offender, along which an offender is moved based on response to correctional programs.

contract labor system A system under which inmates' labor was sold on a contractual basis to private employers, who provided the machinery and raw materials with which they made salable products in the institution.

corporal punishment Punishment inflicted on the body of the offender with whips or other devices that cause pain.

corrections The variety of programs, services, facilities, and organizations responsible for the management of people who have been accused or convicted of criminal offenses.

courtyard style An architectural design by which the functional units of a prison are housed in separate buildings constructed on four sides of a hollow square.

custodial model A model of a correctional institution that emphasizes security, discipline, and order.

day fine A criminal penalty based on the amount of income an offender earns in a day's work.

deinstitutionalization The release of mental patients from mental hospitals and their return to the community.

Depo-Provera A "chemical castration" drug that eliminates sexual response among males.

deserved punishment *See* **retribution.**

determinate sentence A sentence of a fixed period of incarceration imposed by a court. This type of sentence is associated with the concept of retribution or deserved punishment.

deterrence *See* **general deterrence; special deterrence.**

direct supervision A method of correctional supervision in which staff members are in direct physical interaction with inmates throughout the day.

discretion The authority to make decisions without reference to specific rules or facts, using instead one's own judgment; allows for individualization and informality in the administration of justice.

discretionary release The release of an inmate to community supervision from incarceration at the discretion of the parole board within the boundaries set by the sentence and the penal law.

diversion An alternative to adjudication by which the defendant agrees to conditions set by the prosecutor (such as to undergo counseling or drug rehabilitation) in exchange for withdrawal of charges.

domain The limited sphere of an organization's authority and responsibility.

domain conflict Competition between two or more organizations in attempts to carry out the same goal; or disagreement as to the appropriate goal for a given organization.

drug abuser A person whose use of a chemical substance disrupts normal living patterns to the extent that social problems develop, often leading to criminal behavior.

drunk tank *See* **lockup.**

due process of law Law in its regular course of administration through courts of justice, as guaranteed in the United States by the Constitution and the Bill of Rights.

due process (procedural) The constitutional guarantee that no agent or instrumentality of government will use any procedures to arrest, prosecute, try, or punish any person other than those procedures prescribed by law.

Enlightenment (Age of Reason) During the eighteenth century in England and France, concepts of liberalism, rationality, equality, and individualism dominated social and political thinking.

equal protection The constitutional guarantee that the law will be applied equally to all persons, without regard for such individual characteristics as gender, race, and religion.

exchange A mutual transfer of resources; hence, a balance of benefits and deficits that flow from behavior based on decisions as to the values and costs of alternatives.

expiration release The release of an inmate from incarceration after full service of a sentence or after reduction for earned good time credits. Supervision in the community is not required.

expungement A legal process that results in the removal of a conviction from official records.

false positive An individual incorrectly classified because of imperfections in the method used.

federalism A system of government in which power and responsibilities are divided between a national government and state governments.

fee system A system by which jail operations are funded by a set amount paid for each prisoner held per day.

forfeiture Seizure by the government of property and other assets derived from or used in criminal activity.

formal organization A structure established for the purpose of influencing behavior in order to achieve particular ends.

galley slavery Forced rowing of large medieval ships, called galleys.

general deterrence Punishment of criminals intended to serve as an example to the general public and thus to discourage the commission of offenses.

goal displacement The replacement of an organization's formally stated or prescribed goals by less visible but perhaps more crucial unstated or latent goals.

good time A reduction of time to be served in a correctional institution awarded at the discretion of correctional officials to inmates whose behavior conforms to the rules or whose activities deserve to be rewarded.

hands-off policy A judicial policy of noninterference in the internal administration of prisons.

holding tank *See* **lockup.**

house arrest A sentence requiring the convicted offender to remain inside his or her home during specific periods.

hulks Abandoned ships converted by the English to hold convicts during a period of prison crowding between 1776 and 1790.

incapacitation Deprivation of capacity to commit crimes against society by detention in prison.

indefinite sentence *See* indeterminate sentence.

indeterminate sentence A period of incarceration set by a judge as a minimum term that must be served before a decision on parole eligibility is made and a maximum term at the conclusion of which the sentence has been completed (for example, five to ten years). This type of sentence is closely associated with the rehabilitation concept, which holds that the time necessary for treatment cannot be predetermined.

individual deterrence *See* special deterrence.

inherent powers The authority of the judiciary to take such actions as are necessary to carry out its responsibilities under the Constitution.

inmate code A set of rules of conduct that reflect the values and norms of the prison social system and help to define for inmates the image of the model prisoner.

intensive probation supervision Probation granted as an alternative to incarceration under conditions of strict reporting to a probation officer with a limited caseload.

intermediate sanctions A variety of punishments that are more restrictive than traditional probation but less stringent and less costly than incarceration.

jail A facility authorized to hold pretrial detainees and sentenced misdemeanants for periods longer than forty-eight hours. Most jails are administered by county governments; sometimes they are part of the state government.

judicial reprieve A practice under English common law whereby a judge might suspend imposition or execution of a sentence on condition of good behavior on the part of the offender.

just deserts model A model of the criminal sanction that emphasizes deserved punishment: criminals should be punished because they have infringed the rights of others; the severity of the sanction should fit the seriousness of the crime.

lease system A variation on the piece-price system in which the contractor provided prisoners with food and clothing as well as raw materials. In some southern states, under this system prisoners were leased to agricultural producers to perform field labor.

least restrictive methods Means of ensuring a legitimate state interest (such as security) that impose fewer limits to prisoners' First Amendment rights than alternative means of securing that end.

lex talionis Law of retaliation; the principle that punishment should correspond in degree and kind with the offense, as an eye for an eye, a tooth for a tooth.

line personnel Employees who are directly concerned with furthering the institution's goals; persons in direct contact with clients.

lockup A facility authorized to hold persons prior to court appearance for periods of up to forty-eight hours. Most lockups (also referred to as drunk tanks or holding tanks) are administered by local police agencies.

mandatory release The required release to community supervision of an inmate from incarceration upon the expiration of a certain time period, as stipulated by a determinate sentencing law or parole guidelines.

mandatory sentence A sentence required by statute to be imposed and executed upon certain offenders.

master An official appointed by a court to administer an activity under judicial direction.

maximum security prison A prison designed and organized to minimize the possibility of escapes and violence; to that end it imposes strict limitations on the freedom of inmates and visitors.

mediation Intervention in a dispute by a third party to whom the parties in conflict submit their differences for resolution and whose decision (in the correctional setting) is binding on both parties.

medical model A model of corrections based on the assumption that criminal behavior is caused by biological or psychological conditions that require treatment.

medium security prison A prison designed and organized to prevent escapes and violence but in which restrictions on inmates and visitors are less rigid than in facilities for more dangerous offenders.

mentally handicapped offender A person whose limited mental development prevents adjustment to the rules of society.

mentally ill offender A person whose criminal behavior may be traced to diminished capacity to think or reason as a result of psychological or neurological disturbance, or who exhibits such diminished capacity while under correctional authority.

minimum security prison A prison designed and organized to permit inmates and visitors as much freedom as is consistent with the concept of incarceration.

model A representation; an ideal description of something that cannot be visualized, permitting generalized statements to be made about it and its strengths and weaknesses to be evaluated.

new-generation jail A facility of podular architectural design and management policies that emphasizes interaction of inmates and staff and provision of services.

normative power The ability to obtain compliance by manipulation of symbolic rewards.

null strategy The strategy of doing nothing to relieve crowding in prisons on the assumption that the problem is temporary and will disappear in time.

ombudsman A public official who investigates complaints against government officials and recommends corrective measures.

paradigm A model; a set of assumptions about the boundaries, theories, methodologies, and research tools supporting a field of inquiry.

pardon An action of the executive branch of state or federal government excusing an offense and absolving the offender from the consequences of the crime.

parens patriae The "parent of the country"; the state as guardian and protector of all persons (particularly juveniles) who are unable to protect themselves.

parole The conditional release of an inmate from incarceration under supervision after a portion of the prison sentence has been served.

penitentiary An institution intended to isolate prisoners from society and from one another so that they could reflect on their past misdeeds, repent, and thus undergo reformation.

people processing The application of methods and systems for the provision of services to clients in a public bureaucracy.

piece-price system A labor system under which a contractor provided raw materials and agreed to purchase goods made by prison inmates at a set price.

podular unit Self-contained living areas, for twelve to twenty-four inmates, composed of individual cells for privacy and open areas for social interaction. "New-generation jails" are made up of two or more pods.

population-reduction strategy A strategy to reduce or at least hold constant the prison population by reducing new admissions to prisons through alternatives to incarceration and by releasing inmates to parole and community corrections before the expiration of their terms.

population-sensitive flow-control strategy A strategy of linking sentencing to the availability of prison space, releasing prisoners when

facilities become crowded, and allocating specific amounts of space to judges and prosecutors.

positivist school An approach to criminology and other social sciences based on the assumption that human behavior is a product of biological, economic, psychological, and social factors, and that the scientific method can be applied to ascertain the causes of the behavior of any individual.

presentence investigation (PSI) An investigation and summary report of the background of a convicted offender, prepared to help the judge decide on an appropriate sentence.

pretrial diversion An alternative to adjudication in which the defendant agrees to conditions set by the prosecutor (for example, to receive counseling or drug rehabilitation) in exchange for withdrawal of charges.

preventive detention Detention of an accused person in jail for the purpose of protecting the community from crimes the accused is considered likely to commit if set free pending trial.

principle of interchangeability The intrusiveness of different forms of intermediate sanctions can be calibrated to make them equivalent as punishments despite their differences in approach.

principle of least eligibility The doctrine that prisoners ought to receive no goods or services in excess of those available to persons who live within the law.

prison An institution for the imprisonment of persons convicted of serious crimes. See also maximum security prison, medium security prison, and minimum security prison.

prisonization The process by which a new inmate absorbs the customs of the prison society and learns to adapt to the environment.

prison program Any formal, structured activity that takes prisoners out of their cells and sets them to instrumental tasks.

probation A sentence the offender serves in the community while under supervision.

procedural due process *See* due process (procedural).

PSI *See* presentence investigation (PSI).

Prozac A drug that reduces depression.

public account system A labor system under which a prison bought machinery and raw materials with which inmates manufactured a salable product.

public works and ways system A labor system under which prison inmates work on public construction and maintenance projects.

radial design An architectural plan by which a prison is constructed in the form of a wheel, with "spokes" radiating from a central core.

reality therapy Treatment that emphasizes personal responsibility for actions and their consequences.

recognizance A formally recorded obligation to perform some act (such as keep the peace, pay a debt, or appear in court when called) entered by a judge to permit an offender to live in the community, often upon posting a sum of money as surety, which is forfeited by nonperformance.

regional jail Facility operated under a joint agreement by two or more governmental units, usually with a jail board drawn from representatives of the participating jurisdictions with varying authority over policy, budget, operations, and personnel matters.

rehabilitation The process of restoring a convicted offender to a constructive place in society through some form of vocational, educational, or therapeutic treatment.

rehabilitation model A model of a correctional institution that emphasizes the provision of treatment programs designed to reform the offender.

reintegration Rehabilitation of the offender by supervision in the community, undertaken in the belief that criminal behavior results from a lack of opportunity to succeed legitimately in the community, and therefore such opportunities must be made available.

reintegration model A model of a correctional institution that emphasizes maintenance of the offender's ties to family and the community as a method of reform, in recognition of the fact that the offender will be returning to the community.

release on recognizance (ROR) Pretrial release granted on the defendant's promise to appear in court because the judge believes that the defendant's ties in the community are sufficient to guarantee the required appearance.

remunerative power The ability to obtain compliance in exchange for material resources.

restitution Compensation for financial, physical, or emotional loss caused by an offender, in the form of either a payment of money to the victim or work at a service project in the community, as stipulated by the court.

retribution Punishment inflicted on a person who has infringed the rights of others and so deserves to be penalized to a degree commensurate with the crime.

ROR *See* release on recognizance (ROR).

secular law The law of the civil society, as distinguished from church law.

selective incapacitation The strategy of making optimum use of expensive and limited prison space by targeting for incarceration those individuals whose incapacitation will do the most to reduce crime.

self-report study An investigation of behavior (such as criminal activity) based on subjects' responses to questions concerning activities in which they have engaged.

sentence disparity Divergence in the lengths and types of sentences imposed for the same crime or for crimes of comparable seriousness when no reasonable justification can be discerned.

sentencing guidelines An instrument developed to indicate to judges the usual sanction given in the past in particular types of cases.

separate confinement A penitentiary system developed in Pennsylvania in accordance with which each inmate was held in isolation from other inmates. All activities, including craftwork, were carried on in the cells.

separation of powers The division of authority among the executive, legislative, and judicial branches of government.

sex offender A person who has committed a sexual act prohibited by law. Such acts may be committed for a variety of reasons, including economic, psychological, and even situational.

situational offender A person who in a particular set of circumstances has violated the law but who is not given to criminal behavior in normal circumstances and is unlikely to repeat the offense.

social control Actions and practices of individuals and social institutions designed to induce conformity to social norms and rules.

social therapy Treatment that attempts to make the institutional environment supportive of prosocial attitudes and behaviors.

span of control A management principle holding that a supervisor can effectively oversee only a limited number of subordinates.

special deterrence (specific or individual deterrence) Punishment administered to criminals with the intent to discourage them from committing crimes in the future.

specific deterrence *See* special deterrence.

staff personnel Employees who provide services in support of line personnel (for example, training officer, accountant).

stakes The potential losses to victims and to the system if offenders fail; stakes include

injury from violent crime and public pressure resulting from negative publicity.

stand bail The practice, by a private citizen, of posting bail for a defendant and promising to make certain that the defendant will appear for trial.

state use system A labor system under which goods produced by prison industries are purchased by state institutions and agencies exclusively and never enter the free market.

status offenders Juveniles who are made subjects of the juvenile court due to behavior that, while not criminal, calls for the supervision of official authorities.

stratified subculture A subculture in which members form a social hierarchy, with some assuming leadership roles and others becoming followers.

street-level bureaucrats Public service workers who interact directly with citizens in the course of their work, granting access to government programs and providing services within them.

system A complex whole consisting of interdependent parts whose operations are directed toward goals and influenced by the environment within which they function.

technical violation The revocation of the probation sentence due to the probationer's failure to abide by the rules and conditions of probation specified by the judge.

technology A method of applying scientific knowledge to practical purposes in a particular field.

telephone-pole design An architectural plan for a prison

calling for a long central corridor crossed at regular intervals by structures containing the prison's functional area.

therapeutic community A treatment facility in which all aspects of programming are designed to reinforce the adoption of socially acceptable behaviors by the inmate.

Thorazine A drug used to control violent or aggressive behavior caused by psychiatric problems.

token economy A type of behavior therapy that uses payments (such as tokens) to reinforce desirable behaviors in an institutional environment.

total institution An institution (such as a prison) that completely encapsulates the lives of the people who live and work within it. Behavior is governed by rules and the group is split into two parts, one of which controls all aspects of the lives of the other.

totality of conditions The aggregate of circumstances in a correctional facility that, when considered as a whole, may violate the protections guaranteed by the Eighth Amendment, even though such guarantees are not violated by any single condition in the institution.

transactional analysis Treatment that focuses on how a person interacts with others, especially on patterns of interaction that indicate personal problems.

transportation The practice of removing offenders from the community to another region or land, often a penal colony.

unity of command A management principle holding that a subordinate should report to only one superior.

utilitarianism The doctrine that the aim of all action should be the greatest possible balance of pleasure over pain; hence, the belief that a punishment inflicted on an offender must achieve enough good to outweigh the pain inflicted.

wergild "Man money"; money paid to the relatives of a murdered person or to the victim of a crime as compensation and to prevent a blood feud.

widening the net Increasing the scope of corrections by applying a diversion program to persons charged with offenses less serious than those of the persons the program was originally intended to serve.

work release Release of a sentenced inmate from a correctional institution for work during the day; the inmate must spend nights and weekends in the facility.

work release center A facility that allows offenders to work in the community during the day, while residing in the center during nonwork hours.

Index

Boldface numbers in this index refer to the page on which the term is defined.

A

Abate, Catherine, 154–155
Abbott, Jack Henry, 438
Accountability system for sentences, 212–213
Adler, Freda, 285
Administration building assignments for officers, 339
Adoption, 303
AFL-CIO, 340
Against Our Will (Brownmiller), 111
Age of Reason, **38–39,** 72
Agricultural production, 320
AIDS
 detainees with, 156
 direct supervision and, 167
 housing inmates with, 126
 issues involving, 26
 legal issues involving, 126–127
 medical care for inmates with, 126
 offenders with, 124–127, 252
 prevention of, 124–126
 prostitutes and, 113
 release of inmates with, 126
Alabama prison system, 243
Alcohol abusers, **117–118,** 119
 Antabuse, use of, 199, **498**
 detention of, 155–156
 detoxification centers for, 156
 supervision strategies for, 199
Alcoholic beverages in prison, 266
Alcoholics Anonymous (AA), 117–118, 345

Alderson, West Virginia Federal Reformatory for Women, 290, 297
Alexander, Myrle, 242
Alexander, Wayne B., 236, 252–253
Alien offenders, private facilities for, 249
Alternative Incarceration Center, Torrington, Connecticut, 208
American Civil Liberties Union prisoners' rights, 388
 Prison Project, 376–377
American Correctional Association, 57
American Federation of State, County, and Municipal Employees (AFSCME), 340
American Prison Association, on discretionary release, 408
American Revolution, 34
Andenaes, Johannes, 75
Anglican Code, 48–49
Anglo-Saxon societies, 31
Antabuse, 199, **498**
Appeals from capital punishment, 486–487
Architecture of prisons, 243–246
Arkansas State Prison, Cummins Farm Unit, 324, 382
Aryan Brotherhood, 273
Assessment centers, **517**
Atlanta prison, 271
Attica prison, 247, 271
Auburn prison, New York, 53–54, 244, 335
 job assignments at, 338
 women prisons, 288
Augustus, John, 172, 174–175, 203

Austin, James, 350
Australia, transportation of
    offenders to, 34, 36
Authority, types of, 193
Autonomous parole boards,
    417, 421
Aversive conditioning, 357

B

Bail, **157–158**
    alternatives to, 158
    Eighth Amendment rights,
        381–382
    stand bail, **172**
Bainer, LaNelle Marie, 305
Baldus, David, 489
Banishment in American
    colonies, 49
Barefield v. *Leach,* 303
Barfield, Thelma, 487–488
Barfoot, Joel, 418–419
Bartley-Fox gun control law,
    Massachusetts, 83
Bates, Sanford, 242
Baunach, Phyllis Jo, 303–304
Baxter v. *Palmigiano,* 385
Beccaria, Cesare, 39–40, 48, 50, 72
Bedford Hills Correctional Facility,
    New York, 284, 299, 302
    nursery facility at, 304
Behavior therapy, **355–357**
    as abusive, 357
    cognitive restructuring, **356**
    token economy, **356**
Bell v. *Wolfish,* 157, 382, 386
Bendix, 369
Benefit of clergy, **31**, 173
Benign neglect, **275**
Bennett, James, 242
Bensinger, Peter, 322
Bentham, Jeremy, 39, 40, 41–42,
    44, 50, 55, 72
Beto, George, 330
Bias. *See* Discrimination
Bible study, 345
Bill of Rights, 379
Birmingham Borough Prison, 56
Black Guerrilla Family, 273
Black Muslim religion, 322, 380
Black offenders. *See* Minority
    offenders
Blackstone, Sir William, 433–444
Blackwell Island, Women's
    Workhouse on, 290
Block officers, 338
Body searches, 381
Bondsman, **157–158**
Bonfire of the Vanities, The
    (Wolfe), 102

Boot camps, **88–89**, 222–223
Booth, Maud, 289
Boston Prison Discipline
    Society, 244
Bowker, Lee, 276
Branding. *See* Corporal punishment
Bridewell houses, 33
Brierton, David, 323
Brockway, Zebulon, 57, 58–59,
    60–61, 64, 288–289, 347, 406
Brodsky, Annette, 305
Brokerage in probation, 203–204
Bronson, George D., 316–319
Bronstein, Alvin, 103
Brownmiller, Susan, 111
Brubaker, 324, 382
Brute Force, 466
Building-tender system, 274, 394,
    395–396
Bureau of Justice Statistics
    actual time served, 86
    on prison overcrowding, 472
    on prison population, 250–251,
        463–464
Burger, Warren E., 235, 387,
    389, 397
Burnout of wardens, 319
Burris, Judy, 269
Bush, George, 445

C

Cales, Gloria, 304
California correctional system, 16
California Institute for Women,
    Frontera, 297
Calvinist doctrine of predestina-
    tion, 49
Campbell Soup Company, 248
Campus style prisons, **246**
Camus, Albert, 489
Cannon, Joseph, 322
Capital punishment, 80, 90–91,
    477–495, 487–490
    in American colonies, 49
    under Anglican Code, 49
    appeals process, 486–487
    constitutionality of, 482–487
    continuing debate on, 491
    death row inmates, 487–490
    executioner, discussion with,
        492–493
    habeas corpus process, 487
    history of, 480–482
    and insane offenders, 484
    justification for, 478–480
    for juvenile offenders, 485–486
    mentally retarded offenders, 486
    opposition arguments, 479–480

presentence investigation (PSI)
    and, 190
    states, distribution among,
        488–489
    supporting arguments, 479
Captains, 338
Career criminals, **108–110**
Carey, Hugh, 341
Carey, Matthew, 54
Carlson, Norman, 242
Carroll, Leo, 258
Carvalho, Philip, 310, 330,
    331–335
Case planning for supervision, 198
Casework/control strategies, 194
Cell searches, 381
Chain of command, **313**
Chase, Jerusha, 174
Chattanooga, Tennessee private
    prison, 249
Chicano offenders. *See* Minority
    offenders
Child molesters, 111–113
Children. *See also* Juvenile offenders
    women offenders, children
        and, 303–305
Chirico, Ted G., 445
Chivalry factor, **285**
Christie, Nils, 503–504
Church of the New Song, The, 362
Cigarettes, 266, 267–269
Cincinnati Declaration of
    Principles, 57–58, 61, 288
Cincinnati National Prison
    Association, 288
Civil commitment of drug
    offenders, 117
Civil disabilities, **360–361**
    of parolees, 451
Civil liability, **376**
Civil Rights Act of 1871, 162, 376,
    377, 378
    suits by prisoners under, 389
    women offenders and, 303
Civil rights movement, 238
    Illinois prison reform and, 322
Civil service, vs. professionalism,
    516–517
Classical School of criminology,
    39–40
Classification committee, 349
Classification process, **347–350**
    factors used in, 351
    labels on inmates, 350–352
    models of, 350
    objective systems, 350
Classifying offenders, 131–134
    problems with, 132–133

Clear and present danger, **379**
Clemmer, Donald, 258, 259
Clergy, benefit of, **31**, 173
Clerical jobs in prison, 368, 369
Client-specific planning, 190–191
Clinton, Bill, 485
Co-corrections, 301–302
Coercive power, **311**
Coercive therapy, **353**
Coffin, Rhoda M., 289
Cognitive restructuring, **356**
Cohen, Albert, 277
Cohen, Stanley, 496, 505
Coleman, Roger, 478
Coleman v. *Thompson*, 387
Colonial period, United States,
    48–49
Commissaries, 266
Community, release to, 422–424
Community correctional
    centers, **444**
Community corrections, **67**,
    227–232
  future of, 232
  legislation, 228–232
  list of states with acts for, 230
  payback system, 230
  prisons, impact on, 237–238
  private services and, 248
  Rikers Island, New York,
      154–155
Community protection. *See*
    Surveillance
Community service, **88**, 213,
    217–218
  as jail alternative, 162
Community supervision, 429. *See
    also* Parole officers and agen-
    cies; Residential programs
  bureaucracy of, 439–443
  dimensions of organization
      policy, 441
  hidden conditions of, 438
  levels of, 439–440
  structure of, 434–436
Compelling state interest, **379**
Compliance, **311**
Comprehensive Community
    Corrections Act, Minnesota,
    229
Conditional pardons, 405–406
Conditions of release, **428–429**,
    430
Condoms, 124–125
Conflict of corrections goals, 15
Congregate system, **53**
Conjugal visits, 265
Conley, John A., 35–36, 363

Connecticut Halfway Houses, Inc.,
    228–229
Con politician role, 261
Consolidated parole boards,
    417, 421
Constitutional rights, 377,
    378–379
  capital punishment and, 482–487
  Eighth Amendment rights,
      381–382
  First Amendment rights, 379–381
  Fourteenth Amendment rights,
      383, 384–385
  Fourth Amendment rights, 381
  state constitutional rights,
      377–378
Contact supervision standards, 198
Continuing Criminal Enterprise
    Act (CCE), 88
Continuing education units
    (CEU), **516**
Continuum of sanctions, **210**,
    214–215
Contract labor system, **363**
Contract of consent, 403
Convict role, 299
Convict subculture, 262
Cook County Jail, Chicago, 323
Cool role, 298–299
Cooper v. *Pate*, 376, 378, 385–386
Co-optation of corrections officers,
    328–329
Corporal punishment, **382**. *See also*
    Capital punishment
  under Anglican Code, 49
  history of, 37
  in Middle Ages, 32
Corrections, **5**. *See also* History of
    corrections
  administration of, 12–14
  assessment centers, **517**
  budget for, 7
  civil service, vs. professionalism,
      516–517
  classification in, 348–349
  co-corrections, 301–302
  complexity of, 8–9
  continuing education units
      (CEU), **516**
  cost dilemma of, 512–513
  de-escalation of, 519–520
  demystification of, 520–521
  devaluation of, 521–522
  development of, 522–523
  federalism and, **8–9**
  funding for, 13
  goals of, 14–15, 18

  implementation of programs,
      18–19, 21
  insider vs. outsider promo-
      tions, 518
  interconnectedness of, 23
  intermediate sanctions and,
      222–223
  for mentally ill offenders,
      120–122
  methods dilemma of, 510
  mission dilemma of, 509
  organizations of, 11
  paradigms of, **10**
  personnel dilemma of, 511–512
  principle of least eligibility
      and, **347**
  professional issues, 513–519
  purpose of, 72–79
  rediscovering rehabilitation
      in, 362
  structure dilemma of, 510–511
  technologies of, **18–19**, 518–519
  women, career opportunities
      for, 517–518
Corrections Corporation of
    America, 249
Corrections director, 25–26
Corrections officers, 330–341. *See
    also* Parole officers and agen-
    cies; Probation officers
  administration building
      assignments, 339
  assessment centers, **517**
  block officers, 338
  civil service, vs. professionalism,
      516–517
  continuing education units
      (CEU), **516**
  co-optation of, 328–329
  custodial force, 323
  industrial shop/school
      officers, 339
  inmate guards, 274
  insider vs. outsider promo-
      tions, 518
  labor unions for, 318, 340
  prison violence involving,
      275–276
  problems with role of, 340
  professional issues, 513–519
  ranks of, 338
  recruitment of, 335–336
  relief officers, 340
  Ruiz v. *Estelle* affecting, 395–396
  staffing goals, 511–512
  technology and, 518–519
  training programs for, 336
  unionism, 318, 340

wall post assignments, 339
women, career opportunities
for, 336–337, 517–518
work detail supervisors,
338–339
work perspective on, 331–335
yard officers, 339
Corrections system, **10–11**
employees of, 6–7
Philadelphia County,
Pennsylvania, corrections
system, 11, 12
Cosmetology programs, 299
Cost dilemma of corrections,
512–513
Courtyard style prisons, **245–246**
Crawford, William, 51
Cressey, Donald R., 95–98,
261–262, 297
Crime control model, 68–69
Criminal sanctions. *See also*
Punishment
forms of, 79–91
incarceration, 80–86
CRIPS gang, 273
Crofton, Sir Walter, 55, 405, 424
Cross, Robert W., 368
Cross-visiting, 264–265
Crouch, Ben M., 338–339
Cruz v. *Beto*, 380
Cullen, Francis, 362
Cummins Farm Unit, Arkansas
State Prison, 324, 382
Custodial model, **239**

D

Damiens, Robert-François, 30, 48
Daronco, Richard J., 79
Datesman, Susan, 304
Davis, Katherine Bennett, 290
Day fines, **217**
Day reporting centers, 218
Death penalty. *See* Capital
punishment
Death rates in prisons, 271
De Beaumont, Gustave Auguste,
47, 51, 53
Declaration of Independence, 50
Declaration of Principles,
Cincinnati, 57–58, 61, 288
De-escalation of corrections,
519–520
Deinstitutionalization, **120**, **122**
and mentally handicapped
offenders, 122, 124
Delinquent children, 64–65
Demystification of corrections,
520–521

Denver County Jail, Colorado, 153
Dependent and neglected children,
64–65
Depo-Provera, 112, **498**
Deputy wardens, 312–313
management by, 319, 320
Deserved punishment, **74–75**
Design of prisons, 243–246
Desk assignments, 369
Detention, 152–160
bail, **156–157**
for federal offenders, 242
legal needs during, 156–157
medical needs during, 156
mental health problems and,
153–155
pretrial diversion, **159–160**
preventive detention, **158–159**
release from, 157–160
release on recognizance
(ROR), 158
of substance abusers, 155–156
suicide during, 152–153
Determinate sentences, **81**, 83
and crime control model, 68
mandatory release and, 412–413
Deterrence, **74–75**
effectiveness of, 75
De Tocqueville, Alexis, 47, 51, 53
Detoxification centers, 156
Detroit House of Correction, 303
Devaluation of corrections,
521–522
Dickens, Charles, 53
DiIulio, John J., Jr., 318, 325,
329–330, 466, 475
Direct supervision, in jails,
167–168
Discipline in prisons, 277–279
Discretionary release, **403**,
408–411
computing eligibility for, 409
consequences of, 411
criteria for, 410
Discrimination. *See also* Minority
offenders
intermediate sanctions and,
225–226
Disorganized criminal role, 263
Disparity of sentences, **94**
District of Columbia Women's
Reformatory, Occoquan,
Virginia, 298
Doing time, 263
Double celling, 383, 386
Drug controls as surveillance,
498–499

Drug offenders, **113–117**
booked arrestees, drug use
by, 114
community correctional
centers, 444
detention of, 155–156
forfeiture by, **88**
mandatory prison terms for, 82
methadone, use of, 199
parole requirements, 418
pretrial diversion programs, 216
prison population and war on
drugs, 468–469
probation for, 202
rehabilitation and, 78
rehabilitative programs for, 359
supervision strategies for,
198,199
treatment programs for, 117
women as, 296
Drug tests, 500
Drunk drivers, 117
Drunk tanks, 144
Due process, **384**
in prison discipline, 384–385
Dukakis, Michael, 445
Durkheim, Emile, 6

E

Eastern Penitentiary, Philadelphia,
48, 50, 51, 237
design of, 244
Eastham Unit, Texas, 329,
395–396
Ecclesiastical punishments, 31
Eclectic Communications, Inc., 248
Eden, William (Lord Auckland),
433–444
Education
of corrections professionals,
514–516
direct supervision and programs
for, 167
prison programs, 359–360
women offenders, programs for,
299–301
Edward VI, 33
Ego states, 354
Ehrlich, Isaac, 479
Ehrlichman, John, 192
Eighth Amendment, 381–382
insane offenders, execution
of, 485
mentally retarded offenders,
execution of, 486
selected interpretations of, 383
totality of conditions, **382**

Elderly offenders, 127–128
in prison population, 251
Electric fence surveillance, 500
Electronic monitoring, 87–88,
221–222. *See also* Surveillance
technology for, 499–500
video surveillance, 499–500
Elizabeth I, 32, 33, 37
Elmira Reformatory, 56, 58–59
classification process, **347–350**
indeterminate sentences at, 64
parole in, 406
Emergency powers acts (EPA), 414
Employment of parolees, 451–452
Enlightenment, **38–39**, 72
*Enquiry into the Effects of Public
Punishment on Criminals, An*
(Rush), 52
Environmental structure strategies,
194
Equal protection, **384**
AIDS, inmates with, 127
United States Supreme Court
on, 385
Equal Rights Amendment, 303
Essay on Crimes and Punishments
(Beccaria), 39
Estelle v. *Gamble*, 383
Ethical standards for corrections
professionals, 514
Etzioni, Amitai, 311, 312
Exchange concept, **19, 21**
Executions. *See* Capital
punishment
Executive branch probation
administration, 178
Expiration release, **403**
Expungement of criminal records,
452
Extended parole, 401

F

Fairfax County jail, Virginia, 153
Fairness dilemma of correc-
tions, 510
False positives, **77**
Family
house arrest and, 221
jails, contact in, 161
visiting programs, 305
Farming as prison industry,
364–365
Farnham, Elizabeth, 287
Fatal Shore, The (Hughes), 36
Fauver, William, 330
FBI drug offense data, 468
Federal Bureau of Prisons,
240–242

detention facilities, 144
institutions of, 241
rehabilitation and, 65
women staff, 336–337
Federal Correctional Institution,
Fort Worth, Texas, 301
Federalism, **8–9**
administration of corrections
under, 12
Federal Parole Commission revo-
cation guidelines, 433
Federal Prison Industries
Corporation, 368–369
Federal prisons, 12, 240–242
Federal Reformatory for Women,
Alderson, West Virginia,
290, 297
Federal Sentencing Guide-
lines, 224
Feedback systems, 177
Fee system in jails, **145**
Female offenders. *See* Women
offenders
Ferracuti, Franco, 273
Field parole services, 421
Fifty-First Psalm, 173
Fifty Years of Prison Service
(Brockway), 58
Finckenauer, James, 226, 249
Fines, 6, 87
under Anglican Code, 49
day fines, **217**
as intermediate sanctions,
216–217
as jail alternative, 162
in Middle Ages, 32
Firearms, use of, 82
First Amendment, 379–381
selected interpretations of, 380
First International Prison Congress,
1846, 55
Fishman, Joseph, 257
Florida correctional system, 16
Folsom prison, California, 312
Food service
in prisons, 248
programs for women offenders,
299
Ford v. *Wainwright*, 484–485
Forer, Lois G., 96–97
Forfeiture, **88**
Formal organization for prison
management, **311**
Fort Worth, Texas Federal
Correctional Institution, 301
42 U.S.C. 1983, 377, 389
legal assistance, 394

ombudsman alternative, 393
prisoners' litigation under,
389–390
Fourteenth Amendment, 303, 383,
384–385
selected interpretations of, 385
Fourth Amendment, 381
selected interpretations of, 382
Fox, James, 299
Franklin, Benjamin, 51
French Code of 1791, 430
Freud, Sigmund, 66, 176
Frontera, California Institute for
Women, 297
Fry, Elizabeth Gurney, 41, 287,
288, 289
Fulwood v. *Clemmer*, 380
Furloughs, 423
in Vermont, 20
Furman v. *Georgia*, 482–483

G

Galley slavery, **32**
Gangs
classification process and, 349
direct supervision and, 167
in prison, 258, 273–274
protective custody, 274–275
in Stateville prison, 322–323
in Texas, 275
Garland, Bonnie, 72, 78, 79
Gaylin, Willard, 72
General deterrence, **74–75**
General Dynamics, 369
General equivalency degree
(GED), 360
Gettinger, Stephen, 488–489
Giallombardo, Rose, 297
Gilbert, Karin, 362
Gittlemacker v. *Prasse*, 380
Glaser, Daniel, 360, 437–438
Gleaning, 263
Glick, Ruth, 300
Glorious Revolution in England, 38
Glover v. *Johnson*, 303
Goals of corrections, 14–15, 18
Goffman, Erving, 309, 310
Goldberg v. *Kelly*, 278
Good News Regeneration
House, 231
Good time, **84**, 86
actual time served, effect on, 86
Gorczyk, John, 20
Governing Prisons (DiIulio), 318
Grace/privilege concept of
parole, 403
Graterford, Pennsylvania prison,
245

Great Law, The, 48
Great Society, 177
Green Haven Prison, New York, 266, 270
Greenwood, Peter, 75
Greenwood, Peter W., 109
Gregg v. *Georgia*, 483
Grievance procedures, 277, 391–392
   three-step process for, 392
   time limits on, 391–392
   wardens and, 317
Group psychotherapy, 355
Guards. *See* Corrections officers
Guided group interaction, 355
Guilt, 5
Guilty plea, 180

H

Habeas corpus, 387
   in capital punishment cases, 487
Habitual Offender Act, Alabama, 418
Hacks, Blacks, and Cons (Carroll), 258
Hair testing for drugs, 500
Halfway houses. *See* Residential programs
Hammurabic Code, 31
Hand, Judge Learned, 477
Hands-off policy, **376–377**
Hanging. *See* Capital punishment
Harriman and Straussman, 388
Harris, Jean, 106
Harris, Louis, 330
Harris, Mary Belle, 290
Harris, Thomas, 346
Haskell, Martin R., 108
Haviland, John, 52, 244
Hawes-Cooper Act, 366
Hawk, Kathleen, 242
Hedin, Tricia, 264–265
Hedonic calculus, 41
Heffernan, Esther, 297, 298
Helber, Norman, 203
Hennessey, Michael, 141
Henry VIII, 37
Herrera, Leonel, 487
Herrera, Raul, Sr., 487
Herrin, Richard, 72, 78, 79
High school equivalency diplomas, 160
Hinckley, John, 120
Hispanic offenders. *See* Minority offenders
History of corrections
   capital punishment, 480–482
   Colonial period, United States, 48–49

community corrections, **67**
corporal punishment, **37**
crime control model, 68–69
Damiens, Robert-François, 30
development of corrections, 30–31
Enlightenment/Age of Reason in, **38–39**
galley slavery, **32**
incarceration, 236–238
industrial programs, 363
jails, 142–143
juvenile corrections, 59–60
medical model, **65–67**
   in Middle Ages, 31–32
   in New York, 53–54
parole, 404–407
penitentiaries, 49–51
Penitentiary Act of 1779, 43–44
Positivist school, **62**
prisons in, 32–34
probation, 172–177
Progressiveness, 61–65
reformatory movement, 55–61
reform in, 37–44
women offenders, 287–292
Holding tanks, 144
Home surveillance, 26
Homosexuals
   AIDS in prisons, 125
   in male prisons, 299
   rape, 273
   in womens' prisons, 297–298
Horner, Henry, 316
Horton, Willie, 445
House arrest, **87–88**, 221
   as jail alternative, 162
Housekeeping programs, 299
House of Shelter, Detroit, 288–289
Howard, John, 33, 39, 41, 42–44, 50, 52, 55, 243, 287
Howe, Samuel Gridley, 54
"How Far May We Abolish Prisons?" (Brockway), 59
Howkins, Gordon, 475
Hubbell, Gaylord, 56–57, 406
Huber Law, Wisconsin, 444
Hudson, Keith, 375
Hudson v. *Palmer*, 381, 382
Hughes, Robert, 36
Hulks, **36**
Human immunodeficiency virus (HIV), 124. *See also* AIDS
   testing prisoners for, 125
Hutto v. *Finney*, 382
Hypodermic needles, 124

I

I Knew Them in Prison (Harris), 290
Immigration and Naturalization Service (INS), 249
I'm OK, You're OK (Harris), 346
Incapacitation, **75–77**
   false positives, **77**
   selective incapacitation, **76–77**
Incarceration, 80–86, 235–255. *See also* Prisons
   benefits of, 474–475
   costs of, 474–475
   goals of, 238–240
   intermittent incarceration, 177
   of mentally handicapped offenders, 124
   shock incarceration, 177
   state prison systems, 242–243
   unnecessary imprisonment, 209
   of women, 283–308
Indefinite sentences. *See* Indeterminate sentences
Indeterminate sentences, **81**
   Progressive period and, 64
   Index crimes by gender, 285, 286
Individual deterrence, **74–75**
Individual psychotherapy, 353–355
Industrial production, 320
Industrial programs, 362–365
   contract labor system, **363**
   farming, 364–365
   lease system, **363**
   piece-price system, **363**
   public account system, **364**
   public works and ways system, **365**
   sample list of prison industries, 367
   space age for, 368–369
   state use system, **364–365**
   trends in, 365–367
Industrial Revolution, 53–54
Industrial schools, 60
Industrial shop officers, 339
Inmate Classification Manual, 348
Inmate code, **259**
Inmate lawyers. *See* Jailhouse lawyers
Institutional management. *See* Prison management
Intensive probation supervision (IPS), **89**
   as jail alternative, 162
Intensive supervision probation (ISP), 219, 221

Intensive Treatment Unit, RCA
    Corporation, 248
Interchangeability, principle of, **224**
Interconnectedness of correc-
    tions, 23
Intermediate sanctions, **80**, 86–89.
    See also Fines
    accountability system for sen-
        tences, Delaware, 212–213
    agency problems, 210–211
    boot camp, **88–89**
    community service, **88**
    continuum of sanctions
        concept, **210**
    corrections-administered pro-
        grams, 222–223
    and corrections professionals,
        226–227
    evaluation of, 223–227
    fines as, 216–217
    forfeiture, **88**
    future of, 232
    house arrest, **87–88**
    intensive probation supervision
        (IPS), **89**
    judicial programs, 215–217
    justice and, 209–210
    limited risk management,
        214–215
    and minority offenders,
        225–226
    offender issues, 211–212
    principle of interchangeability,
        224
    probation and, 209
    problems with, 210–214
    reasons for, 208–210
    restitution, **88**
    selection of offenders, 224–225
    shock incarceration, 88–89
    stakes issue, **211–212**
    target group for, 224–225
    types of, 214–223
    unnecessary imprisonment, 209
    widening the net and, 213–214
    women offenders and, 225
Intermediate system, 55
Intermittent incarceration, 177
International Brotherhood of
    Teamsters, 340
Interstate sales of prison
    products, 366
In the Belly of the Beast (Abbott), 438
In the life role, 298, 299
*Introduction to the Principles of Morals
    and Legislation* (Bentham), 40

Investigation function of
    probation. *See* Presentence
    investigation (PSI)
Irrational authority, 193
Irwin, John, 258, 261–262, 297,
    298–299, 318

J

Jackson, Georgia prison, 245
Jackson, Michigan prison,
    243, 266
Jacobs, James B., 316
Jailhouse lawyers, 376
    legal assistance, 393–394
Jailing, 263
Jails, 140–170. *See also* Detention
    administration of, 12–13,
        144–145
    alternatives to, 162
    in American colonies, 49
    binding standards for, 163
    in California, 16
    capacity of, 144
    characteristics of population of,
        143–144
    in colonial America, 142–143
    credit for time in, 86
    crowding of, 165–166
    defined, **13**
    direct supervision, **167–168**
    facilities, 166–168
    fee system, **145**
    future of, 168
    interconnectedness of correc-
        tions and, 23
    legal liability for, 162–163
    legal rights of detainees,
        156–157
    lockups, **144**
    management issues of, 162–168
    medical needs of detainees,
        156–157
    new-generation jail, **166–168**
    in New York, 17
    origins of, 142–143
    overcrowding in, 165–166
    personal experience of, 148–152
    personnel issues, 163, 165
    podular units, **166–167**
    politics and, 145–147
    pretrial diversion, **159–160**
    principle of interchangeability
        and, **224**
    regional jails, **147**
    sentenced inmates in, 160–161
    services and facilities of, 161
    standards for, 163

    turnover in population, 141
    voluntary guidelines for, 163
    work details in, 160–161
    working conditions in, 165
Jail-time credit, 86
Janitorial jobs in prison, 370
Jarratt, Grady, 492–493
Johns Hopkins Hospital, 112
Johnson, Frank M., Jr., 382
Johnson, Lyndon, 177
Johnson v. *Avery*, 376
Jones, Maxwell, 357
Judges
    Forer, Lois G., 96–97
    intermediate sanction programs,
        215–217
    plea bargaining and, 93–94
    probation administration by, 178
    sentences and, 92–93
    sentencing guidelines for, 84
    wardens and, 317
Judicial reprieve, **173**
Julius, Nicholas, 51
Jung, Carl, 66
Junior Chamber of Commerce
    meetings, 345
Justice, Department of. *See* Capital
    punishment
Justice, William W., 395
Justice System, 13
Juvenile corrections
    in California, 16
    in Florida, 16
    Mack, Julian W., 63
    in New York, 16
    parens patriae doctrine, **60**
    reformatory movement and,
        59–60
    in Texas, 17
Juvenile courts, 130
    Progressiveness and, 64–65
Juvenile offenders, 128–131
    behavior therapy for, 356–357
    delinquent offenders, 128–129
    execution of, 485–486
    private facilities for, 249
    status offenders, **128–130**
    therapeutic communities for, 359
    violent offenders, 130–131

K

Kahane v. *Carlson*, 380
Kalinich, David, 266
Kant, Immanuel, 72, 73
Kassebaum, Gene, 297
Kerle, Kenneth E., 140
Killing of Bonnie Garland, The
    (Gaylin), 72

Kirchheimer, Otto, 32, 37
Kitchen jobs in prison, 370
Klockars, Carl B., 434–435
Knoll, Michael, 148–152, 260–261, 267–269, 446–449
Korn, Richard, 329
Kross, Anna, 330

L

Labor. *See* Industrial programs
Labor unions
    for corrections workers, 318, 340–341
    industrial programs and, 366
La Neustra Familia, 273
Langan, Patrick, 465, 466, 467, 468, 469
Lavin, Marvin, 109
Lease system, **363**
Least eligibility principle, **347**
    vocational programs and, 360
Least restrictive methods, **379**
Leavenworth radial design, 244
Leeke, William, 330
Lee v. *Downs*, 382
Legal assistance, 393–394
Legal rights. *See also* Constitutional rights; Prisoners' rights
    AIDS, inmates with, 126–127
    benefit of clergy and, 173
    of capital punishment, 482–487
    of detainees, 156–157
    judicial reprieve, **173**
Legislation
    community corrections legislation, 228–232
Legislature
    probation administration by, 178
    sentencing and, 95–98
Levin, Martin A., 93
Lex talionis, **31**
Liability issues. *See also* Prisoners' rights
    AIDS, inmates with, 127
    civil liability, **376**
Library jobs in prison, 370
Licensing corrections professionals, 513
Lieutenants, 338
Limited risk management, 214–215
Limit-setting strategies, 194
Limits to Pain (Christie), 503–504
Line personnel, **313–314**
Lipsky, Michael, 21, 337, 439
Lockdowns, 270
Locke, John, 38
Lockups, **144**
Logan, Charles, 240, 249, 456

Lombardo, Lucien, 337, 338
Los Angeles County Department of Adoptions v. *Hutchinson*, 303
Los Angeles County Men's Central Jail, 144
Louis XV, 30
Louisiana, death penalty in, 481–482
Lynds, Elam, 53

M

McCleary, Richard, 439
McCleskey v. *Kemp*, 483–484
McCleskey v. *Zant*, 387, 487
McCorkle, Lloyd W., 329
MacDougall, Ellis, 268
Machismo, 273
Mack, Julian W., 63
Maconochie, Alexander, 56, 405, 406, 424
Maddox, Lester, 101
Mahan, Sue, 295
Maintenance programs, 367–370
Maison de Force (Ghent), 33–34
    Howard, John, on, 43
Malinow, George, 270
Management of prisons. *See* Prison management
Mandatory release, **403,** 411–414
    determinate sentencing and, 412–413
    emergency powers acts (EPA), 414
    guidelines for, 412
Mandatory sentences, **83**
    jurisdictions requiring, 82, 83
Manson, Charles, 407
Marion, Illinois prison, 242, 245
Marion Adjustment Center, Kentucky, 249
Mark system, 55
    at Elmira Reformatory, 59
Marshall, Thurgood, 485
Marshals Service, 242
Martinson, Robert, 68, 353, 362, 456
Maslow, Abraham, 507
Massachusetts Reformatory Prison for Women in Framingham, 289, 291
Mauer, Marc, 462
Maximum security prisons, **246–247**
    as total institution, 310
Meachum, Larry, 468
Media and wardens, 319
Mediation, **393**
Medical care
    AIDS, inmates with, 126

    of detainees, 156
    for elderly offenders, 128, 251
    for women offenders, 302
Medical model, **65–67**
    Patuxent Institution, Maryland, 66–67
    probation and, 176
Medium security prisons, **247**
Megaprison, 239
Mempa v. *Rhay*, 200
Menard Penitentiary, Illinois, 258, 259
Menninger, Karl, 66
Mens rea, 484
Mentally handicapped offenders, **122–124**
    execution of, 486
Mentally ill offenders, **118–122**
    deinstitutionalization of, **120, 122**
    detention problems of, 153–155
    execution of, 484–485
    medical model and, 66
    Prozac, **500**
    Rush, Benjamin and, 52
    supervision strategies for, 198
    Thorazine, **498–499**
Methadone, 199
Methods dilemma of corrections, 510
Metropolitan Correctional Center, New York City, 386
Michigan Department of Corrections rules of conduct, 326
Michigan House of Correction, 58
Middle Ages, 31–32
    punishments in, 31
    secular law in, **32**
Milan House of Correction, 33–34, 48
Milieu therapy, 357
Military prisons, 242
Millbank, England, 51
Miller, Jerome, 359
Milwaukee House of Corrections, 153
Minimum security prisons, **247–248**
Minority offenders. *See also* Prisoners' rights
    civil rights movement and, 238
    classification process and, 349
    equal protection rights, 385
    in gangs, 273–274
    intermediate sanctions and, 225–226
    patterns involving, 103–104
    percentage of, 102–103
    in prison population, 104–105, 465–466

Minority offenders *(continued)*
  in prison society, 258, 259–260
  prison violence and, 273
  sentencing and, 93
Minors. *See* Children
Misdemeanor sentences, 92
Mission dilemma of corrections, 509
Model system of case management, 197–198
Monroe County Penitentiary, New York, 58
Montesquieu, 38
Montgomery County Detention Center, Maryland, 153
Morris, Norval, 207, 208, 475
Moyer, Imogene, 297–298
Murder. *See also* Capital punishment
  parole requirements, 418
  rehabilitation and, 78
  situational offenders, 108
Murton, Tom, 324, 382
Muslims, 362, 380
Mutilation. *See* Corporal punishment
Mutual Welfare League, 315

N

Nagel, William G., 246
Narcotics abusers. *See* Drug offenders
National Advisory Commission
  on classification, 348
  on fines, 87
  on probation, 178
  productive work in prisons, 366
National Association for the Advancement of Colored People's Legal Defense Fund, 376–377
National Council on Crime and Delinquency, 468
  on prison construction, 472
National Guard, 327
National Institute of Corrections
  model system of case management, 197–198
  on private prison costs, 249
  rehabilitation programs, 362
National Institute of Justice, 366
National Jail Census, 143
National Jail Center, National Institute of Corrections, Colorado, 165
National Moratorium on Prison Construction lobby, 472
National Prison Association, 57, 288, 406

National Prison Project (ACLU), 103
National sentencing system, 95
Neck verse (Fifty-First Psalm), 173
Neto, Virginia, 300, 305
Nettles, John S., 420
Newgate Prison, London, 53, 287, 288
New-generation jail, **166–168**
New Jersey State Maximum Security Prison, 258, 259
New Jersey State Prison, 327
  sickout of corrections officers, 341
New Jersey State Reformatory for Women at Clinton, 290
Newman, Donald J., 346
Newman v. *Alabama*, 303
New South Wales, transportation to, 34, 36
New York
  arguments for system, 54–55
  correctional system, 16–17
  history of corrections system in, 53–54
New York Children's Aid Society, 60
New York City Probation Department, 172
New York State Lunatic Asylum for Insane Convicts, 120
NIMBY Syndrome, 246
  and community correctional centers, 444
Nixon, Richard, 191
Nordheimer, J., 220
Norman conquest, 31
Normative power, **311**
Null strategy, **469**

O

Objective classification systems, 350
Observations in Visiting, Superintendence and Government of Female Prisons (Fry), 288
Occoquan Women's Reformatory, 298
O'Connor, Judith C., 419–420
O'Connor, Sandra Day, 375, 379
Offenders. *See also specific offenders*
  with AIDS, 124–127, 252
  average time served, 86
  career criminals, **108–110**
  child molesters, 111–113
  classifying offenders, 131–134
  false positives, **77**

  intermediate sanctions, issues of, 211–212
  postrelease life of, 445–452
  prostitutes, 113
  rapists, 111
  sentencing guidelines for, 84
  situational offenders, **106, 108**
  supervision of probationers, 194–195
  surveillance, resistance to, 504–505
  widening the net, **159–160**
Offense, 5
Ogilvie, Richard, 322
Okeechobee School for Boys, Florida, 249
O'Lone v. *Estate of Shabazz*, 380
Ombudsmen, 277, **392–393**
On Punishing Murder by Death (Rush), 52
On the Diseases of the Mind (Rush), 52
Oregon Parole Guidelines, 412, 413, 414
Osborne, Thomas Mott, 314, 315
Outlaw role, 261
Overcrowding. *See also* Prison overcrowding
  in jails, 165–166
Overdetermination, 245
Oxenbridge, Judge Peter, 174

P

Packer, Herbert, 72–73
Panopticon, 41–42
Paradigms, **10**
Pardons, **452**
  conditional pardons, 405–406
Parens patriae doctrine, **60**
Parole, **401–403**. *See also*
  Community supervision;
  Parole officers and agencies
  AIDS, release of inmates with, 126
  barriers to success after, 450
  civil disabilities of parolees, 451
  classification process and, 131–132, 352
  community, release to, 422–424
  conditions of release, **428–429,** 430
  consequences of, 414–415
  contract of consent, 403
  custody concept, 403
  decision for, 407–416
  dimensions of organization policy, 441
  discretionary release, **403,** 408–411

effectiveness of, 455–456
effect on sentencing, 415–416
emergency powers acts
(EPA), 414
employment of parolees, 451–452
experiences of offenders,
445–452
extended parole, 401
grace/privilege concept, 403
history of, 404–407
mandatory release, **403,** 411–414
New York creating, 16
prerelease programs, 423–424
probation combined with, 179
Progressiveness and, 64
revocation of, 429–433
technical violations of, 429, 432
termination of parole, 455
typing parolees, 439
violations, 23
of women offenders, 305
Parole boards
Alabama Parole Board, backgrounds on, 418–420
appointment to, 421–422
autonomous boards, 417, 421
consolidated boards, 417, 421
field services, 421
full-time vs. part-time
members, 421
organization of, 417–422
qualifications for membership
on, 422
Parole officers and agencies,
436–439
accountability and, 452–455
advocacy agencies, 442–443
broker agencies, 442
civil service vs. professionalism,
516–517
constraints on, 443
dimensions of organization
policy, 441
hidden conditions of supervision, 438
liability of, 193–194
paperwork problems, 454
philosophy of, 440–442
professional issues, 513–519
revocation of parole by, 431–432
roles of, 436–437
staffing goals, 511–512
technology and, 518–519
uncertainties affecting, 453–454
Pate, Frank, 322
*Pathway of Mattie Howard to and
From Prison, The* (Harris), 290

Patuxent Institution, Maryland,
66–67, 132
Pedophilia, 112
Penitentiaries. *See also* Prisons
arrival of, 49–51
congregate system, **53**
defined, **50**
separate confinement, **51–52**
Penitentiary Act of 1779, England,
43–44, 51
Penn, William, 48, 227
Pennsylvania
arguments for system of, 54–55
penitentiary system, 51–53
Penry, Johnny Paul, 486
Pentonville, England, 51
Personnel dilemma of corrections,
511–512
Petersilia, Joan, 109
Philadelphia County, Pennsylvania
corrections system, 11, 12
Piece-price system, **363**
Plato, 77
Plea bargaining, 93–94
presentence investigation (PSI)
recommendation for, 190
Podular units, **166–167**
Police and prison management, 327
Politics
jails and, 145–147
wardens and, 318–319
Population-reduction strategy, **470**
Population-sensitive flow-control
strategy, **470–471**
Positive peer culture, 357
Positivist school, **62**
Powell, Lewis, 483
Predestination, 49
Pregnant women inmates,
302–303
Prejean, Dalton, 486
Prerelease programs, 423–424
Presentence investigation
(PSI), **180**
contents of, 188–189
disclosure in, 190
illustration of, 181–186
information overload in, 189
private PSIs, 190–191
purpose of, 188
rearrested probationers compared
to recommendations, 191
recommendations in, 189–190
redundant information in, 189
verification of validity, 189
Presentence report, 94–95
President's Commission of 1967,
67, 324

on jails, 145
on parole, 440
Pressure artists, 349
Pretrial detention. *See* Detention
Pretrial diversion, **159–160,**
215–216
widening the net, **159–160**
Pretrial release programs, 104
Preventive detention, **158–159**
Pride Inc., 220
Principle of interchangeability, **224**
Principle of least eligibility. *See*
Least eligibility principle
Prison Community (Clemmer), 258
Prisoners' litigation, 388–390
alternatives to, 390–394
grievance procedures, 391–392
masters, appointment of, 389
mediation alternative, **393**
ombudsman alternative, **392–393**
pro se actions by prisoners, 389
Prisoners' rights. *See also*
Constitutional rights
attorney error and, 387
compliance problem, 387–388
constitutional rights, 381
Eighth Amendment rights,
381–382
federal statutory rights, 378
First Amendment rights, 379–381
foundations of, 377–378
Fourteenth Amendment rights,
383, 384–385
hands-off policy, **376–377**
impact of movement, 394, 397
objective vs. subjective criteria
for, 387
Ruiz v. *Estelle,* effect of, 394,
395–396
state constitutional rights,
377–378
state statutory rights, 378
Prison fever, 42
Prison Health Services
Incorporated, 248
Prison Industries Enhancement
(PIE) program, 366
Prison industry. *See* Industrial
programs
Prisonization, **258**
Prison management. *See also*
Deputy wardens; Wardens
chain of command, **313**
coercive power, **311**
compliance, **311**
continuum for, 312
custodial employees, 314
force, use of, 327

Prison management *(continued)*
formal organization, **311**
goals of, 312
leadership of inmates, 329
line personnel, **313–314**
literature on, 325
Michigan Department of
Corrections' rules of conduct, 326
normative power, **311**
prison directors, role of, 329–330
remunerative power, **311**
reward/punishment system, 328
span of control, **313**
staff personnel, **314**
structure for, 312–325
total institution, **310**
total power, defects of, 327
unity of command, 313
Prison overcrowding
co-corrections, 301–302
cost dilemma and, 513
double celling, 383, 386
Eighth Amendment rights
and, 383
impact of, 472–474
principle of interchangeability,
224
Prison population. *See also* Prison
overcrowding
arrest rates and, 466
construction of prisons and,
467–468
construction strategy, **471–472**
crisis, dealing with, 469–472
demographic change and,
464–465
drugs, effect of war on, 468–469
null strategy, **469**
population-reduction strategy,
470
population-sensitive flow-
control strategy, **470–471**
regional factors, 464
selective incapacitation strategy,
469–470
sentencing practices and,
466–467
trends in, 463–469
Prison programs, **345.** *See also*
Industrial programs;
Rehabilitative programs
educational programs, 361–362
maintenance programs, 367–370
prerelease programs, 423–424
principle of least eligibility
and, **347**

recreation programs, 370–371
religious programs, 361–362
security and, 346–347
types of activities for, 371
Prison rats, 349
Prison reform, 265
Prisons, 6, 11. *See also* Good time;
Industrial programs;
Intermediate sanctions; Jails;
Mandatory sentences; Prison
programs; Women offenders
agricultural production, 320
AIDS and, 124–126, 252
average time served, 86
Bridewall houses, 33
campus style prisons, **246**
child molesters in, 111, 113
classification of, 246–248
community corrections, 67
construction of, 467–468,
471–472
cost dilemma and, 513
courtyard style prisons, **245–246**
custodial model, **239**
defined, **13**
design of, 243–246
discipline in, 277–279
elderly prisoners, 252
federal prisons, 12, 240–242
food services in, 248
history of, 32–34
incapacitation and, 76–77
industrial production, 320
leadership of inmates, 329
location of, 246
male versus female subcultures,
298–299
manuals, 277–278
maximum security prisons, **247**
medical model and, 66
medium security prisons,
247–248
minimum security prisons, **248**
in New York, 17
NIMBY Syndrome, 246
offense characteristics of
inmates, 251
operation of, 240–243
population of, 250–252
possessions of prisoners, 265–266
private prisons, 248–250
protective custody, 274–275
radial design, **244–245**
rehabilitation model, **239**
reintegration model, **239–240**
rule violations, 277–279
sanctions for rule viola-
tions, 279

self-government by inmates,
317–318
sexual assaulters, 111
sociodemographic characteristics
of inmates, 251
state prison systems, 242–243
telephone-pole design, **245**
in Texas, 17
as therapeutic community, 358
tickets for violations, 278
in Vermont, 20
Prisons and Common Sense
(Osborne), 315
Prison society, 257–263
adaptive roles, 262–263
contraband goods in, 270
economy of, 263–271
fish, 250
inmate code, **259**
merchants in, 266–270
Prison violence, 271–277
gangs, 273–274
inmate characteristics, 272–273
institutional structure and, 276
officer-prisoner violence,
275–276
prevention of, 277
prisoner-officer violence, 275
prisoner-prisoner violence,
271–275
protective custody, 274–275
racism and, 273
sexual assaults, 273
Private prisons, 248–250
Probation, 6, 80, **89–90**, 171–206
administration of, 178
alternatives, 225
brokerage in, 203–204
in California, 16
centralization/decentralization
of, 177–178
in community corrections, 67
day reporting centers, 218
for drug offenders, 202
dual role of, 180, 187
future of, 202–204
history of, 172–177
intensive probation supervision
(IPS), **89**
interconnectedness of corrections
and, 23
intermediate sanctions and, 209
judicial reprieve, **173**
jurisdictional arrangements
for, 178
law enforcement model of, 176
medical model and, 176

modernization of, 175–177
parole combined with, 179
procedures for revocation of,
201–202
Progressiveness and, 63–64
psychology and, 176
rates of revocation for typical
probationers, 201
reparative probation, 20
revocation of, 199–202
special conditions of, 195–196
split sentences, 177
strategies for supervision,
194–195
supervision phase, 180
technical violations of, **199–200**
in Texas, 17
violations, 23
Probation centers, 218
Probation fee, 176–177
Probation officers, 11
for alcohol abusers, 117
authority, types of, 193
chief probation officer, 203
civil service vs. professionalism,
516–517
intensive probation supervision
(IPS), **89**
liability of, 193–194
professional issues, 513–519
size of caseload by state, 197
street police officers, pairing
with, 199
supervision by, 192–194
technology and, 518–519
Probation Subsidy Act, California,
228, 231
Procedural due process, **384**
Procunier v. *Martinez,* 380
Professional issues, 513–519
Progressiveness, 61–65
history of corrections, 62
reforms of, 62
Pro se actions by prisoners, 389
Prostitution, 113
Protective custody, 274–275
Protestant Reformation, 33
Prozac, **499**
PSI. *See* Presentence investigation
(PSI)
Psychological authority, 193
Psychology. *See also* Psychotherapy
medical model and, 66
probation and, 176
theories, 10
treatment programs, 352–355
Psychopaths, 118
public attention to, 132

Psychotherapy, 352
behavior therapy, **355–357**
coercive therapy, **353**
defined, 353
group psychotherapy, 355
individual psychotherapy,
353–355
reality therapy, **354**
social therapy, **357–359**
transactional analysis, **354–355**
Public account system, **364**
Public works and ways
system, **365**
Pugh v. *Locke,* 382
Punishment, 5. *See also* Capital
punishment; Corporal
punishment; Fines;
Rehabilitation; Sentences
definition of, 72–73
deterrence, **74–75**
false positives, **77**
forfeiture, **88**
in French history, 30
incapacitation, **75–77**
in Middle Ages, 31, 32
overlapping of, 78–79
retribution, **74–75**
selective incapacitation, **76–77**
Punitive conditions of probation, 195
Puritans, 48

Q

Quaker Code, 48
Quaker principles, 44, 48–49, 54
community corrections and, 227
penitentiaries and, 51–53
women offenders and, 287, 288
Quinlan, Michael, 242

R

Racial minorities. *See* Minority
offenders
Racial segregation, 385
Racketeer Influence and Corrupt
Organizations Act (RICO), 88
Radial design of prison, **244–245**
Rafter, Nichole, 285, 291, 292
Ragen, Joseph E., 314–315,
316–317, 321–323
Rahway Prison, New Jersey, 226
parole issues, 411
radial design, 244
Rand Corporation
of intensive supervision proba-
tion, 219
on prison population, 250
probation violation study, 200
Randolph, Ross, 321

Rapists, 111
Rational authority, 193
RCA Corporation Intensive
Treatment Units, 248
Reaffirming Rehabilitation
(Cullen & Gilbert), 362
Reagan, Ronald, 120, 468
Reality therapy, **354**
guided group interaction, 355
token economy as, **356**
Recidivism
in Auburn, New York State
prison, 54
in California and Kentucky, 200
cumulative rates of, 433
as measure of success, 455–456
three-year rates of, 456
three years, parolees returned
after, 433
of young parolees, 431
Reckless, Walter, 110
Recognizance, **174**
release on recognizance
(ROR), **158**
Records room jobs, 368
Recreation programs, 370–371
Rector, Rickey Ray, 485
Reentry programs, 429
Reeves, 142
Reform
sentencing and, 95–98
warden's action for, 317
Reformatories, 16
Reformatory movement, 55–61
Elmira Reformatory, 56, 58–59
juvenile corrections and, 59–60
women prisoners, 288–289, 290
Regional jails, **147**
Rehabilitation, **77–78**
in crime control model, 68
deemphasis on, 10
medical model of corrections,
65–67
parole and, 402
probation and, 176
warden's action for, 317
of women offenders, 291–292
Rehabilitation model, **239**
Rehabilitative programs, 352–362
classification programs in, 348
educational programs, 359–360
rediscovery of, 362
religious programs, 361–362
security and, 346–347
vocational rehabilitation,
359–361
Rehnquist, William, 386, 397, 486
Reintegration idea, 67

Reintegration model, **239–240**
Relapse Prevention Program,
  Vermont, 500
Release. *See also* Parole
  discretionary release, **403**
  expiration release, **403**
  mandatory release, **403**
Release on recognizance (ROR),
  158, 165
Relief officers, 340
Religion, 10. *See also* Quaker
  principles
  ecclesiastical punishments, 31
  First Amendment rights of
    prisoners, 379–380
  prison programs, 361–362
Remunerative power, **311**
Reparative probation, 20
Repeat offenders, 108–110
Reports. *See also* Presentence inves-
  tigation (PSI)
  presentence report, 94–95
Residential programs, 11, 443–445
  community correctional
    centers, **444**
  Connecticut Halfway Houses,
    Inc., 228–229
  work release centers, **444–445**
Restitution, **88**, 217–218. *See also*
  Fines
  as jail alternative, 162
Restitution centers, 218
Retribution, **73**
Revocation
  of parole, 429–433
  of probation, 199–202
Rhodes v. *Chapman*, 383, 386
Ridley, Bishop Nicholas, 33
Right guy role, 261
Rikers Island, New York, 154–155
Riots. *See* Prison violence
Riveland, Chase, 25–26
Rockefeller drug law, New York, 83
Roesing, Peter, 208
Roosevelt, Franklin, 366
Rosecrance, John, 95
Rosett, Arthur, 95–98
Rothman, David, 49, 61–62,
  64, 143
Roulet, Sister Elaine, 284
Rubin, Sol, 411
Ruffin v. *Commonwealth*, 375
Ruiz v. *Estelle*, 274, 383, 394,
  395–396
Rüsche, Georg, 32, 37
Rush, Dr. Benjamin, 51, 52, 55

S

Sacks, Howard, 456
Salvation Army, 289
Sanborn, Franklin, 57, 406
Sanctions. *See also specific sanctions*
  continuum of sanctions, **210**
  for prison rule violations, 279
San Francisco, jails in, 141
Santa Cruz County Jail, California,
  148–152
Santa Fe, New Mexico prison, 271
Satter, Robert, 71
Saxbe v. *Washington Post*, 380
Scared straight program, 226
School officers, 339
Schrag, Clarence, 261
Search and seizure in prisons, 381
Section 1983. *See* 42 U.S.C. 1983
Secular law, **32**
Security
  classification policy and, 350
  recreation programs and,
    370–371
  and rehabilitative programs,
    346–347
  time management and, 346–347
Selective incapacitation, **76–77**,
  469–470
Selective intervention strategies,
  194
Self-government by inmates,
  317–318, 329
Self report studies, **103**
Sentence disparity, **94**
Sentences. *See also* Determinate
  sentences; Good time;
  Indeterminate sentences;
  Mandatory sentences; Parole;
  Presentence investigation
  (PSI); Probation;
  Rehabilitation
  accountability system,
    Delaware, 212–213
  actual time served versus, 86
  administrative context of, 93–94
  deterrence and, 75
  interconnectedness of corrections
    and, 23, 24
  judges and, 92–93
  judicial reprieve, **173**
  minority offenders and, 104
  modification of, 177
  national sentencing system, 95
  politics and reform, 95–98
  presentence report, 94–95
  principle of interchangeability,
    224

prison population and, 466–467
process of sentencing, 91–95
recognizance, **174**
reform and, 95–98
sentence disparity, **94**
sentencing guidelines, **83–84**
split sentences, 177
types of sentence imposed, 92
for women offenders, 285
Sentencing guidelines, **83–84**
  grid used in Minnesota for, 85
Sentencing Project, The, 474
Separate confinement, **51–52**
  decline in, 53
Sergeants, 338
Service Employees International
  Union (SEIU), 340
Severity-softening-severity
  process, 95
Sewing programs, 299
Sex in Prison (Fishman), 257
Sex offenders, **111–113**
  Depo-Provera, **498**
  parole requirements, 418
  probation officers and, 193–194
  relapse prevention programs,
    500–501
  supervision strategies for, 198
Sexual assaults
  prevention of, 276
  in prison, 273
Sexual aversion therapy, 112
Shakedowns, 346
Sheehan, Susan, 266, 270
Sheriffs, 142
Shires, 142
Shivs, 276
Shock incarceration, **88–89**,
  177, 222
  probation substitute, 213
Shock probation, 90
Sickouts by corrections officers, 341
Sigler, Maurice, 410
Sing Sing, 247
  Hubbell, Gaylord, 56–57
  Osborne, Thomas Mott, 315
  parole in, 406
  women's wing at, 287
Situational offenders, 106, 108
Slavery
  African slaves, 34, 36
  galley, **32**
Smith, Sarah, 289
Social control, **5**
Social life
  of elderly offenders, 128
  recreation programs, 370–371

Social therapy, **357–359**

Society and Prisons (Osborne), 315

Society for Alleviating the Miseries of Public Prisoners, 51

Society of Captives, The (Sykes), 258

Sociopaths, 118

Soledad prisons, California, 329

Sommers Prison, Connecticut, 112, 245

  violations, classes of, 278

Southern United States, prisons in, 237

Southwest Detention Facilities, 249

Span of control, **313**

Special deterrence, **74–75**

Specific deterrence, **74–75**

Speedy trials, 165

Spenkelink, John, 488

Spierenburg, Pieter, 29

Split sentences, 90, 177

Spouses of prisoners, 264–265

Square John role, 261, 298, 299

Staff personnel, **314**

Stakes, **211–212**

Standard conditions of probation, 195

Stand bail, **172**

Stanford v. *Kentucky,* 485

State of Prisons and of Child-Saving Institutions in the Civilized World, The (Wines), 57

State of the Prisons in England and Wales, The (Howard), 39, 43

State prison systems, 242–243

State use system, **364–365**

Stateville (Jacobs), 316–317

Stateville Penitentiary, Illinois, 247, 321–323, 358–359

  Ragen, Joseph E., 314–315, 321–323

Statistical risk assessment, 197–198

Status offenders, **128–130**

Statutory rights of prisoners, 378

Street-level bureaucrats, **21–23**

Strikes by corrections officers, 341

Structure dilemma of corrections, 510–511

Substance abusers. *See also* Alcohol abusers; Drug offenders

  detention of, 155–156

  supervision strategies for, 198–199

Suicide

  in jails, 152–153

  in prisons, 271

Sullivan, Robert Austin, 488–489

Supervised release, 165

Supervision, 180, 191–197. *See also* Intensive probation supervision (IPS)

  administration of, 195–196

  case management systems, 197–198

  case supervision plan illustration, 187

  effectiveness of, 197–199

  intensive supervision probation (ISP), 219, 221

  intermediate sanctions and, 217–222

  model system of case management, 197–198

  by probation officers, 192–194

  responses to, 194–195

  size of caseload by state, 197

  special conditions of probation, 195–196

  special programs for, 198–199

Supreme Court. *See* United States Supreme Court

Surveillance, 226, 497–498

  benefits of, 505–506

  drug controls, 498–499

  goals of, 501–502

  growth of, 497–498

  home surveillance, 26

  human response to, 504–505

  human surveillance, 500

  limits of, 503–505

  in maximum security prisons, **247**

  moral and ethical limits to, 505

  politics of, 502–503

  programmatic controls, 500–501

  technologies and, 504

  video surveillance, 499–500

Sykes, Gresham, 258, 259, 260–261, 327

System, **10–11** *See also* Corrections system

Systematic needs assessments, 198

Szasz, Thomas S., 118, 352

T

Taft, William Howard, 63

Talarico, Susette, 410

Target group for intermediate sanctions, 224–225

Tarnower, Dr. Herman, 106

Tax revenues, 13

Technical violations

  of parole, 429, 432

  of probation, **199–200**

Technology, **18–19**

  and corrections profession, 518–519

Telephone-pole design for prisons, **245**

Texas

  correctional system, 17

  prison gangs in, 275

Texas Department of Correction, 395–396

Texas Syndicate, 273

Therapeutic community, 357–358

  for juvenile offenders, 359

Theriault v. *Carlson,* 380

Thief role, 299

Thief subculture, 262

Thomas, Charles, 249

Thompson, William Wayne, 485

Thompson v. *Oklahoma,* 485

Thorazine, **498–499**

Tickets, 338

Tickets-of-leave, 55, 404–405

Time management, 345–347. *See also* Prison programs

  security and, 346–347

Toch, Hans, 271, 350

Token economy, **356**

Tonry, Michael, 95, 207, 208

Torrington, Connecticut Alternative Incarceration Center, 208

Torture. *See* Corporal punishment

Total institution, **310**

Totality of conditions, **382**

Transactional analysis, **354–355**

Transportation, **34**

  hulks, transport on, **36**

  incapacitation and, 76

  parole and, 405

Treatment conditions of probation, 195–196

Treatment model, 78

Treatment programs

  for alcohol abusers, 117–118

  day reporting centers, 218

  Intensive Treatment Unit, RCA, 249

  in jails, 160

  in prisons, 240

  psychological treatment programs, 352–355

  total institution and, 310

  in Vermont, 20

Trenton State Prison, New Jersey, 236

  radial design, 245

Truman, Harry, 366

Turner v. *Safley,* 379, 380

Twomey, John, 321

U

UNICOR, 368–369
Uniform Crime Reports, 285, 296
Uniform Parole Reports, 305
Unions. *See* Labor unions
United States Board of Parole, 407
United States Constitution. *See* Constitutional rights
United States Corrections Corporation, 249
United States Industrial Commission, 366
United States Marshals Service, 242
United States Supreme Court. *See also specific cases*
    on capital punishment, 480, 482
    on discipline in prison, 278
    on double celling, 383
    due process in prison discipline, 384–385
    on jailhouse lawyers, 376
    judicial reprieve, 173
    on pretrial detainees' rights, 157
    on prisoners' rights, 375
    probation, revocation of, 201–202
United States v. *Bailey,* 385
United States v. *Hitchcock,* 382
Unity of command, **313**
Urine tests for drug offenders, 199, 202, 500
Utilitarianism, 40, **41**
    deterrence and, 75

V

Vacaville Correctional Medical Facility, HIV-infected inmates at, 126
Vagrancy Act of 1597, 34
Vagrancy in history, 35–36
Van den Haag, Ernst, 478
Vaux, Robert, 52–53
Vehicular homicide, 117
Vermont correctional system, 20
Vietnam War, 67
Violent crimes. *See also* Prison violence
    by juvenile offenders, 130–131
Visitation
    conjugal visits, 265
    parole, visitation prior to, 423
Vocational rehabilitation, 359–361
    for women, 299
Voltaire, 38

W

Wackenhut Corrections Corporation, 249

Waldo, Gordon, 445
Walla Walla prison, Washington, 329
Wall post assignments for officers, 339
Walnut Street Jail, Philadelphia, 51
Walpole State Prison, Massachusetts, 247
Ward, David, 297
Wardens, 314–319. *See also* Deputy wardens
    burnout, 319
    paperwork and, 319
    and politics, 318–319
    role of, 312–313
    work perspective for, 316–319
Warren, Earl, 387
Wasson, Billy, 214–215
Watkinson Foundation, 228
Weaversville private facility, 248
Wergild, **31**
Western Penitentiary, Pittsburgh, 51
Wheeler, Martha, 300–301
Whipping. *See* Corporal punishment
White, Byron, 386
Whitley v. *Albers,* 383
Widening the net, **159–160**, 162
    intermediate sanctions and, 213–214
Wilder, Governor L. Douglas, 478
Wilkes, Judith, 456
Wilkins v. *Missouri,* 485
William of Orange, 38
Williams, Charles (Prisoner Number 1), 48
Williams v. *New York,* 190
Wilson, James Q., 68, 76, 430
Wilson v. *Seiter,* 387
Wines, Enoch Cobb, 57, 61
Within Prison Walls (Osborne), 315
Wives of inmates, 264–265
Wolfe, Tom, 102
Wolff v. *McDonnell,* 278, 385, 386
Wolfgang, Marvin, 273
Women. *See also* Women offenders
    career opportunities for, 517–518
    corrections officers, 336–337
Women offenders
    adaptive roles of, 298
    benign neglect of, **275**
    characteristics of, 293, 296
    chivalry factor, **285**
    co-corrections, 301–302
    correctional facilities for, 293
    crimes of, 296
    on death row, 487–488

drug use, 296
    history of, 287–292
    incarceration of, 283–308
    intermediate sanctions and, 225
    male versus female subcultures, 298–299
    mothers and children, 303–305
    population of, 284–285
    pregnant women inmates, 302–303
    programs for, 299–300
    reformatory movement and, 288–289, 290
    rehabilitative programs for, 291–292
    release of, 305
    services for, 302–303
    subculture of women's prisons, 296–298
Women's Workhouse, Blackwell Island, 290
Work assignments, 235
Work detail supervisors, 338–339
Work furlough, 445
Workload accounting in supervision, 198
Work release
    as jail alternative, 162
    centers, **444–445**

Y

Yablonsky, Lewis, 108
Yale Law Journal, 300
Yard officers, 339
Yelaja, Shankar, 193
Young, Robert, 452
Youth. *See* Juvenile corrections
Yuma prison, Arizona, 247

Z

Zedlewski, Edwin, 474–475
Zephyr Products, Inc., 366
Zimmer, Lynn, 337
Zimring, Franklin, 475

Photo Credits

Part I Opener Linda Rosier/Impact Visuals; p. 8 ©Bob Daemmrich/ Stock Boston; p. 9 ©Joseph Schuyler/Stock Boston; p. 11 ©Donna Ferrato/Black Star; p. 18 ©Alan Carey/The Image Works; p. 22 ©Martin J. Dain/Magnum Photos; p. 31 Private Collection; p. 33 Bettmann/Hulton; p. 34 Federal Bureau of Prisons; p. 42 Historical Pictures Stock Montage; p. 49 Historical Society of Pennsylvania; p. 50 American Correctional Association; p. 51 American Correctional Association; p. 54 Reproduced from *Warden Cassidy on Prisons and Convicts,* Michael J. Cassidy. Used with permission of the ACA; p. 56 Courtesy New York Department of Correction. Used with permission of the ACA; p. 59 Courtesy Indiana Department of Correction. Used with permission of the ACA; p. 80 ©David Burnett/Contact Press Images; p. 87 UPI/Bettmann; p. 89 ©Jerry Berndt/Stock Boston; p. 90 The Bettmann Archive; p. 94 AP/ Wide World Photos; p. 106 UPI/ Bettmann; p. 113 ©Andrew Lichtenstein/Impact Visuals; p. 120 ©Andrew Lichtenstein/Impact Visuals; p. 127 ©Abbas/Magnum Photos; p. 129 ©James L. Shaffer/Photo Edit; **Part II Opener** The Bettmann Archive; p. 143 ©Philip Taft/Black Star; p. 147 ©Frank Fournier/Contact Press Images; p. 160

©Danny Lyon/Magnum Photos; p. l66 ©Mark Ludak/Impact Visuals; p. 167 Ricci Associates; p. 174 Courtesy of the Bostonian Society Old State House; p. 179 Brooks/Cole Publishing Company; p. 192 (top) ©Gilles Peress/Magnum Photos; p. 192 (bottom) ©Frank Siteman/Stock Boston; p. 194 ©Ray Ellis/Photo Researchers; p. 216 Szaba Photography; p. 218 ©Andrew Lichtenstein/Impact Visuals; p. 223 ©Linda Rosier/Impact Visuals; p. 231 ©George Cohen/Impact Visuals; p. 237 ©Barry Halkin; p. 239 Federal Bureau of Prisons; p. 244 ©Susan Meiselas/ Magnum Photos; p. 247 ©Susan Meiselas/Magnum Photos; p. 248 Courtesy Hellmuta, Obata, Kassabum, Inc.; p. 258 ©Danny Lyon/ Magnum Photos; p. 262 ©Urlike Welsch; p. 272 ©Ruth Morgan; p. 289 Courtesy American Correctional Association; p. 296 ©Neil Leifer/Time Magazine; p. 300 ©Frank Fournier/Contact Press Images; p. 302 ©Gary Wagner/ Impact Visuals; p. 304 ©Gary Wagner/Impact Visuals; p. 314 Robert Harbison/©1992 The Christian Science Monitor; p. 324 UPI/Bettmann; p. 327 ©Neil Leifer/Time Magazine; p. 337 UPI/Bettmann; p. 339 ©Dilip Mehta/Contact Press Images; p. 348 ©Cathy Cheney/ Stock Boston; p. 354 The Bettmann

Archive; p. 359 ©Gale Zucker/ Stock Boston; p. 361 ©George Cohen/Impact Visuals; p. 365 ©Black Star; p. 370 ©Alex Webb/ Magnum Photos; p. 376 ©Alon Reininger/ Contact Press Images; p. 378 ©Ethan Hoffman/Picture Project; p. 381 UPI/Bettmann; p. 394 ©Alex Webb/Magnum Photos; p. 402 ©Kent Reno; p. 403 © Alain McLaughlin/Impact Visuals; p. 407 UPI/ Bettmann; p. 408 ©Bob Daemmrich/The Image Works; p. 421 UPI/Bettmann; p. 432 ©Vernon Merritt/Black Star; p. 438 UPI/ Bettmann; p. 442 ©Bruce Kliewe/Jeroboam; p. 444 ©Michael Weisbrot/Stock Boston; p. 450 ©Terrence McCarthy for the *New York Times;* p. 453 ©Chiasson/ Gamma Liaison; **Part III Opener** ©Gale Zucker; p. 466 Photofest; p. 468 ©Evan Johnson/Impact Visuals; p. 471 ©Nancy Shia/ Impact Visuals; p. 479 (left) UPI/Bettmann; p. 479 (right) UPI/Bettmann; p. 483 ©Impact Visuals; p. 486 UPI/Bettmann; p. 499 ©Chiasson/Gamma Liaison; p. 502 ©Leonard Freed/Magnum Photos; p. 504 ©Charles Gatewood/Magnum Photos; p. 514 ©Harvy Finkle/Impact Visuals; p. 517 ©Bob Daemmrich/Stock Boston.

KALAMAZOO VALLEY
COMMUNITY COLLEGE

Presented By

Jeff Shouldice

continued from
inside front cover

1900 – present

**CORRECTIONAL
THOUGHT**

1916	Thomas Mott Osborne, *Society and Prison*
1929	National Commission on Law Observance and Enforcement (Wickersham Commission)
1939	Georg Rusche, *Punishment and Social Structure*
1958	Gresham Sykes, *The Society of Captives*
1967	President's Commission on Law Enforcement and Administration of Justice

**CORRECTIONAL
PRACTICE**

1924	Congressional authorization of Federal Bureau of Prisons
1925	Prison at Stateville, Illinois, based on Bentham's pantopticon design
1927	Mary Belle Harris, warden, opens federal institution for women in Alderson, West Virginia
1930	Thirty states and federal government use probation
1935	Execution of 199 offenders in U.S.; highest rate in 20th century
1965	California Probation Subsidy Act

LAW

1925	Federal Probation Act
1964	*Cooper* v. *Pate*: State prisoners may sue officials in federal courts
1967	In re *Gault*: Requires counsel for juveniles
1968	Congress passes omnibus Crime and Safe Streets Act
1970	*Holt* v. *Sarver*: Declares Arkansas prison system unconstitutional

**AMERICAN
SOCIETY**

1903	Wright brothers' flight
1914–1918	World War I
1920	First scheduled radio program broadcast Amendment 18 goes into effect, beginning prohibition
1927	Charles T. Lindbergh flies nonstop from New York to Paris
1928	First color motion pictures
1929	"Black Thursday" stock market crash
1935	Social Security Act